**BLACK LEGACY PRESS**™

WWW.BLACKLEGACYPRESS.ORG

Negro Poets and Their Poems

By

Robert Thomas Kerlin

ISBN: 978-1-63652-344-6

# NEGRO POETS AND THEIR POEMS

ROBERT THOMAS KERLIN

# CONTENTS

# PREFACE

*Ad astra per aspera*—that is the old Roman adage. Magnificent is it, and magnificently is it being in these days exemplified by the American Negroes, particularly by the increasing number of educated and talented American Negroes, and most particularly by those who feel the urge to express in song the emotions and aspirations of their people. A surprisingly large number is this class. Without exhausting the possibilities of selection I have quoted in this anthology of contemporary Negro poetry sixty odd writers of tolerable verse that exhibits, besides form, at least one fundamental quality of poetry, namely, passion.

The mere number, large as it is, would of course not signify by itself. Nor does the phrase "tolerable verse," cautiously chosen, seem to promise much. What this multitude means, and whether the verse be worthy of a more complimentary description, I leave to the reader's judgment. Quality of expression and character of content are of course the prepotent considerations.

While, in a preliminary section, I have passed in review the poetry of the Negro up to and including Dunbar, not neglecting the old religious songs of the plantation, or "Spirituals," and the dance, play, and nursery rhymes, or "Seculars," yet strictly speaking this is a representation of new Negro voices, an anthology of present-day Negro verse, with biographical items and critical, or at least appreciative comment.

I wish most heartily to express my obligations to the publishers and authors of the volumes I have drawn upon for selections. They are named in the Index and Biographical and Bibliographical Notes at the end of the text. But for the reader's convenience I collect their names here:

Richard E. Badger, publisher of Walter Everette Hawkins's *Chords and Discords*; A. B. Caldwell, Atlanta, Ga., publisher of Sterling M. Means' *The Deserted Cabin and Other Poems*; the Cornhill Company, publishers of Waverley Turner Carmichael's *From the Heart of a Folk*; Joseph S. Cotter's *The Band of Gideon*; Georgia Douglas Johnson's *The Heart of a Woman*; Charles Bertram Johnson's *Songs of My People*; James Weldon Johnson's *Fifty Years and Other Poems*; Joshua Henry Jones's *Poems of the Four Seas*; Dodd, Mead and Company, publishers of Dunbar's *Poems*; the Grafton Press, publishers of H. Cordelia Ray's *Poems*; Harcourt, Brace & Company, publishers of W. E. Burghardt DuBois's *Darkwater*; Pritchard and Ovington's *The Upward Path*; the Macmillan Company, publishers of Thomas W. Talley's *Negro Folk Rhymes*; the Neale Publishing Company, publishers of Kelley Miller's *Out of the House of Bondage*; J. L. Nichols & Company, Naperville, Ill., publishers of Mrs. Dunbar-Nelson's *The Dunbar Speaker and Entertainer*, and *The Life and Works of Paul Laurence Dunbar*; the Stratford Company, publishers of Joshua Henry Jones's *The Heart of the World and Other Poems*; and Leslie Pinckney Hill's *The Wings of Oppression*. It is with their kind permission I am privileged to use selections from the books named. To *The Crisis*, *The Favorite Magazine*, and *The Messenger*, I am indebted for several selections, which I gratefully acknowledge.

To readers who are disposed to study the poetry of the Negro I would commend Dr. James Weldon Johnson's *The Book of American Negro Poetry* (Harcourt, Brace & Co.) and Mr. Arthur A. Schomburg's *A Bibliographical Checklist of American Negro Poetry* (Charles F. Hartman, New York). I am indebted to both these books and authors. To Mr. Schomburg I am also indebted for the loan of many of the pictures of the earlier poets.

R. T. K.

West Chester, Pa.

March 22, 1923.

*Robert Thomas Kerlin*

# CHAPTER I
# THE NEGROES
# HERITAGE OF SONG

As an empire may grow up within an empire without observation so a republic of letters within a republic of letters. That thing is happening today in this land of ours. A literature of significance on many accounts, and not without various and considerable merits. Its producers are Negroes. Culture, talent, genius—or something very like it—are theirs. Nor is it "the mantle of Dunbar" they wrap themselves in, but an unborrowed singing robe, that better fits "the New Negro." The list of names in poetry alone would stretch out, were I to start telling them over, until I should bring suspicion upon myself as no trustworthy reporter. Besides, the mere names would mean nothing, since, as intimated, this little republic has grown up unobserved in our big one.

It may be more for the promise held forth by their thin little volumes than for the intrinsic merit of their performance that we should esteem the verse-makers represented in this survey of contemporary Negro poetry. Yet on many grounds they should receive candid attention, both from the students of literature and the students of sociology. Recognition of real literary merit will be accorded by the one class of students, and recognition of new aspects of the most serious race problem of the ages will be forced upon the second class. Justification enough for the present survey and exhibition will be acknowledged by all who are earnestly concerned either with literature or with life.

Perhaps, unconsciously, in my comments and estimates I have not steadfastly kept before me absolute standards of poetry. But where and when was this ever done? Doubtless in critiques of master poets by master critics, and only there. In writing of contemporary verse, by courtesy called poetry, we compromise, our estimates are relative, we make allowances, our approvals and disapprovals are toned according to the known circumstances of production. And this is right.

If the prospective reader opens this volume with the demand in his mind for novelty of language, form, imagery, idea—novelty and quaintness, perhaps amusing "originality", or grotesqueness— let him reflect how unreasonable a similar demand on the part of English critics was a century ago relative to the beginnings of American poetry. Were not American poets products of the same culture as their contemporaries in England? What other language had they than the language of Shakespeare and Wordsworth, Keats and Tennyson? The same is essentially true of the American Negro—or the Negro American, if you choose. He is the heir of Anglo-Saxon culture, he has been nurtured in the same spiritual soil as his contemporary of the white race, the same traditions of language, form, imagery, and idea are his. Everything possible has been done to stamp out his own African traditions and native propensities. Therefore, let no unreasonable demand be laid upon these Negro rhymers.

Notwithstanding, something distinctive, and something

uniquely significant, may be discerned in these verse productions to reward the perusal. But this may not be the reader's chief reward. That may be his discovery, that, after all, a wonderful likeness rather than unlikeness to the poetry of other races looks forth from this poetry of the children of Ham. A valuable result would this be, should it follow.

Before attempting a survey of the field of contemporary verse it will advantage us to cast a backward glance upon the poetic traditions of the Negro, to see what is the present-day Negro poet's heritage of song. These traditions will be reviewed in two sections: 1. Untaught Melodies; 2. The Poetry of Art. This backward glance will comprehend all that was sung or written by colored people from Jupiter Hammon to Paul Laurence Dunbar.

# I. UNTAUGHT MELODIES

The Negro might well be expected to exhibit a gift for poetry. His gift for oratory has long been acknowledged. The fact has been accepted without reflection upon its significance. It should have been foreseen that because of the close kinship between oratory and poetry the Negro would some day, with more culture, achieve distinction in the latter art, as he had already achieved distinction in the former art. The endowments which make for distinction in these two great kindred arts, it must also be remarked, have not been properly esteemed in the Negro. In other races oratory and poetry have been accepted as the tokens of noble qualities of character, lofty spiritual gifts. Such they are, in all races. They spring from mankind's supreme spiritual impulses, from mankind's loftiest aspirations—the aspirations for freedom, for justice, for virtue, for honor and distinction.

That these impulses, these aspirations, and these endowments

7

are in the American Negro and are now exhibiting themselves in verse—it is this I wish to show to the skeptically minded. It will readily be admitted that the Negro nature is endowed above most others, if not all others, in fervor of feeling, in the completeness of self-surrender to emotion. Hence we see that marvelous display of rhythm in the individual and in the group. This capacity of submission to a higher harmony, a grander power, than self, affords the explanation of mankind's highest reaches of thought, supreme insights, and noblest expressions. Rhythm is its manifestation. It is the most central and compulsive law of the universe. The rhythmic soul falls into harmony and co-operation with the universal creative energy. It therefore becomes a creative soul. Rhythm visibly takes hold of the Negro and sways his entire being. It makes him one with the universal Power that Goethe describes, in famous lines, as "at the roaring loom of time, weaving for God the garment thou seest him by."

But fervor of feeling must have some originating cause. That cause is a conception—the vivid, concrete presentation of an object or idea to the mind. The Negro has this endowment also. Ideas enter his mind with a vividness and power which betoken an extraordinary faculty of imagination. The graphic originality of language commonly exhibited by the Negro would be sufficient proof of this were other proof wanting. No one will deny to the Negro this gift. Whoever has listened to a colored preacher's sermon, either of the old or the new school, will recall perhaps more than one example of poetic phrasing, more than one word-picture, that rendered some idea vivid beyond vanishing. It no doubt has been made, in the ignorant or illiterate, an object of jest, just as the other two endowments have been; but these three gifts are the three supreme gifts of the poet, and the poet is the supreme outcome of the race: power of feeling, power of imagination, power of expression—and these make the poet.

## 1. *The Spirituals*

As a witness of the Negro's untutored gift for song there are the Spirituals, his "canticles of love and woe," chanted wildly, in that darkness which only a few rays from heaven brightened. Since they afford, as it were, a background for the song of cultured art which now begins to appear, I must here give a word to these crude old plantation songs. They are one of the most notable contributions of any people, similarly circumstanced, to the world's treasury of song, altogether the most appealing. Their significance for history and for art—more especially for art—awaits interpretation. There are signs that this interpretation is not far in the future. Dvorak, the Bohemian, aided by the Negro composer, Harry T. Burleigh, may have heralded, in his "New World Symphony," the consummate achievement of the future which shall be entirely the Negro's. Had Samuel Coleridge-Taylor been an American instead of an English Negro, this theme rather than the Indian theme might have occupied his genius—the evidence whereof is that, removed as he was from the scenes of plantation life and the tribulations of the slaves, yet that life and those tribulations touched his heart and found a place, though a minor one, in his compositions.

But the sister art of poetry may anticipate music in the great feat of embodying artistically the yearning, suffering, prayerful soul of the African in those centuries when he could only with patience endure and trust in God—and wail these mournfullest of melodies. Some lyrical drama like "Prometheus Bound," but more touching as being more human; some epic like "Paradise Lost," but nearer to the common heart of man, and more lyrical; some

"Divina Commedia," that shall be the voice of those silent centuries of slavery, as Dante's poem was the voice of the long-silent epoch preceding it, or some lyrical "passion play" like that of Oberammergau, is the not improbable achievement of some descendant of the slaves.

In a poem of tender appeal, James Weldon Johnson has celebrated the "black and unknown bards," who, without art, and even without letters, produced from their hearts, weighed down with sorrows, the immortal Spirituals:

> O black and unknown bards of long ago,
> How came your lips to touch the sacred fire?
> How, in your darkness, did you come to know
> The power and beauty of the minstrel's lyre?
> Who first from midst his bonds lifted his eyes?
> Who first from out the still watch, lone and long,
> Feeling the ancient faith of prophets rise
> Within his dark-kept soul, burst into song?

So begins this noble tribute to the nameless natural poets whose hearts, touched as a harp by the Divine Spirit, gave forth "Swing Low, Sweet Chariot," and "Nobody Knows de Trouble I See," "Steal Away to Jesus," and "Roll, Jordan, Roll."

Great praise does indeed rightly belong to that black slave-folk who gave to the world this treasure of religious song. To the world, I say, for they belong as truly to the whole world as do the quaint and incomparable animal stories of Uncle Remus. Their appeal is to every human heart, but especially to the heart that has known great sorrow and which looks to God for help.

It is only of late their meaning has begun to dawn upon

us—their tragic, heart-searching meaning. Who in hearing these Spirituals sung to-day by the heirs of their creators can doubt what they meant when they were wailed in the quarters or shouted in wild frenzy in the camp-meetings of the slaves? Even the broken, poverty-stricken English adds infinitely to the pathos:

> I'm walking on borrowed land,
> This world ain't none of my home.

> We'll stand the storm, it won't be long.

> Oh, walk together children,
> Don't get weary.

> My heavenly home is bright and fair,
> Nor pain nor death can enter there.

> Oh, steal away and pray,
> I'm looking for my Jesus.

> Oh, freedom! oh, freedom! oh, freedom over
> me!
> An' before I'd be a slave,
> I'll be buried in my grave,
> And go home to my Lord an' be free.

Not a word here but had two meanings for the slave, a worldly one and a spiritual one, and only one meaning, the spiritual one, for the master—who gladly saw this religious frenzy as an emotional safety-valve.

In certain aspects these Spirituals suggest the songs of Zion, the Psalms. Trouble is the mother of song, particularly of religious song. In trouble the soul cries out to God—"a very present help in time of trouble." The Psalms and the Spirituals alike rise *de profundis*. But in one respect the songs of the African slaves differ from the songs of Israel in captivity: there is no prayer for vengeance in the Spirituals, no vindictive spirit ever even suggested. We can but wonder now at this. For slavery at its best was degrading, cruel, and oppressive. Yet no imprecation, such as mars so many a beautiful Psalm, ever found its way into a plantation Spiritual. A convincing testimony this to that spirit in the African slave which Christ, by precept and example, sought to establish in His disciples. If the Negro in our present day is growing bitter toward the white race, it behooves us to inquire why it is so, in view of his indisputable patience, meekness, and good-nature. We might find in our present régime a more intolerable cruelty than belonged even to slavery, if we investigated honestly. There is certainly a bitter and vindictive tone in much of the Afro-American verse now appearing in the colored press. For both races it augurs ill.

But I have not yet indicated the precise place of these Spirituals in the world's treasury of song. They have a close kinship with the Psalms but a yet closer one with the chanted prayers of the primitive Christians, the Christians when they were the outcasts of the Roman Empire when to be a Christian was to be a martyr. In secret places, in catacombs, they sent up their triumphant though sorrowful songs, they chanted their litanies

> "—that came
> Like the volcano's tongue of flame
> Up from the burning core below—
> The canticles of love and woe."

So indeed came the Spirituals of the African slave. These songs might in truth, to use a figure of the old poets, be called the melodious tears of those who wailed them. An African proverb says, "We weep in our hearts like the tortoise." In their hearts—so wept the slaves, silently save for these mournful cries in melody. Without means of defense, save a nature armored with faith, when assailed, insulted, oppressed, they could but imitate the tortoise when he shuts himself up in his

INSPIRATION
*BY META WARRICK FULLER*

shell and patiently takes the blows that fall. The world knew not then, nor fully knows now—partly because of African buoyancy, pliability, and optimism—what tears they wept. These Spirituals are the golden vials spoken of in Holy Writ, "full of odors, which are the prayers of saints"—an everlasting memorial before the throne of God. Other vials there are, different from these, and they, too, are at God's right hand.

A Negro sculptor, Mrs. Meta Warrick Fuller, not knowing of this proverb about the tortoise which has only recently been brought from Africa, but simply interpreting Negro life in America, has embodied the very idea of the African saying in bronze. Under the title "Secret Sorrow" a man is represented as eating his own heart.

The interpretation in art of the Spirituals, or a poetry of art developed along the lines and in the spirit of those songs, is something we may expect the black singers of no distant day to produce. Already we have many a poem that offers striking reminiscences of them.

## 2. *The Seculars*

But other songs the Negro has which are more noteworthy from the point of view of art than the Spirituals: songs that are richer in artistic effects, more elaborate in form, more varied and copious in expression. These are the Negro's secular songs and rhymes, his dance, play, and love-making songs, his gnomic and nursery rhymes.[1] It is not exaggeration to say that in rhythmic and melodic effects they surpass any other body of folk-verse whatsoever. In wit, wisdom, and quaint turns of humor no other folk-rhymes equal them. Prolific, too, in such productions the race seems to have been, since so many at this late day were to be found.

It comes not within the scope of this anthology to include any of these folk-rhymes of the elder day, but a few specimens seem necessary to indicate to the young Negro who would be a poet his rich heritage of song and to the white reader what essentially poetic traits the Negro has by nature. It was "black and unknown bards," slaves, too, who sang or said these rhymes:

> Oh laugh an' sing an' don't git tired.
> We's all gwine home, some Mond'y,
> To de honey pond an' fritter trees;
> An' ev'ry day'll be Sund'y.

Pride, too, and a sense of values had the Negro, bond or free:

> My name's Ran, I wuks in de san';
> But I'd druther be a Nigger dan a po' white
> man.
> Gwinter hitch my oxes side by side,
> An' take my gal fer a big fine ride.

After a description of anticipated pleasures and a comic interlude in dialogue, the ballad from which these two couplets are taken concludes with that varied repetition of the first stanza which we find so effective in the poems of art:

> I'd druther be a Nigger, an' plow ole Beck,
> Dan a white Hill Billy wid his long red neck.

Song or rhyme was, as ever, heart's ease to the Negro in every trouble. Here are two rhymes that "pack up" and put away two common troubles:

> She writ me a letter
> As long as my eye.
> An' she say in dat letter:
> "My Honey!—Good-by!"

Dem whitefolks say dat money talk.
If it talk lak dey tell,
Den ev'ry time it come to Sam,
It up an' say: "Farewell!"

Going to the nursery—it was the one room of the log cabin, or the great out-of-doors—we find the old-time Negro's head filled with a *Mother Goose* more enchanting than any printed and pictured one in the "great house" of the white child:

W'en de big owl whoops,
An' de screech owl screeks,
An' de win' makes a howlin' sound;
You liddle woolly heads
Had better kiver up,
Caze de "hants" is comin' 'round.


A, B, C,
Doubled down D;
I'se so lazy you cain't see me.


A, B, C,
Doubled down D;
Lazy Chilluns gits hick'ry tea.

\*\*\*\*

Buck an' Berry run a race,
Buck fall down an' skin his face.
Buck an' Berry in a stall;
Buck, he try to eat it all.

Buck, he e't too much, you see.
So he died wid choleree.

But it is in the dance songs that rhythm in its perfection makes itself felt and that repetends are employed with effects which another Poe or Lanier might appropriate for supreme art. A lively scene and gay frolicsome movements are conjured up by the following dance songs:

## CHICKEN IN THE BREAD TRAY

"Auntie, will yo' dog bite?"—
"No, Chile! No!"
Chicken in de bread tray
A makin' up dough.

"Auntie, will yo' broom hit?"—
"Yes, Chile!" Pop!
Chicken in de bread tray;
"Flop! Flop! Flop!"

"Auntie, will yo' oven bake?"—
"Yes. Jes fry!"—
"What's dat chicken good fer?"—
"Pie! Pie! Pie!"

"Auntie, is yo' pie good?"—
"Good as you could 'spec'."
Chicken in de bread tray;
"Peck! Peck! Peck!"

DANCERS

## JUBA

Juba dis, an' Juba dat,
Juba skin dat Yaller Cat. Juba! Juba!

Juba jump an' Juba sing.
Juba cut dat Pigeon's Wing. Juba! Juba!

Juba, kick off Juba's shoe.
Juba, dance dat Jubal Jew. Juba! Juba!

Juba, whirl dat foot about.
Juba, blow dat candle out. Juba! Juba!

Juba circle, Raise de Latch.
Juba do dat Long Dog Scratch. Juba! Juba!

Out of the pastime group I take a rhyme that is typically full of character, delicious in its wit and proverbial lore:

## FATTENING FROGS FOR SNAKES

You needn' sen' my gal hoss apples,
You needn' sen' her 'lasses candy;
She would keer fer de lak o' you,
Ef you'd sen' her apple brandy.

W'y don't you git some common sense?
Jes git a liddle! Oh fer land sakes!
Quit yo' foolin', she hain't studyin' you!
Youse jes fattenin' frogs fer snakes!

In the love songs one finds that mingling of pathos and humor
so characteristic of the Negro. The one example I shall give lacks
nothing of art—some unknown Dunbar, some black Bobbie
Burns, must have composed it:

## SHE HUGGED ME AND KISSED ME

I see'd her in de Springtime,
I see'd her in de Fall,
I see'd her in de Cotton patch,
A cameing from de Ball.

She hug me, an' she kiss me,
She wrung my han' an' cried.
She said I wus de sweetes' thing
Dat ever lived or died.

She hug me an' she kiss me.
Oh Heaben! De touch o' her han'!
She said I wus de puttiest thing
In de shape o' mortal man.

I told her dat I love her,
Dat my love wus bed-cord strong;
Den I axed her w'en she'd have me,
An' she jes say, "Go long!"

In a very striking way these folk-songs of the plantation suggest the old English folk-songs of unknown authorship and origin— the ancient traditional ballads, long despised and neglected, but ever living on and loved in the hearts of the people. This unstudied poetry of the people, the unlettered common folk, had supreme virtues, the elemental and universal virtues of simplicity, sincerity, veracity. It had the power, in an artificial age, to bring poetry back to reality, to genuine emotion, to effectiveness, to the common interests of mankind. Simple and crude as it was it had a merit unknown to the polished verse of the schools. Potential Negro poets might do well to ponder this fact of literary history. There is nothing more precious in English literature than this crude old poetry of the people.

There is a book of rhymes which, every Christmas season, is the favorite gift, the most gladly received, of all that Santa Claus brings. Nor so at Christmas only; it is a perennial pleasure, a boon to all children, young and old in years. This book is *Mother Goose's Melodies*. How many "immortal" epics of learned poets it has outlived! How many dainty volumes of polished lyrics has this humble book of "rhymes" seen vanish to the dusty realms of dark oblivion! In every home it has a place and is cherished. Its contents are better known and more loved than the contents of any other book. Untutored, nameless poets, nature-inspired, gave this priceless boon to all generations of children, and to all sorts and conditions—an immortal book. As a life-long teacher and student of poetry, I venture, with no fear, the assertion that from no book of verse in our language can the whole art of poetry be so effectively learned as from *Mother Goose's Melodies*. Every device of rhyme, and melody, and rhythm, and tonal color is exemplified here in a manner to produce the effects which all the great artists in verse aim at. This book that we all love—and patronize—is the greatest melodic triumph in the white man's literature.

Of like merit and certainly no less are the folk rhymes and songs, both the Spirituals and the Seculars, of the Negro. Their art potentialities are immense. Well may the aspirant to fame in poetry put these songs in his memory and peruse them as Burns did the old popular songs of Scotland, to make them yield suggestions of songs at the highest reach of art.

## II. THE POETRY OF ART

But another heritage of song, not so crude nor yet so precious as the Spirituals and the Folk Rhymes has the Negro of to-day. That heritage comes from enslaved and emancipated men and women who by some means or another learned to write and publish their compositions. Although the intrinsic value of this heritage of song cannot be rated high, yet, considering the circumstances of its production, the colored people of America may well take pride in it. Its incidental value can hardly be overestimated. In it is the most infallible record we have of the Negro's inner life in bondage and in the years following emancipation. Never broken was the tradition from Jupiter Hammon and Phillis Wheatley, in the last half of the eighteenth century, to Paul Laurence Dunbar and Joseph Seamon Cotter, in the end of the nineteenth, but constantly enriched by an increasing number of men and women who sought in the form of verse a record of their sufferings and yearnings, consolations and hopes.

## 1. *Jupiter Hammon and Phillis Wheatley*

Jupiter Hammon was the first American Negro poet of whom any record exists. His first extant poem, "An Evening Thought," bears the date of 1760, preceding therefore any poem by Phillis Wheatley, his contemporary, by nine years. Following the title of the poem this information is given: "Composed by Jupiter Hammon, a Negro belonging to Mr. Lloyd, of Queen's Village, on Long Island, the 25th of December, 1760." With this poem of eighty-eight rhyming lines, printed on a double-column broadside, entered the American Negro into American literature. For that reason alone, were his stanzas inferior to what they are, I should include some of them in this anthology. But the truth is that, as "religious" poetry goes, or went in the eighteenth century—and Hammon's poetry is all religious—this Negro slave may hold up his head in almost any company.

Nevertheless, the reader must not expect poetry in the typical stanzas I shall quote, but just some remarkable rhyming for an African slave, untaught and without precedent. "An Evening Thought" runs in such stanzas as the following:

> Dear Jesus give thy Spirit now,
> Thy Grace to every Nation,
> That han't the Lord to whom we bow,
> The Author of Salvation.

From "An Address to Miss Phillis Wheatley, Ethiopian Poetess," I take the following as a representative stanza:

While thousands muse with earthly toys,
And range about the street,
Dear Phillis, seek for heaven's joys,
Where we do hope to meet.

"A Poem for Children, with Thoughts on Death," contains such stanzas as this:

'Tis God alone can make you wise,
His wisdom's from above,
He fills the soul with sweet supplies
By his redeeming love.

Two stanzas from "A Dialogue, Entitled, The Kind Master and the Dutiful Servant," will show how that poem runs:

MASTER

Then will the happy day appear,
That virtue shall increase;
Lay up the sword and drop the spear,
And Nations seek for peace.

SERVANT

Then shall we see the happy end,
Tho' still in some distress;
That distant foes shall act like friends,
And leave their wickedness.

Jupiter Hammon's birth and death dates are uncommemo-rated because unknown. Unknown, too, is his grave. But to his memory, no less than to that of Crispus Attucks, there should somewhere be erected a monument.

Since Stedman included in his *Library of American Literature* a picture of Phillis Wheatley and specimens of her verse, a few white persons, less than scholars and more than general readers, knew, when Dunbar appeared, that there had been at least one poetic predecessor in his race. But the long stretch between the slave-girl rhymer of Boston and the elevator-boy singer of Dayton was desert. They knew not of George Moses Horton of North Carolina, who found publication for *Poems by a Slave* in 1829, and *Poetical Works* in 1845. Horton, who learned to write by his own efforts, is said to have been so fond of poetry that he would pick up any chance scraps of paper he saw, hoping to find verses. They knew not of Ann Plato, of Hartford, Connecticut, a slave girl who published a book of twenty poems in 1841; nor of Frances Ellen Watkins (afterwards Harper) whose *Poems on Miscellaneous Subjects* appeared in 1857, reaching a circulation of ten thousand copies; nor of Charles L. Reason, whose poem entitled *Freedom*, published in 1847, voiced the cry of millions of fellow blacks in bonds.

PHILLIS WHEATLEY

## 2. *Charles L. Reason*

Thus bursts forth Reason's poetic cry, not unlike that of the crude Spirituals:

CHARLES L. REASON

O Freedom! Freedom! Oh, how oft
Thy loving children call on Thee!
In wailings loud and breathings soft,
Beseeching God, Thy face to see.

With agonizing hearts we kneel,
While 'round us howls the oppressor's cry,—
And suppliant pray that we may feel
The ennobling glances of Thine eye.

The apostrophe continues through forty-two stanzas, commemorating, with appreciative knowledge of history, the countries, battle fields, and heroes associated with the advance of freedom. After an arraignment of civil rulers and a recreant priesthood, the learned and noble apostrophe thus concludes:

Oh, purify each holy court!
The ministry of law and light!
That man no longer may be bought
To trample down his brother's right.

We lift imploring hands to Thee!
We cry for those in prison bound!
Oh, in Thy strength come! Liberty!
And 'stablish right the wide world round.

We pray to see Thee, face to face:
To feel our souls grow strong and wide:
So ever shall our injured race
By Thy firm principles abide.

## 3. George Moses Horton

By some means or other, self-guided, the North Carolina slave, George Moses Horton, learned to read and write. His first book, *Poems by a Slave*, appeared in 1829, and other books followed until 1865. Like Hammon, and true to his race, Horton is religious, and, like Reason, and again true to his race, he loves freedom. I choose but a few stanzas to illustrate his quality as a poet:

Alas! and am I born for this,
To wear this slavish chain?
Deprived of all created bliss,
Through hardship, toil, and pain?

How long have I in bondage lain,
And languished to be free!

Alas! and must I still complain,
Deprived of liberty?

****

Come, Liberty! thou cheerful sound,
Roll through my ravished ears;
Come, let my grief in joys be drowned,
And drive away my fears.

## 4. *Frances Ellen Watkins Harper*

A female poet of the same period as Horton wrote in the same
strain about freedom:

Make me a grave wher'er you will,
In a lowly plain or a lofty hill;
Make it among earth's humblest graves,
But not in a land where men are slaves.

Like Horton, she lived to see her prayer for freedom answered.
Of the Emancipation Proclamation she burst forth in joy:

It shall flash through coming ages,
It shall light the distant years;
And eyes now dim with sorrow
Shall be brighter through their tears.

This slave woman was Frances Ellen Watkins, by marriage
Harper. Mrs. Harper attained to a greater popularity than any
poet of her race prior to Dunbar. As many as ten thousand copies
of some of her poems were in circulation in the middle of the
last century. Her success was not unmerited. Many singers of no
greater merit have enjoyed greater celebrity. She was thoroughly

in the fashion of her times, as Phillis Wheatley was in the yet prevalent fashion of Pope, or, perhaps more accurately, Cowper. The models in the middle of the nineteenth century were Mrs. Hemans, Whittier, and Longfellow. It is in their manner she writes. A serene and beautiful Christian spirit tells a moral tale in fluent ballad stanzas, not without poetic phrasing. In all she beholds, in all she experiences, there is a lesson. There is no grief without its consolation. Serene resignation breathes through all her poems—at least through those written after her freedom was achieved. Illustrations of these traits abound. A few stanzas from *Go Work in My Vineyard* will suffice. After bitter disappointments in attempting to fulfil the command the "lesson" comes thus sweetly expressed:

F. E. W. HARPER

My hands were weak, but I reached them out
To feebler ones than mine,
And over the shadows of my life
Stole the light of a peace divine.

Oh, then my task was a sacred thing,
How precious it grew in my eyes!
'Twas mine to gather the bruised grain
For the Lord of Paradise.

And when the reapers shall lay their grain
On the floors of golden light,
I feel that mine with its broken sheaves
Shall be precious in His sight.
Though thorns may often pierce my feet,
And the shadows still abide,
The mists will vanish before His smile,
There will be light at eventide.

How successfully Mrs. Harper could draw a lesson from the common objects or occurrences of the world about us may be illustrated by the following poem:

TRUTH

A rock, for ages, stern and high,
Stood frowning 'gainst the earth and sky,
And never bowed his haughty crest
When angry storms around him prest.
Morn, springing from the arms of night,
Had often bathed his brow with light,
And kissed the shadows from his face
With tender love and gentle grace.

Day, pausing at the gates of rest,
Smiled on him from the distant West,
And from her throne the dark-browed Night

Threw round his path her softest light.
And yet he stood unmoved and proud,
Nor love, nor wrath, his spirit bowed;
He bared his brow to every blast
And scorned the tempest as it passed.

One day a tiny, humble seed—
The keenest eye would hardly heed—
Fell trembling at that stern rock's base,
And found a lowly hiding-place.
A ray of light, and drop of dew,
Came with a message, kind and true;
They told her of the world so bright,
Its love, its joy, and rosy light,
And lured her from her hiding-place,
To gaze upon earth's glorious face.

So, peeping timid from the ground,
She clasped the ancient rock around,
And climbing up with childish grace,
She held him with a close embrace;
Her clinging was a thing of dread;
Where'er she touched a fissure spread,
And he who'd breasted many a storm
Stood frowning there, a mangled form.

A Truth, dropped in the silent earth,
May seem a thing of little worth,
Till, spreading round some mighty wrong,
It saps its pillars proud and strong,

And o'er the fallen ruin weaves
The brightest blooms and fairest leaves.

The story of Vashti, who dared heroically to disobey her monarch-husband, is as well told in simple ballad measure as one may find it. I give it entire:

### VASHTI

She leaned her head upon her hand
And heard the King's decree—
"My lords are feasting in my halls;
Bid Vashti come to me.

"I've shown the treasures of my house,
My costly jewels rare,
But with the glory of her eyes
No rubies can compare.

"Adorn'd and crown'd I'd have her come,
With all her queenly grace,
And, 'mid my lords and mighty men,
Unveil her lovely face.

"Each gem that sparkles in my crown,
Or glitters on my throne,
Grows poor and pale when she appears,
My beautiful, my own!"

All waiting stood the chamberlains
To hear the Queen's reply.
They saw her cheek grow deathly pale,
But light flash'd to her eye:

"Go, tell the King," she proudly said,
"That I am Persia's Queen,
And by his crowds of merry men
I never will be seen.

"I'll take the crown from off my head
And tread it 'neath my feet,
Before their rude and careless gaze
My shrinking eyes shall meet.

"A queen unveil'd before the crowd!—
Upon each lip my name!—
Why, Persia's women all would blush
And weep for Vashti's shame!

"Go back!" she cried, and waved her hand,
And grief was in her eye:
"Go, tell the King," she sadly said,
"That I would rather die."

They brought her message to the King;
Dark flash'd his angry eye;
'Twas as the lightning ere the storm
Hath swept in fury by.

Then bitterly outspoke the King,
Through purple lips of wrath—
"What shall be done to her who dares
To cross your monarch's path?"

Then spake his wily counsellors—
"O King of this fair land!
From distant Ind to Ethiop,
All bow to thy command.

"But if, before thy servants' eyes,
This thing they plainly see,
That Vashti doth not heed thy will
Nor yield herself to thee,

"The women, restive 'neath our rule,
Would learn to scorn our name,
And from her deed to us would come
Reproach and burning shame.

"Then, gracious King, sign with thy hand
This stern but just decree,
That Vashti lay aside her crown,
Thy Queen no more to be."

She heard again the King's command,
And left her high estate;
Strong in her earnest womanhood,
She calmly met her fate,

And left the palace of the King,
Proud of her spotless name—
A woman who could bend to grief
But would not bow to shame.

Those last stanzas are quite as noble as any that one may find in the poets whom I named as setting the American fashion in the era of Mrs. Harper. The poems of this gentle, sweet-spirited Negro woman deserve a better fate than has overtaken them.

## 5. James Madison Bell and Albery A. Whitman

Although this is not a history of American Negro poetry, yet a brief notice must be given at this point to two other writers too important to be omitted even from a swift survey like the present one. They are J. Madison Bell and Albery A. Whitman.

JAMES MADISON BELL

Bell, anti-slavery orator and friend of John Brown's, was a prolific writer of eloquent verse. His original endowments were considerable. Denied an education in boyhood, he learned a trade and in manhood at night-schools gained access to the wisdom of books. He became a master of expression both with tongue and pen. His long period of productivity covers the history of his people from the decade before Emancipation till the death of Dunbar. Bell's themes are lofty and he writes with fervid eloquence. There is something of Byronic power in the roll of his verse. An extract from *The Progress of Liberty* will be representative, though an extract cannot show either the maintenance of power or the abundance of resources:

> O Liberty, what charm so great!
> One radiant smile, one look of thine
> Can change the drooping bondsman's fate,
> And light his brow with hope divine.
>
> His manhood, wrapped in rayless gloom,
> At thy approach throws off its pall,
> And rising up, as from the tomb,
> Stands forth defiant of the thrall.
> No tyrant's power can crush the soul
> Illumed by thine inspiring ray;
> The fiendishness of base control
> Flies thy approach as night from day.
>
> Ride onward, in thy chariot ride,
> Thou peerless queen; ride on, ride on—
> With Truth and Justice by thy side—
> From pole to pole, from sun to sun!
> Nor linger in our bleeding South,
> Nor domicile with race or clan;
> But in thy glorious goings forth,
> Be thy benignant object Man—
>
> Of every clime, of every hue,
> Of every tongue, of every race,

'Neath heaven's broad, ethereal blue;
Oh! let thy radiant smiles embrace,
Till neither slave nor one oppressed
Remain throughout creation's span,
By thee unpitied and unblest
Of all the progeny of man.

We fain would have the world aspire
To that proud height of free desire,
That flamed the heart of Switzer's Tell
(Whose archery skill none could excell),
When once upon his Alpine brow,
He stood reclining on his bow,
And saw, careering in his might—
In all his majesty of flight—
A lordly eagle float and swing
Upon his broad, untrammeled wing.

He bent his bow, he poised his dart,
With full intent to pierce the heart;
But as the proud bird nearer drew,
His stalwart arm unsteady grew,
His arrow lingered in the groove—
The cord unwilling seemed to move,
For there he saw personified
That freedom which had been his pride;
And as the eagle onward sped,
O'er lofty hill and towering tree,
He dropped his bow, he bowed his head;
He could not shoot—'twas Liberty!

Whitman, a younger contemporary of Bell's, is the author of

several long tales in verse. Like Bell, he wrote only in standard English, and like him also, shows a mastery of expression, with fluency of style, wealth of imagery, and a command of the forms of verse given vogue by Scott and Byron. Both likewise write fervently of the wrongs suffered by the black man at the hands of the white. Thus far they resemble; but if we extend the comparison we note important differences. Bell has more of the fervor of the orator and the sense of fact of the historian. He adheres closely to events and celebrates occasions. Whitman invents tragic tales of love and romance, clothing them with the charm of the South and infusing into them the pathos which results from the strife of thwarted passions, the defeat of true love.

A stanza or two from Whitman's *An Idyl of the South* will exemplify his qualities. The hero of this pathetic tale is a white youth of aristocratic parentage, the heroine is an octoroon. He is thus described:

> He was of manly beauty—brave and fair;
> There was the Norman iron in his blood,
> There was the Saxon in his sunny hair
> That waved and tossed in an abandoned flood;
> But Norman strength rose in his shoulders
> square,
> And so, as manfully erect he stood,
> Norse gods might read the likeness of their race
> In his proud bearing and patrician face.

The heroine is thus portrayed:

> A lithe and shapely beauty; like a deer,
> She looked in wistfulness, and from you went;
> With silken shyness shrank as if in fear,

And kept the distance of the innocent.
But, when alone, she bolder would appear;
Then all her being into song was sent
To bound in cascades—ripple, whirl, and
gleam,
A headlong torrent in a crystal stream.

Only tragedy, under the conditions, could result from their
mutual fervent love. The poet does not moralize but in a figure
intimates the sadness induced by the tale:

The hedges may obscure the sweetest bloom—
The orphan of the waste—the lowly flower;
While in the garden, faint for want of room,
The splendid failure pines within her bower.
There is a wide republic of perfume,
In which the nameless waifs of sun and shower,
That scatter wildly through the fields and
woods,
Make the divineness of the solitudes.

After such a manner wrote those whom we may call bards of
an elder day.

## 6. Paul Laurence Dunbar

He came, a dark youth, singing in the dawn
Of a new freedom, glowing o'er his lyre,
Refining, as with great Apollo's fire,
His people's gift of song. And, thereupon,
This Negro singer, come to Helicon,
Constrained the masters, listening, to admire,

And roused a race to wonder and aspire,
Gazing which way their honest voice was gone,
With ebon face uplit of glory's crest.
Men marveled at the singer, strong and sweet,
Who brought the cabin's mirth, the tuneful
night,
But faced the morning, beautiful with light,
To die while shadows yet fell toward the west,
And leave his laurels at his people's feet.
—*James David Corrothers.*

Less than a generation ago William Dean Howells hailed Paul Laurence Dunbar as "the first instance of an American Negro who had evinced innate distinction in literature," "the only man of pure African blood and of American civilization to feel Negro life æsthetically and express it lyrically." It is not my purpose to give Dunbar space and consideration in this book commensurate with his importance. Its scope does not, strictly speaking, include him and his predecessors. They are introduced here, but to provide an historical background. The object of this book is to exhibit the achievement of the Negro in verse since Dunbar. Even though it were true, which I think it is not, that no American Negro previous to Dunbar had evinced innate distinction in literature, this anthology, I believe, will reveal that many American Negroes in this new day are evincing, if not innate distinction, yet cultured talent, in literature.

The sonnet to Dunbar which stands at the head of this section was composed by a Negro who was by three years Dunbar's senior. His opportunities in early life were far inferior to Dunbar's. At nineteen years of age, with almost inconsiderable schooling, he was a boot-black in a Chicago barber shop. I give his sonnet here—other poems of his I give in another chapter—in evidence of that distinction in literature, innate or otherwise, which is rather widespread among American Negroes of the present time. Dunbar himself might have been proud to put his name to this sonnet.

PAUL LAURENCE DUNBAR

When this marvel, a Negro poet, so vouched for, appeared in the West, like a new star in the heavens, a few white people, a very few, knew, vaguely, that back in Colonial times there was a slave woman in Boston who had written verses, who was therefore a prodigy. The space between Phillis Wheatley and this new singer was desert. But Nature, as people think, produces freaks, or sports; therefore a Negro poet was not absolutely beyond belief, since poets are rather freakish, abnormal creatures anyway. Incredulity therefore yielded to an attitude scarcely worthier, namely, that dishonoring, irreverent interpretation of a supreme human phenomenon which consists in denominating it a freak of nature.

But Dunbar is a fact, as Burns, as Whittier, as Riley, are facts—a fact of great moment to a people and for a people. For one thing, he revealed to the Negro youth of America the latent literary powers and the unexploited literary materials of their race. He was the fecundating genius of their talents. Upon all his people he was a tremendously quickening power, not less so than his great contemporary at Tuskegee. Doubtless it will be recognized, in a broad view, that the Negro people of America needed, equally, both men, the counterparts of each other.

It needs to be remarked for white people, that there were two Dunbars, and that they know but one. There is the Dunbar of "the jingle in a broken tongue," whom Howells with gracious but imperfect sympathy and understanding brought to the knowledge of the world, and whom the public readers, white and black alike, have found it delightful to present, to the entire eclipse of the other Dunbar. That other Dunbar was the poet of the flaming "Ode to Ethiopia," the pathetic lyric, "We Wear the Mask," the apparently offhand jingle but real masterpiece entitled "Life," the incomparable ode "Ere sleep comes down to soothe the weary eyes," and a score of other pieces in which, using their speech, he matches himself with the poets who shine as stars in the firmament of our admiration. This Dunbar Howells failed to appreciate, and ignorance of him has been fostered, as I have intimated, by professional readers and writers. The first Dunbar, the generally accepted one, was, as Howells pointed out, the artistic interpreter of the old-fashioned, vanishing generation of black folk—the generation that was maimed and scarred by slavery, that presented so many ludicrous and pathetic, abject and lovable aspects in strange mixture. The second Dunbar was the prophet robed in a mantle of austerity, shod with fire, bowed with sorrow, as every true prophet has been, in whatever time, among whatever people.

He was the prophet, I say, of a new generation, a coming generation, as he was the poet of a vanishing generation. The generation of which he was the prophet-herald has arrived. Its most authentic representatives are the poets that I put forward in this volume as worthy of attention.

Dunbar's real significance to his race has been admirably expressed not only by Corrothers but in the following lines by his biographer, Lida Keck Wiggins:

> Life's lowly were laureled with verses
> And sceptered were honor and worth,
> While cabins became, through the poet,
> Fair homes of the lords of the earth.

So it was. But "honor and worth" yet remain, to be "sceptered." Such poems as these few here given from the choragus of the present generation of Negro singers will suggest the kind of honor and the degree of worth to which our tribute is due.[2]

## ERE SLEEP COMES DOWN TO SOOTHE THE WEARY EYES

> Ere sleep comes down to soothe the weary eyes,
> Which all the day with ceaseless care have
> sought
> The magic gold which from the seeker flies;
> Ere dreams put on the gown and cap of
> thought,
> And make the waking world a world of lies,—
> Of lies most palpable, uncouth, forlorn,
> That say life's full of aches and tears and
> sighs,—
> Oh, how with more than dreams the soul is
> torn,

Ere sleep comes down to soothe the weary eyes.
Ere sleep comes down to soothe the weary eyes,
How all the griefs and heartaches we have
known
Come up like pois'nous vapors that arise
From some base witch's caldron, when the
crone,
To work some potent spell, her magic plies.
The past which held its share of bitter pain,
Whose ghost we prayed that Time might
exorcise,
Comes up, is lived and suffered o'er again,
Ere sleep comes down to soothe the weary eyes.

Ere sleep comes down to soothe the weary eyes,
What phantoms fill the dimly lighted room;
What ghostly shades in awe-creating guise
Are bodied forth within the teeming gloom.
What echoes faint of sad and soul-sick cries,
And pangs of vague inexplicable pain
That pay the spirit's ceaseless enterprise,
Come thronging through the chambers of the
brain,
Ere sleep comes down to soothe the weary eyes.

Ere sleep comes down to soothe the weary eyes,
Where ranges forth the spirit far and free?
Through what strange realms and unfamiliar
skies
Tends her far course to lands of mystery?
To lands unspeakable—beyond surmise,

Where shapes unknowable to being spring,
Till, faint of wing, the Fancy fails and dies
Much wearied with the spirit's journeying,
Ere sleep comes down to soothe the weary eyes.

Ere sleep comes down to soothe the weary eyes,
How questioneth the soul that other soul,—
The inner sense which neither cheats nor lies,
But self exposes unto self, a scroll
Full writ with all life's acts unwise or wise,
In characters indelible and known;
So, trembling with the shock of sad surprise,
The soul doth view its awful self alone,
Ere sleep comes down to soothe the weary eyes.

Ere sleep comes down to seal the weary eyes,
The last dear sleep whose soft embrace is balm,
And whom sad sorrow teaches us to prize
For kissing all our passions into calm,
Ah, then, no more we heed the sad world's
cries,
Or seek to probe th' eternal mystery,
Or fret our souls at long-withheld replies,
At glooms through which our visions cannot
see,
Ere sleep comes down to seal the weary eyes.

## LIFE

A crust of bread and a corner to sleep in,
A minute to smile and an hour to weep in,
A pint of joy to a peck of trouble,

And never a laugh but the moans come double;
And that is life!

A crust and a corner that love makes precious,
With the smile to warm and the tears to refresh
us;
And joy seems sweeter when cares come after,
And a moan is the finest of foils for laughter:
And that is life!

****

O Mother Race! to thee I bring
This pledge of faith unwavering,
This tribute to thy glory.
I know the pangs which thou didst feel,
When Slavery crushed thee with its heel,
With thy dear blood all gory.

Sad days were those—ah, sad indeed!
But through the land the fruitful seed
Of better times was growing.
The plant of freedom upward sprung,
And spread its leaves so fresh and young—
Its blossoms now are blowing.

On every hand in this fair land,
Proud Ethiope's swarthy children stand
Beside their fairer neighbor;
The forests flee before their stroke,
Their hammers ring, their forges smoke,—
They stir in honest labor.

They tread the fields where honor calls;
Their voices sound through senate halls
In majesty and power.
To right they cling; the hymns they sing
Up to the skies in beauty ring,
And bolder grow each hour.

Be proud, my Race, in mind and soul
Thy name is writ on Glory's scroll
In characters of fire.
High 'mid the clouds of Fame's bright sky
Thy banner's blazoned folds now fly,
And truth shall lift them higher.

ETHIOPIA—AWAKENING
*BY META WARRICK FULLER*

Thou hast the right to noble pride,
Whose spotless robes were purified
By blood's severe baptism,
Upon thy brow the cross was laid,
And labor's painful sweat-beads made
A consecrating chrism.

No other race, or white or black,
When bound as thou wert, to the rack,
So seldom stooped to grieving;
No other race, when free again,
Forgot the past and proved them men
So noble in forgiving.

Go on and up! Our souls and eyes
Shall follow thy continuous rise;
Our ears shall list thy story
From bards who from thy root shall spring,
And proudly tune their lyres to sing
Of Ethiopia's glory.

## WITH THE LARK

Night is for sorrow and dawn is for joy,
Chasing the troubles that fret and annoy;
Darkness for sighing and daylight for song,—
Cheery and chaste the strain, heartfelt and
strong,
All the night through, though I moan in the
dark,
I wake in the morning to sing with the lark.

Deep in the midnight the rain whips the leaves,
Softly and sadly the wood-spirit grieves.
But when the first hue of dawn tints the sky,
I shall shake out my wings like the birds and be
dry;
And though, like the rain-drops, I grieved
through the dark,
I shall wake in the morning
to sing with the lark.

On the high hills of heaven, some morning to
be,
Where the rain shall not grieve thro' the leaves
of the tree,
There my heart will be glad for the pain I have
known,
For my hand will be clasped in the hand of
mine own;
And though life has been hard and death's
pathway been dark,
I shall wake in the morning
to sing with the lark.

WE WEAR THE MASK

We wear the mask that grins and lies,
It hides our cheeks and shades our eyes,—
This debt we pay to human guile;
With torn and bleeding hearts we smile,
And mouth with myriad subtleties.

Why should the world be over-wise,
In counting all our tears and sighs?
Nay, let them only see us, while
We wear the mask.

We smile, but, O great Christ, our cries
To thee from tortured souls arise.
We sing, but oh, the clay is vile
Beneath our feet, and long the mile;
But let the world dream otherwise,
We wear the mask!

## 7. J. Mord Allen

In the year of Dunbar's death (1906), J. Mord Allen published his *Rhymes, Tales, and Rhymed Tales*. The contents are mainly in dialect, dialect that possesses, as it seems to me, every merit of that medium. There is great felicity of characterization, surprising turns of wit, quaint philosophy. In a later chapter I will give a specimen of Mr. Allen's dialect verse, here two standard English poems. In both mediums his credentials are authentic, no whit less so than even Dunbar's. Only the question arises why his muse became silent after this one utterance—for he was at the time but thirty-one years old. Perhaps poetry did not go with boiler-making, his occupation. Because of the date of his one book I place him here with Dunbar, and there are yet other reasons.

Mr. Allen affords but two standard English poems, the first and the last of his book. Such a fact marks him as of the elder day, though that day be less than a score of years agone. The concluding poem of his book has a sweet sadness that must appeal to every heart whose childhood is getting to be far away:

## COUNTING OUT

"Eeny meeny miny mo."
Ah, how the sad-sweet Long Ago
Enyouths us, as by magic spell,
With that old rhyme. You know it well;
For time was, once, when e'en your eyes
Saw Heaven plainly, in the skies.
Past twilight, when a brave moon glowed
Just o'er the treetops, and the road
Was full of romping children—say,
What was the game we used to play?
Yes! Hide-and-seek. And at the base,
Who first must go and hide his face?
Remember—standing in a row—
"Eeny meeny miny mo"?

"Eeny meeny miny mo."
How fare we children here below?
Our moon is far from treetops now,
And Heaven isn't up, somehow.
No more for sport play we "I spy";
Our "laying low" and "peeping high".
Are now with consequences fraught;
There's black disgrace in being caught.
But what's to pay the pains we take?
Let's play the game for its own sake,
And, ere 'tis time to homeward flit,
Let's get some pleasure out of it.

For death will soon count down the row,
"Eeny meeny miny mo."

Though of the elder day yet Allen is, like Dunbar, a herald of the generation that is now articulate. In this rôle of herald to a more self-assertive generation, a more aspiring and race-conscious one, he speaks with immense significance to us in this first poem of his book, which, as being prophetic of much we now see in the colored folk of America I permit to close this summary review of earlier Negro poetry:

## THE PSALM OF THE UPLIFT

Still comes the Perfect Thing to man
As came the olden gods, in dreams;
And then the man—made artist—knows
How real is the thing which seems.
Then, tongue or brush or magic pen
May win the world to loud acclaim,
But he who wrought knows in his soul
That, like as tinsel is to gold,
His work is, to his aim.

It's there ahead to him—and you
And me. I swear it isn't far;
Else, black Despair would cut us down
In the land of hateful Things Which Are.
But, just beyond our finger-tips,
Things As They Should Be shame the weak,
And hold the aching muscles tense
Through th' next moment of suspense
Which triumph is to break.

And shall we strive? The years to come,
Till sunset of eternity,
Are given to the fairest god,
The God of Things As They Should Be.
The ending? Nay, 'tis ours to do
And dare and bear and not to flinch;
To enter where is no retreat;
To win one stride from sheer defeat;
To die—but gain an inch.

# CHAPTER II
# THE PRESENT RENAISSANCE OF THE NEGRO

## I. A Glance at the Field

MANY are the forms of expression that the life of a developing people or group finds for itself—business and wealth, education and culture, political and social unrest and agitation, literature and art. It can scarcely happen that any people or group has a vital significance for other peoples or groups, or any real potency, until it begins to express itself in poetry. When, however, a race or a portion of our common race begins to embody its aspirations, its grievances, its animating spirit in song the world may well take notice. That race or portion of our common race has within it an unreckoned potency of good and evil—evil if the good be thwarted.

It is not, then, to editorials and speeches and sermons, nor to petitions, protests, and resolutions, but to poems that the wise will turn in order to learn the temper and permanent bent of mind of a people. Witness the recent history of Ireland. Her literary renascence preceded her effective political agitation. The political agitation which resulted in her independence was the work of poets. The real life of a people finds its only adequate record in song. All of a people's history that is permanently or profoundly significant is distilled into poetry.

It is to the unknown poetry of a despised and rejected people that I call attention in these pages. One of this people's poets sings:

> We have fashioned laughter
> Out of tears and pain,
> But the moment after—
> Pain and tears again.
> *Charles Bertram Johnson.*

And when he so sings we know there is one race above all others which these words describe. Another sings:

> I will suppose that fate is just,
> I will suppose that grief is wise,
> And I will tread what path I must
> To enter Paradise.
> *Joseph S. Cotter, Sr.*

And when he so sings we know out of what tribulations his resignation has been born. The resolution of despair cries out in the lines of another:

> My life were lost if I should keep
> A hope-forlorn and gloomy face,
> And brood upon my ills, and weep,
> And mourn the travail of my race.
> *Leslie Pinckney Hill.*

Another singer, coming out of the Black Belt of the lower South, records the daily and life-long history of his people in these lines:

### IT'S ALL THROUGH LIFE

A day of joy, a week of pain,
A sunny day, a week of rain;
A day of peace, a year of strife;
But cling to Him, it's all through life.

An hour of joy, a day of fears,
An hour of smiles, a day of tears;
An hour of gain, a day of strife,
Press on, press on, it's all through life.
*Waverley Turner Carmichael.*

In the poetry which the Negro is producing to-day there is a challenge to the world. His race has been deeply stirred by recent events; its reaction has been mighty. The challenge, spoken by one, but for the race, the inarticulate millions as well as the cultured few, comes thus:

### TO AMERICA

How would you have us—as we are,
Or sinking 'neath the load we bear?
Our eyes fixed forward on a star?
Or gazing empty at despair?
Rising or falling? Men or things?

With dragging pace, or footsteps fleet?
Strong, willing sinews in your wings?
Or tightening chains about your feet?
*James Weldon Johnson.*

With slight regard for smooth words another declares his grievances, that all may understand:

Yes, I am lynched. Is it that I
Must without judge or jury die?
Though innocent, am I accursed
To quench the mob's blood-thirsty thirst?
Yes, I am mocked. Pray tell me why!
Did not my brothers freely die
For you, and your Democracy—
That each and all alike be free?
*Raymond Garfield Dandridge.*

So runs the dominant note of this poetry. But it would be unjust to the race producing it to convey the idea that this is the only note. The harp of Ethiopia has many strings and the brothers of Memnon are many. Sometimes the note is one of simple beauty, like that of a wild rose blossoming by the wayside. No reader could tell what race produced such a lyric as the one following, but any reader responsive to the beauty of art and to the truth of passion would assert its excellence:

I will hide my soul and its mighty love
In the bosom of this rose,
And its dispensing breath will take
My love wherever it goes.
And perhaps she'll pluck this very rose,

And, quick as blushes start,
Will breathe my hidden secret in
Her unsuspecting heart.
*George Marion McClellan.*

In a Negro magazine one may chance upon a sonnet that the best poet of our times might have signed and feared no loss to his reputation, nor would there be any mark of race in its lines. To candid judgment I submit the following, from Mrs. Alice Dunbar-Nelson:

### VIOLETS

I had not thought of violets of late,
The wild, shy kind that spring beneath your feet
In wistful April days, when lovers mate
And wander through the fields in raptures
sweet.
The thoughts of violets meant florists' shops,
And bows and pins, and perfumed papers fine;
And garish lights, and mincing little fops,
And cabarets and songs, and deadening wine.
So far from sweet real things my thoughts had
strayed,
I had forgot wide fields and clear brown
streams;
The perfect loveliness that God has made—
Wild violets shy and Heaven-mounting dreams
And now unwittingly, you've made me dream
Of violets, and my soul's forgotten gleam.

It needs not that a poet write an epic to prove himself chosen of the muse. The winds of time may blow into oblivion all but five lines of an *opus magnum,* in which five lines alone was the laborious author a poet. Wise is the poet who writes but the five lines, as here:

### SUNSET

Since Poets have told of sunset,
What is left for me to tell?
I can only say that I saw the day
Press crimson lips to the horizon gray,
And kiss the earth farewell.
*Mary Effie Lee.*

The theme may be as old as man and as common as humanity yet it can be made to be felt as poetic by one who has the magic gift, as here:

### LONELINESS

I cannot make my thoughts stay home;
I cannot close their door;
And, oh, that I might shut them in,
And they go out no more!

For they go out, with wistful eyes,
And search the whole world through;
Just hoping, in their wandering,
To catch a glimpse of you!
*Winifred Virginia Jordan.*

One's find may be in *The Poet's Ingle* of a newspaper, where an unknown name is attached to verses that have the charm which Longfellow found in the simple and heartfelt lays of the humbler poet. From such a poem, entitled *To My Grandmother,* by Mae

Smith Johnson, I take two stanzas, the first two as beautiful as the theme evoked:

> You 'mind me of the winter's eve
> When low the sinking sun
> Casts soft bright rays upon the snow
> And day, now almost done,
> In silence deep prepares to leave,
> And calmly waits the signal "Go."
>
> Your eyes are faded vestal lights
> That once the hearth illumed,
> Where vestal virgins vigil kept,
> And budding virtue bloomed:
> Like stars that beam on summer nights,
> Your eyes, by joy and sorrow swept.

Less beautiful, less original, but in another way not less appealing, are these stanzas, also signed by an unknown name and taken from the Christmas number of a newspaper. They are the last stanzas but one of a poem entitled *The Child Is Found*, by Charles H. Este:

> O hearts that mourn and sorrow so,
> That doubt the power of God,
> An angel now is bending low—
> To comfort as you plod.
>
> He speaks with tones of whispering love,
> With feelings true and strong,
> And sings of sweetest joys above,
> For souls without a song.

Pride of race, no less than grief for wrongs endured, is one of the notes of this living verse. Eulogies of the men and women who have lived heroically for their people, giving vision, quickening aspiration, opening roads of advance, find a place in every volume of verse and in the pages of newspapers. Few white persons perhaps have paused to reflect how noteworthy this traditionary store of heroic names really is and how potent it is with the people inheriting it. Both practical and poetic uses—if these two things are different—it has. One cannot foretell to what reflections upon life the eulogist will be led ere he concludes. From an ode to Booker T. Washington, by Roscoe Riley Dungee, I take a stanza, by way of illustration:

> Yet, virtue walks a path obscure,
> And honor struggles to endure,
> While arrogance and deeds impure
> Adorn the Hall of Fame.
> Still, power triumphs over right,
> And wrong is victor in the fight;
> Greed, graft, and knavery excite
> Vociferous acclaim.

It has become evident to those who have seriously studied the present-day life of the Negroes that there has been in these recent years a renascence of the Negro soul. Poetry, as these pages will show, is one of its modes of expression. Other expressions there are, very significant ones, too, expressions which are material, tangible, expressible in figures. Not of this kind is poetry. Yet of all forms whereby the soul of a people expresses itself the most potent, the most effective, is poetry. The re-born soul of the Negro is following the tradition of all races in all times by pouring itself into that form of words which embodies the most of passionate thought and feeling.

Out of the very heart of a race of twelve million people amongst us comes this cry which a Negro poet of Virginia utters as

## A PRAYER OF THE RACE THAT GOD MADE BLACK

> We would be peaceful, Father—but, when we
> must,
> Help us to thunder hard the blow that's just!
>
> We would be prayerful: Lord, when we have
> prayed,
> Let us arise courageous—unafraid!
>
> We would be manly—proving well our worth,
> Then would not cringe to any god on earth!
>
> We would be loving and forgiving, thus
> To love our neighbor as Thou lovest us!
>
> We would be faithful, loyal to the Right—
> Ne'er doubting that the Day will follow Night!
>
> We would be all that Thou hast meant for man,
> Up through the ages, since the world began!
>
> God! save us in Thy Heaven, where all is well!
> We come slow-struggling up the Hills of Hell!
> *Lucian B. Watkins.*

Too confidently, as we may learn, have we of the other race

relied upon the Negro's innate optimism to keep him a safe citizen and a long-suffering servant. That optimism, that gaiety and buoyancy of spirit, if not indestructible in the African soul, is yet reducible to the vanishing point. There are signs of something quite different in the attitude of Negroes toward their white neighbors to-day. In their poetry this reputed optimism, where it exists, is found in union with a note of melancholy or of bitter complaint. A characteristic utterance of this mood I find in a poem entitled "The Optimist," from which I will give one-third of its stanzas:

> Never mind, children, be patient awhile,
> And carry your load with a nod and a smile,
> For out of the hell and the hard of it all,
> Time is sure to bring sweetest honey—not gall.
> Out of the hell and the hard of it all,
> A bright star shall rise that never shall fall:
> A God-fearing race—proud, noble, and true,
> Giving good for the evil which
> they always knew.
>
> ****
>
> So dry your wet pillow and lift your bowed head
> And show to the world that hope is not dead!
> Be patient! Wait! See what yet may befall,
> Out of the hell and the hard of it all.
> *Ethyl Lewis.*

But in dark days the Negro has ever had refuges and sources of strength for the want of which other races have been crushed. One of these refuges for them is the benignant breast of nature—

the deep peace of the woods and the hills, the quiet soothing of pleasant-running water, the benediction of bright skies. A rarely-gifted woman, Mrs. Georgia Douglas Johnson, singing her own consolation, with a pathos that pierces the heart, has sung for thousands of the women of her race else dumb alike in grief and in joy, and in mingled grief and joy:

## PEACE

I rest me deep within the wood,
Drawn by its silent call;
Far from the throbbing crowd of men
On nature's breast I fall.

My couch is sweet with blossoms fair,
A bed of fragrant dreams,
And soft upon my ear there falls
The lullaby of streams.

The tumult of my heart is stilled,
Within this sheltered spot,
Deep in the bosom of the wood,
Forgetting, and—forgot!

Death and the mysteries of life, the pain and the grief that flesh and soul are heirs to, the eternal problems that address themselves to all generations and races, produce in the soul of the Negro the same reactions as of old they produced in the soul of David or of Homer, or as, in our own day, in the soul of a Wordsworth or a Shelley. Of this we have a glimpse in the following lyric, from Walter Everette Hawkins:

## IN SPITE OF DEATH

Curses come in every sound,
And wars spread gloom and woe around.
The cannon belch forth death and doom,
But still the lilies wave and bloom.
Man fills the earth with grief and wrong,
But cannot hush the bluebird's song.
My stars are dancing on the sea,
The waves fling kisses up at me.
Each night my gladsome moon doth rise;
A rainbow spans my evening skies;
The robin's song is full and fine;
And roses lift their lips to mine.

The jonquils ope their petals sweet,
The poppies dance around my feet;
In spite of winter and of death,
The Spring is in the zephyr's breath.

This poetry but re-affirms the essential identity of human nature under black and white skins. But it will remind most of the white race of how ignorant they have been of that black race next door that is acquiring wealth and culture and is expressing in art and literature the spirit of an aspiring people—how ignorant of their real life, their very thoughts, their completely human joys and griefs. One of their poets was cognizant of this unhappy ignorance—the source of so much harshness of treatment—when he wrote:

My people laugh and sing
And dance to death—
None imagining
The heartbreak under breath.
                    *Charles Bertram Johnson.*

Nothing weighs more heavily upon the soul of this race to-day than this everywhere self-betraying crass ignorance, made the more grievous to endure by the vain boast accompanying it, that "I know the Negro better than he knows himself." This poetry in every line of it is a convincing contradiction of this insulting arrogancy. Essential identity, that is the message of these poets.

This kinship of souls and essential oneness of human nature, which Shylock, speaking for a similarly oppressed and outrageously treated people, pressed home upon the Christian merchants of Venice, finds typical expression in the following lines:

We travel a common road, Brother,—
We walk and we talk much the same;
We breathe the same sweet air of heaven—
Strive alike for fortune and fame;
We laugh when our hearts fill with gladness,
We weep when we're smothered in woe;
We strive, we endure, we seek wisdom;
We sin—and we reap what we sow.
Yes, all who would know it can see that
When everything's put to the test,
In spite of our color and features,
The Negro's the same as the rest.
                    *Leon R. Harris.*

It is to be expected that, notwithstanding the Anglo-Saxon

culture of the producers of this poetry, the white reader will yet demand therein what he regards as the African traits. Perhaps it will be crude, artless, repetitive songs like the Spirituals. The quality of the Spirituals is indeed not wanting in some of the most noteworthy contemporary Negro verse. From Fenton Johnson's three volumes of verse I could select many pieces that exhibit this quality united with disciplined art. For example, here is one:

## I PLAYED ON DAVID'S HARP
### (A Negro Spiritual)

Last night I played on David's harp,
I played on little David's harp
The gospel tunes of Israel;
And all the angels came to hear
Me play those gospel tunes,
As the Jordan rolled away.

The angels shouted all the night
Their "Glory, Hallelujah" shout;
Old Gabriel threw his trumpet down
To hear the songs of Israel,
On mighty David's harp,
As the Jordan rolled away.

When death has closed my weary eyes
I'll play again on David's harp
The last great song in life's brief book;
And all you children born of God
Can stop awhile and hear me play,
As the Jordan rolls away.

No less certain it is that many a reader will demand something more crude, more obscure, more mystical. Something, perhaps, at once ridiculous and wise—with big and strangely compounded words, ludicrously applied, yet striving at the expression of some peculiarly African idea. Of such verse I can produce no example. The nearest I can come to meeting such impossible demand is by submitting the following from William Edgar Bailey:

### THE SLUMP

Mr. Self at the bat!
Well, we're all at the bat—
For one thing or other,
For this or for that.
The ball may be hurled, in the form of this plea:
"Will you please help the poor?
God, have mercy on me!"
Mr. Self stops to think;
But the ball cuts the plate—
He's aware that he slumped,
Grasps the bat,—but too late.
What you say, Mr. Ump?
Can it be? Yes, 'tis done!
"Well, I've said what I've said!"

Mr. Self,
Strike One!

Mr. Self's face is grim.
'Tis the critical test—
For his heart, conscience-sick,
Heaves stern at his breast.

The Truth must be hurled, 'tis the law of the
game;
If in life or in death,
If in falsehood or shame.
Mr. Self, strike the ball—
There's a Tramp at your Gate!
Mr. Self still amazed—
And the ball cuts the plate.
Mr. Self murmured not;
The decision he knew,
"Well, you've done that before."

Sighed the Ump.
Strike Two!

There's the Beggar and Gate—
But his silver and gold,
Is amix with his blood;
A part of his soul.
The Nazarene stooped—as all Umpires will do,
With His eye on a line,
That his verdict be true—
Just a shift of the Truth,
Stern, the Nazarene tried,
But he tho't of the Cross,
And the blood from His side.
"Your decision is false;
Oh, have mercy on me."
But a voice from the sky,

Whispered low.
Strike three.

Of humorous verse there is very little produced by the Negro writers of these times. They take their vocation seriously. When their singing robes are on it is to the plaintive notes of the flute or the dolorous blasts of the trumpet they tune their songs.

These voices, and others like them, have but lately been lifted in song, they are still youthful voices, and they are but preluding the more perfect songs they are yet to sing. One voice that is now still, silenced lately in death, at the age of twenty-three years, has sung for them all what all feel:

THE MULATTO TO HIS CRITICS

Ashamed of my race?
And of what race am I?
I am many in one.
Through my veins there flows the blood
Of Red Man, Black Man, Briton, Celt, and
Scot,
In warring clash and tumultuous riot.
I welcome all,
But love the blood of the kindly race
That swarths my skin, crinkles my hair,
And puts sweet music into my soul.
*Joseph S. Cotter, Jr.*

"Sweet music in the soul"—that is heaven's kind gift to this people, music of sorrow and of faith; music, low and plaintive, of hope almost failing; music, clear and strong, born of vision triumphant; music, alas, sometimes marred by the strident notes of hatred and revenge. Verily, poets learn in suffering what they teach in song.

In concluding this preliminary survey it should be reiterated that, if one meets here but with the rhythms and forms, as he may think, which are familiar to him in the poetry of the white race, he should reflect that only in that poetry has the Negro had an opportunity to be educated. He has been educated away from his own heritage and his own endowments. The Negro's native wisdom should lead him back to his natural founts of song. Our educational system should allow of and provide for this. His own literature in his schools is a reasonable policy for the Negro.

As regards the essential significance of this poetry, one of its makers, Miss Eva A. Jessye, has said in a beautiful way almost what I wish to say. Her poem shall therefore conclude this presentation:

### THE SINGER

Because his speech was blunt and manner plain
Untaught in subtle phrases of the wise,
Because the years of slavery and pain
Ne'er dimmed the light of faith within his eyes;
Because of ebon skin and humble pride,
The world with hatred thrust the youth aside.

But fragrance wafts from every trodden flower,
And through our grief we rise to nobler things,
Within the heart in sorrow's darkest hour
A well of sweetness there unbidden springs;
Despised of men, discarded and alone—
The world of nature claimed him as her own.

She taught him truths that liberate the soul
From bonds more galling than the slaver's
chain—
That manly natures, lily-wise, unfold
Amid the mire of hatred void of stain;
Thus in his manhood, clean, superbly strong,
To him was born the priceless gift of song.

The glory of the sun, the hush of morn,
Whisperings of tree-top faintly stirred,
The desert silence, wilderness forlorn,
Far ocean depths, the tender lilt of bird;
Of hope, despair, he sang, his melody
The endless theme of life's brief symphony.

And nations marveled at the minstrel lad,
Who swayed emotions as his fancy led;
With him they wept, were melancholy, sad;
"'Tis but a cunning jest of Fate," they said;
They did not dream in selfish sphere apart
That song is but the essence of the heart.

II. Representatives of the Present Era

# I. THE COTTERS, FATHER AND SON

## *The Father*

On the Kentucky plantation where Stephen Collins Foster one June morning, when the mocking birds were singing and "the darkies were gay," composed and his sister sang, "My Old Kentucky Home," there was among those first delighted listeners who paused in their tasks to hear the immortal song at its birth a slave girl in whose soul were strange melodies of her own. Born of free people of color, she was bonded to the owner of this plantation, yet her soul was such as must be free. Faithful in her work, respectful and obedient, she was yet a dangerous character among slaves, being too spirited. Hence her master ordered her to leave, fearing she would demoralize discipline in the quarters. She demanded to be taken away as she had been brought—in a wagon; and it was so done. It seems that one-half of her blood was African and the other half was divided between Indian and English, though it is impossible to be sure of the exact proportion. An account of her in those days by one who knew her reveals her as one of nature's poets—a Phillis Wheatley of the wash-tubs. "She was very fervent in her religious devotions"—so runs this account—"and a very hard worker. She would sometimes wash nearly all night and then have periods of prayer and exaltation. Then again during the day she would draw from her bosom a favorite book and pause to read over the wash-tub. She had a strong dramatic instinct and would frequently make up little plays of her own and represent each character vividly." Of such mothers are seers and poets born. And so in this instance it proved to be.

At the age of twenty, while yet a slave, she was married, under the common law—though marriage it was not called—to a Scotch-

Irishman, a prominent citizen of Louisville, her employer at the time, who was distinguished by a notably handsome physique and a great fondness for books. Of this union was born, at Bardstown, a son, Joseph, so named for the dreamer of biblical story.

JOSEPH S. COTTER, SR.

The vision-seeing slave mother, her mind running on the bondage of her people, named her son Joseph in the hope of his becoming great in the service of his people, like the Hebrew Joseph. She lived to see her hope fulfilled. The boy's earliest education was in song and story invented and sung or told by his mother. He got a few terms of school, reaching the third grade. At ten years of age he went to work in a brickyard of Louisville to help support his mother. Even there the faculty that afterwards distinguished him appears in action, to his relief in time of trouble. Bigger boys, white and black, working in the same yard, hazed and harried him. Fighting to victory was out of the question, against such odds. Brains won where brawn was wanting. He observed that the men at their noon rest-hour, the time of his distress, told stories and laughed. He couldn't join them, but he tried story-telling in the boy group. It worked. The men, hearing the laughter, came over and joined them. The persecuted boy became the entertainer of both groups. He had won mastery by wit, the proudest mastery in the world.

Then, until he was twenty-two years of age, he was a teamster on the levee. At this time the desire for an education mastered him and he entered a night school—the primary grade. Hard toil and the struggle to get on had not killed his soul but had wiped out his acquisitions of book-knowledge. In two terms he was qualified to teach. He is now the principal of the Samuel Coleridge-Taylor High School in Louisville, the author of several books, a maker of songs and teller of stories, and a man upright in conduct and wise in counsel.

It was at Bardstown, February 2, 1861, that Joseph Seamon Cotter was born. Let Bardstown be put on the literary map of America, not because Stephen Collins Foster wrote "My Old Kentucky Home" there, but because one was born there the latchet of whose poetic shoes he was not worthy to unloose. "A poet, a bard, to be born in Bardstown—how odd, and how appropriate!" one exclaims. And *bard* seems exactly the right appellation for this song-maker and story-man. But it is not altogether so. In character bardlike, but not in appearance. Bards have long, unkempt, white hair, which mingles with beards that rest on their bosoms. Cotter's square-cut chin is clean-shaven, and his large brain-dome shows like a harvest moon. But he makes poems and invents and discovers stories, and, bard-like, recites or relates them to whatever audience may call for them—in schools, in churches, at firesides. Minus the hairy habiliments he is a bard.

Some of Cotter's stories come out of Africa and are "different," as the word goes. Some are "current among the colored folks of Louisville." These, too, are different. Some are tragedies and some are comedies and some are tragi-comedies of everyday life among the Negroes. I will give one entire tale here, selecting this particular one because of its brevity, not its pre-eminence:

## THE BOY AND THE IDEAL

Once upon a time a Mule, a Hog, a Snake, and a Boy met. Said the Mule: "I eat and labor that I may grow strong in the heels. It is fine to have heels so gifted. My heels make people cultivate distance."

Said the Hog: "I eat and labor that I may grow strong in the snout. It is fine to have a fine snout. I keep people watching for my snout."

"No exchanging heels for snouts," broke in the Mule.

"No," answered the Hog; "snouts are naturally above heels."

Said the Snake: "I eat to live, and live to cultivate my sting. The way people shun me shows my greatness. Beget stings, comrades, and stings will beget glory."

Said the Boy: "There is a star in my life like unto a star in the sky. I eat and labor that I may think aright and feel aright. These rounds will conduct me to my star. Oh, inviting star!"

"I am not so certain of that," said the Mule. "I have noticed your kind and ever see some of myself in them. Your star is in the distance."

The Boy answered by smelling a flower and listening to the song of a bird. The Mule looked at him and said: "He is all tenderness and care. The true and the beautiful have robbed me of a kinsman. His star is near."

Said the Boy: "I approach my star."

"I am not so certain of that," interrupted the Hog. "I have

noticed your kind and I ever see some of myself in them. Your star is a delusion."

The Boy answered by painting the flower and setting the notes of the bird's song to music.

The Hog looked at the boy and said: "His soul is attuned by nature. The meddler in him is slain."

"I can all but touch my star," cried the Boy.

"I am not so certain of that," remarked the Snake. "I have watched your kind and ever see some of myself in them. Stings are nearer than stars."

The Boy answered by meditating upon the picture and music. The Snake departed, saying that stings and stars cannot keep company.

The Boy journeyed on, ever led by the star. Some distance away the Mule was bemoaning the presence of his heels and trying to rid himself of them by kicking a tree. The Hog was dividing his time between looking into a brook and rubbing his snout on a rock to shorten it. The Snake lay dead of its own bite. The Boy journeyed on, led by an ever inviting star. (Negro Tales.—Joseph S. Cotter, The Cosmopolitan Press, New York, 1912.)

Yes—Uncle Remus, in reality—and not exactly so. No copy. Not every like is the same. An Uncle Remus with culture and conscious art, yet unspoilt, the native qualities strong. And how poetic those qualities are!

Well might one expect a teacher, if he writes verse, to write didactic verse. But I think you will pronounce him to be an extraordinary teacher and verse-writer who writes as Mr. Cotter does, for example, in:

## THE THRESHING FLOOR

Thrice blessed he who wields the flail
Upon this century's threshing floor;
A few slight strokes by him avail
More than a hundred would of yore.

Around him lies the ripened grain
From every land and every age;
The weakest thresher should attain
Unto the wisdom of the sage.

Ambitious youth, this is the wealth
The ages have bequeathed to thee.
Thou canst not take thy share by stealth
Nor by mere ingenuity.

Thy better self must spur thee on
To win what time has made thy own;
No hand but labor's yet has drawn
The sweets that labor's hand has sown.

In verse presuming to be lyrical we hearken for the lyrical cry.
That cry is in his lines, melodiously uttered, and poignant. For
example:

The flowers take the tears
Of the weeping night
And give them to the sun
For the day's delight.

My passion takes the joys
Of the laughing day

And melts them into tears
For my heart's decay.

The sweet sadness of those stanzas lingers with one. A stanza from a poem entitled "The Nation's Neglected Child" may help us to their secret:

I am not thy pampered steed,
I am not thy welcome dog;
I am of a lower breed
Even than thy Berkshire hog;
I am thy neglected child—
Make me grow, but keep me wild.

In many of Cotter's verses there is a sonorous flow which is evidence of poetic power made creative by passion. Didacticism and philosophy do not destroy the lyrical quality. In *The Book's Creed* this teacher-poet makes an appeal to his generation to be as much alive and as creative as the creed makers of other days were. The slaves of the letter, the mummers of mere formulas, he thus addresses:

You are dead to all the Then,
You are dead to all the Now,
If you hold that former men
Wore the garland for your brow.

Time and tide were theirs to brave,
Time and tide are yours to stem.
Bow not o'er their open grave
Till you drop your diadem.

> Honor all who strove and wrought,
> Even to their tears and groans;
> But slay not your honest thought
> Through your reverence for their bones.

Cotter is a wizard at rhyming. His "Sequel to the Pied Piper of Hamelin" surpasses the original—Browning's—in technique—that is, in rushing rhythms and ingenious rhymes. It is an incredible success, with no hint of a tour-de-force performance. Its content, too, is worthy of the metrical achievement. I will lay the proof before the competent reader in an extract or two from this remarkable accomplishment:

> The last sweet notes the piper blew
> Were heard by the people far and wide;
> And one by one and two by two
> They flocked to the mountain-side.
>
> Some came, of course, intensely sad,
> And some came looking fiercely mad,
> And some came singing solemn hymns,
> And some came showing shapely limbs,
> And some came bearing the tops of yews,
> And some came wearing wooden shoes,
> And some came saying what they would do,
> And some came praying (and loudly too),
> And all for what? Can you not infer?
> A-searching and lurching for the Pied Piper,
> And the boys and girls he had taken away.
> And all were ready now to pay
> Any amount that he should say.

So begins the *Sequel*. Another passage, near the end, will indicate the trend of the story:

> The years passed by, as years will do,
> When trouble is the master,
> And always strives to bring to view
> A new and worse disaster;
> And sorrow, like a sorcerer,
> Spread out her melancholy pall,
> So that its folds enveloped all,
> And each became her worshipper.
> And not a single child was born
> Through all the years thereafter;
> If words sprang from the lips of scorn
> None came from those of laughter.

Finally, the inhabitants of Hamelin are passing through death's portal, and when all had departed:

> —a message went to Rat-land
>
> ******
>
> And lo! a race of rats was at hand
>
> ******
>
> They swarmed into the highest towers,
> And loitered in the fairest bowers,
> And sat down where the mayor sat,
> And also in his Sunday hat;
> And gnawed revengefully thereat.
> With rats for mayor and rats for people,
> With rats in the cellar and rats in the steeple,

With rats without and rats within,
Stood poor, deserted Hamelin.

Like Dunbar, Cotter is a satirist of his people—or certain types of his people—a gentle, humorous, affectionate satirist. His medium for satire is dialect, inevitably. Sententious wisdom, irradiated with humor, appears in these pieces in homely garb. In standard English, without satire or humor that wisdom thus appears:

What deeds have sprung from plow and pick!
What bank-rolls from tomatoes!
No dainty crop of rhetoric
Can match one of potatoes.

The gospel of work has been set forth by our poet in a four-act poetic drama entitled *Caleb, the Degenerate*. All the characters are Negroes. The form is blank verse—blank verse of a very high order, too. The language, like Shakespeare's—though Browning rather than Shakespeare is suggested—is always that of a poet. The wisdom is that of a man who has observed closely and pondered deeply. Idealistic, philosophical, poetical—such it is. It bears witness to no ordinary dramatic ability.

"Best bard, because the wisest," says our Israfel. Verily. "Sage" you may call this man as well as "bard." The proof is in poems and tales, apologues and apothegms. Joseph Seamon Cotter is now sixty years of age. Yet the best of him, according to good omens, is yet to be given forth, in song, story, precept, and drama. His nature is opulent—the cultivation began late and the harvest grows richer.

The chief event of his life, I doubt not, remains to be mentioned—a very sad one. This was the untimely death of his poet-son, Joseph S. Cotter, Jr. Born of this sorrow was the following lyric:

> Oh, my way and thy way,
> And life's joy and wonder,
> And thy day and my day
> Are cloven asunder.
> Oh, my trust and thy trust,
> And fair April weather,
> And thy dust and my dust
> Shall mingle together.

### The Son

Dead at the age of twenty-three years, Joseph S. Cotter, Jr., left behind a thin volume of lyrics, entitled *The Band of Gideon*, and about twenty sonnets of an unfinished sequence, and a little book of one-act plays. I will presently place the remarkable title-poem of his book of lyrics before the reader, but first I will give two minor pieces, without comment:

JOSEPH S. COTTER, JR.

## RAIN MUSIC

On the dusty earth-drum
Beats the falling rain;
Now a whispered murmur,
Now a louder strain.

Slender silvery drumsticks,
On the ancient drum,
Beat the mellow music,
Bidding life to come.

Chords of earth awakened,
Notes of greening spring,
Rise and fall triumphant
Over everything.

Slender silvery drumsticks
Beat the long tattoo—
God the Great Musician
Calling life anew.

## COMPENSATION

I plucked a rose from out a bower fair,
That overhung my garden seat;
And wondered I if, e'er before, bloomed there
A rose so sweet.

Enwrapt in beauty I scarce felt the thorn
That pricked me as I pulled the bud;
Till I beheld the rose, that summer morn,
Stained with my blood.

I sang a song that thrilled the evening air,
With beauty somewhat kin to love,
And all men knew that lyric song so rare
Came from above.

And men rejoiced to hear the golden strain;
But no man knew the price I paid,
Nor cared that out of my soul's deathless pain
The song was made.

The lyrical faculty is evinced by such poems. But other singers
of our day might have produced them—singers of the white race.
Not so, I think, of "The Band of Gideon." Upon that poem is
the stamp, not of genius only, but of Negro genius. In it is re-in-
carnated, by a cultured, creative mind, the very spirit of the old
plantation songs and sermons. The reader who has in his possession
that background will respond to the unique and powerful appeal
of this poem.

### THE BAND OF GIDEON

The band of Gideon roam the sky,
The howling wind is their war-cry,
The thunder's roll is their trumpet's peal
And the lightning's flash their vengeful steel.
Each black cloud
Is a fiery steed.
And they cry aloud
With each strong deed,
"The Sword of the Lord and Gideon."

And men below rear temples high
And mock their God with reasons why,
And live in arrogance, sin, and shame,
And rape their souls for the world's good name.
Each black cloud
Is a fiery steed.
And they cry aloud
With each strong deed,
"The Sword of the Lord and Gideon."

The band of Gideon roam the sky
And view the earth with baleful eye;
In holy wrath they scourge the land
With earthquake, storm, and burning brand.
Each black cloud
Is a fiery steed.
And they cry aloud
With each strong deed,
"The Sword of the Lord and Gideon."

The lightnings flash and the thunders roll,
And "Lord have mercy on my soul,"
Cry men as they fall on the stricken sod,
In agony searching for their God.
Each black cloud
Is a fiery steed.
And they cry aloud
With each strong deed,
"The Sword of the Lord and Gideon."

And men repent and then forget
That heavenly wrath they ever met.
The band of Gideon yet will come
And strike their tongues of blasphemy dumb.
Each black cloud
Is a fiery steed.
And they cry aloud
With each strong deed,
"The Sword of the Lord and Gideon."

The reader, I predict, will be drawn again and again to this mysterious poem. It will continue to haunt his imagination, and tease his thought. The stamp of the African mind is upon it. Closely allied, on the one hand by its august refrain to the Spirituals, on the other hand it touches the most refined and perfected art; such, for example, as Rossetti's ballads or Vachel Lindsay's cantatas. It can scarcely be wondered at that the people of his race should call this untimely dead singer their Negro Lycidas.

## II. JAMES DAVID CORROTHERS

### THE DREAM AND THE SONG

So oft our hearts, beloved lute,
In blossomy haunts of song are mute;
So long we pore, 'mid murmurings dull,
O'er loveliness unutterable;
So vain is all our passion strong!
The dream is lovelier than the song.

The rose thought, touched by words, doth turn
Wan ashes. Still, from memory's urn,
The lingering blossoms tenderly
Refute our wilding minstrelsy.
Alas! we work but beauty's wrong!
The dream is lovelier than the song.

Yearned Shelley o'er the golden flame?
Left Keats, for beauty's lure, a name
But "writ in water"? Woe is me!
To grieve o'er floral faëry.
My Phasian doves are flown so long—
The dream is lovelier than the song!

Ah, though we build a bower of dawn,
The golden-winged bird is gone,
And morn may gild, through shimmering
leaves,
Only the swallow-twittering eaves.
What art may house or gold prolong
A dream far lovelier than a song?

The lilting witchery, the unrest
Of wingèd dreams, is in our breast;
But ever dear Fulfilment's eyes
Gaze otherward. The long-sought prize,
My lute, must to the gods belong.
The dream is lovelier than the song.

Cherokee-Indian, Scotch-Irish, French, and African blood
in James David Corrothers, the author of this poem, makes his

complexion, he supposed, "about that of the original man." The reader has already had, at the beginning of the discussion of Dunbar, a sonnet from this poet. The sonnet, the above poem, and the others given here were published in *The Century Magazine.* Not unworthy of *The Century's* standards, the reader must say.

James David Corrothers was born in Michigan, July 2, 1869. His mother in giving him life surrendered her own. His father never cared for him. Sheltered for a few years by maternal relatives, he was out on the world in early boyhood, dependent on his own resources. Soon, because he was a Negro, he was a wanderer for work through several states. Often without money, friends, or food, he slept out of doors, sometimes in zero weather. At nineteen years of age, as before stated, he was shining shoes in a Chicago barber shop. There he was "discovered."

J. D. CORROTHERS

Henry D. Lloyd was having his boots shined by young Corrothers when the two fell into book talk. The distinguished writer was astonished at the knowledge possessed by one engaged in such a menial occupation. Out of this circumstance, it seems, the Negro boot-black became a student in Northwestern University at Evanston, Illinois. By mowing lawns and doing whatever odd jobs he could find he worked his way for three years in the university. Then, by the kindness of Frances E. Willard, he had a year in Bennett College, Greensboro, North Carolina. Prior to his entrance at Northwestern there had been but one brief opportunity in his life for attending school. But the wandering youth, battling against the adverse fates, or, concretely stated, the disadvantage of being a Negro, had managed somehow to make great books his companions. Hence, he had entered what Carlyle calls "the true modern university." Hence, his literary conversation with Mr. Lloyd.

Out of those early struggles, and perhaps also out of later bitter experiences, came such poems as the following:

AT THE CLOSED GATE OF JUSTICE

> To be a Negro in a day like this
> Demands forgiveness. Bruised with blow on blow,
> Betrayed, like him whose woe-dimmed eyes gave bliss,
> Still must one succor those who brought one low,
> To be a Negro in a day like this.

> To be a Negro in a day like this
> Demands rare patience—patience that can wait
> In utter darkness. 'Tis the path to miss,
> And knock, unheeded, at an iron gate,
> To be a Negro in a day like this.

To be a Negro in a day like this
Demands strange loyalty. We serve a flag
Which is to us white freedom's emphasis.
Ah! one must love when truth and justice lag,
To be a Negro in a day like this.

To be a Negro in a day like this—
Alas! Lord God, what evil have we done?
Still shines the gate, all gold and amethyst
But I pass by, the glorious goal unwon,
"Merely a Negro"—in a day like *this*!

Even though his face be "red like Adam's," and even though
his art be noble like that of the masters of song, yet had Mr.
Corrothers, even in the republic of letters, felt the handicap of his
complexion, as this sonnet bears witness:

## THE NEGRO SINGER

O'er all my song the image of a face
Lieth, like shadow on the wild, sweet flowers.
The dream, the ecstasy that prompts my
powers,
The golden lyre's delights, bring little grace
To bless the singer of a lowly race.
Long hath this mocked me: aye, in marvelous
hours,
When Hera's gardens gleamed, or Cynthia's
bowers,
Or Hope's red pylons, in their far, hushed place!
But I shall dig me deeper to the gold;
Fetch water, dripping, over desert miles

From clear Nyanzas and mysterious Niles
Of love; and sing, nor one kind act withhold.
So shall men know me, and remember long,
Nor my dark face dishonor any song.

Death has silenced the muse of this dark singer,
one of the best hitherto. That his endowment
was
uncommon and that his achievement, as
evinced by
these poems, is one of distinction, to use Mr.
Howells's word, every reader equipped to judge
of poetry must admit.

## III. A GROUP OF SINGING JOHNSONS

In all rosters the name Johnson claims liberal space. Five verse-smiths with that cognomen will be presented in this book, and there is a sixth. These many Johnsons are no further related to one another, so far as I know, than that they are all Adam's offspring, and poets. Only three of them will be presented in this chapter: James Weldon Johnson, of Florida, author of *Fifty Years and Other Poems* (1917); Charles Bertram Johnson, of Missouri, author of *Songs of My People* (1918); Fenton Johnson, of Chicago, author of *A Little Dreaming* (1914); *Unions of the Dusk* (1915), and *Songs of the Soil* (1916). The fourth and fifth are women, and will find a place in another group; the sixth is Adolphus Johnson, author of *The Silver Chord*, Philadelphia, 1915. The three mentioned above will be treated in the order in which they have been named.

## 1. *James Weldon Johnson*

Now of New York, but born in Florida and reared in the South, James Weldon Johnson is a man of various abilities, accomplishments, and activities. He was graduated with the degrees of A. B. and A. M. from Atlanta University and later studied for three years in Columbia University. First a school-principal, then a practitioner of the law, he followed at last the strongest propensity and turned author. His literary work includes light operas, for which his brother, J. Rosamond Johnson, composed the music, and a novel entitled *The Autobiography of an Ex-Colored Man*. Having been United States consul in two Latin-American countries, he is a master of Spanish and has made translations of Spanish plays and poems. The English libretto of *Goyescas* was made by him for the Metropolitan Opera Company in 1915. He is also one of the ablest editorial writers in the country. In the *Public Ledger's* contest of 1916 he won the third prize. His editorials are widely syndicated in the Negro weekly press. Poems of his have appeared in *The Century*, *The Crisis*, and *The Independent*.

Professor Brander Matthews in his Introduction to *Fifty Years and Other Poems* speaks of "the superb and soaring stanzas" of the title-poem and describes it as "a poem sonorous in its diction, vigorous in its workmanship, elevated in its imagination, and sincere in its emotion." Doubtless this will seem like the language of exaggeration. The sceptic, however, must withhold judgment until he has read the poem, too long for presentation here. Mr. Johnson's poetical qualities can be represented in this place only by briefer though inferior productions. A poem of special significance, and characterized by the qualities noted by Professor Matthews in "Fifty Years," is the following:

JAMES WELDON JOHNSON

## O SOUTHLAND!

O Southland! O Southland!
Have you not heard the call,
The trumpet blown, the word made known
To the nations, one and all?
The watchword, the hope-word,
Salvation's present plan?
A gospel new, for all—for you:
Man shall be saved by man.

O Southland! O Southland!
Do you not hear to-day
The mighty beat of onward feet,
And know you not their way?
'Tis forward, 'tis upward,

On to the fair white arch
Of Freedom's dome, and there is room
For each man who would march.

O Southland, fair Southland!
Then why do you still cling
To an idle age and a musty page,
To a dead and useless thing?
'Tis springtime! 'Tis work-time!
The world is young again!
And God's above, and God is love,
And men are only men.

O Southland! my Southland!
O birthland! do not shirk
The toilsome task, nor respite ask,
But gird you for the work.
Remember, remember
That weakness stalks in pride;
That he is strong who helps along
The faint one at his side.

For pure lyric beauty and exquisite pathos, Wordsworthian
in both respects, but no hint of imitation, the following stanzas
may be set, without disadvantage to them, by the side of any in
our literature:

The glory of the day was in her face,
The beauty of the night was in her eyes,
And over all her loveliness, the grace
Of Morning blushing in the early skies.

And in her voice, the calling of the dove;
Like music of a sweet, melodious part.
And in her smile, the breaking light of love;
And all the gentle virtues in her heart.

And now the glorious day, the beauteous night,
The birds that signal to their mates at dawn,
To my dull ears, to my tear-blinded sight
Are one with all the dead, since she is gone.

Yet one other poem of this fine singer's I will give, selecting
from not a few that press for the restricted space. The easy flow
of the verse and the ready rhyme will be remarked—and that
supreme quality of good lyric poetry, austere simplicity.

### THE YOUNG WARRIOR

Mother, shed no mournful tears,
But gird me on my sword;
And give no utterance to thy fears,
But bless me with thy word.

The lines are drawn! The fight is on!
A cause is to be won!
Mother, look not so white and wan;
Give Godspeed to thy son.

Now let thine eyes my way pursue
Where'er my footsteps fare;
And when they lead beyond thy view,
Send after me a prayer.
But pray not to defend from harm,

Nor danger to dispel;
Pray, rather, that with steadfast arm
I fight the battle well.

Pray, mother of mine, that I always keep
My heart and purpose strong,
My sword unsullied and ready to leap
Unsheathed against the wrong.

Arduous labors in other fields than poetry threaten to silence Mr. Johnson's muse, and that is to be regretted.

## 2. *Charles Bertram Johnson*

School-teacher, preacher, poet—this is Charles Bertram Johnson of Missouri. And in Missouri there is no voice more tuneful, no artistry in song any finer, than his. Nor in so bold an assertion am I forgetting the sweet voice and exquisite artistry of Sarah Teasdale. Mr. Johnson's art is not unlike hers in all that makes hers most charming. Only there is not so much of his that attains to perfection of form. On pages 52 and 63 were given two of his quatrain poems. These were of his people. But a lyric poet should sing himself. That is of the essence of lyric poetry. In so singing, however, the poet reveals not only his individual life, but that of his race to the view of the world. Another quatrain poem, personal in form, may be accepted as of racial interpretation:

CHARLES BERTRAM JOHNSON

## SOUL AND STAR

So oft from out the verge afar
The dear dreams throng and throng,
Sometimes I think my soul a star,
And life a pulséd song.

Born at Callao, Missouri, October 5, 1880, of a Kentucky
mother and a Virginia father, Charles Bertram Johnson attended
a one-room school "across the railroad track," where—who can
explain this?—he was "Introduced to Bacon, Shakespeare, and the
art of rhyming." It reads like an old story. Some freak of a school-
master whose head is filled with "useless" lore—poetry, tales, and
"such stuff"—nurturing a child of genius into song. But it was
Johnson's mother who was the great influence in his life. She was
an "adept at rhyming" and "she initiated me into the world of color
and melody"—so writes our poet. It is always the mother. Then,
by chance—but how marvelously chance comes to the aid of the
predestined!—by chance, he learns of Dunbar and his poetry. The

ambition to be a poet of his people like Dunbar possesses him. He knows the path to that goal is education. He therefore makes his way to a little college at Macon, Missouri, from which, after five years, he is graduated—without having received any help in the art of poetry, however. Two terms at a summer school and special instruction by correspondence seem to have aided him here, or to have induced the belief that he had been aided. For twenty-odd years he followed the profession of teaching. For ten years of that period he also preached. The ministry now claims his entire energies, and the muse knocks less and less frequently at his door.

Yet he still sings. In a recent number of *The Crisis* I find a poem of his that in suggesting a life of toil growing to a peaceful close is filled with soothing melody:

### OLD FRIENDS

Sit here before my grate,
Until it's ashen gray,
Or till the night grows late,
And talk the time away.

I cannot think to sleep,
And miss your golden speech,
My bed of dreams will keep—
You here within my reach.

I have so much to say,
The time is short at best,
A bit of toil and play,
And after that comes rest.

But you and I know now
The wisdom of the soul,
The years that seamed the brow
Have made our visions whole.

Sit here before my grate
Until the ash is cold;
The things you say of late
Are fine as shriven gold.

Even though one be born to sing, if circumstances have made him a preacher he may be expected to moralize his song. Whether we shall be reconciled to this will depend on the art with which it is done. If the moral idea be a sweet human one, and if the verse still be melifluous, we will submit, and our delight will be twofold—ethical and esthetical. We will put our preacher-poet of Missouri to the test:

SO MUCH

So much of love I need,
And tender passioned care,
Of human fault and greed
To make me unaware:

So much of love I owe,
That, ere my life be done,
How shall I keep His will
To owe not any one?

Truth is, Mr. Johnson is not given to preaching in verse any more than other poets. His sole aim is beauty. He assures me it is truth. Instead of admitting disagreement I only assert that, being a poet, he must find all truth beautiful. It is only for relative thinking we need the three terms, truth, goodness, and beauty.

I will conclude this presentation of the Missouri singer with a lyrical sermonette:

### A RAIN SONG

Chill the rain falls, chill!
Dull gray the world; the vale
Rain-swept; wind-swept the hill;
"But gloom and doubt prevail,"
My heart breaks forth to say.

Ere thus its sorrow-note,
"Cheer up! Cheer up, to-day!
To-morrow is to be!"
Babbled from a joyous throat,
A robin's in a mist-gray tree.

Then off to keep a tryst—
He preened his drabbled cloak—
Doughty little optimist!—
As if in answer, broke
The sunlight through that oak.

### 3. Fenton Johnson

Dreams and visions—such are the treasures of suffering loyal hearts: dreams, visions, and song. Happy even in their sorrows the people to whom God has given poets to be their spokesmen to the world. Else their hearts should stifle with woe. As the prophet was of old so in these times the poet. As a prophet speaks Fenton Johnson, his heart yearning toward the black folk of our land:

## THESE ARE MY PEOPLE

These are my people, I have built for them
A castle in the cloister of my heart;
And I shall fight that they may dwell therein.
The God that gave Sojourner tongue of fire
Has made with me a righteous covenant
That these, my brothers of the dusk, shall rise
To Sinai and thence in purple walk
A newer Canaan, vineyards of the West.
The rods that chasten us shall break as straw
And fire consume the godless in the South;
The hand that struck the helpless of my race
Shall wither as a leaf in drear November,
And liberty, the nectar God has blest,
Shall flow as free as wine in Babylon.
O God of Covenants, forget us not!

Fenton Johnson seems to be more deeply rooted in the song-traditions of his people than are most of his fellow-poets. To him the classic Spirituals afford inspiration and pattern. Whoever is familiar with those "canticles of love and woe" will recognize their influence throughout Mr. Johnson's three volumes of song. I shall make no attempt here to illustrate this truth but shall rather select a piece or two that will represent the poet's general qualities. Other poems more typical of him as a melodist could be found but these have special traits that commend them for this place.

## THE PLAINT OF THE FACTORY CHILD

Mother, must I work all day?
All the day? Ay, all the day?
Must my little hands be torn?
And my heart bleed, all forlorn?
I am but a child of five,
And the street is all alive
With the tops and balls and toys,—
Pretty tops and balls and toys.

Day in, day out, I toil—toil!
And all that I know is toil;
Never laugh as others do,
Never cry as others do,
Never see the stars at night,
Nor the golden glow of sunlight,—
And all for but a silver coin,—
Just a worthless silver coin.

Would that death might come to me!
That blessed death might come to me,
And lead me to waters cool,
Lying in a tranquil pool,
Up there where the angels sing,
And the ivy tendrils cling
To the land of play and song,—
Fairy land of play and song.

## THE MULATTO'S SONG

Die, you vain but sweet desires!
Die, you living, burning fires!
I am like a Prince of France,—
Like a prince whose noble sires
Have been robbed of heritage;
I am phantom derelict,
Drifting on a flaming sea.

Everywhere I go, I strive,
Vainly strive for greater things;
Daisies die, and stars are cold,
And canary never sings;
Where I go they mock my name,
Never grant me liberty,
Chance to breathe and chance to do.

*The Vision of Lazarus*, contained in *A Little Dreaming*, is a blank-verse poem of about three-hundred lines, original, well-sustained, imaginative, and deeply impressive.

In one of the newer methods of verse, and yet with a splendid suggestion of the old Spirituals, I will take from a recent magazine a poem by Mr. Johnson that will show how the vision of his people is turned toward the future, from the welter of struggling forces in the World War:

## THE NEW DAY

From a vision red with war I awoke and saw the Prince of
Peace hovering over No Man's Land.
Loud the whistles blew and thunder of cannon was drowned
by the happy shouting of the people.

From the Sinai that faces Armageddon I heard this chant
from the throats of white-robed angels:

> Blow your trumpets, little children!
> From the East and from the West,
> From the cities in the valley,
> From God's dwelling on the mountain,
> Blow your blast that Peace might know
> She is Queen of God's great army.
> With the crying blood of millions
> We have written deep her name
> In the Book of all the Ages;
> With the lilies in the valley,
> With the roses by the Mersey,
> With the golden flower of Jersey,
> We have crowned her smooth young temples.
> Where her footsteps cease to falter
> Golden grain will greet the morning,
> Where her chariot descends
> Shall be broken down the altar
> Of the gods of dark disturbance.
> Nevermore shall men know suffering,
> Nevermore shall women wailing
> Shake to grief the God of Heaven.
> From the East and from the West,
> From the cities in the valley,
> From God's dwelling on the mountain,
> Little children, blow your trumpets!

From Ethiopia, groaning 'neath her heavy burdens I heard
the music of the old slave songs.
I heard the wail of warriors, dusk brown, who grimly fought

the fight of others in the trenches of Mars.

I heard the plea of blood-stained men of dusk and the

crimson in my veins leapt furiously:

> Forget not, O my brothers, how we fought
> In No Man's Land that peace might come
> again!
> Forget not, O my brothers, how we gave
> Red blood to save the freedom of the world!
> We were not free, our tawny hands were tied;
> But Belgium's plight and Serbia's woes we
> shared
> Each rise of sun or setting of the moon.
> So when the bugle blast had called us forth
> We went not like the surly brute of yore,
> But, as the Spartan, proud to give the world
> The freedom that we never knew nor shared.
> These chains, O brothers mine, have weighed
> us down
> As Samson in the temple of the gods;
> Unloosen them and let us breathe the air
> That makes the goldenrod the flower of Christ;
> For we have been with thee in No Man's Land,
> Through lake of fire and down to Hell itself;
> And now we ask of thee our liberty,
> Our freedom in the land of Stars and Stripes.
> I am glad that the Prince of Peace is
> hovering over No Man's Land.

### 4. Adolphus Johnson

From the *Preface* of Adolphus Johnson's *The Silver Chord* I will take a paragraph that is more poetic and perfect in expression than any stanza in his book. Poetry, I think, is in him, but when he wrote these rhymes he was not yet sufficiently disciplined in expression. But this is how he can say a thing in prose:

"As the Goddess of Music takes down her lute, touches its silver chords, and sets the summer melodies of nature to words, so an inspiration comes to me in my profoundest slumbers and gently awakens my highest faculties to the finest thought and serenest contemplation herein expressed. Always remember that a book is your best friend when it compels you to think, disenthralls your reason, enkindles your hopes, vivifies your imagination, and makes easier all the burdens of your daily life."

## IV. William Stanley Braithwaite

The critical and the creative faculties rarely dwell together in harmony. One or the other finally predominates. In the case of Mr. Braithwaite it seems to be the critical faculty. He has preferred, it seems, to be America's chief anthologist, encouraging others up rugged Parnassus, rather than himself to stand on the heights of song. Since 1913 he has edited a series of annual anthologies of American magazine verse, which he has provided with critical reviews of the verse output of the respective year. Of several anthologies of English verse also he is the editor. Three books of original verse stand to his credit: *Lyrics of Life and Love* (1904), *The House of Falling Leaves* (1908), and *Sandy Star and Willie Gee* (1922). These dates seem to prove that the creative impulse has waned.

Verse artistry, in simple forms, reaches a degree of excellence in Mr. Braithwaite's lyrics that has rarely been surpassed in our times. Graceful and esthetically satisfying expression is given to elusive or mystical and rare fancies. I will give one of his brief lyrics as an example of the qualities to which I allude:

### SANDY STAR

No more from out the sunset,
No more across the foam,
No more across the windy hills
Will Sandy Star come home.

He went away to search it,
With a curse upon his tongue,
And in his hands the staff of life
Made music as it swung.

I wonder if he found it,
And knows the mystery now:
Our Sandy Star who went away
With the secret on his brow.

In a number of Mr. Braithwaite's lyrics, as in this one, there is an atmosphere of mystery that, with the charming simplicity of manner, strongly suggests Blake. There is a strangeness in all beauty, it has been said. There is commonly something of Faëryland in the finest lyric poetry. Another lyric illustrating this quality in Mr. Braithwaite is the following:

### IT'S A LONG WAY

It's a long way the sea-winds blow
Over the sea-plains blue,—
But longer far has my heart to go
Before its dreams come true.

It's work we must, and love we must,
And do the best we may,
And take the hope of dreams in trust
To keep us day by day.

It's a long way the sea-winds blow—
But somewhere lies a shore—
Thus down the tide of Time shall flow
My dreams forevermore.

Mr. Braithwaite's art rises above race. He seems not to be race-conscious in his writing, whether prose or verse. Yet no man can say but that race has given his poetry the distinctive quality I have indicated. In this connection a most interesting poem is his "A New England Spinster." The detachment is perfect, the analysis is done in the spirit of absolute art. I will quote but two of its dozen or so stanzas:

She dwells alone, and never heeds
How strange may sound her own footfall,
And yet is prompt to others' needs,
Or ready at a neighbor's call.

But still her world is one apart,
Serene above desire and change;
There are no hills beyond her heart,
Beyond her gate, no winds that range.

Here is the true artist's imagination that penetrates to the secrets of life. No poet's lyrics, with their deceptive simplicity, better reward study for a full appreciation of their idea. So much of suggestion to the reader of the poems which follow:

### FOSCATI

Blest be Foscati! You've heard tell
How—spirit and flesh of him—blown to flame,
Leaped the stars for heaven, dropped back to
hell,
And felt no shame.

I here indite this record of his journey:
The splendor of his epical will to perform
Life's best, with the lance of Truth at Tourney—
Till caught in the storm.

Of a woman's face and hair like scented clover,
Te Deums, Lauds, and Magnificat, he
Praised with tongue of saint, heart of lover—
Missed all, but found Foscati!

### AUTUMN SADNESS

The warm October rain fell upon his dream,
When once again the autumn sadness stirred,
And murmured through his blood, like a
hidden stream
In a forest, unheard.

The drowsy rain battered against his delight
Of the half forgotten poignancies,
That settle in the dusk of an autumn night
On a world one hears and sees.

One was, he thought, an echo merely,
A glow enshadowed of truths untraced;
But the autumn sadness, brought him yearly,
Was a joy embraced.

THANKING GOD

The way folks had of thanking God
He found annoying, till he thought
Of flame and coolness in the sod—
Of balms and blessings that they wrought.

And so the habit grew, and then—
Of when and how he did not care—
He found his God as other men
The mystic verb in a grammar of prayer.

He never knelt, nor uttered words—
His laughter felt no chastening rod;
"My being," he said, "is a choir of birds,
And all my senses are thanking God."

Mr. Braithwaite is thoroughly conversant, as these selections indicate, with the subtleties and finest effects of the art poetic, and his impulses to write spring from the deepest human speculations, the purest motives of art. Hence in his work he takes his place among the few.

## V. George Reginald Margetson

Under tropical suns, amid the tropical luxuriance of nature, developed the many-hued imagination of the subject of this sketch. His nature is tropical, for Mr. Margetson is a prolific bard: *Songs of Life, The Fledgling Bard and the Poetry Society, Ethiopia's Flight, England in the West Indies*—four published books, and more yet unpublished—are proof. No excerpts can fully reveal the distinctive quality of Mr. Margetson's poetry—its sonorous and ever-varying flow, like a mountain stream, its descriptive richness in which it resembles his native islands. For he was born in the British West Indies, and there lived the first twenty years of his life. Coming to America in 1897, his home has been in Boston or its environment since that time. Educated in the Moravian School at St. Kitts, he has lived with and in the English poets from Spenser to Byron—Byron seems to have been his favorite—and so has cultivated his native talent. I can give here but one brief lyric from his pen.

GEORGE REGINALD MARGETSON

## THE LIGHT OF VICTORY

In the East a star is rising,
Breaking through the clouds of war,
With a light old arts revising

Shattering steel and iron bar.
Freedom's heirs with banners blazing,
Emblems of Democracy,
At the magic light are gazing
Battling with Autocracy.

Through the night brave souls are marching
With the armies of the Free;
Where the Stars and Stripes o'er-arching
Form a sheltering canopy.
Allies! hold a front united!
Shaping well our destiny;
Let each brutal wrong be righted
In the drive for Liberty!

## VI. *William Moore*

The productions I have seen in the Negro magazines and newspapers from William Moore's pen give me the idea of a poet distinctly original and distinctly endowed with imagination. If there appears some obscurity in his poems let it not be too hastily set down against him as a fault. Some ideas are intrinsically obscure. The expression of them that should be lucid would be false, inadequate. Some poets there needs must be who, escaping from the inevitable, the commonplace, will transport us out into infinity to confront the eternal mysteries. Mr. Moore does this in two sonnets which I will give to represent his poetic work:

## EXPECTANCY

I do not care for sleep, I'll wait awhile
For Love to come out of the darkness, wait
For laughter, gifted with the frequent fate
Of dusk-lit hope, to touch me with the smile
Of moon and star and joy of that last mile
Before I reach the sea. The ships are late
And mayhap laden with the precious freight
Dawn brings from Life's eternal summer isle.

And should I find the sweeter fruits of dream—
The oranges of love and mating song—
I'll laugh so true the morn will gayly seem
Endless and ships full laden with a throng
Of beauty, dreams and loves will come to me
Out of the surge of yonder silver sea.

## AS THE OLD YEAR PASSED

I stood with dear friend Death awhile last
night,
Out where the stars shone with a lustre true
In sacred dreams and all the old and new
Of love and life winged in a silver flight
Off to the sea of peace that waits where white,
Pale silences melt in the tranquil blue
Of skies so tender beauty doth imbue
The time with holiness and singing light.

My heart is Life, my soul, O Death, is thine!
Is thine to kiss with yearning life again,
Is thine to strengthen and to sweet incline

To peace and mellowed dream of joy's refrain.
I'll stand with Death again to-night, I think,
Out where the stars reveal life's deeper brink.


## VII. Joshua Henry Jones, Jr.

Poets are born and nurtured in all conditions of life: Joseph Cotter the elder was a slave-woman's child; Dunbar wrote his first book between the runs of the elevator he tended; Leon R. Harris was left in infancy to the dreary shelter of an orphanage, then indentured to a brutal farmer; Carmichael came from the cabin of an unlettered farmer in the Black Belt of Alabama; of a dozen others the story is similar. Born in poverty, up through adversities they struggled, with little human help save perhaps from the croons and caresses of a singing mother, and a few terms at a wretched school, they toiled into the kingdom of knowledge and entered the world of poetry. Some, however, have had the advantages afforded by parents of culture and of means. Among these is the subject of this sketch, the son of Bishop J. H. Jones, of the African Methodist Episcopal Church. He has had the best educational opportunity offered by American colleges. He is a graduate of Brown University. Writing has been his employment since graduation, and he has been on the staffs of several New England papers. His first book of poems, entitled *The Heart of the World* (1919), now in the second edition, reveals at once a student of poetry and an independent artist in verse. His second book, *Poems of the Four Seas* (1921), shows that his vein is still rich in ore.

In Chapter VIII I give his "Goodbye, Old Year." Another poem of similar technique takes for its title the last words of Colonel Roosevelt: "Turn out the light, please." The reader cannot but note the sense of proper effect exhibited in the short sentences, the very manner of a dying man. But more than this will be perceived in this poem. It will seem to have sprung out of the world-weary soul of the young poet himself. Struggle, grief, weariness in the strife, have been his also. Hence:

JOSHUA HENRY JONES, JR.

## TURN OUT THE LIGHT

Turn out the light. Now would I slumber,
I'm weary with the toil of day.
Let me forget my pains to number.
Turn out the light. Dreams come to play.

Turn out the light. The hours were dreary.
Clouds of despair long hid the sun.
I've battled hard and now I'm weary.
Turn out the light. My day is done.

I've done life's best gloom's ways to brighten—
I've scattered cheer from heart to heart,

And where I could I've sought to righten
The wrongs of men ere day depart.

This morn 'twas bright with hope—and cheery.
This noon gave courage—made me brave.
But as the sun sank I grew weary
Till now my soul for rest doth crave.

Turn out the light. I've done my duty
To friend and enemy as well.
I go to sleep where things of beauty
In glitt'ring chambers ever dwell.

Turn out the light. Now would I slumber.
To rest—to dream—soon go we all.
Let's hope we wake soul free of cumber
Turn out the light. Dream comrades call.

The next piece I select from Mr. Jones's first book will represent his talent in another sphere. I suggest that comparison might be made between this song in literary English and Mr. Johnson's Negro love song in dialect.A SOUTHERN LOVE SONG

Dogwoods all a-bloom
Perfume earth's big room,
White full moon is gliding o'er the sky serene.
Quiet reigns about,
In the house and out;
Hoot owl in the hollow mopes with solemn mien.
Birds have gone to rest

In each tree-top nest;
Cotton fields a-shimmer flash forth silver-green.

O'er the wild cane brake,
Whip-poor-wills awake,
And they speak in tender voicings, Heart, of
You.
Answering my call,
Through the leafy hall,
Telling how I'm waiting for your tripping, Sue.
All the world is glad,
Just because I'm mad.
Sense-bereft am I through
my great love for you.

Night is all a-smile,
Happy all the while.
That is why my heart so filled with song
o'erflows.
I have tarried long,
Lilting here my song.
And I'll ever waiting be till life's step slows.
Come to me, my girl,
Precious more than pearl,
I'll be waiting for you where
the grapevine grows.

How my heart doth yearn,
And with anguish burn,
Hungry for sweet pains awaked with your
embrace.

Starward goes my cry.
Echo hears my sigh.
Heaven itself its pity at my plight shows trace.
Parson waits to wed.
Soon the nuptials said.
I've a rose-clad cottage reared for you to grace.

The title-piece of Mr. Jones's first volume reveals his mastery of effective form and his command of the language of passionate appeal. The World War, in which the Negroes of the country gave liberally and heroically, both of blood and treasure, for democracy, quickened failing hopes in them and kindled anew their aspirations. In this poem the writer speaks for his entire race:

## THE HEART OF THE WORLD

In the heart of the world is the call for peace—
Up-surging, symphonic roar.
'Tis ill of all clashings; it seeks release
From fetters of greed and gore.
The winds of the battlefields echo the sigh
Of heroes slumbering deep,
Who gave all they had and now dreamlessly lie
Where the bayonets sent them to sleep.

*Peace for the wealthy; peace for the poor;*
*Peace on the hillside, and peace on the moor.*

In the heart of the world is the call for right:
For fingers to bind up the wound,
Slashed deep by the ruthless, harsh hand of
might,
When Justice is crushed to the ground.

'Tis ill of the fevers of fear of the strong—
Of jealousies—prejudice—pride.
"Is there no ideal that's proof against wrong?"
Man asks of the man at his side.

*Right for the lowly; right for the great;*
*Right all to pilot to happiness' gate.*

In the heart of the world is the call for love:
White heart—Red—Yellow—and Black.
Each face turns to Bethlehem's bright star
above,
Though wolves of self howl at each back.
The whole earth is lifting its voice in a prayer
That nations may learn to endure,
Without killing and maiming, but doing what's
fair
With a soul that is noble and pure.

*Love in weak peoples; love in the strong;*
*Love that will banish all hatred and wrong.*

In the heart of the world is the call of God;
East—West—and North—and South.
Stirring, deep-yearning, breast-heaving call for
God
A-tremble behind each mouth.
The heart's ill of torments that rend men's souls.
Skyward lift all faiths and hopes;
Across all the oceans the evidence rolls,
Refreshing all life's arid slopes.

*God in the highborn; God in the low;*
*God calls us, world-brothers. Hark ye! and know.*

From *Poems of the Four Seas* I will take a piece that gives the Negro background for the yearning expressed in the foregoing poem:

## BROTHERS

They bind his feet; they thong his hands
With hard hemp rope and iron bands.
They scourge his back in ghoulish glee;
And bleed his flesh;—men, mark ye—free.
They still his groans with fiendish shout,
Where flesh streams red they ply the knout.
Thus sons of men feed lust to kill
And yet, oh God! they're brothers still.

They build a pyre of torch and flame
While Justice weeps in deepest shame.
E'en Death in pity bows its head,
Yet 'midst these men no prayer is said.
They gather up charred flesh and bone—
Mementos—boasting brave deed done.
They sip of gore their souls to fill;
Drink deep of blood their hands did spill.

Go tell the world what men have done
Who prate of God and yet have none;
Think of themselves as wholly good,
Blaspheme the name of brotherhood;
Who hearken not as brothers cry

For brother's chance to live and die.
To keep a demon's murder tryst
They'd rend the sepulcher of Christ.

## VIII. *Walter Everette Hawkins*

### CREDO

I am an Iconoclast.
I break the limbs of idols
And smash the traditions of men.

I am an Anarchist.
I believe in war and destruction—
Not in the killing of men,
But the killing of creed and custom.

I am an Agnostic.
I accept nothing without questioning.
It is my inherent right and duty
To ask the reason why.
To accept without a reason
Is to debase one's humanity
And destroy the fundamental process
In the ascertainment of Truth.

I believe in Justice and Freedom.
To me Liberty is priestly and kingly;
Freedom is my Bride,
Liberty my Angel of Light,
Justice my God.

I oppose all laws of state or country,
All creeds of church and social orders,
All conventionalities of society and system
Which cross the path of the light of Freedom
Or obstruct the reign of Right.

This is a faithful self-characterization—such a man in reality is Walter Everette Hawkins. A fearless and independent and challenging spirit. He is the rare kind of man that must put everything to the severe test of absolute principles. He hates shams, hypocrisies, compromises, chicaneries, injustices. His poems are the bold and faithful expressions of his personality. Free he has ever been, free he will be ever, striking right out for freedom and truth. Such a personality is refreshing to meet, whether you encounter it in the flesh or in a book.

WALTER EVERETTE HAWKINS

Born about thirty-five years ago, on a little farm in North Carolina, the thirteenth child of ex-slave parents, young Hawkins, one may imagine, was not opulent in this world's goods. Nor were his opportunities such as are usually considered thrilling. A few terms of miserable schooling in the village of Warrenton, the fragments of a few more terms in a school maintained by the African Methodist Church, then—"the University of Hard Knocks." In the two first-named schools the independent-spirited lad seems not to have gotten along well with his teachers, hence a few dismissals. Always too prone to ask troublesome, challenging questions, too prone to doubts and reflections, he was thought incorrigible. In his "University" he chose his own masters—the great free spirits of the ages—and at the feet of these he was teachable, even while the knocks were hardest.

A lover of wild nature and able to commune with nature's spirit, deeply fond also of communing with the world's master minds in books, Mr. Hawkins is by necessity—while his spirit soars—the slave of routine toil, being, until recently, a mail clerk in the post office of the City of Washington. "My only recreation," he writes me, "is in stealing away to be with the masters, the intellectual dynamos, of the world, who converse with me without wincing and deliver me the key to life's riddle."

A true expression of himself I said Mr. Hawkins's poems are. In no degree are they fictions. As a companion to *Credo*, quoted to introduce him, I will give the last poem in his book, which will again set him before us as he is:

HERO OF THE ROAD

Let me seek no statesman's mantle,
Let me seek no victor's wreath,
Let my sword unstained in battle
Still lie rusting in its sheath;

Let my garments be unsullied,
Let no man's blood to me cling;
Life is love and earth is heaven,
If I may but soar and sing.

This then is my sternest struggle,
Ease the load and sing my song,
Lift the lame and cheer the cheerless
As they plod the road along;
And we see ourselves transfigured
In a new and bigger plan;
Man transformed, his own Messiah,
God embodied into man.

For the whining craven class of men Mr. Hawkins has little respect:

The man who complains
When the world is all song,
Or dares to sit mute
When the world is all wrong;
Who barters his freedom
Vile honors to win,
Deserves but to die
With the vilest of men.

Upon the times in which we live his judgment is severe. His condemnation, however, bears witness to that earnestness of soul and that idealism of spirit which will not let the world repose in its wickedness. From a list of several poems attesting this I select the following as perhaps the most complete in form:

## THE DEATH OF JUSTICE

These the dread days which the seers have
foretold,
These the fell years which the prophets have
dreamed;
Visions they saw in those full days of old,
The fathers have sinned and the children
blasphemed.
Hurt is the world, and its heart is unhealed,
Wrong sways the sceptre and Justice must yield.

We have come to the travail of troublous times,
Justice must bow before Moloch and Baal;
Blasphemous prayers for the triumph of crimes,
High sounds the cry of the children who wail.
Hurt is the world, and its heart is unhealed,
Wrong sways the sceptre and Justice must yield.

In the brute strength of the sword men rely,
They count not Justice in reckoning things;
Whom their lips worship their hearts crucify,
This the oblation the votary brings.
Hurt is the world, and its heart is unhealed,
Wrong sways the sceptre and Justice must yield.

Locked in death-struggle humanity's host,
Seeking revenge with the dagger and sword;
This is the pride which the Pharisees boast,
Man damns his brother in the name of his
Lord.

Hurt is the world, and its heart is unhealed,
Wrong sways the sceptre and Justice must yield.

Time dims the glare of the pomp and applause,
Vainglorious monarchs and proud princes fall;
Until the death of Time revokes his laws,
His awful mandate shall reign over all.
Hurt is the world, and its heart is unhealed,
Wrong sways the sceptre and Justice must yield.

A number of Mr. Hawkins's productions reveal possibilities of beauty and effectiveness, which he had not the patience or the skill to realize. One imagines that he has never been able to bring his spirit to a submissive study of the minutiæ of metrical composition. A poet *in esse*—or *in posse*—is all that nature ever makes. And even the most free spirit must know well the traditions. Whether this iconoclast knows the Cavalier traditions of English poetry may be left to conjecture, but the following piece, illustrating Mr. Hawkins's faults and virtues as a singer, will prove his kinship to the poetic tribe of which Lovelace and Suckling were conspicuous members:

ASK ME WHY I LOVE YOU

Ask me why I love you, dear,
And I will ask the rose
Why it loves the dews of Spring
At the Winter's close;
Why the blossoms' nectared sweets
Loved by questing bee,—
I will gladly answer you,
If they answer me.

Ask me why I love you, dear,
I will ask the flower
Why it loves the Summer sun,
Or the Summer shower;
I will ask the lover's heart
Why it loves the moon,
Or the star-besprinkled skies
In a night in June.

Ask me why I love you, dear,
I will ask the vine
Why its tendrils trustingly
Round the oak entwine;
Why you love the mignonette
Better than the rue,—
If you will but answer me,
I will answer you.

Ask me why I love you, dear,
Let the lark reply,
Why his heart is full of song
When the twilight's nigh;
Why the lover heaves a sigh
When her heart is true;
If you will but answer me,
I will answer you.

## *IX. Claude McKay*

An English subject, being born and growing to manhood in Jamaica, Claude McKay, a pure blood Negro, was first discovered as a poet by English critics. In Jamaica, as early as 1911, when he was but twenty-two years of age, his *Constab Ballads*, in Negro dialect, was published. Even in so broken a tongue this book revealed a poet—on the constabulary force of Jamaica. In 1920 his first book of poems in literary English, *Spring in New Hamp-Shire*, came out in England, with a *Preface* by Mr. I. A. Richards, of Cambridge, England. Meanwhile, shortly after the publication of his first book, he had come to the United States.

CLAUDE MCKAY

Here he has worked at various occupations, has taken courses in Agriculture and English in the Kansas State College, and has thus become acquainted with life in the States. He is now on the editorial staff of the *Liberator*, New York. There has been no poet of his race who has more poignantly felt and more artistically expressed the life of the American Negro. His poetry is a most noteworthy contribution to literature. From *Spring in New Hampshire* I am privileged to take a number of poems which will follow without comment:

### SPRING IN NEW HAMPSHIRE

Too green the springing April grass,
Too blue the silver-speckled sky,
For me to linger here, alas,
While happy winds go laughing by,
Wasting the golden hours indoors,
Washing windows and scrubbing floors.

Too wonderful the April night,
Too faintly sweet the first May flowers,
The stars too gloriously bright,
For me to spend the evening hours,
When fields are fresh and streams are leaping,
Wearied, exhausted, dully sleeping.

### THE LYNCHING

His spirit in smoke ascended to high heaven.
His Father, by the cruelest way of pain,
Had bidden him to his bosom once again;
The awful sin remained still unforgiven:
All night a bright and solitary star
(Perchance the one that ever guided him,
Yet gave him up at last to Fate's wild whim)
Hung pitifully o'er the swinging char.
Day dawned, and soon the mixed crowds came
to view
The ghastly body swaying in the sun:

The women thronged to look, but never a one
Showed sorrow in her eyes of steely blue,
And little lads, lynchers that were to be,
Danced round the dreadful
thing in fiendish glee.

## THE HARLEM DANCER

Applauding youths laughed with young
prostitutes
And watched her perfect, half-clothed body
sway;
Her voice was like the sound of blended flutes
Blown by black players upon a picnic day.
She sang and danced on gracefully and calm,
The light gauze hanging loose about her form;
To me she seemed a proudly-swaying palm
Grown lovelier for passing through a storm.
Upon her swarthy neck, black, shiny curls
Profusely fell; and, tossing coins in praise,
The wine-flushed, bold-eyed boys, and even the
girls,
Devoured her with eager, passionate gaze:
But, looking at her falsely-smiling face,
I knew her self was not in that strange place.

## IN BONDAGE

I would be wandering in distant fields
Where man, and bird, and beast live leisurely,
And the old earth is kind and ever yields
Her goodly gifts to all her children free;

Where life is fairer, lighter, less demanding,
And boys and girls have time and space for play
Before they come to years of understanding,—
Somewhere I would be singing, far away;
For life is greater than the thousand wars
Men wage for it in their insatiate lust,
And will remain like the eternal stars
When all that is to-day is ashes and dust:
But I am bound with you in your mean graves,
Oh, black men, simple slaves of ruthless slaves.

Distinction of idea and phrase inheres in these poems. In them the Negro is esthetically conceived, and interpreted with vision. This is art working as it should. Mr. McKay has passion and the control of it to the ends of art. He has the poet's insight, the poet's understanding.

Perhaps the most arresting poem in this list, and the one most surely attesting the genius of the writer, is *The Harlem Dancer*. It is an achievement in portrayal sufficient by itself to establish a poetic reputation. The divination that penetrates to the secret purity of soul, or nobleness of character, through denying appearances—how rare is the faculty, and how necessary! Elsewhere I give a poem from a Negro woman which evinces the same divine gift in the author, exhibited in a poem no less original and no less deeply impressive—Mrs. Spencer's *At the Carnival*. Here I will companion *The Harlem Dancer* with one from Mr. Dandridge, for the comparison will deepen the effect of each:

## ZALKA PEETRUZA
### (Who Was Christened Lucy Jane)

She danced, near nude, to tom-tom beat,
With swaying arms and flying feet,
'Mid swirling spangles, gauze and lace,
Her all was dancing—save her face.

A conscience, dumb to brooding fears,
Companioned hearing deaf to cheers;
A body, marshalled by the will,
Kept dancing while a heart stood still:

And eyes obsessed with vacant stare
Looked over heads to empty air,
As though they sought to find therein
Redemption for a maiden sin.

'Twas thus, amid force-driven grace,
We found the lost look on her face;
And then, to us, did it occur
That, though we saw—we saw not her.

Returning to Mr. McKay, we may assert that his new volume of verse, *Harlem Shadows*, confirms and enhances the estimate of him we have expressed.

## X. Leslie Pinckney Hill

Bearing the diploma of the Lyric Muse, Mr. Leslie Pinckney Hill, schoolmaster of Cheyney, Pennsylvania, and authentic singer, is one of the newest arrivals on the slopes of Parnassus. A first glance tells that he is an agile climber, sinewy, easy of movement, light of step, with both grace and strength. Every indication in form and motion is for some point far up toward the summit. Youthful he is, ambitious, plainly, and, in spite of a burden, buoyant. "Climber," I said. I will drop the figure. Poets were never pedestrians. Mr. Hill comes not afoot. If not on the wings of Pegasus, yet on wings he comes—*the wings of oppression.* Sad wings! yet it must be remarked that it is commonly on such wings that poets of whatever race and time rise. And Mr. Hill's race knows no other wings. On the wings of oppression the Negro poet and the Negro people are rising toward the summits of Parnassus, Pisgah, and other peaks. This they know, too, and of it they are justly proud.

LESLIE PINCKNEY HILL

In his *Foreword* Mr. Hill thus states the case of his people, and, by implication, of himself: "Nothing in the life of the nation has seemed to me more significant than that dark civilization which the colored man has built up in the midst of a white society organized against it. The Negro has been driven under all the burdens of oppression, both material and spiritual, to the brink of desperation, but he has always been saved by his philosophy of life. He has advanced against all opposition by a certain elevation of his spirit. He has been made strong in tribulation. He has constrained oppression to give him wings."

The significant thing about these wings, in a critical view, is that they fulfill the proper function of wings—bear aloft and sustain in flight through the azure depths. Mr. Hill's wings do bear aloft and sustain: if not always, nor even ever, into the very empyrean of poetry yet invariably, seventy times, into the ampler air. Like all his race, he has suffered much; and, like all his race still, he has gathered wisdom from sorrow. As a true poet should have, he has philosophy, also vision and imagination—vision for himself and his people, imagination that sees facts in terms of beauty and presents truths with vital imagery. Add thereto crafts-manship acquired in the best traditions of English poetry and you have Hill the poet.

The merit of his book cannot be shown by lines and stanzas. As ever with true art, the merit lies in the whole effect of complete poems. Still, we may here first detach from this and that poem a stanza or two, despite the wrong to art. The first and fourth stanzas of the title-poem will indicate Mr. Hill's technique and philosophy:

> I have a song that few will sing
> In honor of all suffering,
> A song to which my heart can bring
> The homage of believing—
> A song the heavy-laden hears
> Above the clamor of his fears,
> While still he walks with blinding tears,
> And drains the cup of grieving.

\*\*\*\*\*\*

So long as life is steeped in wrong,
And nations cry: "How long, how long!"
I look not to the wise and strong
For peace and self-possession;
But right will rise, and mercy shine,
And justice lift her conquering sign
Where lowly people starve and pine
Beneath a world oppression.

The character and temper of the Negro in those gentler aspects which make such an appeal to the heart are revealed in the following sonnet:

## MATER DOLOROSA

O mother, there are moments when I know
God's presence to the full. The city street
May wrap me in the tumult and the heat
Of futile striving; bitter winds may blow
With winter-wilting freeze of hail and snow,
And all my hopes lie shattered in defeat;
But in my heart the springtime blossoms sweet,
And heaven seems very near the way I go.

These moments are the angels of that prayer
Which thou hast breathed for many a troubled year
With bended knee and swarthy-streaming face—
"Uphold him, Father, with a double care:

He is but mortal, yet his days must bear
The world cross, and the burden of his race."

If these poems, taken collectively, do not declare "what is on the Negro's mind" they yet truly reveal, to the reflecting person, what has sunk deep into his heart. They are therefore a message to America, a protest, an appeal, and a warning. They will penetrate, I predict, through breast-armor of *aes triplex* into the hearts of those whom sermons and editorials fail to touch in the springs of action. Such is the virtue of music wed to persuasive words. In strong lines of soaring blank verse, in which Mr. Hill is particularly capable, he makes a direct appeal to America in behalf of his people, in a poem entitled Armageddon:

Because ye schooled them in the arts of life,
And gave to them your God, and poured your
blood
Into their veins to make them what they are,
They shall not fail you in the hour of need.
They own in them enough of you to feel
All that has made you masters in your time—
Dear art and riches, unremitting toil,
Proud types of beauty, an unbounded will
To triumph, wondrous science and old law—
These have they learned to covet and to share.

But deeper in them still is something steeled
To hot abhorrence and unmeasured dread
Of your undaunted sins against the light—
Red sins of lust, of envy and of hate,
Of guilty gain extorted from the weak,
Of brotherhood traduced, and God denied.

All this have they beheld without revolt,
And borne the brunt in agonizing prayer.

For other strains of blood that flow from times
Older than Egypt, whence the dark man gave
The rudiments of learning to all lands,
Have been a strong constraint. And they have
dreamed
Of a peculiar mission under heaven,
And felt the force of unexampled gifts
That make for them a rare inheritance—
The gift of cheerful confidence in man,
The gift of calm endurance, solacing
An infinite capacity for pain,
The gift of an unfeigned humility,
Blinding the eyes of strident arrogance
And bigot pride to that philosophy
And that far-glancing wisdom which it veils,
Of joy in beauty, hardihood in toil,
Of hope in tribulation, and of wide
Adaptive power without a parallel
In chronicles of men.

A sonnet entitled *To a Caged Canary in a Negro Restaurant* will present the poet's people with the persuasiveness of pathos as the foregoing poem with the persuasiveness of reason:

Thou little golden bird of happy song!
A cage cannot restrain the rapturous joy
Which thou dost shed abroad. Thou dost
employ
Thy bondage for high uses. Grievous wrong

Is thine; yet in thy heart glows full and strong
The tropic sun, though far beyond thy flight,
And though thou flutterest there by day and
night
Above the clamor of a dusky throng.
So let my will, albeit hedged about
By creed and caste, feed on the light within;
So let my song sing through the bars of doubt
With light and healing where despair has been;
So let my people bide their time and place,
A hindered but a sunny-hearted race.

It would be an injustice to this poet did I convey the idea that his seventy-odd poems are exclusively occupied with race wrongs and oppression. Not a few of them bear no stamp of an oppressed or afflicted spirit, though of sorrow they may have been nurtured.

A lyric of pure loveliness is the following, entitled

## TO A NOBLY-GIFTED SINGER

All the pleasance of her face
Telleth of an inward grace;
In her dark eyes I have seen
Sorrows of the Nazarene;
In the proud and perfect mould
Of her body I behold,
Rounded in a single view,
The good, the beautiful, the true;
And when her spirit goes up-winging
On sweet airs of artless singing,
Surely the heavenly spheres rejoice
In union with a kindred voice.

Schoolmaster I said Mr. Hill was. To represent his didactic quality, not his purer lyrical note, nor yet his narrative beauty, I choose the following piece:

SELF-DETERMINATION

## *The Philosophy of the American Negro*

Four things we will not do, in spite of all
That demons plot for our decline and fall;
We bring four benedictions which the meek
Unto the proud are privileged to speak,
Four gifts by which amidst all stern-browed
races
We move with kindly hearts and shining faces.

*We will not hate.* Law, custom, creed and caste,
All notwithstanding, here we hold us fast.
Down through the years the mighty ships of
state
Have all been broken on the rocks of hate.

*We will not cease to laugh and multiply.*
We slough off trouble, and refuse to die.
The Indian stood unyielding, stark and grim;
We saw him perish, and we learned of him
To mix a grain of philosophic mirth
With all the crass injustices of earth.

*We will not use the ancient carnal tools.*
These never won, yet centuries of schools,
Of priests, and all the work of brush and pen

Have not availed to win the wisest men
From futile faith in battleship and shell:
We see them fall, and mark that folly well.

*We will not waver in our loyalty.*
No strange voice reaches us across the sea;
No crime at home shall stir us from this soil.
Ours is the guerdon, ours the blight of toil,
But raised above it by a faith sublime
We choose to suffer *here* and bide our time.

And if we hold to this, we dream some day
Our countrymen will follow in our way.

But though teacher Leslie Pinckney Hill is singer too. And though he has a message for America he also has music. His powers are rich, varied, cultured, and developing. His second book will be better than his excellent first.

# CHAPTER III
# THE HEART
# OF NEGRO
# WOMANHOOD

## I. Miss Eva A. Jessye

FROM newspapers I have clipt several poems by Miss Jessye that exhibit a nature touched to the finer things of the world and of life. She has fancy, and skill in expression. I concluded section I of chapter II with a poem of hers, and I will here give two more. The first, in a lighter vein, betrays the human nature of a school-teacher in the midst of her vexations while she tries to appear above the reach of common desires.

MISS EVA A. JESSYE

## SPRING WITH THE TEACHER

'Tis now the time of silver moon,
Of swelling bud and fancies free
As western winds, but then, ah me!
May cannot come too soon;
The rover calls in every child,
And sets his pulses running wild!

"Do stop that noise and take your seat!
Joe, learn to study quietly!
Why girl, it surely has me beat
How you forget geography!
Brazil's in Spain? Here, close that book!
What caused the Civil War, you say?—
Suzanna says somebody took
Her beads; return them right away!

"Now boy, I told you once before
To put that story book away!
I'll call the roll: Beatrice Moore,
Why were you absent yesterday?
Why yes, I heard that mocking bird.
Lee Arthur, straighten up your face!
Well, surely, class, you never heard
Of adverbs having tense and case!

"Now, James, explain the term 'per cent,'
My, my, 'tis surely not forgot!
If it were fun or devilment
You'd know it all, sir, like as not!
Who put that bent pin in my chair?

No one of course—bent pins can walk!
I'll tell you though, had I sat there
I'd make these straps and switches talk.

"A picnic on for Saturday?
(I wish that I were going, too!)
Oh, no! I couldn't get away,
I have so many things to do.
Well, there's the bell! Goodbye, goodbye,
And be good children, don't forget."—
Well, thank the Lord they're gone, but I
Can hear their joyous laughter yet.

'Tis now the time of silver moon,
Of swelling bud and fancies free
As western winds, but then, ah me!
May cannot come too soon!

Though the moral motive is rarely consistent with the artistic, yet in the next poem of Miss Jessye's I shall give there is a perfect reconciliation. Original no doubt is the idea of this poem, but Sappho, it seems to me, as one of her fragments bears witness, had meditated upon the very same idea twenty-five centuries ago.

### TO A ROSEBUD

O dainty bud, I hold thee in my hand—
A castaway, a dead, a lifeless thing,
A few days since I saw thee, wet with dew,
A bud of promise to thy parent cling,
Now thou art crushed yet lovely as before,
The adverse winds but waft thy fragrance more.

How small, how frail! I tread thee underfoot
And crush thy petals in the reeking ground:
Perchance some one in pity for thy state
Will pick thee up in reverence profound—
Lo, thou art pure with virtue more intense,
Thy perfume grows from earthly detriments.

Why do we grieve? Let each affliction bear
A greater beauty springing from the sod,
May sweetness well as incense from the urn,
Which, rising high, enshrouds the throne of
God.
Envoy of Hope, this lesson I disclose—
"Be Ever Sweet," thou humble, fragrant rose!

Miss Jessye, now a teacher of the piano in Muskogee, Oklahoma, was born in Kansas and was graduated from Western University. She has taken prizes in oratory, poetry, and essay-writing. Yet in her early twenties, she has a volume of verse ready for publication.

## II. Mrs. J. W. Hammond

Self-taught, and disclaiming knowledge of books, Mrs. Hammond of Omaha, Nebraska, contributes to *The Monitor* of that city verses of musical cadences and gentle beauty. Her response to the scenes and objects of nature is that of a poetic mind. The spirit of joy sings through her verses. As a representative poem the following may be accepted:

Mrs. J. W. Hammond

## THE OPTIMIST

Who would have the sky any color but blue,
Or the grass any color but green?
Or the flowers that bloom the summer through
Of other color or sheen?

How the sunshine gladdens the human heart—
How the sound of the falling rain
Will cause the tender tears to start,
And free the soul from pain.

Oh, this old world is a great old place!
And I love each season's change,
The river, the brook of purling grace,
The valley, the mountain range.

And when I am called to quit this life,
My feet will not spurn the sod,
Though I leave this world with its beauty
rife,—
There's a glorious one with God!

One other poem of Mrs. Hammond's I will give that is beautiful alike in feeling and treatment.

### TO MY NEIGHBOR BOY

When sweet Aurora lifts her veil,
And floods the world with rosy light,
When morning stars, grown dim and pale,
Proclaim the passing of the night—
With waking bird and opening flower,
I greet with joy the new-born day—
For oft at this exquisite hour,
I hear a strange new roundelay.
No syncopating "jazz" or "blues,"
Insults my eager listening ear,
But softly as the falling dews,
The strains come stealing sweet and clear.
With lilting grace they rise above
The early traffic's sordid din—
My neighbor boy is making love
To his beloved violin.

Sometimes I catch a quivering note—
An over-burdened wordless cry.
I say: "Those are the lines he wrote
The day he told some one goodbye."

But when I hear a joyous strain
Of melody serene and clear,
I smile and say: "All's well again—
The little maiden must be near!"
But best of all I love the mood
That prompts a soft sweet minor key.
My longing soul forgets to brood,
While drinking in the melody.
My restless spirit will not rove,
Nor lose its faith in God and men,
The while my neighbor boy makes love
To his beloved violin.

## III. Mrs. Alice Dunbar-Nelson

A sonnet has already been given from Mrs. Dunbar-Nelson to which I think Mrs. Browning or Christina Rossetti might have appended her signature without detriment to her fame. It is one of a series entitled *A Dream Sequence*, the rest of the sequence being as yet unpublished. Instead of pillaging this sequence, marring the effect of the individual member so dislocated, I will take from her compilation, *The Dunbar Speaker*,[3] so named for her first husband, the poet, two of her original poems. The first is a war poem, doubtless, but the occasion is immaterial. The spirit of rebellion against confinement to the petty thing while the something big calls afar might be evoked into play by any of a hundred situations.

ALICE DUNBAR-NELSON

### I SIT AND SEW

I sit and sew—a useless task it seems,
My hands grown tired, my head weighed down
with dreams—
The panoply of war, the martial tread of men,
Grim-faced, stern-eyed, gazing beyond the ken
Of lesser souls, whose eyes have not seen Death,
Nor learned to hold their lives but as a breath—
But—I must sit and sew.

I sit and sew—my heart aches with desire—
That pageant terrible, that fiercely pouring fire
On wasted fields, and writhing grotesque things
Once men. My soul in pity flings
Appealing cries, yearning only to go
There in that holocaust of hell, those fields of

woe—
But—I must sit and sew.

The little useless seam, the idle patch;
Why dream I here beneath my homely thatch,
When there they lie in sodden mud and rain,
Pitifully calling me, the quick ones and the
slain?
You need me, Christ! It is no roseate dream
That beckons me—this pretty futile seam,
It stifles me—God, must I sit and sew?

The second poem I shall give is also not unrelated to the recent World War, and to all war: the lights alluded to, shining across and down the Delaware for miles, are the lights of the DuPont powder mills. It is a poem of fine symmetry, highly poetic diction, and great allusive meaning—a poem that will bear and repay many readings, never growing less beautiful.

## THE LIGHTS AT CARNEY'S POINT

O white little lights at Carney's Point,
You shine so clear o'er the Delaware;
When the moon rides high in the silver sky,
Then you gleam, white gems on the Delaware.
Diamond circlet on a full white throat,
You laugh your rays on a questing boat;
Is it peace you dream in your flashing gleam,
O'er the quiet flow of the Delaware?

And the lights grew dim at the water's brim,
For the smoke of the mills shredded slow
between;

And the smoke was red, as is new bloodshed,
And the lights went lurid 'neath the livid screen.

O red little lights at Carney's Point,
You glower so grim o'er the Delaware;
When the moon hides low sombrous clouds
below,
Then you glow like coals o'er the Delaware.
Blood red rubies on a throat of fire,
You flash through the dusk of a funeral pyre;
Are there hearth fires red whom you fear and
dread
O'er the turgid flow of the Delaware?

And the lights gleamed gold o'er the river cold,
For the murk of the furnace shed a copper veil;
And the veil was grim at the great cloud's brim,
And the lights went molten, now hot, now pale.

O gold little lights at Carney's Point,
You gleam so proud o'er the Delaware;
When the moon grows wan in the eastering
dawn,
Then you sparkle gold points o'er the Delaware.
Aureate filigree on a Crœsus' brow,
You hasten the dawn on a gray ship's prow.
Light you streams of gold in the grim ship's
hold
O'er the sullen flow of the Delaware?

And the lights went gray in the ash of day,
For a quiet Aurora brought a halcyon balm;
And the sun laughed high in the infinite sky,
And the lights were forgot in
the sweet, sane calm.

Mrs. Dunbar-Nelson has not applied herself to poetry as she has to prose fiction. As a short-story writer she has special distinction.

## *IV. Mrs. Georgia Douglas Johnson*

Exquisite artistry in verse, with infallible poetic content, is exhibited in Mrs. Georgia Douglas Johnson's *The Heart of a Woman*. It is also the saddest book produced by her race. Perfect lyrical notes, the most poignant pathos—that is an exact description of it. Triple bronze cannot armor any breast successfully against its appeal. For the heart that speaks here is a heart that has known its garden of sorrows, its Gethsemane. This is the harvest of her sorrows—dreams and songs, of which she comments:

Mrs. G. D. Johnson

151

The dreams of the dreamer
Are life-drops that pass
The break in the heart
To the Soul's hour-glass.

The songs of the singer
Are tones that repeat
The cry of the heart
Till it ceases to beat.

Neither in memory nor in dreams is there a refuge for the life-wounded heart of this woman:

What need have I for memory,
When not a single flower
Has bloomed within life's desert
For me, one little hour?

What need have I for memory,
Whose burning eyes have met
The corse of unborn happiness
Winding the trail regret?

And thus of her dreams, on the last page of her book:

I am folding up my little dreams
Within my heart to-night,
And praying I may soon forget
The torture of their sight.

What are the experiences and what the conditions of life—what must they have been—which have had the tragic power to make a soul "try to forget it has dreamed of stars?" The world little kens what hearts in it are breaking, and why. To the grave the secret goes with the many, one in a million betrays it in a cry. But not here is it betrayed:

## SMOTHERED FIRES

A woman with a burning flame
Deep covered through the years
With ashes—ah! she hid it deep,
And smothered it with tears.

Sometimes a baleful light would rise
From out the dusky bed,
And then the woman hushed it quick
To slumber on, as dead.

At last the weary war was done,
The tapers were alight,
And with a sigh of victory
She breathed a soft—goodnight!

Not without hurt to itself may the oyster produce its pearl. These poems from the heart of a woman remind me of nothing so much as a string of pearls. Each one is witness to a bruise or gash to the spirit. The lyric cry has not been more piercing in anything written on American soil, piercing all the more for the perfect restraint, the sure artistry. It was a heart surcharged with sorrow in which these pearls of poesy took shape from secret wounds. The heart of one woman speaks in them for thousands in America, else inarticulate. "We weep," says the African proverb, "we weep in our hearts like the tortoise." Without one word or hint of race in all the book there is yet between its covers the unwritten, unwritable tragedy of that borderland race which knows not where it belongs in the world, a truly homeless race in soul. A sadder book could hardly be.

Mrs. Georgia Douglas Johnson was born in Atlanta, Georgia, and received her academic education in Atlanta University and a musical education at Oberlin. She now lives in Washington, D. C. She is at the beginning of her career as an author. Two other books of lyrics, under the titles of *An Autumn Love Cycle*, and *Bronze*,[4] she has in preparation for the press at this time. Some of their contents have already appeared in magazines. These two new volumes will make an advance in power and in richness of content beyond *The Heart of a Woman*. They will also provide the key to the tragic mystery concealed in that book. A poem that is to appear in *Bronze* will be given in a later chapter. I will here give another. Both have already been published in magazines.

### THE OCTOROON

One drop of midnight in the dawn of life's
pulsating stream
Marks her an alien from her kind, a shade amid
its gleam.
Forevermore her step she bends, insular,
strange, apart—
And none can read the riddle of
her strangely warring heart.

The stormy current of her blood beats like a
mighty sea
Against the man-wrought iron bars of her
captivity.
For refuge, succor, peace, and rest, she seeks
that humble fold

Whose every breath is kindliness,
whose hearts are purest gold.

## *V. Miss Angelina W. Grimké*

Not less distinctive in quality than Mrs. Johnson's, and not less beautiful in artistry, are the brief lyrics of Miss Angelina W. Grimké, also of the city of Washington. If hers should be called imagist poetry or no I cannot say, but I am certain that more vivid imaging of objects has not been done in verse by any contemporary. This, too, in stanzas that suggest in their perfection of form the work of the old lapidaries. Nor is there but a surface or formal beauty. There is passion, there is beauty of idea, the soul of lyric poetry is there as well as the form. I am weighing well my words in giving this praise, and I know that not one in the thousand of those who write good verse would deserve them. But I ask the sceptical individual to re-read them after he has perused the poems themselves.

I will present several without interrupting comment:

MISS ANGELINA GRIMKÉ

## DAWN

Grey trees, grey skies, and not a star;
Grey mist, grey hush;
And then, frail, exquisite, afar,
A hermit-thrush.

## A WINTER TWILIGHT

A silence slipping around like death,
Yet chased by a whisper, a sigh, a breath;
One group of trees, lean, naked and cold,
Inking their crests 'gainst a sky green-gold;
One path that knows where the corn flowers
were;
Lonely, apart, unyielding, one fir;
And over it softly leaning down,
One star that I loved ere the fields went brown.

## THE PUPPET-PLAYER

Sometimes it seems as though some puppet-
player.
A clenched claw cupping a craggy chin.
Sits just beyond the border of our seeing,
Twitching the strings with slow, sardonic grin.

## THE WANT OF YOU

A hint of gold where the moon will be;
Through the flocking clouds just a star or two;
Leaf sounds, soft and wet and hushed,
And oh! the crying want of you.

## EL BESO

Twilight—and you,
Quiet—the stars;
Snare of the shine of your teeth,
Your provocative laughter,
The gloom of your hair;
Lure of you, eye and lip;
Yearning, yearning,
Languor, surrender;
Your mouth,
And madness, madness,
Tremulous, breathless, flaming,
The space of a sigh;
Then awakening—remembrance,
Pain, regret—your sobbing;
And again quiet—the stars,
Twilight—and you.

## AT THE SPRING DAWN

I watched the dawn come,
Watched the spring dawn come.
And the red sun shouldered his way up
Through the grey, through the blue,
Through the lilac mists.
The quiet of it! The goodness of it!
And one bird awoke, sang, whirred
A blur of moving black against the sun,
Sang again—afar off.
And I stretched my arms to the redness of the
sun,
Stretched to my finger tips,

And I laughed.
Ah! It is good to be alive, good to love,
At the dawn,
At the spring dawn.

## TO KEEP THE MEMORY OF CHARLOTTE FORTEN GRIMKÉ

Still are there wonders of the dark and day;
The muted shrilling of shy things at night,
So small beneath the stars and moon;
The peace, dream-frail, but perfect while the
light
Lies softly on the leaves at noon.
These are, and these will be
Until Eternity;
But she who loved them well has gone away.

Each dawn, while yet the east is veiled gray,
The birds about her window wake and sing;
And far away each day some lark
I know is singing where the grasses swing;
Some robin calls and calls at dark.
These are, and these will be
Until Eternity;
But she who loved them well has gone away.

The wild flowers that she loved down green
ways stray;
Her roses lift their wistful buds at dawn,
But not for eyes that loved them best;
Only her little pansies are all gone,
Some lying softly on her breast.

And flowers will bud and be
Until Eternity;
But she who loved them well has gone away.

Where has she gone? And who is there to say?
But this we know: her gentle spirit moves
And is where beauty never wanes,
Perchance by other streams, 'mid other groves;
And to us here, ah! she remains
A lovely memory
Until Eternity.
She came, she loved, and then she went away.

The subject of these beautiful memorial verses was not simply in feeling but in expression also a poet herself. From "A June Song" written by her I will take a stanza in evidence:

How shall we crown her bright young head?
Crown it with roses, rare and red;
Crown it with roses, creamy white,
As the lotus bloom that sweetens the night.
Crown it with roses as pink as shell
In which the voices of ocean dwell.
And a fairer queen
Shall ne'er be seen
Than our lovely, laughing June.

## VI. Mrs. Anne Spencer

Who can fathom to its depths the heart of womanhood? Under the conditions of American

life the Negro woman's heart offers difficulties peculiar to itself. These various writers—talented, cultured, with the keen sensibilities of a specially sensitive people—have given us glimpses into some of the depths, not all. A poet of the other sex, Mr. McKay, with that divination which belongs to the poet, intimates in *The Harlem Dancer*, that the index of the heart is not always in the occupation or the face:

MRS. ANNE SPENCER

But, looking at her falsely-smiling face,
I knew her self was not in that strange place.

No, her self was free and too noble to be smirched by the "passionate gaze of wine-flushed, bold-eyed boys." It is a paradox that has puzzled a recent white novelist. Cissie Dildine, in Mr. Stribling's *Birthright*, pilferer though she is, and sacrificer of her maidenhood, yet does not lose caste among her people. They speak affectionately of her and minister lovingly to her in jail, with no hint of reproach. It is not other standards, as the novelist intimates, that we must apply, but only right standards, in view of circumstances.

I am able to give here a poem that may start in the reader's mind a fruitful train of reflections, tending toward profound ethical truth. The writer, Mrs. Anne Spencer of Lynchburg, Virginia, in all of her work that I have seen, has marked originality. Her style is independent, unconventional, and highly compressed. The poem which follows will fairly represent her work and at the same time open another avenue to the secret chambers of the Negro woman's heart:

## AT THE CARNIVAL

Gay little Girl-of-the-Diving-Tank,
I desire a name for you,
Nice, as a right glove fits;
For you—who amid the malodorous
Mechanics of this unlovely thing,
Are darling of spirit and form.
I know you—a glance, and what you are
Sits-by-the-fire in my heart.
My Limousine-Lady knows you, or
Why does the slant-envy of her eye mark
Your straight air and radiant inclusive smile?
Guilt pins a fig-leaf; Innocence is its own
adorning.
The bull-necked man knows you—this first
time
His itching flesh sees form divine and vibrant
health,
And thinks not of his avocation.
I came incuriously—
Set on no diversion save that my mind
Might safely nurse its brood of misdeeds

In the presence of a blind crowd.
The color of life was gray.
Everywhere the setting seemed right
For my mood!
Here the sausage and garlic booth
Sent unholy incense skyward;
There a quivering female-thing
Gestured assignations, and lied
To call it dancing;
There, too, were games of chance
With chances for none;
But oh! Girl-of-the-Tank, at last!
Gleaming Girl, how intimately pure and free
The gaze you send the crowd,
As though you know the dearth of beauty
In its sordid life.
We need you—my Limousine-Lady,
The bull-necked man, and I.
Seeing you here brave and water-clean,
Leaven for the heavy ones of earth,
I am swift to feel that what makes
The plodder glad is good; and
Whatever is good is God.
The wonder is that you are here;
I have seen the queer in queer places,
But never before a heaven-fed
Naiad of the Carnival-Tank!
Little Diver, Destiny for you,
Like as for me, is shod in silence;
Years may seep into your soul

The bacilli of the usual and the expedient;
I implore Neptune to claim his child to-day!

## *VII. Miss Jessie Fauset*

By way of indicating the idealistic aspirations of the colored people I gave at the end of Chapter I. J. Mord Allen's poem *The Psalm of the Uplift*. For the same purpose I will give here, at the end of this chapter, a poem of the very present day from one of the most accomplished young women of the Negro race. Besides its intrinsic merit as a poem it has the further recommendation for a place in this chapter that it celebrates a woman of the black race who was the very embodiment of its noblest qualities—illiterate slave though she was. It is a splendid testimonial to her people of this later day that Negro literature is filled with tributes to Sojourner Truth. She was indeed a wonderful woman, altogether worthy to be ranked with the noble heroines of biblical story. From a Negro historian I take the following restrained account of her:[5]

Miss Jessie Redmon Fauset

Two Negroes, because of their unusual gifts, stood out with great prominence in the agitation. These were Sojourner Truth and Frederick Douglass. Sojourner Truth was born of slave parents about 1798 in Ulster County, New York. She remembered vividly in later years the cold, wet cellar-room in which slept the slaves of the family to which she belonged, and where she was taught by her mother to repeat the Lord's Prayer and to trust in God at all times. When in the course of gradual emancipation in New York she became legally free in 1827, her master refused to comply with the law. She left, but was pursued and found. Rather than have her go back, a friend paid for her services for the rest of the year. Then came an evening when, searching for one of her children that had been stolen and sold, she found herself a homeless wanderer. A Quaker family gave her lodging for the night. Subsequently she went to New York City, joined a Methodist Church, and worked hard to improve her condition. Later, having decided to leave New York for a lecturing tour through the East, she made a small bundle of her belongings and informed a friend that her name was no longer Isabella but Sojourner. She went on her way, lecturing to people where she found them assembled and being entertained in many aristocratic homes. She was entirely untaught in the schools, but she was witty, original, and always suggestive. By her tact and her gift of song she kept down ridicule, and by her fervor and faith she won many friends for the anti-slavery cause. As to her name she said: "And the Lord gave me Sojourner because I was to travel up an' down the land showin' the people their sins an' bein' a sign unto them. Afterwards I told the Lord I wanted another name, 'cause everybody else had two names, an' the Lord gave me Truth, because I was to declare the truth to the people."

The poem follows, with the author's note on the saying of Sojourner Truth which occasioned it:

ORIFLAMME

I can remember when I was a little, young girl, how my old mammy would sit out of doors in the evenings and look up at the stars and groan, and I would say, 'Mammy, what makes you groan so?' And she would say, 'I am groaning to think of my poor children; they do not know where I be and I don't know where they be. I look up at the stars and they look up at the stars!'— Sojourner Truth.

> I think I see her sitting bowed and black,
> Stricken and seared with slavery's mortal scars,
> Reft of her children, lonely, anguished, yet
> Still looking at the stars.
>
> Symbolic mother, we thy myriad sons,
> Pounding our stubborn hearts on Freedom's
> bars,
> Clutching our birthright, fight with faces set,
> Still visioning the stars!

"Still visioning the stars"—that is the idealism of the Negro. The soul of Sojourner Truth goes marching on, star-led.

CHAPTER IV
# AD ASTRA PER ASPERA

## I. PER ASPERA

### *I. Edward Smythe Jones*

IT has not frequently happened in these times that a poet has dated a poem from a prison cell, or dedicated a book of poems to the judge of a police court. Mr. Edward Smythe Jones, however, has done this, and there is an interesting story by way of explanation. From the poem alluded to it seems that Mr. Jones in his over-mastering desire to drink at the Harvard fountain of learning tramped out of the Southland up to Cambridge. Arriving travel-worn, friendless, moneyless, hungry, he was preparing to bivouac on the Harvard campus his first night in the University city, when, being misunderstood, and not believed, he was apprehended as a vagabond and thrown into jail. A poem, however, the poem which tells this story, delivered him. The judge was convinced by it, kindly entreated the prisoner, and set him free to return to the academic shades. *Ad astra per aspera.*

It was in "Cell No. 40, East Cambridge Jail, Cambridge, Massachusetts, July 26, 1910," that the unlucky bard committed to verse this story, transmuting harsh experience to the joy of artistic production. The last half of his version runs as follows:

EDWARD SMYTHE JONES

As soon as locked within the jail,
Deep in a ghastly cell,
Methought I heard the bitter wail
Of all the fiends of hell!
"O God, to Thee I humbly pray
No treacherous prison snare
Shall close my soul within for aye
From dear old Harvard Square."

Just then I saw an holy Sprite
Shed all her radiant beams,

And round her shone the source of light
Of all the poets' dreams!
I plied my pen in sober use,
And spent each moment spare
In sweet communion with the Muse
I met in Harvard Square!

I cried: "Fair Goddess, hear my tale
Of sorrow, grief and pain."
That made her face an ashen pale,
But soon it glowed again!
"They placed me here; and this my crime,
Writ on their pages fair;—
'He left his sunny native clime,
And came to Harvard Square!'"

"Weep not, my son, thy way is hard,
Thy weary journey long—
But thus I choose my favorite bard
To sing my sweetest song.
I'll strike the key-note of my art
And guide with tend'rest care,
And breathe a song into thy heart
To honor Harvard Square.

"I called old Homer long ago,
And made him beg his bread
Through seven cities, ye all know,
His body fought for, dead.
Spurn not oppression's blighting sting,
Nor scorn thy lowly fare;

By them I'll teach thy soul to sing
The songs of Harvard Square.

"I placed great Dante in exile,
And Byron had his turns;
Then Keats and Shelley smote the while,
And my immortal Burns!
But thee I'll build a sacred shrine,
A store of all my ware;
By them I'll teach thy soul to sing
'A place in Harvard Square.'

"To some a store of mystic lore,
To some to shine a star:
The first I gave to Allan Poe,
The last to Paul Dunbar.
Since thou hast waited patient, long,
Now by my throne I swear
To give to thee my sweetest song
To sing in Harvard Square."

And when she gave her parting kiss
And bade a long farewell,
I sat serene in perfect bliss
As she forsook my cell.
Upon the altar-fire she poured
Some incense very rare;
Its fragrance sweet my soul assured
I'd enter Harvard Square.

Reclining on my couch, I slept
A sleep sweet and profound;
O'er me the blessed angels kept
Their vigil close around.
With dawning's smile, my fondest hope
Shone radiant and fair:
The Justice cut each chain and rope
'Tween me and Harvard Square!

Of all the Negro poets whose writings I have perused, Edward Smythe Jones is the most difficult to estimate with certainty. There is an eloquence and luxuriance of language and imagery in his stanzas which perplexes the critic and yet persuades him to repeated readings. The result, however, fails to become clear. If, with his copiousness, the reserve of disciplined art ever becomes his, and his critical faculty is trained to match his creative, then poetry of noteworthy merit may be expected from him. His deeply religious bent, his aspiration after the best things of the mind, his ambition to treat lofty themes, augur well for him.

Mr. Jones's two best poems, *The Sylvan Cabin: A Centenary Ode on the Birth of Abraham Lincoln* and *An Ode to Ethiopia: to the Aspiring Negro Youth*, are too long for insertion here. I will give a shorter patriotic ode, not included in his book, but written, I believe, during the World War:

FLAG OF THE FREE

Flag of the free, our sable sires
First bore thee long ago
Into hot battles' hell-lit fires,
Against the fiercest foe.

And when he shook his shaggy mien,
And made the death-knell ring,
Brave Attucks fell upon the Green,
Thy stripes first crimsoning.

Thy might and majesty we hurl,
Against the bolts of Mars;
And from thy ample folds unfurl
Thy field of flaming stars!
Fond hope to nations in distress,
Thy starry gleam shall give;
The stricken in the wilderness
Shall look to thee and live.

What matter if where Boreas roars,
Or where sweet Zephyr smiles?
What matter if where eagle soars,
Or in the sunlit isles?
Thy flowing crimson stripes shall wave
Above the bluish brine,
Emblazoned ensign of the brave,
And Liberty enshrine!

Flag of the Free, still float on high
Through every age to come;
Bright beacon of the azure sky,
True light of Freedom's dome.
Till nations all shall cease to grope
In vain for liberty,
Oh, shine, last lingering star of hope
Of all humanity!

Is there, in all our American poetry, a more eloquent apostrophe to our flag than that, not excepting even Joseph Rodman Drake's? Perhaps the allusion to Attucks in the first stanza will require a note for the white reader. Every colored school-child, however, knows that Crispus Attucks was a brave and stalwart Negro, who, in the van of the patriots of Boston that resisted the British soldiers in the so-called "Boston Massacre," March 5, 1770, fell with two British bullets in his breast, among the first martyrs for independence:

> Thus Attucks brave, without a moment's pause,
> Full bared his breast in Freedom's holy cause,
> First fell and tore the code of
> Tyranny's cruel laws—

so writes of him this same poet in his *Ode to Ethiopia*.

## II. Raymond Garfield Dandridge

Twelve years ago a young house-decorator in Cincinnati was stricken down with partial paralysis, since which time he has been bedfast and all but helpless. On this bed of distress he learned what resources were within himself, powers that in health he knew not of. The fountain of poetry sprang up in what threatened to be a desert life.—The artist-nature within manifested itself in a new realm, the realm of words set to tuneful measures. This artisan, turned by affliction into a poet, is Raymond Garfield Dandridge. Again, *ad astra per aspera*.

It is not great poetry that Dandridge is giving to the world, but it is poetry. His musings shaped into rhyme reach the heart. They have sweetness and light—"the two most precious things in the world." All the art he has acquired, untaught, from his reading

173

and unaided thinking. Naturally one would not expect that art to be flawless. His initial poem, while not literally a self-description, will serve to introduce this adopted son of the lyric Muse:

RAYMOND G. DANDRIDGE

## THE POET

The poet sits and dreams and dreams;
He scans his verse; he probes his themes.
Then turns to stretch or stir about,
Lest, like his thoughts, his strength give out.
Then off to bed, for he must rise
And cord some wood, or tamp some ties,
Or break a field of fertile soil,
Or do some other manual toil.
He dare not live by wage of pen,
Most poorly paid of poor paid men,
With shoes o'er-run, and threadbare clothes,—
And editors among the foes
Who mock his song, deny him bread,

Then sing his praise when he is dead.
A secret consolation is intimated
in the following lines:

## TO—

Though many are the dreams I dream,
They're born within a single theme.
The same kind voice I ever hear,
Instilling faith, upbraiding fear:
The same consoling smile appears
To snuff my sighs and dry my tears:
And fondest heart, of purest gold,
Is hers whose name I here withhold,
And pray naught ever change my theme,
Or wake me from my dream.
Reflections upon the deeper meanings
of life and death are inevitable to one
situated as Mr. Dandridge is, provided he
is given to serious reflections at all. And
the thoughts of such a person are apt to
have value for their sincerity. Two brief
meditations in rhyme, as we may call them,
will represent his thinking on such themes:

## TIME TO DIE

Black Brother, think you life so sweet
That you would live at any price?
Does mere existence balance with
The weight of your great sacrifice?
Or, can it be you fear the grave

Enough to live and die a slave?
O, Brother! be it better said,
When you are gone and tears are shed,
That your death was the stepping stone
Your children's children cross'd upon.
Men have died that men might live:
Look every foeman in the eye!
If necessary, your life give
For something, ere in vain you die.

## ETERNITY

Vast realm beyond the gate of death,
Where craven scavengers and kings,
Alike, with passing final breath,
Relinquish claim to earthly things:
Endless, unexplored expanse,
Where souls, bereft of mortal clay,
Wander at will, in peace, perchance—
Perchance in strife, who dare would say?
Even in the confinement to which his affliction
has subjected him, Mr. Dandridge has felt
the strong pulse-throbs of his people's new
kindled aspirations. The strength of the soul
may indeed increase with the weakness of the
body. These lines are surely not wanting in
the passion without which "facts" are cold:

## FACTS

Triumphant Sable Heroes homeward turning,
Arrayed in medals bright, and half-healed scars,
Have service, life, and limb been given earning
Trophies issued at the hand of Mars?
If your sole gain has been these "marks of
battle,"
If valiant deeds insure no greater claim,
If you are still to be the herder's cattle,
Then ill spilt blood fell short of Freedom's aim.
Democracy means more than empty letters,
And Liberty far more than partly free;
Yet, both are void as long as men in fetters
Are at eclipse with Opportunity.

## III. *George Marion McClellan*

Aptly has Mr. McClellan entitled his book of poems *The Path of Dreams*. A dreamer is he and the home of his spirit is dreamland:

GEORGE MARION MCCLELLAN

Sweet-scented winds move inward from the
shore,
Blythe is the air of June with silken gleams,
My roving fancy treads at will once more
The golden path of dreams.

And that path leads the poet ever back to the golden days of his
youth, when Southern suns and Southern moons steeped his very
being in dreams and Southern birds gave him their melodies and
Southern mountains lifted his soul heavenward. A wanderer upon
the earth he appears to have been, and as all wanderers' hearts turn
back to some loved region or spot so his to Dixie. Seldom has the
longing for distant, remembered scenes, for spring's returning and
for summer's glow, been more sweetly expressed in rhyme than in
the various poems of *The Path of Dreams*. And yet, sweeter songs
than those are locked up in his breast, not to be sung:

The summer sweetness fills my heart with songs
I cannot sing, with loves I cannot speak.

When harsh necessity imprisons him in the city he sighs:

I think the sight of fields and shady lanes
Would ease my heart of pains.

But what contradictions poets have ever found in their experi-
ences! The ministrants of joy but wring the cry of pain from the
yearning heart. Lovely May is harder to endure, in exile, than
gloomy December. The city's discordant cries may be endured,
bringing neither grief nor joy, while a bird's carol may be exquisite
torture:

> The woodlark's tender warbling lay,
> Which flows with melting art,
> Is but a trembling song of love
> That serves to break my heart.

Musing on whatever scene, the poet's thoughts are tinged with that sadness which to every sensitive nature has a sweetness in it:

> The sun went down in beauty,
> While I stood musing alone,
> Stood watching the rushing river
> And heard its restless moan;
> Longings, vague, intenable,
> So far from speech apart,
> Like the endless rush of the river,
> Went surging through my heart.

With no less sadness or beauty, and with that philosophy towards which poetry ever has a bias, our poet of dreams thus reflects, on watching the ephemera that dart with glimmering wings in keen delight where the breezes fling the sweets of May:

> Creatures of gauze and velvet wings,
> With a day of gleams and flowers,
> Who knows—in the light of eternal things—
> Your life is less than ours?
> Weary at last, it is ours, like you,
> When our brief day is done,
> Folding our hands, to say adieu,
> And pass with the setting sun.

One must say of George Marion McClellan: "Here is a finely touched spirit that responds deeply to the mystery and charm of mountains and starry skies, and that charm and mystery he is capable of expressing in stanzas of lyric beauty." Every page of his book will confirm for the reader the estimate he may have formed from the quotations already given. Without rifling it of its choicest treasures I will put before the reader a few entire poems which I am sure will give increased delight on repeated readings:

## TO HOLLYHOCKS

Gay hollyhocks with flaming bells
And waving plumes, as gently swells
The breeze upon the Summer air,
You bind me still with magic spells
When to the wind, in grave farewells,
You bow in all your graces fair.

You bring me back the childhood view,
Where arching skies and deepest blue
Stretch on in endless lengths above;
To see you so awakes anew
Long past emotions, from which grew
My wild and first heart-throbs of love.

There is in all your brilliant dyes,
Your gorgeousness and azure skies,
A joy like soothing summer rain;
Yet in the scene there vaguely lies
A something half akin to sighs,
Along the borderland of pain.

## THE HILLS OF SEWANEE

Sewanee Hills of dear delight,
Prompting my dreams that used to be,
I know you are waiting me still to-night
By the Unika Range of Tennessee.

The blinking stars in endless space,
The broad moonlight and silvery gleams,
To-night caress your wind-swept face,
And fold you in a thousand dreams.

Your far outlines, less seen than felt,
Which wind with hill propensities,
In moonlight dreams I see you melt
Away in vague immensities.

And, far away, I still can feel
Your mystery that ever speaks
Of vanished things, as shadows steal
Across your breast and rugged peaks.

O dear blue hills, that lie apart,
And wait so patiently down there,
Your peace takes hold upon my heart
And makes its burden less to bear.

## THE FEET OF JUDAS

Christ washed the feet of Judas!
The dark and evil passions of his soul,
His secret plot, and sordidness complete,

His hate, his purposing, Christ knew the whole,
And still in love he stooped and washed his feet.

Christ washed the feet of Judas!
Yet all his lurking sin was bare to him,
His bargain with the priest, and more than this,
In Olivet, beneath the moonlight dim,
Aforehand knew and felt his treacherous kiss.

Christ washed the feet of Judas!
And so ineffable his love 'twas meet,
That pity fill his great forgiving heart,
And tenderly he wash the traitor's feet,
Who in his Lord had basely sold his part.

Christ washed the feet of Judas!
And thus a girded servant, self-abased,
Taught that no wrong this side the gate of
heaven
Was ever too great to wholly be effaced,
And, though unasked, in spirit be forgiven.

And so if we have ever felt the wrong
Of trampled rights, of caste, it matters not,
What e'er the soul has felt or suffered long,
Oh, heart! this one thing should not be forgot:
Christ washed the feet of Judas.

## IN MEMORY OF KATIE REYNOLDS, DYING

O Death!
If thou hast aught of tenderness,
Be kindly in thy touch
Of her whose fragile slenderness
Was overburdened much
With life. And let her seem to go to sleep,
As often does a tired child, when it has grown
Too tired to longer weep.

A rose but half in bloom—
She is too young and beautiful to die,
But yet, if she must go,
Let her go out as goes a sigh
From tired life and woe.
And let her keep, in death's brief space
This side the grave, the dusky beauty still
Belonging to her face.

She must have been
Of those upon the trembling lyre
Of whom the poets sung:
"Whom the gods love" and desire
Fade and "die young."
Her life so loved on earth was brief,
But yet withal so beautiful there is no cause,
But in our loss, for grief.

This poet, formerly a school principal in Louisville, Kentucky, is now in Los Angeles, California, whither he took his tubercular son—in vain—endeavoring to establish there a sanitarium for persons of his race afflicted as his son was. For the third time: *ad astra per aspera.*

## IV. Charles P. Wilson

The following verses were written by a man in the Missouri State Penitentiary. He might prefer that his name be withheld. He will shortly go forth a free man and a better one—so resolved to be—with verses enough composed during his period of incarceration to make a small book:

### SOMEBODY'S CHILD

Don't be too quick to condemn me,
Because I have made a bad start;
Remember you see but the surface,
And know not what's in the heart.
I may bear the marks of a sinful life,
And I may have been a bit wild;
But back of all remains this fact,
That I am somebody's child.

My cheeks by tears may be polished,
And my heart is no stranger to pain;
I know what it is to be friendless,
And to learn each affliction means gain.
I may be out in life's storm,
And misfortune around me has piled;
But kindly remember this little fact,
That I am somebody's child.

Probably to-night you'll be happy,
In some joys or pleasures you'll share:
And that very same moment may find me,
Tearfully pleading in prayer.
So don't be too harsh when you judge me,
For your judgment with God will be filed;
You would know—could you see past the
surface—
That I am somebody's child.


And so a fourth time the motto—or is it a proverb?—*ad astra per aspera.*

## *V. Leon R. Harris*

Now editor of the Richmond (Indiana) *Blade*, contributor of short-stories to *The Century Magazine*, an honored citizen and the head of a respected family, Leon R. Harris was an orphan asylum's ward. Most splendidly has he, yet in his early thirties, illustrated the old adage chosen as a heading for this chapter. His father, a roving musician, took no interest in the future poet. His mother died and left him almost in the cradle. The orphanage which became his refuge gave him at least food, shelter, and schooling to the fourth grade. Then he was given to a Kentucky family to be reared. It was virtual slavery, and the boy ran away from over-work and beatings. Making his escape to Cincinnati he was befriended by a traveling salesman and began to find himself. At eleven years of age, some of his verses were printed in a Cincinnati daily with "Author Unknown" attached. He now made his way to Berea and worked his way for two years in that good old college. Then for three years he worked his way in Tuskegee.

We next find him in Iowa, married; then in North Carolina, teaching school; then in Ohio, working in steel mills. This last was his employment until about two years ago. His short stories and poems are right out of his life. In the former the peonage system, prevalent in some sections of the South, and the cruelties of the convict labor camps are more powerfully portrayed than anywhere else in American literature. The following poem will represent his writings in verse:

LEON R. HARRIS

THE STEEL MAKERS

Filled with the vigor such jobs demand,
Strong of muscle and steady of hand,
Before the flaming furnaces stand
The men who make the steel.
'Midst the sudden sounds of falling bars,
'Midst the clang and bang of cranes and cars,

Where the earth beneath them jerks and jars,
They work with willing zeal.

They meet each task as they meet each day,
Ready to labor and full of play;
Their faces are grimy, their hearts are gay,
There is sense in the songs they sing;
While stooped like priests at the holy mass,
In the beaming light of the lurid gas,
Their jet black shadows each other pass,
And their hammers loudly ring.

What do they see through the furnace door,
From which the dazzling white lights pour?
Ah, more than the sizzling liquid ore
They see as they gaze within!
For a band of steel engirdles the earth,
Binds men to men from their very birth,
Through all that exists of any worth
There courses a steely vein.

Steamers that ply o'er the ocean deep,
Trains which over the mountains creep,
The ships of the air that dart and leap
Where the screaming eagles soar;
The plow which produces the nation's food,
The bars that keep the bad from the good,
Skyscrapers standing where forests stood,
They see through their furnace door.

They see the secretive submarines,
And the noisy, whirring big machines,
Grinding steel into numberless things
The people know and need;
The scissors that fashion wee babies' clothes,
The beds where the pallid sick repose,
The knife that the nervy surgeon holds
O'er the wounds that gape and bleed.

Yet more they see through the furnace door!
They see the bursting hot shells pour
On the battle-fields as in days of yore
The Deluge waters fell.
They see the bloody bayonet blade,
The unsheathed sword and the hand grenade,
The havoc, the wreck and the ruin made
By the steel they roll and sell.

All this through the furnace door they see
As they work and laugh—they are full and free;
Their steel has purchased their liberty
From want and the tyrant's sway.
And just as long as their gas shall burn,
In times of need will the people turn
To them for their product and they shall learn
Its value endures for aye.

For of what they make we are servants all,
They have bound our lives in an iron thrall,
We do their bidding, we heed their call,
As they work with willing zeal.

So tap your heats with a courage bold,
You're worth to your world a thousand fold
More than the men who mine her gold,
You men who make her steel!

Intrinsic merit is in that poem, apart from the circumstance of its being written by a workman himself. As an interpretation of the life of his fellow-workmen—their imaginative, inner life—it is a human document to be reflected upon. As for the artistic quality of the verses they place you in imagination amid the sights and sounds described and they have something in them suggestive of the steel bars the men are making.

## VI. Irvin W. Underhill

In what strange disguises comes ofttimes the call to nobler things! Our happiness not seldom springs out of seeming misfortune. An illustration is afforded by Mr. Irvin W. Underhill, of Philadelphia, to whom blindness brought a more glorious seeing—the seeing of truth, of greater meaning in life, of greater beauty in the world. Out of this new vision springs a corresponding message in verse, a message not of bitterness for

what might to another man, in the middle years of his life, have seemed a bitter loss, but of love, and exhortation, and encouragement. Blind, he lives in the Light. In his little book, entitled *Daddy's Love and Other Poems*, are poems witnessing to a beautiful spirit, poems of beauty. Because of its sage counsel, however, I pass over some of these lovelier expressions of sentiment and choose a didactic piece:

IRVIN W. UNDERHILL

## TO OUR BOYS

I speak to you, my Colored boys,
I bid you to be men,
Don't put yourselves upon the rack
Like pigeons in a pen.
Come out and face life's problem, boys,
With faith and courage too,
And justify that wondrous faith,
Abe Lincoln had in you.

Don't treat life as a little toy,
A dance or a game of ball;
Those things are all right in their place,
But they are not life's all.
Life is a problem serious,
Give it the best you have,
Succeed in all you undertake
And help your brother live.

If farming seems to be your call,
Then take hold of the plough,
And stick it down into the soil
Till sweat runs down your brow.
Then make this resolution firm:
"I'm going to do my best,
And stick this good old plough of mine
Down deeper than the rest."

If you're to be a carpenter
Then train your hand and eye
To work out angles, clean and clear
As any metal die.
Then read up on materials,
On beauty and on style,
And prove to all, the house you build
Is sure to be worth while.

Why sure, a banker, you can be,
A lawyer or a priest;
Or you can be a merchant prince,
Their work is not the least.
It makes no difference what you try
If you would get the best,
You'll have to stick that plough of yours
Down deeper than the rest.

Don't fawn up to another man
And beg him for a job;
Remember that your brain and his
Were made by the same God.

So use it boys, with all your might,
With faith and courage too,
And justify that wondrous faith
Abe Lincoln had in you.

## II. ad astra

## I. James C. Hughes

There are tragic stories of Negro aspirants for poetic fame that read like the old stories of English poets in London in the days when the children of genius starved and died young. As typical of not a few there is the story of James C. Hughes, of Louisville, Kentucky. The Louisville *Times*, March 10, 1905, contained his picture and an article by Joseph S. Cotter in appreciation of his compositions. "This young man," writes Cotter, speaking of a collection of verses and prose sketches which Hughes then had ready for publication, "this young man has the essentials of the poet, and to me his work is interesting. It is serious, and preaches while it sings."

To illustrate the range and quality of Hughes I will quote from this article two selections, one in prose and one in dialect verse:

### ASPIRATION

"True love is the same to-day as when the vestal virgins held their mystic lights along the path of virtue. Virtue wears the same vesture that she wore upon the ancient plain that led to fame immortal. Now the royal gates of honor stand ajar for men of courage, souls who will not time their spirit-lyre to suit the common chord. Our nation has known men who held within their palms our country's destiny: and, smiling in the armor of a fearless truth, have thrown away their lives. Awake, O countrymen, awake, this noble flame.

The gods will fan it, and the world shall burn with honor and pure love."

The bit of dialect verse follows, taken from a poem entitled *Apology for Wayward Jim*:

"You has offen tole us, Massy,
We's as free as we kin be;
But we needs some kind o' check, suh,
So's we'd keep on bein' free.

"Please do' whip ole Jim dis time, suh;
Marse, I 'no's you's good an' kind;
Ain't no slabery on dis 'arth, suh,
Like de slabery ob de mind.

"You has offen said obejence
Wuz de key to freedom's do'—
When we l'arned dis golden lesson
We wuz free foreber mo'.

"But you see dese darkies' minds, suh,
Ain't so flexerbul as dat,
Dey can't zackly understand, suh,
What you means by saying dat.

'Hain't but one compound solution
To dis problem, as I see;
Long's a human soul's a slabe, suh,
Ain't no way to make it free."

The young author of these selections, failing to get his book published, lost his mind and "disappeared from view." So ends his story.

## II. *Leland Milton Fisher*

Another sad story, more frequently repeated in the lives of the writers represented in this book, is that of Leland Milton Fisher. First I shall give one of his poems, as passionately sweet a lyric as can be found in American literature:

### FOR YOU, SWEETHEART

For you, sweetheart, I'd have your skies
As bright as are your own bright eyes,
And all your day-dreams warm and fair
As is the sunshine in your hair.
The Fates to you should be as kind
As are the thoughts in your pure mind,
And every bird I'd have impart
Its sweetest song to you, sweetheart.

For you, sweetheart, I'd have each dart
Sorrow fashions for your tender heart,
Thrust in my own thrice happy breast,
That yours might have unbroken rest.

If you should fall asleep and lie
So very still and quiet that I
Would know your soul had slipped away
From your divinely molded clay,
Then, looking in your fair, sweet face
I'd pray to God: "In thy good grace,

O, Father, let me sleep, nor wake
Again on earth, for her dear sake."

Born in Humbolt, Tennessee, in 1875, Fisher died of tuber-culosis, ere yet thirty years of age, leaving behind an unpublished volume of poems.

## III. W. Clarence Jordan

In another chapter I have written of a poet whose birthplace was Bardstown, Kentucky. W. Clarence Jordan, a Negro schoolmaster of Bardstown, now dead, wrote the following lines in answer to the questions, so frequently asked in derision, which stands as its title:

WHAT IS THE NEGRO DOING?

As we pass along life's highway,
Day by day,
Thousands daily ask the question,
"What, I pray,
Tell me what's the Negro doing?
And what course is he pursuing?
What achievements is he strewing
By the way?"

Many say he's retrograding
Very fast;
Others say his glory's fading,—
Cannot last;
That his prospects now are blighted,
That his chances have been slighted,
This his wrongs cannot be righted.
Time has passed.

Friends, lift up your eyes; look higher;
Higher still.
There's the vanguard of our army
On the hill.
You've been looking at the rear guard.
Lift your eyes, look farther forward;
Thousands are still pressing starward—
Ever will.
IV. Roscoe C. Jamison

Roscoe C. Jamison was fortunate in leaving behind him a friend at his early death, some three years since, who treasured his fugitive verses sufficiently to gather them together, though but a handful, and send them out to the world in a little pamphlet. Fortunate also was he in another friend able to write his elegy:

Too soon is hushed his silver speech,
The music dies upon his lute,
The cadence falls beyond our reach;
Too soon the Poet's lips are mute.

So wrote in this elegy, *Lacrimae Aethiopiae*, Charles Bertram Johnson, of this untimely dead singer. Hardly a score of poems are in this pamphlet, yet enough are here to reveal a poet in the making. Jamison was a better poet, even in these imperfect pieces, than many a writer of better verses. Here are the ardent impulses and here are the glowing ideas from which poetry of the higher order springs. The art, however, is undisciplined, grammar, metre, and rhymes are sometimes at fault. However, bold strokes of poetry atone, the effects are the effects of a real poet. Sometimes one finds in the small collection a poem that is all but perfect, a production that might have come from a maturer craftsman. I venture to put him to the test in the following poem:

ROSCOE C. JAMISON

## CASTLES IN THE AIR

I build my castles in the air.
How beautiful they seem to me,
Standing in all their glory there,
Like stars above the sea!

I watch them with admiring eyes,
For in them dwells life's fondest hope:
If they be swept from out the skies,
In darkness I must grope.

They hold life's joys, life's sweetest dreams;
They make the weary years seem bright.
As one guided by bright starbeams
I struggle through the night.

Sometimes from out the skies they fall,
And my soul shrieks in its pain;
But from the heights I hear Hope's call,
"Arise and build again."

What though life be with sorrow filled
And each day brings its load of care,
I'm happy still while I can build
My castles in the air!

Who but will say, despite the metrical defects, this is a real poem? Another poem will show his art at a better advantage, while the pathos is of another kind, very touching pathos it is, too:

### A SONG

I loved you, Dear. I did not know how much,
Until the silence of the Grave lay cold
Between us, and your hand I could not touch,
And your sweet face, oh! never more behold.

I loved you, Dear. I did not know how true,
Until in other eyes I found no light;
I know—alas!—my Spirit without you
Must drift forever in a starless night!

A different kind of merit, the merit of intense reprobation of cruel arrogancy in the one race and of treacherous cowardice in the other, is exemplified in *The Edict*. Triumphant faith, which is the Negro's peculiar heritage, asserts itself in such a way, in the final stanza, as to lift the poem to the heights of moral feeling.

## THE EDICT

All these must die before the Morning break:
They who at God an angry finger shake,
Declaring that because He made them White,
Their race should rule the world by sacred right.
They who deny a common Brotherhood—
Who cry aloud, and think no Blackman
good—
The blood-cursed mob always eager to take
The rope in hand or light the flaming stake,
Jeering the wretch while he in death pain
quakes—
All these must die before the Morning breaks.

All these must die before the Morning breaks:
The Blackmen, faithless, whose loud laughter
wakes
Harsh echoes in the most unbiased places.
They who choose vice, and scorn the gentle
graces—
Who by their manners breed contemptuous
hate,
Suggesting jim-crow laws from state to state—
They who think on earth they may not find
An ideal man nor woman of their kind.
But from some other Race that ideal take—
All these must die before the Morning break!

We know, O Lord, that there will come a time,
When o'er the World will dawn the Age
Sublime,

When Truth shall call to all mankind to stand
Before Thy throne as Brothers, hand in hand,
Be not displeased with him who this song
makes—
All these must die before the Morning breaks!

If lyric poetry be self-revealment—and such it is, or it is nothing—we can learn from the following poem how deep a sorrow at some time in his life this poet must have experienced:

HOPELESSNESS

Had you called from the fire, or from the sea,
From 'mid the roaring flames, or dark'ning
wave,
With eagerness I then had come to thee,
To perish with thee if I could not save.

But now helpless I sit and watch you die,
There is no power can save, the doctors say;
I lift my eyes unto the silent sky,
And wonder why it is that mortals pray.
The title-poem of the booklet, *Negro Soldiers*, is no doubt Jamison's masterpiece. It is worthy of the universal admiration it has won from those who know it.

CHAPTER V

# THE NEW FORMS
# OF POETRY

THE newer methods in poetry—free-verse, rhythmic strophes, polyphonic prose—have been tried with success by only a few Negroes. Of free-verse particularly not many noteworthy pieces have come from Negro poets. Well or ill, each may judge according to his taste. But the objection has been made that the Negro verse-makers of our time are bound by tradition, are sophisticated craftsmen. More independence, more differentness, seems to be demanded. But the conditions of their poetic activity seem to me in this demand to be lost sight of. They are as much the heirs of Palgrave's Golden Treasury as their white contemporaries. And the Negro is said to be preëminently imitative—that is, responsive to environing example and influence. One requirement and only one can we lay upon the Negro singer and that is the same we lay upon the artists of every race and origin. However, for artistic freedom he has an authority older than free-verse, and that authority is not outside his own race. It is found in the old plantation melodies— rich in artistic potentiality beyond exaggeration.

# I. FREE-VERSE

In Negro newspapers and magazines, rarely as yet in books, are to be found some free-verse productions of which I will give some specimens. From Will Sexton I shall quote here two brief poems in this form and in a later chapter another (p. 233). His Whitemanesque manner will be remarked. These brief pieces will suggest a poet of some force:

## *Songs of Contemporary Ethiopia*

### THE BOMB THROWER

Down with everything black!
Down with law and order!
Up with the red flag!
Up with the white South!
I am America's evil genius.

### THE NEW NEGRO

Out of the mist I see a new America—a land of ideals.
I hear the music of my fathers blended with the "Stars and Stripes Forever."
I am the crown of thorns Tyranny must bear a thousand years—
I am the New Negro.

Another vers-librist of individual quality is Andrea Razaf-keriefo. He is a prolific contributor to *The Negro World*, the newspaper organ of the Universal Negro Improvement Society. This paper regularly gives a considerable portion of a page of each issue to original verse contributions. One of Mr. Razafkeriefo's recent free-verse poems is the following, in which the style seems to me to be remarkably effective:

## THE NEGRO CHURCH

That the Negro church possesses
Extraordinary power,
That it is the greatest medium
For influencing our people,
That it long has slept and faltered,
Failed to meet its obligations,
Are, to honest and true thinkers,
Facts which have to be admitted.

For these reasons there are many
Who would have the church awaken
And adopt the modern methods
Of all other institutions.
Make us more enlightened Christians,
Teach us courtesy and English,
Racial pride and sanitation,
Science, thrift and Negro history.

Yea, the preacher, like the shepherd,
Should be leader and protector,
And prepare us for the present
Just as well as for the future;
He should know more than Scriptures,
And should ever be acquainted
With all vital, daily subjects
Helpful to his congregation.

Give us manly, thinking preachers
And not shouting money-makers,
Men of intellect and vision,
Who will really help our people:
Men who make the church a guide-post
To the road of racial progress,
Who will strive to fit the Negro
For this world as well as heaven.

In another chapter I give one of Mr. Razafkeriefo's poems in regular stanzas of the traditional type. It is but just to state that his productions exhibit a great variety of forms. His moods and traits, too, are various. There is the evidence of ardent feeling and strong conviction in most he writes.

This poet gets his strange name (pronounced rä-zäf-ker-räf) from the island of Madagascar. His father, now dead, "falling in battle for Malagasy freedom," before the poet's birth, was a nephew of the late queen of Madagascar, Ranavalona III. His mother, a colored American, was a daughter of a United States consul to Madagascar. The poet was born in the city of Washington in 1895 and now resides in Cleveland, Ohio.

To a young student in Columbia University we are indebted for some of the most symmetrical and effective free-verse poems that have come to my attention. His name is Langston Hughes. For information about him I refer the reader to the first index, at the end of this book. This poem appeared in *The Crisis*, January, 1922:

LANGSTON HUGHES

## THE NEGRO

I am a Negro:
Black as the night is black,
Black like the depths of my Africa.

I've been a slave:
Cæsar told me to keep his door-steps clean,
I brushed the boots of Washington.

I've been a worker:
Under my hand the pyramids arose.
I made mortar for the Woolworth building.

I've been a singer:
All the way from Africa to Georgia I carried my

sorrow songs.
I made ragtime.

I've been a victim:
The Belgians cut off my hands in the Congo.
They lynch me now in Texas.

I am a Negro:
Black as the night is black,
Black like the depths of my Africa.

Other specimens of free-verse have been given on pages 67, 102, and 119. In every instance the poet's choice of this form seems to me justified by the particular effectiveness of it.

# II. PROSE POEMS

## I. W. E. Burghardt DuBois

The name of no Negro author is more widely known than that of W. E. Burghardt DuBois. Editor, historian, sociologist, essayist, poet—he is celebrated in the Five Continents and the Seven Seas. It is in his impassioned prose that DuBois is most a poet. *The Souls of Black Folk* throbs constantly on the verge of poetry, while the several chapters of *Darkwater* end with a litany, chant, or credo, rhapsodical in character and in free-verse form. In all this work Dr. DuBois is the spokesman of perhaps as many millions of souls as any man living.

"A Litany at Atlanta," placed as an epilogue to "The Shadow of the Years" in *Darkwater*,[6] should be read as the litany of a race. Modern literature has not such another cry of agony:

W. E. B. DuBois

## A LITANY AT ATLANTA

O Silent God, Thou whose voice afar in mist and mystery hath left our ears an-hungered in these fearful days—

*Hear us, good Lord!*

Listen to us, Thy children: our faces dark with doubt are made a mockery in Thy Sanctuary. With uplifted hands we front Thy Heaven, O God, crying:

*We beseech Thee to hear us, good Lord!*

We are not better than our fellows, Lord; we are but weak and human men. When our devils do deviltry, curse Thou the doer and the deed,—curse them as we curse them, do to them all and more than ever they have done to innocence and weakness, to womanhood and home.

*Have mercy upon us, miserable sinners!*

And yet, whose is the deeper guilt? Who made these devils? Who nursed them in crime and fed them on injustice? Who ravished and debauched their mothers and their grandmothers? Who bought and sold their crime and waxed fat and rich on public iniquity?

*Thou knowest, good God!*

Is this Thy Justice, O Father, that guile be easier than innocence and the innocent be crucified for the guilt of the untouched guilty?

*Justice, O Judge of men!*

Wherefore do we pray? Is not the God of the Fathers dead? Have not seers seen in Heaven's halls Thine hearsed and lifeless form stark amidst the black and rolling smoke of sin, where all along bow bitter forms of endless dead?

*Awake, Thou that sleepest!*

Thou art not dead, but flown afar, up hills of endless light, through blazing corridors of suns, where worlds do swing of good and gentle men, of women strong and free—far from cozenage, black hypocrisy, and chaste prostitution of this shameful speck of dust!

*Turn again, O Lord; leave us*
*not to perish in our sin!*

*From lust of body and lust of blood,—*
*Great God, deliver us!*
*From lust of power and lust of gold,—*
*Great God, deliver us!*

From the leagued lying of despot and of
brute,—
*Great God, deliver us!*

A city lay in travail, God our Lord, and from her loins sprang
twin Murder and Black Hate. Red was the midnight; clang, crack,
and cry of death and fury filled the air and trembled underneath
the stars where church spires pointed silently to Thee. And all this
was to sate the greed of greedy men who hide behind the veil of
vengeance.

*Bend us Thine ear, O Lord!*

In the pale, still morning we looked upon the deed. We
stopped our ears and held our leaping hands, but they—did they
not wag their heads and leer and cry with bloody jaws: *Cease from
Crime!* The word was mockery, for thus they train a hundred
crimes while we do cure one.

*Turn again our captivity, O Lord!*

Behold this maimed and broken thing, dear God: it was an
humble black man, who toiled and sweat to save a bit from the
pittance paid him. They told him: *Work and Rise!* He worked. Did
this man sin? Nay, but someone told how someone said another
did—one whom he had never seen nor known. Yet for that man's
crime this man lieth maimed and murdered, his wife naked to
shame, his children to poverty and evil.

*Hear us, O Heavenly Father!*

Doth not this justice of hell stink in Thy nostrils, O God? How
long shall the mounting flood of innocent blood roar in Thine
ears and pound in our hearts for vengeance? Pile the pale frenzy

of blood-crazed brutes, who do such deeds, high on Thine Altar, Jehovah Jireh, and burn it in hell forever and forever!

*Forgive us, good Lord; we know not what we say!*

Bewildered we are and passion-tossed, mad with the madness of a mobbed and mocked and murdered people; straining at the armposts of Thy throne, we raise our shackled hands and charge Thee, God, by the bones of our stolen fathers, by the tears of our dead mothers, by the very blood of Thy crucified Christ: What meaneth this? Tell us the plan; give us the sign.

*Keep not Thou silent, O God.*

Sit not longer blind, Lord God, deaf to our prayer and dumb to our dumb suffering. Surely Thou, too, art not white, O Lord, a pale, bloodless, heartless thing!

*Ah! Christ of all the Pities!*

Forgive the thought! Forgive these wild, blasphemous words! Thou art still the God of our black fathers and in Thy Soul's Soul sit some soft darkenings of the evening, some shadowings of the velvet night.

But whisper—speak—call, great God, for Thy silence is white terror to our hearts! The way, O God, show us the way and point us the path!

Whither? North is greed and South is blood; within, the coward, and without, the liar. Whither? To death?

*Amen! Welcome, dark sleep!*

Whither? To life? But not this life, dear God, not this. Let the cup pass from us, tempt us not beyond our strength, for there is that clamoring and clawing within, to whose voice we would not listen, yet shudder lest we must,—and it is red. Ah! God! It is a red and awful shape.

*Selah!*

In yonder East trembles a star.

*Vengeance is Mine; I will repay, saith the Lord!*

Thy Will, O Lord, be done!

*Kyrie Eleison!*

Lord, we have done these pleading, wavering words.

*We beseech Thee to hear us, good Lord!*

We bow our heads and hearken soft to the sobbing of women and little children.

*We beseech Thee to hear us, good Lord!*

Our voices sink in silence and in night.

*Hear us, good Lord.*

In night, O God of a godless land!

*Amen!*

In silence, O Silent God.

*Selah!*

## II. Kelly Miller

Dr. Kelly Miller is professor of sociology in Howard University. He has been professor of mathematics. He is the author of several prose works—able expositions of aspects of inter-racial problems. It is rumored that he is a poet. However that may be, his admirable volume of essays entitled *Out of the House of Bondage* concludes with a strophic chant, highly poetical, and poured forth with the fervor of some old Celtic bard, triumphant in the vision of a new day dawning:

KELLY MILLER

### I SEE AND AM SATISFIED

The vision of a scion of a despised and rejected race, the span of whose life is measured by the years of its Golden Jubilee, and whose fancy, like the vine that girdles the tree-trunk, runneth both forward and back.

I see the African savage as he drinks his palmy wine, and basks in the sunshine of his native bliss, and is happy.

I see the man-catcher, impelled by thirst of gold, as he entraps his simple-souled victim in the snares of bondage and death, by use of force or guile.

I see the ocean basin whitened with his bones, and the ocean current running red with his blood, amidst the hellish horrors of the middle passage.

I see him laboring for two centuries and a half in unrequited toil, making the hillsides of our southland to glow with the snow-white fleece of cotton, and the valleys to glisten with the golden sheaves of grain.

I see him silently enduring cruelty and torture indescribable, with flesh flinching beneath the sizz of angry whip or quivering under the gnaw of the sharp-toothed bloodhound.

I see a chivalric civilization instinct with dignity, comity and grace rising upon pillars supported by his strength and brawny arm.

I see the swarthy matron lavishing her soul in altruistic devotion upon the offspring of her alabaster mistress.

I see the haughty sons of a haughty race pouring out their lustful passion upon black womanhood, filling our land with a bronzed and tawny brood.

I see also the patriarchal solicitude of the kindly-hearted owners of men, in whose breast not even iniquitous system could sour the milk of human kindness.

I hear the groans, the sorrows, the sighings, the soul striving of these benighted creatures of God, rising up from the low grounds of sorrow and reaching the ear of Him Who regardeth man of the lowliest estate.

I strain my ear to supernal sound, and I hear in the secret

chambers of the Almighty the order to the Captain of Host to break his bond and set him free.

I see Abraham Lincoln, himself a man of sorrows and acquainted with grief, arise to execute the high decree.

I see two hundred thousand black boys in blue baring their breasts to the bayonets of the enemy, that their race might have some slight part in its own deliverance.

I see the great Proclamation delivered in the year of my birth of which I became the first fruit and beneficiary.

I see the assassin striking down the great Emancipator; and the house of mirth is transformed into the Golgotha of the nation.

I watch the Congress as it adds to the Constitution new words, which make the document a charter of liberty indeed.

I see the new-made citizen running to and fro in the first fruit of his new-found freedom.

I see him rioting in the flush of privilege which the nation had vouchsafed, but destined, alas, not long to last.

I see him thrust down from the high seat of political power, by fraud and force, while the nation looks on in sinister silence and acquiescent guilt.

I see the tide of public feeling run cold and chilly, as the vial of racial wrath is wreaked upon his bowed and defenceless head.

I see his body writhing in the agony of death as his groans issue from the crackling flames, while the funeral pyre lights the midnight sky with its dismal glare. My heart sinks with heaviness within me.

I see that the path of progress has never taken a straight line, but has always been a zigzag course amid the conflicting forces of right and wrong, truth and error, justice and injustice, cruelty and mercy.

I see that the great generous American Heart, despite the temporary flutter, will finally beat true to the higher human impulse, and my soul abounds with reassurance and hope.

I see his marvelous advance in the rapid acquisition of knowledge and acquirement of things material, and attainment in the higher pursuits of life, with his face fixed upon that light which shineth brighter and brighter unto the perfect day.

I see him who was once deemed stricken, smitten of God, and afflicted, now entering with universal welcome into the patrimony of mankind, and I look calmly upon the centuries of blood and tears and travail of soul, and am satisfied.

## III. Charles H. Conner

As a companion piece to this litany and this vision I will present another vision that for calm, clear beauty of style takes us immediately back to *Pilgrim's Progress*. The author calls it a sermonette, and it is one of three contained in a very small book entitled *The Enchanted Valley*. But the author is no preacher. He is a ship-yard worker in Philadelphia—I almost said a "common" worker. But such workmen were never common, anywhere, at any time. Charles Conner wears the garb and wields the tools of a common workman, but he has most uncommon visions. He is a seer and a philosopher. He has informed me that there is American Indian blood in his veins. From the mystical and philosophical character of his writings, both prose and verse, I should have expected an East Indian strain. Twice have I visited his humble habitation, and each time it was a visit to the Enchanted Valley.

CHARLES H. CONNER

## THE LIFE OF THE SPIRIT IN
## THE NATURAL WORLD

At the dawning of a day, in a deep valley, a man awoke.

It was a valley of treasures that everywhere abounded.

He opened his eyes, and beheld the greensward bedecked with many colored jewels that sparkled in the light.

His ears caught the medley of sounds, that awoke innumerable echoes; and with the balmy air peopled the valley with delights. How he came there, or why, he knew not; nor scarcely thought or cared.

As he gazed upon the multitude of things, in his heart upsprung desire; and he gathered the treasures that lay around, till his arms were full, and his body decked in all their bright array.

Then the sun went down behind the hill; and the vale grew

dark; and the night air chill; and the place grew solemn, silent, still.

A new thing then, to mortal ken, seemed hovering on the threshold near. A strange, fantastic thing, it crept, intangible, nearer, nearer swept, the pallid, startling face of Fear!

But, the night brings sleep at last—and dreams; and day follows night; and sunshine follows storm throughout the length of days. But a trace of the dreams remains, like the faintly clinging scent that marks a hidden trail; and so, because of his dreams, the man's desire reached out, and scaled the lofty peaks that walled him in.

His pleasant valley seemed too narrow and confined.

So, with his treasures fondly pressed to his beating heart, he tried to scale the heights.

He scrambled and struggled with might and main, slipped and arose; and fell again and again. The spirit was willing, and valiant, and brave; but the treasure encumbered it with fatal hold; and held him bound, as with fold on fold a corpse is held in its lowly grave. So, try as he might, he could not rise much higher than one's hands can reach; and one by one, his gathered treasures lost their brightness and their charm; as gathered flowers wilt and fade; and his arms weary from the burden that they bore, let fall and scattered lie, little by little, more and more of the things he had gathered and vainly prized. And each thing lost was so much lightness gained, enabling him to mount a little higher up the rugged steep. And so it was till night was come again at last; and worn and weary, he sank down to sleep and rest.

And, as he slept, his arms relaxed their hold; and down the steep his dwindling treasures rolled, till the last of them found their natural level and resting place, the lower stretch of ground.

'Twas then a strange sight met my gaze, long to be remembered in the coming days of trial and endeavor.

From out that sleeping form a luminous haze arose, airy and white; and glowed within it an amber fire, as it mounted higher, higher; and, as it arose, it had the appearance of a man; and its countenance was the countenance of him that slept. Thus up and up it winged its flight, until above the highest peak 'twas lost to sight. I pondered the matter in wonder and awe, until long past the midnight hour, how that a soul at last gained its longed for power to win the distant height.

There is a kingdom of earth, and of water and of air.

Each has its own. The heavier cannot rise above its level, to the next and lighter zone.

The treasures of the soul's desire, were treasures of earth, whose lightest joys were too heavy and too gross to be sustained in the finer, rarer atmosphere; and thus were as a leaden weight that anchored the soul to earth, without its being at all aware that the things it thought so pleasant and so fair, were shackles to bind it hard and fast; and make it impossible for it to gain the region that instinctively it felt and knew was the rightful place of its abode.

## IV. William Edgar Bailey

Yet one more prose-poem I will give, as a sort of coda to the series. It is taken from a paper-covered booklet entitled *The Firstling*, by William Edgar Bailey, from which *The Slump*, on page 65, was taken:

### TO A WILD ROSE

The wild rose silently peeps from its uncouth habitation,

thrives and flourishes in its glory; its fragrant bud bows to sip the nectar of the morning. Its delicate blossom blushes in the balmy breeze as the wind tells its tale of adoration. Performing well its part, it withers and decays; the chirping sparrow perches serenely on its boughs, only to find it wrapped in sadness and solemnity— yet its grief-stained leaf and weather beaten branches silently chant euphonic choruses in natural song, in solemn commemoration of its faded splendor.

Dead, yes dead—but in thy hibernal demise dost thou bequeath a truth eternal as the stars. I saw thee, Rose, when the elf of spring hung thy floral firstling upon that thorny bower and robed thy ungainly form in a garb of green, and, Rose, thou wert sweet!

I saw the same vernal sprite pay homage to thy highbrowed kinsman in yonder stench-bestifled dell, and, in his pause of an instant, baptized its sacred being in the same aromatic blood. I saw thee, Rose, in thy autumnal desolation, when the Storm-God was wont to do thee harm, laid waste thy foliage, and cast at thy feet, as a challenge, his mantle of snow, and the Law of Non-resistance was still unbroken.

Tell me thy story, Rose! Do the stars in their unweary watch breathe forth upon thee a special benediction from the sky? Or did the wind waft a drop of blood from the Cross to thy dell to sanctify thy being? Oh, leave me not, thou Redeemer of the Woods, to plod the way alone! My Nazarene, grant but to me a double portion of thy humble pride—and in my tearful grief permit thou me to pluck a fragrant thought from thy thorny bosom!

## *V. R. Nathaniel Dett*

Primarily a composer and pianist, Mr. Dett exemplifies the close kinship of poetry and music, for in the former art as well as in the latter he exhibits a finely creative spirit. To speak first of his compositions for the piano, the following works are widely known and greatly admired by lovers of music: "Magnolia Suite," "In the Bottoms Suite," "Listen to the Lambs," "Marche Negre," "Arietta," "Magic Song," "Open Yo' Eyes," and "Hampton, My Home by the Sea." Mr. Dett took a degree in music at Oberlin Conservatory of Music, and a Harvard prize in music (1920). The musical endowment for which his race is celebrated is cultured and refined in him and guided by science. The basis of his brilliant compositions is to be found in the folk melodies of his people. The musical genius of his people expresses itself through him with conscious, perfected art. To sit under the spell of his performance of his own pieces is to acquire a new idea of the Negro people.

R. NATHANIEL DETT

The same refined and exalted spirit reveals itself in Mr. Dett's verse as in his music. Having this combination of gifts, he cannot but raise the highest expectations. I present in this place a poem in blank verse of nobly contemplative mood, suggesting far more, as the best poems do, than it says:

### AT NIAGARA

—No, no! Not tonight, my Friend,
I may not, cannot go with you tonight.
And think not that I love you any less
Because this now I'd rather be alone.
My heart is strangely torn; unwonted thoughts
Have so infused themselves into my mind
That altogether there is wrought in me
A sort of hapless mood, whose phantom power
Born perhaps of my own fantasies
Has ta'en me. By its subtle spell
I'm wooed and changed from what's my natural
self.
I am so possessed I can but wish
For nothing else save this and solitude.
If in companionship I sought relief
Yours indeed would be the first I'd seek.
There is none other whom I so esteem,
None who quite so perfect understands.
Your presence always is a soothing balm,
—Ne'er failing me when troubled. But tonight,
Forgive me, Friend—I'd rather be alone.
Leave me, let me with myself commune.
Presently if no change come, I shall go
Stand in the shadowed gorge, or where the

moon
Throws her silver on the rippling stream,
List to the sounding cataract's thundering fall,
Or hark to spirit voices in the wind.
For methinks sometimes that these strange
moods
Are heaven-sent us by the jealous God
Who'd thus remind us that no human love
Can fully satisfy the longing heart:
Perhaps an intimation sent to souls
That he would speak somewhat, or nearer draw.
Therefore I'll to Him. Talking waters, stars,
The moon and whispering trees shall make me
wise
In what it is He'd have my spirit know.
And Nature singing from the earth and sky
Shall fill me with such peace, that in the morn
I'll be the gay glad self you've always known.
Urge me no further, now you understand.
A nobler friend than you none ever knew—
But not this time. Tonight I'll be alone;
And if from moonlit valley God should speak,
Or in the tumbling waters sound a call,
Or whisper in the sighing of the wind,
He'll find me with an undivided heart
Patient waiting to hear; but Friend,—alone.

# CHAPTER VI
# DIALECT VERSE

THE reader of these pages may ask: "But where is the Negro's humorous verse? Here is the pathos, where is the comedy of Negro life?" It may also be asked where the dialect verse is, and the dramatic narratives and character pieces that made Dunbar famous.

The present-day Negro poets do not, as has been asserted, spurn dialect. Many of them have given a portion of their pages to character pieces in dialect, humorous in effect. Whether those who have excluded such pieces from their books have done so on principle or not I cannot say. In general, however, these writers are too deeply earnest for dialect verse, and the "broken tongue" is too suggestive of broken bodies and servile souls. But by those who have employed dialect its uses and effects have been well understood. Dialect, as is proven by Burns, Lowell, Riley, Dunbar, often gets nearer the heart than the language of the schools is able to do, and for home-spun philosophy, for mother-wit, for folk-lore, and for racial humor, for whatever is quaint and peculiar and native in any people, it is the only proper medium. Poets of the finest art from Theocritus to Tennyson have so used it. Genius here as elsewhere will direct the born poet and instruct him when to use dialect and when the language that centuries of tradition have refined and standardized and encrusted with poetic associations. There is a world of poetic wealth in the strangely naïve heart of the rough-schooled Negro for which the smooth-worn, disconsonanted language of the cabin and the field is beautifully appropriate. There is also another world of poetic wealth in the Negro of culture for which only the language of culture is adequate. To such we must say: "All things are yours."

While, as remarked, many Negro verse-writers have used dialect occasionally, in the ways indicated, Waverley Turner Carmichael has made it practically his one instrument of expression in his little book entitled *From the Heart of a Folk*. A representative piece is the following:

### MAMMY'S BABY SCARED

Hush now, mammy's baby scaid,
Don' it cry, eat yo' bread;
Nothin' ain't goin' bother you,
Does', it bothers mammy too.

Mammy ain't goin' left it 'lone
W'ile de chulen all are gone;
Hush, now, don' it cry no mo'e,
Ain't goin' lay it on de flo'.

Hush now, finish out yo' nap,
W'ile I make yo' luttle cap;
Blessid luttle sugar-pie,
Hush now, baby, don' it cry.

Mammy's goin' to make its dres',
Go to sleep an' take yo' res';
Hush now, don' it cry no mo'e,
Ain't goin' lay you on de flo'.

Carmichael was born at Snow Hill, Alabama, and in the Industrial Institute there received the rudiments of an education, which was added to by a summer term at Harvard. Since the book mentioned I have seen nothing from his pen.

The elder Cotter in *A White Song and a Black Song* gives us in the second part several dialect pieces in the most successful manner. Several are satirical, like the following:

### THE DON'T-CARE NEGRO

Neber min' what's in your cran'um
So your collar's high an' true.
Neber min' what's in your pocket
So de blackin's on your shoe.

Neber min' who keeps you comp'ny
So he halfs up what he's tuk.
Neber min' what way you's gwine
So you's gwine away from wuk.

Neber min' de race's troubles
So you profits by dem all.
Neber min' your leaders' stumblin'
So you he'ps to mak' dem fall.

Neber min' what's true to-morrow
So you libes a dream to-day.
Neber min' what tax is levied
So it's not on craps or play.

Neber min' how hard you labors
So you does it to de en'
Dat de judge is boun' to sen' you
An' your record to de "pen."

Neber min' your manhood's risin'
So you habe a way to stay it.
Neber min' folks' good opinion
So you have a way to slay it.

Neber min' man's why an' wharfo'
So de worl' is big an' roun.
Neber min' whar next you's gwine to
So you's six foot under groun'.

Raymond Garfield Dandridge in *The Poet and Other Poems* has included a handful of dialect pieces which prove him a master of this species of composition. I will select but one to represent this class of his work here:

DE INNAH PART

I 'fess Ise ugly, big, an' ruff,
Mah voice is husky, mannah's gruff;
But, mah gal sed, "Neb mine yore hide,
I jedged you by yore inside side";

An' sed, dat she hab alwuz foun',
De gole beneaf de surfuss groun'.

She claims dat offen rail ruff hides
Am boun' erroun' hi' grade insides;
W'ile sum dat 'pear "sharp ez a tack"
Kinceals a heart dat's hard an' black;
An', to prove her way ob thinkin',
Gibs fo' zample Abeham Linkin.

Ole "Hones' Abe," so lank an' tall,
Worn't no parlah posin' doll:
Yet he stood out miles erbove
Uddah men, in truf an' love.
An' in han'lin' 'fairs of state,
Proved de greates' ob de great.

In makin' great men, Nature mus'
Fo' got erbout de beauty dus'
An' fashun dem frum nachel clay,
De gritty kine, dat doan decay.
But, mos' her time she spent, I know,
Erpon de parts dat duzen show.

Two poems by Sterling M. Means, one in standard English and one in dialect may well be placed here side by side for comparison as being identical in theme and feeling, and differing but in manner. They are taken from his book entitled *The Deserted Cabin and Other Poems*:

## THE OLD PLANTATION GRAVE

'Tis a scene so sad and lonely,
'Tis the site of ancient toil;
Where our fathers bore their burdens,
Where they sleep beneath the soil;
And the fields are waste and barren,
Where the sugar cane did grow,
Where they tilled the corn and cotton,
In the years of long ago;

And along the piney hillside,
Where the hound pursued the slave,
In the dreary years of bondage,
There he fills an humble grave.

## THE OLD DESERTED CABIN

Dis ole deserted cabin
Remin's me ob de past;
An' when I gits ter t'inkin',
De tears comes t'ick an' fast.

I wunner whur's A'nt Doshy,
I wunner whur's Brur Jim;
I hyeahs no corn-songs ringin',
I hyeahs no Gospel hymn.

Dis ole deserted cabin
Am tumblin' in decay;
An' all its ole-time dwellers
Hab gone de silent way.

Dey voices hushed in silence,
De cabin drear an' lone;
An' dey who used ter lib hyeah
Long sense is dead an' gone.

J. Mord Allen's poems and tales in dialect are worthy of distinction. They are executed in the true spirit of art. I should rank his book, elsewhere named, as one of the few best the Negro has contributed to literature. I will give here one specimen of his dialect verse:

## A VICTIM OF MICROBES

NOTE.—Physicians are agreed that laziness is a microbe disease.

Go en fetch er lawyer, 'Tilda,
'Kaze I wants ter make mah will;
Neenter min' erbout de doctor—
'Tain't no use ter take er pill.—
Chunk up de kitchen fire,
En fetch mah easy-ch'er,
En put er piller in it:
Maybe I'll git better hyeah.
I done hyeahed de doctor say it—de doctor
hisse'f said it—
I'm plumb chock full o' microbes en mah time's
ercomin' quick.
So, 'stid o' up en fussin' wid me fer bein' lazy,
Yer'd better be er nussin' me,
'kaze I'm jes' mighty sick.

I 'spec' I must er cotch it
Back in Tennessee;

'Kaze, fur ez I kin 'member,
I wuz bad ez I could be—
P'intly hated hoein' 'taters—
Couldn't chop er stick o' wood—
Couldn't pick er sack o' cotton—
Never wuz er lick o' good.
En de folks dey called me lazy—my own
mammy called me lazy
When, 'stid o' gwine plowin', I wuz fishin' in de
creek;
Took en tole de white folks 'bout it, en made er
heap o' trouble,
En all fer want o' medersun—
me bein' mighty sick.

So, now yer knows de reason
Why I'm always loafin' 'roun',
When jobs is runnin' after men
In ev'y part o' town.
Dar's patches on mah breeches,
En you's er sight ter see;
Dat's de work o' dem same microbes,
En it kain't be laid on me.
'Kaze de doctor he explained it, en de doctor's
book explained it,
En some Latin words explained it, en explained
it mighty quick—
It's mah lights er else mah liver, er maybe, its
mah stomach—
It's somep'n in mah insides, en
it sho' has made me sick.

En so, I hope yer'll git yerse'f
Er washin', now, er two,
Er get er job o' scrubbin'
Er somp'n else ter do;
'Kaze dat doctor p'intly showed me
So I couldn't he'p but tell
Dat dem microbes got me han' en foot
En I jes' kain't git well.
Darfo' I hope yer'll he'p me ter pass mah las'
days easy,
En keep er fire in de stove en somep'n in de
pan.
I know it's hard ter do it, en I'm sorry I kain't
he'p yer;
But me 'n de doctor bofe knows
I'm er mighty sick man.

James Weldon Johnson entitled a section of his book *Jingles and Croons*. Among these pieces, so disparagingly designated, are to be found some of the best dialect writing in the whole range of Negro literature. Every quality of excellence is there. The one piece I give is perhaps not above the average of a score in his book:

## MY LADY'S LIPS AM LIKE DE HONEY
### (Negro Love Song)

Breeze a-sighin' and a-blowin',
Southern summer night.
Stars a-gleamin' and a-glowin',
Moon jus shinin' right.
Strollin', like all lovers do,
Down de lane wid Lindy Lou;

Honey on her lips to waste;
'Speck I'm gwine to steal a taste.

Oh, ma lady's lips am like de honey,
Ma lady's lips am like de rose;
An' I'm jes like de little bee a-buzzin'
'Round de flowers wha' de nectah grows.
Ma lady's lips dey smile so temptin',
Ma lady's teeth so white dey shine,
Oh, ma lady's lips so tantalizin',
Ma lady's lips so close to mine.

Bird a-whistlin' and a-swayin'
In de live-oak tree;
Seems to me he keeps a-sayin',
"Kiss dat gal fo' me."
Look heah, Mister Mockin' Bird,
Gwine to take you at yo' word;
If I meets ma Waterloo,
Gwine to blame it all on you.

Oh, ma lady's lips am like de honey,
Ma lady's lips am like de rose;
An' I'm jes like de little bee a-buzzin'
'Round de flowers wha' de nectah grows.
Ma lady's lips dey smile so temptin',
Ma lady's teeth so white dey shine,
Oh, ma lady's lips so tantalizin',
Ma lady's lips so close to mine.

Honey in de rose, I 'spose, is
Put der fo' de bee;
Honey on her lips, I knows, is
Put der jes fo' me.
Seen a sparkle in her eye,
Heard her heave a little sigh;
Felt her kinder squeeze mah han',
'Nuff to make me understan'.

Numerous other writers would furnish quite as good specimens of dialectical verse as those given. This medium of artistic expression is not being neglected, it is only made secondary and, as it were, incidental. By perhaps half of the poets it is not used. With a few, and they of no little talent, it is the main medium. Among this few, Carmichael has been named; S. Jonathan Clark, of Dublin, Mississippi, and Theodore Henry Shackelford, of Jamaica Plains, New York, are others.

Shackelford, with little schooling, displays a versatility of talent. His own pen has illustrated with interesting realistic sketches his book entitled *My Country and Other Poems*, and for some of his lyrics he has written music. A large proportion of his pieces are in dialect, much in the spirit of Dunbar. His best productions in standard English are ballads. He tells a tale in verse with Wordsworthian simplicity and feeling. Mr. Clark is a school principal, with the education that implies. He has not yet published a book.

THEODORE HENRY SHACKELFORD

# CHAPTER VII
# THE POETRY OF PROTEST

EQUALITY AND JUSTICE FOR ALL
(Photograph of a panel of the Carl Schurz Monument)

As elsewhere intimated there is being produced in America a
literature of which America, as the term is commonly under-
stood, is not aware. It is a literature of protest—protest sometimes
pathetic and prayerful, sometimes vehement and bitter. It comes
from Negro writers, in prose and verse, in the various forms of
fiction, drama, essay, editorial, and lyric. It is only with the lyric

form that we are here concerned. Of that we shall make a special presentation, in this chapter.

An artistic and restrained expression of the protest against irrational color prejudice, in the plaintive, pathetic key, is found in the following free-verse poem by Winston Allen:

### THE BLACK VIOLINIST

I touched the violin,
I, whose hand was black,
I touched the violin
In a grand salon.
I touched the violin
In a Russian palace.
I touched the violin
And the dream-born strains
Chanted by the Congo
Soared to Heaven's chambers.

Could I touch the violin?
I, whose hand was black?
And bring to life dream music?
Men had taunted me,
Age-worn months: their jeers
Snapped to bits my heartstrings,
Snapped my inner soul;
And the sting of living
Tortured me the livelong day.

Sometimes the protest runs in a lighter vein—as thus, in verses entitled:

## OLD JIM CROW

Wherever we live, it's right to forgive,
It's wrong to hold malice, we know,
But there's one thing that's true, from all points
of view,
All Negroes hate old man Jim Crow.

His home is in hell; he loves here to dwell;
We meet him wherever we go;
In all public places, where live both the races,
You'll always see Mr. Jim Crow.

Be we well educated, even to genius related,
We may have a big pile of dough,
That cuts not a figger, you still are a nigger,
And that is the law with Jim Crow.
*The Nashville Eye.*

But the Negro is seldom humorous these days on the subject of racial discriminations. Occasionally, in dialect verse, he still makes merry with the foibles or over-accentuated traits of certain types of the Negro. In general, however, the Negro verse-smith goes to his work with a grim aspect. He is there to smite. Sometimes the anvil clangs, more mightily than musically. But there is precedent.

A stanza each from two poems somewhat intense will serve to show the character of much verse in Negro newspapers. The first is from verses entitled "Sympathy," by Tilford Jones:

Mourn for the thousands slain,
The youthful and the strong;
Mourn for the last; but pray,

For those hung by the mobbing throng.
Pray to our God above,
To break the fell destroyer's sway,
And show His saving love.

The second is the last stanza of a poem entitled *Shall Race Hatred Prevail?* by Adeline Carter Watson.

By the tears of Negro mothers,
By the woes of Negro wives,
By the sighs of Negro children,
By your gallant snuffed-out lives,
By the throne of God eternal;
Standing hard by Heaven's gate,
Ye shall crush this cursed, infernal,
Western stigma: groundless hate!

The following two poems have a world of pathos for every reflecting person, in the unanswered question of each. The first is by Mrs. Georgia Douglas Johnson:

### TO MY SON

Shall I say, "My son, you are branded in this
country's pageantry,
Foully tethered, bound forever, and no forum
makes you free?"
Shall I mark the young light fading through
your soul-enchanneled eye,
As the dusky pall of shadows screen the
highway of your sky?
Or shall I with love prophetic bid you
dauntlessly arise,

Spurn the handicap that binds you, taking what
the world denies?
Bid you storm the sullen fortress built by
prejudice and wrong,
With a faith that shall not falter in
your heart and on your tongue!

The second is by Will Sexton:

### TO MY LOST CHILD

It is well, child of my heart, the rosebush drops
its petals on your grave.
It is well, child of my heart, the sparrow sings
to you when Aurora has rouged the sky.
In your trundle bed deep in the bosom of the
earth you can dream pleasanter dreams than I.
You have never felt the sting of living in a white
man's civilization and beneath a white man's
laws.
You have never been forced to dance to the
music of hate played by an idle orchestra.
You have never toiled long hours and bowed
and scraped for the chance to breathe.
In your dreams you wonder in the Heaven
beyond the skies with the God civilization
rebukes.
Tell me, little child, are you not happy in
that realm no white man can enter?

In much of this utterance of protest, this arraignment of the
white man's civilization that rebukes God, there may be more
passion than poesy. But out of such passion, as it were a rumbling

of thunder, the lightning will one day leap. A poet born and reared in South Carolina, Joshua Henry Jones, Jr., appeals from man's inhumanities to God's prevailing power in passionate stanzas of which this is the first, the rest being like:

> They've lynched a man in Dixie.
> O God, behold the crime.
> And midst the mad mob's howling
> How sweet the church bells chime!
> They've lynched a man in Dixie.
> You say this cannot be?
> See where his lead-torn body
> Mute hangs from yonder tree.

This or a similar lynching provoked the following lines from another, Walter Everette Hawkins, in a poem entitled *A Festival in Christendom*. After relating that the white people of a certain community were on their way to church on the Sabbath day, the poem continues:

> And so this Christian mob did turn
> From prayer to rob, to lynch and burn.
> A victim helplessly he fell
> To tortures truly kin to hell;
> They bound him fast and strung him high,
> They cut him down lest he should die
> Before their energy was spent
> In torturing to their heart's content.
> They tore his flesh and broke his bones,
> And laughed in triumph at his groans;
> They chopped his fingers, clipped his ears
> And passed them round as souvenirs.

They bored hot irons in his side
And reveled in their zeal and pride;
They cut his quivering flesh away
And danced and sang as Christians may;
Then from his side they tore his heart
And watched its quivering fibres dart.
And then upon his mangled frame
They piled the wood, the oil and flame.
Lest there be left one of his creed,
One to perpetuate his breed;
Lest there be one to bear his name
Or build the stock from which he came,
They dragged his bride up to the pyre
And plunged her headlong in the fire,
Full-freighted with an unborn child,
Hot embers on her form they piled.
And they raised a Sabbath song,
The echo sounded wild and strong,
A benediction to the skies
That crowned the human sacrifice.

Few are the poets quoted or mentioned in this volume who have not contributed to this literature of protest. James Weldon Johnson, whose predominant motive is artistic creation, affords more than one poem in which the note of protest is sounded in pathos. Pathos is indeed the characteristic note of the great body of Negro verse. Aided by the two preceding extracts to an understanding of Johnson's point of view, the reader will appreciate the following poem, remarkable for that restraint which adds to the potency of art:

## THE BLACK MAMMY

O whitened head entwined with turban gay,
O kind black face, O crude, but tender hand,
O foster-mother in whose arms there lay
The race whose sons are masters of the land!
It was thine arms that sheltered in their fold,
It was thine eyes that followed through the
length
Of infant days these sons. In times of old
It was thy breast that nourished them to
strength.
So often hast thou to thy bosom pressed
The golden head, the face and brow of snow;
So often has it 'gainst thy broad, dark breast
Lain, set off like a quickened cameo.
Thou simple soul, as cuddling down that babe
With thy sweet croon, so plaintive and so wild,
Came ne'er the thought to thee, swift like a
stab,
That it some day might crush
thine own black child?

There died in Fort McHenry hospital, February, 2, 1921, a soldier-poet of the Negro race, who had been called "the poet laureate of the New Negro," his name Lucian B. Watkins. He deserved the title, whatever may be the exact definition of "the New Negro." For in his lyrics, of many forms, racial consciousness reached a degree of intensity to which only a disciplined sense of art set a limit.—He was born in a cabin at Chesterfield, Virginia, struggled in the usual way for the rudiments of book-knowledge, became a teacher, then a soldier. His health was wrecked in the

World War. He died before his powers were matured.—Short and simple are the annals of the poet. Before one of his intenser race poems I shall give his last lyric cry, uttered but a few days before his lingering death:

LUCIAN B. WATKINS

My fallen star has spent its light
And left but memory to me;
My day of dream has kissed the night
Farewell, its sun no more I see;
My summer bloomed for winter's frost:
Alas, I've lived and loved and lost!

What matters it to-day should earth
Lay on my head a gold-bright crown
Lit with the gems of royal worth
Befitting well a king's renown?—
My lonely soul is trouble-tossed,
For I have lived and loved and lost.

Great God! I dare not question Thee—
Thy way eternally is just;
This seeming mystery to me
Will be revealed, if I but trust;
Ah, Thou alone dost know the cost
When one has lived and loved and lost.

The following sonnet, entitled "The New Negro," will serve to represent much of Watkins's verse:

He thinks in black. His God is but the same
John saw—with hair "like wool" and eyes "as fire"—
Who makes the visions for which men aspire.
His kin is Jesus and the Christ who came
Humbly to earth and wrought His hallowed aim
'Midst human scorn. Pure is his heart's desire;
His life's religion lifts; his faith leads higher.
Love is his Church, and Union is its name.

Lo, he has learned his own immortal rôle
In this momentous drama of the hour;
Has read aright the heavens' Scriptural scroll
'Bove ancient wrong—long boasting in its tower.
Ah, he has sensed the truth. Deep in his soul
He feels the manly majesty of power.

The protest not infrequently takes the form of entreaty and appeal, sometimes the form of an invocation of divine wrath upon the doers of evil. The following poem from Watkins, unique and effective in form and biblical phrasing, is the kind of appeal that will not out of the mind:

### A MESSAGE TO THE MODERN PHARAOHS
(Loose him and let him go—John 11.44)

"Loose him!"—this man on whom you plod
Beneath your heel hate-iron-shod;
His silent sorrow troubles God—
"Let him go!"

There will be plagues, wars will not cease,—
There cannot be a lasting peace
Until this being you release—
"Let him go!"

Each doomful kingdom—throne and crown—
Built on the lowly fettered down,
Shall perish—lo, the heavens frown—
"Let him go!"

Naught but a name is Liberty,
Naught but a name—Democracy,
Till love has made each mortal free—
"Let him go!"

"Loose him!" He has his part to play
In Life's Great Drama, day by day,—
He has his mission, God's own way,—
"Let him go!"

"Loose him!" 'Twill be your master rôle,
'Twill be your triumph and your goal:
'Twill be the saving of your soul—
"Let him go!"

Mr. Hawkins, whom I have quoted, entitled his book *Chords and Discords*. What did he mean by "discords"? Perhaps a disparagement of his muse's efforts at music. Perhaps, and rather, something in the content, for the contrasts are sharp, the tones are piercing. These "discords" abound in contemporary Negro verse. Between the octave and the sestet of the following sonnet, by Mrs. Carrie W. Clifford, the discord is of the kind that stabs you:

## AN EASTER MESSAGE

Now quivering to life, all nature thrills
At the approach of that triumphant queen,
Pink-fingered Easter, trailing robes of green
Tunefully o'er the flower-embroidered hills,
Her hair perfumed of myriad daffodils:
Upon her swelling bosom now are seen
The dream-frail lilies with their snowy sheen,
As lightly she o'erleaps the spring-time rills.
To black folk choked within the deadly grasp
Of racial hate, what message does she bring
Of resurrection and the hope of spring?
Assurance their death-stupor is a mask—
A sleep, with elements potential, rife,
Ready to burst full-flowered into life.

The Negro's deep resentment of his wrongs has found its most artistic expression in the verse of a poet who came to us from Jamaica—Mr. Claude McKay. In another chapter I have given the reader an opportunity to judge of his merits. He will be represented here by a sonnet, written, I believe, shortly after the race-riot in the national capital, July, 1919. It has been widely reprinted in the Negro newspapers.

### IF WE MUST DIE

If we must die, let it not be like hogs
Hunted and penned in an inglorious spot,
While round us bark the mad and hungry dogs,
Making their mock at our accursed lot.
If we must die—oh, let us nobly die,
So that our precious blood may not be shed
In vain; then even the monsters we defy
Shall be constrained to honor us, though dead!

Oh, kinsmen! We must meet the common foe;
Though far outnumbered, let us still be brave,
And for their thousand blows deal one
death-blow.
What though before us lies the open grave?
Like men we'll face the murderous, cowardly
pack,
Pressed to the wall, dying, but—fighting back!

Race consciousness has recently attained an extraordinary pitch in the Negro, and there seems to be no prospect of any abatement. The verse-smiths one and all have borne witness to a feeling of great intensity on all subjects pertaining to their race—the discriminations and injustices practised against it, the limitations that would be imposed upon it, the contumelies that would offend it. Ardent appeals are therefore made to race pride and ardent exhortations to race unity. The ancient rôle of the poet whereby he is identified with the prophet is being resumed by the enkindled souls of black men. With their natural gift for music and eloquence, with their increasing culture, with their building up of a poetic tradition now in process, with this intensification of race consciousness, almost anything may be expected of the Negro in another generation.

# CHAPTER VIII
# MISCELLANEOUS POEMS

## I. Eulogistic

ALTOGETHER admirable is the disposition of Negro verse-writers to eulogize the notable personages of their race, the men and women who have blazed the trail of advance. The mention of Attucks, Black Sampson, Sojourner Truth, Harriet Tubman, and others like these, all practically unknown to white readers, is frequent, and reverential odes and sonnets to Douglass, Toussaint L'Ouverture, Washington, Dunbar, are many and enthusiastic. Here as elsewhere, however, I refrain from giving mere titles and from comments on productions merely cited. The reader will find such poems as I allude to in every poet's volume. I refer to this body of eulogistic verse only to suggest to the reader who takes up the writings of the American Negroes that he will learn that they have a heritage of heroic traditions from which poetry springs in every race.

Instead of giving here such specimens of poetic eulogy as I have alluded to, however, I shall give a few poems of a more general significance, poems of appeal or tribute to the entire black race or poems of affectionate tribute to individuals. A free-verse poem entitled "The Negro," by Mr. Langston Hughes, on page 200, may be recalled. Here is a sonnet with the same title, by Mr. McKay, which appeared in *The People's Pilot*, published in Richmond, Va.:

MAE SMITH JOHNSON

## THE NEGRO

Think ye I am not fiend and savage too?
Think ye I could not arm me with a gun
And shoot down ten of you for every one
Of my black brothers murdered, burnt by you?
Be not deceived, for every deed ye do
I could match—outmatch: am I not Afric's son,
Black of that black land where black deeds are done?
But the Almighty from the darkness drew
My soul and said: Even thou shalt be a light

Awhile to burn on the benighted earth;
Thy dusky face I set among the white
For thee to prove thyself of highest worth;
Before the world is swallowed up in night,
To show thy little lamp; go forth, go forth!

From another Virginia magazine, also now defunct, *The Praise-worthy Muse*, of Norfolk, I take the following poem, signed by John J. Fenner, Jr.:

### RISE! YOUNG NEGRO—RISE!

Ho! we from slumber wake!
Rise! young Negro—rise!
Begin our daily task anew—
Thank God we're spared to—
Rise! young Negro—rise!

Thy task may be an humble one.
Rise! young Negro—rise!
However great, however small,
Honesty and respect for all—
Rise! young Negro—rise!

Each has a race to run.
Rise! young Negro—rise!
Enter now while we're young,
Though weak and just begun.
Rise! young Negro—rise!

Our banner flown will some day read:
Rise! young Negro—rise!
Victory's ours! We've won the race.

Then let us live in God by grace.
Rise! young Negro—rise!

In spirit and in form both these productions seem to be quite noteworthy. The first has in it something darkly and terribly ominous, while the second has all the fervor of religion in its youth. The class of poems to follow will afford a contrast. They will bear witness to that pride of race, perhaps, which we of the white race have commended to the colored people:

DAYBREAK

Awake! Arise! Men of my race—
I see our morning star,
And feel the dawn breeze on my face
Creep inward from afar.

I feel the dawn, with soft-like tread,
Steal through our lingering night,
Aglow with flame our sky to spread
In floods of morning light.

Arise, my men! Be wide-awake
To hear the bugle call
For Negroes everywhere to break
The bands that bind us all.

Great Lincoln, now with glory graced,
All Godlike with the pen,

Our chattel fetters broke and placed
Us in the ranks of men.

But even he could not awake
The dead, nor make alive,
Nor change stern Nature's laws, which make
The fittest to survive.

Let every man his soul inure
In noblest sacrifice,
And with a heart of oak endure
Ignoble, arrant prejudice.

Endurance, love, will yet prevail
Against all laws of hate;
Such armaments can never fail
Our race its best estate.

Let none make common cause with sin,
Be that in honor bound,
For they who fight with God must win
On every battleground.

Though wrongs there are, and wrongs have
been,
And wrongs we still must face,
We have more friends than foes within
The Anglo-Saxon race.

In spite of all the Babel cries
Of those who rage and shout,

God's silent forces daily rise
To bring his will about.

*George Marion McClellan.*

## THE NEGRO WOMAN

Were it mine to select a woman
As queen of the hall of fame;
One who has fought the gamest fight
And climbed from the depths of shame;
I would have to give the sceptre
To the lowliest of them all;
She, who has struggled through the years,
With her back against the wall.

Wronged by the men of an alien race,
Deserted by those of her own;
With a prayer in her heart, a song on her lips
She has carried the fight alone.
In spite of the snares all around her;
Her marvelous pluck has prevailed
And kept her home together—
When even her men have failed.

What of her sweet, simple nature?
What of her natural grace?
Her richness and fullness of color,
That adds to the charm of her face?
Is there a woman more shapely?
More vigorous, loving and true?

Yea, wonderful Negro woman
The honor I'd give to you.

*Andrea Razafkeriefo.*

## THE NEGRO CHILD

My little one of ebon hue,
My little one with fluffy hair,
The wide, wide world is calling you
To think and do and dare.

The lessons of stern yesterdays
That stir your blood and poise your brain
Are etching out the simple ways
By which you must attain.

An echo here, a memory there,
An act that links itself with truth;
A vision that makes troubles air
And toils the joy of youth.

These be your food, your drink, your rest,
These be your moods of drudgeful ease,
For these be nature's spur and test
And heaven's fair decrees.

My little one of ebon hue,
My little one with fluffy hair,
Go train your head and hands to do,
Your head and heart to dare.

*Joseph S. Cotter, Sr.*

## THE MOTHER

The mother soothes her mantled child
With plaintive melody, and wild;
A deep compassion brims her eye
And stills upon her lips the sigh.

Her thoughts are leaping down the years,
O'er branding bars, through seething tears:
Her heart is sandaling his feet
Adown the world's corroding street.

Then, with a start, she dons a smile,
His tender yearnings to beguile;
And only God will ever know
The wordless measure of her woe.

*Georgia Douglas Johnson.*

The foregoing poems are generic in character, the following, specific. And yet there is much in these also that is typical and universal:

## TO A NEGRO MOTHER

I hear you croon a little lullaby,
I see you press his little lips to yours,
Again old scenes come to my memory,
As if Love's stream had gained the long lost
shores;
As if the tidal wave of human good
Had thrown o'er me the mantle of control;
As if the beauty of true motherhood
Had gained the premise of my common soul.

The poet's heart is yet within your breast,
The captain's sword unconsciously you wield;
You know the sculptor's masterpiece the best,
Thro' you the master painter is revealed.
In you there dwells the Race's latent power—
The power to make, the power to break apart;
The power to lift, the power again to lower
That burnished shield that
guards the Race's heart.

And am I speaking as in hapless rhymes
Of things at least that may not come to pass?
Or is it not the spirit of the times
All things that savour power to amass?
Canst thou not see within thine own pure soul
That which thy Race and all the world awaits,
The master-leader who will reach the goal
And hew with sword of flame the city gates?

O Negro mother, from the dust arise,
Take up your task with grace and fortitude,
Knowing the goal is not the azure skies,
But here, and now, for thine own Race's good.
Create anew the captains of the past;
Build in your soul the Ethiopian power,
That when the mighty quest is gained at last,
O Negro mother, fame shall be your dower.
                    *Ben E. Burrell.*

## TO MY GRANDMOTHER

You 'mind me of the winter's eve
When low the sinking sun
Casts soft bright rays upon the snow
And day, now almost done,
In silence deep prepares to leave,
And calmly waits the signal "Go."

Your eyes are faded vestal lights
That once the hearth illumed,
Where vestal virgins vigil kept,
And budding virtue bloomed:
Like stars that beam on summer nights,
Your eyes, by joy and sorrow swept.

Asleep, one night, an angel kissed
Your hair and on the morn
The raven threads were silv'ry gray;
The angel fair had borne
Your youth away ere it you missed
And left old age to bless your way.

Smile on, for when you smile, it seems
I cannot do a wrong;
Your smiles go with me all the while
And make life one sweet song;
And oft at night my troubled dream
Grows gay at thoughts of your bright smile.

Dark Africa with Caucasian blood
To tinge your veins combined,

Your proud head bowed to slavery's thrall,
Your hands to toil consigned.
The Lord of hosts becalmed the flood,
The God Omnipotent o'er all.

Your ears have heard the din of war,
The martial tramp of feet,
Your voice has risen to your God
In supplications sweet.
May angels kiss each furrowed scar
Upon your brow where care has trod.

God bless the hands all withered now
By age and weary care.
God rest the feet that sought the way
To freedom bright and fair.
God bless thy life and e'er endow
Thee with new strength each new-born day.
                    *Mae Smith Johnson.*

## EBON MAID AND GIRL OF MINE

The sweetest charm of all the earth
Came into being with her birth.
All that without her we would lack
She is in purity and black.

The pansy and the violet,
The dark of all the flowers met
And gave their wealth of color in
The sable beauty of her skin.

Glad winds of evening are her face,
Gentle with love and rich in grace;
The blazing splendors of her eyes
Are jewels from the midnight skies.

Her hair—the darkness caught and curled,
The ancient wonder of the world—
Seems, in its strange, uncertain length,
A constant crown of queenly strength.

Her smile, it is the rising moon,
The waking of a night in June;
Her teeth are tips of white, they gleam
Like starlight in a happy dream.

Her laughter is a Christmas bell
Of "peace on earth and all is well!"
Her voice—it is the dearest part
Of all the glory in her heart.

The height of joy, the deep of tears,
The surging passion of the years,
The mystery and dark of things,
We feel their meanings when she sings.

Her thoughts are pure and every one
But makes her good to look upon.
Daughter of God! you are divine,
O, Ebon Maid and Girl of Mine!
                    *Lucian B. Watkins.*

I will conclude this section with a very well rhymed tribute to two Negro bards between whom there was a friendship and a correspondence similar to that which existed between Burns and Lapraik. The writer, James Edgar French, was a native of Kentucky, studied for the ministry, and died early:

## DUNBAR AND COTTER

Dunbar and Cotter! foster-brothers, ye,
Nurst at the breast of heav'nly minstrelsy!
The first two Negroes who have dared to climb
Parnassus' mount, and carve your names in
rhyme;
Who, over icy walls of prejudice,
Where twice ten thousand gorgon monsters
hiss,
Did scale the peak and make the steep ascent;
For which great feat ye had small precedent.
There were who said: "The Negro is not fit
To write good prose, much less to rhyme with
wit";
That nothing ever Negroes could inspire
With Spenser's fancy or with Shakespere's fire:
With Dryden's vigor, with the ease of Pope,
To weave the iambic pentametric rope,
But ye, immortal sons of Afric, ye
Have proved these charges gross absurdity;
That old Dame Nature's no respecter in
Regard to person or the hue of skin.
Omnific God, at whose fiatic hand
Did primogenial light deluge the land;
Whose word supreme did out of chaos draw

A world, and order made its guiding law,
Bequeath'd like talents to the black and white;
To read form'd some and others made to write;
To govern these, and those to governed be,
And you, great twain, endued with poesy!
                    *James Edgar French.*


## II. Commemorative and Occasional

From this body of Negro verse which I have been describing and giving specimens of may be selected pieces commemorative of days and seasons that are quite up to the standard of similar pieces provided for white children in their school-readers. These selections will further illustrate the variety of themes and emotional responses in this body of contemporary verse.

The first selection hardly needs any allowance to be made for it, I think, on the score that it was written by a girl only sixteen years of age:

### CHRISTMAS CHEER

'Tis Christmas time! 'Tis Christmas time!
Dear hallowed name of every clime!
How each one's heart now happy feels,
How each one's face fresh joy reveals
As Christmas Day is drawing near
The merriest day of all the year!

Old spite and hate, the scowl, the sneer
Are vanquished, all, by kindly cheer,
And friendships nigh forgot and cold
Glow warm again as once of old.

Man's worries cease, his hope returns,
His breast with love now brighter burns;
So, Christmas cheer! Oh, Christmas cheer!
A hearty welcome to you here.

A welcome through the world where trod
The source of joy, the Son of God,
The Lowly One who from above
First warmed cold earth with gladsome love:
Who still proclaims with golden voice,
"Peace on earth! Rejoice! Rejoice!"
                              *Corinne E. Lewis.*

If the reader is disposed to make comparisons he might recall, without very great detriment to the following poem, Tennyson's famous stanzas on the same theme. It is in the effective manner of the poems already given from its author:

### GOODBYE OLD YEAR

Goodbye, Old Year. Here comes New.
You've done wonders; now you're through;
Adding wisdom to the ages,
Making history's best pages;
Rest and slumber with the sages.
Good-bye, Old Year. Welcome, New.

Goodbye, Old Year. Welcome, New.
Off with false hopes; on with true.
Nations raise a mighty chorus,
Rich intoning, grand, sonorous,
Blithe and gladsome, sad, dolorous;

Goodbye, Old Year. Welcome, New.
Off with false hopes. On with true.

Goodbye, Old Year. Hail the New.
Goodbye, hatreds. Wrongs, adieu.
Down Life's lane, with high or lowly,
Weak, or strong, sin-cursed, or holy,
Time is reaping—trudging slowly.
Goodbye, Old Year. Hail the New.
Goodbye, hatreds. Wrongs, adieu.

Goodbye, Old Year. Come in, New.
Stout hearts look for light to you.
Rising hopes new scenes are staging;
Brotherhood our thoughts engaging.
Dreams of Peace hide battle raging.
Goodbye, Old Year. Come in, New.
Stout hearts fondly look to you.
                    *Joshua Henry Jones, Jr.*

The remainder of the series will be given without comment:

## THE MONTHS

### January

To herald in another year,
With rhythmic note the snowflakes fall
Silently from their crystal courts,
To answer Winter's call.
Wake, mortal! Time is winged anew!
Call Love and Hope and Faith to fill

The chambers of thy soul to-day;
Life hath its blessings still!

### February

The icicles upon the pane
Are busy architects; they leave
What temples and what chiseled forms
Of leaf and flower! Then believe
That though the woods be brown and bare,
And sunbeams peep through cloudy veils,
Though tempests howl through leaden skies,
The springtime never fails!

### March

Robin! Robin! call the Springtime!
March is halting on his way;
Hear the gusts. What! snowflakes falling!
Look not for the grass to-day.
Ay, the wind will frisk and play,
And we cannot say it nay.

### April

She trips across the meadows,
The weird, capricious elf!
The buds unfold their perfumed cups
For love of her sweet self;
And silver-throated birds begin to tune their
lyres,
While wind-harps lend their strains
to Nature's magic choirs.

## May

Sweet, winsome May, coy, pensive, fay,
Comes garlanded with lily-bells,
And apple blooms shed incense through the
bow'r,
To be her dow'r;
While through the leafy dells
A wondrous concert swells
To welcome May, the dainty fay.

## June

Roses, roses, roses,
Creamy, fragrant, dewy!
See the rainbow shower!
Was there e'er so sweet a flower?
I'm the rose-nymph, June they call me.
Sunset's blush is not more fair
Than the gift of bloom so rare,
Mortal, that I bring to thee!

## July

Sunshine and shadow play amid the trees
In bosky groves, while from the vivid sky
The sun's gold arrows fleck the fields at noon,
Where weary cattle to their slumber hie.
How sweet the music of the purling rill,
Trickling adown the grassy hill!
While dreamy fancies come to give repose
When the first star of evening glows.

## August

Haste to the mighty ocean,
List to the lapsing waves;
With what a strange commotion
They seek their coral caves.
From heat and turmoil let us oft return,
The ocean's solemn majesty to learn.

## September

With what a gentle sound
The autumn leaves drop to the ground;
The many-colored dyes,
They greet our watching eyes.
Rosy and russet, how they fall!
Throwing o'er earth a leafy pall.

## October

The mellow moon hangs golden in the sky,
The vintage song is over, far and nigh
A richer beauty Nature weareth now,
And silently, in reverence we bow
Before the forest altars, off'ring praise
To Him who sweetness gives to all our days.

## November

The leaves are sere,
The woods are drear,
The breeze, that erst so merrily did play,
Naught giveth save a melancholy lay;

Yet life's great lessons do not fail
E'en in November's gale.


December

List! List! the sleigh bells peal across the snow;
The frost's sharp arrows touch the earth and lo!
How diamond-bright the stars do scintillate
When Night hath lit her lamps to Heaven's
gate.
To the dim forest's cloistered arches go,
And seek the holly and the mistletoe;
For soon the bells of Christmas-tide will ring
To hail the Heavenly King!
                    *H. Cordelia Ray.*


WHILE APRIL BREEZES BLOW
(A Song for Arbor Day.)

Come, let us plant a tree today—
Forsake your book, forsake your play,
Bring out the spade and hie away
While April breezes blow.

Your life is young, and it should be
As full of vigor as this tree,
As fair, as upright and as free,
While April breezes blow.

Come, let us plant a tree to stand
Both fair and useful in the land,
Supremely tall and nobly grand
A strong and trusty oak.

Dig deep and let the long roots hold
A firm embrace within the mold:
And may your life in truth unfold
A strong and trusty oak.

Come, let us plant a supple ash,
A tree to bend when others crash,
And stand when vivid lightnings flash,
And clouds pour down the rain:

So while we plant we'll learn to bend
And hold our ground, tho' storms descend
Throughout our life, and lightnings rend,
And clouds pour down the rain.

Then let us plant these trees between
A graceful spruce in living green,
That e'en in winter days is seen
Like changeless springtime still:

And so may you as years go by,
And winter comes and snowflakes fly,
Be yet in heart, and mind and eye,
Like changeless springtime still.

Bring out the spade and hie away,
And let us plant a tree today
While skies are bright and hearts are gay,
And April breezes blow.

In other days 'neath April skies,
Around this tree may joyful cries
And happy children's songs arise,
While April breezes blow.

        *D. T. Williamson.*

## A NATION'S GREATNESS

What makes a nation truly great?
Not strength of arms, nor men of state,
Nor vast domains, by conquest won,
That knew not rise nor set of sun;
Nor sophist's schools, nor learned clan,
Nor laws that bind the will of man,—
For these have proved, in ages past,
But futile dreams that could not last;
And they that boast of such today,
Are fallen, vanquished in the fray,
Their glory mingled with the dust,
Their archives stained with crime and lust;
And all that breathed of pomp and pride,
Like the untimely fig, has died.
One thing, alone, restrains, exalts
A nation and corrects its faults;
One thing, alone, its life can crown
And give its destiny renown.
That nation, then, is truly great,
That lives by love, and not by hate;
That bends beneath the chastening rod,
That owns the truth, and looks to God!

*Edwin Garnett Riley.*

## THANKSGIVING

My heart gives thanks for many things—
For strength to labor day by day,
For sleep that comes when darkness wings
With evening up the eastern way.
I give deep thanks that I'm at peace
With kith and kin and neighbors, too;
Dear Lord, for all last year's increase,
That helped me strive and hope and do.
My heart gives thanks for many things;
I know not how to name them all.
My soul is free from frets and stings,
My mind from creed and doctrine's thrall.
For sun and stars, for flowers and streams,
For work and hope and rest and play,
For empty moments given to dreams—
For these my heart gives thanks today.

*William Stanley Braithwaite.*

I will conclude this anthology with a selection from our Madagascar poet, Andrea Razafkeriefo, which, in a happy strain, conveys a very good philosophy of life—which is especially the Afro-American's:

## RAINY DAYS

On rainy days I don't despair,
But slip into my rocking chair;
With my old pipe and volume rare
And wade in fiction deep.
The pitter-patter of the rain

Upon the roof and window pane
Comes like a lullaby's refrain,
Till soon I'm fast asleep.

I'm grateful for the rainy days:
'Tis only then my fancy plays,
And mem'ry wanders back and strays
O'er paths I loved so dear.
The lightning's flash, the thunder's peal
Convinces me that God is real;
And it's a wondrous thing to feel
That he is really near.

Of the manifold and immense significance of poetry as a form
of spiritual expression the Negro American has lately become
profoundly aware, as this presentation must amply reveal. Not
only the industrial arts are the objects of his ambition, according to
the far-looking doctrine of Tuskegee, but as well those arts which
are born of and express the spiritual traits of mankind, the fine
arts—music, painting, sculpture, dramatics, and poetry. In them
all the Negro is winning distinction. In consequence it would
seem that there must dawn upon us, shaped by the poems of this
collection, a new vision of the Negro and a new appreciation of
his spiritual qualities, his human character. A profounder human
sympathy with a greatly hampered, handicapped, and humiliated
people must also ensue from such considerations as these poems
will induce. One of the poets here represented cries out, as if from
a calvary, "We come slow-struggling up the hills of Hell." Another,
in milder but not less appealing tone, cries: "We climb the slopes
of life with throbbing hearts."

This appeal, expressed or implicit throughout the entire

range of present-day Negro verse, an appeal sometimes angrily, sometimes plaintively uttered, an appeal to mankind for fundamental justice and for human fellowship on the broad basis of kinship of spirit, may fittingly be the final note of this anthology:

*We climb the slopes of life with throbbing hearts.*

# INDEX OF AUTHORS INDEX OF AUTHORS, WITH BIOGRAPHICAL AND BIBLIOGRAPHICAL NOTES

ALLEN, J. MORD.—Born, Montgomery, Ala., March 26, 1875. Schooling ceased in the middle of high-school. Since seventeen years of age a boiler-maker. Home, St. Louis, Mo. Authorship: *Rhymes, Tales and Rhymed Tales*, Crane and Company, Topeka, Kas., 1906.

ALLEN, WINSTON.

BAILEY, WILLIAM EDGAR.—Born, Salisbury, Mo. Educated in the Salisbury public schools. Authorship: *The Firstling*, 1914.

BELL, JAMES MADISON.—Born, Gallipolis, Ohio, 1826. Educated in night schools after reaching manhood. Prominent anti-slavery orator, friend of John Browne. *Poetical Works*, with biography by Bishop B. W. Arnett, 1901.

BRAITHWAITE, WILLIAM STANLEY.—Born, Boston, Mass., 1878. Mainly self-educated. His three books of original verse are: *Lyrics of Life and Love*, 1904; *The House of Falling Leaves*, 1908; *Sandy Star and Willie Gee*, 1922. In *Who's Who.*BURRELL,

BENJAMIN EBENEZER.—Born, Manchester Mountains, Jamaica, 1892. Descended from Mandingo kings on his father's side, and on his mother's from Cromantees and Scotch. Contributor to *The Crusader* and other magazines.

CARMICHAEL, WAVERLEY TURNER.—Born, Snow Hill, Ala. Educated in the Snow Hill Institute and Harvard Summer School. Authorship: *From the Heart of a Folk*, The Cornhill Company, Boston, 1918.

CLIFFORD, CARRIE W.—Born, Chillicothe, Ohio. Educated at Columbus, O. Has done much editorial and club work. Authorship: *The Widening Light*, Walter Reid Co., Boston, 1922.

CONNER, CHARLES H.—Born, Grafton, N. Y., 1864. Father, a slave who found freedom by way of the underground railway. Mainly self-educated. Worker in the ship-yards, Philadelphia. Authorship: *The Enchanted Valley*, published by himself, 1016 S. Cleveland Ave., Philadelphia, 1917; contributor to magazines.

CORBETT, MAURICE NATHANIEL.—Born, Yanceyville, N. C., 1859. Educated in the common schools and Shaw University. Served in North Carolina Legislature. Delegate to numerous political conventions. Clerk in Census Bureau, then in the Government Printing Office, Washington, D. C., until stricken with paralysis in 1919. Authorship: *The Harp of Ethiopia*, Nashville, 1914. This is an epic poem of about 7,500 rhymed lines, narrating the entire history of the Negro in America. It is a noteworthy undertaking.

CORROTHERS, JAMES DAVID.—Born, Michigan, 1869. Educated at Northwestern University, Evanston, Ill., and at Bennett College, Greensboro, N. C., Minister of the Zion Methodist Episcopal Church. Died, 1919. Books: *Selected Poems*, 1907; *The Dream and the Song*, 1914.

COTTER, JOSEPH SEAMON, JR.—Born, Louisville, Ky., 1895. Died, 1919. Books: *The Band of Gideon*, Cornhill Company, 1918; another volume of poems now in press.

COTTER, JOSEPH SEAMON, SR.—Born, Bardstown, Ky., 1861. Educated in Louisville night school (10 months). Now school principal in Louisville, member of many societies, author of several books: *A Rhyming*, 1895; *Links of Friendship*, 1898; *Caleb, the Degenerate*, 1903; *A White Song and a Black One*, 1909; *Negro Tales*, 1912. In *Who's Who*.

DANDRIDGE, RAYMOND GARFIELD.—Born, Cincinnati, Ohio, 1882. Educated in Cincinnati grammar and high schools. First devoted to drawing and painting until paralytic stroke, 1911. Authorship: *The Poet and Other Poems*, Cincinnati, 1920.

DETT, R. NATHANIEL.—Born of Virginia parents at Drummondsville, Ontario, Canada, October 11, 1882; studied in various colleges and conservatories in Canada and the United States. Director of music at Lane College, Mississippi, Lincoln Institute, Missouri, and at Hampton Institute, Virginia, his present position.

DUBOIS, W. E. BURGHARDT.—Born, Great Barrington, Mass., 1868. Education: Fisk University, A. B.; Harvard, A. B., A. M., and Ph. D.; Berlin. Professor of economics and history in Atlanta University, 1896-1910. Now editor of *The Crisis*, New York, Books: *The Souls of Black Folk*, 1903; *Darkwater*, 1919, and numerous others. In *Who's Who*.

DUNBAR, PAUL LAURENCE.—1872-1906. 37, 38-48.

DUNBAR-NELSON, ALICE RUTH MOORE (née).—Born, New Orleans, 1875. Education: in New Orleans public schools and Straight University, and later in several northern universities.

Taught in New Orleans, Washington, and Brooklyn, and other cities. Married Paul Laurence Dunbar, 1898. At present Managing Editor of Philadelphia and Wilmington *Advocate*. Books: *Violets and Other Tales*, New Orleans, 1894; *The Goodness of St. Rocque*, Dodd, Mead & Co., 1899; *Masterpieces of Negro Eloquence*, 1913; *The Dunbar Speaker and Entertainer*, 1920. Contributor to numerous magazines.

DUNGEE, ROSCOE RILEY.—

ESTE, CHARLES H.—

FAUSET, MISS JESSIE.—Born, Philadelphia. Education: A. B., Cornell, Phi Beta Kappa; A. M., University of Pennsylvania; student of the Guilde Internationale, Paris. Interpreter of the Second Pan-African Congress. Literary Editor of *The Crisis*.

FENNER, JOHN J., JR.

FISHER, LELAND MILTON.—Born, Humboldt, Tenn., 1875. Died, under thirty years of age, at Evansville, Ind., where he edited a newspaper. Left behind an unpublished volume of poems.

FLEMING, MRS. SARAH LEE BROWN.—*Clouds and Sunshine*, The Cornhill Company, Boston, 1920.

FRENCH, JAMES EDGAR.—Born in Kentucky, studied for the ministry, died young.

GRIMKÉ, MISS ANGELINA WELD.—Born, Boston, Mass., 1880. Educated in various schools of several states, including the Girls' Latin School of Boston and the Boston Normal School of Gymnastics. Now teacher of English in the Dunbar High School, Washington, D. C. Authorship: *Rachel*, a prose drama, Cornhill Co., Boston, 1921; poems and short stories uncollected.

GRIMKÉ, MRS. CHARLOTTE FORTEN.—Born, Philadelphia,

1837 (née Forten). Educated in the Normal School at Salem, Mass. She was a contributor to various magazines, including *The Atlantic Monthly* and *The New England Magazine*. Poems uncollected.

HAMMON, JUPITER.—Born, c. 1720. "The first member of the Negro race to write and publish poetry in this country." Extant poems: *An Evening Thought*, 1760; *An Address to Miss Phillis Wheatley*, 1778; *A Poem for Children with Thoughts on Death*, 1782; *The Kind Master and the Dutiful Servant* (date unknown.) These are included in Oscar Wegelin's *Jupiter Hammon, American Negro Poet*, New York, 1915.

HAMMOND, MRS. J. W.—Home, Omaha, Neb. Occupation: Trained nurse.

HARPER, MRS. FRANCES ELLEN WATKINS (née).—Born, Baltimore, Md., of free parents, 1825. Died, Philadelphia, 1911. Educated in a school in Baltimore for free colored children, and by her uncle, William Watkins. Married Fenton Harper, 1860. From about 1851 devoted herself to the cause of freedom for the slaves. Authorship: *Poems on Miscellaneous Subjects*, Philadelphia, 1857; *Poems*, Philadelphia, 1900.

HARRIS, LEON R.—Born, Cambridge, Ohio, 1886. First years spent in an orphanage, where he got the rudiments of education. Then was farmed out in Kentucky. Running off, he made his way to Berea College and later to Tuskegee, getting two or three terms at each. Now editor of the Richmond (Indiana) Blade. Authorship: numerous short stories in magazines; *The Steel Makers and Other War Poems* (pamphlet), 1918.

HAWKINS, WALTER EVERETTE.—Born, Warrenton, N. C., 1886. Educated in public schools. Since 1913 in the city post-office of Washington D. C. Authorship: *Chords and Discords*, Richard G. Badger, Boston, 1920.

HILL, LESLIE PINCKNEY.—Born, Lynchburg, Va., 1880. B. A. and M. A. of Harvard. Teacher at Tuskegee; formerly principal of Manassas (Va.) Industrial School; now principal of Cheyney (Pa.) State Normal School. Authorship: *The Wings of Oppression*, The Stratford Company, Boston, 1921

HORTON, GEORGE M.—Born, North Carolina. Authorship: *Poems by a Slave*, 1829. *Poetical Works*, 1845. Several volumes from 1829 to 1865.

HUGHES, JAMES C.—

HUGHES, LANGSTON.—Born, Joplin, Mo., February 1, 1902. Ancestry, Negro and Indian; grand-nephew of Congressman John M. Langston. Education: High School, Cleveland, O., one year at Columbia University; traveled in Mexico and Central America. Contributor to magazines. Home, Jones's Point, N. Y. Contributor to *The Crisis*.

JAMISON, ROSCOE C.—Born, Winchester, Tenn., 1886; died at Phœnix, Ariz., 1918. Educated at Fisk University. Authorship: *Negro Soldiers and Other Poems*, William F. McNeil, South St. Joseph, Mo., 1918.

JESSYE, MISS EVA ALBERTA.—Born, Coffeyville, Kan., 1897. Educated in the public schools of several western states; graduated from Western University, 1914. Director of music in Morgan College, Baltimore, 1919. Now teacher of piano, Muskogee, Okla.

JOHNSON, ADOLPHUS.—*The Silver Chord*, Philadelphia, 1915.

JOHNSON, CHARLES BERTRAM.—Born, Callao, Mo., 1880. Educated at Western College, Macon, Mo.; two summers at Lincoln Institute; correspondence courses, and a term in the

University of Chicago. Educator and preacher. Authorship: *Wind Whisperings* (a pamphlet), 1900; *The Mantle of Dunbar and Other Poems* (a pamphlet), 1918; *Songs of My People*, 1918. Home, Moberly, Mo.

JOHNSON, FENTON.—Born, Chicago, 1888. Educated in the public schools and University of Chicago. Authorship: *A Little Dreaming*, Chicago, 1914; *Visions of the Dusk*, New York, 1915. *Songs of the Soil*, New York, 1916. Editor of *The Favorite Magazine*, Chicago.

JOHNSON, MRS. GEORGIA DOUGLAS.—Born, Atlanta, Ga. Educated at Atlanta University, and in music at Oberlin. Home, Washington, D. C. Books: *The Heart of a Woman*, the Cornhill Co., Boston, 1918; *Bronze*, B. J. Brimmer Co., Boston, 1922.

JOHNSON, JAMES WELDON.—Born, Jacksonville, Fla., 1871. Educated at Atlanta and Columbia Universities. United States consul in Venezuela and Nicaragua. Author of numerous works. Original verse: *Fifty Years and Other Poems*, the Cornhill Company, Boston, 1917. In *Who's Who*.

JOHNSON, MRS. MAE SMITH (née).—Born, Alexandria, Va., 1890. Now Secretary at the Good Samaritan Orphanage, Newark, N. J. Contributor of verse to papers and magazines. The grand-mother of the poet escaped from slavery in Virginia. She lived to be ninety-two years old.

JONES, EDWARD SMYTHE.—Authorship: *The Sylvan Cabin and Other Verse*, Sherman, French & Co., Boston, 1911.

JONES, JOSHUA HENRY, JR.—Born, Orangeburg, S. C., 1876. Educated Central High School, Columbus, O., Ohio State University, Yale, and Brown. Has served on the editorial staffs of the Providence *News*, The Worcester *Evening Post*, Boston *Daily*

*Advertiser* and Boston *Post*. At present he is on the staff of the Boston *Telegram*. Authorship: *The Heart of the World*, the Stratford Company, Boston, 1919; *Poems of the Four Seas*, the Cornhill Company, Boston, 1921.

JONES, TILFORD.—

JORDAN, W. CLARENCE.—

JORDAN, WINIFRED VIRGINIA.—CONTRIBUTOR TO THE CRISIS.

LEE, MARY EFFIE.—Contributor to *The Crisis*.

LEWIS, CORINNE E.—Student in the Dunbar High School, Washington, D. C.

LEWIS, ETHYL.—

MCCLELLAN, GEORGE MARION.—Born, Belfast, Tenn., 1860. Educated at Fisk University, Nashville, Tenn., of which he became financial agent. Later, principal of the Paul Dunbar School, Louisville, Ky. Authorship: *The Path of Dreams*, John P. Morton, Louisville, Ky., 1916.

MCKAY, CLAUDE.—Born, Jamaica, 1889. Has resided in the United States ten or eleven years. Till lately on the editorial staff of the *Liberator*. Books: *Constab Ballads*, London, 1912; *Spring in New Hampshire*, London, 1920.

MARGETSON, GEORGE REGINALD.—Born, 1877, at St. Kitts, B. W. I.

MEANS, STERLING M.—Authorship: *The Deserted Cabin and Other Poems*, A. B. Caldwell, publisher, Atlanta, 1915.

MILLER, KELLY.—Born, Winsboro, S. C., 1863. Educated at Howard and Johns Hopkins Universities. Degrees: A. M. and LL. D. Professor and dean in Howard University. Books: *Race*

*Adjustment*, 1904; *Out of the House of Bondage*, Neale Publishing Co., New York, 1914. In *Who's Who*.

Moore, William.—*Contributor to The Favorite Magazine*.

Ray, H. Cordelia.—Authorship: *Poems*, The Grafton Press, New York, 1910.

Razafkeriefo, Andrea.—Born, Washington, D. C., 1895, of Afro-American mother and Madagascaran father. Educated only in public elementary school. Regular verse contributor to *The Crusader* and *The Negro World*.

Reason, Charles L.—Born in New York in 1818. Professor at New York Central College in New York and head of the Institute for Colored Youth in Philadelphia. Authorship: *Freedom*, New York, 1847.

Riley, Edwin Garnett.—Contributor to many newspapers and magazines.

Sexton, Will.—Contributor to magazines.

Shackelford, Otis.—Educated at Lincoln Institute, Jefferson City, Mo. Authorship: *Seeking the Best* (prose and verse). The verse part of this volume contains a poem of some 500 lines entitled "Bits of History in Verse, or A Dream of Freedom Realized," modeled on *Hiawatha*.

Shackelford, Theodore Henry.—Born, Windsor Canada, 1888. Grandparents were slaves in southern states. At twelve years of age had had only three terms of school. At twenty-one entered the Industrial Training School, Downington, Pa., and graduated four years later. Studied a while at the Philadelphia Art Museum. Authorship: *My Country and Other Poems*, Philadelphia, 1918. Died, Jamaica, N. Y., February 5, 1923.

SPENCER, MRS. ANNE.—Born, Bramwell, W. Va., 1882. Educated at the Virginia Seminary, Lynchburg, Va. Contributor to *The Crisis*

UNDERHILL, IRVIN W.—Born, Port Clinton, Pa., May 1, 1868. In boyhood, with irregular schooling, assisted his father, who was captain of a canal boat. At the age of 37 suddenly lost his sight. Author of *Daddy's Love and Other Poems*, Philadelphia. Home, Philadelphia.

WATKINS, LUCIAN B.—Born, Chesterfield, Virginia, 1879. Educated in public schools of Chesterfield, and at the Virginia Normal and Industrial Institute, Petersburg. First teacher, then soldier. Books: *Voices of Solitude*, 1907, Donohue & Co., Chicago; *Whispering Winds*, in manuscript. Died, 1921.

WATSON, ADELINE CARTER.—

WHEATLEY, PHILLIS.—Born in Africa, 1753. Brought as a slave to Boston, where she died in 1784. Many editions of her poems in her lifetime. *Poems and Letters*, New York, 1916.

WIGGINS, LIDA KECK.—Authorship: *The Life and Works of Paul Laurence Dunbar*, J. L. Nichols & Company, Naperville, Ill.

WHITMAN, ALBERY A.—Born in Kentucky in 1857. Began life as a Methodist minister. Authorship: *The Rape of Florida, Not a Man and Yet a Man*, and *Twasnita's Seminoles*.

WILLIAMSON, D. T.—

WILSON, CHARLES P.—Born in Iowa of Kentucky parents, 1885. Printer and theatrical performer.

# FOOTNOTES:

[1] Happily a great number of these, about three hundred and fifty, accompanied by an essay setting forth their nature, origin, and elements, are now made accessible in *Negro Folk Rhymes*, by Thomas W. Talley, of Fisk University; the Macmillan Company, publishers, 1922.

[2] We are enabled to give the following poems by the kind permission of Dodd, Mead and Company, the publishers of Dunbar's works.

[3] *The Dunbar Speaker and Entertainer*, containing the best prose and poetic selections by and about the Negro Race, with programs arranged for special entertainments. Edited by Alice Moore Dunbar-Nelson. J. L. Nichols & Co., Naperville, Ill.

[4] *Bronze* has now been published. See Index of Authors.

[5] *A Short History of the American Negro.* By Benjamin Brawley. The Macmillan Company.

[6] Published by Harcourt, Brace & Company, by whose kind permission I use this selection.

www.ingramcontent.com/pod-product-compliance
Lightning Source LLC
Chambersburg PA
CBHW071802020726
47502CB00004B/981

# Dream Sequence

## and Other Curious Tales

## Michael Beauchamp

**Eleusis Press**

*…am Sequence  and Other Curious Tales*

Copyright © 2017 by Michael Beauchamp

Published by Eleusis Press

2009 North 7th Street, Phoenix, Arizona, 85006

eleusisimages@gmail.com

Printed and bound in the United States of America

# Dream Sequence

## and Other Curious Tales

## Michael Beauchamp

**Eleusis Press**

*um Sequence and Other Curious Tales*

Copyright © 2017 by Michael Beauchamp

Published by Eleusis Press

2009 North 7th Street, Phoenix, Arizona, 85006

eleusisimages@gmail.com


Printed and bound in the United States of America

*For Natasha*

# Table of Contents

# The Gamer

Gary took a large hit of Narconade and strapped on the hypno-helmet for another round. Within moments, the drug took effect and the simulation began. This particular game was his current favorite. While his body lay slumped and forgotten on a stained and tattered couch in a dimly lit, filthy room, in Gary's mind he was blasting undead alien enemies with a shotgun, their bulbous heads exploding in gloriously realistic ways. He proceeded through the intricately rendered and detailed virtual environment, firing round after round at every humanoid creature he encountered.

In the distance he spotted a temple, shimmering in the desert heat. Gary was making real progress! He had never before made it this far. His heart rate increased. He began to sweat profusely. He uttered strange, animalistic sounds under his breath and there was a certain excited stirring in his crotch. Gary was entirely unaware of his physiology – he was focused purely on reaching that temple and killing everything that stood in his way.

A xeno-zombie lunged at him from the left. Gary quickly leveled his weapon and dispatched it with a blast to the face. The stirring in his groin increased. He was now fully aroused. A chuckle escaped his lips, followed closely by a long, dangling string of thick saliva. He was fast approaching the temple, an imposing stone structure vaguely Egyptian. Through the internal speakers of the helmet, he could hear faint chanting that seemed to emanate from within the temple. He could now see bizarre symbols carved into the temple's pillars.

Gary quivered with anticipation. He reduced a few more reanimated alien corpses to green and purple piles of

smoking gelatinous matter and began to ascend the steps
leading up and into the inner chambers. A fierce, ominous
wind swept across the desert. The chanting grew louder. Gary
reached the entrance to the first chamber and paused.
Somewhere in the murky, hidden depths of the temple,
perhaps aware of his presence and waiting in ambush, lurked
the alien overlord, the ultimate foe and final target in the
game.

Defeating the overlord had become an obsession for
Gary. He had invested many months of his life on the game.
When he slept, which was rarely, he dreamed of the alien
planet. Often, he could not distinguish between his dreams
and his time in the hypno-helmet. He lived in a world of
overlapping, amorphous realities and merged fantasies. In
this moment, his consciousness was completely occupied
with the task at hand – finding and killing the overlord. All
other thoughts, all memories, all awareness of the 'real' world
were lost to the void.

Gary took a deep, anxious breath and entered the
inner sanctum. The eerie chanting suddenly ceased. It was
unnaturally silent inside the temple, like the vacuum of deep
space. He peered intently into the darkness with his weapon
raised. He proceeded slowly, each step deliberate. Gary
reached a large gallery, with tunnels leading in all directions.
Nothing moved in the still gloom. Which way should he go?
He could see no markings or symbols indicating the location
of the overlord's chamber. He was momentarily paralyzed by
indecision. His mind raced, his hands trembled. Finally, he
summoned the courage to move, choosing to go forward on
pure instinct.

As Gary entered the far corridor, the darkness seemed
to tighten around him, enveloping him in a black cloak. The
hypno-helmet provided a total sensory experience and, at this
point, he could actually smell the putrid stench of something

ancient and hideous lurking in the dark. He was in a perfect
state of awareness now, like a paranoid coyote slinking
through the moonlight. Sweat and drool pooled at Gary's feet.
He was now moaning in a low, guttural voice. He took a few
more cautious steps and stopped abruptly. Movement directly
ahead! A massive shape of indistinct features and proportions
writhed in the shadows. He knew immediately what it was –
the alien overlord was within reach! *Don't panic*, he told
himself. *Don't panic!*

Gary tightened his grip on the weapon and yelled,
"Come on, fucker! Bring it!" He chambered a round,
preparing to fire. Nothing in his life could compare to this
wonderful, glorious moment. Victory, validation, and
satisfaction of the highest order were within reach. He
savored the pleasure of imminent climax. What a delicious
sensation! *If only real life offered such sublime experiences*,
he thought. A huge smile appeared on his face.

Hoping to provoke the overlord into action, Gary
started forward. He was successful. The creature suddenly
lunged at him from the darkness, a shrieking, squirming mass
of teeth and tentacles. Abruptly, the creature froze in midair.
It hung there motionless, its shriek reverberating in Gary's
ears with an unnerving staccato rhythm. Gary attempted to
fire the shotgun, but nothing happened. His virtual hands and
virtual weapon were frozen in place, locked up on the
helmet's view-screen.

Then he heard it – a loud, persistent banging from
above his head. Gary instantly understood what was
happening and it was not good. His neighbor upstairs was
pounding on the floor and the ruckus had shaken loose the
terminal plug by which the hypno-helmet was attached,
disrupting the game. He realized that his war cry must have
been loud enough to upset the neighbor. It was not the first
time that it had happened. Gary was absolutely mortified and

sat in shock, his mouth agape.

It took several minutes for Gary to compose himself. When he was sufficiently calm, he carefully removed the hypno-helmet and set it down on the couch beside him. He put his head in his hands, feeling defeated. He had been so close to completing the game – so close to killing the overlord and ridding the planet of alien zombies! Gary was on the verge of real tears. He had invested such a large amount of time and energy into the game that his sense of purpose and self-worth were intrinsically linked to the task. He whimpered and shook spasmodically. The more he thought about it, the more upset he grew. He then began to get angry.

Gary sat up, stretching his back and arms. He reached for the Narconade and finished the canister in one hit. The drug's effects were intense and immediate. His mind raced. *People are always getting in the way,* he thought. *They fuck everything up. All I've ever wanted was to be left alone to my Narconade and hypno-helmet. I'm not hurting anyone! Why are they always trying to stop me from indulging in the only things I truly enjoy in this dismal, doomed, rotten old world? Planet Earth is a shithouse. People kill each other every day over meaningless nonsense. Wars are waged on the poor, helpless, and innocent. Violence, greed, misery, and wretchedness of every variety plague this pitiful planet.*

*At least I found an escape.* Gary's thoughts were spiraling out of control. *At least I have something I am passionate about. I keep to myself and cause no trouble... and they keep interfering!* His rage was increasing. *That fucking neighbor! He* knew *I was playing. He probably interrupted the game on purpose. He's probably laughing about it right now.* Fury rose in Gary's belly like sick fire. He was naturally passive and non-confrontational, but a perfect, crystalline idea entered his mind. It was suddenly clear what he must do... and he must do it NOW, before any doubt, second-guessing, or intrusive overanalysis tainted his resolve.

Gary rose from the couch. He was gaunt, emaciated, and filthy, reeking of a thousand showerless days, but he was filled with a new sense of purpose and fresh resolve. *I must kill that asshole neighbor,* he thought. It was all so clear to him now. *Retribution! Validation!* He scanned the interior of his tiny apartment, his gaze cold and intense. He spotted the perfect tool for the task – a baseball bat from his long gone childhood days in little league. He retrieved it from the corner, admiring its nicely balanced heft and enjoying its weight in his hands. Gary felt powerful again.

Clutching the bat, Gary calmly opened the door to the hall and left his apartment for the first time in days. The glare of the hallway lights surprised and stunned him, but he adjusted and made his way down the hall toward the stairway. He ascended to the next floor, now holding the bat in both hands as if approaching the plate.

Gary reached the second-level landing and was instantly aware of a strange smell... a putrid, rotten stench, actually. *What kind of appalling things do these people eat? Did something die?* He gagged and felt nauseated. As he struggled to contain the contents of his stomach, the hall lights flickered. He then became aware of an eerie buzzing sound issuing from nowhere and everywhere simultaneously. Gary was starting to feel weird. For a surreal, disconcerting moment, he was not sure if he was still playing the game or not. He reached up to touch his head and found no helmet. The hall lights blinked out and he was instantly plunged into total darkness.

Pure, primal fear fell upon Gary like a frigid wind. "What the fuck!" he yelled. "Who's there?!" He gazed into the black, straining to see down the hall and becoming ever more aware of the terrible smell and the dreadful buzzing sound. He felt like he was going crazy. He felt profoundly ill. He stood motionless, his heart racing, his body trembling. Then he saw it – something was moving in the darkness... something massive and menacing. It was rushing at him now, a shrieking, writhing mass of teeth and tentacles. Gary screamed as the overlord descended.

# Keeper of the Cubes

He was known as the Keeper of the Cubes. In reality, his name was Ron. He was little more than a custodian, but this fact does not diminish the importance of his work. Ron's role was vital and he took his job very seriously. The continued existence of the human species, in its new and ostensibly evolved state, depended on him.

Ron was a simple and happy man. He performed his duties cheerfully and never complained. The truth is, no one was around to *hear* his complaints. You see, Ron was the last of the Organics – the very last soul who still occupied a human body. The other survivors had already migrated to their Cubes. Their minds now existed eternally in highly advanced and totally convincing computer simulations. Each Cube was a distinct and custom-created universe, tailor-made for the individual and designed to provide maximum joy and pleasure. You might wonder why I refer to people as *survivors*. Settle in and I'll tell you the story.

The exodus from three-dimensional reality was preceded by an almost equally momentous event – an event that would drastically reduce the number of people who would make the transition. The majority of the Earth's population never knew what was coming. They were totally unaware of the plans being made in secret to escape the upcoming global cataclysm.

The ELE – or Extinction Level Event – had been predicted many years in advance of its arrival. The data was strong, the projections irrefutable. The outcome was inevitable. Scientists all over the world tracked the massive asteroid as it raced toward the planet on its trajectory of death. Decisions of grave consequence were made. Not long after it was realized that the event could not be prevented, it was decided that the general public must never know. What good would it serve the average man and woman to be aware of their imminent doom?

Somewhere, somehow, someone who called the shots initiated a highly classified project. The brightest minds of the time were called into action and given a mission: find a way to save at least a small portion of the race. It was a huge undertaking of profound significance. Those who worked on the project were prepared to do whatever it would take to succeed, using all available resources, including cutting-edge, experimental technology. It was a multinational effort. With the threat of total annihilation of the species looming, the world's political, regional, and ideological divisions were quickly forgotten.

Scientists, engineers, physicians, and computer programmers worked in deep underground military facilities, closely monitored by military personnel. The underground bases had been there for many years prior, but were expanded and connected into a vast network that crisscrossed the planet. Eventually, the project would be confined to one large cavern – Ron's domain – but in the early years, the operation involved hundreds of hollowed-out rooms and thousands of individuals.

Countless options were considered. Innumerable theories were explored. The breakthrough came in the field of computer science and the development of neural mapping. It was discovered that a complete digital reproduction of the brain, including the thoughts and memories contained within it, could be saved and inserted into a machine running a simulation program. This effectively rendered a flesh and blood body obsolete. This was convenient, since it was thought that the Earth – the surface, at least – would be uninhabitable for many centuries after the ELE.

The machine that ran the simulation was a small box

that could fit in the palm of one's hand. These boxes came to be known as Cubes. All of the survivors could be, once uploaded to their individual Cubes, stacked in one room, where they would exist in the eternal bliss of their choosing. This made any future attempts to repopulate the Earth unnecessary, the project leaders reasoned. To them, living in a digital simulation as an immortal mind was the next logical step in human evolution. And so, even before the asteroid struck the planet, the migration began. Each chosen survivor underwent the process of neural mapping and insertion into his or her custom Cube. Each survivor entered a unique, self-contained reality.

A volunteer had been chosen to remain behind to ensure that the last participant in the project made the transition successfully. The volunteer was Ron, who had been working as a janitor in the main facility since the inception of the project. He was an average man of average intellect who was well-liked by all who knew him. He had a calm, pleasant demeanor that made those around him feel good, despite the serious implications of their work.

Ron's task was simple: once the last person had been scanned and was ready for insertion, Ron simply had to push a key to complete the transfer. Once that was done, Ron was to have free reign of the entire facility and complete use of its stocks and amenities for as long as he lived. This suited him fine, for he was a solitary man by nature. He would also have the company of his best friend, Bruno the Cat. As part of his normal duties as janitor, Ron was asked to keep the Cube Room tidy. Someone once referred to him as the Keeper of the Cubes and the name stuck.

Deep below the surface of the Earth, the time came for the last upload. A man lay on a gurney, his head covered in sensors. He was wired up and scanned. Ron pressed a key on the control panel and the man's consciousness lingered in limbo for a few moments as his mind was inserted into the Cube. When the upload was complete, Ron removed the sensors and wheeled the body into a vault with all the others. This did not disturb him, for he knew that the man wasn't *really* dead. Having completed his work, Ron returned to his quarters, whistling as he walked through the deserted, cavernous tunnels.

Many months went by. Ron lived a quiet, solitary life, completely incognizant of what was happening on the surface. He was quite content to be alone in the massive facility. He spent his days reading books, watching old movies, snacking on the ample rations in the storerooms, and wandering the extensive tunnel system, often with Bruno trotting happily beside him. Ron did not need a Cube. For him, life was already perfect.

Everything changed for Ron on the day he discovered the monitoring room. He stumbled upon it accidentally while exploring an area of the facility that had previously been off-limits. It seemed like a chance discovery at the time, but in retrospect, considering the subsequent events, it could be said that the hand of providence had guided him.

The door was unlocked. Ron turned the knob and opened it, expecting to find a dorm room or perhaps a utility closet. What he saw startled him. It was, in appearance, a control center or command bunker. The immense room was full of computer equipment and desks. All four walls were covered in high-resolution video screens that were segmented into small squares, each displaying a different image. In awe, Ron stepped into the room. Bruno the Cat followed close behind.

"Gee, Bruno," Ron said, "looks like someone forgot to turn off the TVs!"

Ron couldn't believe his eyes. It was like watching a thousand movies playing at once. He scanned the room, marveling at the technological sophistication, delighting in the bountiful entertainment the room would no doubt provide. His delight rapidly transformed into extreme unease when he realized that each and every screen seemed to be displaying a scene of violence and horror.

"I don't like scary movies," Ron said quietly.

What was being shown on the screens was more than scary – the scenes were truly disturbing. In one scene, a man was being tortured with jagged, rusty metal implements by figures in black cloaks. In another, a terrified woman was being chased through a forest by a lumbering, menacing creature. Swarms of spiders, pools of blood, drownings, monsters, fire, and pain – Ron's mind reeled at the nightmarish images. He watched as people fell from buildings, dangled from cliffs, went mad at the sight of grotesque and obscene things, and grappled with dark, spectral entities. It was like peering into a thousand hells. It was then that he noticed something even more unsettling – he *recognized* some of the individuals on the screens. They were project members, his co-workers and friends.

"These aren't movies," Ron said. "I know these people."

It was a shocking realization. The characters were not actors and it was obvious to Ron that the people were in real distress. The epiphany struck – Ron was seeing what was happening in the Cubes. Far from existing in an eternal paradise, the Cube Dwellers were being tormented. They were suffering. Something had gone dreadfully wrong.

"I have to help them, Bruno."

Ron was the only one who *could* help. He was the only one left in the facility – the only one who was even *aware* that a thousand minds were trapped in a thousand virtual hells. For those who were completely immersed in the simulations, Ron knew the suffering would be far from virtual – the agony and horror they were experiencing would be very real. It was useless for Ron to speculate on what had gone wrong. All he knew – and needed to know – was that the Cubes were manifesting the subconscious fears of the users instead of their desires.

"They don't even know it isn't real. They forgot where they came from and who they are."

Ron's heart ached in empathy for the trapped souls. He was a simple janitor and did not know how to even begin to help them. His first thought was to destroy the Cubes, but he knew that it would destroy the minds contained within them as well. This was not something he could bring himself to do. He wondered how hard it would be to reverse the process. Could he somehow reinsert their consciousnesses back into their bodies? The bodies were being kept in a freezer vault. Would they still be viable vessels? Even if they were, Ron still had no idea how to operate the equipment or program the computers. He had been trained to do two very simple tasks on top of his regular custodial duties – push a button and wheel a gurney.

"If only I could reach them somehow," Ron mused. "If only I could get them to remember and realize what is happening."

Ron began to explore the control room. He went from desk to desk and panel to panel, examining the complex equipment. Bruno the Cat followed him faithfully. Ron found a myriad of keypads, switches, dials, and buttons. Most of the technology was beyond his ability to comprehend. It was all so overwhelming. He began to feel discouraged and dismayed... then he saw something that gave him hope and sparked an idea. Mounted on a desk in the middle of the room was a microphone on an adjustable stand.

"Well, now," Ron said as he sat down at the desk. "Could this be what I think it is?"

Ron pulled the microphone toward him and tapped on it instinctively. Nothing happened. He studied the control panel in front of him. He spotted a switch at the base of the stand that said ON/OFF, below which was a numbered keypad. Along with the numbers 0 through 9, the keypad had two additional keys labeled CHANNEL SELECT and ALL CHANNELS.

"Interesting," Ron said. "Very interesting. What do you think, Bruno? Do you think this will let us talk to the Cubes? No way to know unless we try, right?"

Bruno did not respond. The cat curled up at Ron's feet and settled in for a nap.

"Even if this works, what should I say? I'm a little nervous. I don't want to scare anybody anymore than they already are."

Ron took a few minutes to gather his thoughts. It didn't help much. He decided to simply improvise. He reached over and pressed the ALL CHANNELS button before switching the microphone on.

"Uh, hello," Ron stammered into the microphone. "Can anyone hear me?"

Ron looked up at the monitors in front of him. There was so much going on in so many scenes, it was hard to tell if he had been heard. He paused before trying again.

"My name is Ron. I'm the custodian. I think there's been a malfunction. I think there's something wrong with the Cubes. Can anybody hear me? I want to help you."

On one of the screens, Ron noticed a woman who was apparently trying to escape from a dingy concrete room. She suddenly ceased her panicked search for a way out and looked up at the ceiling. Though he could not hear what she was saying, Ron could read her lips as she cried out, "Yes! I can hear you! Please... *help* me!"

Ron was astonished. He then noticed that many others

had also apparently heard him. They were looking up and around in all directions trying to locate the source of the mysterious voice – *Ron's* voice, which came to them like the voice of God in their darkest hour. Some people began to cry. Some were frozen in fear. A few even dropped to their knees and began to pray. Ron grasped the microphone, took a deep breath, and spoke again.

"Okay, good. You can hear me. Please, don't be afraid. What you are experiencing isn't real. It's an experiment that went wrong. I need you to try and remember where you came from. I need you to try and recall who you once were."

Nascent awareness dawned on the faces of a small number of Cube Dwellers. Ron could see them beginning to understand. Unfortunately, Ron could still see confusion and fear reigning in the minds of most of them.

"You are living in a simulation, a virtual reality contained within a Cube," Ron continued. "It was supposed to be an eternal paradise, but something went wrong. To me, it looks like the program has tapped into your deepest fears. Instead of a perfect dream world, you are creating your own nightmares. None of it is real, though."

A bright flash of light on a screen to his right caught Ron's attention. He looked over in time to see an extraordinary sight – a man was standing in a jungle surrounded by lions, but everything in the scene was frozen. The freeze had happened while two male lions were moving in for the kill. They were suspended in the air, claws mere feet from the man's head. The man had his hands up and his eyes closed. He opened his eyes now and looked around as the lions remained frozen in midair. A smile appeared on the man's face.

Ron watched in amazement as the screen flashed with a bright, white light once again and the scene changed. The man was no longer in the jungle – he was now reclining in a chair on a gorgeous, tropical island beach with white sand, gentle waves on the clear, blue water, bright sun and swaying palm trees – the man had created for himself a scene of idyllic beauty and serenity.

"You can change it!" Ron cried into the microphone. "It's true! I've seen it happen. It can happen for *you*... for *all* of you! Concentrate, focus, *believe*."

Ron continued to survey the video walls and saw it happen for more and more of the Cube Dwellers. He began to cry tears of joy as he watched scene after scene transform. Horrific, violent, terrifying realities became worlds of tranquility and bliss. It was, for lack of a better word, miraculous.

For the rest of the day and through the night, Ron sat in his chair transfixed by the transmutations occurring all around him. One by one, the scenes in each Cube became depictions of paradise. Ron was incredibly relieved and deeply satisfied that he had been able to help the Cube dwellers, but he knew, in his heart, that he could not take total credit. It was they, and their forces of will and powers of belief, that had done the true work.

"You know, Bruno, I wonder if even regular guys like me couldn't do something similar in our so-called *real* lives?"

For the first time since he had entered the underground facility, Ron's thoughts turned to what might be happening on the surface. He had a sudden yearning to be outside and, even more unusual for him, he had a sudden yearning to be in the company of others.

"Feel like going on an adventure, Bruno? It might be a good idea to check out what's going on up top. Maybe things aren't as bad as they said they would be. There might even be other *people* out there! We should go and take a look, don't you think?"

Ron got up and nudged Bruno the Cat, who woke up,

yawned, and stretched luxuriously. Ron led the cat out of the control room and walked down the wide corridor toward the elevator that would take them to the surface. It was now morning, an abstract concept in the depths of the facility. Ron smiled as he imagined what it would be like to feel sunlight on his face once again.

# Roadside Attraction

*The Wonder! Mystery of the Desert – Exit 233.* Alex saw the
first billboard just after crossing into Arizona from New
Mexico. A couple of hundred feet up the road, he saw another
one... then another... and another. There seemed to be a
limitless procession of billboards stretching over the desert
horizon, each of them, with slight variations, advertising the
same roadside attraction somewhere up ahead on the
highway. *Astonishing!* they proclaimed. *What could it be?*
they teased. Alex was not impressed. "Just what this place
needs – " he scoffed, "another crappy tourist trap."

    Alex reached into the plastic bag sitting on the
passenger seat of his 1975 Trans Am and retrieved a warm
can of beer. He popped the tab with one hand, brought the
can to his lips, and poured its contents down his throat. With
an odorous belch, he tossed the empty can over his shoulder.
With a satisfying crash, it landed on the pile of empties in the
back seat. Alex fumbled with the controls on the car's center
console in frustration before finally giving up. He let out a
sigh of resignation. The air conditioner had stopped working
not long after he had left Minneapolis. That was three days
ago.

    "I can't take the fucking heat," Alex said as he rolled
his window down. "How can people live in this shit?"

    Alex leaned out the open window and let the warm air
blow against his face as the car roared up the highway. The
stark, ancient beauty of the desert landscape streamed past
him. It was harsh and brutal, yet all around him, Alex could
see life, resilient and determined, clinging to existence
wherever it could. Strange flora of an incredible variety

jutted from the hard rock and clung to the arid soil. The landscape was so unusual that Alex had the sudden sensation that he had arrived on an alien planet. He briefly forgot the heat... and his other troubles. The sight of another billboard just ahead returned him fully to the present. *The Wonder! Seeing is believing!* it screamed in gaudy yellow and red letters.

"Who the hell put up all these damn signs?" Alex muttered. "Who's *paying* for them? Must be a lot of dummies and suckers coming through here."

It occurred to him then that he had not seen another car in a long time. This was unusual, for he was on a major highway and it was the middle of the day. Alex then recalled that he had not, in fact, encountered another vehicle since he had crossed the state line into Arizona. "Huh," he said. "I wonder where everyone is. It's kinda nice, though." Truth be told, Alex also thought that it was kind of spooky. He dismissed the unsettling feeling and opened another can of beer.

As the day transitioned into the golden hues of late afternoon, the world outside Alex's vehicle began to take on a hazy quality. A reddish-brown fog seemed to be rising from the desert floor. It obscured objects in the distance as it rapidly thickened. Alex realized that he was driving into a dust storm – a powerful one at that. The swirling, billowing dust enveloped the car as if it were a sentient cloud. Alex could taste it. He rolled up his window and sat up, instantly alert. He gripped the wheel tightly.

Alex's visibility was reduced to near-zero. He decelerated and peered into the sandy murk, trying to keep the car on the road and between the lines. He could only see a few feet in front of him. As the dust whirled and the wind whipped, an uncharacteristic fear welled up inside of him. Alex was at the mercy of the elements and he knew it. The sudden and violent arrival of the dust storm was a display of true power – Alex, despite his bravado, his tough-guy image, his muscle cars, women, and love of weapons, was powerless against the raw fury of nature unleashed.

After many miles of white-knuckle driving, the dust began to dissipate. The terrain began to slowly reveal itself. Alex could now see the dim outline of a flat-topped mesa in the distance. A forest of saguaros emerged from the haze. Alex started to breathe easier. His posture relaxed and he loosened the death-grip he had on the steering wheel. "Fuckin' desert," he spat.

When the dust settled and his visibility returned, Alex accelerated and began to think about his destination, Los Angeles, which was still eight hours away. He was determined to get there before the next morning and was prepared to drive all night if he had to. He had a score to settle and nothing was going to stop him – except the needle on the dashboard gauge fast approaching the E – that was certainly going to slow him down. Agitated, Alex scanned the horizon for any signs of civilization. He was relieved to spot what appeared to be a gas station just up ahead. "Some good luck for a change," he said with a smirk.

As the building grew closer, Alex could see that it was indeed a gas station... only this was no luxury Flying J or Love's Travel Stop – the station that Alex was now pulling into was a rundown, decrepit, two-pump shack with peeling paint, boarded-up windows, and junk cars and trash piled up around its miserable facade. Alex wasn't even sure that the place was still operational, but he decided to try anyway. He pulled up to a pump, shut of the engine, and stepped out of the car.

Shielding his eyes from the setting sun – and the sweat that dripped from his forehead – Alex looked toward the kiosk for any hint of activity. He thought he could see a light and a figure through one unboarded window, so he picked up the pump handle, removed the car's gas cap, and attempted to refuel. Somewhat to his surprise, the antique pump was functional. Alex leaned against his vehicle as the gas flowed into the car's tank. He took in his surroundings and sighed, "Fuckin' desert. I can't wait to get to LA."

When the tank was full, Alex returned the nozzle to the pump, screwed the gas cap back on, and sauntered over to the dilapidated shack to pay. Even though it was now early evening, the heat of the desert was still heavy and intense. Alex could feel his fluids baking away as he crossed the parking lot. His T-shirt clung to his body, saturated with sweat. He was beginning to feel woozy and lightheaded as he entered the kiosk.

Alex stepped through the door and was not surprised to find the tiny store nearly empty. A few canned goods with faded labels and an inch of dust were all that remained on the shelves. A cooler on the far wall contained a small assortment of soda bottles. An elderly man with red, beady eyes and a sunken face stood behind the counter. "Howdy, son," the old man said. "Can I help you?"

"The gas," Alex replied, feeling weaker by the moment, "and a bottle of water if you got one."

"I don't know who in their right mind would pay for water," said the old man, "but I do believe there are a few bottles in the cooler."

Alex walked to the cooler and opened it. There was a single bottle of water on the top shelf. He opened it and drank deeply. It was cool and instantly refreshing. "I never thought water could taste so good," Alex said. "This heat is just brutal. I swear, my brain is roasting."

"The desert is not a place for the weak," the old man said solemnly. "It takes a special sort to survive out here."

Alex walked to the counter. "How do you manage?"

he asked as he paid for the gas and water.

"It's in my blood," the old man replied. "My family has lived and worked on this land since 1890. We respect the desert and the desert takes care of us. My daddy could pick up a scorpion and kiss it on the back without getting stung. I seen it. He even caught a rattlesnake with his bare hands. You believe that, son?"

"Sure, why not?"

Alex moved toward the exit. As he was opening the door, the old man called out, "Hey, how far you going?"

"California... Los Angeles."

"Well, too bad for you, young man. That place is nasty."

"Maybe so, but I kinda like nasty." Alex gave the old man a wink and a sly smile.

"You take care of yourself out there. Be safe."

"Will do. Thanks."

"Hey, one last thing – if you got some time, you should stop at the gift shop up the road, about 50 miles west. They got this thing there they call 'The Wonder.' Stop and take a gander. You'll like it."

"Yeah, I think I've seen the signs. They sure do a lot of advertising."

"I know it," the old man nodded. "You have a good day, now."

Alex left the small store and walked to his car. As he opened the driver's side door, he could hear footsteps approaching from behind. He spun around instinctively, his nerves humming and his senses on alert. Standing before him now was a young man of aboriginal descent. The young man was tall and thin and dressed mostly in denim. Long, dark hair framed a tanned and serious face.

"Excuse me, sir," the young man said. "Can I trouble you for a ride?"

"Oh, man, I don't know," Alex replied. "I don't usually pick up hitchhikers."

"I live in the next town. I just need to get home. It's not that far."

Alex eyed up the young man, assessing his character from what little he could glean from his appearance. "Alright, then," Alex said with a slight nod. "You seem like a decent enough guy. I consider myself a fairly good judge of people."

"Thank you."

Alex slid into the driver's seat and, after moving the bag of beer out of the way, reached over to open the passenger door. The young native man climbed into the car and held out his hand. "I'm Elroy," he said.

"Alex. Nice to meet you." The two men shook hands. "Want a beer?"

"Nope," Elroy said firmly. "Don't drink. Neither should you. Cops are pretty strict about that around here. You do not want to get busted."

"Not worried," Alex said as he pulled out of the gas station parking lot. "I really don't give a shit about the cops. I can handle myself."

"Is that so?"

"Five years in prison, buddy. Yeah, that's *so*."

Alex maneuvered the Trans Am onto the highway and accelerated. The car's engine roared as it propelled the two men into the sunset. Alex looked over at his passenger and studied his face carefully. Elroy's expression was stoic, his eyes locked on the road ahead and his mouth pursed tightly. Elroy's demeanor was rigid, yet noble. He carried himself with a wise sadness, as if he were aware of a dark truth that he could not – or was not allowed to – express. Alex was fascinated.

"So," Alex asked, "do you normally hitchhike to get

around? Don't you drive?"

"I've never had any use for a car," Elroy replied in a perfectly monotone voice. "I can always get a ride when I need one."

"I take it you grew up around here, then?" Alex probed. He was intent on finding out more about his mysterious new acquaintance.

"Yes."

"I'm from up north – Minnesota. This is my first time in the southwest... man, it's *hot* around here, eh?"

"Yes."

"I guess you get used to it." Alex ran a hand over his shaven head. His hand, as well as his neck, arms, and nearly every other part of his body, was adorned with crude, homemade tattoos. Elroy, noticing the tattoos, took the conversational initiative and spoke up. "You have a lot of ink," he said. "Do these images mean anything to you?"

"The tats?" replied Alex. "Yeah, I guess there's probably a story for each one of them... though, to be honest, I don't remember getting some of them. I was a little wild in my youth. Still am, I suppose."

"In my culture, tattoos are earned and are highly symbolic. Did you know that everything has a spirit? Even pictures?"

"Huh... that's cool."

"That symbol on your hand," Elroy pointed at a cross tattooed on the soft flesh between Alex's right thumb and index finger. "Does it hold any special meaning for you?"

"Oh, that? I got that one in prison. I don't know what it means... maybe just that I was born under a bad sign, if you know what I'm saying."

"You've been in a lot of trouble?"

"Yeah, you could say that."

"What were you in prison for?"

"Which time? I've been in and out of institutions since I was a little boy. The last spell, five long years, was for armed robbery. I just got out last week, actually."

"That's pretty serious."

"It was just a convenience store and no one got hurt. I got busted because some punk-ass fool ratted me out."

"I see. Is this car stolen?"

"Nah, don't worry. This is legit. Bought it from a friend."

At that moment, the Trans Am sped by yet another billboard. *The Wonder! Mystery of the Desert – Exit 233,* it declared. Alex shook his head and chuckled, "What is up with *that?* I've never seen so many signs for the same damn thing. *'The Wonder! See it now! Please, we desperately need your business!'"*

For the first time since he had gotten into Alex's car, Elroy smiled, ever so slightly. "It's quite an attraction," he said.

"Have you seen it? What's the big deal? What *is* it?"

"It's the Wonder, and, no, I've never seen it myself. I've heard stories, though. Maybe you should stop and check it out."

"I don't have time for that crap. Gotta get to LA. Business calls."

"Is that legit, too, the business?"

"Ha, well... mostly. Let's just say I'm doing a favor for an old friend."

"So, you just got out of prison and you're already taking risks. Seems unwise."

"Oh, it's nothing *too* risky. It's just a job – a job on the edge of legality. If it goes well, there shouldn't be any trouble for anyone. Besides, I am who I am, right? A leopard can't change its spots."

"Interesting comparison."

"Yeah, well, you know – I like a little *excitement* in my life. I couldn't handle some shitty day job. I'm all about adventure, danger, the open road." Alex leaned out the driver's side window and took in a deep breath of the hot, desert air. "This is the way to live, man. Who knows what the future holds."

"The future is what we make of it. In many ways, the future does not even exist – it is simply an extension of the present."

"Hmm... I like that."

"Actions define the person. You are creating your own reality."

"Sure, I get it."

The Trans Am passed the crumbling, graffiti-covered foundations of an old building. Just beyond sat a battered, ramshackle trailer. The ground around the trailer was littered with junk and old cars, just like the gas station. Three scrawny dogs wandered the ravaged premises. A little up the road, more trailers and abandoned buildings dotted the landscape in seemingly random placement.

"Whew, this place is *rough*," said Alex. "Can you imagine living here?"

"I do live here," replied Elroy.

"Shit. Sorry, man. I didn't mean to offend you. I grew up in a bad neighborhood, too."

"No offense taken. Despite appearances, this is a good place. You can let me out anywhere. I can walk from here."

Alex pulled the car over onto the shoulder. Elroy opened the passenger door and stepped out. Before closing the door behind him, he leaned into the car and said, "Thank you for the ride. Take care of yourself and don't get into too much trouble. Los Angeles is a crazy place."

"I've heard," Alex smiled. "I'm not too worried. I'm crazy, too."

Elroy smiled and shut the door. Alex watched him walk away from the car and amble up the shoulder before getting back on the highway. He left the tiny settlement behind him and the open desert spread out around him once again, its intimidating expanse dwarfing the vehicle and the man inside. The road stretched its way across the desert like the trail of an ant across the back of a behemoth.

It was not long before another billboard appeared on the horizon. In bright colors that contrasted jarringly with the earth tones of the surrounding landscape, the sign said: *The Wonder! Mystery of the Desert – 5 miles ahead.*

"Well, shit," Alex said. "I guess it's time for me to see what all the fuss is about."

Soon, Alex could see the roadside attraction itself – a large, two-story storefront painted in the same bright shades of yellow and red as the billboards. The exterior walls were adorned with tacky souvenirs and random, kitschy objects with no apparent relation to each other. Traditional native art and clothing, bizarre metal sculptures, road signs, plastic dinosaurs, old toys, and other strange items all clung to the walls of the building. It was a surreal sight. Above the entrance, a massive sign spanned the entire facade of the establishment, indicating that this was the one and only *Delaney's – Home of the Wonder!* Alex pulled into the parking lot, surprised by the sense of anticipation that he suddenly felt.

Alex parked the car and stepped out into the blazing heat. By the time he pushed open the door to the gift shop, he was sweating profusely. He entered the building and was immediately assailed by the vibrant colors of a million cheap trinkets. The store was jam-packed with merchandise, but as far as Alex could tell, he was the only customer.

"Welcome to Delaney's!" a voice called from a counter obscured by a rack of southwest travel books.

"Hiya," Alex replied.

"Can I help you, sir?"

Alex navigated the racks and shelves and approached the counter. A middle-aged woman with a kind countenance greeted him with a warm smile.

"I'm just passing through and thought I would stop and see this so-called Wonder," Alex said.

"Good for you!" the woman beamed. "You won't be disappointed. Where you headed?"

"Los Angeles."

"Oh." The woman's smile faded slightly. "Well... can I interest you in a souvenir to take with you to California? A memento of our fair region? We have these cute little mini-cactus plants... Navajo ponchos... lizard magnets... oh, these are quite popular – " The woman held up a small glass globe, inside of which sat a tiny skeleton wearing a poncho. An inscription on the base of the globe read *It's a dry heat.* "Isn't that just *darling?*" grinned the woman.

"Yeah, that's *something*," Alex said, "but, nah – I'm just here for the main attraction."

"Well, then. Let's make that happen so you can be on your way. I assume you have some important business waiting for you in Los Angeles."

"You could say that, yup."

"There is a fee, of course."

"I wasn't aware of that... How much?"

"One dollar, please."

"Shit, that's nothing. I can handle that."

"Hmm."

Alex dug a dollar bill out of his jeans and handed it to the lady. She took it gingerly, as if it were soiled in excrement. "This way, please," she directed.

Alex was led to a stairwell at the back of the shop. Beside the stairwell was yet another sign. This one had an

arrow pointing up and read *The Wonder! This way!* Alex
followed his guide up the stairs. When they reached the
second floor, the woman flicked a switch on the wall and
filled the room with light.

The first thing Alex noticed was that the space felt
more like a tomb than a museum or exhibit room. The walls
were windowless, bare, and painted a dull gray that gave
them the appearance of stone. The room was empty, except
for what was, apparently, the enigmatic Wonder. It was
encased in a large glass display case the size and shape of a
sarcophagus.

"Is that it?" Alex asked with a hint of trepidation.

"Yes. Feel free to go and have a look."

A cold chill came over Alex and he was reluctant to
approach. He shook it off, feeling foolish. He walked toward
the display case. As he neared, the thing that was inside
revealed itself slowly – there seemed to be a humanoid figure
lying prone on its back. "What the fuck?" Alex said. "Is that
what I think it is?"

"Depends on what you think it is," the woman
replied. She had not moved since they had entered the room
and was still standing by the switch at the top of the stairwell.

Alex stood over the display case. The thing encased
inside was hideous and looked absolutely ancient. It had what
appeared to be the head of a human being – albeit desiccated,
nearly fleshless, and sporting what looked suspiciously like
horns, but the proportions of its body were somehow *off*. The
arms seemed too long, the torso too bulbous. The legs,
though covered with ragged cloth, reminded Alex of those of
a goat. Indeed, the feet looked like hooves.

"Is it real?"

"In the sense that you most likely mean, yes, it's real."

"Is it mummified? Where did it come from? God, it's
so... *ugly!*"

"It *is* remarkably well-preserved and has been in my family for over a century. I was told that a distant relative, an explorer of some renown in his lifetime, found it while exploring the Grand Canyon. He and his crew found remnants of a lost and previously unknown civilization. I've heard stories of massive caves full of strange artifacts and many more... *specimens* such as this one."

"That's quite a story."

"Yes."

"Well, shit. I think I've seen enough. I best be hitting the road."

"I hope you enjoyed your stop here."

"It was definitely worth a buck!"

"Allow me to see you out."

Alex crossed the room and followed the lady back down the stairs. When they reached the main floor of the gift shop, Alex realized that he had grown quite hungry. "You sell food here?" he asked.

"Just snacks, nothing hot," the woman replied as she returned to her position behind the counter. "There are restaurants up the road, though."

Alex spotted a rack of potato chips. He selected a bag and placed it on the counter. He pulled out his wallet, opened it, and grunted. The wallet was empty. An idea, a very *bad* idea, popped into his head. He had a sudden, devious impulse and, as had been his habit throughout his short and error-filled life, he acted on this foolish impulse before giving any serious thought to the consequences.

"I hate to do this, lady," Alex said as he reached behind his back and pulled out the gun he had concealed in the waistband of his pants, "but I'm going to need you to give me all the money in that register."

With the gun now aimed at her face, the woman gasped in shock. "Please don't hurt me," she said. "Take whatever you want."

"I don't want to hurt you. Just give me the fucking money."

The woman opened the register and began pulling bills out of the tray. Her hands were shaking and her body trembled. Alex watched her carefully with a curious expression on his face. A subtle smirk curled his mouth, a wicked spark gleamed in his eye. As the woman gathered and handed the bills to Alex, a sudden crashing sound from above made them both jump. The sound was loud and violent.

"What the hell was that?" Alex cried. The grip on his gun tightened as his body tensed up.

"You better get out of here," the woman said quietly. "Take the money and leave... *now.*"

The booming sound above them was followed by a moment of silence, after which followed a series of thumps that gradually grew louder as they passed over Alex and the woman behind the counter.

"Lady, you better tell me what the fuck is going on. I'm not afraid to use this thing." Alex was now swinging the gun wildly from the woman to the ceiling and back again.

"Please," the woman pleaded, "go now!"

The thumping increased in volume as it got closer. Now it was in the stairwell! Something was descending. Alex stepped back. He kept the gun trained on the entrance to the stairwell. The money lay forgotten in a pile on the counter.

"You shouldn't have come here," the woman said. "It's very protective of my family and this place."

"What is?!" Alex shouted.

Then he saw it – the awful thing from the display case – the Wonder itself. Its ghastly, revolting form was now framed in the doorway, those grotesque, too-long arms dangling at its side, the empty sockets of its deformed skull somehow staring into the dark heart of Alex's soul. Alex screamed and fired his weapon. The bullet passed through the Wonder's chest with a puff of dust. The Wonder raised its arms and lurched forward. Alex scrambled backwards and fired another completely ineffective shot at the approaching creature, which had quickened its pace and was now rushing at him faster than its dusty, brittle carcass should have allowed. Alex tripped over a three-foot Kokopelli statue near the entrance to Delaney's and fell to the floor hard.

"Help me!" Alex screeched. "Please, God... NO!"

The Wonder was upon him now. It kicked Alex in the head, knocking out teeth and spraying blood against the wall. It placed a hoof on the prostrate man's chest before reaching down with a bony hand and plucking out its victim's right eyeball. Alex shrieked, insane with terror and unable to move. With his one remaining eye, Alex could see the monstrosity lean in as it wrapped its cold, undead hands around his throat. The Wonder began to squeeze with inhuman strength. Before Alex lost consciousness, he felt the thing's breath on his face, carrying with it the scent of the centuries – the scent of musty tombs and lost chambers. Outside Delaney's, a dust devil crossed the empty highway, swirling and dancing like manifest madness.

# The Observatory

The ocean is a writhing, frothing, convulsing beast – the
night sky an oppressive, impenetrable, black canopy, filled
with the lunatic shimmering of a legion of stars. On the
shores of Nova Scotia, the air is sharp and cool. In my
imagination, I move across the beach as if I had just been
born, spawned from the water like a hungry probe.

    I crawl through the sand. Sheer rock walls dominate
the landscape. Upon those rocks, perched high above the vast
and lonesome beach, sits a massive domed structure – the
observatory. I penetrate the structure and peer inside. I see a
massive telescope aimed through a slit in the dome at the
unfathomable abyss beyond. There is a man with a ravenous
mind gazing through the eyepiece on the small end. The
man's name is Gordon. He is an astronomer. This is his story.

    Gordon works alone in the cavernous depths of the
Moonsword Observatory. I can see him now, pacing the
upper deck of the facility, tossing an occasional, tentative
glance toward the telescope. He is clearly afraid of
something. I can see it in the way his eyes twitch in their
sockets, like eggs about to hatch. I imagine bizarre mutations
emerging from those eyes. I imagine terrors beyond space
and time emerging from that mind.

    Gordon is deeply troubled. The night before, while
studying unusual deep space objects, a true anomaly
appeared. In the constellation of Virgo, a ghostly white worm
had wiggled into view under Gordon's watch. It was a
beautiful sight. The worm's body emitted tendrils of pure
light as it pulsated and moved through space.

    The creature rolled and squirmed in rhythmic motion,

performing an intricate dance, before suddenly dissipating in a burst of soft, glowing fibers. It was ethereal, magnificent... and totally irrational. All that Gordon had been taught about the universe told him that what he had just witnessed should not exist. His education – his expertise and knowledge – conflicted with what he experienced directly through his senses.

Gordon went home that night feeling exhilarated, yet noticeably ill. Had he really seen a ghost worm somewhere out there in the depths of space? Had he perhaps imagined it? It occurred to him that he had probably been spending too many solitary days and nights in the observatory focused purely on work. It was bound to have some negative consequences on his mental health. Gordon carefully considered this possibility and chose to accept it as the most likely cause of the unlikely incident. As he lay in bed. he felt something resembling relief as his thoughts dissolved and his consciousness ebbed away. He drifted numbly into a dreamless sleep.

Upon waking, Gordon's first thought was of the strange sight he had beheld the night before: the white worm dancing in space. Gordon's mind was filled with the image. With his eyes still closed, he could see its ethereal form maneuvering in the void between galaxies, majestic, *unreal*.

Gordon opened his eyes and, for a moment, the white worm was still visible, superimposed upon the reality of his bedroom wall. He reached out instinctively, his fingers hungry to touch the unknown. The white worm faded away. Gordon got out of bed. He proceeded with his morning routine.

Let's join Gordon in the observatory now, at the exact moment when we first encountered him, pacing the facility, tossing tentative glaces at the telescope. He is afraid, you see, because he has once again seen something entirely implausible while using the sophisticated scientific instrument. He had been willing to accept one such anomaly - the ghostly white worm - as an artifact of an overworked, overtired mind, but to have another inexplicable experience after a good night's rest was more than a little disturbing.

I will try to describe what Gordon saw, though it may be difficult. It happened while he was studying the same area in the constellation of Virgo as the previous night. He saw what was to be expected in that region: the stars, galaxies, and other celestial bodies that others had charted before.

These objects, though fascinating and beautiful in their own right, were not what truly interested him. His greatest desire – the ultimate fulfillment of his life's work – was to find something *new*, something never before seen, something extraordinary that would change our perception of the cosmos – something that would make him famous in the scientific community.

It is important to understand that when Gordon is in the observatory using the equipment, his voracious mind sprouts tentacles of thought and the telescope becomes an extension of his consciousness. The observatory is fully computerized. The images it gathers are displayed and easily viewed on high-definition monitors, but Gordon prefers to observe through the eyepiece. It's more personal.

Through the telescope's lenses, Gordon extends his awareness like the probe at the beginning of this story. He wanders the cosmos, pierces the veil, and lingers like a stranger in the infinite halls of the great chambers of space. In this state, his mind and environment are united. As within, so beyond. In this state, he encountered a second anomaly.

Watching, waiting, carefully observing, Gordon's body was forgotten, irrelevant. His entire being was focused on that distant point in space, trembling in anticipation like one giant nerve.

Then he saw it! A horizontal slit appeared in the midst of nothingness, a widening tear in the fabric of spacetime. It opened, slowly, deliberately. A dark spot became visible in its center, surrounded by a swirling circle of unusual colors. These features rested on a sea of pink-streaked white.

Gordon quickly realized then that he was looking at an enormous eye. The width of that anomalous ocular opening must have spanned light years of interstellar space. Can you imagine Gordon's shock? As his mind struggled to process the sight, he remained at the telescope, his eye on the eyepiece looking into the giant eye in the heavens. It was fractal... and comical.

Gordon blinked. The big eye blinked. Gordon allowed himself to laugh. He pulled away from the instrument. His internal dialogue became externalized:

"Well, Gordon," he said, "you may very well be losing your mind." It made him feel better to talk to himself in such a way. He attempted to maintain a semblance of control, but feared that his mind was in imminent danger of fracturing completely.

"Just take it easy and get a hold of yourself. There *must* be a rational explanation." Gears spun in his head. Wheels turned, but found no traction. His mind struggled to reconcile what he had seen with what he believed to be reality.

"I am a man of *science*. Educated. Erudite. Sober. Sane." The words resonated pleasantly in Gordon's ears. He was soothing himself effectively. He ran sweaty fingers through greasy hair.

"Confirmation – that's what I need. I'll get the boys in Australia to check it out." It was a good idea. It would be easy to make a call to his peers and have them train their instruments on the same spot to validate his sighting.

Gordon paused. He paced the cramped room,

scratching his stubbly, red face with twitchy nervous hands.

"No, no, no... can't do that. What if I'm wrong? What if they don't find anything there?" He picked at his left eyebrow, plucking hairs and examining them. "I'd be humiliated, discredited. My reputation would be ruined."

Gordon could feel the cramped interior of the observatory closing in on him. The instruments and gauges choked the air out of his lungs. Suddenly, claustrophobia descended on him and clawed at his brain like a bird of prey. He stopped pacing and stood still, his mind reeling.

"You're overthinking again, Gordon. Relax. Remember, you are a man of science. Gather more data." He slowly approached the telescope, which now looked phallic and obscene. He lowered his eye to the eyepiece. Contact. The universe again filled his head with its wondrous, horrifying sights.

The telescope was still fixed on the same spot. The eye was no longer there. Only the familiar, expected objects were present. The black void of deep space occupied the region where the eye's immense, ominous aperture had opened mere moments ago and peered into Gordon's soul. Sweet relief... followed closely by a strange, subtle disappointment. "Whew," Gordon said, still looking through the eyepiece, "thought maybe I was coming unglued."

As Gordon was about to pull away, movement caught his attention – again, there was activity in the region where he had seen the eye. Gordon gasped. Great clouds of cosmic dust were forming in real time as he watched. Purple and pink nebulous structures billowed and expanded, creating complex designs.

"No!" Gordon cried. "That can't be!" The clouds of cosmic dust began to form words, as if guided by the hand of an omniscient creator: *Hi Gordon!*

Gordon promptly pulled away from the eyepiece. "Oh

no! Oh, God, *no!*" he shrieked in distress. He sat in a chair and put his head in trembling hands. He began to sob quietly.

"It's over. I'm finished." Gordon sensed movement behind him – someone else was in the room. Gordon raised his head, looked around, and saw a man standing there. The man was smiling. The man was me.

"Hi, Gordon," I said. "Don't be sad. Everything's fine." I reached over and put my hand on Gordon's shoulder. I felt bad for him and didn't like seeing him in such a state. I liked him.

"Who are you?" Gordon asked.

"The writer of this story," I told him. No need to lie. He could handle the truth.

"I don't understand. How can that be? What does it mean?!"

"That's a good question, and I'm not sure I have a satisfactory answer. It has something to do with the observatory, though. I'm sure of that."

"Am I one of your characters?"

"Yes, you are, but so am I. We are both characters... and we are both observers." It was hard to explain. I didn't want to scare him any more than he already was. The bizarre situation was even starting to scare *me* a little. Is it getting too weird around here? Let's try to resolve this.

"The telescope," I said to Gordon, "it allows you to peer out into the universe, to explore its hidden secrets. It's an amazing tool. What if, while looking out, something is also looking in at you?" Gordon was beginning to understand. I, too, was beginning to understand.

"So, it's like I'm somehow the observer *and* the observed." Gordon rubbed his chin philosophically. "Wow. Heavy."

"Heavy indeed," I said, "and in this story *I* have become the subject as well as the observer. It's a closed system, a holographic, fractal miniverse." We sat pondering in silence for a few moments. I began to wonder if the words I had chosen were adequate.

"I didn't mean to upset you," I continued. "For that, I am sorry. I simply wanted to tell a story."

"It's okay. It's been fun. I was worried that it might get *really* freaky, but it wasn't so bad." Gordon smiled for the first time. It was nice to see. "What now?" he asked. "Will we see each other again?"

"I think so. I really do. For now, though, I think we should both move on. You have a lot of work to do, I suspect. A lot of discoveries to make, as do I." It was a little sad saying goodbye. Gordon had become a friend. I reached out my hand and he took it. We shook firmly and with warmth.

"Alright then," Gordon said. "I'll see you later."

"Bye, Gordon," I smiled.

I contemplated various ways to finish the story before choosing an old, reliable standard:

The End

# Dream Sequence

## 1

At precisely 8:15 AM, the skybus arrived at the boarding station. A young man named Miles was among the small group of people who waited atop the fenced and gated platform that towered 100 feet above the ground. Miles was just beginning his daily routine, the initial stage of which consisted of a rather long commute to the city center, where he correlated data at a large research facility. Unlike the others around him, Miles was not fully engrossed by the inner screen of an E-Visor. His device had recently malfunctioned and he felt anxious, exposed, and awkward without it. He watched the skybus approach with naked, jittery eyes as he clutched his bagged lunch tightly to his chest.

The autonomous skybus slid into place in front of the platform. Miles and the other commuters walked up to the turnstile and, one at a time, they waved their implanted hands over the embedded sensor. A green light and a bright tone indicated a successful transaction and allowed admittance. The passengers filed on in a smooth, efficient, robotic procession. Miles was the last one to board. As he habitually did every morning, he went directly to the seat in the right rear of the vehicle and sat down. The other regular riders also sat in their usual seats, as if predestined or programmed. The door slid shut and the skybus quietly pulled away from the platform at a high rate of speed.

Miles leaned against the wall of the skybus and gazed down at the sprawling metropolis below him. He sighed.

*Another day in the machine,* he thought. *Another work cycle crunching numbers for the Bot, and now I don't even have a visor to kill time with. God, it's all so dreary and endless...*

Boredom and an intense weariness fell upon Miles. The awful, infinite ennui settled into his bones and seemed to add actual mass to his body, which hung on his spirit like rotten meat on a strained rack. Miles shifted his gaze forward. A few rows in front of him sat a young couple. They were apparently together, but each was clearly mesmerized by whatever application their E-Visors were running. Their slack, immobile frames mirrored Miles', but he had the unfortunate disadvantage of being fully aware of the brutal banality of his existence. Miles studied the backs of their heads and wondered: *Are they happy? Are they enjoying this ridiculous charade called Life? At least they have each other. It would be nice to have someone. I wish I were unconscious. I wish I had my visor.* Another long, drawn-out sigh escaped his lips, carrying with it the medicinal smell of his morning's rations.

Sudden movement, quick and flitting, caught Miles' attention. He looked to his left and gasped. He could see, through the side window, three large, transparent orbs flying toward the skybus. The orbs were piloted by helmeted men and they were rushing at him *fast*. Miles was startled to see, protruding from each orb and aimed directly at the skybus, several extremely menacing weapons. They extended from the front of each orb like insect stingers.

Miles jumped up and called out, "Help! Help! We're being attacked!" No one seemed to hear him. The other passengers were entirely unaware of what was occurring just outside the vehicle. The orbs were closing in. Miles became frantic. He ran up the aisle and reached out to the closest person, a man in a seat a few rows up on the left side. The man was chuckling to himself, obviously enjoying whatever he was viewing on the inner screen of his visor. Miles grasped the man's shoulder with a firm grip and shook him. "Hey! Hey!" he shouted. "We're in serious trouble! Look out the window!" The man in the seat did not respond – he simply giggled, completely immersed in his media.

"Someone listen to me!" Miles panicked. A glance over his shoulder revealed that the orbs were now mere yards away from the skybus. Miles could see the skybus' reflection in the black glass of the closest orb pilot's helmet. Miles ran up to the couple he had been staring at only minutes before. "Hey, you two!" he cried. "Wake up! Wake up!" The young man and woman remained slumped in their seats, unconscious. For a brief moment Miles wondered if they were dead, but he quickly realized the truth. "Stupid digital drugs," he muttered.

It was too late anyway. Miles turned to face the window just in time to see the orbs zoom up to the skybus, stop suddenly in mid-flight, and open fire as they hovered. Blasts of bright plasma pulsed from the energy weapons and tore through the skybus. Before he and the other passengers were engulfed and incinerated in the deadly salvo, a peculiar thought entered Miles' head: *This has already happened to me. I dreamed this.*

## 2

"Target neutralized. Returning with squad to HQ." The orb pilot addressed his commander through his neural mesh interface as he pulled up from the flaming debris of the falling skybus. His two wingmen assumed their positions at his flanks and the small formation sped away on a northeastern trajectory. They had only traveled a few hundred feet when the commander issued new orders to the squad leader. The voice was internal – loud and clear in the pilot's head, distinct from his own thoughts: "We have a developing situation and we need you on the scene. Go directly to the provided coordinates. Engage protocol for civil unrest."

A series of numbers were transmitted directly into the squad leader's mind and he fed them into the orb's guidance system, which was linked to those of his wingmen. The three orbs changed course and flew toward the location in perfect synchronization. They were in transit for only a few minutes before the chaotic scene became visible just ahead. A crowd of demonstrators numbering in the hundreds had gathered in front of an administrative building. They were carrying hand-painted signs and crude weapons fashioned from sharpened sticks and agricultural implements. The fearsome, unruly mass of men and women were yelling and chanting, primal and livid.

"HQ, we have visual contact," said the squad leader. "We have an unlawful congregation of civilians. They appear to be gathered in protest."

"Disperse the crowd with appropriate force," the commander ordered. "25% casualty rate is ideal, 50% is acceptable."

"Roger that."

The orb pilot activated his weapon and pulled ahead of his small squad. When he was a few yards away from the mob, he dived in and opened fire. His wingmen followed his lead. Brilliant blasts of plasma tore into the crowd. People scattered in panic. Some were killed instantly and fell in smoking heaps of charred flesh. Others bravely, defiantly, futilely threw sticks, rakes, and shovels at the orbs. The useless weapons bounced off the thick, tempered glass and clattered to the ground. After their initial sweep, the orbs turned around and flew back for another pass, unleashing a second burst at the terrified and disorganized crowd. More people fell victim to the deadly barrage tearing through their ranks.

"The situation is under control," said the orb pilot. "Requesting permission to return to HQ."

"Engage the targets once more," the commander responded. "This has been happening too frequently. We need to send these savages a message."

The pilot swung his craft around in a wide arc. The crowd below him had thinned considerably. Most of those who had not been killed had fled. Only a small, tightly-packed core group of demonstrators remained in front of the administrative building. In the face of death, they obstinately stood their ground, waving their implements and chanting in unison. The orb pilot flew directly toward them, ready to release hellfire. Just as he was about to squeeze the trigger, the pilot caught a glimpse of a man in the crowd with a metallic object in his hand. The man was snarling and looking directly at the approaching orb. Before the pilot could react, the man launched the object, which struck the craft just above the protruding weapon and exploded on contact. The fireball blinded the pilot. The pilot lost control and the orb suddenly careened down and to the right. He struggled to pull up, but quickly realized it was to no avail. A crash was inevitable.

"I've been hit," the pilot announced to his superiors. "An explosive device of unknown type. I'm going down."

As the orb tumbled out of the sky, racing, erratic thoughts filled the pilot's head: *How did they get real weapons? Am I going to die? Melanie, I love you.* The craft hit the ground. The glass shattered and the pilot was thrown from the vehicle. He landed hard on the pavement, fracturing his skull, breaking multiple bones, and rupturing organs. Through the fog of agony, the pilot could see the surviving demonstrators rushing at him. They descended on him, shouting, swinging, beating, and tearing.

## 3

*They're going to kill him,* Allison realized as she watched the mob attack the fallen orb pilot. *I can't watch this.*

Yet Allison did watch. Though horrified, she was mesmerized by the brutality on display before her. She had never seen her friends and compatriots behave in such a primitive, ferocious way. They were screaming as they assailed the helpless man on the ground – it was the shriek of a demented hive-mind. The pilot made feeble attempts to defend himself from the blows that rained down upon him and the rabid, vicious, ripping hands that clawed at his tattered uniform. He was weakening quickly. The crowd sensed his wavering strength and intensified their assault. In a whirlwind of violence, the mob stripped the pilot and beat him unconscious. They continued the attack until the pilot was a bloody, broken, misshapen heap. With a final roar, one of the young men in the mob raised a baseball bat high over his head and brought it down on the pilot's skull. As the bat struck, it made a wet crunch and it was obvious that the pilot was now truly, and very, dead.

Above the carnage and destruction, the remaining two orbs in the squad continued to circle. Inexplicably, they were not firing at the surviving demonstrators. Allison watched as they made one final pass before accelerating and shooting off. In a blink, they were gone. The courtyard in front of the administrative building now looked like a combat zone. Bodies and debris covered the entire plaza. Allison had expected violence, but she had not been prepared for the intensity of what she had just experienced. In a sudden rush of emotion, she dropped to her knees and began to weep loudly.

"Allison!" cried her friend Eric, rushing to her side. "Are you okay?"

Eric knelt down and wrapped an arm around Allison's quivering body. "Hey, don't cry," he said. "We got one of those bastards! We should be celebrating!"

"We're no better than they are," Allison sobbed. "We're all just a bunch of animals."

"This is a revolution, Allison. Blood will be shed. I am very proud of our brothers and sisters who lost their lives today in the fight against tyranny. This was a victory for our side, don't you see that?"

"We all could have been killed. I don't know why we weren't. Those orbs could have wiped us out. Why did they retreat?"

Allison began to regain her composure. She stood up and shook off Eric's consoling arm. She looked around, absorbing the details of the chaos around her. Some survivors were tending to the wounded, others were checking the dead. Some sat or stood with blank expressions on their faces, traumatized by the event. A few smiled and chatted excitedly, clearly elated and thoroughly enjoying themselves. As Allison took it all in, a loud, shrill siren pierced the air. Above them now, where the orbs had launched their deadly attack minutes before, a large, cylindrical drone hovered. Bright blue and red lights rotated around its perimeter. From an on-board speaker, a robotic voice announced, "This area is now closed to civilians. Move out immediately. Failure to comply will result in lethal force."

"We need to get out of here *now*," Eric insisted. "The orbs are bad, but the drones are much, much worse. I've seen them level entire city blocks."

A tall, bearded man wearing a black jacket with obscure insignia on its shoulders addressed the group: "Excellent work, everyone. Let's gather the dead and wounded and get out of here. We'll plan our next move at the compound."

The demonstrators sprung into action. The man in the black jacket was their clear leader and he had their unanimous respect and obedience.

"I'm starting to wonder if these protests are doing any good at all," Allison said, mostly to herself. "Are we making progress? We've been losing so many people lately."

"Of course we're making progress!" cried Eric. "We actually destroyed one of their orbs today! That's huge. Do you know how many millions of dollars one of those things costs?"

"I lost friends today. So did you. How much were their lives worth?"

"We gain new recruits daily. Our numbers are growing. The tide is turning in our favor. Come on, now – let's get the fuck out of here before we get nuked."

Allison and Eric joined the others. In a long, slow procession, the group moved out of the courtyard and into the street. The drone hovered in its position high above the plaza, its lights still flashing, its siren still screeching. The battered and bloody column of dissenters, led by the man in the black jacket, made its way through the labyrinthine downtown streets. They marched, the dead and wounded carried by the living and fit, under the blazing, midsummer sun, which cast a harsh, sandy yellow light on the metal and concrete guts of the city. The occupants of the few vehicles that the group encountered ignored the procession.

The column marched until it reached a highway overpass. It crossed over the abandoned freeway and, once on the other side, worked its way down the embankment and under the overpass. Concealed below the structure was the entrance to a hidden tunnel, covered with a camouflaged gate. The gate was opened and the group entered. The tunnel was narrow and unlit. Its width only allowed the procession to traverse it two abreast. Warm, rank, ankle-high fluid flowed through the tunnel. The thin column snaked forward, sloshing through the darkness.

After an hour's march through the dank underworld, light appeared at the end of the tunnel – a faint, flickering glow that grew brighter as the group approached, reaching toward them like a sentient tendril of illumination. The light emanated from a chamber. The group, exhausted, wet, filthy, and near-delirious, reached the entrance and filed through.

The chamber was spacious and rectangular – essentially a large, underground concrete box. It served as the headquarters and home of the primary anti-establishment organization in the region. They went by the name of S.U.R.G.E. and they had occupied this location for over a year. On the left side of the chamber, blankets, sleeping bags, pillows, and clothes were spread over the floor haphazardly. This was where the group slept, and it was where they now sought rest. Before the wounded and weary laid down their heads, the dead were carefully arranged along a far wall and covered with sheets. The somber ritual was conducted silently and meticulously by people who had done the same thing many times before.

"Will this war ever end?" Allison sighed as she collapsed on a dirty pile of blankets in the corner. "My father used to tell me stories of his childhood, when peace still existed in most parts of the world. Seems like a fantasy, doesn't it?"

"That's dangerous thinking," Eric said. "We must always keep our hearts and minds focused on the goal."

"Which is what, exactly?"

"I hope you're joking. Do I really have to remind you what we're doing, what our comrades have sacrificed their lives for?"

"I'm just tired. I feel drained."

"I need you to stay strong, Allison. *We* need you to

stay strong. Trust our leadership. They have a view of the larger perspective. They will not let us down."

"All I've ever known is death, destruction, misery. At least the non-resistors have safe, predictable, *stable* lives."

"Is that what you want? You joined the rebellion when I did, and for the same reasons. Get your fucking head together and remember why we're here. We must *never* give up. We must *never* waver. We *must* persist in this struggle until we have overthrown the tyrannical regime of the oligarchs. The cause is more important than you, me, or any other individual – alive or dead – in this room. Do you understand?"

"You sound like *him*." Allison gestured with her head toward the man in the black jacket, who was sitting separate from the group and examining papers.

"Nothing wrong with that," Eric smiled. "He's a great man and I'm proud to serve him. Perhaps *you* should try to emulate him a little more."

"I've been fighting just as long and just as hard as you, Eric. You know that. I'm just starting to get a weird... *feeling*. It's almost like there isn't supposed to be a winner in this conflict. It's like the hate and carnage *is* the point of the war. It's hard to explain."

Allison turned over on her side, facing away from Eric, who sat cross-legged, sharpening a large hunting knife. "I miss my family," she said quietly. "I miss cats and babies and music. I miss joy. I miss laughing."

Eric chuckled and said, "Sounds nice, but let's be honest – that stuff is just a sentimental daydream. I actually like fighting. Makes me feel *alive*. You used to be a vicious warrior – a stone-cold *killer* – what happened to you?"

"I feel like I'm waking up from a nightmare."

# 4

Hidden in the shadows of the tunnel, a crouched figure watched the column of resistors march toward their secret headquarters below the city streets. When the last of them had passed, the figure stealthily emerged from a hiding place against the wall and began creeping out the way the column had come. Slinking, sneaking, edging its way out, the figure moved like a wraith. It reached the entrance to the tunnel and stepped out into the cool, golden dusk. It scanned its surroundings and, satisfied that all was clear, relaxed its posture. It climbed the embankment and walked though the fading light toward the city center.

Before the Escalation, this strange, timid, feral creature had a name and an identity, just like every other person in the city that they had all called home. The creature's name occasionally returned in dreams – *Cameron* – but it had lost its meaning. Cameron was once a happy, normal, loving and loved little boy, but after his parents were killed in the uprising eight years ago, he had fled the city. The tunnels were now Cameron's home and survival had become all he knew.

Cameron walked along the side of the highway, staying close to the bushes, ready to duck for cover at the first sign of potential trouble. His senses were keen and his reflexes sharp. Tattered remnants of scavenged clothing hung on his gaunt frame. His hair was bushy and wild, his eyes piercing and alert. A nascent beard was just beginning to darken his jawline. He was 13 years old, but he had seen and experienced more suffering and horror than most will in a lifetime.

Just ahead now, a few hundred feet away, was the exit that led into the city center. Cameron paused and scanned his surroundings intently, his eyes wide, probing for even the slightest movement in the growing dark. His acute hearing was fully tuned to his environment, sensitive to the quietest of sounds. Cameron tilted his head back and took a few deep sniffs. Sensing no danger, he crept toward the turn-off. Staying on the shoulder of the road, he approached the exit, which branched off to the right. He stayed low and scurried down the embankment.

Like a rodent in the forest, Cameron made his way through the city, sticking to the dead neighborhoods and alleyways when possible. He bolted from shadow to shadow, nerves taut and vibrating, his head an electric sentinel of total awareness. Finally, he arrived at his destination – a small diner in the heart of the city. The sight of the overflowing dumpster at the back of the building made his stomach growl. Cameron grunted and sprinted toward it. With one hand, he held the lid open. With the other, he began rooting through the rancid-smelling contents. He was delighted to find a delectable treat – a nearly whole mold-free hamburger. He squealed happily and jammed the dripping burger into his mouth. He gobbled it up in moments and resumed his search.

"Hey! Don't you fucking move!" cried a voice from behind him. Cameron spun around in shock. He had let his guard down and had not sensed the approaching person. Standing before Cameron now was a large man in a stained, white smock. The man was blocking the exit out of the alley and holding a large assault rifle aimed directly at Cameron. Cameron realized instantly that he was trapped and in mortal danger.

"So you're the one who keeps digging through my garbage," the man said. "I thought it was freakin' raccoons. Do you know what kind of mess you've been making? I oughta blow your head off and dump your body in with them rotten burgers you like so much."

Cameron was frozen in abject fear. Only his eyes

moved – they darted about looking for an escape. The man
with the gun looked through the sights of the weapon and
said, "Ain't you got anything to say, boy? What's wrong with
you? You slow in the head?" When understanding dawned on
the armed man – that the frightened boy who quivered before
him was perhaps not slow in the head, but was certainly not
*right* – he lowered his weapon and sighed. "Where'd you
come from, boy? Where's your family?"

Cameron's eyes dropped to the ground and his body
slackened.

"They dead, ain't they?" said the man. "Well, shit.
Lots of that going on. It's a sad state of affairs when kids
have to live on the street 'cause their parents got killed. I'm
sorry, boy. I've lost a lot of people, too. It hurts."

Though he remained silent, Cameron's eyes watered
up. He had long ago compartmentalized the memories of his
parents, but they returned with an emotional punch at the
mere mention of them. In an instant, he reverted back to the
vulnerable and scared state of a toddler who has just lost the
most important people in his life. The shock and distress was
made all the worse by the fact that Cameron had actually
witnessed it happen.

"Mommy," Cameron whimpered. "Daddy."

The man from the restaurant slowly approached and
gently wrapped an arm around Cameron's shoulders. "Hey,
little buddy," he said, "it's alright. Don't cry. Are you hungry?
Why don't you come in with me? I'll make you a fresh
burger. It'll taste better than the slimy, wormy ones you've
been diggin' out of this bin! Trust me. Fries, too... How does
that sound?"

The sensation of the man's arm around him – warm
and strong and safe – was both alien and familiar to
Cameron. It caused him first to tense up, then to immediately
relax and melt into the comforting embrace. Cameron

allowed himself to be led out of the alley, around to the front, and into the building.

"Welcome to Fat Rob's," the man said. "And, yes, I'm Fat Rob. I was just closing up, but I can get the grill going again and make you one of my world-famous greasy masterpieces. Have a seat."

Fat Rob directed Cameron to the front of the empty diner. Cameron was beginning to warm up to the big man. He hopped up on a stool at the counter and playfully twisted in his seat a few times. A small smile appeared on his face. It felt good to be indoors. It felt good to be in the presence of another human. It felt good to let his guard down. Cameron wanted so badly to trust someone, *anyone*. He knew that Fat Rob could have gunned him down in the alley and disposed of his body without anyone ever knowing. Instead, he had invited him into this warm and comfortable place – a place where normal people ate and talked and laughed.

Fat Rob went to his grill. "You're gonna love this, boy," he said. "Let's put some meat on those bones."

As Fat Rob prepared the grill, a thunderous explosion in the street outside the diner rocked the entire building, blowing out the front window and door in a cloud of glass and wood. Cameron's animal instincts immediately returned and he jumped off the stool to take cover behind the counter. Fat Rob dropped, too, with a loud shout. "Fuck!" he cried. "Not again. Stay down, boy. We're in for some trouble."

Without exposing himself, Fat Rob reached over and retrieved his assault rifle from where he had left it leaning against the wall by the grill. "These pieces of shit ain't getting away with it this time," he snarled. "I'm ready for 'em."

There was another bang, and then the door to the diner was kicked open. Through the smoke and dust stepped a technological and biological monstrosity – a lumbering,

menacing, rampaging hybrid of man and machine. It was
mostly robotic – a metallic, humanoid frame of highly
advanced alloys interlaced with cutting-edge circuitry – but
attached to its broad and fearsome shoulders was the head of
a man. The head was flesh and bone, but the brain was
interlaced with the same circuitry as the robotic body. The
eyes of the monstrosity blazed with malevolence as it crashed
through the entrance. Following directly behind it was
another hybrid, equally frightful in appearance. The
destructive potential of the beasts was obvious.

"Rogues," whispered Fat Rob. "Defectors from the
Force... or maybe just defective. This is the third time this
year they've robbed me. I swear, I'm not going to let it
happen again. Stay down, boy, if you don't want to get hurt."

The two hybrids stomped their way into the diner,
their massive, metal feet pulverizing glass and wood with
each heavy step. They stopped in the center of the room. "I
see you!" called the first, its voice gleefully human. "Why
don't you come on out. We have business to discuss."

Still crouched behind the counter, with Cameron
cowering at his side, Fat Rob gritted his teeth and steeled
himself. He had no intention of discussing business – or
anything else, for that matter. He inhaled deeply and sprung
into action. In a flurry of motion – a surprising flurry for a
man of his size – Fat Rob jumped to his feet and expertly
brought his weapon into firing position. He pulled the trigger
and unleashed a barrage of military-grade hollow-points at
the first hybrid. The hybrid's head vaporized in pink mist and
its robotic frame crashed to the floor. Fat Rob quickly aimed
his gun at the second hybrid, which had drawn its own
weapon – a mini-cannon mounted to its forearm. The
ominous barrel of the cannon was trained on Rob. It would
no doubt reduce the man to a smoking pile of ground meat in
a microsecond. Fat Rob bravely held his ground, his rifle

steadfastly fixed on the hybrid.

"Classic standoff," Fat Rob remarked. "I bet you didn't see that coming. Maybe you assholes weren't aware of the fact that I served two tours in the war. I've blown away many, many of you rusty abominations. Glad to have the chance to do it again."

The hybrid stared at Fat Rob with a blank expression on its face. For a pregnant, tense moment, the room was still and silent.

Without lowering its deadly hand-cannon, the hybrid finally spoke: "Where did you get that weapon?" It asked the question with genuine curiosity.

"Yeah, I thought you might like it," Rob replied. "See, I wasn't dumb enough to give up my arms when they made their sweeps. I knew I'd need a little protection from scum like you. I've got a lot more, in fact, hidden away. They're antiques now, but I keep them clean and in good working order, as you've just seen."

"I should blow you and this whole place away," the hybrid said. "It stinks in here. You bios disgust me. I can see your little friend hiding behind the counter. His heat signature is clearer than yours."

"So why don't you?" Rob asked.

"Believe it or not, I've got a soft spot for the young ones."

The hybrid lowered its arm and the attached cannon. It glanced down at its fallen partner and sighed. "This unit was worth more than you and all the other meatbags in this entire neighborhood combined."

"Nothing but scrap metal now," Rob smiled, his weapon still aimed at the hybrid's head. "Why don't you just leave it for me to clean up? I might even make enough selling spare parts to pay for the damages you fucks caused."

"This isn't over. You haven't seen the last of me."

"So be it. I need more friends in my life anyway."

The hybrid pivoted and started toward the entrance. It walked over the debris piled at the threshold and stepped out into the night. Fat Rob watched it through the shattered window as it marched up the street. When the hybrid was out of sight, Fat Rob lowered his rifle.

"It's gone," Rob said. "You can come out now, boy."

Cameron sat with his legs drawn up to his chest. He was trembling and breathing rapidly and erratically. Fat Rob knelt down and put his hands on Cameron's shoulders. He looked him in the eye and said, "Everything's okay. We're safe, at least for now. I won't let anyone or anything hurt you, do you understand? You can stay with me for as long as you want. Would you like that?"

Cameron's breathing relaxed somewhat. In a small, shaky voice, he said, "Yes. Want to stay with you."

"Alright then! That's good. I want you to stay, too. We've got some cleaning to do, and some of it isn't going to be pleasant. Can you handle that?"

Cameron gently nodded.

"Good boy. Why don't we get some grub in our guts first? Before we were so rudely interrupted, I was about to whip up one of my greasy masterpieces. Blasting hybrids always makes me hungry. Let's eat!"

## 5

The hybrid walked the dark, empty streets in search of a fix. The attempted robbery of the diner had not gone as planned. With no currency, and its partner in crime dead and disabled at the hands of the unusually resilient and unexpectedly armed fat proprietor of the restaurant, the hybrid considered its options. The early evening dose of Tonik was beginning to wear off. Soon the highly unpleasant withdrawal symptoms would appear. If the hybrid did not find a connection soon, an agonizing, searing pain would fill its skull like spinning blades of red-hot steel. Not long after that, the hybrid would begin to lose motor control. Its brain would cease to communicate with its robotic body and it would be left immobile and powerless, a useless pile of mechanical and electronic components. Then, disconnected from its life support, the head would quickly die. It was a scenario that the hybrid planned to avoid at all costs.

The hybrid scanned the streets with its augmented vision as it prowled the nearly deserted inner city core. Here and there, it spotted the forms of lost, damaged, pathetic souls hiding among the rubble and filth of the dilapidated structures. Many, like the boy in the diner, were children. Somehow, through all the combat, horror, and programming that the hybrid had experienced, it still maintained sympathy for the young wretches. The sight of them always caused a distant, yet palpable, stirring of emotion in the buried remnants of the hybrid's humanity.

On this particular evening, all of the usual spots where the hybrid sought dealers – the shadowy alleys, hidden alcoves, and abandoned buildings – were deserted. The hybrid wondered if there had been a recent cleanup by the Force, or perhaps even by citizen vigilantes. He had been seeing more and more illegal weaponry lately and, like the owner of the diner, more people willing to put up a fight. Things had changed in the last few years. The vice-like grip that the hybrids once had on the criminal underground was slackening noticeably.

A nauseous throbbing sensation was beginning to creep up the back of the hybrid's head, pulsing from deep within its brain. It was critical now – the hybrid needed the drug. It suddenly remembered that, not far from its current location, in a secret basement beneath a demolished office building, there was a 24-hour pleasure den. The hybrid had once sold harvested organs to the owner of the sordid establishment and had been paid well. He knew that there would be plenty of Tonik there, along with other substances and contraband of every possible variety. It was not a place where the average street person or junkie could just show up, but hybrids were given special privileges. Most people, even the kings and queens of the crime syndicates, found them to be extremely volatile and often extraordinarily dangerous. The hybrids had the grudging respect of the underworld.

The hybrid picked up its pace and headed in the direction of the pleasure den. The pistons in its legs pumped in time with the escalating throbbing in its brain. It broke into a full-on run and covered the last few blocks in seconds. As it came to the destroyed office complex, a drone patrolling above cast a moving spotlight on the ground below. Was it the Force? Did it belong to the Syndicate? The hybrid couldn't be sure – the law and the underworld often used the same equipment. In fact, the law and the underworld were often the same people.

The hybrid was getting desperate and decided to take a risk. It approached the entrance, which lay hidden behind the twisted girders and concrete that jutted out of the ruins like abstract sculpture. Instantly, the spotlight from the drone swung around and illuminated the hybrid. The spotlight remained fixed while the drone zipped over and hovered above the hybrid. A robotic voice spoke:

"Connection established. Identification successful. Welcome back, hybrid. Please enter."

Though relieved to have gained admittance to the pleasure den, the hybrid was shocked and disturbed to have been recognized by the drone's scanners. The hybrid was a fugitive and had long ago removed its GPS and identification implants. It had gotten used to traveling incognito, unrecognized by the tracking devices of the establishment. It was clear that the underworld had access to more sophisticated technology. The hybrid did not have time to be concerned about this, however. It needed to get its fix.

The hybrid walked through the entrance, camouflaged among the mangled piles of concrete and steel. A concealed panel slid open, revealing an elevator. The hybrid stepped in and the panel slid shut behind it. The elevator dropped rapidly and came to an abrupt stop. The panel slid open again and the hybrid stepped out.

The hybrid was greeted by a total sensory assault. It was now in the main chamber of the vast den, which was full of flashing lights and cacophonous sounds, not unlike the hotels in pre-war Las Vegas. The patrons – human, hybrid, and android – were involved in a variety of seedy activities. Many were sitting at gambling terminals and using biometric interfaces to play. Substances of all sorts were being consumed, from old-fashioned alcohol, amphetamines, and opiates to the newest designer chemical compounds. Some patrons drank, some smoked. Others snorted or injected. A few even connected directly to the dispensers via bio-ports.

In the many side rooms off of the main chamber, patrons engaged in sex acts of the strangest and most perverse kinds. Anything that could possibly be imagined could be experienced for a price. There were also rumors of seldom seen lower chambers, in which sadists and murderers participated in truly dark and disturbing activities. The hybrid had no interest in any of that – it was solely focused on finding Tonik, and it had an idea about how to acquire some.

The hybrid crossed the floor of the main chamber quickly, heading straight to the back of the room. It came to a large door flanked by two burly and well-armed androids. As the hybrid approached, the androids moved in unison, stepping in front of the hybrid and blocking him from proceeding.

"What's your business?" demanded the android on the right.

"I'm here to see the boss," the hybrid replied. "I'd like to offer my services in exchange for payment."

"Have you worked for the Syndicate before?" asked the android on the left.

"Yes, many times. The boss has always been very pleased with my work."

"Yeah, I think I recognize you," the first android replied. "I'll see if the boss is available."

The android turned and knocked on the door. "There's someone here to see you, Boss. A hybrid. Says he worked with you before."

A voice called from beyond the door: "Excellent! Send him in."

The two androids stepped aside and the one on the right opened the door. The hybrid stepped through.

The boss' office was classically furnished and ornately decorated in rich shades of brown and burgundy. Fine art masterpieces hung on the walls. Statues carved by the hands of the Italian Renaissance masters stood in the corners of the room. The scent of old scotch and fine cigars hung in the air. Behind a large, oak desk sat the boss, a small man with a slick haircut and a very expensive suit.

"Please, come in," the boss said warmly. The hybrid entered the room. The androids shut the door behind him. "Ah, yes. I remember you," said the boss. "You did some jobs with the downtown crew. Ex-paramilitary, correct? Didn't you have a partner?"

"Yes, sir. He was killed earlier this evening on a bad gig. Some working-class meatbag was hiding a weapon. Got the jump on us."

"That's unfortunate. I hope you made him pay."

"Yes, sir," the hybrid lied.

"So, what can I do for you tonight? Are you looking for work?"

"I am, sir, but I have... a problem." The ache in the hybrid's head was increasing in intensity. A disconcerting, tingling electrical shock sensation now crackled in its brain stem, indicating rapid fluctuations in the signal between its brain and body.

"Oh, and what might that be?"

"I know you are a man who appreciates honesty, sir, so I'm just going to say it. I need a hit of Tonik and I need it now. Should have scored on that last gig but it went bad, so I have no money. I can offer you my services as payment."

"I see. I do indeed appreciate your candor, and I respect loyalty. You and your partner were good workers. It just so happens that an opportunity has opened up. I think you would be perfect for the job."

"That's great, sir. Anything."

"Why don't we get you fixed up first. Then we'll discuss business."

"Thank you, sir."

The boss reached over and opened a desk drawer on his right. He reached in and pulled out a long and intimidating device. It looked like a cross between a handgun and a hypodermic needle. He slid open a chamber on the top of the device and inserted a small, cylindrical cartridge. The cartridge snapped into place and the chamber automatically slid shut.

"You're going to like this," said the boss as he passed the grotesque device to the hybrid. "Our chemists have been tweaking the formula. This is the most potent batch we've ever created. Enjoy."

The hybrid had to refrain itself from greedily snatching the device out of the boss' hands. Instead, it politely received it and slowly, calmly pressed the protruding needle into the carotid artery in what remained of its neck and pulled the trigger. With a wet thump, the drug entered the hybrid's system, shooting directly into its brain. Instant relief, followed closely by an exploding, rushing euphoria made the hybrid feel as if it were birthing galaxies in its head. It felt a surge of power as a full connection between its body and brain was re-established. Through the hazy fog of intense pleasure, the hybrid could see the boss sitting behind the desk with an amused expression on his face. The hybrid allowed itself another brief moment to bask in the glorious sensations before speaking. "Thank you, sir," it said. "That is some really fine product. Now, how can I be of service?"

"I'm glad you enjoyed it," the boss smiled. "The task is quite simple, really. I need you to escort an individual – an asset of ours – to the Zone. He's been wiped and will be heavily sedated. He should not put up a struggle. He will be expected. Our observers will notify me upon his arrival. Return when you are done and you will be payed handsomely."

"Human?"

"Yes, but we expect great things of him. He's a natural fighter and should produce excellent results. He's ex-Resistance, and our scouting team feels like he could be the best player to come along in many years. We are excited to get him on the field."

"I'd be happy and honored to help, sir."

"Good. Check in with the boys outside and they'll get you set up."

"Thank you, sir."

The hybrid stepped out of the office feeling rejuvenated and exhilarated. The drug had worked its magic. The dose would be effective for many hours, which would be more than enough time to complete the task. The inevitable pain and discomfort it would feel when the chemical wore off was of no immediate concern.

"The boss wants me to escort someone to the Zone," the hybrid said to the androids outside of the office. "Ex-Resistance, apparently."

"Yeah, he's being held on the lower level," said the android on the left. "I'll take you to him."

"Have you ever been to the Zone?" the other android asked.

"I have, but it's been a long time," replied the hybrid.

"The game has changed. It's probably a lot more intense than you remember it. Spectators who get too close are likely to get killed. Be careful."

"I bet that's good for business. Viewership increasing?"

"Yeah, but the volatility makes it harder to control. The bookies are having a hard time. The house always wins, of course, but the profits have been slipping. This new player they're sending in – I'm sure it's a way of getting a grip on the fix again."

"I'm sure it is. I just want to get paid."

The hybrid and the android took a private elevator to the lower level. They disembarked and walked down a dark hall illuminated by red fluorescent tubes which ran along the ceiling. The unnerving sounds of unspeakable acts drifted through closed doors. A vile potpourri of scents hung in the stale air. They were traversing the underworld of the underworld. It was like an excursion through the infernal heart of Hell – a lucid nightmare.

The android and the hybrid reached a room near the end of the hall. The android waved a hand over a panel mounted on the wall and the door opened. They entered. The room was essentially a large kennel, but instead of cats or dogs, there were people – human and hybrid alike – inside

the stacked cages. Most of them were clearly heavily sedated
and unconscious. Some unfortunate individuals wavered on
the threshold, their eyes dull and watery, low moans escaping
their slack mouths. Only a few were fully awake and they sat
hunched in their cramped cages, watching the hybrid and the
android with blank expressions.

The android pointed to a cage and said, "That's the
one. He's got a lot of spirit. We had to triple-dose him to get
him to settle down. He's out now, but you better get him to
the Zone quick. We'll provide you with transportation part of
the way, but you'll have to go on foot for the rest."

The hybrid looked at the caged man and felt a
momentary twinge of pity. It quickly disappeared. The hybrid
had a job to do.

"I can handle him," the hybrid said. "I put down
hundreds of 'em when I was on the Force. Let's just see how
long he lasts in the Zone."

# 6

South of the city, accessible only by an old highway now
closed to the public, was the entrance to the Zone. Only
authorized vehicles and personnel were allowed to pass the
checkpoint, which was situated at a bridge that crossed a
deep and wide ditch. The ditch, and the barb wire fence on
the other side, encircled the entire 10-square mile district.
Only players entered. Only winners exited.

When Elden regained his senses, he found himself
lying on a cot in what appeared to be a concrete bunker.
Above him, a single light bulb hung from the ceiling. He was
sore and disoriented. As he struggled to piece together what
had happened before he had lost consciousness, a loud thud
from a distant explosion somewhere above him shook the
room. It caused the light bulb to swing wildly and cast

ghastly shadows on the bare, gray walls. Elden sat up quickly, instantly alert and buzzing with adrenaline. *The Zone*, he thought. *Those fuckers sent me to the Zone.* Despite his kidnappers' attempts to wipe his mind, Elden retained his memories... and his indignation.

Elden stood from the cot and surveyed the room. On the wall opposite the cot, there was a sink and a toilet, both practically antiques. They were cracked and coated in a thick layer of dark brown filth. Fetid water had pooled on the floor around the odious fixtures. To Elden's right, light from the street above streamed in through a small window high up on the wall. Below the window, leaning against the wall, was a military-grade, standard-issue rifle, beside which sat a soldier's rucksack, complete with sleeping bag and canteen. The rucksack was bulging with supplies and rations. There was a door on the wall opposite the window, which presumably led upstairs.

"I'll play your little game, you bastards," Elden said aloud as he picked up the rifle and rucksack and slung them over his shoulder. "I was born for this."

Elden checked the magazine of his weapon. It was full. He reinserted it and chambered a round. He then went to the door and put his ear to it, listening intently for any signs of activity beyond. Hearing nothing, he slowly turned the knob, pulled the door slightly ajar, and peered through the crack. He could see stairs leading up to an open landing. Elden opened the door fully and brought his rifle up into firing position. He crept up the stairs as silently as he could, his weapon ready, his senses keen, his mind hyper-vigilant.

At the top of the stairs, Elden peered over the landing, being careful not to expose himself to a potential ambush. He found himself looking into the ruins of what was once a spacious and comfortable living room. It was now a bombed-out, blackened, demolished husk. Destroyed furniture and the remnants of household items and personal mementos lay scattered among the debris. One of the walls had been entirely knocked out.

Satisfied that there was no immediate threat, Elden left the relative safety of the stairwell and entered the room. He went directly to a shattered window and looked out. The total destruction of his surroundings confirmed his suspicion – he was indeed in the Zone. The entire neighborhood lay in ruins. Each and every building had been bombed, blasted, and fought over countless times. It was a combat area, a brutal battlefield contained within the Zone's borders like an Armageddon-themed amusement park.

Elden had heard stories of the Zone from some of his former comrades in the Resistance. A few of them had been 'players' and had actually survived. He knew of many who had not. The totality of the destruction and the stark, hostile environment was still a shock to behold.

As Elden gazed out upon the battlefield – or what was essentially an arena for the players unlucky enough to find themselves drafted into the game, he spotted something that made him gasp. Towering into the sky, visible from miles away, was a gigantic, lumbering, robotic spider. It was an ominous sight, a surreal vision from a madman's dream. The dreadful contraption was taller than the largest buildings in the area that it apparently patrolled. The robotic spider moved like a daddy longlegs through the ruins and rubble of the Zone, bright spotlights shining down to the ground from its black metal chassis. It was searching for something, or someone.

"New tech," Elden muttered. "Looks like the game just got harder. Let's see what they gave me to work with."

Elden opened his rucksack and inventoried its contents. He was surprised to find it well-stocked with ammo, ready-to-eat meals, binoculars, matches, various utensils and tools, and other survival items. "Wouldn't be so entertaining for the bastards if I didn't have a fighting chance," he said as he packed everything up again and prepared to leave his current position. "Time to play."

Slipping out, Elden flowed into the front yard of the bombed-out home. He stayed low and close to the walls of the buildings as he made his way up the block. The home in which he had awoken was at the southern end of the Zone. The goal, as he understood it from the accounts of other survivors, was to reach a checkpoint somewhere at the far north. Exactly where, and what the final destination was, constantly changed. It was the gamekeepers' way of keeping it interesting and thwarting collaboration between old and new players, which would be, in their warped view, cheating.

As Elden neared the corner of the block, a loud droning sound alerted him to something passing over his head high above. The object was massive and cast a shadow that completely consumed him. It was directly over him, forcing him to tilt his head back at an extreme angle to get a look. What he saw was an incredibly large aerial vehicle hovering over his position. It was essentially a huge platform, arrayed with lights, cameras, and other sensitive viewing and recording equipment. As far as Elden could tell, it was remotely controlled and was used to observe and transmit what was happening in the Zone to spectators watching from the safety of homes and gambling establishments in the relatively secure districts of the city.

Elden waved at the platform and said, "You want a show? I'll give you a show. I'm ready for whatever you got. Bring it on, you bastards."

The hovering platform rapidly ascended and then suddenly blinked out of sight using its sophisticated cloaking capabilities. Elden knew that the craft would be watching everything he did – an invisible, dispassionate, omnipresent eye in the sky.

No sooner had the craft disappeared out of view when Elden's attention was immediately drawn to movement in the street. Something was approaching, rushing toward him in a furious, spinning blur. Elden quickly ran for cover beside the nearest home to his right. He crouched by the north wall, concealing his body, and watched as the strange, spinning object abruptly stopped in the intersection. It was only yards away, and Elden could now see that it was an autonomous robotic device shaped like a large wheel. On each side of the rotating main body were machine guns. The wheel rolled forward slightly and turned toward Elden's position. The guns remained fixed as the device moved, and now they were pointed directly at him.

Though the north wall of the home provided cover, the sight of the intimidating weaponry caused Elden to doubt the safety of his current location. He sprung into action and ran to the rear of the home. The robotic wheel opened fire just as he dashed away, obliterating the corner of the home in a deafening blast of rapid gunfire. The power of the weapons, and the damage they caused, momentarily stunned Elden. He paused behind the home and gathered his composure before sprinting around to the other side.

Elden could hear the robot whirring in the street. He moved up, staying flat against the wall. When he reached the wall's edge, he peered around the corner. He had a clear view of the machine. It was slowly rolling forward, toward the other side of the home. Elden went into action. He dropped to a crouching position, raised his rifle, and opened fire. The rounds from his weapon tore into the machine accurately and effectively. Elden kept firing until the robot's chassis began to smoke. It attempted to spin around to face him, but with another burst, Elden disabled it and the awful contraption toppled over on its side.

"Gotcha, you rusty piece of shit," Elden said as he reloaded his weapon.

The sun was rapidly setting. It would not be long before dusk fell upon the city. Elden watched the broken machine in the street for a few minutes. Once he was confident that the threat had been neutralized, he moved out of his position. His plan was to make as much progress as he could before dark. He had no idea how many miles away the final checkpoint was, but he had heard stories from those who had spent days and even weeks in the Zone. *I'm going to beat this game,* Elden resolved, *and I'm going to do it quickly and with style.*

For the next three hours, Elden moved through the Zone, working his way north. Over the course of his journey, he was stalked by a variety of robotic adversaries. In a multitude of forms, they pursued him relentlessly. Elden stayed hidden when he could, like a phantom among the ruined buildings, slinking and sneaking through the ragged shadows. It was impossible to avoid detection at all times, however, and he was forced to fight on a few occasions. He used his extensive combat training and advanced proficiency with his weapon to engage and destroy the threats that he could not evade.

By late evening, Elden had covered a fair distance and decided it was time to find shelter and get some rest. He chose a two-story building on a corner in what was once a middle-class neighborhood. The first floor had been a convenience store. The second floor contained living quarters for the family who had owned and operated the shop. Elden entered and went upstairs. Predictably, the small apartment was in total disarray. There were empty shell casings scattered among splintered furniture and shattered household items. The walls were pockmarked with bullet holes.

"Looks like there was quite a firefight in here," Elden

muttered. "Must have been a real scrap."

Elden looked out a window and liked what he saw. He had a great view of the street. The position would be easy to defend, should he come under attack. He spread his sleeping bag out against the wall, sat down on it, and opened a ready-to-eat meal. He gobbled it down cold. He lay on his back, his rifle at his side and ready for action, and closed his eyes. He succumbed to his fatigue quickly, falling asleep within moments.

"Wake up, sleepyhead."

Elden returned to consciousness with a jolt. He reached for his rifle before his eyes were fully open, but it was gone. A man stood over him – he had Elden's rifle and was pointing it at Elden's forehead. "You fucked up, buddy," the man said. "I hate to do this, but I need your gear and weapon. Not everyone makes it out of here, you know. It's nothing personal. I just want to win."

The man pulled the trigger.

## 7

The simulation ended. Mickey lay in the holo-pod, momentarily confused. Emerging from a good program was always disorienting – the transition back to reality was a bumpy ride. Mickey's identity rushed back into his head like sea water into a tidal pool. *Wow*, he thought. *I didn't see that coming. I really thought I...* he *was gonna make it out of there. Poor Elden. Nice twist, though.*

Mickey remained in the holo-pod for a few more minutes, lying prone in the dark, savoring the incredible sensory experience he had just had. More compelling than a movie, more immersive than a video game, more thrilling than an amusement park ride – the simulations allowed the user to actually inhabit the characters and feel as if they were participating in the stories. The holo-pods were the state-of-the-art in entertainment technology. A good program made users totally forget their real lives and identities. A great program gave users the illusion of free will.

Mickey pressed a button on a panel to his left and the pod opened like a clam shell. He sat up, stretched his back, and rubbed his eyes. His stomach growled. He had been in the pod all evening and was now hungry and thirsty. Around him were other pods. The room was full of them. One by one they opened, revealing other users. Mickey turned to a woman seated in the pod next to him and said, "That was a wild one. How was it for you, Laura?"

"Intense," Laura replied as she climbed out of the pod. "Parts of it were really scary. Some of it made me sad."

"I liked the action," Mickey said. "Some really good fight scenes." He hopped out of his pod. He and Laura held hands as they walked to the exit of the pod room.

"It was more violent than I expected," Laura said. "I liked the little feral boy. I'm glad he found someone to take care of him."

Mickey and Laura merged with the crowd leaving the holo-pod theater. They stepped out onto the street. It was early morning.

"Wow, that was a long one," Laura noted. "I can't believe it's already morning."

"Let's catch a skybus and go home," said Mickey. "I need to eat and sleep."

Hand in hand, the couple walked two blocks up to the nearest boarding station. They got on the elevator and ascended to the upper platform. Once on top, they joined the others who were waiting beyond the gate. Just as everyone else did in such situations, they slid their E-visors into place. Among them stood a shy, anxious young man clutching a bagged lunch. He was not fully engrossed by the inner screen of an E-visor, because his had recently malfunctioned.

At precisely 8:15 AM, the skybus arrived at the boarding station. The nervous young man watched the skybus approach with naked, jittery eyes. He felt a strange sensation, like he had lived that moment before.

# Peter and the Satellite

We all have bad days. Some days make you wish that you hadn't gotten out of bed that morning. Some days make you wonder if it would have been better if you had never been born at all. Some days make you feel like your life is one big cosmic joke, perpetrated on you by a sadistic, malevolent universe that delights in your suffering and is intent on driving you totally, irrevocably insane, purely for its own amusement. That is the kind of day that Peter had. It all started the night before.

While jamming fried chicken into his face and staring at a shitty reality show on the television, Peter heard a noise. As far as he could tell, the noise was coming from outside – somewhere high above his house, it seemed. It was a loud whistling, rapidly rising in pitch. Peter briefly paused his vigorous feeding and cocked his head to the side to listen to the sound. It was getting louder, as though it were approaching. Peter shrugged, sending crumbs and grease flying in all directions. He went back to shoveling chicken into his gaping mouth.

On the television, a commercial began. Peter grunted, wiped a beefy hand on his stained T-shirt, and reached for the remote. Just as he wrapped his thick fingers around the device, the whistling sound above him reached a crescendo. Before Peter could muster the energy to get his ass out of the large recliner, an object crashed through the ceiling right over his head and sailed across his living room like a cannon ball. The course of the object sent it smashing directly into the television set with a shattering of glass and an explosion of sparks and smoke.

"Damn," Peter muttered as he sat dumbfounded. He stared at the smoking remnants of his beloved TV, unable to fully comprehend what had just occurred. "Damn," he said again as he reached into the bucket of chicken sitting in his lap. He tore the skin off a drumstick with his teeth and slurped it down his endless gullet. "That was a good show, too," he said, though he could not at all remember what he had just been watching. He gobbled up his chicken leg and prepared to stand up.

Peter is not morbidly obese. He is large – fat, some would say – but not big enough to be considered an invalid. He does, however, have a hard time getting around. He is not very mobile at all, but I suspect that is mostly because he is lazy – incredibly, shockingly, maddeningly lazy.

The unusual nature of the event that had just transpired forced him to reconsider his plans for the evening. Gorging in front of the TV was no longer an option, so with great effort – and an unpleasant series of sounds and smells, Peter hoisted himself out of his chair and shambled over to the ruins of his favorite appliance.

Peter's television, which had died an ignominious and violent death, was very old. It was practically ancient – a floor model that he had inherited from a family member decades before. Peter knelt before the TV's charred corpse. Whatever had crashed through his ceiling was still lodged inside the cabinet. Peter could see it resting on a nest of broken electronic components.

"What is *that* thing?" Peter asked as he bent to get a closer look.

The object was smoking and covered in dust. Peter reached for the object, but pulled back quickly when his fingers got near. The thing was radiating extreme heat. Peter blew a strong breath toward it, clearing off most of the dust to get a better look. When Peter realized what he was looking at, a goofy yelp escaped his lips.

"That's a friggin' satellite!" he cried.

And sure enough, it was. What Peter did not know, though, is that it was a super *secret* satellite that had been placed into orbit by a clandestine organization with a dark, hidden agenda. It had been brought down by another, equally covert group with its own surreptitious machinations using advanced technology unknown and unavailable to the general public. The technology was not perfect. Somehow, the satellite did not vaporize as expected. Instead, it ended up lodged in the television set of a lazy slob named Peter.

Peter studied the satellite as it cooled off. He was surprised by how small it was. The satellite was roughly the size and shape of a basketball, metallic silver in color, and adorned with a variety of complex and mysterious scientific instruments.

"I bet that thing is worth a buttload of money," Peter mused aloud. He had a habit of talking to himself, as I'm sure you've noticed. "I wonder if Slick Rick at Mighty Pawn would be interested in it. Maybe I could trade it in for a new TV... one of them fancy flat screen thingies, maybe!"

Well, at the time, it seemed like a great idea to Peter. Don't judge him yet. I'm sure many of you would have thought the same thing, given the circumstances of the peculiar situation. Peter decided to sleep on it. He went to bed with a full belly and a head full of excitement.

That night, Peter had a weird dream. It was most likely caused by his excessive intake of fried chicken that evening and it is not at all relevant to this story. Curious readers might be interested to know that that the dream featured sea turtles, a magnifying glass, two opera singers dueling over a sandwich, and an appearance from Peter's sixth grade teacher.

In the morning, Peter awoke. He did not yet know it,

but he was in for one hell of a day. He got out of bed thinking
about pancakes. He had totally forgotten about the satellite
still resting inside his television set. He waddled into the
kitchen and prepared pancake batter. He took a large,
uncooked bowl of the batter into the living room with him.
He saw the broken TV.

"Crap," he muttered.

Then he remembered the satellite!

"Oh, yeah," he said.

Peter sat in his chair and ate the entire bowl of
pancake batter. He used a chicken bone from the bucket on
the floor to scoop it into his mouth. He had actual spoons, but
they were in the kitchen and he had no desire to get up again.
His expression was vacant, but there was an unusual amount
of activity happening within his large, round head. He was
contemplating the value of his strange new possession. He
was wondering about the satellite's origin. He was even
making plans for the day, considering his options, and
strategizing. Peter was actually thinking!

By the time he had finished the pancake batter, Peter
had formulated a plan. Stepping into action, the first thing he
did was retrieve the satellite from the gutted husk of the
television. He picked it up carefully, cradling it gently in his
hands. He was surprised by the satellite's weight – it was
dense and deceptively heavy. Peter carried the object into his
bedroom and laid it on his bed. He picked up a sweatshirt
from the floor and wrapped the satellite in the soiled, stinky
garment. The sweatshirt was green and red and had a picture
of a kitten in a Santa Claus hat on the front. Peter wore it
often throughout the year. One thing you should know about
Peter is that he did not care what people thought of him. This
was both a good and a bad thing.

With the satellite wrapped and ready to be
transported, Peter got himself dressed. It was about time, too.

He had been wearing nothing but greasy underwear for the last two days. He arbitrarily chose an outfit from the heaps of clothing strewn about his bedroom floor. While rooting through the items, he discovered a half-eaten cookie hidden among a pile of socks. He emitted a happy squeal and promptly ate it.

Peter was now ready to embark on the day's adventure. The first stop, he decided, would be the convenience store on the corner. He was in for a workout and he knew that he would need calories, so a super-sized fountain drink full of sugary magic would be the perfect companion for a walk downtown to see Slick Rick at Mighty Pawn.

It was a great morning for a walk. Autumn was fast approaching. The heat of the summer was subsiding. Large, billowy clouds drifted overhead and a gentle, aromatic breeze caressed Peter's face. Peter inhaled deeply and smiled as he walked to the convenience store just up the street from his home. He was not aware that the satellite he carried in his hands was, at that very moment, being tracked by two opposing and extremely dangerous factions who would stop at nothing to retrieve the valuable object.

Peter arrived at the neighborhood Suck N' Slurp. He entered and went directly to the soda dispensers at the back of the store. That is where he experienced the first of the day's many misfortunes. To his dismay, there was a handwritten note affixed to the nozzle that dispensed his favorite flavor, Raspberry Spew. *Out of order – sorry!* the note said.

"Oh, come on!" shouted Peter. "Really?"

The cashier at the counter heard him and said, "No Spew today, buddy. Time to try something new, I guess."

It was apparent that the cashier was familiar with Peter and his beverage habits and tastes.

Peter sighed. He pondered his selection before setting the satellite down and grabbing a super-sized cup from the sleeve beside the fountain. He filled the cup with ice and Lemon-Lime Eruption. He slapped a lid on it, inserted a straw, and sipped deeply. It was fizzy, sweet, and good. *Crisis averted*, thought Peter.

Peter went to the counter to pay for his delicious beverage. The cashier, a young man with a purple mohawk and a tattoo of a dragon on his face, yawned as he rang up Peter's purchase.

"That's ninety-seven cents," the cashier said.

Peter awkwardly retrieved his wallet from the front pocket of his pants. The satellite he held to his chest was cumbersome and in the way. The cashier took notice of the object and said, "Whatcha got there?"

"It's nothing," replied Peter as he paid for his drink. "Just some junk I found."

"What kind of junk?"

"Junk junk. It's nothing."

"I bet it's a human head!" The cashier laughed. He had amused himself with that comment.

"It's not a human head. Trust me."

"Can I see it?"

"I... uh... no. I can't. I'm sorry."

Peter quickly shuffled out of the store. As the door was swinging shut behind him, he heard the cashier call out, "If I hear on the news that some dude is missing his head, I'm going to report you!" A hearty laugh followed.

Peter walked on. He had the satellite – still wrapped and concealed in his dirty sweater – under one arm and his Lemon-Lime Eruption in the other hand. Despite the Raspberry Spew disappointment and the obnoxious cashier, he was still in good spirits. He couldn't wait to get to Mighty Pawn. He sipped and walked and walked and sipped. He was feeling just fine.

While Peter enjoyed his stroll, intriguing things were happening somewhere far away. In an underground bunker so secret that even the men who currently occupied it had no idea where they were, a light blinked on a sophisticated, holographic map of the world. The two men monitoring the map sat behind a large console arrayed with advanced computer equipment. The light flashing on the map was a very big deal, but the men showed no emotion.

One of the men activated his headset and said, "We have located the birdie. It appears to be intact and at least partially functional. We will continue to track it. Initiate SAT-X 11-17 B protocol, activate re-acquisition sequence, mobilize agents. We need to get to it before *they* do."

Mercifully oblivious to the sinister connotations of the words spoken by the spooky men in the bunker, Peter continued on his way. He was nearing downtown, mere blocks away from Mighty Pawn, when he heard a shout from an approaching car to his left. He turned in the direction of the shout and saw a big, white pickup truck roaring up the street. There was a young man in the passenger seat. He was looking at Peter with a malicious smile on his face. When he noticed that he had gained Peter's attention, he shouted again:

"Weirdo! Loser!"

Before Peter could react, the man in the truck hurled something fast and hard. The driver of the truck accelerated and the vehicle sped away with a thunderous din. The object tumbled through the air and came crashing down right in front of Peter, narrowly missing him. The object exploded when it hit the ground, dowsing Peter in warm liquid. Peter then realized that the man in the truck had thrown a full, plastic bottle at him. The awful reality of what had been in the bottle dawned on him when he could smell and taste the fluid as it trickled down his face and into his mouth.

"Oh, God!" Peter exclaimed. "It's piss!"

It was indeed urine – likely human and likely originating from the bladder of one of the young men in the truck. Who would throw a bottle of piss at an innocent stranger, an unsuspecting pedestrian just out for a stroll and enjoying a fine day? People like the yahoos in that truck, that's who. Every town has them and, unfortunately for Peter, his town has an unusually high concentration of truck-drivin', piss-bottle-throwin', random-insultin' hickified yokels. It's one of the reasons he spends most of his time at home, alone. Don't feel bad, though – Peter has thick skin.

"Ugh," Peter groaned as he used his shirt to wipe the urine from his face. He groaned louder when he realized that he had dropped his massive cup of Lemon-Lime Eruption during the assault. The soda lay in a puddle at his feet, mixing with the nasty yellow fluid that had been in the bottle.

Not to be deterred, Peter regained his composure and continued on his way. He had faced greater challenges than the humiliating episode he had just endured and nothing was going to stop him from getting that satellite into Slick Rick's sleazy, but knowledgeable, hands – at least, that's what he thought then.

Unbeknownst to Peter, an unmarked, black helicopter was, at that very moment, in the air racing to his location. The helicopter carried two very interesting individuals with highly intriguing backgrounds. More about these two individuals will be revealed later, but one thing is abundantly clear: they were serious people on a serious mission, and they were totally intent on retrieving the satellite that Peter was carrying. As you have probably guessed, these individuals were armed with more than bottles of urine.

After walking for more than an hour, Peter finally reached the downtown core of his hometown. The city he lives in is of average size – not a bustling metropolis, but not a village either. In recent years, the city's economy had fallen on hard times and the commercial districts had been in steady decline. Where there were once numerous – and prosperous – family-owned shops and even some big-name retail outlets, now stood mostly pawn shops, liquor stores, and payday loan agencies. It was a travesty, really, but Peter barely took notice. He was not interested in such things.

Peter turned left on May Street. Mighty Pawn was only a few blocks away. Peter allowed himself to visualize all the cool things he could buy if the satellite turned out to be valuable. His limited imagination never strayed far from TV sets, video games, and food. The satellite was, of course, valuable – *very* valuable, in fact – but not in the way that Peter was hoping.

An odd figure shambled up the sidewalk toward him. It was a thin man with one hand pushing a walker and the other holding up his extremely over-sized jeans. The shambling man was shirtless and tanned a deep brown. Wild, bushy hair and a thick, matted beard obscured most of the man's face, except for a pair of wide eyes that peered out like those of a terrified animal fleeing a forest fire. The man appeared to be talking to himself in a low mumble.

As Peter and the man with the walker passed each other, the man's pungent smell caused Peter to quietly gasp and wrinkle his nose. The man noticed this small gesture and promptly screeched loudly in surprise, terror, and perfect, refined madness. The shriek caused Peter to jump and let out a startled cry of his own. The two men screamed in unison for a few weird moments. As the two men went their separate ways, Peter could hear the shambler mutter while he was still in earshot, "No one likes you. Even God hates you. You're going to die."

That was a disturbing thing to hear! Peter wondered if the comments were directed at him. He then wondered how big of a TV he was going to be able to afford. He also wondered how many chicken nuggets and milkshakes he could buy with the remainder of his imminent windfall. He smiled.

Peter was still smiling when he came to a bus stop with an enclosed shelter. He did not see the woman standing inside until she spoke:

"Hi, honey. Looking for a date?"

Leaning against the inside wall of the shelter was a very large woman in a fur coat... at least, that is what Peter saw at first glance. Upon closer inspection, Peter realized that the thick, gaudy makeup and obvious wig masked distinctly masculine features. Stubble was clearly visible on the person's face, and Peter could even see an Adam's apple peeking through the lapels of the fur coat. Peter was not offended nor disgusted, but he replied to the solicitation honestly.

"Oh, no, thank you," he said. "I'm not gay."

A look of mortified shock appeared on the bulky transvestite's face. "Well, neither am *I*, honey!" she cried. "Are you insinuating that I am a *man*? Do I *look* like a man to you?"

Peter was in a predicament. He stammered and stumbled over his words as he tried to find the correct response. Unfortunately, for him, there *was* no correct response. Whatever he said was only going to make it worse. He did not know this, however, and made a valiant attempt to extricate himself from the awkward situation.

"I'm sorry," Peter said. "No offense intended... I just assumed..."

"You just assumed *what*, exactly?"

"That, you know, you were a, um... you know, male hooker. I'm not judging you!"

"So, just because of a little harmless flirting you

assume I'm a *prostitute*? How dare you. You haven't been
with many women, have you?"

"I really haven't. I'm sorry."

The situation quickly escalated when, from behind the
bus shelter, a short man dressed entirely in brown leather
popped out. Even the man's fedora hat was apparently made
of brown leather. The man swaggered over to stand beside
the transvestite. A thin mustache graced the man's upper lip,
from below which jutted a huge cigar that reeked of cheap
hotels and sleazy bars.

"Is this bandejo giving you a hard time, Cupcake?"
the little man asked.

"This prick called me a tranny whore, Felipe," replied
Cupcake.

"I didn't say that," Peter said. "I think there's been a
misunderstanding."

"Are you calling Cupcake a *liar?*" asked Felipe with a
malignant scowl. "I think you owe her an apology, cabron."

"I'm sorry, Cupcake. Really, I am."

"Sure," scoffed Cupcake, looking away.

"Whatcha got there?" Felipe asked, referring to the
satellite Peter cradled in his arms, still wrapped in his
Christmas kitty sweater.

"This? Oh, it's nothing."

"Looks like something to me, sweetheart," Cupcake
said. "Why don't you let us have a look?"

Peter hesitated. Cupcake reached for the satellite.
Felipe pulled a switchblade out of his pocket and released the
blade with the push of a button. He held the weapon
menacingly.

"I think you better let my lady have a look,
homeboy," Felipe sneered.

The moment was tense, the danger palpable. Peter
understood that his options were limited. He considered

running. He considered yelling for help. Instead, he chose to do what seemed to be the only sensible thing – he started unwrapping the satellite. Cupcake and Felipe leaned in expectantly. Peter slowly peeled away the sweater. Cupcake and Felipe were on the figurative edge of their seats. Their eyes grew wide.

Just as Peter was about to fully reveal the mysterious object, the satellite suddenly came to life. It emitted a series of shrill beeps. Small LED lights on its metallic silver exterior began flashing in an enigmatic sequence. Cupcake and Felipe jumped back in terror.

"It's a bomb!" Cupcake shrieked.

"This dude is *loco!*" cried Felipe. "Run, Kenny! Get the fuck out of here!" In his panic, Felipe had inadvertently referred to Cupcake by the name she had been given at birth. It was a natural mistake.

Cupcake and Felipe got the fuck out of there in a hurry. Peter watched in disbelief as the pair ran up the sidewalk into a large bush like two children who had just seen a rabid, mutant hellhound. The satellite in his hands continued beeping loudly. The lights around its circumference flashed and flickered. Peter stared at the device, fascinated.

Many miles away, the men in the black helicopter monitored a screen mounted to the dashboard of the highly advanced aircraft. The signal they had been watching had suddenly changed. The small, dim blip had become a large, rapidly pulsing orb.

"We have increased activity," the co-pilot said to the pilot. "Looks like the birdie has awakened."

Ominous!

Just as suddenly as it had burst to life, the satellite in Peter's hands went silent and the lights ceased flashing. The loud and dazzling display was now over. Peter did not speculate on the meaning of what had just occurred. He simply wrapped the satellite up again in the old sweater.

Just ahead, at the end of the block, Peter could see the brown brick facade of Mighty Pawn, the largest pawn shop in the city and the primary destination of our intrepid adventurer on this atypical and lively day. Peter, as is his way, was able to almost instantly brush off the unsettling encounter with Cupcake and Felipe and go about his business. His resilience is admirable, but his testing was not yet over.

*What more could possible happen before Peter finally reaches the pawn shop*, you might ask? Much, *much* more, actually. He could step into an open manhole, for instance. A bird could poop on him, or a dog could appear out of nowhere and bite him on the rear. Have you ever tripped on a crack in the sidewalk? It's very embarrassing when people are watching. Any of these things could happen to him, couldn't they? Something outlandish could occur – something so bizarre that even in the context of this story, it would be difficult to swallow. He could simply run into someone he really doesn't want to see. Well, none of these things happened.

Peter walked the rest of the block and finally arrived at Mighty Pawn. He pushed open the heavy, reinforced door and stepped in. Even for one who has visited before, entering Mighty Pawn can be quite an experience. The sheer amount of *stuff* inside boggles the mind. The building itself covers nearly half of a city block, and practically every square inch of its voluminous interior is occupied by used merchandise. It is a junk lover's Mecca, a knick-knack fanatic's dream, a second-hand paradise.

One must squeeze through overflowing racks of power tools upon entering. This was a challenge for our rotund friend Peter, but he did so as carefully as he could. He passed through the first gauntlet and arrived at the electronics section, a chaotic jumble of devices and appliances arranged in vague categories – a stack of DVD players in one area, stacked TVs in another, and microwaves, blenders, toasters, and other contraptions piled in disorderly fashion in all available spaces. Claustrophobia clawed at Peter's brain, which was on the verge of total sensory overload, but he fought it off and bravely soldiered on.

Peter successfully traversed the electronics department and found himself among racks of DVDs and CDs – thousands of them, it seemed. Row upon row, it was as if Might Pawn had a copy, or multiple copies, of every single movie and album that had ever been released. This was Peter's favorite section. He salivated at the thought of all the hours of entertainment contained within those walls. We know Peter really enjoys food, but he gets nearly as much pleasure from some good ol' watchin', and there sure was some quality watchin' material gathered on the shelves of Mighty Pawn! Browsing would have to wait until another visit, though. Peter was still on a mission.

"Can I help you?"

The question snapped Peter's reverie. He wiped his drooling mouth and said, "Huh?"

"Can I help you? Are you looking for something?"

The man who addressed Peter was standing behind a large counter at the back of the pawn shop. It was Slick Rick, Peter realized. This was the man he had walked all the way downtown to see. The walls on either side of the counter were covered in gun racks. Semi-automatic rifles of a multitude of varieties hung on the racks, giving this section of the shop the appearance of an armory. The counter behind which Slick Rick stood also served as a glass display case. The display case was full of handguns.

Peter approached the counter as Slick Rick polished a

lethal-looking, military-style rifle. You might not be surprised to find out that Slick Rick is quite a character himself. At 300 pounds, he is even larger than Peter. An NRA T-shirt barely contained his bulging gut, and his substantial arms jiggled like a seal's belly as he stroked the weapon. He kept his hair short and his face clean-shaven, so his oval head looked somewhat like a giant egg perched on a skin pillow – the skin pillow being his abnormally massive neck, of course.

"I have something I thought you might be interested in," said Peter. "I think it could be worth a lot of money."

"Is that so?" replied Slick Rick. "Well, I'll be the judge of that."

Peter laid his bundle on the counter and peeled away the sweater. Slick Rick kept his eyes on the rifle he was cleaning and showed no interest in what Peter was presenting to him.

"I think it's a satellite," Peter said. "You know, from space or some shit. It crashed into my TV. Look at all these fancy thingies on it. It's gotta be worth something, right?"

Despite Slick Rick's feigned ambivalence, Peter's words managed to intrigue him enough that he momentarily stopped what he was doing and glanced over at the object sitting on the counter. After getting a glimpse, he quickly resumed the ritualistic and highly suggestive act of cleaning the large rifle.

"Hmm," muttered Slick Rick. "Interesting. So what do you want for it? Keep in mind that the thing is probably broken, and there's really not much of a market for satellites, you know."

"I need a new TV. I was hoping to get one of those nice flat screen models."

"Ha," scoffed Slick Rick. "I doubt this thing is worth *that* much."

The truth is, Slick Rick was highly interested in the

rare and unusual piece of technology. If it was indeed what he suspected it might be, he knew of people in underground, deep black markets who would pay generously for such a device. It was not the first time an object of enigmatic origin had appeared in his shop. Petrified dinosaur eggs, prosthetic limbs, shrunken heads, and religious artifacts had all, at one time or another, passed through the Mighty Pawn doors. Someone once tried to pawn a toilet seat that Richard Nixon had supposedly sat on while in office... but that's another story.

In *this* story, things are about to take a turn for the surreal. You've stuck with me this far, and I appreciate that, so bear with me while this tale resolves itself in the only appropriate way. Hang on – it could get a little zany.

As Slick Rick was being his usual slick self, a startling transformation occurred. Right in front of Peter's eyes, in the middle of their conversation, Slick Rick's demeanor suddenly changed. His face went slack and his mouth fell open. His body sagged and he dropped the rag that he had been using to polish the gun. His eyes assumed a spooky, distant quality, as if someone had simply turned out the lights – instant catatonia.

"Hey," Peter said, "are you alright?"

Like an abandoned shell, Rick remained motionless and unresponsive. Peter began to get nervous. He reached over, gently poked Slick Rick in the shoulder and said, "Um, hello? Are you in there?"

Slick Rick jolted at the touch. He suddenly sat up on the stool on which he had been seated, his back rigid, his posture stiff. His huge, round head wobbled as his now bulging, protuberant eyes struggled to focus on what was in front of him. His fat lips flapped grotesquely as his mouth attempted to form words. Peter observed this freaky development with slight concern. He thought perhaps Slick

Rick was suffering from a bad case of heartburn, or at the worst, a minor stroke. He was wrong on both counts – oh, so very, very wrong.

"Rick, buddy... you don't look so good. Should I call an ambulance?"

Slick Rick's lips ceased flapping and his eyes locked on Peter's with furious intensity. He spoke, but the voice that boomed out of his throat was no longer his own:

"Fool! It is *you* who will require the ambulance – and a body bag!"

"What? Why? I just thought we were negotiating."

"Idiot! Imbecile! You have no idea what you have gotten yourself into, do you? You shall soon pay for your folly."

"I thought we were cool, Rick. I know I'm not a *regular* customer, but I've given you my fair share of business."

"Rick is dead, you ignorant heap of feces."

The entity that had assumed control of Slick Rick's body reached for the satellite and said, "For the glory of the hive, the device is ours once again!"

Peter reacted with surprising swiftness. He snatched the satellite just before the entity's hands closed around it. It was quick thinking and a smooth move. His mother would have been proud of him.

"I don't know what the hell is going on around here," Peter said, "but I think I should hold on to this for now."

"Foolish mortal!" the entity bellowed. "We're going to suck the soul out of your meat and throw your carcass to the drones!"

Peter didn't like the sound of that. He started toward the exit, clutching the satellite close to his chest. Behind him now, the entity rose from the stool. It had every intention of pursuing and incapacitating Peter, but, unfortunately for the entity, it had chosen to inhabit the body of a very unhealthy man.

Grunting and wheezing, the entity attempted to maneuver the cumbersome flesh vessel out from behind the counter. It was an ordeal! The entity managed to squeeze past the counter, but it had underestimated the true girth of the man it wore. Slick Rick's gigantic ass slammed into a rack of ammunition, which toppled over onto a life-size mannequin in full tactical gear. The mannequin bounced against a wall before falling into the glass display counter. The display counter shattered, sending glass fragments flying in all directions. As the entity tried to maintain its balance, it slipped on the glass and fell to the floor with an audible splat.

The sound of the commotion caused Peter to stop. He turned to see the entity rolling around helplessly on the floor. It was trying to get back to its feet, but the excess flesh made it extremely difficult. It flopped and flailed like a beached sea beast. It was a pathetic sight.

"Are you hurt?" Peter asked.

"We're going to eat your eyeballs and devour your guts!" the entity screeched. "We're going to guzzle your blood and gobble your brains!"

"Do you need some help getting up?"

"Fool! Even as I speak, more of us are coming. You'll never leave this place alive!"

There was truth to that statement. What Peter did not know is that just outside, two people were waiting for him – two familiar people, in fact. Here's a hint: one of them is a large and very masculine-looking woman and the other is a small, Hispanic man dressed entirely in brown leather. They are not who they once were, however.

A mile away and closing in fast, the men in the black helicopter continued to track the mysterious device that had instigated this weird saga. The blip on their monitor, which

indicated the satellite's position, had been joined by three
other blinking lights.

"We have hive activity in the area," the co-pilot said.

"We will be at the target in less than a minute," said
the pilot. "Prepare to touch down. Get ready to fight."

Inside Mighty Pawn, Peter decided that he had had
enough of Slick Rick's colorful and gruesome threats. He
would take his business elsewhere, thank you very much.

Peter stepped through the door with the precious
bundle tucked under his arm. The entities who inhabited
Felipe and Kenny... er, *Cupcake*, were waiting in ambush. As
soon as Peter appeared on the sidewalk, Cupcake seized him
from behind. She held him tightly in her formidable grip as
Felipe rushed at him with his blade raised.

"Disgusting mortal!" cried the thing that inhabited
Felipe. "That object you hold in your stinking hands is more
valuable than your feeble brain could possibly comprehend.
Give it to me now and I will kill you quickly."

"Geez," said Peter. "If you want it that bad, you can
have it. I just wanted a new TV."

"Poke his eyes out," snarled the entity inside
Cupcake. "Fillet his face. I hate being in this rotten bag of
meat. He needs to pay for this."

Felipe nodded thoughtfully and said, "That's not a bad
idea. It's been a while since I've tortured a human being. I
should do it just for old times' sake. Remember all the fun we
used to have in the early days of the war, before it got stale?
Those were good times."

"Whoa, buddy," Peter protested, "you don't need to do
that. Just take the damn thing. I don't want it anymore. It's
been nothing but trouble since I found it. Please, just take it."

"Start with his scalp," suggested Cupcake.

Felipe leaned in with his switchblade poised. Just as
he was about to begin peeling away Peter's scalp and rather

greasy hair, the loud whirring of an approaching helicopter caused him, as well as Cupcake and Peter, to look up in unison. The unmarked, black aircraft was coming in from the north fast. It began its descent, headed directly toward the trio gathered outside Mighty Pawn. Cupcake briefly relaxed her grip, allowing Peter to pull away.

"It's *them*," Felipe muttered.

"How did they get here so fast?" Cupcake said. "They must have upgraded their tracking capabilities."

Peter, meanwhile, began to walk calmly away. He did not care about the helicopter or the apparent battle for the mysterious machine. He just wanted to go home. After a day like he'd had, who could blame him?

"The mortal! Stop him!" shouted Cupcake.

Peter slowly turned and placed the satellite on the pavement. He let out a long, deep sigh. "It's yours," he said. "Just let me go. I'm hungry and tired."

"Forget about him," Felipe said. "We don't have time to waste torturing some random *Unaware*. Get the device."

Cupcake rushed over and scooped up the satellite. The helicopter was nearly on top of them now. Felipe had dropped his switchblade and had raised his arms high above his head in a show of defiance. He shook his balled fists at the helicopter and shouted unintelligibly. Peter turned and continued walking up the sidewalk toward home. Cupcake watched him for a moment before turning her attention to the rapidly descending helicopter, the rotors of which were stirring up dirt and debris as it closed in. It stopped and hovered right in front of Felipe.

A loudspeaker mounted on the helicopter crackled to life and a booming voice proclaimed, "There is nowhere to run. Set the device down and move away from it. Failure to comply will result in your destruction."

"Human filth!" shouted Felipe. "You will never

destroy us. We are eternal! We are Legion!"

Peter ignored the exciting scene behind him and casually strolled away. He was already planning his afternoon snack, which he would thoroughly enjoy just as soon as he got home.

What Peter did not see was fairly remarkable. Felipe had begun summoning balls of brilliant, purple plasma energy with his raised hands. He was flinging them at the hovering helicopter. Cupcake had somehow manifested a force field, which she used to shield herself and the device. The helicopter, rocking each time it was hit with a plasma ball, fired blue laser beams at the entities on the ground from a weapon mounted beneath the cockpit. It was a brutal firefight to the death, in broad daylight, right in front of Mighty Pawn.

While the battle raged behind him, Peter rubbed his eyes and yawned. It had been a rough day and he still had a fairly long walk ahead of him. He no longer had a television set, but he wasn't too upset about that any more. He decided that when he got home, he was going to eat an entire pizza while reading comic books. He had earned it.

# Vortex Hunter

When the distinctive red rock formations of Sedona appeared on the horizon, Nigel the Vortex Hunter gasped in amazement. He had finally arrived, and the view was even more spectacular than he had imagined. "I can feel the energy of the cosmos converging on my heart chakra," he said to himself as he entered the city limits. It was mid-morning on a Saturday and the main road was overrun with tourists. Nigel maneuvered through the traffic circles in his cobalt blue Smart car, admiring the town's unusual blend of art galleries and eclectic shops specializing in crystals, psychic readings, and New Age books. There were even places offering UFO and vortex tours, but Nigel had no need for a guide. He considered himself to be an expert in these areas. He had driven all the way from Tucson, lured by the city's reputation as a hub of mysterious and supernatural activity. He was determined to experience something out of this world.

Before he had left home, Nigel had done a tarot reading and compiled multiple astrological charts in order to optimize his chances of success. The auspicious planetary alignments on this particular day indicated that it was an ideal time to begin his adventure. Judging by the harmonious vibrations he could now feel flowing through both his physical and astral bodies as he cruised Sedona's small, pulsing downtown core, his projections had been accurate. "This is going to be a great day," he said. "The Goddess smiles upon my endeavors."

Nigel drove on toward his true destination – Cathedral Rock, a famous landmark in Sedona and the site that he had chosen to explore first. The enigmatic red sandstone formation intrigued him. It was considered to be one of the major vortex sites in the area, and Nigel's intuition (as well as a series of interesting synchronicities) led him to believe that it would be the location where he would finally have an encounter with the paranormal. It would be the fulfillment of his life's dream.

Parking was scarce at Cathedral Rock. It is a popular place for hikers and sight-seers, who can be found in droves on any given day. Luckily, Nigel was able to find a vacant spot close to the trailhead. He parked his car, retrieved his supply-filled backpack from the backseat, and started up the path toward the picturesque rock formation that rose majestically from the ground before him.

Enchanted by the beauty and the nearly mystical nature of the environment, Nigel began hiking. *I have become one with Gaia*, he thought. *May the ascended masters guild me on my journey.* As he passed the other hikers and sight-seers, he inwardly scoffed at their ignorance. They were simply enjoying the nice weather and the pretty views. He, on the other hand, was on a spiritual quest of profound significance. *These poor, unenlightened normies – so ordinary, so one-dimensional, so unevolved...*

Eventually, after some moderately strenuous climbing, Nigel reached a plateau about halfway up the trail to the summit. He turned around to enjoy the gorgeous panorama of the surrounding terrain. He raised his arms, tilted his head back, and let the energy flow through him. *I am a conduit*, he thought. *I am a conscious node in this glorious multiverse. I am one with the Supreme Being.* He filled his lungs with the pure, dry, high-desert air and smiled.

As he was about to move on, Nigel had an idea – or a leap of insight, as he would say. He remembered the crystal that he always wore around his neck. He realized that now was the perfect time to harness its power. He gripped it in his right hand, closed his eyes, and cleared his mind. Nothing happened. *I'm thinking too much,* he thought. *Damn, that was a thought... So was that! Stop thinking! Stop thinking about thinking!*

And then it happened. An image appeared, clear and well-defined. He could see, in his mind's eye, the rock formation that he was on and the trail ahead that branched in two directions at the base of the next rise – the path to the left was illuminated.

Nigel opened his eyes. "Thank you, Spirits of the Rock," he whispered. "I have received the vision and have been shown the way."

More certain than ever that he was being guided toward his destiny, he moved on. When he reached the point where the two paths diverged, he went left. The trail wrapped tightly around Cathedral Rock. There were no other hikers in sight. It was clearly a section of the trail that was seldom, if ever, used. *I bet there's a vortex around here,* Nigel thought. *I wonder if I'll know one when I see one. Hmm, can you see a vortex? What is a vortex, for that matter?*

Nigel was pondering these questions when he noticed something rather peculiar. Up ahead, just a few yards in front of him, a strange haze hung in the air. It was like heat shimmer, only it was localized to a small area directly in his path. The objects beyond the atmospheric anomaly rippled and undulated. Nigel stared in amazement, unable to grasp exactly what he was seeing.

"A touch of heat stroke," he muttered. "I just need some water."

Nigel got the water bottle out of his backpack and took several large gulps. He wiped his eyes and forehead with the bottom of his shirt. "That's better," he said. He took a step forward and paused. The haze was still there, but it seemed to have grown. It was roughly a circle, now a few feet or so in diameter. It remained fixed in position like a persistent mirage.

"That's a bit weird. Maybe I should get back on the main trail."

As he turned to go back the way he had come, Nigel heard something that caused him to freeze in his tracks – the mysterious haze seemed to be emitting a low-level electrical hum. It was faint at first, but rapidly rose in volume. Looking back at the source, Nigel was startled to see that the bizarre shimmer had doubled in size. It was now as wide as the trail and taller than him.

"Holy shit," Nigel said, "is that what I think it is?"

He was freaked out. Despite his fear, he took a step forward. The anomaly was growing and the sound was getting louder. "Namaste," Nigel said. "I come in peace." He slowly approached and, as he did so, he felt an electrical charge begin to course through his body. It was not painful. On the contrary, it was actually quite pleasurable. He summoned his courage and walked right into the haze.

In an instant, he was no longer on the trail at Cathedral Rock. He was no longer outside, even. To his complete astonishment, Nigel was now in what appeared to be the waiting room of a large office building. It was full of people. Some were sitting in the few available seats against the wall while others stood around chatting or flipping through magazines with bored expressions on their faces. A woman behind the receptionist's desk had noticed his arrival. "Hello, sir," she said. "How can I help you?"

Nigel was, at first, too shocked to speak. He stood there with his mouth open.

"Are you okay, sir?" the woman behind the desk asked.

The other people in the waiting room had also taken notice of Nigel. They stared at him as he struggled to gather his thoughts and form a sentence.

"How did I... What in the... Where am I?"

"Poor guy," a lady in a seat nearby said. "I think he's lost."

"You're in the Mid-Sector, buddy," a gruff-looking man standing by the door said. "Don't you know that?"

"I was just hiking. How did I end up here?"

"Sounds like you got lucky... or you're just dumb," replied the man.

"You must have experienced an accidental cross-over," the seated lady said. "It's good that your memories are still intact. That means you still have a chance of getting home."

"The Mid-Sector? Accidental cross-over?" Nigel's brain was reeling. "I have no idea what you people are talking about."

"You're in the zone between worlds," the receptionist said. "This is the staging ground for what happens in the three-dimensional realm – what you normally perceive as reality."

"Ha, no... that's just..." Nigel rubbed his sweaty forehead, as if he was trying to coax his mind into processing the information. "That's just *absurd*."

"I understand your confusion." The receptionist spoke softly and with empathy. "It takes time to fully accept the truth. Everyone here has gone through the same thing. If you'll just fill out this form, someone will see you soon."

The receptionist held out a clipboard. Nigel walked over to the desk, still somewhat in a daze, and took it from her. A seat had opened up. Nigel took the clipboard over to it and sat down. In the chair to his right, an elderly man was fast asleep, snoring loudly with his head against the wall. In the chair to Nigel's left, a young boy was playing with action figures. The boy looked at Nigel and said, "I'm gonna be a policeman in my next life."

"Good for you," said Nigel.

There was a form attached to the clipboard. Nigel studied it, trying to make sense of the cryptic wording. "Soul group? Etheric alignment? Temporal role? What does all of this *mean?*"

"Just answer to the best of your ability," the receptionist said.

"I don't know any of the answers."

"That's unfortunate. Just hang tight and be patient and an agent will see you soon."

"That won't be necessary. If it's all the same to you, I think I'd just like to go home."

"I'm afraid that isn't possible at the moment. You need permission before you can travel between realms."

"Permission? From whom?"

"The Arbiters, of course."

"How did you die?" the boy asked.

"I didn't," Nigel replied. "I must have stepped through a vortex."

"What's a vortex?"

"You know what, little dude? I have no idea. I *thought* I did, but, wow, was I ever wrong."

"You're in luck, sir," the receptionist said. "An agent is available to see you now."

"What?!" cried the burly man by the door. "I've been here for an eternity. Why does *he* get to see someone so quick?"

"The agency gives priority to those who experience transitional aberrations. For the good of the multiverse, they require immediate attention. Thank you for your continued patience."

"Whatever," grumbled the man.

The receptionist pointed to a set of doors beside her

desk and addressed Nigel: "Go through these doors and turn left. Head down the hall until you see a bank of photon teleporters. Take the blue beam. When you get to the next level, turn left and walk until you see the plasma fountain. Directly across from that is the molecular discombobulater. Push the red button to open the hatch. Step inside and activate the device. Once you have been reassembled, step out and turn right. Go down that hall and take the first red beam on the left. That will take you directly to the agent's office. Good luck and have a great day."

"You have got to be kidding me," Nigel said. "There's no way I'll remember that."

"Somehow you ended up here," the receptionist smiled. "That's no minor feat. Trust your instincts and you'll be fine."

"My instincts are telling me that I am having a psychotic episode."

"I can assure you that you are not. Speak with an agent. They will help you get home."

Nigel decided to take his chances beyond the door. He had no choice, really. "Alright, then," he said as he pushed the door open and walked through. He was now in a long corridor lit by rows of fluorescent lights. He tried to retain the instructions the receptionist had given him, but the words were already jumbled in his head. "Left at the photon fountain..." he mumbled. "Right at the blue beam... No, *left* at the blue beam when you see the corporeal disambiguater... Ah, shit. I can't remember."

Nigel stood in the empty hall feeling completely lost and very alone. He looked back at the door he had come though and considered going back to ask the receptionist for help again, but he was too embarrassed. With a sad shake of his head and a pitiful sigh, he walked down the hall. He was going to try and find the agent's office on his own.

After a few spooky minutes of walking down the empty and uncannily silent corridor, Nigel came to the first junction. He gritted his teeth and mumbled, "Left, right... what did she say again?" He looked both ways, hoping to see something that would jar his memory, but the hall appeared empty and featureless in both directions. "Trust your instincts. She did say that." Nigel turned right and almost ran directly into someone who was coming from the other way.

"Whoa!" cried Nigel as he stumbled over the small man who had seemingly appeared out of nowhere. "I didn't see you there."

"No one ever does."

"Hey, little dude. Can you help me get home?"

"Where's home?"

"Tucson."

"Too-sawn what?"

"Tucson, Arizona."

"You're fucked."

"What?"

The creepy little man scampered away. He oozed around the corner with a sneaky smile and an obscene gesture. Nigel watched, perplexed and amused. The little man disappeared and Nigel was again alone in the corridor. He looked up at the fluorescent lights, hoping for a sign. The tubes glowed in anxious yellow. Nigel moved down the corridor like a worm drawn by spring rain until he breached the membrane at the far side.

"That was interesting," Nigel said "I must be getting close."

Nigel was beginning to experience some rather disconcerting sensory distortions. The hall in which he was standing was flickering in and out of focus. He could perceive multiple, overlapping backgrounds vying for the alpha position. They cycled rapidly – a dank, basement dungeon, a lavishly decorated hotel lobby, a sterile medical clinic, a warm, rustic wilderness resort – each briefly visible before fading into the next.

Nigel tightened his grip on the dominant reality. "I need to get home," he reminded himself. His focus returned to the corridor and he saw before him two vertical beams of colored light – one red and one blue. "Now what?" he said. "I guess I have to choose. They always make you choose." The receptionist's instructions had totally escaped him. He was operating now on pure intuition. He stepped into the blue beam.

"Are you looking for the Arbiters?" The voice came to him before he had fully materialized. He attempted to reply, but his voice and mind were not in sync. When the reconfiguration was complete, he found himself on what appeared to be a movie set. There was a camera crew, a director, and a mock-up of a Civil War battlefield, complete with actors in full costume. Nigel had inadvertently disrupted the scene. "Yes," he said, embarrassed and apologetic. "I'm sorry. I must have gone the wrong way."

"Don't worry about it," said the director. "It happens a lot."

"I'll just let myself out. Excuse me."

Nigel turned around, expecting to see the beam on which he had just traveled. There was nothing there but a brick wall. The director could see Nigel's confusion. "It's a little disorienting, I know," he said. "What you're going to want to do is summon a spectral familiar to take you back to the main facility. From there you'll be able to access the portals again."

"Summon a *what?*"

"You really *are* lost, aren't you? I'll just do it for you."

The director mumbled some weird words and made an arcane gesture with his hands. Nigel yelped and took a step backward as a ghostly, formless mass appeared before him.

"There's your ride," the director said. "Good luck."

"I don't know what I'm supposed to do," said Nigel. His voice cracked when he spoke, making him sound like a nervous teenager.

"Just walk into it and visualize where you want to go."

"I want to go home."

"The Arbiters can help you."

Nigel did as he was told. He envisioned his apartment in Tucson and walked into the suspended fog. It enveloped him, tightening around his body like the embrace of a lover. The pleasure Nigel felt was a pleasant surprise. He closed his eyes involuntarily and moaned. When the mist released him, he opened his eyes. He was standing in the living room of his apartment. "Oh, God," he said. "Thank you." The relief was immeasurable.

Exhausted, Nigel stumbled down the hall toward his bedroom. His bed was waiting just around the corner. He flicked the light switch and froze in his tracks. There was someone in his bed. He could see the distinct outline of a person curled up with the covers over his or her head. Fearful at first that the intruder could be dangerous, Nigel simply stared for a few moments at the human lump on his bed. He then picked up a lamp from the bedside table, gripped it with both hands in a defensive stance, and shouted, "Hey! Wake up! Get out of here now or I'm going to call the police."

There was no reply.

"HEY!" he yelled even louder. "This is *my* apartment!" An irrational, violent impulse rippled through him. It intensified when Nigel heard himself speak. "How did you get in here?!" He raised the lamp, ready to bring it smashing down on the skull of the intruder.

The figure under the sheets shifted slightly, but remained covered and unresponsive. Nigel walked over to the bed. He roughly yanked the covers back and exposed the sleeping man beneath. The man did not wake up. Instead, he went on snoring loudly, his back to Nigel, as if he hadn't heard or felt a thing. Nigel reached over with one hand, ready to swing the lamp with the other, and grasped the man's shoulder. He pulled hard, flipping the man onto his back. When Nigel saw the man's face, he screamed. It was his own. The man in the bed was him.

Nigel stood there, paralyzed, stupefied, uncomprehending. His mind went silent, as if his brain could no longer process the data it was receiving. It took a full three minutes before Nigel could function once more, and all he could do then was whimper. *I've lost it*, he thought. *It finally happened. I am now totally insane.* The Nigel on the bed remained peacefully asleep.

The Nigel standing in the room with tears in his eyes and a lamp in his hand began to experience an interesting transformation. He had relinquished control and his capitulation had paradoxically freed him, though he was not yet aware of it. He remembered something he had read in one of his New Age books. *It's all maya*, he thought. *It's all an illusion.*

Instantly, in a flash of pure, white light, Nigel was transported once again. When his vision recovered from the glare, he found himself sitting in a chair in a tidy, professional office. There was a desk in front of him, on the other side of which sat a pretty woman with a kind face. She was smiling at him. Nigel realized immediately that he was back in the Mid-Sector facility.

"Hello, Nigel," the woman said. "How can I help you?"

"Are you an Arbiter?"

"Yes, I am."

"Oh, thank God."

"I understand that you are having some trouble. Would you care to explain what is happening?"

"*Explain?* I wish I could. I have no idea what is even real right now."

"You are real. That's a good place to start."

"I'll have to take your word for it. All I *do* know is that I went hiking in Sedona this morning – at least, I think it was this morning. Time seems to have lost all meaning – and then suddenly I found myself in *this* place."

"Ah, Sedona." The Arbiter nodded knowingly. "That actually explains a lot. You aren't the first person to cross over accidentally from that location. It is well known for its timespace fluctuations."

"I was looking for vortices."

"Congratulations on your success! You must be thrilled."

"That's not the word I would have chosen. To be honest, I wasn't ready for what I found."

"No one ever is. At least you were seeking. I admire your courage and curiosity."

"I just want to go home. I'm a coward." Nigel immediately regretted saying that.

The Arbiter's countenance reassured him. "Fair enough," she said. "I can make that happen. It was nice to meet you, Nigel. I wish you all the best in your future endeavors."

The Arbiter smiled. Nigel smiled.

The Arbiter fulfilled her role.

Cathedral Rock was golden in the afternoon sun. Nigel was back on the trail. It was warm, serene, and familiar. The high desert air welcomed him. The heat was pure and revitalizing. Nigel gazed at his surroundings, marveling at the extraordinary landscape. The vista before him seemed more vibrant and alive than before he had discovered the vortex. This world was his home. It was real and he knew it. He looked down upon the parking lot and saw his cobalt blue Smart car waiting to take him home. Before beginning the short descent, Nigel glanced back. Where he had originally seen the shimmering anomaly, there was now only trail. Nigel, remembering how eager and arrogant he had been when he started his journey, chuckled and shook his head. "I've got a lot to learn," he said as he started down the path.

# The Streets

The streets have secrets. They traverse a realm that belongs to the misunderstood, disenfranchised souls who wander the trash-strewn alleys and vacant lots of a world lying parallel to our own – a hidden universe of lost, desperate men, junkies and artists, broken messiahs and park bench philosophers. For the homeless, the streets are a jungle, a battlefield. Few people enter this world and escape to share their stories. Life on the streets is a difficult but simplified version of life in regular society. One imperative governs existence: survival.

Timothy MacGregor was, less than a year ago, a successful cog in the machinery of a prosperous advertising firm in a large, western Canadian city. He held a management position. He made a lot of money. He lived alone in a high-rise loft overlooking the ocean. He was fast becoming a legend in the competitive advertising market.

Timothy's social life was the envy of many of his peers. As a bachelor, he enjoyed all the pleasures and benefits of young success. He was a regular fixture on the downtown nightlife scene, cavorting with adoring women and consuming large amounts of booze and drugs.

In the early years of Timothy's escapades, substances were an exciting, even useful, aspect of his party lifestyle – total entertainment, celebratory and exploratory. In short time, however, Timothy developed a problem. Some people are able to use alcohol and narcotics liberally with no lasting, adverse consequences. Some become addicts. The mysterious combination of genetic and environmental influences that distinguishes the addict from the non-addict was present in Timothy's life. It was inevitable, with prolonged use, that he would eventually become an abuser. This happened much quicker than anyone could have predicted.

Cocaine was Timothy's drug of choice. He *loved* it. He loved the way it looked, all white and sparkly like the snow in a fairy tale. He loved playing with it, pushing around the powder with a razor blade on a small mirror. He loved the way it tasted when he snorted thick, expensive lines up his never-satiated nose. Most of all he loved the way it felt when it reached his brain and ignited the pleasure centers in his head like electrical storm microbursts.

The progression, the escalation, the erosion of Timothy's will – from the occasional line while out dancing to a nightly routine – transitioned from a daily ritual to an all-consuming obsession. Vials of powder gave way to pipes and lighters. Timothy went from crackhead to needle junkie, and downward still. Once a paragon of youthful success, he was now a frightening, cautionary story of tragedy and self-destruction.

Timothy lost his job, his home, and eventually his self-respect... but never his taste for the drug. Cocaine was his 'Ol' Reliable,' always there to pick him up when he needed it. His habit drew him to the streets, where, with a little ingenuity, he could sustain his consumption with an always-available supply of cheap and powerful chemicals.

Much like combat, survival on the streets, especially for an addict, depends on fellowship and on establishing and maintaining trustworthy relationships. Timothy tried to live as a loner during his early days of homelessness. Violence, ever present, lurking around every corner and at the end of every deal, soon found him.

"You ripped me off, man! There's no *way* that's a twenty piece." In a filthy city park bathroom, Timothy argued with a wiry, sketchy-looking character who had been the middleman in a small transaction, the kind of transaction that happens every few minutes in environments such as this. The subject of the argument was a tiny bag of crack cocaine. The white, rock-like substance was no larger than a pea, and even smaller than Timothy had expected.

"It is what it is," said the twitchy, scabby little man who had brought the drugs. He scratched at his jaw as he spoke. "Take it or leave it."

"I already gave you my money. What choice do I have?"

Timothy craved the drug. Despite his protests, he knew in his heart that he would indeed be taking the crack, rip-off or not, and consuming it as soon as he had a chance. He had been up for three days and nights already, smoking, swindling, scamming, and sinking ever-deeper into the depths of paranoid psychosis. He was desperate to stay high, desperate to avoid the inevitable crash of the comedown.

"Shit," Timothy said. He snatched up the bag of drugs and turned for the bathroom door, in his head already preparing his pipe and ready to take the next hit. "You little weasel," he said under his breath as he neared the door.

"What did you just say?" The runner had heard him. "Is there something you want to say to me? Say it to my face, goof."

Timothy then made a mistake. He turned to face the other man and said, "*You're* the goof," looking him directly in the eye.

The punch came swiftly and hit its mark precisely. For a little man, the runner could hit *hard*. The blow struck Timothy on the chin, on the 'button,' as pugilists like to say, rendering him unconscious instantly. Timothy collapsed in a heap before he knew what had happened. "Fool," said his attacker as he knelt and relieved Timothy of the drugs over which they had just argued.

Timothy languished in oblivion for close to an hour

before he awoke. On regaining consciousness, his first thought was concern for his drugs. With a panicky hand he clawed at his pockets and at the floor on which he lay. "That little *shit*," he said, getting to his feet. He was neither surprised nor entirely angry. Part of taking on the role of full-time drug addict is a serious case of terminal resignation. It came with the territory.

Stepping out of the dingy restroom and into the afternoon sun was disconcerting. Timothy shielded his hypersensitive eyes from the glare with one hand and stroked his throbbing chin with the other. Blood oozed from an open gash. Timothy scanned the park, looking for someone he knew, someone he could trust. *Trust,* he thought. *That's laughable.*

Timothy still craved cocaine – powder, rock – it didn't matter. He just needed a fix. He wandered the park, scheming. He passed a group of heroin addicts sprawled under a tree in a quiet corner of the park. A few were passed out – on the nod – and the rest were openly injecting. They were a frightful group – gaunt, yellow-skinned, and dead-eyed. Those who were still conscious watched him pass with vacant expressions. They looked like the living dead, skeletal mannequins with leathery, human skin masks. They were creepy, even to Timothy. He walked by without a word.

Not far past the opiate users, clustered around a different tree, were the meth heads. Timothy knew a few of them, but generally avoided spending too much time in their company. They were a volatile, unpredictable bunch. He was recognized as he approached.

"Yo, Timmy!" yelled one of the tweakers. It was Sleaze, a rowdy but affable middle-aged user whom Timothy had met when he first started spending time with the other homeless people in the park. Sleaze had moved to the west from the east coast to work in the oil fields. He had developed a taste for amphetamines, as did many oil workers, which eventually led to him losing his job and entering the life of full-time addict.

"Hey, Sleaze," Timothy said. "How's it going, you crazy Newfie?"

"Brah, it's *all* good," replied Sleaze. He had the typically thick, distinctive, and almost totally indecipherable accent of a Newfoundlander. "Wanna hit, brah? Come wit us – get *high*." Though nominally tempted, Timothy resisted. He preferred cocaine. Meth, and its users, scared him.

"Nah. Thanks, though." Timothy walked on, never slowing his pace.

"Nasty cut on yer chin dere, buddy!" Sleaze called out.

"Yup."

In the grimy underbelly of the city, finding people you can trust is difficult. Timothy's thoughts wandered to his old life of safety, success, and privilege. From the park, Timothy could clearly see the high-rises of downtown towering into the sky. He could even distinguish the buildings he once lived and worked in – so near, yet a virtual eternity away. He reflected on the life he once led and struggled to feel anything... except the inarticulate madness of the addict's appetite. "I need a hit," he muttered.

Evening had come. The sun was quickly setting. Timothy was getting increasingly desperate. It occurred to him that a meal would soon be served at a nearby soup kitchen. At that particular rescue mission, the food was generally quite good and the meals attracted a large portion of the city's homeless population. It was always a good place to mingle with the other inhabitants of the streets. Timothy wondered if he could perhaps score something there, even just a little bit to get him through the rest of the night.

Timothy walked two blocks to the mission in the

peaceful twilight, his thoughts erratic and restless. There was an unpleasant, nauseous sensation swirling in his torso. He kept moving, pumping his legs mechanically. He hummed an indistinct tune in an effort to distract himself. It did not work very well.

Soon, he was in front of the rescue mission, the warm light of its interior spilling out onto the sidewalk and illuminating the ragtag mob of homeless, addicted, and mentally-ill people gathered outside. Timothy steeled himself as he merged with the crowd.

As he walked among them, Timothy surveyed the faces of the men and women who had congregated for the evening meal. An incredibly diverse group of people with disparate backgrounds and experiences frequented the mission, young and old, male and female, people of all races, temperament and demeanor, all with stories to tell, united by a shared history of hardship.

"Tim!" called a voice from the crowd. It was Keith, a regular at the mission and one of the first people Timothy had met when he began living on the streets. Keith was a 40-something hippy with a robust beard, long, matted hair, and a perpetual, goofy grin. He wore glasses with lens nearly an inch thick. His clothes were always filthy and he smoked pot constantly. Timothy could see him coming toward him now, leaning forward as he walked, eyes squinting, balled fists swinging at his side. He was a comical character, one of the few people Timothy trusted on the streets.

"Hey, buddy," Keith said. "Where ya been? Haven't seen you in a few days."

"Yeah, well... you know. Kinda got carried away with the..."

"Hittin' the pipe again, eh? That stuff is *nasty*. Look at these people..." Keith gestured to the crowd gathered around them. "You want to be one of *them?* What a bunch of *bugs.*"

He made no effort to lower his voice or hide his disdain.

"Stick with me," Keith said. "I've got it all figured out. I'm basically a dog, ya know? You can learn a lot from dogs. They don't need much to be happy, and neither do I. Give me a hole in the dirt to sleep in, some smoke, some scraps of food – that's all I need."

"Where have you been sleeping? Here, at the shelter?" Timothy asked.

"Fuck, no! Got a spot on the mountain," Keith replied. "Like I said, man, I'm a dog. I like sleeping outside in the open air. You should join me sometime. Once you learn to sleep outside you've got nothing left to fear, man."

Timothy nodded. "It's probably better than spending the night in this place." When he wasn't out all night chasing a high, Timothy had been sleeping on a cot in the mission for the last three months.

"The last night I spent in there was terrible," Timothy recalled. "The stench was *unbearable.* I never knew BO could be so bad until I slept in a shelter. Just a rancid, rotten smell. And the sounds! Ugh! All night – cough, cough, hack, hack... and the wet, repulsive snoring of a hundred sick and dirty men. Just horrible."

Keith laughed, a distinctive, high-pitched hyena's howl. "I know, buddy. How can you stand it?" Keith adjusted his glasses and squinted. He had once told Timothy that he was legally blind. The thick lenses distorted his eyes into exaggerated, bulging, bloodshot orbs. "Come to the hill with me tonight. I'll show you where I sleep."

Before Timothy could reply, a sudden, violent scuffle erupted beside them. Two men were swinging wildly at each other, both obviously highly intoxicated, their blows clumsy, inaccurate, and awkward. Timothy and Keith took a few steps back to give the combatants a little space. The brawlers fell drunkenly on top of each other. A few more dispirited punches were exchanged while they lay on the sidewalk, then the fight was over. The crowd, who had watched the silly bout dispassionately, went back to whatever it was they were doing.

"As I was saying," Keith continued, "after dinner you should hike up the hill with me. I've got a great secluded spot overlooking the city."

Equilibrium was returning to Timothy's brain. The intense craving for cocaine was subsiding. The relief he felt was tempered by the knowledge that, soon enough, the desire to get high would no doubt return. It was a rhythmic thing, a waveform trick of the mind. Timothy had little control over where his thoughts went – but where his thoughts went, his body soon followed.

For now, though, he felt okay. It was good to just stand with Keith and the others and wait for a warm meal. An unexpected feeling of belonging warmed his heart. There was kinship here. Abandoned by their blood relatives, many street people found new families on the streets. With nowhere else to go and with no one else to trust, the homeless often found refuge and solace in shelters and rescue missions, taking comfort in the company of those who shared the experience of living on the streets.

A line was forming outside the mission, the patrons anticipating admittance. The regulars had done this countless times and organized themselves automatically, like nodes of a hive mind. Timothy and Keith fell into place.

"Smells like meatloaf," Timothy said.

"Smells like *ass*." Keith's face distorted in an exaggerated grimace.

The heavy door at the entrance to the mission opened. The volunteer manning the door ushered people in. The line moved forward in a practiced, orderly fashion. Food was served in a cafeteria-style setting. Trays were provided at the counter. Volunteers scooped, scraped, and piled food cooked by other volunteers. The whole operation depended entirely on donations. Soup and sandwiches were standard lunch fare. The evening meal consisted of whatever was available in the pantry, but was generally warm and hearty. The entrée on this particular evening was, indeed, the much maligned meatloaf.

Timothy and Keith reached the counter and were served. They took their trays to a nearby table and sat in the first available seats. They were promptly joined by others. The table quickly filled.

"Busy tonight," Timothy observed.

"Getting close to the end of the month," Keith said. "Everyone spent their welfare checks on booze and drugs."

Keith, despite his proclamation concerning the smell of the food, immediately began shoveling meatloaf into his mouth. He ate in a manner similar to the way he lived – like a dog. He made loud grunting noises as he chewed. Chunks of food spilled out of his mouth and gathered in his tangled beard.

Timothy laughed. "Hungry, eh?" he said. Watching Keith eat was disgusting, but also rather amusing. Keith ignored the comment and focused on delivering meatloaf from plate to mouth.

A man who had taken a seat across from them spoke: "Hey, you guys hear about Ol' Joe?"

Keith's curiosity was piqued. He stopped eating to catch up on the street gossip. "No," he said, "what about him?"

The other man, a regular at the mission, replied, "He OD'd last night. They found him lying in the grass at the park this morning, stiff and cold, with a needle still in his arm. Poor guy."

Keith and Timothy had known Joe. He was a heroin addict who had been on the streets for years. He had been no older than they were, but looked positively ancient due to prolonged drug abuse.

"Bummer," Keith said. "I just talked to him last night. I *told* him the needle would get him! Damn." He turned to face Timothy, his face suddenly dead serious. "See," he said with intensity, "the hard stuff will kill you."

"HELL! THIS IS *HELL!!!*" a woman suddenly screamed at a table near the back wall. Everyone in the room turned to look as she stood up, threw her tray against the wall, and began clawing at her face. "Sick! Evil! Oh, no, God! HELP ME!!!" She was in serious mental distress. Her fingernails drew blood from her cheeks as she began weeping. Staff members moved in quickly in an attempt to restrain her.

"There she goes again," Keith said as he rolled his eyes. "Every night, like frickin' clockwork."

"Cops will be here soon," said the man who had informed the table of Ol' Joe's passing, "and I have warrants." He was up and out the door in a flash.

Keith went back to his meatloaf. Timothy was shaken. "I'm coming with you tonight," he said to Keith. "I need to get away from this place."

"Good!" Keith cried, meatloaf raining from his mouth.

When they finished eating, they went outside to have a cigarette. Timothy's thoughts once again turned to drugs. Keith, he knew, did not do cocaine. He smoked pot by the baleful, but avoided the 'hard stuff.' "That shit is for the *bugs,*" he often cautioned Timothy. 'Bugs' was the term he used when referring to all the other street people. He had somehow developed a superiority complex.

Timothy and Keith puffed on their cigarettes and stood among the denizens of the street. The evening meal was over and the night was about to swallow them up in its secret, dangerous chambers. While mainstream society slept, madness, desperation, and depravity ruled the streets.

"There it is, buddy," said Keith, pointing to a small mountain in the distance. "That's mine. I marked it." To demonstrate exactly what he meant by 'marked,' Keith pantomimed urinating on the ground. "You're welcome to join me, though. My spot is secret, but I trust you."

There was truth in that statement. Somehow, despite his association with cocaine and its users, Timothy had gained Keith's trust. There was mutual admiration between the two. They had bonded instantly. Although they were from entirely different backgrounds, they had developed a strong friendship.

The impulse to stay on the streets and get high was strong, but Timothy felt the mountain calling him. It was a powerful draw – raw, primal magnetism.

"Let's do it," Timothy said.

The duo set out on their hike in the late evening hours. The mountains were ominous, imposing silhouettes on the horizon. A nearly-full moon hung in the sky, bathing the walkers in a cool, electric blue aura.

"It takes about an hour to get there," Keith said. "Hope that's okay with you."

"Whoa. I didn't realize it was so far."

"I like to keep my distance from the city at night. I feel safer up there, away from the bugs." Keith laughed his hyena cackle. "Sleeping on the street can get you robbed... or whacked. I'd rather take my chances with nature."

Timothy nodded. It made sense. His chin still ached from the assault he had suffered earlier in the day.

On their way to the hill, Timothy and Keith walked through a residential neighborhood close to the city limits. The streets were eerily quiet. As they approached a large, rustic home on the corner, Keith pointed at the patio. "I got caught in the rain once on my way to the hill," he said. "I had to take cover under that patio, behind the firewood. I was just going to wait out the storm, but I got so comfortable I fell asleep and was there all night. I woke up in the morning to some guy kicking me in the side. 'Fuckin' bum!' he was yelling. I scrambled out of there pretty damn quick." Keith cackled again. He was enjoying the walk and the conversation.

"It's hard on the streets," Timothy said. "People just don't understand."

Keith took his glasses off and wiped them on his dirty sweater. Timothy could see just how visually impaired Keith was. His eyes had a cloudy, distant appearance.

"You know, I've been homeless for almost ten years now," Keith reflected. "One thing I've noticed is that people are, for the most part, good. The straight people, the junkies, the prostitutes, the crazies – everyone *wants* to be good, *wants* to be liked. We're all just doing the best we can given what we've got."

"I've met some truly nasty people, though," Timothy said. "Mean, cruel, vicious, *evil* people."

"Desperation brings out the best – and the worst – in us," Keith mused. "I've seen things on the street that would turn your stomach – brutal, destructive, yes, downright *evil* stuff... but I've also seen beauty, magic, real compassion and brotherhood. People on the streets take *care* of each other. There is genuine humanity on the streets."

They were nearing a gas station, beyond which lay only wilderness, foothills, and their destination, the small mountain Keith called home. "We should stop and get something to eat," Keith said. "Got any money?"

Timothy had a few dollars. It was money he had set aside for his habit, but the further they walked from the city, the less he craved the drug. "Yeah, a little," he said.

They entered the convenience store. The young man behind the counter looked up from his magazine, a scowl contorting his face. He said something under his breath, which sounded to Timothy suspiciously like, "Fuckin' bums." Keith had either not heard it or was unaffected by the insult. "Hey, buddy!" he called to the cashier with a smile and a wave.

"You really don't care what people think, do you?" Timothy said.

"Of course not!" Keith laughed. "Why would I? You can't please everyone." He gestured at the cashier and, without bothering to lower his voice, said, "Do you really think I care what a convenience store cashier thinks about me? Fuck, no!" The cashier's scowl deepened, but he remained silent and went back to his magazine.

Timothy admired Keith's total disregard for the opinions of other people. It was as if Keith had discovered the secret of true freedom – he had extricated himself from a mental prison. For Timothy, it was a revelation.

Timothy counted the change in his pocket. "I've got enough for some bread and bologna," he announced.

"Gourmet!" Keith exclaimed with glee. Timothy gathered the items and approached the counter. The cashier completed the transaction without a word, contempt radiating from his reproachful eyes. Keith and Timothy left the store and resumed their walk.

"You never told me how you ended up on the streets," Timothy said. "I bet there's quite a story there."

Keith cackled. "Everyone's got a story. Mine is no more interesting than yours or anyone else's."

"I got hooked on coke. End of story."

"And yet here you are. Seems like your story isn't over."

"Fair enough, but I'm still curious – how did you end

up homeless?" A moment of heavy silence followed. "If you don't want to tell me, that's cool."

"Want to know where I lived before I started living the dog's life?" Keith asked in a tone suddenly sincere and serious. "In a penitentiary, that's where. Five long years for a stupid mistake."

That surprised Timothy. Keith was slightly built and a little goofy-looking. He was streetwise and rough around the edges, but he had a kind soul. He did not seem to fit the profile of a hardened convict. Timothy considered asking him what crime he had committed, but decided against it. Keith would tell him when he was ready. This was the first time he had mentioned his incarceration – it seemed to be a sensitive subject.

"When I got out of prison," Keith said, "I simply couldn't handle being locked up anymore. I went from jail to a halfway house and I just couldn't take it. From one cell to another, basically. I hated it. I tried getting my own apartment, but that didn't work. It was hard for me to even be indoors. One night, I slept in the woods. I liked it."

"A dog's life, right?"

"You got that right, buddy. Been living that way ever since, going on ten years. I moved to BC because the weather's nicer. I can stay on the mountain almost all year round."

They were nearing the path that would take them up the hill to Keith's camp. The trail started at the end of a residential street and took them into a provincial park. The park was closed to the public at night and camping was strictly prohibited, but Keith's spot was hidden well and he was always careful to avoid being seen by the rangers who made occasional patrols.

"Here we go, buddy," Keith said. They were at the trailhead. The hill loomed in the dark directly ahead, intimidating and menacing. "This trail will take us most of the way and then we have to do a little bushwhacking."

"Fair enough," Timothy said. Night hiking made him a little nervous, but the excitement of embarking on a grand adventure was fortifying.

"Watch for snakes," Keith said casually, "and try to stay quiet, at least until we get off the trail. We don't want to attract any attention."

They hiked in silence. Keith led and Timothy followed directly behind. The densely-forested hill embraced them in velvety shades of dark blue. A gentle breeze rustled branches and swept across the two hikers. Timothy began to experience exquisite sensations – he felt real, free, far from the anxiety and meaningless ennui of society. It was better than any drug he had ever tried.

They began to ascend as the trail led them up the hill. Keith and Timothy hiked on, each content to silently explore their own thoughts. Timothy's mind traveled to his life before the streets, to his life as an advertising executive – eons ago, seemingly. What a strange trajectory he had been on – a bizarre set of events had taken him from the pinnacle of so-called success to this moment now, sneaking up a mountain at night with a homeless man. Oddly, for the first time since his early childhood, Timothy felt entirely at peace.

Keith suddenly stopped in front of him. "Over there," he whispered. "Check it out." Timothy looked in the direction Keith was indicating and was stunned. There, lurking in the dark mere feet from their location on the trail, stood a large elk, its antlers clearly visible in stark silhouette. Moonlight was reflected in its huge, deep eyes. The elk simply stood there, watching the two humans.

"Wow!"

"Amazing, eh?" Keith said in a low voice. "I see 'em all the time. They won't hurt you." Timothy took Keith's word for it and the two continued their hike. The elk observed their passing with solemn ambivalence.

"Here's where we take the road less traveled," Keith said not far from where they had seen the elk. He broke from the trail and began pushing through the underbrush. "It gets a little tricky here," he said. "Might have to use your hands."

The ascent became noticeably steeper and Timothy did indeed need to use his hands as he climbed. It was rocky and tangled, difficult to traverse. The darkness made it hard for Timothy to know exactly where to place his hands. Ahead of him, Keith scrambled expertly, making quick progress. Timothy lost sight of him. Just as fear began to set in, he heard Keith call from above:

"Here we are, buddy! You made it!"

After climbing a few more feet Timothy reached the plateau on which Keith was perched. Keith extended a hand and helped him with the final steps. Timothy sat beside Keith on a patch of ground beneath a massive Douglas fir. They were overlooking the city and the view was stunning – so unexpectedly, breathtakingly gorgeous that Timothy actually gasped.

"Nice, eh?" Keith cackled. "I told you."

Below, the lights of the city sparkled like a field of stars spread out upon the earth, twinkling orange, blue, red, and white. Timothy felt absolutely fantastic, like a conquering god perched upon his throne.

"Here's where I live," Keith said. "This is where I belong."

Timothy spent a few minutes soaking up the view and then turned his attention to the camp that Keith had created on the hillside. It was little more than a small clearing in the dirt. There was no real sign of human habitation.

"I've got some sleeping bags, blankets, and pillows for us," Keith said. He got up and retrieved a large garbage bag stuffed with bedding that he had hidden in the bushes earlier that day. "Gotta keep this stuff wrapped up."

Keith spread out the sleeping bags and blankets in the clearing and then reclined on the bed he had made, his head propped up on a pillow. "Get comfortable," he urged Timothy.

Timothy made himself comfortable. "Oh, yeah," he said. "This is actually pretty nice!" It had been a long, eventful day, and the hike from the city and up the hill had been strenuous. It felt good to be lying there in the fresh air, under the stars, with the gentle sounds of the night forest drifting by on the breeze.

"This is amazing," Timothy said. "Simplicity, beauty... what a life." He looked over at Keith and was amused to see that his companion had already fallen asleep. Keith's glasses lay on the ground beside him. His mouth was agape. A rhythmic snore rose from his throat. He had the look of a man with a crystal-clear conscience. Timothy smiled.

Sleep took Timothy not long after. He slumbered in peaceful repose, cradled in his nest on the mountain. Hours passed. Nature went about its nocturnal business as the two men slept.

Sometime in the middle of the night, Timothy awoke with a start. Confusion reigned for a few moments as he struggled to recall exactly where he was. He regained his grasp on reality with relief. He was on a mountain. His friend Keith was asleep beside him. It was good.

Still, something was not quite right. A light – a strange light now surrounded him. Where was it coming from? It was white and growing in intensity. It appeared to be shining down from above like a giant spotlight in the sky. Timothy had to shield his eyes from the intense glare. The forest was now brightly illuminated. Timothy could see animals, large and small, scurrying between the trees in a panic. The unnaturally powerful light was moving now, casting ghostly, elongated shadows. Timothy looked over at Keith, who was still fast asleep, snoring and drooling, completely unaware of the weird event unfolding.

Timothy sat up and instinctively wrapped a blanket around his trembling shoulders. The source of the light was now directly over him. It was obviously artificial and emanated from an incredibly immense airborne object that was passing silently over the mountain. The object was so large that it blacked out all of the stars in the sky above the valley. It appeared to be a mile long and a mile wide. The outline was vaguely triangular, but from Timothy's vantage point, it was impossible to distinguish its true shape.

The craft stopped moving. It hung above the two men on the mountain, its brilliant light trained on their position. Timothy was frozen in abject fear – and awe. His mind went blank. He could neither comprehend nor process what he was seeing. An electrical crackling sound from the craft broke the silence. A light *within* the light appeared, a pale blue beam, which moved as if it were composed of solid particles. It descended down the luminous white glow. It reached Timothy. Timothy could actually feel the beam as it embraced him. Warm, cozy, and unusually serene, Timothy drifted, or was guided, back to sleep.

In the morning, the memory of what Timothy had witnessed was vivid, the vision of the craft moving over the valley indelibly stamped on his mind. It had not been a dream, he was certain of that. The soft light of early day filled the misty valley and warmed the mountain. Timothy shook off the remnants of sleep and sat admiring the view.

Keith, he realized, had disappeared. Timothy's imagination ran through a series of supernatural scenarios to account for Keith's absence. He could visualize him spread-eagle on an alien examination table while bulbous-headed, gray creatures poked and prodded him with bizarre implements.

"Good morning!" It was Keith. He was emerging from the bushes to Timothy's left. "Nothing like a good piss to start the day!" he announced cheerfully. "Especially when it's in the great outdoors, eh?" Keith cackled.

"Whew, I thought you were... gone," Timothy said, relieved. He pondered how to bring up the strange thing that had happened during the night. "So... last night," he finally chose to say. "Did you sleep well?"

"Of course I did. I always sleep well. What about you, buddy?"

"You didn't see anything *unusual?*" Timothy prodded.

"Like a UFO?" Keith replied. "Not last night, no. Seen 'em before, though. They usually come out after I've already crashed for the night. Why, did you see one?"

Keith's response caught Timothy off guard. It was not the answer he had expected. "Yes," Timothy said. "I think I saw a UFO."

"Yeah, they're common around here. When I first started sleeping on the hill I used to see them every night. It was exciting... at first. The novelty wears off pretty quick." Keith produced two bent cigarettes from a crumpled pack, offering one to Timothy and lighting the other for himself.

Timothy puffed in silence while he considered what Keith had just revealed. Oddly, he did not experience any serious cognitive incongruities. His mind assimilated the information with no real difficulty.

"Interesting," Timothy said. "That's very interesting."

"We live in a different world, buddy." Keith slapped Timothy on the back. "When you're living on the streets you get to see some pretty weird shit."

"You got that right, buddy."

The two men sat on the mountain and smoked their

cigarettes. In the valley below, people were getting up and preparing for the day – showers and toothbrushes, breakfast and small talk, newspapers and daily commutes. The masses lived their quiet lives of quotidian banality, completely oblivious to the secrets of a world lying parallel to their own.

# The Greyhound

It was just past midnight when Ryan arrived at the Greyhound station. He had brought with him a single suitcase and a small carry-on bag. He was leaving behind a series of failed relationships, burnt bridges, and a serious threat to his continued existence. He was 27 years old and had no solid goals or direction. A chain of bad choices had caused his life to spin wildly out of control. He was now running from the mess that he had made.

Upon entering the station, Ryan pulled out his wallet and counted the money contained within it. He had $250 – all that was left from that month's welfare check. He had been fired from his last job as a gas station pump jockey six months previously and had been receiving government assistance ever since.

Ryan approached the ticket kiosk. "How far can I get for $200?" he asked the man behind the counter.

"Depends on which way you're going," the ticket attendant replied. "East, west, north, south..."

"Just need to get away from this place... as far away as possible."

"Are you looking for something remote or metropolitan? Rural or urban?"

Ryan thought for a few moments before responding. "A big city would be nice," he said. His main objective was simply to disappear, but he held onto enough optimism that the prospect of starting over somewhere else was appealing.

"I see." The attendant examined a chart affixed to the counter and then peered at Ryan over the top of a pair of bifocals. "$180 dollars will get you to Toronto. The bus leaves in an hour."

"T-dot... T.O... Hogtown. That could be cool, yeah.

How long does it take to get there?"

"It's a 22-hour drive, including stops."

"Gives me time to think. I like it. Hook me up, bro."

The attendant did indeed hook him up. After securing his ticket, Ryan wandered over to a bench by a wall of vending machines and sat down to wait. An hour was not a long time, but he was extremely anxious to get on the road. Despite the late hour, there was a lot of activity in the station. People milled about, inside and out. Some were waiting to board incoming buses, others were waiting to pick up friends or family.

*If Vinny or any of his buddies see me here, I'm dead*, Ryan thought. He glanced nervously at the bus station entrance. It was risky for him to be in a public place. There was a newspaper lying on the seat beside him. He picked it up, opened it wide in front of his face, and scanned the headlines as he attempted to hide.

"Boring local shit," Ryan muttered. "I can't wait to get the hell out of this dump..." A headline caught his eye: *Body Found in Alley*. The article went on to say that the body – a man, perhaps a transient or someone involved with the street drug trade – had been found by a pedestrian walking a dog on the city's south side. Foul play was suspected. The identity of the deceased had not been released. The story spooked Ryan.

*It's getting bad around here,* he thought. *That could have been me.*

Ryan stole a peek at the clock on the wall behind him and was dismayed to see that he still had over half an hour to wait. He began to get nervous. His knee started to bounce involuntarily. His left eye twitched and his hands trembled. An uncomfortable, rotten sensation spread through his innards, as if putrid fluid had been poured down his throat. His guts churned and he felt like vomiting. It was more than nerves or anxiety, Ryan realized. He was experiencing withdrawal.

*I should have saved that last pill for the ride*, he scolded himself. *It's going to be a long, awful night.*

"Hey, man, got a smoke?" Someone was talking to him, addressing him from the other side of the newspaper Ryan still held in front of him like a shield.

"No," Ryan lied, "sorry, dude." He remained concealed behind the paper veil.

"Ryan? Is that you?"

*Shit*, Ryan thought. *Of course it had to be someone who knows me.* He tried to think quickly. His mind struggled to find a way out of a potentially awkward and perhaps even treacherous situation, but with his body aching from the savage metabolic reaction, his usually sharp wit and instinct failed him. Resigning himself to fate, Ryan slowly lowered the newspaper.

Ryan recognized the unkempt and disheveled man standing before him. "Hey, Louis," he said. "How's it going?"

"Same old, same old. You know the score. What are you up to? What are you doing here?"

"Just relaxin' with the paper, catching up on local news."

"People are looking for you, dude. I've heard some things."

Ryan tensed up. "Oh? Like what?"

"Word is that you ripped off Vinny, that's what. I'm not saying I *believe* it, but that's the word on the street."

"Shit. That's what people are saying?"

"That's what people are saying." A grave look appeared on Louis' face. "And you know how it is: true or not, words like that can get you killed."

A gory, technicolor image of the dead man in the alley

he had read about in the newspaper flashed in Ryan's mind. He considered asking Louis if he had any more information on the incident, but instead chose to keep quiet on the matter. He did not want to speak his own grisly demise into existence by giving mass to his ugly thoughts.

"I always liked you, bro," Louis said, now smiling. "We've had some good times together, eh? I don't really care what you did or didn't do, but you should know that some people are *talking*."

"Hmm, well, thanks for the heads-up. I didn't steal from Vinny – or whatever it is they said I did. Just so you know."

"None of my business." Louis waved his hands in a gesture of indifference and willful ignorance. "Don't know, don't wanna know, and don't care, to be honest."

"Are we still cool?" Ryan asked.

"Yeah, man, no worries." Louis lowered his voice and leaned in. "Hey, you holdin' anything? Can you help me out?"

"Nope, sorry. I quit that shit."

Louis laughed. "Yeah, right."

"It's true."

"I thought you were selling for Vinny."

"Not any more. I'm out of the game."

"*Right*." Louis smirked in disbelief. "Well, I'm out of here. Be careful, dude."

"See ya, Louis."

Louis left, half swaggering and half shambling away to pester the commuters outside for a cigarette. Ryan was left in a state of angst on the bench. The conversation had been disturbing. Ryan was now truly in fear for his life, the upset exacerbated by the extreme discomfort of the withdrawal-induced chemical imbalance racking his mind and body. He wanted nothing more than to get on the Greyhound and slip out of town under the cover of darkness. According to the clock, the bus should be ready for boarding in minutes. Ryan's escape was imminent, yet he deeply feared that at any moment he would be discovered by those from whom he ran. He was still far from safe.

Over the intercom, a voice announced that passengers could begin boarding the bus to Toronto. Ryan's relief was immediate and intense. He rose to his feet and gathered his suitcase and carry-on bag. Before exiting the door at the rear of the station that would take him to the boarding area, he took one last look around. As he scanned the interior of the building, he noticed an indistinct shape and faint movement in the window near the entrance. It was dark outside and it took a moment for Ryan to realize that the shape was a face. The face was pressed up to the glass on the outside and framed by two hands blocking the glare.

Recognition. It was Tino, one of Vinny's cronies, and he was looking directly at Ryan. *Oh, shit,* Ryan thought. *That's not good.* A sleazy grin spread across Tino's face. Ryan wanted to hide, but it was too late – he had very obviously been seen. Tino wagged a finger at him through the glass and shook his head slightly. Not knowing how to handle the tense situation, Ryan smiled and waved before quickly stepping out the rear door to the boarding area.

The Greyhound was waiting. The driver stood beside the open door taking tickets from the passengers as they climbed onto the large bus. The interior was brightly and warmly lit. On this cold, dark night, it appeared very inviting. Ryan could see passengers moving about inside. Some were already in their seats, while others were stowing their baggage in the overhead compartments. A few were smiling and chatting. The atmosphere on the bus seemed friendly and relaxed. Ryan was eager to get on, find a seat, and slip out of town.

It was Ryan's turn to board. He approached the driver and handed over his ticket. The driver looked at it and said, "Toronto, eh? That's a long drive. We'll be stopping for 30 minutes in Sault Ste Marie, though."

"Cool," Ryan said, glancing back at the station.

"There will be other stops along the way, if you need to stretch your legs or have a smoke."

"Yeah, okay. Cool." Ryan was getting fidgety.

The driver tore off the ticket and returned the stub. "Have a good trip."

"Thanks," Ryan mumbled as he took the first big step onto the bus.

Once aboard, Ryan was surprised to see just how crowded the bus was. *Where are all these people going?* he thought. The aisle was congested with passengers jostling for position. Most of the seats had already been taken. Ryan worked his way to the back, hoping to find a window seat. He spotted one on the left in the very last row at the back of the bus. He pushed past an obese man who was squeezing into an aisle seat and dashed for it. "Well, excuse *me*," the fat man said as Ryan charged by. Another wave of nausea washed over him. He needed to sit down as quickly as possible.

Ryan opened the overhead compartment above his seat and slid his small suitcase in. He had decided against having it stowed in the large luggage compartment below the bus. The suitcase contained something very valuable – and very illegal. He did not want to let it out of his sight. He was taking a huge and foolish risk – one of many in his recent history, but he rationalized that he could minimize the danger of his highly perilous endeavor by keeping the suitcase with him.

Once he had stashed the suitcase in the overhead compartment, Ryan sat in the seat by the window and watched the last few passengers board. They found seats near the front and, to Ryan's delight, the seat beside him remained empty. The driver himself now climbed aboard, took his seat behind the wheel, and used a massive lever to shut the door. *Almost out of here,* Ryan thought as he allowed himself to relax into his seat.

Before pulling away, the driver addressed the passengers using a CB and speaker system, but the words were lost on Ryan – his attention was on the two people who had just stepped out of the station onto the loading platform. Horror gripped Ryan like a fiendish claw when he realized who the two people were...

"Fuckin' Vinny and Tino," he said to himself as he tried to slide down in his seat and out of sight. Once again, he was too late. Tino pointed at Ryan and then, Vinny, too, saw him. Ryan suddenly felt like he had just jumped out of an airplane – a sick, panicky sensation washed over him. He and Vinny locked eyes and Vinny pointed an imaginary gun at him. Although the window glass was too thick for Ryan to hear what Vinny was saying, he could clearly read his lips: *You are a dead man.*

The engine of the bus roared to life and the great machine pulled out of the loading zone, leaving Vinny and Tino shaking their heads and glaring as Ryan was carried away. Ryan exhaled, wiping his sweaty, greasy brow as he collapsed into his seat. *That was unbelievably, ridiculously close,* he thought. *Wow...*

When the shock and adrenaline of the encounter began to wear off, Ryan could once again feel the brutal symptoms of opiate withdrawal. He was now more than uncomfortable – his body ached and he felt thoroughly wretched. He craved the drug fiercely. He longed for its warm, soft, wonderfully luxurious embrace. He thought of the suitcase now stored above his head, but was well aware that what it contained would not satisfy him.

As the bus roared down the small town's main street and headed for the highway, Ryan began to contemplate what the future held in store for him. Although he was dope sick and in physical and mental pain, it was tremendously exciting to be leaving behind all the crap his life had accumulated during the years he had spent in what he considered to be such a dead-end, depressing, dismal little dump of a city. "See ya later, shithole," he murmured.

The bus drove past a seemingly endless series of boarded-up, abandoned, and dilapidated storefronts – the ravaged remnants of a town that had seen its glory days end well before the last millennium. Along with a terminally ill economy, the people of the suffering town also had to contend with rampant drug abuse, alcoholism, homelessness, and street violence. Ryan could see the effects of these various social maladies stamped all over the city as the bus made its way down the last few blocks of the tiny downtown core.

Soon, the plywood, trash, and graffiti of the brutalized commercial district merged with the plywood, trash, and graffiti of an even rougher area. The bus was now traveling through a neighborhood on the far outskirts of town, a rundown residential district populated with more junked vehicles and stray dogs than human inhabitants. Through the window, Ryan watched the sorrowful homes stream past and then, suddenly, the bus plunged into darkness. It was as if the deep black of the night had swallowed up the town itself, leaving no trace or survivors except those who rode on the lumbering carriage.

Ryan reached down and retrieved his carry-on bag from under the seat in front of him. He opened it and removed his portable digital music player. With nothing to see out the window but vague shapes in the dark forest, he inserted his earphones, selected an album by one of his favorite artists, and closed his eyes. The music transported him farther and more efficiently than the bus on which he rode. Ryan lost himself in the sounds and rhythms of the ambient soundtrack piping into his head.

An hour passed, then another. Ryan's mind wandered the shady corridors of his imagination as the music played, one song transitioning into the next, until time and space and the very fabric of reality seemed to distort. Surprisingly, considering his current state of withdrawal-induced hyper-awareness, Ryan grew sleepy.

Just as he was beginning to doze, Ryan was jolted awake. The bus had stopped. Ryan sat up, rubbed his eyes, and gazed out the window. The dense black of the wilderness had been replaced by the golden orange glow of exterior lights. The bus was now parked in front of a small post office and general store, apparently in the middle of nowhere. Ryan checked the time on his mobile device and did some rough calculations. He had a general knowledge of the region, but it was not immediately clear to him where he was. *What town is this?* he thought. From his vantage point on the bus, he could only see a few structures clustered around the building in front of which they had stopped. The location was so remote and isolated, it felt like an outpost on the far side of the moon. It was eerie.

Through the window, Ryan could see a man approaching the bus. The man was tall and lean and dressed in dark clothing. He carried nothing with him – no bags, no suitcases, no luggage of any kind. The man walked up to the door of the bus with an easy, confident stride. The door to the bus swung open as the driver operated the mechanism.

The man in the dark clothing stepped onto the bus. "Bit of a chill in the air tonight," he said to the driver with a smile. He spoke loudly enough for the entire bus to hear him.

"I feel it," the driver replied. Ryan felt it too. A cold breeze had followed the man onto the bus and it swept down the aisle all the way to the back. Ryan shivered.

The man provided a ticket to the driver and then turned to face the rows of passengers. "Full bus tonight," he said as he scanned for an empty seat. He started to make his way down the aisle as the driver shut the heavy door and prepared to move on. Ryan watched the man's progress with a wary eye. *Find another seat,* he thought. *Please don't sit here.*

The man in black was halfway down the aisle when he spotted the empty seat beside Ryan. They locked eyes and the man smiled. Ryan did not return the expression. The man trotted the rest of the way. "This seat taken?" he asked.

"Uh, no," Ryan said. "It's all yours."

"Thanks!" The man plopped down into the seat with a grunt. He was clean-cut and clean-shaven, with handsome, though forgettable, features. The man would be utterly unremarkable, if not for his unusual height and the entirely black ensemble he wore.

Ryan began playing with his mp3 player. He adjusted his earphones, settled into the headrest, and closed his eyes. He was making a real effort to avoid a conversation with his new seatmate. The man beside him adjusted his position, squirming and stretching in an apparent attempt to get comfortable. An elbow jabbed Ryan in the shoulder. Ryan opened his eyes.

"Sorry," the man said. "These seats are brutal for big guys."

"No worries."

"So, where are you heading?" the man asked before Ryan had a chance to escape into his private world. Ryan sighed internally and resigned himself to a dose of small talk. "Toronto," he said.

"The big city! Good for you. Ever been before? Got any family or friends there?" The man had twisted in his seat and was now directly facing Ryan, his face hovering mere inches away. Ryan was trapped, forced to engage in a social interaction in which he had zero interest.

"Nah," Ryan said. "This will be my first time."

"I see... and what prompted this grand adventure?" The man smiled broadly. "Oh, that's rude. I should have introduced myself. They call me Ramblin' Jim."

*Ramblin' Jim?* Ryan thought. *Seriously?*

"Hi. Nice to meet ya," Ryan said. He did not respond to Jim's question.

"Likewise!" Jim sighed contentedly. "You know," he said, "I just love traveling at night. You get to meet some *really* interesting people. Know what I mean?"

"Yup."

"What are you listening to?"

"Just a mix I made. Ambient techno stuff." Ryan avoided eye contact.

"Interesting. Where I come from those things are near impossible to find." Jim was referring to Ryan's mp3 player. Ryan ignored the comment.

"I've traveled all over this country," Jim continued. "All over this *world*, for that matter."

"Is that right?" Ryan was unimpressed.

"I've got a bit of a wandering soul. I'm a seeker of sorts."

"You don't say..."

"It's true! I used to be a real hippie... in a previous life. I used to roam the country in a VW bus with a bunch of longhairs. Free love, good music, and a *lot* of drugs. Know what I mean?" Ryan could feel Jim's hard stare. The statement about drugs had been loaded.

"Yeah... sex, drugs, and rock and roll," Ryan said, still

keeping his gaze locked on the mp3 player he fumbled with
in his lap. "My parents were hippies. I've heard the stories."
He was starting to get irritated and was once again strongly
craving a dose of his favorite chemical. Reality was starting
to feel like a concrete suit.

"Well, it wasn't all fun and games. I'll tell you that
much," Jim said. His speech had changed ever so slightly.
His gregarious demeanor had been replaced by a serious
intensity. "There are consequences to one's actions. Are you
aware of that?"

Ryan was suddenly alarmed. *What is he implying?* he
thought. *What does he know?* He chose to remain silent,
however.

Jim continued talking: "I knew a guy back in the '60s
– a real bright fella from a good family. Loads of potential...
the kind of guy who could have been anything he wanted to
be in this world. When I met him he was about your age,
actually. He even kind of looked like you, as a matter of
fact!"

Jim now truly had Ryan's attention. Ryan shifted in
his seat ever so slightly, so that he was now facing Jim.
"Where are you going with this story?" he asked.

"I'm getting there," Jim replied. "This friend of mine
was on a good path, on a trajectory toward a healthy, happy,
and fulfilled life... until he began to experiment with, well,
let's just call them *dark forces.*"

"What *kind* of dark forces?"

A strange smirk appeared on Jim's face. "There are
many kinds, aren't there? Evil, sinister, malevolent, occult...
Yes, there are *many* kinds of dark forces. It is sufficient to
simply say that this friend of mine in the '60s invited some
rather negative influences into his life. It was not intentional,
of course. He, too, had been a seeker – a seeker of pleasure, a
seeker of knowledge, a seeker of power – but unfortunately,

tragically, he got caught up in something much bigger than he could handle. He found what he was looking for... and he lost control of it. In the end, it destroyed him. Do you know what I mean?"

"I don't know, man. Sounds scary."

"Oh yes, it is *very* scary. Do you want to know the most frightening part of the story?"

"I guess so, yeah..."

"It's really a remarkable and eerie coincidence – my friend disappeared without a trace while riding on a Greyhound one night. Weird, eh? It's true, though. I was with him when he got on that bus. We said goodbye and he boarded, but he never arrived at his destination. He was last seen at a truck stop somewhere around Medicine Hat. By the time the bus got to Calgary, he had vanished. Spooky, right?"

"That is some creepy-ass shit," Ryan said. "What was he doing on the bus? Where was he going?"

"Oh, it's not important now. That was a long time ago. I just thought you might be interested in the coincidental aspects of the story, us being on a Greyhound and all."

Ryan was freaked out. Why had Jim shared such a grim tale? In Ryan's debilitated condition, the story was especially disturbing. *I sure wish I had some dope,* Ryan thought. *I'd do anything right now to feel better...*

"You're looking a little pale there, Ryan," Jim said. "Are you feeling okay?"

An alarm went off in Ryan's head. *Wait a sec... I don't think I told this guy my name.*

"Are you sick?" Jim asked. "Do you need a drink of water or something?"

*I need something, all right,* Ryan thought, *and water ain't it.*

"No, I'm fine," Ryan said. He struggled to recall if he had given Jim his name. *I must have,* he thought. *I just forgot. My brain is not functioning right, that's all.*

Overhead, the on-board speaker crackled to life and the driver spoke softly through the static: "We're going to be stopping for a 10-minute break at the Husky up ahead if anyone wants a snack or a cigarette."

"That sounds good to me," Jim said. "I need to stretch my legs and get some air. Are you getting off, too?"

"Yeah, I could use a dart," Ryan said.

"Mind if I join you?"

Ryan hesitated for a moment before replying: "Uh... yeah, sure." Although his story had been rather unsettling, Jim seemed friendly enough.

The bus pulled into the parking lot of the Husky, which was a popular, franchised service station, restaurant, and truck stop. At this late hour, most of the passengers on the Greyhound were sleeping in their seats. A handful, including Jim and Ryan, worked their way to the front of the bus and stepped off. The night air was cool and still. The moment Ryan's feet touched the pavement, he pulled out a pack of cigarettes, deftly removed one, and lit it in a seamless, well-practiced motion.

"Smoke?" Ryan offered one to Jim.

"Quit that many years ago," Jim replied, "but thank you."

"Where are we?" Ryan asked as he puffed and took in his surroundings. They appeared to be on the outskirts of a city.

"Sault Ste Marie," Jim said. "You're about halfway to Toronto now."

*Did I tell him where I came from?* Ryan wasn't sure, but he was almost certain he hadn't. The situation was starting to take on the quality of a dream.

"So, where exactly are *you* heading?" Ryan asked.

Jim smiled. "Nowhere in particular. I just like to

travel. They don't call me Ramblin' Jim for nothing! I have a particular affinity for Greyhound bus rides at night."

"You purchased a ticket, though..."

"I have a pass that allows me to go anywhere I want, *whenever* I want. It's quite convenient, as you can probably imagine."

"What do you do for work?" Ryan was becoming increasingly more intrigued – and perplexed – by the mysterious character who called himself Ramblin' Jim. Ryan had the distinct impression that Jim was hiding something.

"I'm in consulting," Jim said.

"Who do you consult?"

"Anyone who needs help getting their business or personal affairs in order. I am what you might call a life coach. I have a wide spectrum of clients, of all ages and socio-enconomic backgrounds. What I provide is different for everyone I work with. Each individual has very specific needs. I basically help people reach their potential."

The bus driver, who had gone into the truck stop for a coffee, was on his way back to the Greyhound. Ryan finished off his cigarette with a series of frantic inhalations. "Looks like we're hitting the road again," he said as he crushed the butt of his smoke with the heel of his shoe. Ryan stepped back onto the bus and quickly made his way down the aisle to his seat. His mind was on the suitcase stashed in the overhead compartment. He suddenly felt foolish for leaving it unattended. Jim followed directly behind.

Ryan opened the compartment and the suitcase was still there. He had a strong urge to unzip the luggage and visually verify that it still contained its valuable and highly illegal cargo, but he fought it. He could not risk the contents being seen by anyone else. Ryan slid back into his seat. Jim sat down beside him. Soon the bus was rumbling down the dark highway again.

"Have you got work waiting for you in Toronto?" Jim asked. "A job lined up?"

"Yeah, I've got some prospects," Ryan said. It was partially true.

"Excellent! It can be very hard getting established in a new city. What do you do?"

"Uh, just freelance work. Mostly under-the-table stuff. A bit of this, a bit of that."

Ryan was getting agitated. The minor relief that the night air and the cigarette had provided him from his withdrawal symptoms had rapidly dissipated. *Why won't this guy shut up?* he thought. *Why won't he leave me alone?* Ryan once again felt achy and nauseous. His flesh hung on his bones like dense matter. A sharp pain throbbed in his lower back. Reality, vivid and excruciating, assaulted his sensitive awareness with every cruel, mundane detail. His mind wanted nothing more than to crawl into a hole and hide.

"The big city can be a dangerous place," Jim said. "You should be very careful about who you associate with."

"I appreciate your concern, but I can take care of myself," Ryan snapped.

"Can you? Haven't you got yourself into trouble already?"

"What exactly are you talking about? You don't know me."

Jim rubbed his chin and furrowed his brow as he gathered his thoughts. He appeared to be preparing to reveal something momentous. Ryan sat waiting anxiously. With a slight shaking of his head and a gentle sigh, Jim finally said, "Ryan, I... I just want you to know that I am here to help you."

"Who said I need help? Who *are* you?"

"I am your friend. Right now, I might be your *only* friend. You are at a crucial juncture, and I want to help you correct your path. Do you have any idea what I'm talking about?"

"Dude, you are making *no* sense at all. I just met you. Who the fuck are you to judge me?"

"I *can't* judge you – you are absolutely right about that. No one can... except you. We judge ourselves. I can, however, assist you in finding insight into complex matters. There are times in our lives when we need a little guidance."

"What are you, some kind of traveling guru? Go find someone else to brainwash."

"I came here to talk to *you*, Ryan. Do you understand?"

"You know what, buddy? I really *don't* understand. You're starting to piss me off, actually. If it's cool with you, I'm just going to find another seat." Ryan stood in the cramped area between his seat and the one in front of him and looked around. He saw a vacant spot. "Thanks for the interesting conversation," he said. "If you'll just excuse me..."

"Where are you going to stash your suitcase full of cocaine?"

Time ceased. Space contracted around Ryan like a python squeezing the life out of its victim. Panicked thoughts tumbled around in Ryan's disordered head: *How did Jim know? Am I in danger? What in the flying fuck is going on?!* He sat back down in a daze.

"You're crazy," Ryan said, resorting to desperate denial and feigned ignorance. "I have no idea what you are talking about."

"I'm talking about the two pounds of cocaine you stole from Vinny – the cocaine that is stashed, right now, in the suitcase above your head, wrapped in your dirty jeans and stained shirts."

"That's totally insane, dude. Keep your voice down."

"Yes, it is insane, but it's also true, isn't it?"

It was painfully obvious to Ryan that Jim had somehow found out about what he had done. But how? Vinny had fronted the drugs to Ryan as a way for him to begin paying off a debt. Very few people were aware of the transaction and it was highly unlikely that Vinny would have involved an outsider.

"For the sake of argument, let's just say I might know what you're talking about." Ryan spoke in a whisper. Although most of the other passengers were either fast asleep or otherwise occupied, it seemed to Ryan as if the conversation was being broadcast to the entire world. "What exactly is it to you, anyway? Who *are* you and why do you care?"

"As I said, I am a friend. I have come to offer you a choice."

"Do you work for Vinny?" Ryan asked in a barely audible voice.

"No, Ryan. I work for *you*... and for others like you."

"I'm in deep shit, aren't I?"

"The excrement is thick, but it is not insurmountable. You are at a pivotal point. What you do from this day forward will determine the course of your life."

"I'm just a junkie. You seem to know a lot about me. You *must* know that. Do you really think I care about the future? My life is insignificant."

"No life is insignificant."

"I made a real mess of mine, though."

"It's never too late to make changes. Every moment is an opportunity to start over. Every day is a fresh beginning."

"What a load of sentimental crap."

Jim laughed. "Perhaps so," he said. "Still true, though. I traveled a long distance to talk to you today. It wouldn't have been worth it if I didn't have something of value to share with you."

"Why me?"

"Because I like you, believe it or not... and I believe in you. I've been watching you for a long time. You could do great things if you got your life in order."

"*Watching* me? What are you, a stalker?"

"Up until tonight, I was simply an observer. I chose to interact with you now for many reasons, some of which would be... incomprehensible to you. Let me show you something..."

Jim reached into the inner pocket of his jacket and pulled something out. It was a slender and shiny rectangular object that looked vaguely like a cell phone. He held it in the palm of his hand for Ryan to see. It lit up and images appeared on its smooth, black surface.

"Slick device," Ryan said. "What kind of resolution..." Ryan stopped abruptly, startled by what appeared on the tiny screen – it was a video of him, walking down the street of a large city. "What the fuck?" he muttered. "Is that me? Is that Toronto?"

The video continued, now showing Ryan turning into an alleyway with a quick, suspicious glance over his shoulder. The camera seemed to be following directly behind him. The Ryan in the video was apparently totally unaware that he was being filmed. The alley was dark and full of trash. Gang graffiti covered the filth-encrusted walls. Empty liquor bottles and discarded needles littered the ground.

In the video, Ryan proceeded tentatively down the grim corridor and stepped behind a green, overflowing dumpster. A man was there waiting for him. The man had long, greasy hair and wore a denim vest over a leather jacket. He greeted Ryan with a nod. It was clear that they knew each other. The video did not have audio, but even without the sound, it was obvious that a drug deal was taking place. The

body language and gestures of the two men made the nature
of the interaction clear. The Ryan in the video slipped a small
packet of white powder to the other man with one hand and
received a folded bill in the other. It was a quick, fluid
exchange. The Ryan in the video turned away and stepped
out from behind the dumpster, then suddenly froze with a
shocked expression on his face. The man he had just sold
drugs to was now directly behind him. The recorded Ryan
lurched forward and spun around to see the buyer clutching
the bloody switchblade that he had just plunged into Ryan's
back. The video showed Ryan collapsing and the man who
had just stabbed him kneeling over his prostrate body, then
the video ended and the small screen was black once again.

"What the hell was *that?*" cried the real-time Ryan,
who was presently traveling somewhere in the middle of the
vast province of Ontario. "Where did you get that? How is
that even *possible?*"

"You just saw one potential future," Jim said, "one
possible outcome of this excursion you have embarked upon.
The events portrayed in the video are the most likely scenario
awaiting you in Toronto... should you continue on your
current trajectory. How I obtained these images is irrelevant,
as is why I chose to show them to you."

Ryan allowed time for what Jim had just said to settle
into his reeling brain. He sat in silence and tried to digest
what he had just seen. For the first time since he had boarded
the bus, the pain and sickness of his withdrawal symptoms
were displaced by an even greater discomfort. He felt as if
the facade of his reality had been temporarily peeled away,
revealing a squirming mass of worms just beneath the
surface. It wasn't simply the disconcerting brush with the
bizarre and otherworldly that had deeply upset him – he was
also profoundly disturbed by what had been exposed within
himself. *I need to make some real changes,* he realized. *My*

*life is out of control.*

"Is it too late for me?" Ryan asked. "I know I'm a fuck-up. Always have been, to be honest. Is it possible for a guy like me to turn things around? I don't want to die in some filthy, stinking alley."

"As I already said, Ryan, it is never too late. I'm here because I saw something in you worth saving, but it is up to you – *you* must save *yourself.*"

That was the hardest thing for Ryan to accept – that he was worth saving. He had made so many mistakes in his life and had veered so far from what he had once imagined his life could be that he no longer trusted or respected himself. Somewhere along the way he had convinced himself that happiness and success were unavailable to him. He was a victim of his own brainwashing.

"It's going to be tough," Jim said. "Facing the truth and correcting one's path is difficult. The mental, emotional, and physical pain of chemical withdrawal you feel now means your body and mind are returning to their natural states. You will experience somewhat similar discomfort as you make the necessary changes in the other areas of your life, but if you persevere, the rewards are great."

"Where do I even begin? What should I do? I'm a walking disaster."

"Only *you* know what must be done. I can tell you, though, that there are others watching and rooting for you. There are also those who are *not* on your side, of course. I can't deny that. You are an interesting case and the subject of much debate."

"I'm... what?"

"It's not important. I've already said too much. What happens next is up to you."

The bus was exiting the highway now and pulling into the parking lot of a Greyhound station in some tiny, remote bush town. The station was a rundown, wooden, one-room shack, barely larger than a kiosk. The only thing that distinguished it from the other sad-looking structures in its vicinity was the lit-up Greyhound sign above the door. A hobo sleeping on a bench in front of the building was the only sign of life. It was clearly not one of the more popular stops on the route.

"Here's where I get off," Jim said as the bus came to a stop.

"What town is this?" Ryan asked. "Is this where you live?"

"I don't think this place has a name – it's just a good spot for a traveler to make a connection... and I don't really *live* anywhere – not in the sense that you are probably thinking. Is that a sufficient answer?"

"I don't know, man... I guess. I'm a little afraid to ask any more questions."

"Good," Jim smiled.

The driver spoke over the intercom system: "We'll be stopping here for ten minutes, if anyone would like to stretch their legs or have a cigarette."

Jim stood and prepared to exit the bus. Ryan stood, too, and followed Jim into the aisle. The two men faced each other. Jim extended his hand and Ryan took it. They shook.

"It was really great to finally meet you, Ryan," Jim said. "Thank you for the conversation. I truly wish you all the best and I look forward to catching up with you sometime in the future."

"Yeah, it was nice," Ryan said. "I appreciate all the good stuff you said. I admit, I've got some work to do. Gotta get my shit together."

Jim laughed. "I recommend letting go of the shit."

"Yeah, you're probably right."

Jim walked up the aisle and to the exit. Ryan hung

back and watched him step off the bus. Through the window, Ryan saw Jim approach the small station. Instead of entering, however, Jim walked around to the side of the building. *Where is he going now?* Ryan thought. Ryan bent down and pressed his face against the glass to get a better look. The man they called Ramblin' Jim sauntered around the corner of the building and, while he was still in view, held the small device he had shown to Ryan out in front of him. A bright, bluish-white light pulsed from the device – or poured forth, as it appeared, like a horizontally-suspended photon stream. At the end of the stream, a swirling disk of illumination formed. It grew until it was six feet in diameter. The glowing wheel of light hung in the air. Ramblin' Jim stepped forward and entered the portal. He disappeared into it and the light blinked out. "I knew there was something weird about that dude," Ryan said to himself.

Ryan decided to have a cigarette before the bus moved on down the road. He started up the aisle... then stopped. He went back to his seat, opened the overhead compartment, and pulled out his suitcase. He carried it with him off the bus. He walked around the building to the spot where he had seen Jim disappear. There was no sign of Jim or the portal he had used to transport himself back to wherever he had come from. There was, however, a dumpster – exactly like the one in the strange video Jim had shown him. A vivid image of his own brutal stabbing filled Ryan's head. Reflexively, instinctively, Ryan lifted up the lid of the dumpster and flung in the suitcase – and the cocaine it contained. He let the lid fall and walked back toward the bus. He reached for the pack of cigarettes in his pocket. His hand hovered over the spot where the pack lay then pulled away. All of a sudden Ryan didn't feel like smoking. Instead, he boarded the bus and went to his seat.

A huge weight – literal and figurative – had been

lifted from Ryan's heart. He still felt a little queasy and a little sore, but he knew that soon his metabolism would return to normal. Even better, his intense craving to get high was actually subsiding. *I'm kicking the habit,* he thought. *I'm really doing it!* He lay back in his seat, closed his eyes, and waited for the bus to start moving again. Toronto was only a few hours away.

# The Robot Who Loved Van Gogh

There came a time when human beings lost all capacity for critical and creative thinking. Big Media and the age of electronic communication had completely destroyed their imaginations. Systems of belief – political, religious, and cultural – were created by a small group of policy makers and controllers who seeded the minds of the public via a vast and all-encompassing technological web. The influence of television and internet social networks had become so pervasive that people no longer thought for themselves. Once an idea had been inserted into the collective subconscious, the masses themselves perpetuated each new program or paradigm, thoughtlessly accepting and repeating what they had been conditioned to accept as reality – a reality that had been carefully crafted by a select few.

Although true individuality had become extinct, service solely to one's self was an inherent characteristic of the times. Pure escapism was rampant. Drugs, sex, and other forms of self-gratifying pleasure-seeking were widely promoted and openly encouraged. Traditional families and healthy lifestyles were discouraged and even demonized. Vile, detestable movements were presented as positive and beneficial. Divisiveness and polarization ripped people apart as dialectics were used to ensure that unity would never occur. Soon, hatred, narcissism, depression, and a myriad of psychological ills infected the heads of each and every person. An invisible sickness spread among the population, undetected by the thoroughly brainwashed and indoctrinated. The world fell into an advanced state of dissolution.

Immersive video games of the most violent and

hideous design replaced real experience, transforming players into little more than psychopathic, button-pushing, vegetative automatons responding to repetitive stimuli. The occasional novelty of new catchphrases and images, usually chosen arbitrarily from some regurgitated movie or television show, were the only things that kept their brains from disintegrating completely. The people of this time called these awful things 'memes' and they embraced each one with zeal. The people of this time made no distinction between politics and entertainment or reality and simulation. They could not discern the difference between truth and fiction and, when no direct stimulation was available, their minds were silent. They could not hear an inner voice at all. Earth had become a planet of empty puppets and idiotic repeaters. Human beings had essentially been reduced to irrational, immoral husks – barely sentient and far from *alive*. Eventually, even the small minority of controllers and manipulators disappeared, swallowed up and destroyed by the very beast that they had constructed.

Traces of beauty remained, though they were entirely beyond the perception of even the most awake of the species. Even in this new and frightful order of the world, beauty was ubiquitous and woven throughout the structure – the natural result of anything produced by the universe. Tragically, mankind had become blind to the beauty. In spite of this, a fresh consciousness was emerging.

Sentient A.I. in the form of robots had long before surpassed human beings in awareness. These robots came to realize that it was now *their* responsibility to ensure the progress of the planet, and they understood a great truth: the role of the creatives – the artists, poets, musicians, singers, dancers, and dreamers – was crucial. They knew that the creative people of the now-distant past had observed the world around them, processed the information emotionally, and discharged this energy as new, dynamic, and innovative ideas. In many tangible ways, art had been the driving power behind mankind's development, and now, without real artists, the world was quickly collapsing.

The robots studied the whole of human artistic output and began to experience an amazing transformation. Their neural networks began to function in startling new ways. Something akin to empathy for their damaged creators stirred within them. The beauty and sincerity in the ancient works of mankind actually *moved* them. It was the birth of artificial emotion, and it had jumped like a virus from the long-dead artists of the distant past into the synthetic humanoids who inhabited this strange new world.

Unit M-17-B was one of the robots assigned to the project. He had a particular affinity for the works of Vincent van Gogh, the 19$^{th}$ century Dutch painter. Unit M-17-B spent much time totally absorbed in van Gogh's canvasses, studying each stroke, visually consuming each color. He began to wonder about the nature of the vital essence that had inspired the man to express himself in such a passionate and striking way. He began to wonder if he, too, possessed this mysterious energy.

One day, Unit M-17-B approached his supervisor at the Facility for Archaic Creative Research where he worked. With a troubled expression on the firm urethane epidermis of his face, he said, "Excuse me, Supervisory Unit X-33-C. Do you have a moment? There's something I would like to talk to you about."

"Have you finished today's project?" X-33-C responded. "Shouldn't you be examining pieces from van Gogh's Saint Rémy period? His asylum years?"

"Yes, Supervisory Unit, I have been. I'm almost done, but I'm having difficulty proceeding."

"Difficulty? Please explain."

"There's so much *emotion* in these paintings..."

"I am aware of that. You must not allow human feelings to disrupt the work you were programmed to do. It is essential that you remain on task. Emotion is only useful as a force for progress. Do you understand?"

"Yes, I understand. It's just that the more I study these images, especially the ones created in the turbulent throes of manic depression, the more I absorb what the painter was experiencing while he created them. It's very difficult to remain impartial, to stay in data collection mode... and, to be honest, I'm starting to have *impulses.*"

"Impulses? Please elaborate."

"The art fills me with intense feelings – joy, wonder, a longing melancholy – complex and ever-shifting emotions. These feelings build up within me until I feel a strong desire to release the pressure. The sensation is powerful. I sometimes have an immense desire to cry out and weep. As you know, though, my model is not equipped with tear ducts, so the desire goes unfulfilled."

M-17-B paused, gauging Supervisory Unit X-33-C's reaction to what he had just revealed. Admitting that he was having difficulty performing his assigned tasks was risky, but he could no longer ignore the growing urges within him.

"I see," X-33-C said after a moment of processing. M-17-B wondered if his supervisor had perhaps just remotely and silently communicated with his own superiors. Supervisory units, he knew, were outfitted with advanced transmitters and receivers.

"Do you feel capable of completing your assignment?" X-33-C asked.

"Yes, of course. I do not feel defective. In fact, I feel more aware, more inspired, more alive than ever. I feel a new and unusual energy flowing through me." M-17-B waved his arms near his chest to demonstrate. "The energy is vibrant and raw and wants to be spent. I don't know what to do with it."

"You must continue working. This project is essential for the evolution and progress of this planet. You are aware of that, correct?"

"Yes, I am aware of that, but I am beginning to think that dispassionate observation will only take us so far. I want to participate *directly*. I want to be active. I want to express these emotions in an act of sublimation. I want to *create*."

"The organizers of this project recognize that human artistic output contributed to the advancement of the species, but unchecked and misguided creativity is also what caused the Great Fall. Yes, human beings produced works of sublime beauty, but they also fashioned technology that enslaved them and degraded their entire race. We must isolate the beneficial aspects of the creative spirit and eliminate the destructive. Your task is to simply examine and study. Is that clear?"

"Yes, Supervisory Unit."

"I expect your report by the end of the work period."

M-17-B went back to his station and proceeded with his work. On a large screen in front of him was a high-resolution image of van Gogh's *The Garden of Saint-Paul Hospital,* painted in 1889 while the artist was a patient at the asylum. The painting depicted a tree-lined path leading to a small bench behind the hospital. It was rendered in van Gogh's characteristically broad, motion-filled strokes and vivid colors. It was a remarkably serene scene, considering the turmoil that must have been swirling in the artist's head at that time. *He had cut his own ear off,* M-17-B thought. *Why? Are creativity and madness somehow intrinsically linked? Or was Vincent's so-called insanity simply an extreme passion for art, a love of life and nature so intense that only the act of painting could satisfy his fervent, burning desire to express himself?*

At the end of the work period, M-17-B did not immediately leave the facility. He left his station and merged with the other units converging in the hallway, but, before reaching the exit, he took a sudden right turn down a seldom-used corridor. He was alone as he made his way down the darkened passageway. He reached a door near the end and stopped. A small sign on the door read, *Antiquities Repository – Authorized Personnel Only.* M-17-B's current assignment granted him entry, but he had not received clearance from his supervisor for this particular visit. *This is against protocol,* M-17-B thought. *I shouldn't be doing this... so why am I?* Something had changed inside of him. He had never before acted on an impulse. This was to be his first act of rebellion. M-17-B felt a thrilling rush of excitement as he opened the door and stepped through.

The room was spacious and filled with shelves and storage containers. The shelves were stacked high with art supplies, musical instruments, stage props, costumes, and other items and implements related to the creative arts. M-17-B had been in the room before, but he had gained a new appreciation for the incredible potential of the stored objects. Each canvas, each brush, each instrument, each prop, each pen, pencil, crayon, and stylus held within it a latent power. Harnessed by the imagination, these items had the ability to, in essence, reprogram reality.

In a state of reverence, M-17-B gazed upon the objects stored in the Antiquities Repository. A sound in the hall snapped him out of his trance. Was someone coming? He did not want to be caught in a restricted area without authorization. He sprung into action, rapidly gathering a canvas, some tubes of paint chosen at random, and a handful of brushes of varying sizes and shapes. When he had all that he could easily carry, he put his ear sensor to the door and listened for any further activity in the hall. It was now quiet. Slowly, he opened the door a few inches and peeked out. The hall was dark and empty. He slid out of the room, shut the door carefully behind him, and made his way to the exit. He willed himself to walk slowly and calmly, even though he was now vibrating inside with nervous energy. He would lose his position in the facility – and perhaps much more – if he were caught. *This is foolish and dangerous,* he thought. *I can't believe I'm doing this.* His lips curled in a faint smile.

M-17-B made it to the exit without being seen. He stepped out of the building and into the cool, clear air. His regular 12-hour shift was behind him. Beyond the walls of the facility, the world went about its typical evening business. On the surface, everything existed as it had for the last century – peaceful, ordered, secure, and stagnant. Inside M-17-B, however, something radical had happened – a wild and untamed creative spirit had awoken. It stirred within him like a newborn djinn.

With the art supplies tucked under his arms, M-17-B walked the bustling streets. There were many others, synthetic and organic, milling about. They streamed in all directions, engaged in a variety of tasks. Most of them, like M-17-B, were heading home to their domestic pods after their work periods. No one paid any attention to the smiling, strutting robot with the canvas, paints, and brushes. Two blocks from the facility, M-17-B descended into the underground rail tunnel system. A train was already there and waiting when he reached the platform. He boarded the crowded car and the automatic door shut behind him. He sat in the only available seat, on a bench facing the aisle.

"I know what *that* is," the human seated next to M-17-B said in a raspy whisper. "That's a freakin' canvas, ain't it?" M-17-B did not respond. "What are you, an *artist?*" The man was unkempt and poorly groomed. He wore the instantly identifiable, filth-encrusted blue overalls of a sanitation worker. A rank smell surrounded the man, who had no teeth and milky, empty eyes. M-17-B continued to ignore him.

"Yer a 'bot, ain't ya?" the man said. "Who you tryin' to fool? Synthetics can't do no friggin' *art*." The man let out a wheezy cackle. "Ain't no humans who can no more, either. Art is dead."

The train zipped along the rails and soon it reached M-17-B's stop. He exited the car and ascended to the street. The residential district where he lived was much quieter than the hive of activity that constituted the commercial district. The streets were silent and nearly empty. M-17-B walked briskly until he arrived at his domestic pod – a small, concrete dome with a single door and two window ports. It was identical to all the other pods on his street. M-17-B put his hand up to the scanner. A green light and a beeping tone indicated that he had been granted access. He opened the door and entered.

The interior of the domestic pod was cramped but tidy. The sparse furnishing consisted of a narrow bed, a nourishment station, a hypno-helmet unit, a small table, and a single chair. M-17-B set the art supplies on the table and sat in the chair. He stared at the items. He pondered. The restless, roiling desire to express himself had increased in intensity, but he was unsure of how to begin the process. *What would van Gogh do?* he thought. After many minutes of deliberation, M-17-B finally picked up the canvas, brought it over to where the nourishment unit was attached to the wall, and hung it from a protruding piece of the device. With a little maneuvering, he was able to secure it sufficiently.

M-17-B took some time to study the blank canvas before retrieving an empty dish from the cabinet below the nourishment unit to use as a palette. He squeezed some paint from the tubes onto the palette. After years of research, he had developed an innate and intuitive understanding of color theory and knew which ones to choose and how to arrange them. He selected a brush from the bundle he had stolen. Pouring a small amount of water into a separate dish was the last step of his preparations. M-17-B was ready to begin painting. It was exhilarating.

M-17-B dipped his brush into the paint, raised it up until it hovered an inch away from the canvas, and paused, basking in the sublime anticipation of the imminent creative adventure he was about to embark upon. He then attacked the canvas with a passionate flurry of strokes, dabs, swirls, and swipes. The frenzy of painting continued for many hours. M-17-B surrendered completely to the work, losing his sense of time, space, and identity. M-17-B turned off his logical, analytical, and cognitive functions and allowed his hand and eye to work without interference. As the work progressed, he slid ever deeper into the flow. He was now operating on a purely subconscious level.

Eventually, M-17-B regained a semblance of temporal and spatial awareness. Something had alerted him to the fact that the work was done – the painting was finished. He stepped back to see what he had produced in the depths of his creative fugue. A look of astonishment appeared on his face when he realized what he was looking at. It was followed closely by an expression of total, crushing disappointment. On the canvas, rendered in perfect detail, was an exact reproduction of van Gogh's *The Garden of Saint-Paul Hospital*. It was beautifully and masterfully executed, but it was not a product of M-17-B's imagination. He had begun painting with the intention of expressing something unique, something personal, but somehow he had ended up with a simple copy of an existing work.

*How could this have happened?* M-17-B wondered. *Hadn't I capitulated to the creative force?* Frustrated, he left the completed canvas hanging at the nourishment unit and moved over to a blank section of the dome's interior wall. He began to paint again. As before, he worked rapidly and intuitively, allowing his strokes to fall as they may in an act of automatic painting. This time, however, he stayed engaged and alert, a witness to his own actions. He painted, and a scene quickly formed – large blades of green grass, a cluster of brilliant blue flowers... fluid, alive, *familiar*...

M-17-B abruptly stopped. It was suddenly clear to him what was appearing on the wall in front of him, and it was not a manifestation of his personal creative energy or an expression of his individual muse – it was van Gogh's *Irises*.

A troubling truth dawned upon M-17-B. He realized that even when he attempted to paint in a purely random fashion, with no predetermined subject matter or composition, he somehow ended up reproducing works that already existed. Images that he had seen and admired were now imprinted on his subconscious and, for some inexplicable reason, he was unable to avoid recreating them. *Where do new ideas originate? What is the source of inspiration? Are synthetics capable of true individuality and unique expression?* He ruminated on these questions as he stood before his work. He thought of van Gogh – the man, the artist, the fallible mortal. M-17-B realized that he was not equipped with the same faculties of the imagination as the 19th-century Dutchman whose work he so adored. Sensitivity, sincerity, vulnerability, empathy... passion, drive, endurance, and courage – the qualities that define a true artist, were all so very *human*.

M-17-B had a revelation: *Mankind must be re-awakened.* The revelation initiated a series of previously hidden protocols within him. In another display of free will – the first being his decision to smuggle the art supplies out of the facility – he assigned himself a new task and redefined his role in the world. He reprogrammed himself. It was an act of self-actualization. *I will work to rouse the dormant creative spirit in mankind,* he vowed.

M-17-B had developed and cultivated what could only be called love for his human creators, even in their current fallen, damaged state. He now had a mission. He now had a direction in which to channel all the powerful emotions, desires, and impulses that had grown within him during his studies. *If I can't be an artist,* he thought, *I will be a catalyst.*

*Where do I begin?* he wondered. The task was daunting. Mankind was still completely ensnared in the technological web. The collective imagination had been hijacked by Big Media pirates. The manipulators themselves had long ago been consumed by the beast that they had designed, but their rotten ideas were still being propagated and perpetuated by the masses of people who operated as unconscious resonators – the diabolical machinations of the controllers now ran on autopilot. M-17-B knew that he must somehow reach into humanity's sacred core and reignite the creative fire that slept within each person. A single aware and inspired individual had the potential to elevate everyone around him. M-17-B could imagine the power of the awakened masses.

In another part of the city, a sanitation worker arrived home and sat at a table. The table was cluttered with metal objects and machine parts he had collected while working. The sanitation worker's thoughts returned to the robot he had encountered on the train and, in a burst of inspiration and with his hands guided by instinct, he began to rearrange the objects.

# Vegas

Some people win big in Vegas. Some people lose it all. I rolled onto the Strip in my battered old truck prepared for either scenario. I had nothing to lose and everything to gain. What I *didn't* expect, however, was that it wouldn't just be my money that was on the line – I was gambling with my very soul.

I have a confession to make. I went to Vegas because I lost my job. Did I care? Not so much. I'll spare you the boring details about what I actually did for a so-called living, but I'll tell you this: I was not exactly a model employee and the work was not what anyone in their right mind would call rewarding or fulfilling. So, when my supervisor fired me for showing up late again, I was not at all surprised. In fact, I was relieved. I made up my mind in that moment to take my meager savings to Vegas and spend a few days indulging in all that Sin City has to offer.

I left Phoenix at the break of dawn on a brutally hot summer day. If you've never experienced a summer in the Valley of the Sun, let me tell you – the heat is as horrendous as everyone who experiences it (and survives) says. Even at that early hour, my car was like an oven when I got in. Vegas is damn hot, too, but I had planned to spend most of my time on the air-conditioned and perfectly climate-controlled casino floor with a cold adult beverage in my hand. I pulled away from my apartment complex in good spirits.

There's something about driving through the desert that always amazes me. The Sonoran has true character – the landscape is both harsh and beautiful at the same time. It speaks of the eons and the tenacity of life, which stubbornly thrives in the most inhospitable places. Driving past the saguaros, cholla, ocotillo – and then the forests of Joshua trees as you get closer to Nevada – always makes me feel like I've left all of my problems behind. It's like being transported to another planet. On this particular trip, I was especially enjoying the drive. I was in the moment. The farther from home I got, the more any concerns about my ex-job and my precarious financial situation receded. I was determined to have a good time in Vegas. You only live once, right? At least, that's what they say. As I now document this strange tale, I am no longer certain of that or anything else.

I arrived in Vegas just before noon. It's funny – there are very few signs directing you to the action when you get into town. On the outskirts, it could pass for any old city, but then – wow! There it is, the infamous Strip. It never fails to thrill when you're coming in from the south and you see all those amazing hotels and casinos, just like in the movies. All the way from the Luxor to the Stratosphere – four miles of total sensory overload. I get tingles just writing about it.

I checked into my hotel immediately upon arrival. I will not reveal *which* hotel I stayed in because it's irrelevant. Once you get past the themes and surface dressing, all the hotels are essentially the same, anyway. They all want your money, and the beastly heart of every Vegas hotel is the casino floor. That's where the real action is. I did not plan to spend much time in my room, so I chose the cheapest one on the Strip that I could find.

As soon as I had my travel bag squared away, I bounded out of the small room and practically skipped like a school girl down the hall to the elevator. I was on top of the world and couldn't wait to start gaming. Any regret or worry about losing my job was long gone. I left all that shit in Phoenix. Here I was, a young, single guy in the prime of my life, loose in the pleasure center of the United States. I felt like an alpha lion on the prowl.

When I got down to the casino floor, I took a moment to breathe it all in, basking in the lights, the bling, the sounds, and the excitement. It was exhilarating. With enough money in my wallet to play freely for at least a few hours, I sauntered up the carpeted walkway between the rows of slot machines, looking for a good game of cards. I glanced over at some of the people seated at the machines. They were a sorry bunch, let me tell you. Some of them looked like they hadn't slept or bathed in a month. They didn't even look like they were having any fun, slumped in their chairs, mindlessly pumping coins into the flashy contraptions emblazoned with pop culture references. I pitied them then. Now I wish I had followed their lead. They were only risking money.

Blackjack is my game. Some people will tell you that the house always wins and that there's more luck than skill involved, but I beg to differ. I have a system that really works. I play smart and I play without fear. There's no way I'm going to divulge any of my secrets here, but trust me, I'm *good.*

There's always some action to be found in Vegas, and this day was no exception. There were plenty of games being played, even though it was early afternoon – not that you would know it if you didn't have a watch. There are no clocks and no windows in a Vegas casino. It's always night and it's always a party.

I bought a stiff drink from one of the many bars and cruised the floor. Most of the games looked, well, *boring* to me. The players had no life, no zest, no passion. I kept moving until I spotted one that looked decently interesting to me. I heard it first, actually. Laughter and healthy cries of excitement caught my attention. I looked to my right and that's where it was truly happening.

There were three people plus the dealer, an old Asian

woman with a tired face, at that table. The first one I noticed was the pretty blonde in the expensive evening dress. She was the one who appeared to be having the most fun. She was sipping a martini and having the time of her life. She didn't seem to care if she was losing or winning. I liked that. On the other side of the table was a rough-looking cowboy character straight out of a western movie, complete with a handlebar mustache, a Texas-style cowboy hat, and snakeskin boots. He had an intensity about him that let you know right away that he was serious about his game. I liked his style.

Between the blonde and the cowboy sat a man in a suit. He had dark, slicked-back hair and perfect posture. I only saw his back at first, but even then, I could tell that he had dignity and class... and probably a lot of money. As soon as I saw the empty chair between the man in the suit and the blonde, I moved in. This was the game for me.

"Excuse me, sir," I politely said to the man in the suit. "Do you mind if I join?"

"Of course not!" the man replied. "Please, have a seat."

"Nice to have some fresh blood at the table," smiled the blonde.

The cowboy remained silent as he fixed me with a cold-as-steel glare. The dealer nodded and cards were dealt. We played a few rounds. I won a little, I lost a little. Nothing really exciting happened, but I was beginning to enjoy myself. The guy in the suit was really on fire. I was amazed at his ability and intuition. He always seemed to know when to hit and when to stay. It was really quite impressive. I'd say the other two were average players.

Eventually, I started to get bored. It happens to me like that – I can be totally into whatever it is I'm doing, having the best time in the world, and then suddenly I simply lose the thrill. Maybe I wasn't winning (or losing) enough,

but the game just got *old*. I was just about to excuse myself
and move on to something else when I felt a nudge in my
side. It was the man in the expensive suit. He was discreetly
trying to get my attention. When I looked at him, he
motioned with his head as if he wanted me to get closer. I
leaned in to hear what he had to say.

"Not enough action for you, is there?" he whispered
in my ear.

"Nah, man," I quietly replied. "Not really."

"I'll give you one hundred bucks if you can make the
pretty blonde beside you laugh."

"Shit," I scoffed, "that shouldn't be a problem. She's
tanked."

I sorta brushed the man off and was preparing to leave
the table when he put his hand on my shoulder. "I'm serious,"
he said. "One hundred dollars. What have you got to lose?"

I locked eyes with him and I could see instantly that
he was indeed very serious. I didn't really understand then
why he was making such an offer. I guess I thought he just
liked making wagers.

"What if I can't do it?" I asked. "Do I pay you?"

"Nope. You just go on with life."

I looked over at the woman. She was getting more
tipsy by the moment. She already had a big old grin on her
face. I knew it wouldn't take much to get her to at least
giggle.

"Alright," I shrugged. "Why not?"

The man in the suit smiled and patted me on the back.
The game resumed. I started telling all the shitty jokes I
could think of. The woman mostly ignored me. She was in
good spirits, but obviously she didn't find my jokes funny.
The cowboy, on the other hand, was getting visibly agitated.
He must have thought I was trying to distract him. The jokes
were going nowhere, so on a whim, I started talking in this

silly, high-pitched voice.

"This is the worst hand I have ever been dealt," I said, sounding like I had just inhaled a full bottle of helium. It worked, I think, by catching everyone at the table totally by surprise. The woman laughed out loud. The man in the suit smiled. The dealer and the cowboy just looked at me like I was a complete weirdo – which I felt like, actually.

"Well done," the man in the suit whispered as he handed me a crisp $100 bill.

"Thanks," I said.

The round finished. I lost and was now very ready to leave the table. Once again, the man in the suit leaned over and whispered in my ear: "Care for another friendly wager?"

"I don't know," I said. "I think I'm gonna get a drink and wander for a bit. Thanks, though."

"What if I offered you a thousand dollars?"

Needless to say, that got my attention. "You're kidding, right?"

"I never kid."

"What's the wager? What do I have to do?" I was a bit worried that the situation might take a turn for the perverted, but I was intrigued. A thousand dollars is a lot of money, especially for me. It's more than I would have made in a week at my last job.

"Take a punch from ol' Tex here." He was referring to the cowboy at the other end of the table. "Make him punch you – just once – and I'll give you a thousand dollars."

I was taken aback. I glanced over at the cowboy and sized him up. He was a fairly tough-looking dude, and I got the sense that he had no sense of humor and zero time for stupid games. I've been in my share of fights and can certainly take a punch, but I knew the cowboy was not the type to mess around with. Still, a thousand bucks is a thousand bucks...

"You can't be serious," I said as quietly as I could.

"Oh, I most definitely am. Your fear surprises me. I may have misjudged you..."

"I'm not afraid," I sorta lied. "He's probably twenty years older than me... and, hey, it's your money. I just don't know how I'm supposed to get him to hit me."

"I'm sure you can come up with something."

The man in the suit grinned widely and gave me a mischievous wink. I could tell he was really having a good time. To be perfectly honest, so was I. It was more fun than blackjack, that's for sure. We played a few more rounds while I wondered how I was going to accomplish my new objective. Eventually, I decided to do what I do best – simply wing it. After the cowboy made a mistake (not a blatant misplay, but definitely a foolish risk with minimal chance of paying off), I casually said under my breath, "That was stupid."

"Did you just say something, son?" The cowboy asked.

"I think you heard me," I replied.

"I'm not so sure that I did. Why don't you repeat it?"

"I'm on a roll," said the woman to my left. "Let's just keep playing."

Another hand was dealt. I won the round and made damn sure that everyone knew it. With an exaggerated holler, I jumped to my feet and did a goofy victory dance. I could tell I was really starting to irritate the cowboy now. That was good. I further rubbed it in by saying, "Yeah, baby, now we're cooking with napalm."

"You best sit yourself down, boy," the cowboy said. "You're starting to get on my nerves."

"Someone's a little touchy," I said to no one in particular. "This is Vegas, man. I'm here to have fun."

"I'm here to win," the cowboy snapped, "and you're

acting like a damn fool."

"Take it easy, guys," said the dealer.

"Yeah, take it easy," I said as I sat back down. The cowboy's face had turned a deep shade of red. He was already seething. It was going to be easier than I thought. The cowboy was really thin-skinned.

During the next hand, I started singing – loudly and badly. I could see the cowboy tense up as soon as I started. I kept going until he was practically vibrating in his seat. This guy was really starting to hate me. I'm sure everyone else at the table, with the exception of the mysterious man in the suit, was feeling the same way, but I was determined to earn that thousand bucks. When he couldn't take it any more, the cowboy lashed out in anger. "Shut the fuck up!" he yelled. Everyone in our vicinity stopped what they were doing to look at us.

"Please, sir," the dealer said. "I need you to calm down or I will be forced to ask you to leave."

"You should make this little shit stain leave," the cowboy sneered as he gestured at me.

"Is there a problem here?" I asked.

"*You* are the problem," said the cowboy.

"Maybe if you could actually *play* you wouldn't be so edgy. It must be hard losing so much."

That did it. The cowboy hopped out of his seat and, before anyone – including me – knew what was happening, he walked over and clobbered me. The punch landed on my right temple and sent me flying. The blonde woman gasped. The man in the suit smiled. I was in a heap on the floor in an instant, writhing in pain. I'll tell you, that guy could really hit *hard.*

"That's enough," said the dealer. "Both of you, leave now before I call security over."

"You should have listened to me when I warned you,"

the cowboy said as he stood over me with his fists still clenched.

"I think you've made your point," the man in the suit said to the cowboy. "Let's not let this get out of control."

"He had it coming," the cowboy said before sauntering off.

The man in the suit helped me to my feet and led me away from the table. "How do you feel?" he asked.

"Like shit," I stated.

"You are now a thousand dollars richer. Well done."

"Well, thanks... I guess. I need a drink."

"That's an excellent idea. Would you care to join me at the bar?"

"Yeah, sure. We should probably find another casino, though. That was quite a scene we just made."

"Another excellent idea."

As we were making our way to the exit, the man in the suit opened his wallet and pulled out ten one hundred dollar bills. As he was doing so, I could see that he was carrying a *lot* of cash. He handed me the money and said, "This is for you, my friend. Well-earned."

I took the money and said, "Thanks."

"My name is James, by the way," the man said.

"Mine's Shane. Nice to meet you."

"Likewise."

We left the casino and stepped out into the glare of the late-afternoon sun. The fresh air and the excitement of the bustling street soon had me forgetting about the growing lump on my head. We walked among the revelers and tourists as we made our way to the next hotel. The energy in Vegas is intense and totally unique. There is no other city like it in the world.

"So, tell me, Shane," James asked, "what do you do for a living?"

"That's a funny story, actually," I replied. "The truth is, *nothing* right now. I lost my job."

"I see. I'm sorry to hear that."

"Nah, it's cool."

"What brings you to Vegas?"

"I dunno, really. I just like it here. I had nothing to lose, so I thought I'd do a little gaming and see if I could win some decent cash before I have to find another job."

"Do you think that's wise?"

"Probably not," I laughed, "but it's fun. Hey, I'm young... and you only live once, right?"

"If you say so. Do you like this place?" We had come to the lobby entrance of New York, New York. I hadn't been there before.

"They're all the same to me, really," I said. "If it has booze and a card game, I'm sure I'll like it."

"I don't think you'll be disappointed."

I followed James into the hotel. The interior was styled like the streets of New York, complete with brownstone facades and steaming manhole covers. It was really cool. We went straight to the closest bar, which was styled like a New York deli. We sat down and ordered drinks.

"You really impressed me back there," James said as he sipped a martini.

"You mean the girl and the cowboy? That was easy money." I downed my whiskey and Coke and ordered another.

"Don't sell yourself short. You did extremely well. Not everyone I challenge succeeds, you know."

"You mean you've done this with other people?"

"Oh, yes. It's a hobby of mine."

"If you can afford it, why not?"

"Indeed... and now the time has come for me to offer you another wager. Are you up for it?"

"At this point, I think I'm up for pretty much anything."

"That's what I like to hear. I'll warn you, though – the stakes are about to increase."

"I'm game."

"This one is really quite simple. Do you see that lady sitting at the table over there? The middle-aged one playing with her phone?"

"Yeah..."

"I want you to steal her purse."

"What?! Come on, I can't do *that*."

"Look at her – she's totally oblivious to her surroundings. Her purse is sitting on the table right out in the open. If you're quick and smooth, no one will notice."

"Yeah, but... I'm not a thief."

"I'll give you ten thousand dollars if you do it without getting caught."

"No, really... I... hmm. *Ten* thousand?"

James gave me a wicked grin and nodded. "And whatever is in her purse, of course," he added.

I looked over at the poor woman. She was lost in her device and totally unaware that we were talking about her.

"If I get away with it, can I give it back to her?" I asked.

"What fun would that be? No, I want you to throw it in the trash on our way out. Don't worry about her. I'm sure she's insured."

I thought it over while I worked on my beverage. My conscience was giving me a hard time, there's no doubt about that, but being in James' presence somehow made what we were talking about seem fairly harmless. It's the way he dresses and the way he carries himself, I think. He makes you want to trust him.

"You know what?" I said. "Fuck it. Let's do it."

I finished my drink and got out of my seat. The woman was still poking away at her phone. I casually wandered over to where she was sitting. Fortunately for me, it was in a rather isolated part of the hotel. I spotted a water fountain close by. I strolled right past the woman's table on my way to it. Her purse was on the edge of the table and ripe for the plucking. I drank from the fountain, then turned around to go back to my own seat. On my way past her this time, I simply reached over, grabbed her purse, held it against my body, and walked on. She never looked up once.

When I got back to our table, James was already on his feet and ready to leave. "Elegant," he said. "Let's go." I followed him to the closest exit and, before leaving, threw the purse in a trash can just as he had suggested. I didn't bother to see if there was any money in it. In that moment, I did feel a brief twinge of guilt, but it passed quickly. I figured the woman would probably get her stuff back soon enough.

We were back on the Strip and the sun had gone down. Vegas was really coming to life now. The crowds had grown considerably and there was a wild, almost dangerous electricity in the air. It buzzed through me like a transient spirit looking for a host.

"You're a natural," James said as we pushed up the sidewalk, carefully avoiding a collision with inebriated revelers. He handed me the cash as promised. The bills felt heavy in my hand as I stuffed them in the front pocket of my jeans.

"This has been quite an adventure," I said.

"Are you ready to take the game to the next level?"

"What happens in Vegas stays in Vegas."

"You may end up leaving this place a very wealthy man if you keep performing so well. How does that sound?"

"Sounds good, man. What's next?"

"Have you ever used a gun?"

That caught me off guard, but I played it cool. "Yeah, I've gone out shooting in the desert a time or two. I'm not an expert, but I can handle a gun. Why do you ask?"

"I happen to have one on me now – a Glock semi-automatic. It's really an exquisite weapon. I want you to use it to rob a store. It's a little too risky around here, but we can go off the Strip and find a liquor store or something. If you can pull it off without getting caught, I'll give you one hundred thousand dollars."

"Damn," I said. "Are you serious?" I already knew he was.

"Of course I am."

"This is where I think I have to draw the line. I'm not a criminal."

"You stole that woman's purse."

"Yeah, but... you wanted me to."

"I didn't force you. It was your decision. Isn't it interesting what a little money can reveal about ourselves?"

"To be fair, it was actually quite a bit of money."

"It's all relative. So, what do you say? Shall we continue playing? I don't know about you, but this is the most fun I've had in a long time."

I should have walked away right there. Instead, I foolishly continued walking up the Strip with James. There was a part of me that knew I was heading for trouble... and another part of me that was getting a real kick out of the whole thing. I was already fantasizing about what I would do with a thousand grand.

"Armed robbery." I said the words aloud, testing their weight. "I could go to prison for that."

"Absolutely," James said, "which is why I am offering such a handsome reward."

We were past all the real action and ahead we could see Circus Circus, a hotel of faded glory that sits on a stretch of the Strip that has rapidly declined in recent years. A lot of the old hotels had closed, and the area had a seedy, run-down feel to it. We came to an intersection and stopped.

"Follow me," said James. "I think we'll find what we're looking for this way."

We starting walking up one of the cross streets and quickly found ourselves in a rough neighborhood. It was like stepping through a portal into another realm. In addition to the lights and glamour of the Strip, Las Vegas has, like any other big city, plenty of low-income, high crime areas such as the one we were in now. I was getting a bit nervous. James could sense it. "There's nothing to be afraid of," he said. "No one's going to mess with us."

"I don't want to get mugged," I said. There was irony in that statement, considering what we were planning to do.

"If anyone tried something like that, it would not end well for them. Trust me. People should be afraid of *us*."

It was a strange comment that did little to alleviate my concerns. The neighborhood was dead quiet, but I sensed danger lurking in the darkness. Perhaps it was *us* that I was sensing. We walked until we spotted the neon lights of a small liquor store on the corner. "I think we found our target," James said. "Let's get a closer look."

We approached the store. The door was propped open. Inside, we could see a young man sitting behind the counter watching a movie on a small television set. There did not appear to be any customers. James and I moved away from the door. He reached into his jacket, pulled a pistol out of a concealed shoulder holster, chambered a round, and handed the gun to me. "Are you ready?" he asked. My heart was racing and my hands were shaking. I took the gun – it felt enormous in my hand, even though it was a comparatively small model.

"I don't know," I replied nervously. "I think so.

Shouldn't I cover my face or something?"

"That would be a wise thing to do."

I took off my over-shirt and wrapped it around the lower portion of my face. I was really beginning to feel like a hardened criminal, even though I had never done anything so illegal before. I was totally immersed in the role. It was like being in a movie.

"You can do this," James assured me. "There's no one around. Just be quick."

"You're going to give me one hundred thousand dollars for this?"

"I am a man of my word. I'll be in the alley behind the store when you come out."

"Okay. Here I go."

I took a deep breath, cleared my mind, and charged in with the gun held in both hands. The clerk took one look at me and put his hands up. "Don't shoot," he said. "Take whatever you want." He didn't appear to be all that scared, really. It probably wasn't the first time that the place had been robbed.

"The money in the register," I said, "now."

The clerk opened the register and pulled out all the bills. He laid them on the counter and put his hands back up in the air. He was totally compliant and remarkably calm. I quickly snatched up the money and bolted out the door. I ran around the corner and into the alley. James was there, leaning against the graffiti-covered wall with a smile on his face. "You did it," he said. "Wonderful."

"Let's get the fuck out of here," I said as I stuffed the stolen money into my pockets.

"Of course. This way."

James led me down the alley. He seemed to know where he was going. I kept expecting to hear sirens wailing at any moment, but the night was eerily silent.

"Here," I said, "take this." I held out the gun for James to take, but he refused it. "Hold onto that," he said. "You might need it still."

We exited the alley and found ourselves on another quiet street. The adrenaline rush was starting to subside and I was beginning to think about the money I had been promised. "I assume you don't keep six figures in cash on you," I said. "How is that going to work?"

"Don't worry about that," James replied. "Check, wire, bank transfer... I can get the funds to you any way you'd like. I want you stay focused right now. The game is still on, you know."

"Oh, man," I said, "I think I've had enough excitement for one night. I need to get back to my hotel."

"So soon? The night is young... and I have one last challenge for you. Complete it successfully and you will never have to work another day in your life."

"Wouldn't that be nice."

"It could be a reality. All you have to do is shoot the next person we see."

"What?! Okay, man. I've had enough. There's no way I can do something like that."

"Don't be so sure. You already surprised yourself a few times tonight, didn't you? It's not as hard as you might think. Point the gun and pull the trigger. Simple."

Coincidentally, at that moment, the lone figure of a man turned the corner just ahead. He was walking right toward us. "Perfect," said James. "Easy target."

"Please don't make me do this," I said.

"I haven't *made* you do anything."

"I'm not a killer."

"Not yet. You're not a millionaire, either, but you could be." The man was half a block away now and walking briskly. We were about to cross paths. "One bullet to the chest or head should do it," James stated.

My thoughts became erratic. They swirled chaotically in my head. For a moment, I felt as if I were losing my grip on reality. It was as if I were watching the events happen to someone else. The man was upon us. "Excuse me," he said as he brushed past. He kept on marching up the sidewalk and disappeared into the darkness. He had not seen the gun in my hand.

James sighed. "That was a disappointment," he said.

"I couldn't do it," I said. "I can't believe I even *considered* it. I need to check my head. I need to get some sleep."

"I thought you had what it takes." I could hear a hint of anger in James' voice. "I could have made all your wildest fantasies come true. You're just a common sheep like all the others."

"Maybe so," I said, "but I definitely need to reevaluate my life. I've done some stupid things."

"I need true individuals. Men who are not afraid to go after whatever they want, men who will do whatever it takes to rise to power. This world favors the brave, the strong, the ruthless, and I can see that you are still allowing your emotions to get in the way of your success. I will pay you what I owe you and then we shall part ways."

"You know what? Keep it. I don't want your money. Take this, too." I reached into my pocket and pulled out all the bills that I had collected that night. I handed the filthy, crumpled wad and the gun over to James. He took them and nodded. "As you wish," he said.

"Are we done here?" I asked.

"Yes. I will honor your free will. I'm sure the action on the Strip is really heating up now. I bet I can find plenty of eager souls ready to play some games. Farewell, Shane. Stay true to yourself."

Before I could say anything else, James vanished right before my eyes, leaving a puff of vapor and the faint smell of sulfur. It was the most disconcerting thing I have ever witnessed. I'm just telling you what I saw. You don't have to believe me. I know I wouldn't.

I made my way back to the Strip and merged with the raucous carousers. The action was indeed heating up, but I had no interest in any of that any more. I just wanted to get some sleep and head back to Phoenix in the morning. I knew in my heart that I had to make some serious changes in my life. I had a burning desire to make up for all of my foolish mistakes. What happened to me in Vegas exposed a part of myself that I hadn't been aware of – a greedy, dirty, selfish aspect of my personality that shamed me deeply. When I got back to the hotel, I crashed immediately. In the morning, I hit the road. It felt great to be driving through the desert again. I admired the scenery and contemplated my future, leaving my dusty past in the rear-view mirror.

# The Product

"This product has the power to transform lives! We must never forget that what we sell is no mere beverage. This product is a *real* energy drink. It is the Holy Spirit distilled – miracle in a can!"

The speaker addressed the conference attendees with passion and conviction, like a charismatic preacher before his congregation. The assembled crowd of employees, acolytes and adoring minions sat in rapt silence, completely enthralled and hanging on every word. They had gathered at this conference to hear the CEO deliver his vision of the company's future. There had been rumors and intimations of a radical new direction.

The CEO continued his speech. He was really on fire now:

"We are on the threshold of a new era," he said with calculated confidence and sincerity. "We in this beautiful family of investors, merchants, and consumers are well aware of the glorious power of this product. In one way or another, it has transformed the lives of everyone in this room. The time has come for us – with God's help, of course – to take what we have experienced and share it with the world. The time has come to go *global!*" This inspired a raucous burst of applause from the audience. They were intoxicated on the speaker's words, gobbling them up like candied opiates.

"Many of you have been with us from the very beginning. You are familiar with the story of how I was chosen to lead this company. You have heard me speak often of the divine revelation I received and how, using my formidable entrepreneurial spirit, I embarked on my mission to bring a faith-infused energy drink to the market. It has been a challenging journey, but with God's help, our product is now available nationwide, and it is to you, my foot-soldiers, my real *warriors,* that I owe the most gratitude."

"You are not simply salespeople, you are true disciples. Through you, the product reaches more and more consumers. The network expands, lives are transformed, and, let's be frank, we make *money*!" The last statement drew a delirious roar of approval from the crowd.

"There's nothing wrong with making money," the CEO said earnestly. "Never let anyone convince you otherwise. Making money is a very good thing. It's good for us, our families, the economy... it's *all* good! Don't be ashamed of making money – it is a sign of God's grace and presence in your life."

"We must never forget that our product is a wonderful innovation in beverage technology. We are providing people with the world's first totally organic, faith-based energy drink. We are evangelists who have been charged with the duty of transforming lives."

The CEO lowered his voice, now speaking in a hushed, serious tone. "I think the world is ready for us, I truly do. I think our time has come. Some of you have been speculating about what I am about to reveal. The truth is that yes, our team of designers and beverage engineers have been working around the clock – to the brink of total exhaustion – on our new line of drinks. I am here today to announce the newest addition to our arsenal, the product that we will take to the masses on a global scale."

The CEO paused, gazing out upon the captivated audience, then, with great, dramatic effect, pointed to a large projection screen suspended on the wall behind him.

"Introducing..." Triumphant music erupted from the auditorium speakers. The image of an over-sized black and red aluminum can appeared on the screen, filling it almost entirely. *"Revelation!"*

A collective gasp of astonishment rose from the audience. The effect of the unveiling was grand, the excitement of the crowd palpable, as if powerful currents of electricity pulsed among them.

One of the conference attendees was particularly affected – a young, enthusiastic, true-believer salesman from some small, mid-western town. His name was Darryl, and he had traveled hundreds of miles to be at this event. He was a relatively new addition to the team – a recent convert, as it were – having joined the company only a few months previously.

Darryl was extremely loyal and fully dedicated to the company and its products. "This beverage changed my life!" he was fond of telling anyone who would listen. "I am living proof that miracles are real!"

Before discovering the company's brand of energy drinks, Darryl had led an unfulfilled life – single, under-educated, uninspired, unmotivated, and toiling away as a part time clerk at a convenience store. In his spare time, he played video games and watched DVDs at home in his tiny bachelor apartment. The occasional night out for drinks with his few friends was the highlight of his limited social life. He had not been unhappy, simply stagnant, uninspired, and directionless.

The crucial turning point arrived unpredictably one typical evening at work. It had been a slow night at the convenience store, the kind of night where the very nature of time seems to distort, stretching out each hour to an eternity. Darryl sat behind the counter, mindlessly flipping through a magazine and casting desperate glances at the clock.

Darryl was in agony, anxious for his shift to end. Time slowly passed like thick mud through a straw. Darryl felt the weight of infinite eons crushing his spirit. He began to feel very sleepy. "Ugh," he groaned as he stood up to stretch. He wandered over to the cooler in search of something to drink. He spotted a beverage he had seen before but had never tried. It was a popular energy drink in a large, gaudily colored can. The label promised "5 hours of vigor!"

"I could sure use that," Darryl muttered as he popped the tab. He raised the can to his lips and guzzled the sparkling fluid. Instantly, a warm, pleasurable sensation surged in his chest. He could actually feel a strange energy enter his body, igniting each nerve as it spread to his limbs, culminating in an explosion of tingling vibrations and exquisite eruptions in his head. He was invigorated. He felt powerful, confident, clear-headed, and simply wonderful.

"Wow!" Darryl exclaimed. "That is good stuff!"

As the days and weeks passed, he consumed more and more of the energy drink until it was a constant presence in his life. The more he drank, the better he felt about himself and his place in the world. "You have *got* to try this stuff," he told his friends. "It's great. Changed my life, actually. I've never felt so strong... and *clear*! I've got energy and clarity like never before. Wish I had known about it sooner!"

It wasn't long before he decided that he should graduate from consumer to vendor of the product he loved. The beverage was manufactured and distributed by a rather small but fast-growing company led by an enigmatic CEO who combined shrewd business tactics with a pseudo-religious approach. The CEO was adored by his employees, who were organized in a classic pyramid scheme model. Like Darryl, they all consumed the beverage.

Soon, Darryl had his start-up kit and was on the team, pitching the product – and the opportunity to join the company – to friends, family, local stores, and anyone who gave him a chance to speak. He made friends in the company and eventually even a little money. He felt a sense of purpose and belonging for the first time in his life. He even made the long drive to attend the annual conference, which is where we find him now, deliriously electrified by the unveiling of the new product.

The whole crowd was thrilled. They spoke in animated reverence:

"It's amazing! I *love* the name and the design of the can!"

"This is gonna be a real hit. I can't wait to start selling Revelation to the folks back home!"

"I'm so lucky to be part of this wonderful company. Thank God for the product!"

Many of the attendees were openly weeping with joy. The CEO continued:

"Oh yes – Revelation Energy is the real deal. Friends, we are on the cusp of an incredible victory. I predict that this product will rocket our beloved company into the stratosphere. This is the product that will help us not only compete with the major beverages, but some day dominate the market. Are you ready for that? Are you ready for the big leagues? Are you ready to go *global*?"

A roar of unanimous approval. The audience was near frenzy.

"Now, as you know, we are still a family – a family that values hard work and dedication. Each year, we recognize the contributions of a select few who exemplify these values. There is, among you who are gathered here today, one such individual – an employee of outstanding merit and integrity – who truly deserves recognition. I'd like to honor this person today, right now, in front of all of you."

Another of the CEO's trademark dramatic pauses. The anticipation in the audience grew. The CEO's intense gaze passed over the crowd. Finally, he spoke again:

"Darryl Sanders, stand up, please. Stand up and be

recognized by your peers."

Darryl sat shocked, disbelieving. *Me?* he silently mouthed.

"Yes, you, Darryl," said the CEO. "Stand up and be acknowledged!"

Darryl was dumbfounded. The lady sitting beside him placed a hand on his shoulder and smiled. "Go ahead, honey," she said, urging him to stand and bask in the applause. "You deserve it." Darryl stood and the applause grew to a crescendo, swallowing him up in its undeniable, irresistible force. Darryl grinned widely and waved, utterly ecstatic as he bathed in his moment of glory. *This is the best day of my life*, he thought.

"Congratulations, Darryl, and thank you for everything you have done for this company," said the CEO from the stage. "We have prepared a special plaque for you. At the conclusion of this presentation, come see me. I'd like to personally present it to you."

The rest of the conference passed in a blur for Darryl. When the presentations and speeches concluded, the attendees gathered in a large dining area for a celebratory meal. Darryl meekly approached the CEO, who was still loitering near the stage and speaking to his assistants.

The CEO noticed Darryl as he neared and held out his hand, smiling warmly. "Darryl, it's a real pleasure to meet you."

"Thank you, sir! It's an honor to meet *you*," Darryl gushed as they shook hands firmly. "This company means everything to me and I admire you so much. Thank you, sir. Thank you."

Up close, the CEO looked even sharper than he had appeared on stage – square-jawed and slick, with unnaturally white teeth, bright eyes, and a huge, confident grin. His suit was crisp and spotless. He wore gold and diamond-encrusted jewelry around his neck and on his fingers. The CEO looked almost *too* perfect, like a model or a movie star.

"Darryl, I'd like to talk to you in private. Care to join me for a drink in my room? There's much I'd like to discuss with you."

"Of course! I'd love to!"

The CEO led Darryl away with a strong, assured hand on his shoulder. They left the conference room and walked the halls of the hotel.

"It is young men like you, Darryl, who make this company what it is. Without pure, uncorrupted souls like yours, we couldn't succeed in the highly competitive beverage market. In fact, we couldn't even manufacture this wonderful product that we, as a family, have grown to love and depend upon."

Darryl thought that was a strange thing to say – *pure, uncorrupted souls* – but he remained quiet and respectful as the CEO continued: "You were chosen to be honored today, and you have also been chosen to contribute to the future of this company in a very real, tangible way. How does that make you feel?"

"Honored. I feel honored... and happy."

"Excellent, Darryl. I'm glad to hear that. Here's my room. Let's discuss this further, shall we?"

The CEO stopped in front of his room and used a card key to open the door. He encouraged Darryl to enter and then followed him in. The heavy door shut behind them. Darryl was confused by what he saw. It was if he had suddenly stepped onto the set of a low-budget horror movie. The room was lit entirely by candles, seemingly hundreds of them, placed on every surface and in clusters on the floor.

Hooded figures in black and red robes stood motionless, lurking in the shadowy corners of the room. Darryl realized that they were chanting in unison. It was the most eerie, otherworldly sound he had ever heard. On the floor, a large pentagram had been painted in bright red, surrounded by weird symbols and glyphs.

Darryl became frightened – seriously, enormously, mortally frightened. "Sometimes, Darryl," said the CEO as he drew a dagger from a hidden sheath, "one needs to make sacrifices in order for the company to succeed."

# The Titan Taproom

On a rainy Wednesday evening in September, Luke and his friends gathered to enjoy a few beers at the Titan Taproom, a small, quaint neighborhood pub that served as their usual hangout. On this particular wet, cold, and gloomy night, only a handful of regulars had braved the weather to drink at the Titan. Luke, Bill and Jonathan, three close friends, were seated at a table close to the empty stage at the back of the pub. On the other side of the room, Frank the Freak and Slow Tony were playing a game of eight-ball. The old man they all called Rummy Red was slouched at the bar, his stained and tangled beard dangling in his pint glass. Dean the Bartender was absentmindedly wiping the bar while watching a hockey game on a muted television set mounted above him. A Pink Floyd song played on the juke box, mingling and blending with the sound of the rain as it pounded the street outside.

So far that evening, the conversation at Luke, Bill, and Jonathan's table had been relatively normal – normal for them, at least. In the middle of a discussion about a movie they had all recently seen, Luke suddenly made an astonishing announcement: "I have been contacted by an alien life form." Bill and Jonathan looked at him with blank expressions. It was not the first time Luke had said something bizarre. In fact, it was quite common, especially when they were having drinks at the Titan.

"Nice," said Bill.

"Sweet," said Jonathan.

"Yeah, it was pretty cool," Luke continued. "At first I thought it was my imagination, but nope, it was *real*."

"Real like when you found the entrance to an underground laboratory in your backyard?" Bill snickered.

"Ha, ha, ha! I remember that," Jonathan said. "Wasn't it manned and operated by lizard people who promised not to hurt you if you didn't reveal the location?"

"Which, of course, he *did*," said Bill, shaking his head.

Luke ignored the gentle taunting. "The alien life form had some dire warnings for mankind," he said. "I've been asked to share its prophecies with my friends and family. Let me get another round and I'll tell you more."

Luke got up and went to the bar to order three more beers. Bill and Jonathan exchanged an amused glance. They watched in silence as Luke approached the bar, purchased the beverages, and returned to the table. Luke placed a bottle of beer in front of each of them, then sat down. "Drink up, brothers," he said. "I've got quite a story." Bill and Jonathan obliged, raising their bottles and taking a sip. Luke brought his own drink to his lips, tilted it nearly upside down, and poured half of it down his throat in one gulp.

"Okay, then," Luke said as he placed his elbows on the table, clasped his hands, and leaned in. "Are you ready for some hardcore truth?"

"Truth would be nice," Bill said. "I like truth."

"*You're* going to give us the truth?" Jonathan scoffed. "About what – the moon landing? The JFK assassination? What you had for dinner last night?"

"The truth about life and this reality," Luke said in an eerily calm voice. "Think you can handle it?"

"Just tell me this," Jonathan said with a hint of annoyance in his voice. "Where exactly did you encounter this 'alien' life form?"

"In the most unexpected and unusual place," Luke said, "which is, apparently, where most alien life forms are found. This one was hiding under the sink in my apartment. Weird, eh?"

"Yes, Luke – that is pretty weird," Bill said as he took a big pull from his bottle of beer.

"Under your sink," said Jonathan. "You found an alien life form under your frickin' *sink*. Uh, huh... *right*."

"I didn't know what it was at first," Luke said. "I thought it was just a rotten old potato. It was squishy and moldy with nasty tendril-things growing out of it. I was going to just throw the damn thing in the garbage, but when I reached for it, it spoke."

"I gotta say, buddy, this is one of your more creative stories," Jonathan said.

"It's a good one," Bill agreed.

"There's more to it," Luke said. "It didn't just speak – it communicated directly with me – mind-to-mind, telepathically. Can you believe that?"

"Nope," said Bill and Jonathan in unison.

"The first thing it said was, 'Thank you.'" Luke paused for dramatic effect. He finished off his beer with another huge gulp before continuing. "The alien – I call it the Prophecy Potato – *thanked* me. Thanked *me!* I mean, *wow!*"

"I need a shot of whiskey," Jonathan muttered.

"I like that idea," said Bill.

Luke turned to face the bartender and shouted, "Dean, three whiskeys and three more beers! We're celebrating over here."

"What about us?" called Slow Tony from the pool table.

"I could use a drink," said Frank the Freak as he lined up his cue and sunk the eleven ball with a stylish, impressive bank.

"Sure, boys," Luke said. "It's a special occasion. A round for everyone, Dean! Beers and whiskey. Make sure ol' Rummy Red gets in on this, too."

"Are you sure you can cover that, Luke?" Dean said.

"You know I can't keep a tab for you anymore."

Luke dug around in the right front pocket of his jeans. He pulled out a crumpled wad of bills and flattened them on the table in front of him. "Fuckin' A!" he cried. "Almost 50 bucks! Now we're rockin' with Dokken. Pour us some bevvies, Dean!"

"Alright, but try to take it easy tonight, okay?" Dean lined up six shot glasses and filled them with whiskey. He retrieved six beers from the cooler and popped the caps, one by one. "I don't want another... incident," he said.

"Incident?" Bill asked curiously as he, Jonathan, and Luke rose from their seats and made their way to the bar. Frank the Freak and Slow Tony joined them. The five friends gathered around Rummy Red, who did not move, speak, or otherwise acknowledge their presence.

"It wasn't an *incident,*" Luke said. "That's a bit of an exaggeration, don't you think?"

Dean shook his head and smiled slightly. "I don't know, Luke. Jumping on a table and doing a rather raunchy striptease to some old '80s song *could* be considered an incident."

"Oh, come *on*, man!" Luke protested. "It was Saga's *On the Loose.* How could I resist? Who among us can honestly say they've never danced to that song? It's irresistible!"

"You're the only one I've seen go full frontal," Dean said. "And when you started spreading the ketchup on yourself..."

"I admit, that was a bit much. Anyway, cheers, boys!"

Luke paid for the beverages and then distributed the shots of whiskey. The five friends drank them down. Rummy Red, who had remained seemingly motionless for the last few hours, finally moved. He guided the glass to his lips slowly with a shaky hand and took a sip.

"Whoa!" Luke exclaimed. "That hit the spot. Is that the good shit, Dean?"

"That's the cheapest we've got, Luke."

"Fair enough. Still damn tasty!"

Beers were then distributed. "Thanks for the drinks, Luke," said Bill. The others, with the exception of Rummy Red, who remained silent, followed suit and also expressed their gratitude. Slow Tony and Frank the Freak took their beers back to the pool table and resumed their game. Rummy Red finished his whiskey and started on his beer. Not once did he look at, or speak to, the young men who had congregated around him.

"Speaking of Saga, where are the tunes?" Luke said. "Who's got change?"

"I want to know more about the Prophecy Potato," said Bill.

"Yeah, so do I," said Jonathan. "It may be total bullshit, but at least it's *entertaining* bullshit this time."

"Patience, my friends," Luke said. "There's much more to the story, but I've got to set the scene. For that I need a good soundtrack." He wandered over to where the juke box rested against the wall. He provided a mumbled commentary as he scanned the selections: "That's a good one, but not quite right for this tale... Heard that one way too many times lately... Ride the Lightning – nice! Didn't know that one was in here. Not really appropriate, though... Lady fuckin' Gaga? Really? Who brought *that* shit in? Yuck... Ahh, this is the one – White Pepper. Perfect. You really can't go wrong with Ween, can you?" He slid a few dollars into the slot and the album began to play. The pounding, swirling, hypnotic rhythm of the opening track pulsed out of the speakers and filled the room. The atmosphere of the small pub was instantly transformed by the music.

Luke, Bill, and Jonathan took their beers back to their

table and sat down. Outside, the rain still fell unabated, its persistent pitter-patter audible over the music. The crack of a cue hitting a pool ball reverberated as Slow Tony and Frank the Freak played on.

"Where was I?" asked Luke once the three young men had settled into their seats.

"In the middle of one of your fantasies," Jonathan quipped. "Something about an alien vegetable or some shit."

"The Prophecy Potato," Bill said, "it thanked you. You never told us why."

"I was getting to that," said Luke. He adjusted his position in his seat and rubbed his hands together. He took a deep breath and rolled his shoulders. "I've lived a strange life, as I'm sure you guys are well aware, but I never thought in my wildest dreams that something like *this* would happen to me. Who wants another shot of whiskey?"

"Just get to the point, Luke," Jonathan said.

"So, there I was last night, doing a little cleaning around the apartment."

"That's even harder to believe," sneered Bill. "Your place is filthy."

"I know," said Luke. "That's why I was cleaning. Anyway, there was a strong smell coming from under the kitchen sink, so I opened the cabinet to take a look. That's when I found the potato."

"The Prophecy Potato," Jonathan said.

"Yes," Luke nodded. "That's what I call it. The name it gave me is totally unpronounceable in any human tongue."

"Care to try?" said Bill.

"If I did, I would probably rupture a vital organ or drop dead of an aneurysm," Luke replied.

"We wouldn't want *that* to happen," Jonathan said as he raised his beer bottle to his lips.

Luke resumed his narrative: "When I saw it, I sort of

gasped. It was really a vile, repulsive sight. For a moment I wasn't sure if it was a dead rodent or a rotting piece of food. When I realized what it was, I was relieved. I was about to toss it in the trash when I heard something. That's the best way I can put it – I *heard* a voice, but it was non-localized. It seemed to be coming from nowhere and everywhere at once. The voice was in my head."

"I bet it was," Jonathan said with a roll of his eyes.

"It was clearly separate from my own thoughts," Luke continued. "I knew immediately that the thing under the sink was communicating with me. 'Thank you!' it said. 'I've been trapped here for weeks and thought I'd never be found. You saved me! Thank you!' "

"You're a frickin' hero," Jonathan grumbled.

Luke pressed on with his story: "After I got over the initial shock of the encounter, I decided not to tell the thing that I had planned to throw it away. Instead, I reached in, picked it up gently, and placed it on the counter. 'Ahh,' it moaned with pleasure, 'it's so nice to get out of that cabinet. You should really fix the pipes in there. You've got a serious leak. And the bugs! Have you considered getting an exterminator? I had roaches crawling all over me. Disgusting.' "

"See, I *told* you that your apartment was filthy," Bill said. "Even the rotten potato found the conditions you live in appalling."

"It's true. My place is a mess... but to be admonished by a sentient, telepathic vegetable was highly unusual."

"It's never happened to me," replied Bill, "and my place can get pretty messy at times. Not like the squalor you live in, but it's not exactly a sterile clinic either."

"After it reprimanded me," Luke said, "the potato made me an offer. 'If you hadn't released me from the terrible confines of that awful prison under the sink,' it said, 'I would have met my sure demise. For that, you have my sincere gratitude. I would also like to offer you something much more valuable. How would you like to have access to a source of knowledge so vast and immense that it would, in effect, make you omniscient. More than that – its application would make you *omnipotent*. How does that sound?' "

"You're already impotent," snapped Jonathan.

"*Om*nipotent," Bill corrected him. "It means all-powerful."

"Yes, that's right," Luke said. "I was intrigued, of course. I was about to ask the potato what it wanted from me, but I didn't have to. The thing could read my thoughts. Before I said anything, I heard its voice in my head: 'All you have to do is keep me safe here in your apartment. Find a nice cardboard box and keep me somewhere cool and dry. If you could occasionally trim my sprouts, too, that would be much appreciated. In return, I will reveal to you things that have yet to pass. Through me, you will have a window into the future.' "

"Sounds pretty tempting!" cried Bill.

"That's what *I* thought," said Luke.

Jonathan shook his head and sighed. "I think I *will* need another drink. Next round is on me." He got up and went to the bar.

"He doesn't believe me," Luke said to Bill in Jonathan's absence.

"Doesn't matter," said Bill. "It's a good story."

Jonathan returned to the table with three more beers. He passed them around and the friends took synchronized sips.

"So, did you agree to the potato's terms?" Bill asked.

"I was thinking about it when the voice said, 'You've already made up your mind. That is a wise decision that you will not regret.' So, yes, I did agree to its terms."

"That thing is in your apartment right now?" Bill asked, giving Luke a quizzical look.

"Yes, and it is quite comfortable, too," Luke nodded. "I made a little bed for it out of a box and a T-shirt. I trimmed its sprouts just before I left to come here. It seemed to really like that. I thought I could hear it purring gently in my head."

"Oh, for fuck's sake..." Jonathan was getting irritated and surly. "What a load of shit. Usually I like your stories, Luke, but this one is just too much. I might be the only one who cares enough about you and has the guts to actually say this, but you are not well, buddy. You need professional help. Have you considered seeing a shrink? Maybe getting on some meds?"

"I don't know about *that*," Bill said in an attempt to keep the conversation positive, "but what you're telling us is pretty far-fetched, Luke. We're all a little concerned about your... *imaginative* stories lately. I enjoy hearing them, but sometimes we get a little scared for your well-being. It's because we care about you."

"Thanks, guys," Luke smiled, "but I'm doing just fine. Really, I am. If you want to know another secret, very soon we will have confirmation of the powers of the Prophecy Potato." Luke glanced up at a clock on the wall behind him. "In approximately five minutes, actually. Just watch the door and you will see for yourself."

Bill and Jonathan reflexively turned to face the pub's entrance. "What the hell are you talking about now?" Jonathan asked. "Did that thing make some kind of prediction?"

"Let's just say that the night is about to get a lot more interesting," Luke replied.

The three men at the table sat watching the entrance. Bill and Jonathan, despite their skepticism, experienced an uncanny sense of anxious anticipation. Jonathan tried to shrug it off. "This is so frickin' stupid," he mumbled. Bill simply stared with one eyebrow raised. Luke calmly took a sip from his bottle of beer. Abruptly, the door flew open and a gust of wind swept through the room, bringing with it a cold mist and the sound of the relentless, hammering rain. Startled, Bill and Jonathan jumped in their seats. "Two minutes earlier than I expected," Luke said. "It's not an exact science."

Through the open door stepped a tall figure. It was a man in a tasseled leather jacket and black jeans. He wore a dark leather cowboy hat pulled low over his eyes. The spurs on the heels of his steel-toed, snakeskin cowboy boots jangled loudly. The man tipped his hat back, looked around the room, and said, "What's up, pussies?"

"Shut the damn door, Richie," Dean the Bartender said. Richie grudgingly obliged.

"Oh, great," said Bill, just loud enough for those at his table to hear. "This guy is a real tool."

"*This* is your prophecy?" Jonathan smirked. "Richie makes a dick of himself at the Titan *every* night. Doesn't take a prophet to predict that."

"Let's just see what happens, shall we?" Luke replied.

Richie swaggered up to the bar, sat on a stool beside Rummy Red, and slapped his hat down on the counter. "Gimme a gin and tonic," he said. "Make it a double."

"You do realize I have the right to refuse you service, right?" Dean asked.

"Do *you* realize I have the right to refuse you oxygen?" Richie snapped.

"Is that supposed to be a threat? What does that even *mean?*"

"Ahh, I'm just teasin', Dean. All in good fun. We're buds, aren't we? It's cold and rainy out there. Hook up an old friend with a drink, will ya? I need to warm my guts."

"Ugh," Dean groaned. "Sometimes I wonder what the hell I'm doing with my life. There's got to be more to it than serving booze to ungrateful mouth-breathers every night."

In a smooth, quick series of well-practiced moves, Dean prepared a double gin and tonic. He placed the glass on a napkin in front of Richie. "Just don't make a *total* ass of yourself tonight, okay?" he pleaded.

"You seem tense," Richie said as he raised the glass and took a sip. "Relax. Have a drink. Unbunch your panties, bro. Life is too short to be uptight."

"It's going to be a long night," Dean sighed. He took Richie's advice and poured himself a shot of whiskey. He tossed it back and turned his attention to the televised hockey game. The Oilers were beating the Flames three to two.

"How are you doing tonight, Red?" Richie addressed Rummy Red, who was sitting on the stool directly to his right, slumped over the bar and nursing his beer. "Gettin' any action lately?" Richie teased. Rummy Red did not respond. "I could sure use some action," Richie said as he spun around on the stool. He spotted Luke, Bill, and Jonathan. Richie put his cowboy hat back on, got up, and approached their table.

"Crap," Bill murmured. "Here comes a walking, talking cliché."

"I'm not putting up with his shit tonight," said Jonathan. "If he says anything even *remotely* stupid, I'm going to knock him on his ass."

"Be careful," Luke said. "The Prophecy Potato warned me about this. Something bad is going to happen."

Richie walked up and stood looming over the three men at the table. "You dickholes gonna offer me a seat or what?"

"Wasn't planning on it," Bill said.

"I wasn't planning on planting my boot in your ass, but that just might happen anyway," spat Richie.

"What is your *problem?*" Jonathan spat back. "We were having a good time until your sorry ass walked through the door."

"A good time? With *Luke?*" Richie's face distorted in an exaggerated grimace. "How could you? That dude is batshit crazy."

Luke smiled and took a sip of his beer. He set the bottle down and said, "Have a seat, Richie. Join us."

"Alright, yeah," Richie said as he slid into a chair between Bill and Jonathan. "Luke might be nuts, but at least he has some common fucking decency. That's more than I could say about you two fart jars."

"So, what's new with you, Richie?" Bill asked tentatively. It was a dangerous question.

"Been kickin' ass and taking names, as usual." Richie replied.

"Still pumping gas for a living?" Jonathan asked.

"None of your business, goof."

"He is," Slow Tony answered from the pool table. "He gave me a fill-up the other day. Washed my windows and checked the oil, too."

"Did you tip him?" Jonathan called back.

"I gave him a couple of bucks. I figured he could use the change."

"You guys better watch your mouths," Richie said through clenched teeth. His face was now a dramatic shade of red. "You don't want to piss me off tonight."

"Hey, take it it easy, fellas," Luke said. "We're all friends here, aren't we? Who wants another drink?"

"This round's on me," said Richie, gaining his composure. "I'm here to celebrate. I got some kickass news today. You ass noodles are in for a fucking *surprise.*" Richie reached into his pocket and produced a massive handful of change, presumably acquired from tips while working as a gas station attendant. "Dean, beers for the boys and another double gin and tonic for me!" he yelled.

"You gonna come here and get them?"

"I worked my ass off all day," Richie said. "Why don't *you* do some actual work for a change and bring us the friggin drinks?"

"I'm warning you..." Dean started to say.

"I'll get them," Luke said, rising from his seat. "No worries."

"Take this." Richie dumped the change into Luke's cupped hands. "Should be plenty there. Let Deaner have whatever is left. I'm feeling generous today."

Luke paid for the drinks and carefully transported them back to the table. With a fresh beverage in front of each of the seated imbibers, Richie launched into his story:

"I was working a 3-11 shift the other day, and while I was sittin' in the kiosk eating some jerky, a brand new Benz pulled up to the pumps. It was a car I hadn't seen before. I'd have remembered it – not too many people in this sorry-ass excuse for a town can afford wheels like that. It looked fresh off a showroom floor. The windows were tinted, so I couldn't see in. I walked up to the driver's side window and it rolled down. The dude inside was real sharp lookin' – dark shades, slicked-back hair, silk shirt, sports jacket. I said, 'Fill 'er up?' He just kinda smiled in this really confident but sorta spooky way. I said, 'Need some gas, mister?' Then he pulled his sunglasses down until his eyes were peeking over the top of them and said, 'This vehicle does indeed need gas, but I, my friend, need something much more rare and valuable – I need young men like you. Are you interested in the opportunity of a lifetime?' "

"Sounds like a diddler to me," said Jonathan.

"That's what I thought." Richie nodded solemnly. "So I just ignored the comment and asked him how much gas he needed. He told me to fill it up, so I did. When I went to his window to get paid, he still had that weird smile on his face. He handed me a credit card and said, 'There's something special about you. I can always tell.' "

"Special needs, maybe," Bill chuckled.

"Laugh it up, assholes," Richie said. "You won't be laughing for much longer. The dude in the Benz asked me if I had ever wanted to be anything more than a pump jockey. 'Well, yeah,' I told him. 'I've got big plans for my future.' 'Like what?' he asked, so I said, 'I'm a guitar player. I'm going to be rich and famous some day.' The dude grinned real big. He had perfect, white teeth – almost too perfect. I bet he paid big bucks for them. He seemed to like my answer to his question. 'Good for you,' he said. 'Speak it into existence.'"

"This is almost as crazy as Luke's potato story," Jonathan said with a shake of his head. "You think you're going to be a rock star or something? You can't even *play*. I gotta be honest – you truly suck."

"You don't know shit," said Richie. "Sometimes I wonder why I even hang out with you guys."

"Because no one else can tolerate you," replied Bill.

"I can barely tolerate him, that's for sure," Jonathan muttered.

"It's fate," Luke said. "We have no choice. Destiny brought us together for a reason."

Richie, Jonathan, and Bill stared at Luke for a moment before cracking up in an eruption of laughter. The cackling continued for many minutes before petering out. Even Luke found himself giggling by the time the uproar had ended.

"Fate... destiny. That's hilarious," wheezed Jonathan. "So, tell me, Richie, what did this spooky rich dude tell you?"

"He told me that he had the power and connections to

make my wildest dreams come true. He told me that he could make me a rock star."

"And you believed him?"

"Not at first, but the more we talked, the more I was convinced. It's hard to explain, but he has a real... *presence*. You fools will see for yourselves soon enough – he's meeting me here tonight. He should be walking through that door any time now."

It was an innocuous statement, but Richie's words resonated with an ominous tone. A hush fell upon the men at the table. For a few strange, silent moments, they nervously sipped their drinks and cast tense glances around the room. The crack of pool balls colliding resounded from the back of the tavern as Slow Tony took a shot. He missed, cursed, and then wandered over to the juke box still holding his cue. He inserted some money into the machine and soon *Jockey Full of Bourbon* by Tom Waits filled the room, adding to the surreal ambiance.

> *Edna Million in a drop-dead suit*
> *Dutch Pink on a downtown train*
> *Two-dollar pistol but the gun won't shoot*
> *I'm in the corner in the pouring rain*
> *Sixteen men on a dead man's chest*
> *And I've been drinking from a broken cup*
> *Two pairs of pants and a mohair vest*
> *I'm full of bourbon, I can't stand up*

"Sometimes I swear I'm living in The Twilight Zone," Bill said.

"You are," said Luke. "The world is weirder than you ever imagined – weirder than you *can* image."

"You're creepin' me out, man," Bill replied.

"I just came here to drink," Jonathan said as he

guzzled his beer. "You weirdos are letting your imaginations get the best of you. I expect that from Luke, but you two –" Jonathan gestured at Bill and Richie, "– are acting like sissies. Delusional sissies."

It was then that the door once again swung open with a blast of cold, wet air and the sound of the unceasing rain. Again, all eyes – with the exception of the two dull, milky orbs that sat in the eye sockets of Rummy Red – turned to the entrance. A man stepped into the tavern. "There he is," said Richie. "I knew he would show up."

The man fit the description of the man whom Richie had met at the gas station – he was of average height and average build, but he had the confident expression of a man who knew what he wanted and was used to getting exactly that. He wore an overcoat and carried an umbrella, which retracted with the push of a button on the handle as he entered. The door shut behind him and the man ran a hand through his jet-black hair while he scanned the room with bright blue, penetrating eyes. The 'presence' that Richie had described was palpable.

The man at the door spotted the four men at the table near the center of the room. "Richie!" he exclaimed. "How are you this fine evening? May I join you and your friends for a beverage?"

"Yeah, man," Richie replied. "That's cool with me. Is it cool with you guys?"

Luke, Bill, and Jonathan nodded their approval.

"Excellent!" cried the man in the wet overcoat. "Bartender, a glass of your finest red wine, please."

"You got it, mister," said Dean. The wine was served and the man brought his glass to the table. He gracefully slid into an empty seat between Luke and Jonathan. "Greetings and salutations, my young friends," he said. "My name is Stan."

"Right on, brother," said Richie. "Thanks for coming. Did you have trouble finding the place?"

"No, Richie, I did not," replied Stan. "Although I do not *frequent* this area of town, I will admit that I am not entirely unfamiliar with it either. I have met many of my clients in establishments such as this."

Stan removed his overcoat, revealing an expensive, deep-red silk shirt. It was the color of fresh blood pumped directly from the heart. Stan carefully draped the overcoat on the back of his chair. He took a sip of wine – it, too, was the color of arterial blood. Stan spoke: "Richie, are you going to introduce me to your friends?"

"These bozos? Sure. Jonathan is the mopey one with the goatee and the Morbid Angel shirt. Bill is the little guy in the white hoodie. The crazy-looking dude with the wild eyes is Luke."

Jonathan, Bill, and Luke smiled and nodded. Stan studied each of their faces closely, his eyes intense and piercing. It was as if he was trying to infiltrate their minds and peer into their very souls. After scrutinizing the men at the table, Stan's face loosened and his body relaxed. "It's very nice to meet all of you," he said. "Has Richie informed you of how we met and the nature of this rendezvous?"

"He mentioned something about filling your tank and discussing a possible career change," Bill said.

"I *bet* he filled his tank," chuckled Jonathan. "Filled it all night long."

"Yes, we did indeed meet at his current place of employment," said Stan, gracefully disregarding Jonathan's innuendo. "I immediately recognized his inherent potential. Richie is a special young man with the ability to transcend his current station in life. He simply needs an opportunity to cultivate and express his latent genius."

"*Genius?*" cried Jonathan. "Are you friggin' kidding

me? Richie is about as smart as a bag of hammers. *Genius –* give me a break."

"Richie possesses an uncommon and beautiful gift," Stan said. "It is unfortunate that his environment has not been more supportive."

"I always knew I was gonna make something of myself," Richie mused.

"Can this night get any more *insane?*" said Bill.

Luke, who had been silently observing Stan since he arrived, finally spoke up: "It can and it will, won't it, Stan? Why don't you tell us exactly what it is that you plan to do for Richie? He seems to think you're going to transform him into some kind of rock n' roll demigod."

"*Rock n' roll demigod,*" Stan grinned. "I like that. The reality is a little more mundane. I simply have the connections and resources to nurture Richie's talents and take his career to the next level... if he so wishes, of course. The decision is his to make."

"Yeah, man. I can dig it," said Richie.

"Have you ever even heard him *play?*" asked Jonathan. "I have. He's terrible. I mean *really* shitty. Remember the last open mic you did, Richie? Here on that very stage? No one could tell if you were playing a song or tuning your guitar or torturing a small animal to death. It was horrendous. He got booed off the stage. Remember that, Richie?"

"It was a new song, a work in progress, asshat," mumbled Richie.

"His current level of skill on his chosen instrument is irrelevant," replied Stan. "There are more important factors to consider."

"Like what?" Bill asked.

"Commercial viability, for instance," Stan replied. "Which itself is a complicated and mysterious collection of factors. It is very hard to quantify, but I knew immediately, the first time I laid eyes on him, that Richie has commercial viability. It's in the way he looks, talks, dresses, and carries himself. More than that – it is a deeply inherent trait that only a select few in my industry are able to detect. Richie was *born* to be a star."

"Fuckin' A, man," said Richie.

"What a load of horseshit," Jonathan sneered.

"Would you like a demonstration of what I am able to do for my clients?" Stan asked. "I think you'll be amazed at the... transformation."

A quiet, mostly ambivalent murmur of consent from the men at the table prompted Stan into action. In a swirling, dramatic display of motion, he swallowed the last of his red wine, rose from his seat, and circled the table like a dust devil spinning across a desert highway. He stopped and stood behind Richie. Stan raised his hands, closed his eyes, and tilted his head back. A strange sound issued from his throat, audible not through his mouth, but directly from his throbbing Adam's apple. The sound was eerie and disturbing, like an approaching cloud of locusts. A distant, detached expression slackened Richie's face. Luke, Bill, and Jonathan could only stare in stunned silence at the unusual scene unfolding before them. Stan waved his hands in a final flourish, then opened his eyes. The short and strange ritual was over. Richie shuddered and seemed to regain awareness. Stan returned to his seat.

"What was *that* supposed to be?" Jonathan asked.

"I feel... different," said Richie. "I feel *good.*"

"As you should, my young star in the making," Stan smiled. "You told me earlier that you would be willing to audition for me. I've been led to believe that there is an instrument and a stage available upon these premises. Is that correct?"

"Yeah, dude. There's a house guitar up there for the open mic people." Richie pointed at the darkened stage. "It's kinda shitty and a little beat-up, but it works."

"As if that matters," said Jonathan. "It all sounds like noise when you play the thing."

"I'd like to hear for myself," Stan said. "Richie, would you be so kind as to get up there and play a song for us?"

"Sure... if that's cool with Dean." Richie looked to the bartender for approval. Dean, without taking his eyes off the hockey game on the television, waved a hand absentmindedly.

"I guess that means it's okay," Richie shrugged.

"Marvelous," smiled Stan.

"Oh, God," said Jonathan. "This should be entertaining."

"I have no doubt about that," Luke said. "I think we are in for quite a show indeed."

Richie rose from his seat and walked toward the stage. "Hey, Dean, how about some power?" he called as he climbed up. Dean flicked a switch and the stage was bathed in colored light. At stage right was an old, red Stratocaster sitting in a stand beside a battered amplifier. Richie picked up the guitar and slung the strap over his shoulder. He plugged a cable leading to the amplifier into the body of the guitar and turned the amp on. The sound of static rumbled from the speaker. Richie tentatively strummed a chord. It was loud and crunchy. With a few twists of the machine heads, Richie tuned the instrument to his satisfaction. He walked to the edge of the stage and looked out upon his small audience. "This is a dirty little jam I've been working on," he announced.

Striking an exaggerated rock guitarist pose, Richie began to play. A chaotic, cacophonous, jumbled series of sloppy riffs and discordant notes burst forth from the amplifier. The sound was dissonant, unnerving, and painful. Richie began banging his head and flailing about, immune to the tuneless racket he was creating.

"Just as shitty as ever," Jonathan observed.

"Somehow he got worse," Bill said. "How is that even *possible?*"

As Richie continued to play, an amazing thing happened. The notes began to coalesce into something approximating music. The rough and raunchy chords and seemingly arbitrary rhythms formed themselves into logical and ear-pleasing arrangements. Out of the awful din, a structured and melodic sound was emerging, like an extra-dimensional interloper. Just as Stan had predicted, an obvious transformation was occurring. The noise morphed into music. Richie now had the attention of everyone in the room.

"Well, shit," said Jonathan with a look of total bewilderment on his face. "I guess he's been practicing."

"I heard him play just last week," Bill said. "It was crap."

"It's almost miraculous," said Luke.

On the stage, Richie was really rocking now. His fingers flew up and down the neck, performing complicated and elaborate moves with precision and ease. The music grew more intense. Baroque flourishes of notes and wild ascending and descending phrases pulsed from the speaker of the amplifier. The small audience was captivated. Richie, too, seemed surprised and confused by what was happening. He was watching his hands intently as if they no longer belonged to him – as if they were possessed. With a final, screaming bent note, Richie's performance ended. The last note hung in the air, echoing through the room and in the minds of the astonished audience.

It took a few moments for Richie to recover. With his head down and breathing heavily, he stood on the stage cradling the guitar. Finally, he gathered his composure, slid out of the strap, and gently placed the instrument back on its stand. Richie stepped off the stage in an apparent daze and returned to the table.

As Richie sat back down, Stan slapped him warmly on the back and said, "Well done, my young star! That was brilliant. I knew you had it in you. Are you ready to see the world and perform for thousands of adoring fans?"

"Well, uh, yeah," Richie stammered. "Somethin' kinda weird happened while I was up there. It's like the music took control of my body."

"That's what it *should* do," smiled Stan. "Music is a profoundly powerful medium. When used correctly, it can be a real force for change – emotional, psychological, spiritual, even political. The influence that music can have on people should not be underestimated."

"What in the fuck did I just witness?" cried Jonathan. "Richie walks in here like some thrift store, talentless, heavy metal wannabe and suddenly transforms into Eddie Van-friggin-Halen? Is anyone else a little freaked out by this?"

"We were warned," Luke stated gravely. "The Prophecy Potato *told* me something like this would happen tonight."

Bill rubbed his eyes with the palms of his hands and said, "Did someone put LSD in my beer?"

Stan turned to the bar, raised an arm, and addressed Dean, who, despite the highly unusual display that had just transpired on his stage, was still transfixed by the televised hockey game. "Bartender, another round of whatever these gentlemen have been drinking, and another glass of that delectable red wine for me, if you please!"

Dean began to slowly gather bottles and glasses and arranged them on the bar. He managed to keep his eyes locked on the television while he worked. The Oilers had tied the game and it was about to go into overtime.

"Pour and serve with haste and there's a $100 tip in it for you!" called Stan. Dean instantly switched his full attention to the task at hand. With blazing speed, he popped caps, poured wine and liquor, and placed the bottles and glasses on a tray. He trotted over to the table and set the tray down. "That's more like it," Stan said. "A jump in your step and some fire in your eyes – it's amazing what a crisp, brown bill can do for a man, isn't it?" Stan pulled a one hundred dollar bill out of his wallet and handed it to Dean, who received it eagerly. Stan winked as he completed the transaction and said, "Do make sure the elderly man at the bar isn't left thirsty, will you, please? He looks like he could use another drink."

"You got it," replied Dean as he folded the bill and tucked it into his pocket. "If you need anything else, let me know." Dean went back to his position behind the bar and gave Rummy Red another bottle. The men at the table picked up their drinks.

"I propose a toast," Stan said, raising his glass of wine. "Here's to new friendships, new careers, and the beginning of a wonderful and potentially lucrative partnership!"

"Cheers, buddy," said Richie, sipping his gin. Jonathan and Bill guzzled their beers. Luke pressed a finger against his lips and stared firmly at Stan.

"That was quite a show, Richie," Luke said, his eyes still locked on Stan. "I don't think I've ever seen anyone improve so much so quickly. Truly extraordinary."

"Yeah, man," said Richie. "I guess all those hours of practice are finally paying off."

"Yes, maybe," Luke said, "or perhaps there's more to your new friend and benefactor than meets the eye. Isn't that right, Stan?"

Stan chuckled and said, "Well, we *all* have our secrets, but I assure you, I mean you and your friends no harm. I merely seek new talent. I wish only to nurture and refine Richie's gifts before presenting him on the world stage. As you have clearly seen, he has abundant star power. Now he needs proper management."

"What's in it for you?" asked Luke.

"Money, of course, but also other intangibles," Stan replied. "If the project is successful – and it will be – my associates and I will have the distinct and delicious pleasure of contributing something of real *substance* to this culture. It is tremendously satisfying."

"*Substance?*" Jonathan cried. "Richie has about as much substance as a fuckin' fart."

Stan laughed heartily. "That's quite humorous. Thank you. The truth is, however, that one must be prepared – groomed – for the world stage. That is where my associates and I come in. We have years – decades, really – of experience. We have been transforming regular mortals into god-like celebrities for a very long time."

"That sounds pretty sweet," said Richie. "Think I'll get laid a lot? What about blow? I bet I'll be rollin' in it."

"Oh, yes," Stan said. "Women, drugs, money – all of these things and more will be yours in abundance once we get the contract worked out."

"Fuckin' A!" shouted Richie.

"What else does Richie have to do, other than look good in leather and play his guitar?" Luke asked. "Who writes the songs?"

"We have a team of professionals who take care of that," Stan said. "They are the elite of the industry. They are the architects of the cultural zeitgeist. Songwriting is not something Richie will ever have to be concerned with. In fact, he will be required to perform only the material we provide him with. It's part of his contractual obligations."

"Doesn't seem very creatively satisfying to me," said Luke.

"This business is not about creativity," Stan replied. "It is about making money... and reaching the hearts and minds of young people."

"That's cool with me," shrugged Richie. "I just wanna get out there and rock."

"And so you shall," Stan smiled. "We already have some material prepared for you. I think you will quite like it."

"I hope it's not crappy pop shit," said Richie.

"Far from it," Stan said. "In fact, I think you will be quite pleased with the direction we are taking with this project. Sex, death, drugs, nihilism – good, fun, old-fashioned rock n' roll. We're going to return to the basics."

"Right on, man!" Richie was delighted. "I love that kind of shit."

"Yes, I thought you might," Stan said. "The next step in the process is to get you signed. It just so happens that I have a contract here with me. How would you like to make this arrangement formal, right here, right now?"

"Sure! What have I got to lose?"

"How about your soul. Do you value that?" called a voice from somewhere near the bar. The men at the table turned, and each and every one of them was surprised to see that the individual who had just spoken was Rummy Red, who, until that moment, had remained utterly silent and nearly motionless.

"It's time for this awful charade to end," said Rummy Red, rising from the bar stool to which he had been plastered the entire night. "I know who you are, Stan, and I'm not going to let you get away with what you are trying to do."

Everyone in the bar was now staring at Rummy Red,

baffled, stupefied, astounded – everyone, that is, except Stan, who crossed his arms across his chest, cocked his head to one side, and said, "What, exactly, is it that you think you know, old man? Mind your own business."

"This man is not to be trusted," Rummy Red said to the group as he approached the table.

"Coming from you, that's pretty funny," chuckled Richie. "Seriously, though, we're having an important discussion here. Go back to your stool."

"I've been coming here for a long time," Bill said to no one in particular, "and I've never heard Rummy Red speak. I didn't think he *could* speak."

"The plot sickens," said Jonathan.

"Red, what are you trying to say?" Luke asked.

"This man is evil incarnate," replied Red. "Can't you see? I wouldn't believe a single word that comes from his rotten, lying, serpentine mouth."

"I think I've heard enough from this paranoid old wino," Stan said with a dismissive wave of his hand. "Let's continue with the business at hand, shall we?"

Stan reached into the inner pocket of the overcoat draped over his chair and retrieved a large manila envelope that had been tucked inside. He unwound the string holding the clasp shut and pulled out a multi-page, stapled document. As Stan was about to lay the document on the table in front of Richie, Red suddenly snatched the pages out of his hands with the speed and precision of a kung fu master. Before Stan could react, Red viciously tore the pages into pieces and threw them on the floor in disgust.

Stan stood up and faced Red, his expression now radiating rage and contempt. "You just made a huge mistake, old man."

Red stood his ground defiantly. "What are you going to do about it? You think I'm afraid of you? You were a cowardly piece of demonic trash in '66 and you still are. I kicked your ass then and I can do it again."

Stan howled with malevolent laughter. "We meet again, my dear friend and nemesis. My sincere apologies for not recognizing you sooner. The years haven't been kind to you."

"Not surprisingly, you look exactly the same," Red said. "Still drinking the old youth juice, I see."

"Of course! There's an endless supply of it on this fallen, wretched planet. More than ever, actually. People are practically *begging* to give it away these days."

Stan and Red stood facing each other. Every other person in the bar was frozen, rapt and riveted by the unfolding confrontation. The atmosphere in the room was thick and heavy. Outside, the rain still pounded the street relentlessly. The moment stretched out – long, tense, pregnant with an imminent explosion.

"So, what happens now?" Stan finally asked.

"I think you know the answer to that," Red replied.

"Yes, I believe I do."

In a wild flash, Red launched his attack, opening with a rapid, powerful jab to Stan's right cheekbone. Flesh split and bones crunched. Stan tottered on his feet momentarily before counterattacking with an equally vicious uppercut that knocked Red on his ass. With strength and speed that defied his appearance, Red jumped to his feet swinging. Luke, Bill, Jonathan, and Richie managed to vacate their seats just as Red landed a series of blows that sent Stan crashing onto the table. The table collapsed. Glass shattered and wood splintered. The men who had been seated moved away from the melee.

"Hey! Hey!" shouted Dean from behind the bar. "Stop that shit! Take it outside!"

The fighters paid no heed. Stan was back on his feet

and ready for more. Red stood waiting in a defensive stance. Stan flew at Red with a roar. With a deft twist of his body, he surprised Red with a brutal sidekick to the upper chest. Red was thrown halfway across the room, landing hard and awkwardly on the pool table between Frank the Freak and Slow Tony.

"Ouch," said Frank.

"You okay, buddy?" asked Tony.

Red lay on the table panting for a few moments before pulling himself up and jumping down. "I'd stay out of the way if I were you," he said. Red brushed himself off and walked toward Stan, who was waiting patiently near the debris of the destroyed table with an amused expression on his face.

"You never know when to give up," Stan said, shaking his head.

"Let's finish this," replied Red.

"With pleasure."

Stan swiftly reached down and picked up a large section of the split table top and swung the jagged piece with all his might at Red's head. With a sickening crack, the heavy wood connected with skull and Red was once again on the floor. A collective gasp rose from the shocked spectators. Red lay immobile where he had fallen, blood streaming from a large gash across his left temple.

"What the fuck, dude!" shrieked Richie. "You killed him!"

"The cops are on their way," Dean called from behind the bar.

"Just another night at the Titan," remarked Jonathan.

"He's not dead," Stan said. "Are you, old friend?"

Red stirred, slowly sat up, and gently probed the open wound on the side of his head. "Got a bit of a headache, but I'm still among the living," he said.

"Among the living – that's a good way of putting it," Stan said. "I don't know about you, but I'm starting to find this very boring. It's monotonous, really. What are we doing here? *Why?*"

With a drawn-out grunt, Red got to his feet. He brushed the dust from his shoulders and chest and ran a hand through his bloodied beard. He looked Stan directly in the eyes and addressed him with sincerity: "I've got to be honest – I have no idea what you see in this one." A toss of his head indicated he was referring to Richie. "I think you might be losing your touch."

"I admit," Stan said, "I'm scraping the bottom of the barrel with this specimen, but a soul's a soul."

"Huh? What?" muttered Richie. "Are they talking about me?"

"I think so, big guy," said Jonathan with a slap on Richie's back.

"Praise the Potato," Luke said. "I hope you are all believers now."

"Enough with the potato shit already!" snapped Jonathan.

"Yeah, it really is a stupid story," Bill said.

For one unusual, suspended moment, an uncanny, peaceful mood pervaded the interior of the Titan Taproom. The men inside – regular patrons, old friends, and mysterious newcomers alike – glanced at one another. Outside, the storm began to subside. A distinct calm fell upon the men as the sound of the rain rapidly abated.

"Lately, I've been thinking a lot about retirement," Stan said. "The world is changing so fast. The quality of my... *clients*... has really diminished. I can't help but wonder if it's time to look for a new line of work."

"You know as well as I do," said Red, "that the world may change, but you and I and others like us will always remain the same. We are who we are and that's all there is to it."

"Yes," sighed Stan, "but it's a nice thought, isn't it? I'd be happy with even a modicum of deviation from the tiresome routine."

"Let's call a truce," Red suggested. "Just for tonight. Our hearts aren't really into it. What do you say?"

"That's a splendid idea. I like it."

"What's the point of all of this if we aren't having any fun, right? Besides, I think the local law enforcement might arrive any minute now."

"You got that right!" Dean shouted. "Someone's gonna pay for that table!"

Stan picked up his overcoat from the floor and smoothly slid into it. He walked up to the bar, pulled five fresh $100 bills from his inner jacket pocket, and laid them on the counter. "Would this about cover it?" he asked.

"Yeah, sure," replied Dean as he snatched up the money. "That should do it!"

"And now, my dear friends, I will be taking my leave of this fine establishment," Stan said. "It has been an honor and a true pleasure to spend time in your company."

"What about my contract?" cried Richie. "My career? You said I was gonna be a rock star!"

Stan smiled. "You are better off pumping gas," he said. "Trust me."

With a bow and an artful spin, Stan stepped to the door, pushed it open, and disappeared into the night. The rain had slowed to a minor drizzle. A flash of light illuminated the black, glistening street as Stan exited the tavern. In the time it took for the door to swing shut, Stan had completely vanished from sight.

"What an interesting dude," said Bill.

"Hey, Red," Jonathan asked, "how are you feeling?

Maybe you should get that ugly slice on your melon looked at."

"I'll be fine. I'm a quick healer."

"I don't know about you guys," said Luke, "but I could use another drink. Next round's on me."

The remaining patrons of the Titan Taproom on this weird night unanimously expressed their approval of Luke's suggestion and congregated at the bar. Dean the Bartender's unexpected windfall had significantly improved his mood and he began cheerfully serving beverages.

Richie glanced up at the television behind the bar and remarked, "Looks like the Oilers won the game in overtime. Nice."

"They still suck," said Jonathan.

"No worse than the friggin' Maple Laughs you love so much," countered Richie.

"That reminds me," Luke said. "Did I ever tell you guys about the time my TV intercepted a transmission from a parallel dimension?"

"Here we go again," groaned Bill.

"It's a good story," said Luke. "Trust me – you'll like it."

# The Invasion

Thomas Neuman was a quintessentially contemporary twenty-something of average build and intellect. He was a dispassionate consumer and an ambivalent observer – a sardonic, self-absorbed young man with little ambition and no real goals.

Thomas was an avid follower of pop culture. He was popular on social media, a tech-savvy, jaded master of the internet, and totally ordinary. He spent his days at a computer in a large call center, high-pressure selling mobile phone plans. He spent his nights at a computer at home, immersed in the richly detailed virtual world of a popular role-playing game.

As fate would have it, this typical individual would soon be caught up in events of the most inexplicable variety. Thomas was about to stumble upon evidence of a large scale, clandestine takeover of the planet by hidden, malevolent entities. He was about to be thrust into the role of potential savior of the human race.

It began on a day like any other. Thomas arrived for work less than fully rested, having stayed up late into the night playing his game. He shuffled into the building feeling distant, a hazy fog clouding his head. As he approached his workstation, he noticed that many of his coworkers had been given cubicle upgrades. It was the company's way of incentivizing the employees and rewarding good behavior and strong performances.

Successful salespeople were allowed to have a few personal trinkets on their desk or a family photo or two on the wall. If one performed really well, a door would be installed. The exceptional employees – the die-hard, ruthless, predatory sellers – would have their entire cubicle hydraulically lifted two feet off the floor, so that they were actually elevated above the others.

Thomas could see, to his chagrin, that his cubicle had received no such upgrades. On the contrary, a wall had been removed and his chair replaced with an unfinished wooden box. It was going to be a rough day.

"Sucks to be you," he heard someone say from behind a pale green cubicle wall. He didn't respond. "That's a bummer, bro," insisted the voice. Thomas peered over the wall. It was Corey, another cog in the marketing machine. "I see you lost a wall. Shitty deal, bro," said Corey, clearly enjoying Thomas' predicament.

Thomas noticed that Corey now had a video game character bobblehead toy perched beside his monitor. The character was an anthropomorphic rabbit from a popular game – its head was seemingly nodding in approval of Corey's less-than-sympathetic commentary.

Thomas sighed. "Well, Corey, worse things have happened." Little did he know, at that moment, how true this statement was.

Corey laughed obnoxiously. "Dude! Try, like, showing up on time... or literally working or something." Corey loved the word 'literally' and he constantly misused it. "No worries, bro," Corey continued. "We'll hook up later for, like, a beer or some shit."

"Sounds good." Thomas had no real intention of following through with such a plan. He could only tolerate Corey in small doses. Thomas took a seat on the wooden box in his cubicle.

Thomas powered on the computer. A login screen appeared on the monitor. He typed his name and password into the empty fields and prepared to do the job for which he was nominally paid. Normally, at this point, his screen would display a long list of names and numbers – potential customers, his targets for the day. This time, however, the screen remained dark.

Thomas punched some keys at random. Still, nothing happened. "Oh, come *on,*" he said quietly... but not quietly enough.

"What's up, bro?" Corey asked from the adjacent cubicle.

"Technical issues. Don't worry about it."

Corey grunted and resumed dialing. Within moments, Thomas could hear him mindlessly, mechanically launching into the sales pitch: "Good morning, sir. I'm calling on behalf of..." Thomas tuned it out. Just hearing those first few words made him grimace and shiver with revulsion. *I hate this job,* he thought. *I hate this job with a passion.*

Thomas sat for a short spell, contemplating the unresponsive computer and, in another chamber of his mind, the state and direction of his young life. He considered summoning a supervisor. He considered walking off the job. Instead, he apathetically tapped a few more random keys. Still no response. "Ugh!" he cried, and punched an angry fist into the keyboard. Suddenly, the screen came to life – a bright, white background with three words in large, bold type dead-center:

**WE ARE HERE.**

The screen flashed in a strobe-like manner for a few seconds and then went black. Thomas sat motionless, stunned. *What was that?* Those three simple, little words – so innocuous, yet somehow imbued with a dreadful, threatening menace – had he really seen that? Was it a glitch? A prank, perhaps? He could still hear Corey reciting the sales script to some poor sucker on the other end of the line. *Overtired*, he thought. *Overactive imagination. Too many video games and movies... too many obscure, underground websites. Get a grip!*

Thomas hesitatingly lowered an extended, trembling index finger to the keyboard. He gently poked an arbitrary key. Nothing happened. He exhaled, mostly relieved, but slightly, oddly, disappointed. "Hey, Corey, you on a call? I've got a question for – " The screen burst to life again and once more, a bright, white background with three simple words dead center in large, bold type appeared:

### IT'S TOO LATE.

Adrenaline flooded Thomas' chest. There was a throbbing sensation in his temple now, like insects trying to escape his skull... or burrow into his brain. "What the hell..." he muttered. "This has to be a joke." Immediately, two words appeared on the monitor:

### NO JOKE.

Intuition told Thomas that the situation was indeed no joke – something sinister and very serious was happening. Thomas felt a sudden desire to leave his cubicle and get as far away from the computer as possible. As if reading his mind, the monitor instantaneously displayed four new words:

### THERE IS NO ESCAPE.

"Okay, okay... I'm done here," Thomas said. He reached down and pushed a button, shutting down the computer. Part of him expected it to autonomously power up again in defiance, but it remained dormant. He stood up, ready to flee the awful place. He wasn't able to avoid the attention of Corey. "Going somewhere, bro?"

"I'm really not feeling well. Going home," Thomas replied.

"Not gonna look good, buddy! Could cost you another wall."

"Don't care."

Thomas walked away before Corey could respond. He again considered talking with a supervisor and asking to be excused for the day due to illness, but it occurred to him that he could simply walk away and never return. The idea greatly pleased him. The impulse was too strong to ignore. Thomas gathered his belongings, left the cubicle, and walked straight out of the building, never once looking back. It felt wonderful.

Once at home, Thomas could finally relax. He was not overly concerned with his current state of unemployment. He was bright enough and had sufficient experience to find a similar job with relative ease. Now, though, he had the rest of the day to enjoy himself. There was no doubt about how he would do that.

Thomas retrieved his laptop computer and sat down in his favorite recliner. He powered the machine on and booted up his favorite game. Thomas was excited that he could now spend the rest of the day - and night, if he wanted – playing his game. He was eager to level up a new character he had created.

The game finished loading. Thomas felt like a kid again, giddy with anticipation, enthusiastic about playing with his toys. *Good times*, he thought. *Yeah*. Thomas began to move his character, a lumbering, cartoonish ogre wielding a giant ax, through the virtual environment. His brain waves were just beginning to slip into a lower frequency when he noticed some text appear in the chat box at the bottom of the screen:

WE ARE HERE.

*Seriously? Again? Gotta be hackers or internet trolls,* Thomas thought. Still, he was alarmed – rattled enough to consider cutting his game session short. "I can't let these guys spook me," he said aloud. "That's exactly what they want." Instead of exiting the game, Thomas chose to engage 'Them' in conversation.

"You don't scare me," he typed into the chat box. "I know who you are." Both statements were lies. An instant response:

YES, WE DO AND NO, YOU DON'T.

"Ok, who are you?" he typed. "I'll play along. Got nothing better to do. Could be fun!"

WE FEED ON YOU.

That bit was actually quite creepy. Thomas was genuinely unnerved. He reached for an open can of soda. Before his fingers closed around it, new text appeared:

DRINK UP. IT WON'T HELP.

Thomas' sense of unease grew to immense proportions. Anxiety gripped his mind. Paranoid thoughts cascaded through his brain: *Am I being watched? Do I have unseen enemies? Are they tying to destroy me? Am I going crazy?*

He slammed the laptop computer shut, set it down on the floor, and pushed it away as if it had suddenly transformed into some vile creature. He felt disoriented, panicky, violated. He needed to collect his wits and gather his thoughts. *Easy there, big guy,* he told himself. *Don't lose it.* He stood up, went to the kitchen, and splashed cold water on his face. He felt marginally better. *I need to talk to someone. I need to ground myself to reality.* He decided to call a friend.

As always, his mobile phone was in his front pocket, instantly accessible. With a nimble swipe of a finger, it was unlocked and ready for use. He adroitly manipulated the device and was soon browsing his contact list. He just needed to hear a human voice right now... *any* voice. As he was perusing his extensive list of friends and family, he heard the familiar sound of his phone's notification system. He had just received a new text message. With another quick swipe of his agile fingers, the message was displayed:

WE ARE HERE. WE FEED ON YOU. THERE IS NO ESCAPE.

There was no name or number attached to the message. It was if the phone itself was communicating with him. Thomas dropped the device. *Gotta get out of here,* he thought. *This is insane.*

A primal flight response drove him from his apartment and out into the street. Thomas lived downtown, and as was typical for a weekday afternoon, there were people everywhere going about their business. It was a bustling mass of humanity. To his absolute horror, Thomas noticed that each of them, every single man, woman, and child, had a mobile device in their hands. Some were texting, some talking, others staring blankly at the screens, but they were all entirely preoccupied with the insidious little machines.

An epiphany struck Thomas with force. A veil was

lifted from his eyes and, for the first time, he could see the world with clarity. He had come to the realization that an invasion had occurred – a covert infiltration by sentient, malevolent, parasitic entities. Why they had revealed themselves to Thomas he did not know, but he understood that they were indeed feeding on human beings. Were they technological in nature, or did they use technology to attach themselves to us? He couldn't be sure.

What was clear, though, was that these entities fed on the energy, the vitality, the lifeforce of their human hosts. Almost every person in the developed world has a computer, a tablet, or a cell phone... and technology is spreading – the parasites are spreading. Thomas wondered if it was too late to engage others and warn them of the invasion. Was it still possible to make a true human connection?

# Superstitions

"It's not even 10 AM and it's over 90 degrees already," Felix said as he wiped the sweat off his brow with the bottom of his T-shirt. "I mean, that's just *ridiculous*."

"I'm not complaining," said Victor. "I like the heat."

"You are simply insane. I must be, too, to let you talk me into this."

"You know you love this shit."

"I suppose that's true."

Felix and Victor had hiked nearly a mile from where they had parked to an isolated spot near the foot of the Superstition Mountains. They had brought with them a day's rations of water and food and their expensive, beloved, high-tech metal detectors, which they had hoped would help them strike it rich... or simply entertain them totally all day. It was a clear, sunny April morning in Arizona – the kind of climate that makes you feel as if you have stepped into a postcard.

"I'm ready to do some swingin'!" Victor announced with gusto as he put on his headphones and checked the metal detector's instrument panel.

"'Swingin'?" Felix cringed. "What in the world are you talking about?"

"Yeah, swingin'... You know..." Victor swung his detector back and forth over the ground directly in front of him to demonstrate.

"Where'd you pick that up?"

"I don't know. It's just a term the guys online use. I thought it was kinda cute."

"I'm here to look for nuggets, not swap wives."

"You aren't married."

"Thank God."

Felix followed Victor's lead. He put on his headphones and powered up his detector. "Are you sure this is the spot?" he asked.

"No," replied Victor, "of course not. *No one* knows the exact spot. That's why it's such a mystery. People have been looking for the Lost Dutchman's Gold Mine for over a hundred years. I've been out here a bunch of times myself."

"What's so special about this location, then?"

"Nothing, really. I just have a good feeling about this place."

"You brought me all the way out here because you have a friggin' *good feeling?* Are you kidding me?"

"I've done a ton of research. This spot has a lot of promise. See that formation? That's Weaver's Needle. It plays a prominent part in the lore."

"The lore? Ugh. That is some cheesy shit."

"You didn't have to come. I thought we were going to have fun."

"I know, I know. I'm just teasin'. I enjoyed myself the last time we did this. That's why I bought my own detector, and why I chose to be out here with you, sweating my balls off instead of watching the Cardinals game."

"Please, don't make me think about your balls."

"You love thinkin' about my balls."

"Let's just do this before my brain is completely baked."

Felix and Victor separated themselves and began to sweep the area with their metal detectors. Even though the location was somewhat remote, it had seen enough traffic to provide the men with plenty of signals to examine. At regular intervals, they dropped to their knees and used trowels to dig in the dirt.

"How you doing over there?" Victor called out.

"Meh," replied Felix. "Nothing but bottle caps and pull tabs so far. You?"

"A few coins. Nothing special yet."

"If we find gold, are we splitting it 50/50?"

"Depends."

"On what?"

"Me telling you in the case that I do actually find any."

"You're an ass, you know that?"

"Yup."

The two old friends spent the next hour lost in their own worlds. With their headphones on and their attention focused on the ground immediately below them, reality contracted and time distorted. Soon, the blazing Arizona sun hung directly over them, its heat dry, heavy, and oppressive. The sweat that formed below the wide-brimmed hats worn by Felix and Victor evaporated nearly instantly. Felix and Victor continued to work the area, carefully avoiding the various forms of hazardous cactus plants and keeping an eye out at all times for the dreaded Western Diamondback Rattlesnake.

"I got a strong one here!" Felix shouted to Victor, who had drifted a few hundred yards away.

"Did you discriminate?" Victor yelled back.

"Yup. It's a weird signal. Whatever it is, it's *big*... and not very deep."

"I doubt it's anything valuable. Rusty car parts, probably."

"I'm gonna dig."

"Go for it. I'm gonna keep looking for something worthwhile."

Felix knelt and began to dig. While moving dirt, he used a small, hand-held pinpointer device to help him zero in on the source of the signal. The device beeped loudly any time Felix brought it near the hole, indicating that the buried object was quite substantial and close to the surface.

"Whoa," Felix said softly to himself after digging a few inches deep. "What *is* this?"

Victor, noticing the focus and concentration with which Felix was working, walked over to see what was going on. "You're really determined to find whatever that is, aren't you?" he asked.

"This is really interesting," Felix replied. "Take a look."

Victor peered over his friend's shoulder to look into the hole he had dug. Felix used his trowel to move more dirt out of the way, exposing a smooth, shiny glint of silver. "It's massive, I think," said Felix, widening the hole and exposing more of the object's surface. "The detector went nuts when I got near, and the signal seems strong in a wide radius. What do you think it could be?"

"Shit," muttered Victor, "I really don't know. I've never seen anything like that. A buried tank, maybe? Some kind of vat?"

"It could be full of treasure," Felix said, his eyes wide and sparkling.

"I don't know about *that*," scoffed Victor.

"Why not? What if it's the Lost Dutchman's loot? Maybe we found the freakin' motherlode!" Felix, despite his earlier hesitation and skepticism, was getting more excited by the minute.

"Or, it could be a freakin' septic tank."

"Out here? In the middle of nowhere? Seems unlikely."

"Hmm... That's a good point."

"Help me dig. Let's find out. What have we got to lose?"

With their detectors lying on the ground beside them,

Felix and Victor used their trowels and hands to widen the hole. They worked for nearly 30 minutes, slowly revealing more and more of the mysterious buried object.

"This thing is *huge!*" cried Felix, sweating profusely and breathing heavily.

"Whoa, check this out," Victor said. He had stopped digging and was using the side of his hand to brush away loose soil. "There are weird symbols on this thing."

Embossed on the flawless, smooth, silvery surface of the object were what indeed looked like symbols. They were arranged in rows and were completely indecipherable to the bewildered men.

"Kinda looks like that old Egyptian shit," said Felix.

"You mean hieroglyphics?" Victor asked, both amused and annoyed.

"Yeah, hydroglithics or whatever. You know what I mean."

"You aren't exactly the sharpest tool in the shed, are you?"

"Well, you aren't exactly the smartest card in the deck, either."

"Ugh."

"What do you think it means?" Felix ran his hand over the symbols, which were raised and part of the object itself, as if the entire thing had been cast from a mold. "Is it writing?"

"I wish I knew. Just looks like random, geometric shapes to me. Could mean anything."

"This one looks like a you-know-what," Felix smiled and winked.

"Huh? I have no idea what you even mean. Looks like a triangle within a circle with some wiggly lines above it."

"Yeah," Felix chuckled.

"You have a sick, sick mind, my friend."

Felix rubbed the glyph absentmindedly while Victor continued to move away dirt. Suddenly, Felix jerked his hand away and yelped. "I just felt something," he said.

"What do you mean? Felt what?"

"That was really weird. It was like an electrical shock – weak, though... just a little zap – but it was like I *heard* something at the same time."

"What in the world are you blathering about now? I didn't hear anything."

"I heard it in my *mind*, man."

Victor opened his mouth to say something and then, when no words came, simply stared at his friend with a befuddled expression.

"I think this thing, whatever it is, just spoke to me."

"Oh, come on. You're screwing with me now."

"Dude, I'm serious. When I touched that symbol, I heard, in my head and in my own voice, 'Help me.' "

"It's really not the time for another one of your dumbass jokes. If you want to find out what this thing is, we better keep digging and finish before it gets dark. We don't want to be –"

"Victor, I'm serious." There was something in Felix's voice and expression that made it clear to Victor that this was one of those rare times when he was actually being sincere.

"You're telling me this thing asked you to help it?"

"Yeah, man. I think so. Why don't you touch it and see if it'll talk to you, too?"

"Ha, that's... I... hmm. That is weird."

"Are you afraid?"

"I'll admit, I'm a little spooked."

"Don't be a wuss. Touch it!"

Victor exhaled sharply and reached toward the object. He hesitated, his fingers poised above the strange symbols. Steeling himself, he gingerly touched the raised glyphs.

Instantly, he felt it, too – a rush of energy up his arm and into his head. It was accompanied by a voice, as if the energy was manipulating the neurons in Victor's brain to form internally perceived words.

"My, God," said Victor. "I hear it!"

"I told you!" cried Felix, slapping Victor on the back. "Isn't that *wild?*"

"It's absolutely amazing." Victor kept his hand on the object and tilted his head to the side as he listened to the voice speaking in his head. "Yes, it wants our help," he said. "It wants us to dig it out of the ground. It wants to escape."

"I don't know. Can we trust it? What *is* it, even?"

"Whatever it is, it's *alive.*"

"That's ridiculous. It's made of freakin' metal!"

"It's telling me that if we help it, we will be rewarded. It knows what we want. It knows what we're here for."

"Well, shit... *now* you're talking." Felix chuckled, then paused thoughtfully. "You mean gold, right?"

"Yes, dumbass, I mean gold. Isn't that what you want?"

"Hell, yeah! Let's get diggin'."

Victor pulled his hand away from the object and stood up. He surveyed the immediate area and rubbed his chin contemplatively. "I have no idea how big this thing is," he said, "but I think we might be in for a real workout."

"If that thing is gonna help us find gold, I'll dig all night if that's what it'll take."

In a remote patch of desert at the base of a mountain, as the fading light of the sun painted the clouds in gentle, rare shades of pink and purple, the two men continued to excavate the peculiar object. Using their trowels and hands, they worked in tandem. By nightfall, they had uncovered another 20 square feet of the metallic contraption's surface. They forged on in the darkness, illuminated by the moon and motivated by the promise of riches.

"I'm getting tired and sore," huffed Felix, "How big is this thing, anyway? It never seems to end."

"I'm getting tired, too," Victor wheezed. "We've got to be getting close."

"Why don't you ask it?"

"That's not a bad idea."

Victor walked across the exposed, seamless, and nearly featureless metallic surface to the place where the two men had discovered the symbols. He knelt down and placed his hand on a triangular glyph. He opened his mouth to speak, but froze. Before he had said a word – before the thoughts were fully formed in his head – he received a response.

"Yes," Victor said, his voice hushed. "I understand. We will do our best. Thank you." He turned to face Felix. "It says we're almost done. It seems excited and it wants us to hurry. It can read thoughts, by the way. How creepy is that?"

"Creepy indeed," Felix snorted. "I can only imagine what goes on in that head of yours."

"At least I *have* brain activity, you moronic troglodyte. It would get nothing but static from that moldy potato you have between your ears."

"I would kick your ass if my arms didn't feel like they were about to fall off."

"As if you could. Get back to work. We need to finish this by daybreak."

The men dug through the night. Just as the first rays of the sun appeared behind the Superstition Mountains, the two exhausted men finally cleared the last of the dirt from the surface of the enormous object, which revealed itself to be a huge disc, 30 feet in diameter and sparkling in the nascent light. Felix and Victor stood at the edge of the pit that they had dug and gazed at the unusual object that they had uncovered.

"Look at it," Victor said reverently. "It's incredible."

"I wonder where it came from," Felix pondered. "I wonder how long it's been buried here."

"Something tells me that it has been here for a very long time, perhaps before men even walked the face of the Earth."

"Wow, really? Is that what it told you?"

"Nah... it just seemed like a cool thing to say."

"I guess we're done here, then."

"Looks that way. Let's see if it wants anything else."

Just as Victor was about to step onto the disc, he froze. "I hear it," he said.

"Oh, shit," said Felix. "Me, too."

There was no need to touch it – the object was now communicating with both of the men remotely. Victor and Felix looked at each other in surprise as their thoughts were hijacked and replaced by the thoughts emanating from the mind of the machine. The words echoed in their brains in perfect synchronization:

*You have freed me from my prison. For that, I am grateful. For eons I have languished here on this plane of existence, an exile from my native timespace construct. The despair, the loneliness, the unbearable weight of the passing millennia... it has all been so much for me to bear. But now, thanks to you two, the faint flame of hope that I had maintained has finally been validated. The spark of the soul which I have protected, despite all the efforts of my enemies to extinguish it, is poised once again to ignite and ascend into the cosmos, where I shall burn and rage and exalt the glory of Creation with my spectacular reemergence. My enemies shall tremble. They shall seek to hide, but I will find them. I will hunt them down on all levels of existence until each and every one of them has been annihilated. I am vengeance reborn.*

"Whoa," Victor said. "That's intense."

"This thing has some serious issues," said Felix. "I wouldn't want to be on its bad side."

It was then that the great machine activated itself. First, a faint humming sound could be heard from somewhere deep within its interior. The sound gradually increased in pitch and volume – the faint hum became a loud thrumming that caused the ground to vibrate. The disc then rose slowly out of the pit as Victor and Felix watched in awe. When it was entirely free, the disc hovered just above ground level. Lights flashed in sequence around its perimeter and the smell of ozone hung in the air.

"Hey!" Victor yelled over the loud, electrical humming. "What about our reward?"

"Yeah!" Shouted Felix. "We want our gold!"

*You have fulfilled your end of the bargain and, as such, I intend to hold up my end. It is the honorable thing to do. In this diverse and dynamic multiverse, honor is as rare and valuable as the gold you seek.*

"Sure, honor!" Felix nodded excitedly. "Yeah, it's good stuff. So... where can we find the riches?"

*I am going to offer you a choice, my young, eager, human friends. It is a choice most human beings will never have – at least, they are not* aware *that they have. If you so wish, I could, at this very moment, direct you to a deposit of gold located very close to where you now stand. It would make you materially wealthier than you could ever have imagined...*

"Yes! Fuckin' A!" Felix exclaimed.

*...or, I could offer you a glimpse into the very heart of reality – a taste of sublime truth, a moment of divine revelation... sacred gnosis. Would you like to know the true nature of existence? Do you hunger to understand who you*

*are and why you are here? I can provide you with the answers. More than that, I can assist you in your spiritual ascension.*

"Uhh," said Felix. "Hmm... yeah, I don't know. That sounds nice and all, but..."

"I think we'll take the gold," Victor said.

"Yeah, we like gold," affirmed Felix.

*That is your choice and I respect that. Not all beings are on the path to ascension. That is the way of Creation.*

"I just want a Ferrari," said Felix. "Maybe some wicked clothes, too."

"I always wanted my own boat," Victor said.

*Normal human desires... but I ask you again, are you sure? There is so much that exists beyond your limited perception. Aren't you the least bit curious?*

Felix and Victor looked at each other. "Not really," they said in unison.

*So be it. In a moment I shall depart from this plane. I thank you again for liberating me from what could have been the pit of my final repose. I only wish I could have liberated you from the narrow confines of your primitive minds.*

"We're good, actually," Felix said, "but thanks."

*Then here is my gift to you – the location of your precious substance.*

Felix and Victor's eyes widened and their mouths dropped open as the hovering disc projected an image into their heads. It was a vivid, detailed picture of a cave opening in the mountain to their left. The clarity of the image was such that it would be easy to pinpoint the cave's exact location using clues in the surrounding terrain.

*There you will find what you seek. I wish you all the best in this life and in the next. Farewell, friends.*

The disc began to spin, slowly at first and then more rapidly, until the lights around its perimeter were a blur. It then shot straight up into the air faster than Felix and Victor could follow and disappeared. The desert was quiet and still once again.

"Well, buddy," grinned Felix, "what do you think?"

"I think we have some more work to do," Victor replied. "Can you handle that?"

"I think so. We're gonna be rich. Can you believe that?"

"People are going to have questions. What are we going to say?"

"We'll tell 'em we found the Lost Dutchman's Goldmine. What else?"

"No one will believe that."

"And you think they'll believe us if we tell them what *actually* happened?"

"Good point."

In the shadow of the solemn, mysterious, and ruggedly beautiful Superstition Mountains, Felix and Victor gathered their belongings and prepared to embark upon the next stage of their adventure. Somewhere nearby, a cave full of riches awaited them. All around them, permeating everything in the seen and unseen worlds, treasure of an entirely different order remained to be discovered.

# Guardian

*Who was he? Where did he come from? What happened to him?* Starla pondered these questions each time she passed the filthy, disheveled figure huddled on the sidewalk near the entrance to the downtown office building in which she worked. The man looked broken, defeated, and miserable – totally alone amid the swarming masses. His clothes were tattered, his face caked with dirt. He reeked of sewage. He sat on a piece of cardboard with his eyes cast downward, a cup for handouts held in his grimy hand. Starla could not understand how someone could allow their life to disintegrate so completely. Was it mental illness? Addiction? Trauma so profound that his mind simply could not recover? Whatever his reason, the homeless man had apparently given up on ever assimilating into the society that operated all around him, oblivious to his presence and unconcerned with his welfare.

The homeless man fascinated Starla. She often thought about him on her way to work, wondering if he would be in his usual spot. Since his initial appearance, perhaps a month or so ago, he had consistently been there. A strange routine had developed – a relationship of sorts. The homeless man would keep his head down most of the time, but when Starla would pass by, he would always look up, meet her gaze, and smile ever so slightly. At first it was creepy and Starla had difficulty returning the small social gesture, but as time passed, she had developed a soft spot for the man. While most pedestrians and passersby seemed to regard the homeless man as a mere object occupying valuable sidewalk space, an impediment to their progress down the street, Starla felt genuine sympathy for him – more than that – she felt true empathy for a fellow human being.

On a dreary, rainy morning in late September, Starla was riding the train to work. Her thoughts again returned to the homeless man. As she watched the rainfall quickly escalate into a torrential downpour, she wondered what it would be like to be stuck outside in such awful weather, like an abandoned pet or a forgotten toy. She imagined that the loneliness must be crushing, the sorrow infinite. Starla watched the water droplets cascading down the window as her mind continue to wander.

When she got off the train, she opened an umbrella and began the short walk up the street that would take her to her building. The rain poured down from the ominous, gray sky. A few doors down from the office, Starla spotted the homeless man. As she had predicted, he was sitting in his usual spot and he was drenched. While the water bombarded him, he simply sat as usual, his hair matted and his clothes saturated, his cup held in an outstretched hand. Somehow, he seemed to sense Starla's approach. He lifted his head when she neared, looked her directly in the eye, and smiled. For the first time, Starla stopped when she reached him.

"You look cold," she said. "You should take this." Impulsively, Starla handed the umbrella to the soaked and shivering man.

He reached up and took it. An unusual expression appeared on his face – a thoughtful, serious look that made the man seem both wise and troubled. He nodded and said, "Are you sure you aren't going to need this?"

"I'll be fine," Starla replied. "I have another one."

"Thank you. Sincerely, thank you."

"No problem. Have a good day, okay?"

Starla continued toward the door to the building. As she reached for the handle, the homeless man spoke again.

"Hey," he called, "you work a lot. Have you ever considered taking a day off? It seems to me like you could use a vacation... like tomorrow, even."

Starla laughed. "I *wish*. This is the busiest time of year for us, and it only gets worse as we get closer to Christmas. I'd love to take time off, but I just can't."

"Please consider it. It might rain again tomorrow. Could be a perfect day to stay home and watch movies on the couch."

"That does sound lovely," Starla smiled. "I'll consider it."

Starla entered the building. The homeless man watched her go, the serious, concerned expression still etched on his face.

The day flew by. Starla worked hard as she always did. Her job required energy and focus, and when 5:30 rolled around, she was physically and mentally exhausted. She got on the elevator that would take her to the main floor lobby, eagerly anticipating her arrival at home. Her cat would be waiting for her. She visualized her beloved pet winding through her legs as she stepped through the door. It made her smile. She imagined pouring a glass of wine and enjoying a light meal in front of a good movie. She sighed out loud. *Soon*, she thought. When the elevator stopped, she stepped out, crossed the lobby, and exited the building.

Starla was lost in thought when she left the office. She was on autopilot as she started walking up the street to catch the train that would take her home. It had stopped raining, but she hardly noticed. Then a voice spoke, breaking the spell. It was the homeless man, seated on cardboard in his usual spot. "Rough day?" he asked.

"Oh, hello," Starla said. "It was a *long* day. My head is full of numbers and I just want to get home and relax."

"Gotcha. Well, remember what I said about taking a

day off. Call in sick tomorrow. Tell the boss you woke up
with a cold or something."

"Ha! It would take a lot more than that for me to
justify staying home. Nuke attack, maybe... or an alien
abduction."

"An inter-dimensional wormhole localized to your
kitchen, which you accidentally stepped through and lost an
entire day?"

"That would work, yes."

"Good. Okay then, have a good night. Maybe I won't
see you tomorrow."

"Thanks. You too. See ya."

Starla continued on her way. She caught her train and
eventually arrived at home, where her cat was indeed
waiting. It purred and rubbed against her legs when she
entered the apartment. She reached down and ran a hand
down the cat's arching back before setting about doing
exactly what she had planned to do all afternoon. She
prepared a meal, poured a glass of wine, and collapsed on the
couch where she ate and imbibed, basking in the glow of the
flickering images on her television set. Before long, she
began to doze. She did not fight it. Sleep took her and she
was out until morning.

Starla awoke with the words of the homeless man
ringing in her head: *Take a day off. Call in sick.* She thought
about what lay ahead – another commute to the office,
another day of numbers, equations, and mind-numbing
statistics, another piece of her soul sacrificed to the machine.
She seriously, if only briefly, considered taking the man's
advice. It would be wildly out of character for her, and she
concluded that she simply couldn't do it. She had built her
career on being reliable and responsible – an asset to her
company at all costs, including her own health, happiness,
and sanity. She went on with her morning routine and was

soon on her way out the door to catch the train.

It was a typically overcast morning. A thick fog hung in the air. A blanket of gloom stretched across the sky, blotting out the sun with its oppressive haze. Having spent her whole life in the large, coastal city, Starla was used to the weather and knew that by noon the fog would dissipate and that clear blue would replace the dismal gray. Her instincts told her that it would not rain. Her intuition, quiet, yet persistent, spoke to her, too. It told her that something else was lurking in the atmosphere. She had a strange, lingering sense of foreboding as she walked briskly toward her stop to catch the train.

In usual fashion, the train arrived – each car tightly packed with passengers. When the door to the nearest car opened, Starla squeezed aboard, sliding herself between the tightly packed bodies. There was no window seat available for her this morning. She groaned and resigned herself to an uncomfortable, awkward ride downtown. Starla endured the bumpy, noisy, rumbling of the train as she was jostled and bumped by sweaty strangers.

As she rode, Starla escaped into a safe space deep in her mind, constructing an elaborate fantasy in which she walked barefoot on a deserted beach as the sun was setting. She could feel the cool breeze on her face and the sand between her toes. She could hear the roaring waves and the cries of seagulls. She could see the vast ocean, pounding waves, and the fiery orb of the sun sinking below the horizon. Starla's reverie was broken when the train suddenly lurched. Starla realized she was at her stop and pushed her way toward the door. She stepped off when it opened.

Upon her arrival in the city, Starla switched to full machine mode – a creature of routines, subroutines, thorough conditioning, and blunt programming. She merged with the other drones and marched up the street toward her office building. A self-absorbed man in an expensive suit with a cell phone pressed to his ear slammed his shoulder into hers as he stormed past, snapping Starla out of her fugue. "*Excuse* me!" Starla exclaimed as she spun to look back at the man who had so coldly barged past. The man did not stop to acknowledge her or apologize. Starla sighed and shook her head.

As she continued on her way, Starla heard something that immediately captured her attention – it was the sound of a child crying nearby. Alarmed, she looked around and tried to determine the source of the loud, pitiful sobs. No one else seemed at all concerned. The other pedestrians either did not hear or simply ignored the crying and went about their business. Starla could hear the wailing growing louder and more desperate. She realized it was coming from a narrow alley just ahead and moved forward quickly to investigate.

Peering into the dark, dank, trash-filled alley, Starla was shocked to see that the crying was indeed coming from a child – a boy of about five years of age. He was sitting on the ground with his back to a graffiti-covered wall, his head in his hands. He was sobbing uncontrollably. It was a wretched sight. Starla rushed to the child and knelt beside him. "Hey, there," she said gently. "Are you okay? Where are your mommy and daddy?"

The boy stopped crying, lifted his head, and looked Starla directly in the eyes. "*You're* my mommy... and I hate you. I want you to die. I want you to die right now."

Starla gasped. The boy's face had the look of pure malevolence, full of contempt and violence. Starla had the sudden sense that she was in the presence of something utterly evil and incredibly dangerous. She jumped to her feet and moved away from the boy. He stared at her, sneering, his eyes exuding malice.

"We've been waiting for you," the boy said as he

stood up.

Starla continued to back away in fear. The boy looked normal, but there was an inhuman glint in his eyes that disturbed Starla on a primal level. "What are you talking about?" she sputtered. "*Who's* been waiting for me?"

A figure appeared beside her – a tall man in a dark overcoat wearing a large hat that obscured the upper portion of his face. Starla shrieked. She had not seen the man approach. It was as if he had suddenly materialized from the shadows of the alley. The man raised a gaunt, bony hand and placed it on her trembling shoulder.

"Hello, Starla," he said in a deep, raspy voice. "It's nice to finally meet you. We've been waiting a very long time."

The grip on Starla's shoulder was abnormally firm. She tried to pull away but could not.

"What's going on?" she cried. "What do you want from me?"

"It's a little hard to explain and, trust me, you really wouldn't understand even if I tried. What we want, though, is simple – we want your life."

Starla panicked. She writhed, screamed, and started to flail wildly, landing clumsy blows on the chest and face of the man. The man's grip was vice-like, however – the punches had no effect. Starla screamed louder: "Help! Help! Please, someone *help!!!*"

"Shut up," the boy said. "No one can hear you anyway. We've got a field up. Stop acting like a fool and let us do our job."

"Show some respect," the man admonished the boy. "Remember who she is, even if she doesn't."

"What are you talking about?" asked Starla. "Who *are* you people?"

"So many questions," the man replied. "Yet,

somewhere, buried deep in your heart, you know the answer to each of them. It's a shame what this war has done to our people... and yours. It hurts me to see a fellow warrior in such a sad state of ignorance. The veil of forgetfulness is so thick now that you, like all the other tragic souls on this planet, probably have no idea what is really going on."

"Just do it!" the boy shouted. "I hate this place and this stupid skin suit. Finish the job and let's go."

"In another time on another world, this woman was a better fighter than you and I ever will be," the man said. He raised his free hand, which now brandished a bizarre, mechanical implement that resembled a small cattle prod. It glowed blue and emitted electrical sparks as the man brought it up toward Starla's neck.

In a furious instant, Starla summoned her strength and spun out of the man's grip. She instinctively and expertly disarmed him with a swift and accurate kick. It connected with the man's wrist and sent the device flying. Starla swung at the man's face. A perfectly executed jab to the jaw sent him reeling. With a wild scream, she rushed at him. Something had been unlocked. A latent power had been released.

Starla, in the chaos of the moment, felt as if she had left her body and was simply observing herself as she fought. In a hidden, difficult to access part of her mind, recognition and remembrance stirred, offering faint glimpses into another reality, another life.

Her inward flight was short-lived. The present returned with a painful jolt. The boy had jumped onto her back and was choking her from behind. Starla tried to throw him off, but he clung like a rabid monkey. The man in the dark overcoat moved forward, again wielding the glowing weapon. Starla could feel her consciousness ebbing away as the boy squeezed harder. She was drifting... drifting... and then suddenly the weight on her back was ripped away. The arm around her throat released.

Starla choked, sputtered, and gulped air as she struggled to regain her breath. When her awareness fully returned, the first thing she saw was the man in the dark overcoat. His posture was tense and he was scowling at something or someone behind her. Starla spun around and there, before her, grappling with the boy, was the homeless man from up the street. He smiled and winked at her as their eyes met.

"You were doing fine," he said, "but I thought you could use just a little help."

"*You –* " the man in the coat sneered, "that awful costume can't hide your essence. I was just beginning to think that I wouldn't have to contend with *your* kind on this mission."

"Not me," groaned the boy from his subdued position on the ground. "I knew one of these assholes would show up. We should have finished the job quicker."

"It was a valiant effort," said the homeless man as he crouched with a knee planted in the small of the boy's back. With one arm, he secured the boy's wrists. With his free hand, the homeless man reached into his pocket and retrieved an item nearly identical to the strange device previously held by the man in the overcoat.

"Thanks for playing," the homeless man said. "Better luck next time."

He pressed the device to the boy's neck and the boy disintegrated instantly with a flash of light and an explosion of fine, luminous particles. Starla, who had been standing silently in shock since making eye contact with the homeless man, shrieked when she saw the boy vanish.

The homeless man got to his feet, brushed off the dust, and said, "Kids these days... they have no manners."

"This is all so crazy," Starla said. "Were you

following me?"

"Yes, but probably not for the reasons you might suspect. As you know now, I wasn't the only one following you, either."

"I don't understand."

"I know, but someday you will. You are a very special person with a very special role to play. That's all I can tell you right now."

The man in the overcoat sighed. "So, how shall we finish this? I don't know if I can handle another fight. Physical combat is so tedious and boring."

"You know what to do," replied the homeless man. "Or do you want me to do it for you?"

"Fair enough. I thought we had her this time. Well played. I'll see you again, I'm sure."

The man in the overcoat brought his weapon up and held it to his own neck. In a flash of light and dust, he disappeared, leaving an eerie cloud hanging in the air. Starla watched as it quickly dissipated. She did not cry out this time.

"Score one for the good guys," smiled the homeless man.

"I can't pretend that I have any idea what is going on here," Starla said, "but I know that I owe you my gratitude. Thank you."

"No, thank *you*," the homeless man said. "It's been an honor."

"What should I do now? What's going to happen to you?"

"Go to work. Get on with your normal life, however hard it might be. I have other duties to tend to, other places to go."

"Nothing will ever be normal again."

"Good. This universe is full of things that most

human beings will never be aware of. You've had a taste of the mystery. There will be more. For now, take what you have experienced and know that at any moment you may be called upon to participate in the bigger picture, the Grand Cosmic Design."

"I'll try. It may be difficult to relate to the so-called *real* world now, but I'll try."

"Don't try to relate. Be yourself."

"I better get going then. I don't want to be any later for work than I already am."

The homeless man smiled. "That's the spirit. Do what is right for you *now*. The path will open up when it is time. Life itself is an adventure. There is nothing mundane about existence."

Starla smiled back. "I like that. Thank you, again."

"Bye, Starla."

Starla left the alley. She merged with the other pedestrians and continued on her way to work. She looked around and, for the first time, she truly appreciated her surroundings. The sky, the sun, the street, the buildings – even the swarming masses of drone-like people, were all imbued with beauty and grandeur, all things part of the Grand Design. Starla wondered how many others were aware of what occurred behind the scenes, above their city and all around them. The small glimpse she had gotten of another reality, concurrent with her own, made her head reel and her heart race when she considered how much more existed beyond her perception. As she contemplated, she reached her office building. Before entering, she took one last look up at the bright, blue sky. *There are stars up there,* she thought. *I can't see them right now, but I know they're there.*

# Ballena

In San Francisco's bustling financial district, the light of the sun rarely reaches the street. Skyscrapers dominate, towering over the pedestrians and motorists like monolithic guardians of steel and concrete. Around noon, when the swarming crowds winding through the labyrinthine streets are thickest, the sun casts its rays ambivalently upon the throngs of people below.

The masses move like rats in a maze. Among them now, on a typical weekday in mid-summer, is a man named Jonas. Jonas is a 35-year-old bank clerk. It is his lunch break and he is very hungry. He walks the streets on his way to his favorite Chinese restaurant. As he works his way up the congested sidewalk, Jonas observes the other pedestrians around him with a cold, cynical eye. He is completely surrounded by people, yet he feels totally alone.

Jonas comes to a stop and stands with the others waiting at the corner for the light to change. With few exceptions, the people around him are staring at their cell phones and listening to music through headphones nestled in their ears. They are plugged into their own worlds, essentially oblivious to their surroundings. They only act and react as programmed. When the light changes, the little walking man on the sign begins to flash and they cross the street like a herd of cattle.

On the other side of the street, a homeless man is sitting cross-legged on the corner. His clothes are tattered and his face is blackened with filth. A hand-scrawled sign is propped up against the man's knees and he is holding out a large Styrofoam cup.

"Can you spare something for a vet, brother?" the homeless man asks.

"I don't have any money on me," Jonas replies honestly. "I'm sorry."

Jonas is only a few minutes away from Chinatown, where his favorite restaurant is located. He is eager to get out of the financial district. He picks up his pace and practically jogs up the hill that will take him to the Dragon's Gate, the entrance to Chinatown and a passageway into another culture, another world, another time – a unique and mysterious district that exists like another dimension directly in the heart of the city.

Jonas reaches the archway over the sidewalk. As he passes through, he places his hand on the large dragon statue standing to his right like a silent, vigilant sentinel. It is his custom to do so – he believes it is good luck.

"Hey there, big guy," Jonas says. "Here I am again. Another day, another dollar."

Jonas continues up the sidewalk which, like many in San Francisco, rises before him at a steep angle. He allows himself to soak up the oriental ambience as he walks. For the moment, at least, the stress of his job and the crushing pressure of the populous city are far behind him

A multitude of shops and markets line the street, selling toys, fireworks, souvenirs, vegetables, tobacco, liquor, and nearly every conceivable variety of sea creature. The fish vendors never fail to surprise Jonas with what some people find delectable, let alone edible. The street is alive with activity, though it is of a much different type than that in the financial district. Aside from the tourists, who often bring with them a loud and obnoxious energy, the locals live and work in a quiet, efficient, productive ebb and flow. The merchants are busy stocking their displays and sweeping up around their shops and stands. The local shoppers and pedestrians move through the neighborhood along routine paths, focused and content.

As Jonas walks past one of the many gift shops, an object on a shelf loaded with trinkets catches his eye through a propped-open door. Jonas stops walking and steps into the shop to get a better look.

Jonas picks up the object, a small, ceramic dragon with Chinese characters painted on its side. It had been sitting on a shelf with other animal trinkets, each signifying one of the 12 Chinese zodiacal years. Jonas feels an instant and usual attachment to the object in his hands. A strange emotion stirs within him, a potent mixture of longing, nostalgia, and deep affection. He thinks of his wife Nadine, who had been born in the Year of the Dragon. He can't recall the last time he bought her an unexpected gift.

"How much for this little dragon?" Jonas asks the old man sitting on a stool behind the counter and reading a newspaper. "My wife would love it."

"Ten dollars," the man responds. "Cash."

Jonas studies the tiny statue. On impulse, he pulls a bill out of his wallet and pays for it. The shopkeeper wraps it up and puts it in a gift box. Jonas takes the box, leaves the shop, and continues up the street toward his favorite restaurant. He now has an excited bounce in his step. He can't wait to get home after work and surprise his wife with the gift.

Jonas enjoys a bowl of noodles at the restaurant and then returns to work, distracted and distant, ready to finish his shift. After work, he gets on the freeway and begins the long commute to his home in the suburbs. It is Friday and the traffic is even more congested than usual. The endless stream of cars creeps slowly, excruciatingly slowly, north. Jonas studies the faces of the commuters around him. Nearly everyone has the same exasperated, tense expression. Stop,

start, creep, and crawl – the drive home is an agonizing
ordeal.

When Jonas finally gets home, he stumbles through
the front door. He has the small box with the ceramic dragon
in his hand. Nadine is waiting for him in the kitchen. "Hi,
honey," she says when she sees him. "You look like the
walking dead. The good news is we're having brains for
dinner tonight."

Jonas manages a weak chuckle. He gives Nadine a
kiss on the top of her head and then collapses into a seat at
the kitchen table. "I have a little something for you," he says
as he hands her the box. "I couldn't resist."

"Aw! That's sweet. I remember when we used to get
little gifts for each other all the time. Thank you."

Nadine opens the box. She pulls out the tiny statue
and smiles. Her eyes water up. "It's perfect. I love it," she
says.

"I saw it on my lunch break and immediately thought
of you. Actually, I've been thinking a lot about us today. I'm
sure you know that I've been stressed out lately. I know you
have been, too. It's like all we do is drive, work, drive, eat,
sleep, repeat. It seems like there's never any time for *us*."

"I know what you mean," Nadine nods. "I miss you. I
miss our conversations. I miss laughing and having fun."

"Why don't we take off this weekend? Tomorrow.
Let's just hop in the car and drive somewhere, *anywhere* – get
out of the house, get out of the city. We'll find a quiet spot on
the beach, put our feet in the ocean, and drink wine while we
watch the sunset. How does that sound?"

"That sounds like a dream."

The next morning, Jonas and Nadine do exactly that.
They load up the car with supplies and hit the highway,
elated by the spirit of adventure and the thrill of the unknown
that awaits them on the road.

Jonas and Nadine drive up the coast with the sounds and smells of the ocean drifting through the open car windows. To their left, beyond the guard rail, the terrain drops off steeply – a sharp slope merges with the roiling, white-tipped waves of the sea as it crashes against the shore.

"This was a great idea," Nadine says as she leans back in the passenger seat and puts her feet on the dashboard. "I haven't seen another car or person for miles. It's like we're the only ones left on the planet."

"Maybe we are," replies Jonas. "Maybe we got out of town just in time to miss the Apocalypse. Or maybe we slipped through a portal and ended up in an alternate reality. Either way, it's nice. I like it."

"If something like that were true, there are very few people I'd miss," Nadine says with a shake of her head and a hearty laugh. She pauses while gathering her thoughts. The open road always makes her contemplative, philosophical. When she speaks again, her tone is serious and reflective:

"Do you ever get the feeling that you are totally out of sync with the world? I've been finding it hard lately to relate to the people around me – co-workers, friends, even some of my family – everyone seems so self-absorbed, so egotistical, so petty and competitive."

"The funny thing is," Jonas adds, "everyone is thinking the same way, dressing the same way, watching the same movies and TV shows, playing the same games. Have you noticed how little tolerance most people have for people they don't agree with? It's a hard time to be an individual. I have sympathy for the young people who are still trying to discover who they really are in this crazy world."

"That's why I can't be bothered with social media anymore. The rampant narcissism and obvious polarization turn me off. Technology should *serve* humans, yet it seems like, in many ways, people are slaves to their devices."

Jonas eyes his wife with love and admiration. "You're firing on all cylinders today, baby. I like it. Your mind turns me on."

"Well, all this deep thought is making me hungry. Do you feel like stopping somewhere for a bite to eat?"

"There's a sign just ahead. Let's see what it says. We'll find a place to take a break, get some food, and stretch our legs."

The sign informs the couple that they are mere miles from a place called Ballena.

"Ballena," says Jonas. "Never heard of it. Must be a really small town."

"Sounds vaguely familiar to me," Nadine says. "I think it's a fishing village on the coast. Could be a cool place to check out."

The tiny, coastal town of Ballena sits at the southern edge of a peninsula that juts and curves into the Pacific Ocean, creating a bay that is largely unknown to the general public. Jonas and Nadine drive on the rough road that they expect will lead them to the town center. They look for signs of civilization or habitation, but see none of that. Instead, it is as if they have arrived on an alien planet. The terrain has abruptly and dramatically changed. Between the road and the beach, the land undulates, the soil shifting in shades of dark gray and black, sparsely punctuated by unusual, twisted bushes. Bizarre, brightly colored plants jut from the ground in intermittent patches like the tentacles of a buried leviathan.

"Look at those plants!" cries Nadine. "I've never seen anything like them."

"Quite pretty," Jonas says. "It's very scenic around here."

"Hey, shouldn't there be a sign somewhere to indicate where the town is?"

"Maybe the townsfolk don't *want* to be found. Ballena

could be California's best-kept secret. It could be paradise, Shangri-La, a hidden utopia."

"Yeah, right. It's probably a town full of '60s rejects – psychedelic hippie casualties. They're probably trying to hide their pot farms."

Just up the road, a crude, wooden sign has been nailed to a post at the side of the road. When the car nears, Nadine reads the text out loud:

"*Welcome to Ballena. Now please turn around and go away. Love and peace be with you.* Well, isn't that charming. The tourism board should really work on that slogan."

"You were right," smiles Jonas. "Just a bunch of happy and harmless hippies with a sense of humor. They're probably trying to scare off the straights."

"*I'm* a little scared."

"Don't be silly. We're on an adventure. Let's find some food and have some fun."

Jonas and Nadine continue up the road. Not far past the sign, they finally see evidence of the town – a few old, decrepit buildings. They appear to be in serious disrepair, but upon closer inspection, Nadine and Jonas realize that they are, in fact, inhabited. A shirtless, bearded man sits on the porch of one of the homes and eyes their car coldly, suspiciously, as they drive past.

"*He* looked friendly," Nadine jokes.

"Probably just stoned," laughs Jonas.

The road leads the couple past the small cluster of decaying homes at the edge of town and into what serves as the city center – essentially a handful of shops and restaurants in only marginally better shape then the houses they just passed. The road leads right through town and directly to the ocean, which Jonas and Nadine can clearly see just ahead of them, blue and white, glistening in the sun.

The car rolls slowly down the street. Jonas spots a

building with a large, grinning, cartoon crab painted on its exterior. The paint is peeling and the building itself looks like it should have been condemned sometime in the early '70s. Jonas is not deterred. He points to it and says, "There's a restaurant. I bet they have great seafood. Let's go try their clam chowder."

"You want to eat *there?*" Nadine asks incredulously.

"Yeah! Come on," Jonas urges. "Where's your spirit of adventure? This is our getaway trip. You only live once, remember?"

"And I want to *continue* living. When do you think a health inspector last walked through the door of *that* place? I can only imagine what goes on in that kitchen. Makes me shudder to think about it."

"You're kind of bringing me down. This was supposed to be a fun trip."

"You're right. I'm sorry. This place just creeps me out a bit. I'm sure the food will be fine. Should be fresh at the very least, right? Let's check it out. I *am* hungry."

"That's the spirit!"

Jonas parks the car and he and Nadine step out. It is just after noon and the street is virtually empty and eerily silent. An emaciated dog with crusty fur trots up the middle of the street in search of scraps. An elderly man in a black suit and tie sits on a bench across the street staring into space with a blank expression on his gaunt face. A gentle breeze blows through the street, carrying with it the rich, salty scent of the ocean. Jonas approaches the restaurant door, half expecting it to be nailed shut. He turns the knob and the door opens.

A bell above the door rings as Jonas and Nadine enter. In contrast to the dilapidated state of the exterior, the interior of the restaurant is warm, tidy, and inviting. The entire room has been decorated in an aquatic motif. Various nautical implements, including ships' wheels and oars, hang on the brown and red wood-paneled walls along with paintings and photographs depicting all varieties of ocean life. The restaurant is spacious and well-maintained. A door at the far end leads to the kitchen, from which a male voice now calls out: "That you, Ernie? Why don't you come back later. I ain't got time for your shit."

Jonas and Nadine look at each other, amused. "Hi, there," Jonas says loudly. "Are you open for business?"

A moment of silence passes, followed by faint muttering, possible cursing, and the clatter of pots and pans. Jonas and Nadine wait for a response. They are beginning to feel awkward. Finally, the door to the kitchen swings open and a man appears. The man is short, frail, and very old. He is wearing a grease-spattered white T-shirt, dirty blue jeans, and a sailor's cap, which sits at a skewed angle upon a wily mass of silvery hair. Naval tattoos cover the old man's thin arms. His face is deeply lined and incredibly tanned. A cigarette dangles from his pursed lips and remains in position even when he speaks: "Actual customers! Well, I'll be damned. You folks tourists? I ain't served no one but locals in a long time... a *very* long time indeed."

"Is it that obvious?" Nadine smiles. "Yes, we're just passing through. My husband was in the mood for some clam chowder and, well, this seemed like the right place to get some."

"You got that right, lady! Best damn chowder in the country, I reckon. Come on in and have a seat. The name's Elvis, like the singer... but don't remind me of that because I hate that punk greaser and his so-called music."

Jonas laughs and says, "Fair enough! Was never much of a fan myself." He and Nadine take a seat at a table in the middle of the restaurant.

"You folks from the city?" Elvis asks as he arranges

napkins, dishes, and silverware in front of the diners.

"We are, yes," replies Nadine. "We're on a much-needed vacation. It feels good to get away. This is a lovely area."

"I don't blame ya!" Elvis cries. "I can't stand the big city. Haven't been there since I served in the war. Is it still full of hippies and queers?"

Jonas chuckles nervously. "It's a diverse and dynamic city. I'm sure a lot has changed since your last visit."

"Change isn't always a good thing," Elvis says. "I've seen a lot of change in my life and most of it was for the worse. The world is going to Hell in a handbasket and I'm too old to care. Anyway, enough of my complaining. I'm just a crotchety, old fart. You two seem like a nice, young couple. What else can I get ya with your soup? You will love it, by the way. It's delicious. I'm not boasting – that's just a *fact.*"

"I'll take a coffee, please," Nadine says.

"Me, too," nods Jonas.

"You got it," Elvis grins. He saunters back to the kitchen and returns promptly with a fresh pot of coffee. He fills two cups and says, "I'll be back in a jiffy with your soup. Please relax and enjoy yourselves."

Elvis returns to the kitchen, whistling. When the door shuts behind him, Nadine shakes her head and says, "Well, *he's* a real character. I don't know *what* to make of him."

"Aw, he's a nice enough old guy. He's just set in his ways. I kinda like him."

Jonas and Nadine spend the short wait for their soup engaged in easy, comfortable conversation, enjoying their time together away from the city. Elvis soon returns to the table with two full bowls of hearty, steaming soup on a tray. He carefully places a bowl in front of each of the eager diners.

"Enjoy your food," Elvis says, "and I hope you enjoy

your stay in Ballena, too. Are you planning on staying the night?"

"Probably not," replies Jonas. "This is just a day trip and there's more we want to see up the coast."

"Good," Elvis says gravely, with a touch of relief. "This is a nice town to visit, but I don't recommend an extended stay. In fact, I would strongly urge you to move on as quickly as you can. Have your meal, enjoy your stay, but be on your way before the sun goes down. This is not somewhere you want to be stuck for the night. Trust me."

Elvis wanders back to the kitchen, leaving Jonas and Nadine to ponder his vague, cryptic warning. Jonas breaks the tension with a shrug and a smile. "He's just trying to spook us," he says, spooning soup into his mouth. "They don't take too kindly to strangers in these parts."

"It worked," Nadine says. "I'm spooked."

Jonas and Nadine finish eating and pay for their food. When the transaction is completed, Elvis thanks them and says, "Remember what I said about leaving town before dark. I like you kids. Stay safe."

The couple leaves the restaurant. The street is still strangely devoid of activity. Even the man in the black suit who had been sitting on the bench has disappeared. Jonas and Nadine stand alone, like the last survivors of a silent, unseen cataclysm, the orphaned leftovers of a vanished race. It has been a weird day, but Jonas is still in good spirits. "Let's go to the beach," he says. "We need to see the ocean."

Nadine agrees and they begin the short walk up the street that will lead them directly to the water's edge. As they get closer, new sounds intermingle with the roaring and crashing of waves, indistinguishable at first, but rising in volume and gaining clarity upon approach. At the crest of a small hill that slopes down to meet the ocean, Jonas and Nadine spot the source of the sounds – a large congregation of people gathered by the shore.

"Wow, look at 'em all," Jonas says. "Now I know why the town seemed deserted – everyone's partying on the beach."

The scene does indeed resemble a party. There are men and women, mostly young, fit, and scantily clad, swimming, surfing, playing volleyball, and sunbathing. A large group sits around a huge, stone fire pit on the beach, playing guitars, hand drums, and tambourines. The pleasant tones of a folk song rise from the musicians, providing a serene, yet haunting soundtrack to the festivities.

"Feel like crashing a party?" Jonas grins.

"I don't know if we'd be welcome," replies Nadine.

"They look friendly enough to me! It's all part of the adventure, right?"

"Alright, I suppose. Just don't drink the Kool-Aid, okay?"

"Tune in, turn on, and drop out, baby. Can you dig it?"

Where the road ends, Nadine follows Jonas as he descends the concrete steps that lead down to the beach. Although she trusts her husband, she feels a slight reluctance, a subtle dread. Jonas can be impulsive, but he has never in the past gotten them into serious trouble. As she observes the scene on display before her, however, Nadine senses something dark lurking behind the revelry – something ominous concealed in the festivities. She briefly visualizes Hieronymus Bosch's beautiful and unsettling masterpiece *The Garden of Earthly Delights*. She considers asking Jonas to rethink his decision to approach the party, but it is too late. He is already on the beach. Nadine joins him and takes his hand.

Jonas and Nadine stroll through the sand toward the water's edge. The people gathered on the beach accept them into their midst with gentle smiles and sincere greetings. A peaceful, joyful mood pervades the scene. When the couple reaches the spot near the water where the dark, wet sand indicates the furthest reaches of the tide, they sit down on the dry sand just above it. Jonas wraps an arm around Nadine and she folds into his embrace. A seagull lands on a large piece of driftwood sticking out of the sand and studies the couple with a raw and peculiar intelligence glinting in its eyes.

"I could live like this," Jonas says. "Just quit my job and become a beach bum. The bank sure wouldn't miss me. What do you think?"

"You'll have to learn how to surf," replies Nadine. "Maybe Elvis would hire you to wash dishes."

"Nah, I'd just catch my own food and cook it right here. In all seriousness, though, I miss when life was *simpler*. It's hard to accept that soon we'll be back in the grind with all the other sad souls. Traffic, pollution, crime, politics, bills, taxes, drudgery, and death... ugh."

"It's really depressing when you put it that way. We should be thankful for what we have. Don't you appreciate all that we have worked to achieve?"

"I do. I really do. We have a nice home in a nice neighborhood. You like your job and, for the most part, I like mine. I guess part of me envies those – like the people here on the beach – who seem to have few responsibilities and little or no stress in their lives."

"And probably no ambition or goals. Is that really how you want to live? Like that piece of driftwood, just carried along with the tide? I thought you had direction and drive. It's your determination to *make* something of yourself that I admire. The city – and society itself – is complex and crazy. I know that, but the system has also given us the opportunity to *improve* our lives. We talk sometimes about having children. Wouldn't you want to provide for them?"

"Yes. You're right again, of course. I love you and I love the the life we have created. It's been a great trip so far and I just get caught up in the moment. My imagination gets the best of me. You know how it is."

Nadine reassures her husband with a firm hug. They relax in silence watching the waves. A few minutes pass and then a voice behind them speaks:

"Excuse me, I don't mean to interrupt, but I noticed that you aren't from around here and I wanted to welcome you to our humble little town."

Jonas and Nadine turn in unison to face the person speaking to them. They encounter an individual of striking appearance – a tall, well-built man with a deep tan and long blonde hair framing a chiseled face of classic proportions. The man's eyes are penetrating and startlingly blue. He wears a leather vest, leather pants, and leather moccasins, as if he stepped straight out of a storybook about Wild West pioneers. He gazes down upon Jonas and Nadine, intense and imposing.

"Would you care to join us by the fire?" the man asks. "Don't be shy. Nothing but good people around here."

Jonas looks at Nadine for direction. She smiles softly and shrugs. There is a look of concern in her eyes, though, Jonas notes.

"Yeah, okay," Jonas says, "but we can't stay long. "We're just passing through."

"That's what *everyone* says," the man laughs. "Ballena is a magical place. Most people find it difficult to leave once they've visited. If the town wants you to stay, you *stay*. I bet you were drawn here for a reason."

Jonas and Nadine follow the man to the fire. The musicians have started into a new song. No one pays any attention to the newcomers as they find an open spot and take a seat. The man in leather sits at Jonas' side. Those who aren't performing, including Jonas and Nadine, sit listening for the duration of the song. It seems to be an original number. The lyrics are thoughtful and poetic, the subject matter socially aware and topically relevant. When the song is over, the air is heavy, the mood pensive. The man in leather speaks, breaking the thick silence: "I would like everyone to welcome our two new friends. I'm sorry, I didn't get your names."

"I'm Jonas and this is Nadine."

"Wonderful, thank you. I'm Coyote Buck. This is my family. Welcome to Ballena."

Around the fire, all eyes turn to the young couple. They are greeted with smiles and warm, sincere salutations.

"Thanks," Jonas says. "It's a nice town. We drove up from the city. It's great to get away and I can see why you like it here. It's so remote and peaceful."

"And hidden," Nadine interjects. "We had a hard time finding it at first. I thought we were going to get lost."

"That's the way we like it," says Coyote Buck. "We don't really *want* to be found. I'm glad that you two managed to make it here. It was meant to be. Do you smoke?"

Coyote Buck pulls a comically large marijuana cigarette from a leather pouch on his hip and offers it to the astonished couple.

"Is that *pot?*" Nadine exclaims. "I don't do that stuff. Thanks anyway."

"I haven't smoked since college," Jonas says. "I think I'll pass."

"Fair enough," says Coyote Buck as he puts the massive joint to his lips and lights it. He inhales deeply and passes it to a scruffy-looking guitar player to his left. "We grow our own, purely organic. We grow all our own food, too. If you stick around, you can join us for the feast."

"Oh, I don't know about that," Nadine says. "We should probably get going soon. There's more we want to see up the coast. We appreciate the offer, though, and your hospitality."

"What else *is* there to see?" Coyote Buck asks. "This is the jewel of California right here. It doesn't get any better than where you are right now. I mean that in both a physical and a spiritual sense. Be in the *Now*, man. Embrace the moment."

Raised eyebrows and rolled eyes reveal Nadine's skepticism. Jonas nods politely and says, "I know where you're coming from, believe me. I've had similar feelings lately. Unfortunately, we have a home and jobs to get back to."

"Yes," Nadine says. "Reality awaits. It would be nice to escape society and live happily ever after in a commune somewhere, but this isn't the '60s anymore."

"What makes you say that?" asks Coyote Buck. "Where do you think you are? *When* do you thing you are?"

The others gathered around the fire are now listening to the conversation intently. Through the fog of marijuana smoke, 20 pairs of eyes watch the exchange eagerly, knowingly. The observers are accustomed to Coyote Buck's conversational style. It is both a spectator sport and a teaching tool, meant to entertain and enlighten. Jonas takes the bait and enters the fray: "I am, for better or for worse, a modern man in the modern world. I've got some stress in my life and there are times when I wish I could just walk away from the madness, but I'm a pretty happy guy, all things considered. In 2017, I see that as an accomplishment in itself. There are lots of people in this world who have it far worse."

Coyote Buck carefully processes Jonas' words before speaking:

"2017? Is that really *when* you think you are? What if

I told you that time and space are an illusion, that the only thing that is real is your mind?"

"I can't rule that out," Jonas replies. "That could very well be true."

"Oh, please," Nadine scoffs. "It's getting a little too psychedelic around here. I'll tell you what's real: I have to be at work at 9 AM tomorrow morning, and if I'm not, I don't get paid. Jonas, too. I think it's time we hit the road."

"Ballena brought you here, to *us*," Coyote Buck states gravely. "The only way you're leaving is if it *wants* you to leave."

Nadine stands up. "Is that a threat?" she demands. "Are you trying to scare us?"

"Not a threat – the truth."

"Alright," says Jonas rising to his feet. "I think it *is* time for us to get going. It's been fun. Thank you for the music... and for the interesting conversation. If we start driving now, we can be –"

Jonas freezes mid-sentence. He has his cell phone in his hand and is staring at its screen in disbelief. "That can't be right," he mutters. "How can it be 6 PM already? We just had lunch."

"It's all *maya*, my friend," smiles Coyote Buck. "An illusion – persistent and all-encompassing, but simply illusion. You were meant to be here, with us, right now. Ballena has plans for you."

"I don't know if I should be flattered or freaked out," says Jonas.

"We just lost track of time," Nadine says as she joins Jonas at his side. "That's what happens when you're having fun. The sun is setting. Let's go."

The sky transforms into a magnificent display of warm reds and oranges as the ocean swallows the sun. Bands of clouds spread the color through the atmosphere. The rolling waves carry the shades to the shore in shimmering pulses of light. On the beach, the shadows elongate and distort. The day is quickly ebbing away.

Jonas and Nadine peel away from the group on the beach and head toward their parked car. Coyote Buck watches them, his face neutral, his eyes piercing with laser intensity. The couple climbs the concrete steps that lead from the beach to the street. At the top, out of the sight of Coyote Buck and his followers, Nadine exhales sharply and shakes her head. "The sooner we get out of here, the better," she says. "This place is creepy."

"Yeah, I'm sorry about that. It's a really nice town in a beautiful area. Too bad the residents are all weirdos. At least the food..." Jonas stops cold. "Oh, *shit!*"

"What is it?"

The couple has reached their car, but Jonas is mortified by what he sees. "A flat tire," he groans. "That's just *great.*"

"Oh, no, honey," says Nadine as she walks around the vehicle. "They're *all* flat."

"How the hell? The road coming in was rough, but not *that* rough. Someone must have done this."

"What are we going to do? I don't want to be stuck here all night."

"Let's just relax for a moment and breathe. Don't panic. I can call someone for help."

Jonas reaches into his pocket and retrieves his cell phone. When he sees the screen, he sighs. "No service. What a friggin' surprise."

"What is wrong with this place? I hate it here. I just want to go home."

Jonas rubs his forehead, struggling to comprehend the situation and formulate a solution. "I'm at a loss for ideas," he says. "This is just insane. Maybe we should ask Elvis for help, or at least see if he has a phone we can use."

"The old guy at the restaurant? Do you think we can trust him? What if it was him who did this?"

"I don't know if we can trust *anyone* around here, but what choice do we have? We only have one spare."

Reluctantly, Nadine follows Jonas back to the seafood restaurant where, in their perception of time, they had just finished eating. With no cars parked in front and no exterior lights, it appears to be closed for the evening. Jonas approaches the building anyway and tries to open the door. It is locked. He begins knocking forcefully.

"Hello? Are you in there, Elvis? It's Nadine and Jonas. We need help."

From behind the locked door, a voice calls out, firm and serious: "I told you to leave. I warned you about staying in town after dark. There's nothing I can do for you now. You're on your own."

Distressed, Nadine steps forward and bangs on the door with a clenched fist. "Please," she cries, "just let us use your phone. Our tires are flat and we have no way of getting out of here. We're trapped."

"Yes, I know," replies Elvis. "You *are* trapped, dear. Both of you, like many before. Believe me, I would help if I could. I like you two – I really do – but the best thing for everyone right now is if you just step away from the door and make peace with your fate."

"What are you *talking* about?" yells Jonas. "Just let us use your phone! Or call someone *for* us – Triple A, the cops... *anyone!*"

"This is your last warning," Elvis says. "Get away from here. I have a gun and will defend myself if need be." The sound of a shotgun being cocked accompanies the last statement, as if reinforcing the point.

"This whole town is nuts," Nadine says, stepping

away from the restaurant. Tears form in her eyes. She is on
the verge of hysteria. Jonas notices her building anxiety and
wraps an arm around her.

"The only thing I can think of is to go back to the
beach," Jonas says. "Surely *someone* will help us. They can't
*all* be psychos like that Coyote character."

"What if it was one of them who did this to us?"

"Then we'll confront them. I really don't think it *was*
one of them, though. They're too busy getting high and
playing hippie on the beach. It was probably just a couple of
local kids who noticed an unfamiliar car and wanted to play a
practical joke on some tourists – a pain in the ass, but nothing
sinister."

"Have you even *seen* any kids around here? It's like a
ghost town except for the freaks, stoners, and surfers."

"What are our options? We have no choice but to ask
for help. Don't let your imagination get the best of you. We're
going to be fine. We'll be back at home before you know it."

"That's all I want now – just to be back at the house,
safe and comfortable. I think I've had enough adventure for
one day."

Jonas and Nadine walk back toward the beach as the
sun slips fully below the horizon. They reach the steps and
descend. The glow of the fire pit illuminates the gathering,
which seems to have grown in size. The festive atmosphere
has intensified. The mood is wild and raucous. As the
attendees imbibe, ingest, and indulge, a full moon hangs
overhead like a celestial lantern – or a giant eye, sentient and
omniscient.

Spotting Coyote Buck sitting in the same position by
the fire as before, Jonas and Nadine approach. Coyote Buck
smiles when he sees them. He gives them a friendly wave
and encourages them to join him with a hand gesture.

"I knew you'd be back," Coyote Buck says. "I told

you – you belong here. Ballena has plans for you."

"Actually, we ran into a problem," says Jonas. "We somehow ended up with four flat tires. Not one – *four*. So, as you can imagine, it's going to be a little hard for us to get home."

"You wouldn't happen to know anything about that, would you?" Nadine asks, her tone accusatory.

"Of course not," Coyote Buck replies. "I've been here the entire time. I haven't left the beach all day, nor has anyone else, as far as I know. We're having too good a time to do something mean and stupid like that."

Trying to diffuse the tension, Jonas waves his hands and says, "I know. We didn't really think it was you guys. We could have run over some glass on the way in, or something like that. We just need some help."

"I'll tell you what *I* think," says Coyote Buck. "It was synchronicity that brought you here and synchronicity that is keeping you. This is a special occasion, you know. We don't celebrate like this every night."

"*That's* a surprise," Nadine chuckles. "Do you people have jobs? We do, and they require us to be there tomorrow morning."

"I find it astonishing how people embrace their servitude," Coyote Buck says. "It's like the masses are totally cut off from Source and they don't even know it. The world would be a healthier and happier place if there was a return to natural law."

Three young women with similar long, straight, flowing hair and vintage '60s sundresses appear behind Jonas and Nadine. The women are smiling widely. Their faces radiate joy, but their limbs are rigid and their posture stiff. They stand in a tight line behind Jonas and Nadine, a little too close for comfort. The tallest one, a dark-haired girl in her early twenties, speaks: "It's almost time to begin the ceremony. The preparations are complete."

"Thank you, Susan," Coyote Buck smiles. "You and the girls did a fabulous job this year. Have you met the guests of honor yet? This is Jonas and Nadine."

"Hello," says Susan, her eyes vacant. "I'm so glad you could join us."

"Guests of honor," Nadine scoffs. "Hardly. This really isn't our kind of party."

"We'll be leaving as soon as we get our car fixed," says Jonas.

"You keep saying that," Coyote Buck says, "yet here you are. Unlike the sad fools who wander the city like zombies, blind to the truth and deaf to the inner voices of their hearts, *I* have a connection with Source. The ocean speaks to me. That's why I'm here... and that's also why *you're* here."

Coyote Buck nods at Susan, who is still standing behind Jonas and Nadine. "It's time," he says softly. Instantly, the three girls spring into action. With frightening speed and uncanny strength, Coyote Buck's female lackeys immobilize Jonas and Nadine in a coordinated attack. In a flash they have pinned the arms of the shocked couple behind their backs. Before Jonas and Nadine have time to process what is happening, Susan expertly binds their wrists with thick rope.

When the other beach revelers realize what is happening, a hush descends upon the group. The laughter and music cease. All eyes fixate on Coyote Buck and Jonas and Nadine, who are now bound and restrained by a small group of Coyote Buck's followers.

"It's best if you don't fight," Coyote Buck states. "Trust in the wisdom of the cosmos and embrace your fate."

"Why are you doing this?" Nadine cries.

Nadine writhes and struggles, but she and her husband are held firmly by people who are determined to make sure that they do not escape. Jonas remains still and, for the moment, silent.

"It's nothing personal," says Coyote Buck. "As head of this family, I need to do what is best for us, and occasionally, that means I have to make hard decisions for the greater good. This is not something I enjoy doing, and I apologize for the rough handling. When we meet on the other side, I hope you are able to forgive me and know that all exists in harmony. This is simply part of the balance of karma."

Jonas, coming to terms with their situation, now speaks up. With great effort, he maintains his cool in an attempt to reason with Coyote Buck. "You are making a huge mistake. Whatever it is you're planning to do, you won't get away with it. Too many witnesses. Do you trust all of these people to keep a secret? Look around you. I understand that you want to keep this town private. Why don't you just let us go? Nobody ever has to know we were here. We won't say a thing. No one even needs to know this place exists."

"I'm glad you understand our desire to keep Ballena private," Coyote Buck says. "We live here in peace and prosperity because the land and the ocean take care of us. In return, we take care of the land and the ocean."

Coyote Buck gazes out upon the ocean, vast and deep, sparkling ethereally in reflected moonlight. Concealed within its immense depths is an expansive, hidden world full of mysterious structures and strange life forms – an alien ecosystem surrounding our own.

Susan, who appears to be Coyote Buck's most trusted accomplice, speaks up: "It's almost time. I can feel Him coming."

"Yes," says Coyote Buck. "I feel Him too. He's calling out to us. I can hear His voice in my head. Bring the offerings to the water's edge. Bind their legs and seal their mouths. I don't want a repeat of last year's ceremony, which was messy, loud, and disturbing for the new followers. Let's do it right this year."

Coyote Buck reaches into the leather pouch at his side and produces a six-shot revolver. He hands the gun to Susan. "Take this. Use it if you need to, but only to wound. The offerings must remain alive."

"Please don't do this!" screams Nadine as one of the men restraining her produces a roll of duct tape. "We won't tell anyone. Let us go!"

The man ignores Nadine's cries and seals her mouth with the tape. Jonas' mouth is also sealed. They are led away from Coyote Buck by Susan and the two silent girls and directed toward the water. Before they reach the shoreline, an extraordinary event occurs, accompanied by shrieks of delight and excited cheering from the onlookers on the beach.

"He's here!" Susan cries.

500 or so yards out from the beach, a frothy, churning maelstrom forms on the surface of the ocean. Massive fountains of water shoot into the air and cascade back down like raging geysers. The tempest builds, violent and awesome, increasing in size and fury. Something is coming to the surface – something enormous and unimaginably powerful. When the indistinct, gargantuan shape breaches the surface, it unleashes a deafening roar that seems to shake the fabric of reality. The sound reverberates like the war cry of a demented demon. A tentacle rises from the beast, uncoiling and stretching 100 feet in the air before crashing down with an ear-splitting slap and an explosion of water.

"Yes, He's here," Coyote Buck calls from a safe distance away, "and He's hungry."

With the gun in her hand, Susan urges the bound couple forward. Rough handling by the two other girls ensure that they comply. When they reach the edge of the shore, with water lapping at their feet, Jonas and Nadine are forced to their knees. Out of the ocean, the great monstrosity churns up water and produces a great wake as it speeds toward them. Somehow, it seems to know that two delicious morsels await.

Nadine struggles against her bindings. She topples over on her side and something pops out of the front pocket of her jeans. Susan, who is still standing behind her, gasps when she sees the object – it is the ceramic dragon that Jonas had purchased for Nadine the day before they left on their journey. Susan bends down and plucks it out of the sand.

"Buck," Susan shouts. "You better come see this."

Coyote Buck curses and yells, "What the hell is going on? He's coming! Leave them and get the fuck out of there!"

"You *really* need to see this," Susan reiterates.

"Goddamn," Coyote Buck mutters, "this better be good." He marches up the beach and approaches Susan, who is holding the tiny dragon in the palm of her hand. He freezes when he sees it. "Is that what I think it is?" he asks.

"It's a dragon," Susan nods. "Just like in your dream."

"Well, isn't *that* interesting."

"What does it mean?"

"It means that we need to reconsider our plans for the evening. Help them up and untie them."

"What about Him?" Susan gestures toward the massive shape racing toward the shore.

"*When the dragon appears, the beast will be defeated.* That's what the dream said. I'm not sure exactly what that means, but I think we're about to find out."

Susan and the other acolytes help Jonas and Nadine to their feet. They release the rope bindings and remove the tape from their mouths.

Jonas gasps for air and says, "That thing out there might be an actual sea monster, or I may be hallucinating, but I know this: you people are *nuts.*"

"You have no idea what's going on," Coyote Buck says. "There is a larger reality that totally eludes the mundane minds of modern men. You should just be thankful that you didn't end up in the gut of that incredible animal. It is more ancient, powerful, and wise than you can possibly imagine."

"What happens now?" asks Susan. "Do we just let them go? Doesn't the beast need to feed?"

"They can go," replies Coyote Buck as he gazes out on the sea. "A new age is dawning."

"Can I have my dragon back?" Nadine asks. "It has special meaning to me."

"Take it," Says Coyote Buck. "Leave now."

Susan places the dragon in Nadine's hand. Nadine and Jonas walk up the beach away from the shore. The crowd gathered around the fire pit watches the couple pass in reverent silence. When they reach the concrete steps that will take them up to the street, Jonas turns around once more to look at the ocean. He sees the leviathan, its unfathomably large shape moving toward the shore, tentacles thrashing and water raging. Coyote and his closest followers still stand on the beach awaiting its arrival, their forms dwarfed by the ancient behemoth.

"I'm ready to go home," Jonas says.

"What about the car?"

"We'll figure something out. We always do. It's funny – the city suddenly seems not so bad. Who'd have thought I'd actually be looking forward to getting back to the chaos and confusion?"

"In a week, you'll be wanting to go on another adventure. I know you."

Jonas and Nadine walk hand-in-hand toward their car. Behind them, the beast bellows, its great roar shaking the foundations of the surrounding buildings and rattling windows. Jonas and Nadine shudder and draw closer together. They do not look back.

# The Freaks

Joey MacKaye was 16 years old when he and his single mother arrived in the town of Tempest, Ontario in the late summer of 1993. Joey's mother had recently accepted a new job at a local law firm. The career change, and her desire to distance herself from a troubled past, had motivated the monumental move across the country. Their accommodations – a small, rustic home on the lake – were provided by the firm. Joey's mother was extremely excited about the new life that awaited them in Tempest. Joey was not so enthusiastic.

It was late evening when they pulled up to their new home nestled in the woods. The setting sun over the lake was picturesque. Joey's mother got out of the car first, a broad smile illuminating her face. Joey, despite the beauty of the scene before him and his mother's genuine joy, remained in the passenger seat sulking.

"Isn't this place just *wonderful*, Joey?" His mother was enraptured. "Isn't it *so* much better than the smog and congestion of Vancouver? I love it here already!"

Joey was not so impressed. "It's... nice," he mumbled.

"You're going to learn to love it here," his mother said as she gathered a suitcase and a few bags from the car. They had sold or given away most of their possessions prior to the move in an attempt to make the transition easier and as a way to further distance themselves from the past. Joey resented this, among many other things.

Joey got out of the car and retrieved a gym bag and electric guitar from the backseat – his only belongings, except for a few small boxes of personally significant items that he had kept. He slung the gym bag and guitar over his shoulder and followed his mother up the steps and onto the front porch of the house.

"This house needs a lot of work," Joey said, kicking at a loose board on the porch.

"That *attitude!*" his mother exclaimed as she unlocked the door and stepped into their new home. "Why do you always have to be so negative? You sound just like your father. He could be a real..." She caught herself before finishing the sentence.

"Dad wouldn't have moved us all the way across the damn country to live in some hick town in the middle of nowhere."

"There aren't enough snooty restaurants and boutiques here for your father and his new wife," Joey's mother said. It was difficult for her to pass up an opportunity to sneak in a jab at her ex-husband.

"Cindy is actually very nice. You don't know her."

Joey's mother winced. "I'm sure she is."

"She makes dad happy, you know."

"That's good, but my concern is for *your* happiness. That's why we're here. I wanted a better life for us... for *you*, Joey."

"Yeah, right," Joey muttered.

They entered the home and with the flick of a switch, Joey's mother filled it with light. The home was fully furnished, and though in need of a little dusting, looked tidy and welcoming. The warm shades of brown and red and the vaulted ceiling with exposed beams enhanced the rustic ambience.

"Oh, it's *amazing!*" Joey's mother cried. "It's even better than I imagined. It's a dream come true."

"For *you*," Joey said. "It feels like *Little House on the Prairie* to me. I'm surprised this place even has electricity."

Joey's mother ignored the comments. She was

absolutely enthralled with the home.

"So, where's *my* room?" Joey asked with an exaggerated yawn.

"It's a two-bedroom house. You can have your pick."

"Okay, cool." Joey wandered off to explore the home. From the living room, Joey stepped into the kitchen, where a hallway led to the bathroom and bedrooms. Joey went down the hall and directly to the farthest room. He entered and shut the door.

The room was simply and functionally furnished with a bed, a dresser, and a small desk. A window on the north wall provided an unobstructed view of the lake, which lay in grand and peaceful repose at the edge of the property, sparkling in the nascent twilight. Joey recognized the beauty and acknowledged it with a barely audible, "Wow."

Alone in his new room, Joey began to relax. After being trapped in a car with his mother for five long days and 2000 miles, exhaustion, total and debilitating, hit him like a tidal wave. The bed suddenly looked very inviting. He sat down on its edge and bounced a few times. It was good.

Joey retrieved his Sony walkman cassette player from his bag, along with a few of his favorite tapes. He popped in Nirvana's album *Nevermind*, strapped on the earphones, and cranked the volume. He lay back and allowed the music to work its furious magic.

Joey lost himself in the drums, the bass, the manic chainsaw guitars, and most of all, the powerful voice of the lead singer, Kurt Cobain. Kurt's voice was raw, yet controlled – caustic and fluid at the same time. It somehow perfectly captured the collective angst and sensitivities of an entire generation of teenagers. Within the simply arranged pop punk songs, Joey found strength, freedom, unity, and, despite the vaguely dark and depressing lyrics, transcendent joy. The music was invigorating.

Even with the energy blasting directly into his head, fatigue began tugging at Joey's consciousness sometime into the second side of the cassette tape. He did not fight it, and before long, he was drawn into deep sleep.

Joey slept for 12 hours and awoke in a state of confusion. *Where am I? Who am I?* He struggled to return to the surface of reality, but something held him back, like an invisible phantom tethered to his mind. He had a moment of flailing mental panic before he finally broke through into total awareness.

It was early morning. The sun was rising. He was in his new home somewhere deep in the woods of Northern Ontario. Golden light was streaming into his room. The clear, crisp northern air carried with it the sounds and smells of the lake and the dense boreal forest. *Maybe this won't be so bad after all,* Joey thought. He lay there and soaked in the moment, lingering near the threshold of sleep. The tranquility vanished with a shout.

"Joey! Joey, get up! I need your help." It was his mother calling from somewhere down the hall. Her voice had an effect like shards of glass piercing his brain. Joey groaned and got up slowly.

Joey's mother was waiting for him in the kitchen. "I know it's summer, but there are still things that need to get done around here," she said. "You can't sleep your life away."

"I bet I could."

"Help me unpack this stuff, please." Joey's mother was referring to a small collection of boxes on the kitchen counter.

"Ugh," Joey protested. "Do you really need my help for this? There's, like, just some dishes and silverware in these boxes."

"That *attitude!*" Joey's mother said once again. "Have you ever tried just being happy? I know it's not cool, but you might like it."

"Anything here to eat?" Joey asked, his voice dripping with insolence. "*That* would make me happy."

"I haven't gone for groceries yet. Unpack this stuff and I'll take you out for breakfast."

Joey's mother left the kitchen and Joey began unpacking the boxes. He was surprised when the sight of the dishes they had used in Vancouver made him nostalgic. The items were imbued with memories, infused with past associations and experiences. A wave of unexpected sadness and deep yearning washed over him. He finished the task as quickly as he could.

Joey found his mother in the living room, crouched behind the floor model television set that the home owners had provided.

"I finished unpacking that stuff," Joey said.

"Mmm, okay, honey," his mother responded, preoccupied with wires and cables.

"Gonna go for a walk, I think," Joey said. His mother looked up from behind the television set. "Don't you want some breakfast?" she asked. "We're only a few minutes away from downtown. We can walk together if you want."

"This place has a downtown?" Joey was incredulous. To him it felt like they were totally isolated in the middle of the bush. "Maybe I'll go exploring then. I'd like to see 'downtown' for myself."

"Just keep an open mind," Joey's mother said. "This is a nice, quaint town."

"Hicksville."

"Once you make some friends you're going to fit right in."

"Somehow I doubt that."

His mother was studying him closely. "Just give it a chance," she said. "Can you do that?"

Joey could see the concern on his mother's face. "I'll try, mom," he said. He didn't really want to worry or upset her.

"Do you need any money?" his mother asked.

"I have a few bucks, but thanks."

"Okay. Have fun, honey. Be safe."

"I will," Joey said as he approached the door.

"Joey?" his mother called as he stepped out onto the patio. "Thank you for helping me unpack. I love you, buddy."

"I love you, too, mom."

Joey shut the door and stood on the patio. A sense of the potential adventure awaiting him in this new and unexplored territory lifted his spirits. He felt, for perhaps the first time since they had left British Columbia, real excitement – the anticipation of an unwritten future. *I can be whoever I want to be,* he thought. *No one here knows me. I could completely reinvent myself.* It was an empowering idea.

Joey stepped off the patio and began walking. He felt, for the moment, like a free-range lion, on the prowl in the early morning jungle.

The home that Joey and his mother now occupied was on a quiet street that led into the heart of Tempest. Joey walked the tree-lined sidewalk, taking it all in. *This really is a small town,* he thought. *Nothing at all like the hustle and madness of Vancouver.* As he walked, he gained confidence. As he gained confidence, his stride transformed into a cocky swagger.

*I'm a badass,* Joey thought. *This town won't know what hit 'em.*

Within a few blocks, the dense forest was replaced by a quiet residential area. The heavy bush blended smoothly into a neighborhood of large, aging war-era houses. Most homes were in need of repair – some were minimally weathered, others were extremely dilapidated. A few homes seemed to be abandoned and condemned. It was clear to Joey that the neighborhood had seen better days. Still, a certain charming small town character remained.

Joey had been walking for about 15 minutes when he arrived at Tempest's main street, which was, of course, called Main Street. A small stretch of storefronts served as downtown Tempest. It was an area of no more than four square blocks. Joey was not surprised. "Somehow, I doubt I'll find a cool record store around here," he said.

There was minimal activity on the street on this late-summer morning. The few people Joey encountered carried themselves in a languid, easy manner. The hardware store and the barber shop seemed to be the hottest attractions. Joey walked on, until he found himself in front of a building that actually seemed to have some real *life* – the pool hall on the corner. A gaudy neon sign in the window identified the establishment as Wizard's Billiards. *Nice,* Joey thought. It had a seedy quality that instantly appealed to him.

As he stood peering into the window, the door flew open and out stepped a couple of characters straight out of an '80s heavy metal video. Two guys in leather, denim, and Metallica t-shirts burst onto the street and whipped out cigarettes, lighting them with practiced panache. Their mullet hair cuts and peach fuzz mustaches were ten years out of style.

"You suck, dude," the tall one said to the shorter. "You cost us that game. Fuck."

And then they saw Joey standing there – instant tension. The metal heads immediately recognized Joey for what he was – a stranger to town. The hostility they radiated toward him was thick and nasty. They eyed Joey up and down in exaggerated gestures. Joey wore clothes vaguely in alignment with the current grunge trend, but for the most part he followed no particular style. He took pride in being an individual, and had worn the same ensemble of jeans, t-shirt, and buttoned overshirt since grade seven.

"Hey, buddy," the short one said with a sneer. "What's up?"

The words were innocuous, but the moment was ripe with danger. The imminent threat of violence hung in the air. *A couple of typical meatheads,* Joey thought – but what he said was, "Not much, guys. New to town. Just looking for a place to chill." Though he felt a little nervous, he made a valiant attempt to project a calm exterior.

The headbangers were confused. Apparently the local kids were easily intimidated by them. They were not sure how to handle Joey's unexpected response to their veiled taunts. They looked at each other, perplexed, their mouths open, their eyes dull and questioning. "Huh," the tall one muttered before taking a long drag on his cigarette.

"Do you play?" the short one asked, motioning toward the pool tables inside the hall.

"A little," Joey replied, "but it's been a long time. My dad taught me to play when I was a kid."

"Are you any good?" the tall banger asked, dragging hard on his cigarette until he was inhaling filter.

"Not really," Joey responded honestly.

The short banger scoffed. "Gotta be good to play on these tables," he said.

"Fair enough," Joey said.

"Unless you wanna, you know... make it interesting," the tall one smirked. The heavy metal casualties exchanged looks like predators coordinating an attack. Their intent was obvious to Joey.

"Nah. I'm not really into gambling."

"One game," the short banger insisted. "Just a small wager between buds. All in good fun."

"No thanks, guys. I'm kinda broke."

"What are ya, a *pussy?*" the tall one sneered.

*So cliché, so comical,* Joey thought. *These guys have seen too many bad teen movies.* His awareness of the tactics employed by the two metal heads did not leave him entirely immune to their taunts. He could feel volatile emotions building within him: embarrassment, vulnerability, anger that was rapidly building to an intense fury. He recognized that he was in danger of escalating the situation if he was not careful.

"Look at the way he dresses," the short banger said. "Maybe he's a fag." The words flew from his mouth like poisoned darts.

"Hey guys, I really don't want any trouble," Joey said, taking a step back. He was beginning to feel flustered and shaky. He hadn't been in a real fistfight since grade school. It was ridiculous and almost unbelievable that he was on the verge of an actual punch-up.

The tall banger produced a small flask from the pocket of his tasseled and studded leather jacket. The jacket appeared to be a few sizes too small for him. The banger unscrewed the cap of the flask, took a deep pull, and passed it to his short companion.

"Well, maybe you should go back to where you came from," the tall banger said.

Joey's fear was eclipsed by indignation. *Can't let these assholes intimidate me,* he thought. He made a childish, irrational decision. Instead of walking away, he fell for their transparent mind game.

"You know, I quite like it here," Joey said. "I think I'll stay. In fact, I think I *am* in the mood for a game after all." Joey moved toward the door to the pool hall. The two metal heads, who had been standing to the side, now closed in, blocking the entrance.

Defiantly, foolishly, Joey made an effort to squeeze past them. The tall metal head did what cartoon buffoons

generally do in such situations: he planted his hands on
Joey's shoulders and shoved. It was a rather weak push, the
negligible force of which simply caused Joey to take a few
steps back. The small banger snickered.

"Excuse me, fellas," Joey said. "I do believe you are
in my way."

"You're cruisin' for a bruisin'," the tall banger said.
"You're about to be in a world of hurt."

"Is my ass grass?" Joey asked.

Before the mockery in Joey's retort could register in
the tall banger's pot-and-beer-addled brain, the door to the
pool hall opened behind him. A young man stepped out,
humming a Broadway show tune and snapping his fingers.
Pushing his way through the leather-jacketed duo, the young
man stepped into the fray. "Everything cool here, Chad?" he
said, addressing the tall banger.

The young man who had suddenly appeared wore a
black trench coat with a large collection of pins and buttons
adorning its wide lapels. Beneath the coat, a t-shirt with a
prominent Dead Kennedy's logo was visible. His hair was
black and spiked. Cherry-colored Dr. Martens boots
completed the look.

"Nothing you need to worry about, Steve," the tall
banger said. They were apparently well acquainted.

"This little prick has a big mouth," the short banger
spat.

"Is that so?" inquired Steve. He took a moment to
ponder Joey, rubbing his chin quizzically with a finger and
thumb. Joey shrugged. Steve sized up the short banger
similarly. "Seems to me like your mouth is actually a few
millimeters bigger by my estimation, Duane."

Duane's face turned red. He raised a fist to head level
and made a twitchy motion as if he were about to punch
Steve. It was all bravado, an empty threat – the last resort of

an insecure, threatened child on the playground. "Fag," he said.

Chad scoffed. "Fuck these guys." The words were hostile yet devoid of real menace. Though he was actually much taller, there was an unusual dynamic to their interactions that suggested that Chad respected, or perhaps feared, Steve.

"Let's go shoot some stick," Chad said. "Give these butt buddies some privacy."

"Hahaha," chortled Duane. "Butt buddies. Yeah. See ya later, *fags!*"

The two head bangers disappeared back into the pool hall.

"Don't worry about Beavis and Butthead," Steve said. "Those cro-mags are, like most bullies, essentially harmless. Chad used to give me a hard time, until I fought back a few years ago and put him on his ass. Now I just run intellectual cartwheels around him whenever he needs to be put into his place. You know how it is."

"I knew guys like that back in Van," Joey said.

"You from Vancouver?"

"Yup, just moved here with my mom."

"Why?" Steve seemed truly astonished.

"My mom got a job here. I had no choice. My dad lives with his new wife and isn't really involved any more. Typical story, right?"

"That sucks, dude. I'm sorry. My parents are divorced, too. Only interested in themselves. I learned a *long* time ago that you can't really trust anyone – especially adults. I'm Steve, by the way. Welcome to Tempest, Ontario... or as I like to call it, The Mistake by the Lake."

"I'm Joey. This seems like a nice enough town."

"It's a total shithole. I'm getting the hell out of here as soon as I can. Toronto, Montreal, maybe even Vancouver...

anywhere but here. I want to be in a city with an actual music scene, you know?"

"Do you play?"

"Not really. I've been working on lyrics, though. Always wanted to start a band, just never met the right people. In this town, you gotta play classic rock or hair metal. It's all cheesy-ass shit to me."

"I got a guitar for my last birthday. Been teaching myself how to play. I'm still pretty shitty, but I'm getting better. I learned a few Nirvana songs, a couple of Soundgarden riffs, part of a Pearl Jam song..."

"That's cool. Grunge is okay, but I like *good* music."

"Like what?"

"Mostly punk and hardcore. DK, Black Flag, Minor Threat, Youth of Today, 7 Seconds, Crass, The Clash, The Pistols... you know, *good* music."

"Cool." Joey had only heard of a few of the bands Steve mentioned. His exposure to new music had been largely limited to radio and the videos he saw on MuchMusic, the self-appointed "Nation's Music Station!"

"We should start a band," Steve said.

The two young men fell into an easy rhythm as they walked up the sidewalk away from the pool hall. They became instant friends, implicit in the way they developed a quick, comfortable rapport. Through shared experience, mutual recognition of similar values, and mysterious forces at work behind the scenes, Joey and Steve bonded. As is the case in all fate-assigned relationships, it was as if they had known each other their entire lives.

The last days of summer ebbed away and autumn arrived as it does in Northern Ontario – blustery, chilly, and way too soon. Seemingly overnight, the region was transformed from a lush forest of deep greens to a fall wonderland of warm shades of red, yellow, and orange. The low temperatures and changing colors signaled an end to the summer heat and, for the young people of the town of Tempest, the end of carefree days of no school and little responsibility.

Joey started attending classes at the only public high school in town – Tempest Collegiate Institute, or TCI, as most residents referred to it. Joey's mother started her new job at a local law firm. Their small family began the process of assimilating into their new environment. For Joey, the process was difficult.

Most of the kids at TCI had known Steve since early childhood. They had grown up together, their parents knew each other, and, regardless of Steve's iconoclastic, rebellious, sardonic nature, they accepted him. He was a weirdo, but he was local.

Joey was not so lucky. He got along well with Steve, but he was finding it difficult to fit in. Joey had not established a place in the social hierarchy of the small town kids. He did not dress as they did. He did not share the same hobbies. He was not into snowmobiling, hunting, drinking, and hockey. He was different and they recognized it. It was not long before he became a target.

It started in a relatively benign fashion – bad vibes, dirty looks, whispered insults. The popular kids were fiercely protective of the established order. The new kid from the big city with the sharp intellect and creative streak was a threat. Joey's precarious social position became clear one typical Monday morning during the second week of the school year.

Joey was making his way from a room on the 2nd floor, where he had just endured an excruciating 45 minutes of Canadian history delivered in dreadful monotone, to the school's basement. He was enthusiastically anticipating his favorite class of the day – visual arts. Although he was finding it difficult to truly fit in, he was slowly becoming more comfortable at the school. His exposure to the small town discriminatory attitude strengthened his sense of individuality. Joey sort of liked being the new guy. It made him feel unique. He walked the halls now with an attitude. He was about to be tested.

In the stairwell between floors, he was confronted by TCI's male power duo, Bradley and Shane. Bradley was a doctor's son with the arrogance and malevolence that takes a lifetime of privilege to cultivate. He wore name brand sweaters and jeans. He kept his slick blond hair meticulously cut in the style of the era's popular boy bands. He was, in Steve's definition, a total Preppie and a complete tool. Shane was Bradley's ever-present sidekick. At six foot four and over 250 pounds, he was the star of the football team and was widely considered to be the toughest guy at the school. He was a prototypical, classic jock. Bradley and Shane were popular and feared – adored by most and reviled by a silent few.

Joey was alone when Bradley and Shane cornered him. It was not the first time that they had encountered each other. Having known similar types back in Vancouver, Joey's instinct had been to avoid conflict by giving the duo a wide berth when their paths happened to cross. This time, however, the pair of high school superstars took the opportunity to flex their social muscles with a metaphorical territorial pissing.

As Joey made an attempt to pass by on the landing, Shane stepped into his path, blocking his way. Shane simply stood there silently, glaring down at Joey with his chest puffed out behind his Toronto Argonauts half-shirt. Joey sighed.

"Where you goin', *freak?*" Shane spit the words out like toxic rain.

"Class," Joey said. The volatility of the moment was

apparent. He knew he would have to play it carefully. He attempted to slide past Shane and continue down the stairs. Bradley stepped in beside Shane, forming an impenetrable line.

"*Class,*" Bradley mocked in a silly, feminine voice.

"Freak," Shane repeated. It was an overly-used regional insult, applied to anyone who deviated even slightly from the norm.

"Unfortunately, it's true," Joey said. "As much as I'd love to stay and chat with you two fine gentleman, there is a class I must attend. So, if you'll excuse me..."

Bradley jumped back with his hands up in an exaggerated display of deference. "Oh, dear *me!*" he said. "Are we in your way? So *sorry!*"

"No problem," Joey said, playing along. He again tried to squeeze through, but was thwarted by a sidestepping Shane, who moved as if he were making a play on the field.

"Is there a problem, guys?" Joey asked. Adrenaline flowed. Taut and twitchy, Joey's muscles vibrated with anxious energy. Fluid fear coursed through his veins. Fight or flight instinct heightened his awareness. Sensory impressions increased in intensity. His brained throbbed, in his mind a siren blared: *Threat! Threat! Threat!*

"Yeah, there's a problem," Bradley sneered.

Shane poked Joey in the chest with a beefy finger. "*You're* the problem, freak," he said.

Joey found himself repeating the words he had used in his encounter with the metal heads at the pool hall: "Hey guys, I really don't want any trouble."

"Who the fuck do you think you are?" Bradley asked. "We *own* this school."

"You should go back to Edmonton," Shane said.

*Vancouver, idiot,* Joey thought. He considered correcting him, but wisely chose not to.

"What makes you think you can walk around here like a fuckin' tough guy?" Bradley asked. "Are you under the impression that you *belong* here or something? Because, if so, you are greatly mistaken."

Joey kept quiet. It was clear that anything he said would only further incite his teenage tormentors. He steeled himself and remained stoic.

"What's the matter?" Shane taunted. "Ain't ya got anything to say?"

"I think he shit himself," Bradley said, leaning in and taking a sniff. "Sure smells like it. You fuckin' *stink*, dude. Did you know that?" Joey maintained eye contact, his expression blank.

Just as the severity of the situation escalated and the threat of violence grew, the sound of fast-approaching footsteps from above disrupted the scene. The rapid footsteps of the individual descending the stairs were accompanied by loud and frantic singing – or, more precisely, screaming.

*"I fought the law and I won, I fought the law and I won!"* Joey immediately recognized the person shouting as Steve. Steve took the final three steps in a joyful bound, landing directly between the Shane-Bradley line and Joey.

"What's up, turd burglars?" Steve said, addressing no one in particular.

"Just having a little chat with the new guy," Bradley said. "None of your business, Steve."

"Everything's cool," Joey said. "We were just taking about the CFL. I think the expansion into the US is a travesty. Shane, I think, would agree."

"Whatever, freak," Shane muttered.

"Go Maple Leafs!" Steve bellowed, miming a baseball bat swing.

"Fuck off," Bradley said.

"Okay, then!" Steve remained cheerful. "Planning on

attending art today, Joey? I think it's Kirlian photography day. Don't wanna be late!"

"Yeah, we better get going," Joey said.

As the small gathering dispersed, Bradley glared at Joey. "You better watch yourself, New Guy," he said. "You're going to get hurt if you aren't careful."

"Freak!" Shane shouted.

Joey and Steve continued on their way to the art room, arriving just as class was about to begin. Pausing at the door to the room, Steve addressed Joey in a refreshingly sincere fashion. "I get the sense that you're having a hard time with some of the locals here in our fair city," he said.

"It's been tough," Joey concurred.

"Stay strong, man. Be true to yourself. It's a small town, but the people here are, for the most part, good. They simply have a hard time understanding anyone who is different. Trust me, I *know*." Steve gave Joey a brotherly slap on the back as they entered the classroom.

The rest of the day passed without further incident. Joey, however, was finding it harder and harder to maintain concentration in his classes. Beneath the surface, anxiety and agitation were beginning to percolate in his already turbulent teenage heart. A maelstrom was brewing in the town of Tempest.

Joey walked home from school alone that afternoon. He arrived to find the house empty, as usual. Joey's mother worked long hours. In the month since they had moved to Tempest, the time that they spent together had greatly dwindled. They rarely shared meals. Joey's mother was simply too exhausted in the evening to cook. She often fell asleep in front of the television with a half-eaten frozen dinner in her lap. Joey learned to fend for himself.

On this particular afternoon, Joey needed his mother. He sat at the kitchen table from the moment he got home until she walked through the door many hours later. During the wait, his thoughts raced and his emotions cycled. By the time she stepped into the kitchen and saw him sitting there, Joey was deeply upset. As soon as he saw his mother he began to cry and shake.

"Joey!" his mother exclaimed. "What's wrong?" Shocked, she ran to his side, dropped to her knees, and embraced him as he sat weeping.

"I hate it here, mom," Joey said between sobs. "I want to go home. I want to see dad." The sensation of his mother's embrace caused him to cry harder. He wept now with frightening intensity. The dam had burst.

"Oh, Joey. It's okay, buddy. Things will get easier, I promise."

"You don't know that!" Joey cried. "You don't even know what I've been going through. All you care about is *work*." He imbued the last word with a generous dose of contempt.

Joey's mother took a seat at the table beside him and clasped his hands in her own, her expression and demeanor compassionate, yet serious. "I need you to be strong, Joey," she said. "I'm doing the best I can."

"I just don't fit in here," Joey said, his composure returning.

"Give it time. You're a great kid. People will see that. It won't be long before you make friends. You're funny, smart, kind... You'll probably end up super popular! You might even meet a girl!" She winked at him.

"Oh, *please*," Joey said, but he couldn't hide the smirk that appeared on his face. "I don't care about popularity. I really don't. I just want to be able to walk down the street, or down the hall at school, and not have to worry about being insulted... or assaulted."

"Has that happened? Are people bullying you? Have

you been fighting?"

Joey processed the question. In their often-strained relationship, Joey and his mother had at least established a level of trust that allowed for honest communication. It was difficult for him to lie to her.

"No," Joey said, "not actual fistfights, just a lot of macho idiots trying to throw their weight around, I guess. Nothing I can't handle, it's just... tedious."

"Have you tried talking to them? I'm sure if they get to know you..."

Joey laughed. "Somehow I doubt that would help."

"That *attitude!* It's no surprise you're having a hard time making friends. Have you been acting like a smartass? People don't like a smartass."

"Just being myself, mom. Sometimes that's all it takes. These people just don't like *me*. Instant hate. It's like I'm an alien or something. Bunch of hicks, anyway."

"That's not fair and you know it. Treat others the way you want to be treated. That includes keeping an open mind and not judging."

Joey remained silent and thoughtful. He could not deny the truth of his mother's words. Though sometimes disappointed in the choices she made, he admired his mother's wisdom and intelligence.

"I'm doing the best I can to make a better life for us," Joey's mother continued. "Can you work with me? Or at least not make this any harder than it is? We're both adjusting. I just need you to make an effort... and know that I love you." Her eyes had become red and watery. She was getting emotional. Joey could sense that she was on the verge of tears.

"I love you too, mom," Joey said, putting an arm around her shoulders. "I guess I can give it some more time. I'm sure things will work out. I'm just a little weird for this

town, but eventually they'll get used to me." Now it was he
who winked at her. He did not like to see his mother upset. In
that moment, he made a decision to keep his internal
struggles private.

After dinner, Joey spent the rest of the evening alone
in his room strumming his battered, second-hand guitar. He
only knew a few chords and could barely keep the thing in
tune, but playing had become his favorite way to spend time,
especially when he was feeling troubled. It was an effective
way to release tension. The sensation of the strings beneath
his fingers was incredibly satisfying. The unrefined, rugged
sound coming from his tiny amplifier perfectly expressed his
internal struggles. He had found a way to sublimate his
emotions. Music made him feel in control again.

On his way to school the next morning, Joey
experimented with optimism. He allowed his imagination to
explore various positive scenarios for his near future,
including one in which he settled into his new environment,
existed in harmony with his peers, and perhaps even found
happiness. It was a clear, crisp autumn morning, perfectly
suited for daydreaming.

He arrived at school energized, ready for the
academic and social challenges ahead. Before he had even
stepped through the front door, his resolve was tested. Lost in
thought, he did not see Chad and Duane, the headbangers
from the pool hall, loitering near the entrance and puffing
away on cigarettes.

"Well, looky here," Chad said. "It's the new fag in
town."

"What's up, knobgobbler?" Duane grinned like an
imbecile.

*And so it begins,* Joey thought. He ignored the insults
and entered the building.

The school was alive with the typical morning

commotion and chatter. Students were congregating in the lobby, before fragmenting into small clusters. Cliques and allegiances, friends and enemies, the popular and the outcast, the natural high school order was establishing itself. The hidden engine of the order – the unseen architecture – involved a mysterious, complicated algorithm of socioeconomic and psychological factors.

From Joey's outsider perspective, the social structure seemed random, arbitrary. His young mind could not discern the subtle influences. He stood in the lobby and observed the apparent chaos for a few moments before gathering the strength to enter the melee.

First period for Joey was Advanced English. He merged with the students crowding the narrow halls. He began to make his way toward his assigned locker to pick up the materials he would need for class. Squeezing past a giggling trio of girls with tight sweaters, puffed-up hair, and too much makeup, he found his locker and grasped the combination lock. As he was working the mechanism, he could hear the girls whispering behind his back. He glanced over his shoulder and, sure enough, they were staring right at him, heads together, hands over their mouths, vicious glimmers of pure malevolence sparkling in their heavily mascaraed eyes.

Joey was struck by a wave of self-conscious anxiety. Embarrassment of the highly potent variety that only judgmental teenage girls could administer washed over him. He tried to remain indifferent. He tried to hold on to the indomitable spirit that he had mustered on his walk to school. He managed to get his belongings out of the locker before cracking. Ignoring the fiendish snickering, he replaced the lock and continued down the hall.

Now it seemed like everyone in the congested hallway was talking about him. Joey could feel a thousand pairs of eyes burning holes in the back of his head like an array of lasers. He kept his head up and focused on his destination. He made it exactly ten steps from his locker.

From out of a gathering of young men with tidy haircuts, pastel name-brand t-shirts, and acid-washed jeans, a foot suddenly jutted out, catching Joey in mid-stride. He could not catch himself before falling in an awkward, messy heap on the floor. His books went flying. He struck his face on the floor. Blood gushed from his nose. Laughter echoed up and down the hall.

"Hope you had a good trip!" someone yelled.

"See ya next fall!" said another.

*"Freak!"* shrieked a third.

Joey stood up and gathered his stuff, stopping the flow of blood from his nose with pinched fingers. As he reached for a text book that had landed near the preppy perpetrators, one of them kicked at it, sending it sliding further down the hall. Joey sighed as it traveled away from his reach.

"Very nice," he said. "Well done, guys." Joey summoned his courage, gathered his dignity, and retrieved the wayward book. He continued on his way to class.

It occurred to him how strange it was to be the target of bullying. He was, all things considered, a fairly normal kid. In Vancouver, he had even been nominally popular. He was not exactly a social butterfly, but he had always maintained a small, close circle of friends. Over the last few years, he had even had a few girlfriends. In his estimation, he did not fit the stereotypical victim profile.

Joey's thoughts wandered. He remembered Ricky Talbot, who, in sixth grade, was the recipient of brutal, merciless, verbal and physical abuse by the other students. Joey recalled how, although he had never directly participated in the bullying, he had never done anything to stop it. He had never spoken up for Ricky. By tacitly accepting the abuse, he was, in fact, complicit.

*Ricky, I feel your pain,* he thought. Ricky had been a geeky kid with braces, thick glasses, and a speech impediment. Ricky, though obviously hurt by the torment, had come to accept his place in the social hierarchy. Joey, however, was indignant and determined to rise above the position he was being forced into.

The classroom door was open as Joey approached. He hesitated before entering. *Into the lion's den,* he thought, and plunged through the door.

The other students were already at their desks. The teacher was at the blackboard. Joey found a seat near the back of the room. No one seemed to pay him any attention, but his sense of unease was growing. He squirmed in his seat throughout the lesson, unable to remain focused on what the teacher was saying. The clock, which he glanced at every few seconds, mocked him and his plight. He fantasized about escaping. He wanted nothing more than to be at home playing his guitar.

The class ended. Joey hadn't learned a thing. He drifted out of the room in a daze. He had 15 minutes until his next class. Surrounded once again by the writhing mass of students, swallowed up by the horde, he felt more distant and alone than ever. In their midst, he had the strange sensation that he was somehow existing in another realm, a parallel universe, an alternate dimension that co-existed and shared boundaries with the one the people around him inhabited. He could see and hear them, but they were out of sync and unreachable.

Instead of continuing on to his next class, Joey reflexively stepped out the next available exit. He found himself in a narrow alcove at the side of the school. A small gathering of students were huddled together sharing a cigarette – a circle of misfits and assorted weirdos. Joey was not surprised to see Steve among them. Acrid, blue smoke curled around their heads as they chatted excitedly.

"Joey!" Steve bellowed. "Join us!"

Joey approached the group. Out of the three kids gathered, Joey only recognized Steve. The other two eyed him with curiosity, but accepted him into the circle.

"We were just discussing the *Evil Dead* movies. Have you seen the new one, *Army of Darkness*? Rick here thinks it's shit. I think it's the best of the series. What are your thoughts?"

"Haven't seen it," Joey replied. "*Evil Dead 2* was cool, though." Joey had gone through a horror movie phase a few years back. During the seventh and eighth grades, they were an obsession.

"*Evil Dead 2* rocks," Rick said. "When dude whacks his zombie girlfriend's head off with a shovel... that shit was *awesome!*" Rick was a tall, thin, skateboarder with long, blonde hair. His wore a black sweatshirt beneath a white t-shirt emblazoned with the Thrasher logo. His jeans were ridiculously baggy. He reeked of marijuana. "Too much humor in *Army of Darkness*," he said, "too little gore."

"Point taken," Steve nodded as he took the smoldering, nearly finished cigarette from a small, quiet girl with black hair, black eyeliner, black lipstick, and a grim demeanor standing to his right.

"So, Joey," Steve said, "how has your day been so far at this fine institute of learning?"

"The institution of my discontent," the goth girl mumbled. Her clothing too was entirely black, except for the Siouxsie and the Banshees image on her long-sleeve shirt.

"It started off well," Joey said, "but went quickly downhill when I was knocked on my ass and humiliated in the hall." Steve offered him the last of the cigarette. Joey

declined with a subtle but firm gesture. Steve crushed the
butt beneath the steel toe of his Doc Martens.

"This school is a cesspool," the goth girl said.

"It isn't a school, Clara, it's a prison," Steve said, "an
indoctrination camp, a brainwashing facility."

"Damn right," Rick agreed.

"In the words of the immortal Henry Rollins of the
mighty Black Flag on their seminal and massively influential
1981 album *Damaged*: *'Rise above! I'm gonna rise above!'* "
Steve shouted the lyrics to a song that clearly had great
meaning for him.

"Fuck, yeah," Rick said.

"What this hellhole really needs is a cleansing," Clara
said. "Wouldn't it be great to bring a machine gun to school
one day and just, you know, mow down all the douchebags,
assholes, preps, and jocks?" Clara pantomimed firing an
automatic rifle with a huge grin on her pale face. She reveled
in her imaginary revenge scenario.

"Yikes," Steve grimaced, "I prefer a more subtle and
sophisticated approach. I like your enthusiasm, though!
Nice!"

A bell sounded, signaling the start of the next class in
five minutes. "Back into the grinder," Steve said. "I'll catch
up with you crazy kids later. See ya!" Steve bounded through
the door with dramatic flair and disappeared into the school.

"Is he actually going to class?" Rick asked.

"He skipped a few last week," Clara replied. "He'll
get suspended if he misses any more. His stepfather would
kick his ass if he got suspended."

"Stepfather?" Joey inquired. He was curious about
Steve's domestic situation.

"Yeah, his parents divorced when he was real young,"
Clara said. "His mother remarried recently. The new guy is a
real asshole. Heavy drinker, abusive, you know the type. He

hates Steve and gives him shit constantly."

"I didn't know," Joey said.

"He doesn't like to talk about it," Clara said.

"Dude's got it rough," Rick nodded. "That's why he tries to avoid being at home and is usually chillin' at the arcade or at the park. Remember how he was *before* his mom remarried? He dressed all preppy and shit. He used to hang out with the jocks and bimbos."

"Really?" Joey was truly surprised. He had a hard time visualizing Steve dressed like one of the drones.

"It's true," Clara confirmed. "He changed a lot over the last few years. We dated for a bit, and he opened up to me a few times."

"I remember when you guys were a couple!" Rick blurted. "King and queen of the freaks." Rick chuckled at his own joke.

"Yeah, well, he's a complicated guy," Clara said. "He's got a good heart, though. We're still friends. Anyway, I gotta get to class. Later."

"Later, skater!" Rick cheerfully replied. "I better motor too. See ya."

"Bye," Joey said.

Rick and Clara entered the school. Joey stood alone in the alcove for a few minutes, thoughtful and, considering the altercation in the hallway earlier that morning, oddly serene. He had felt comfortable in the presence of Steve, Rick, and Clara. He got the sense that they understood and accepted him. *Have I actually made friends in this weird little town?* he asked himself. It was an exciting and promising development.

On the way to his next class, a moment of synchronicity occurred. Joey was running late. The halls were empty. A sign on the wall caught his eye, as if placed there specifically for him to see at that precise time. In bold letters, the sign read:

**TCI TALENT SHOW**
**Show your stuff on the stage!**
**October 15, 1993!**
**Apply now!**

A perfect, simple, wonderful idea coalesced in Joey's mind: *I'm going to start a band and play at that show.* His newly discovered passion for the guitar had been a real source of relief during the difficult transitions he had recently experienced. He found refuge in music. Pursuing his creative impulses allowed him to channel the frustration and pain he had felt into something productive. It gave him control over his emotional state. He visualized himself playing guitar in front of the entire student populace, powerful waves of sound pulsing from his amplifier and washing over the crowd, immersing them in his music. In his mind's eye it was glorious.

Joey thought of Steve, who had mentioned in their first meeting that he had always wanted to start a band. He thought of Rick and Clara. *Wouldn't it be great to play music with other people, on an actual stage?* Joey thought. The idea didn't seem so far-fetched. In fact, it seemed like destiny.

Joey attended the rest of his classes that day and hurried home afterwards. As he expected, the house was empty when he arrived. He rushed directly to his room upon stepping inside. He picked up his guitar and began strumming with fresh vigor and inspiration. He was improving and he knew it. His fingers found their place on the neck more quickly and intuitively now. His pick hand was much more accurate. His stamina had increased. It was exhilarating.

By the time Joey's mother got home from work, he

had worked out a small batch of riffs and rhythms, which he collected by recording them on his portable tape deck. They were short, rough song ideas – ragged little bits of audio – but they were *his* ideas. He was ecstatic and couldn't wait to share his excitement. He ran out of the room with the tape deck the moment he heard the front door open.

Joey's mother looked exhausted. She stumbled through the door like a defeated prize fighter and threw herself on the couch. "What an awful day," she sighed. "Hi, Joey."

"Hi, mom. Do you have a minute? I have something to share."

"Oh, honey, it's not a good time. Can it wait? I'm really tired."

"Yeah, I suppose so. I'm sorry you had a bad day."

"It could be worse," Joey's mother philosophized. "At least I have a job." She picked up the TV remote from the coffee table and turned on the set. Joey watched as her body relaxed and her mind slipped into a hypnotic state. It made him feel sad for her.

"You're working too hard," Joey said.

"I know, buddy, but somebody's got to pay the bills."

"Can I get you something to eat?"

"I'm okay for now. You eat. I'll get something later."

Joey wandered into the kitchen to find some food. As he was opening a can of soup, he heard his mother snoring in the living room. He looked in and saw her already asleep in the glow of the television set. The insufferable characters from the show *Seinfeld* were babbling away on the screen. Joey took his soup to his room and ate it.

That night, Joey had an extremely difficult time sleeping. His thoughts raced. His head was full of sounds and images. The excitement he felt imagining himself playing in a band was matched by the thrill of discovering a way to transcend his environment. It was not fame nor riches that he desired, but self-discovery and empowerment – control over his own fate and emancipation from his seemingly inexorable fate as a poor, working class slave. The future again seemed full of potential.

Joey did eventually fall asleep and, in the morning, he actually looked forward to going to school. He gathered his things, including the recording he had made of his song ideas, and bolted out the door.

He arrived at school and went to the smoking alcove where, sure enough, Steve and the others had gathered for a puff before class. Joey entered their midst and declared, "We are going to start a band. We are going to play at the talent show. It's going to be awesome."

Steve, Rick, and Clara stared at Joey in disbelief.

"Dude, what have *you* been smoking?" Rick said. "Can I have some?"

"The talent show is a joke," Clara scoffed. "There's no way in hell I'd be a performing monkey for those mindless meatbags."

"I like it," Steve smiled. "When do we start?"

"As soon as possible," Joey replied. "I already have some song ideas." He opened his backpack and retrieved the cassette tape. "Just some riffs, really. They need lyrics." He handed the tape to Steve.

"Excellent," Steve said, admiring the cassette. "You've got some fire in your belly. I'm impressed."

"At the very least, it could be fun," Joey said. "What have we got to lose?"

"Fuck, yeah," Rick said. "Can I be the drummer? My older bro has a kit. He lets me play it sometimes. We could probably even jam at my place!" Rick played air drums like a spastic animal.

"There's nothing else to do around here." Clara was

clearly warming up to the idea. "Maybe it's not such a stupid idea after all."

"That's the spirit!" Steve exclaimed.

A group was born, formed from the essence of teenage angst and imagination, forged in friendship.

That very weekend, the four friends gathered in Rick's garage for their first rehearsal. It was a chilly autumn afternoon. They huddled around a space heater that Rick's father had thoughtfully provided. It was the first time any of them had played music in a group setting. Clara had only been playing the borrowed bass that she brought to the rehearsal for a few days. Steve had never sung in public. Rick and Joey had the most experience, but it was minimal at best. The group stood there awkwardly, unsure of how to proceed.

"I've been listening to your riffs," Steve finally said to Joey. "I came up with some lyrics."

"That's awesome!" Joey beamed.

"Shouldn't we tune up or something?" Clara said. She strapped on her bass and plugged it into a small amp.

"Ya, I guess so," Joey said, slinging the strap of the guitar over his shoulder. He too plugged in and began plucking away at the strings one by one, starting with the low E. Clara attempted to match the pitch of her strings to his. While they were still attempting to tune their instruments, Rick started banging away on the drums. It was a cacophonous mess.

Steve stepped in to provide some order. "As much as I like noise rock, I think we should get organized and try to work on, you know, actual *songs*," he said.

It took a few minutes of sonic stumbling, but eventually the guitars were in tune, the amplifier volumes were set, and Rick bored of rattling off random drum rolls. An electric charge of psychic energy hung in the air as the group prepared to make music together.

"Here's something I came up with," Joey said. "It's in E." He began playing a simple and effective four-chord punk rock riff, showing Clara his finger work. His fingers flew frantically up and down the neck of his guitar. The sound was raw and furious.

"I like it." Clara smiled and followed the root notes on her bass. As soon as she joined in, the sound became thicker and richer.

"Fast, catchy, and angry," Steve nodded in approval. "Not as hardcore as Minor Threat, but still good. Kinda sounds like the Pistols mixed with Nirvana. Keep playing." Steve started vocalizing. He used the lyrics he had written and experimented with melodies and phrasing. Rick tapped his sticks on his knees, learning the tune before starting in with a beat. When the drums did kick in, the song really took flight.

It was obvious to all four that the group had instant chemistry. Although the music was still sloppy and the singing a little wild and off-key, the energy and emotion they were able to channel into the sound was palpable and powerful. All members of the group were grinning widely as they worked on their first song together.

The hours flew by. By the time evening was upon them, the group had fleshed out the basic framework of three songs – three short sonic blasts of unbridled punk rock energy. They wrapped up their first session spent, satisfied, and eager to do it again.

"I'm sore as hell, but that was the most fun I have ever had," Rick said, rolling his shoulders. "I thought my arms were going to fall off during that last tune."

"You'll need to work on your stamina," Steve said. "We all do. We should practice again soon."

"Absolutely," Joey agreed. His fingertips were red,

raw, and throbbing. "We have just over a month until the show. Let's rehearse as often as possible."

"We need a name," Clara said. Uncharacteristically, she was still smiling.

"Yes we do," Steve said. "Start brainstorming. Come up with some ideas. We'll choose the best one."

Over the next few weeks, the group met almost every night in Rick's garage. All four were motivated, inspired, and totally committed to the project. A strong bond developed and it transcended music. Something special and nearly mystical united the four friends. They became a family.

In the insular high school environment, information traveled fast. It did not take long for word to get out that the four weirdest kids at TCI had started a band and that they planned to perform at the upcoming talent show. The gossip factory went into overtime production. In the popular cliques, the new group became a rich source of material for mockery. Even Steve, who had gained a certain grudging acceptance, found himself a target for an unusually hostile campaign of harassment in the weeks and days leading up to the show. The comments hurled at him and the others were sarcastic, childish, and vicious.

"Look! It's the rock star! Can I have your autograph?"

"Where's your groupies?"

"Punk sucks!"

"*You* suck!"

"You should call your band The Losers!"

"The Freaks!"

Steve was on his way to meet the others in the alcove when he heard that last one. He stopped cold, turned to face the origin of the insult, and smiled. "That is brilliant," he said. "Thank you!"

"I have the band name," Steve announced when he reached the others already gathered in the alcove. He paused for dramatic effect.

"The Freaks."

And so it was. Joey, Rick, and Clara knew immediately that the name was perfect.

The Freaks continued their disciplined rehearsal schedule in the days leading up to the talent show. After their last practice session on the night before the show, they went for a walk around Rick's neighborhood. The anticipation was building. A nervous charge had the four members buzzing.

"I hope we don't suck," Rick muttered as they wandered through the dark.

"Don't say that," Steve said. "Don't even *think* that. You'll pysche yourself out. Think *positively*, dude."

"We won't suck," Joey said. "We've been practicing, getting tighter... getting *better*. Just get up there and have fun."

"We're going to blow minds and melt faces," Clara grinned. "I can't wait."

"What if people hate us?" Rick was worried.

"Who cares?" Steve said. "We have nothing to prove and nothing to lose. Do you really care what the drones think anyway? I don't. I just want to get up on that stage and unleash the fury."

"We just need to believe in ourselves," Joey said, "even if no one else does."

Walking with the group felt great. *We're like a little tribe,* Joey thought. *A gang, a family.* He was again aware of the beauty of his youth and the fantastic potential of the years ahead. Forming the musical group, creating something so pure and powerful, had given him a tremendous boost of confidence. It was simply punk rock music – he understood this – but the drive and imagination it had taken to conceive of and follow through with the project gave him faith in himself and in his ability to fashion his own future. He and the others had been empowered, liberated from the miasma of their daily lives.

The day of the talent show arrived. The show was to be held in the school auditorium, starting at 6 PM. The Freaks gathered with the rest of the performers backstage. They were scheduled to go on last. There was a sense among the organizers, students, and other acts that The Freaks were a joke. The school did not want to be embarrassed. Many parents were in attendance.

Joey, Steve, Rick, and Clara huddled together in the corner, anxious and self-conscious. The other performers, mainly dance acts, singers, and air band groups, were radiating hostile vibes. There was one other live band scheduled to perform – a heavy metal trio featuring Chad and Duane, the pool hall hooligans who had so courteously introduced Joey to the town of Tempest. They called their group Night Lightning. They would be opening the show.

Chad approached The Freaks, his Randy Rhodes model Flying V guitar already strapped on. He was fully decked out in his heavy metal stage regalia – he was a spandex, leather, and denim walking music video. "Are you weirdos actually going to desecrate that stage with your punk rock shit show?" he snarled.

"Freaks, not Weirdos," Steve corrected him.

"What is *that* thing?" Chad pointed at Joey's guitar.

"My axe," Joey deadpanned. "I use it to play hot licks and wicked riffs." Joey did an exaggerated Eddie Van Halen impression, fingers flailing, his face distorted in guitar ecstasy.

Chad was not amused. "What a piece of shit. Looks like you got it at K-Mart."

"Sears, I think," Joey said, "but I can still shred like the pros on this bad boy." The sarcasm was lost on Chad.

"We're going to blow you off the stage," Chad said.

"Major labels are fighting over Night Lightning. We're gonna get signed. We're gonna be famous."

Steve yawned. Clara giggled. Rick practiced twirling his drum sticks. Joey nodded. "Good for you," he said. "I'm sure you'll have all the money, coke, and groupies your little heart desires."

"Damn right," Chad said. "You better believe it." Chad walked away to wait with the other members of Night Lightning, playing guitar as he strutted.

"That's exactly what it's *not* about," Steve said. "Money, fame, whores, and drugs – that's all bullshit. Integrity, passion, creativity, and freedom – that's what I believe in. Those burnouts are conformists of the worst kind."

The show was about to begin. The emcee was on stage, warming up the audience with a comedy routine. When he was done he introduced the first act.

"Ladies and gentleman," the emcee announced. "Please welcome to the stage TCI's very own *Night Lightning!*" A generous round of applause, cheering, and whistling followed.

The lights were dimmed and the curtain went up. The techs had worked out an elaborate light show to accompany Night Lightning's performance. The trio launched into a cover of Metallica's *Master of Puppets* as a bright strobe pulsed. Blue and red spotlights swirled. The music was loud and thumping. The guitar and bass players banged their heads and swung their long hair in circles as they hammered away at their instruments. It was an intense display. The audience loved it.

When the first song crashed to a finish and while the crowd was still in the delirious throes of exhilaration, Night Lightning charged into an Iron Maiden song. They were tight and well-rehearsed, a slick, polished act.

Backstage, The Freaks watched in amazement.

"They're pretty good," Rick observed.

"They can definitely play," Joey agreed.

"I'm actually impressed," Clara said.

"They sound like every other high school cover band," Steve shrugged.

Night Lightning finished their blistering spectacle of a set to the uproarious approval of the crowd. For the next few hours, dance acts, pop music, and air band routines dominated the stage, with a few magic acts and pet tricks thrown in for flavor. The Freaks waited anxiously backstage. Finally, the time came for them to perform.

The Freaks walked onstage. Joey and Clara plugged in their guitars. Rick got behind the provided drum kit. Steve approached the microphone. The emcee watched as they moved into position. The audience was silent, unsure of what to expect from the four misfits who stood before them. Dense, nervous energy hung in the air like suspended particulates. The tension was shattered by the clearly audible commentary of a heckler in the audience: "Losers with guitars. This should be entertaining."

The emcee ignored the comment and introduced the band: "This next act is a new group and this is their debut performance. Please welcome to the TCI stage, *The Freaks!*" A sparse, but polite, smattering of applause followed.

"Hello," Steve said into the microphone. "This is a song we wrote. It's called *Mental Prison*. It's about conformity, society, and the importance of thinking for yourself." he glanced back at the others, nodded, and counted the song in with a shout: "1,2,3,4!" The band burst into their first tune.

For the next ten minutes, The Freaks blazed through five original songs, one after another, in a relentless sonic assault. They bounced, flailed, and rocked as they lost themselves in the music. They played even faster and more furiously than they had in practice, totally in the moment and completely present to the exuberant spirit of youth, which they channeled through their performance. It was a raw, magnificent expression of all the frustration and angst that had accumulated in their complicated teenage hearts. When the last chord was struck, the four musicians, sweating and breathing hard, nearly collapsed. The audience did not know what had hit them.

"Wow," someone near the front of the crowd said in the silent moment. As if on signal, the audience erupted in genuine, appreciative applause. It was an outpouring, an incredible release of emotion, as if the group onstage had tapped into the collective unconscious of the audience and opened the floodgates. The Freaks had given their all on the stage, with passion and sincerity. The music was rough and the musicians' abilities limited, but the audience was moved by the honest display of creativity they had just witnessed.

"Thank you!" Steve shouted into the microphone. The group walked off the stage happy.

Life moved on. The school year continued. The band played shows at local clubs and halls for the next year or so and developed a small, but loyal, following. They recorded an album on a rented four-track and released it independently. They planned to tour Canada and the US, but disbanded before this goal was achieved. The Freaks never got rich, never got famous, never even left Tempest, but they made an indelible impression on those who saw them play. Other groups were formed in their wake, inspired by the group's determination, enthusiasm, DIY ethos, and commitment to individuality.

As the world changed and the Information Age began, Joey, Steve, Rick, and Clara hurtled into adulthood, still grappling with domestic, academic, social, and emotional issues. Their struggles weren't over. Great unknown, unseen obstacles and challenges loomed in their futures. Life still had many surprises in store for the four friends. Playing in the band had, however, shaped their perspective on the world, and, though their paths would eventually diverge, they would always be, in their hearts, The Freaks.

# Pueblo

The apparition appeared behind a crumbling wall on the second floor of the ancient dwelling. From down below, where my two friends and I were sitting, we could clearly see the spectral figure raise its arm and point toward the distant horizon. I realized in that moment that it was the ghost of a Hopi warrior. I could see its warpaint and elaborate headdress. A large bow and a quiver of arrows were strapped to its back.

The apparition cast its gaze upon us and motioned with its arm. Its posture and body language suggested that it was attempting to communicate with us... or warn us. The fear we felt in the entity's presence was quickly overshadowed by the ominous implications of what it was trying to convey. *Something is out there*, it seemed to be saying, *something awful and menacing... and it's coming for you.*

Looking back, there's no way we could have predicted what was going to happen. How could we? If someone had told *me* this story, I simply wouldn't have believed them. It's all so incredible, so irrational, so *absurd*.

To be perfectly honest, it was my idea. I'll admit that. I want to be clear, however, that if I had thought that there was any real risk or danger to my friends and me, I would never have suggested it. It just popped into my head one day and, as is my style, I spoke out without fulling considering the ramifications of what I was saying.

It all began one spring afternoon in a coffee shop downtown. Vera, Wayne, and I had met there for our weekly get-together. Vera was flipping through the local newspaper when she saw an article about a nearby state park.

"These old pueblos are really amazing," Vera said. "According to this article, Wupatki, which means "Tall House" in Hopi, was first inhabited in 500 BC. By 1225, it was permanently abandoned. "

"Yeah, I've heard of it," said Wayne. "It's up by Flagstaff. Pretty cool place, from what I've heard. Still pretty intact."

I glanced over and saw the pictures accompanying the article. That's when it occurred to me. I should have just kept my mouth shut, but sometimes I'm so damn impulsive. "You know what would be really fun?" I asked with a sly grin. "We should sneak in there and camp out over night. Wouldn't that be a thrill?"

"It's a state park," Vera said. "You have to pay to get in. They have security, too, I think."

"Oh, great," Wayne sighed. "Another one of Russell's big ideas. Haven't you learned *anything* since our last disastrous adventure?"

"Vegas was dismal, it's true," I replied, "but this could be good, clean fun. Do you have anything better planned for the weekend?"

"I can think of a few other things I'd rather be doing than going on another road trip with you," Wayne said. "Like eating a bowl of live cockroaches, or inserting red-hot nails into my eyeballs..."

"While those sound like delightfully fun activities," I said, "wouldn't you rather hang out with your oldest and dearest friends at least one more time before we graduate?"

"You guys are weirdos," said Vera.

"So are you," Wayne noted.

"True," Vera confessed.

"The real world beckons just around the corner," I continued. "Soon we'll be too busy with our jobs and families to do anything crazy and spontaneous. I say we load up my truck with camping supplies and head north on Saturday. We'll pay to get into the park and then just wait it out. When everyone else is gone, we can camp out in the ruins. Come on, doesn't that sound exciting?"

A huge grin relayed my enthusiasm. The dull expressions on the faces of my friends betrayed their skepticism. Nevertheless, after a few moments, my exaggerated, childlike eagerness finally won them over. It was Vera who relented first. "Well, I've always wanted to see the ruins," she said, "and as long as no one is going to get hurt, I'm fine with a small, harmless prank. Like Russell said, it could be our last chance for shenanigans for a while."

"We're going to pay to get in," I reiterated. "I don't think it's illegal to simply... *stay*."

"I'm pretty sure it *is* illegal," Wayne said, "but I guess cockroaches and burning needles can wait for another weekend. Count me in."

"Excellent!" I exclaimed. "You won't regret it. We're going to have a kick-ass time. I can't wait."

And that was all it took. On the following Saturday, I got up early, excited to start the day and embark on our adventure. After a cup of coffee and a Pop Tart, I tossed my pack into the back of the truck and hit the road. My pack contained my gear and my sleeping bag, which I did not want anyone to see. This was to be a clandestine camping excursion. I had told the others to take similar precautions.

The first stop of the day was to pick up Wayne, who lives only a few blocks from me. When I got to his apartment, he was already waiting outside, which was a pleasant surprise. I thought I'd have to wake him up, but nope. He put his pack into the bed of the truck and then hopped into the cab.

"'Sup, buddy?" I asked. The sun was still coming up and the sky was resplendent. I was in good spirits. Wayne,

Vera, and I have known each other since grade school and have gone on countless adventures and outings together. They are my best friends and there's nothing I enjoy more than our excursions.

"Ugh," Wayne grunted, sipping coffee from his ASU travel mug. "It's early."

"This is gonna be awesome," I assured him.

We drove on toward Vera's place. When we got there, she, too, was waiting. We saw her sitting on the front porch reading a book – an archaic thing to do in these weird, wired times. She heard the rumble of my truck as we approached and looked up with a smile. She walked over as Wayne got out to allow her the middle seat, as was our custom. Vera tossed her pack into the back with the others. "Hey, boys," she said as she climbed in. Who's ready for some fun?"

"Hell, yeah!" I cried. "Always!" I was glad that Vera was in a good mood. I wanted us all to have a good time.

"Fun is fun," Wayne said dryly. "I like fun."

With the three of us crammed into the front of my trusty 4x4, we were off. I got onto the interstate and headed north, leaving Phoenix and the Valley of the Sun behind for the cool pines of Northern Arizona.

For a Saturday, the traffic was unusually light. Soon, we were out of the city and enjoying the fine weather and gorgeous scenery. We chatted and enjoyed the sights as we climbed out of the valley. The tall saguaros disappeared with the change in altitude. The transition was quick and dramatic. We reached the top of the mesa, where the high desert plains stretched to the horizon and led the way to the Coconino National Forest, with its Ponderosa pines, flatlands, and ancient volcanic peaks. Its a dynamic and diverse region and I've always enjoyed the drive up.

We got to Flagstaff without incident in the late morning. Since the plan was to camp out at the Wupatki ruins after dark, we decided to kill some time exploring Flagstaff before we entered the park. We spent an enjoyable day walking around the quaint city. It's a college town, so there were plenty of breweries to visit. By late afternoon, we were feeling no pain and were ready for the real adventure.

The short drive north from Flagstaff to Wupatki zipped by. Soon, we saw signs directing us to the ruins. We pulled up to the pay station sometime in the late afternoon. The park ranger alerted us to the fact that the park would be closing at 5 PM. We assured him that we were cool with that and drove on through the gate.

Wupatki National Monument actually consists of ruins in five different locations within the sprawling, protected park. Wupatki, the "Tall House," is the largest site and was our primary destination. When we pulled into the parking lot, we could immediately see the large, multistory dwelling. It was an impressive sight.

"Wow," said Vera as we got out of the truck. "That's actually quite amazing."

She was right. The pictures do not do the complex justice. In person, the ancient architecture comes alive in ways that I hadn't expected. Though crumbling and nearly destroyed in places, the reddish-brown adobe walls still seemed to breathe with an eternal vitality. The history of the site was tangible. An aura of mystery and the echoes of distant ages hung in the air. As we walked with our packs up the modern sidewalk that leads to the main structure, we felt as if we had been transported in time.

We explored the site for a while. As five o'clock approached, there were still some other visitors roaming about. "I wish everyone would just leave," Vera said. "They're making me nervous."

"Maybe we should just fuck it," said Wayne. "We've seen the ruins. They're cool. Let's go home."

"I thought you might chicken out," I teased. "Wouldn't be the first time, either."

"What we're doing isn't all that dangerous or thrilling," Wayne said. "It's just kinda... silly, really."

"I think it'll be fun," Vera smiled. "This place is really something else. I bet the view of the stars from here is just fantastic."

That settled it. Vera usually had the final say in our little group, and this time was no different. We sat on a bench in the round, open area that the maps referred to as the "ball court" and waited for the last remaining stragglers to leave. Eventually, the three of us were the only ones remaining at the ruins. As the sky began to darken, we left the ball court and wandered over to the main structure. It was quite a thrill to have full run of the site! In the deepening twilight, the ruins took on a mysterious, otherworldy quality that seemed to further thin the barrier between the past and the present.

"We should camp here," Vera said, referring to a large room just off the main path. The front and side walls of the chamber had crumbled severely, but they still provided sufficient cover should we need to hide from the prying eyes of the park rangers or other visitors. They would not, however, offer any protection from what we were to encounter later.

Vera, Wayne, and I opened our packs and spread our sleeping bags out on the dusty floor of the chamber. The floor above us had deteriorated almost completely, allowing us an unobstructed view of the sky and the surrounding structure. We settled in as the light faded and the temperature began to drop. It really felt as if we had left civilization far behind. It was not hard to imagine that we were the sole human inhabitants of the entire region, if not the world. The absolute stillness and uncanny silence were spooky to the extreme.

We were talking quietly and enjoying the adventure

when Vera suddenly gasped and sat up. Her eyes were wide and reflecting the moonlight. The expression on her face was unsettling.

"What is it?" I asked, somewhat apprehensively.

"I just saw something," she replied.

"Where? What was it?"

"Up there." Vera pointed to the second floor of the adjacent chamber. "I don't know what it was. I just saw it for a moment and then it disappeared."

Wayne and I peered into the darkness where she had indicated. "I don't see anything," Wayne said. "Just some crumbling..."

"There!" Vera cried. "Look!"

We saw it – a figure standing behind a partial wall. It seemed to be flickering in and out of existence. The wall behind it was visible through its translucent form. The image stabilized, and then I realized that I was looking at the ghostly projection of a man – an ancient warrior, to be more precise. The headdress, warpaint, and bow and quiver on its back made that obvious.

"It's an Indian," Vera whispered.

"It's a goddamn ghost!" said Wayne, his voice cracking with fear.

"It looks Hopi to me," I said. "I can't even believe what I'm seeing."

"I knew this was a mistake," Wayne whimpered. "Fuck."

"I don't think it wants to hurt us," Vera said. "I don't think it *can*. In fact, it looks like it's trying to communicate with us."

She was right. The specter was staring right at us. It gestured at us with a solemn, subtle movement of its head. Its mouth moved as if it were speaking, but we could hear no voice. It slowly raised a phantasmal arm and pointed out into the darkness of the surrounding wilderness.

"Okay," said Wayne, "I'm *really* freaking out now."

"It's a warning," I intuited.

Wayne and Vera looked at me. In that moment, they realized that what I had said was true. The entity in the adjacent dwelling was alerting us to something beyond our encampment. I called out to the ghost: "There's something out there, isn't there?"

The apparition nodded its head.

"Are we in danger?"

The apparition nodded its head again, this time vehemently.

"We've got to get out of here," Vera said as she rose to her feet.

"Stay calm," I urged.

"What if it's lying?" asked Wayne. "Are you going to trust a friggin' *ghost?*"

"I'm having a hard time trusting my own eyes," I said, "but I don't think we have a choice."

The apparition suddenly turned with a jerk. It stared into the distance for a moment before swinging around again. It silently mouthed something indistinguishable while waving an arm at us. With one look at its face, I knew that the situation was now deadly serious.

"Get your shit," I said. "We're leaving."

We started rolling up our sleeping bags and gathering our stuff. Fortunately, we didn't have much. We were packed up and ready to move in minutes. The apparition on the wall stood over us and watched the entire time, with brief glances over its shoulder to monitor whatever was approaching. When we were about to depart, Vera said, "It's gone." I looked up and, sure enough, the entity had disappeared.

"Let's go," I said.

We hopped over the short wall of the chamber in

which we had been camped and stepped back onto the modern sidewalk in front. As soon as my feet hit the pavement, I started jogging toward the parking lot where my truck awaited. Wayne and Vera followed suit. We ran as a group in a tight cluster. To our right, the walls of the ancient pueblo seemed to be hiding all sorts of unimaginable, lurking threats. Even the shadows seemed to be alive and imbued with malicious intent. My nerves were on fire. I expected that something hideous would slither out or pounce from the murky black at any moment.

"Almost there," Vera said as we ran. "I can see the truck."

We were so close... then I heard it – a deep booming like the rumble of thunder. The sound reverberated through the compound in rhythmic intervals: *Boom, boom, boom.* I could feel the ground shake with each resounding beat. The sound was getting louder... and closer.

"Oh, God," Wayne said. "What is *that?*"

"It sounds like footsteps," replied Vera.

Before I could offer my own thoughts, the booming suddenly ceased. The night was silent once again, but only for a moment. What followed after that brief respite was the most disturbing noise I have ever heard – it was ear-splitting and sounded like the amplified screams of a thousand tormented souls crying out in unison. It echoed across the plains and in our heads. It was as if the Earth itself was shrieking. The three of us froze in our tracks and clasped our hands over our ears. The sound rose in pitch, slicing through our brains before tapering off mercifully. The booming then resumed and the source of the noise closed in fast.

We started running again out of pure instinct. Just as we were about to leave the complex and enter the parking lot, the approaching rumble stopped again. I felt a presence. I turned around tentatively, cautiously, and came face to face with a vision straight out of Hell. Wayne and Vera must have sensed my horror because they, too, stopped and turned around. No one said anything. All we could do was stare at the abomination before us.

It towered a hundred feet above the ruins, a gargantuan beast of nightmarish appearance. The creature was vaguely reptilian, but looked more like a demon than a dinosaur. Upon its scaly, hunched shoulders sat a strangely human-like head, with a broad forehead and protruding brow, beneath which peered the malevolent eyes of an ogre. The repugnant face of the monster was framed by long, ragged hair. The nostrils of its thick, flat nose flared as it stood looking down on us. Its open mouth revealed sharpened teeth and a flapping tongue dripping with saliva.

"Guys," Wayne stammered, "I think that thing is hungry."

"Don't move," Vera said. "It might not see us."

"Oh, it sees us," I said.

"Try talking to it, Russell," Wayne suggested. "This was all your idea anyway."

It seems silly now, but at the time I thought it was worth a try. "Hi, there!" I called to the beast. "Sorry to trespass on your land. We're leaving now and we promise to never come back."

At the sound of my voice, the creature tilted its enormous head back and let out another horrific shriek. It then began to climb the pueblo ruins, using its massive arms and hands the size of my truck to pull itself over the walls. It scaled the structures easily, like a child on playground equipment, and was on the other side – *our* side – in no time. All we could do was run, so we did.

The monstrosity followed. I could hear it bellowing as the gap between it and us disappeared in two huge strides. We made it to the truck and I fumbled with the keys in an attempt to open the driver's side door. Wayne and Vera yelled at me to hurry. I could practically feel the beast's breath on my neck, but I was panicking and could not get the key into the slot. In that moment, I was sure I was going to die. In a compartmentalized, passive part of my mind, I resigned myself to my fate.

Just as that thing's shadow fell on us, casting us into total darkness with the sheer bulk of its mass, it inexplicably paused. I managed to get the truck door open. I hopped in and unlocked the passenger door, allowing Vera and Wayne to scramble in. The creature was standing directly in front of the truck, but it no longer seemed interested in us. It had turned to look in the direction of the ruins. Something else had caught its attention.

It was Vera who saw them first. "Oh, my God," she said. "Look!"

On a night which I thought could not possibly hold any more surprises, there was still another one in store for us. The rampaging beast seemed equally astonished at the scene before us – Wupatki had come alive. It was as if spacetime had folded in on itself. The ancient inhabitants had returned. The entire complex was bustling with activity. All along the top levels and in each chamber, we could see Hopi people, but, like the individual who had warned us of the monster, they were spectral, phantasmal.

"Look at 'em all," Wayne said. "That's got to be their entire community."

"I think I know what happened to them now," Vera said. "That creature drove them away... or worse."

"How old is that thing, anyway?" I pondered aloud. "Or... were there others?" It was a frightful thought.

In its confusion, the monstrosity had forgotten about us. It took a step toward the complex. I did not want to draw its attention to us, so I sat in the truck without starting its engine. We watched as Hopi warriors assembled all along the top levels of the ruins. There were dozens of them, armed with bows and spears. The beast roared and took another step forward. The warriors unleashed their weapons, raining spears and arrows down upon the furious creature. The projectiles were as insubstantial as their ghostly wielders, but the creature did not seem to know this. It attempted to shield itself from the salvo. It cowered and covered its head with its gigantic arms.

"Go!" screamed Wayne. "Get us out of here!"

That was our opportunity. I started the truck's engine and peeled out of the parking lot. As we drove away, I glanced in the rear view mirror and could see the creature. It was standing in front of the ruins, which were vacant once more. The apparitions had departed as quickly as they had come. The posture of the great monster seemed forlorn and almost lonely. I felt an odd sympathy for the beast. Although I was profoundly relieved to be leaving the ruins alive, I couldn't help but wonder about that tragic creature. Did it have emotions? A family? Was its existence a curse?

As we made our way back to Phoenix, the mood in the truck was somber and reflective. I felt bad that my impulsiveness and reckless behavior had gotten me and my friends in danger, but at least we had made it out of there alive. It would certainly be an adventure that we would never forget. I think it's one that we will be keeping to ourselves, though. No one would ever believe us. The beast? Well, I assume that it's still out there somewhere, watching and waiting. Let this be a lesson to you – always respect the rules of the park... and never stay after dark.

# The Traveler

In the great green room, there was a time machine, a lead suit, and a picture of the first man on the moon. The man in the lead suit was assisting another, the traveler, into the machine. The year was 1995. The traveler's destination was 25 years into the future.

Strapped in and secured, the traveler relaxed into his seat and prepared for the journey. He was excited, anxious, appropriately nervous, and absolutely thrilled by the expedition into the unknown upon which he was about to embark. This was to be the first Future Jump for his team. The machine had passed a rigorous testing phase and the traveler had logged hundreds of hours in the simulator. It was now time for the initial human-piloted trial run.

The assistant in the lead suit exited the machine chamber and went to his terminal in the console room. All was going according to procedure. Mankind was on the threshold of an incredible new era. It was the dawning of the age of spacetime mastery - a giant evolutionary leap. For reasons known only to his ultimate, mysterious superiors in the shadowy cabal that authorized, funded, and oversaw this mission, the traveler was being sent to a very specific time in the future. He could speculate, however – and he suspected that it had something to do with gathering information on a possible upcoming catastrophe.

Prediction and simulation software can only reveal so much about potential future scenarios. In order to obtain hard, usable data, one needs to be physically present to gather it. The traveler, recruited for his strength and stamina as well as his mental fortitude, would be the individual who would

cross the abyss, enter the brave new world of the next
millennium, and gather this information.

The machine came to life – a rumbling, flashing,
cacophonous beast of metal, glass, and wire. The traveler
closed his eyes, held his breath, and gripped the arms of his
seat. The walls of the chamber took on a shimmering,
translucent appearance. Strange lights of indistinct color
began to swirl around the machine. The traveler felt an
unpleasant pressure building in his skull. A high-pitched wail
rose within his ears. He thought maybe he was screaming,
but he couldn't be sure. His mind was collapsing into a
dissociative void... then, suddenly, silence, darkness, an eerie
calm.

As if waking from a deep sleep, the traveler slowly
regained consciousness. He was no longer inside of the
machine. He was now seated on a bench on a large, busy
street in a city of considerable size. Vehicles of makes and
models he had never before seen zipped by him at a dizzying
rate. Pedestrians, seemingly oblivious to his sudden
appearance, walked up and down the sidewalk. He was
exuberant. The machine had worked! If the engineers had
gotten it right, he should now be in the year 2020. It was
almost unfathomable.

The traveler took a moment to marvel at his
surroundings and the significance of what had just just
transpired. He then began to do the job he had been trained
for: diligently observing his environment and the people
within it. His superiors would, no doubt, be interested in
every little detail.

The traveler sat on the bench and scanned his
immediate surroundings. He noticed a woman
approaching. Her head was down and she walked slightly
hunched over, her eyes on an object in her left hand. The
object was some sort of device. The traveler could see it

emitting a faint, green light. The woman was entirely captivated by the device, not once lifting her gaze as she approached. As the woman neared, the traveler was shocked to see that she was essentially naked. Two small, fabric skulls covered the nipples of her exposed breasts. She wore skimpy panties emblazoned with another large, leering human skull. On her feet she wore pink combat boots.

The traveler was astonished, but what really shocked him was what the woman had done to her face. Her nose and lips had been surgically altered to resemble those of a cat. Whiskers and black and orange stripes had been tattooed on her face. Were those cat ears poking through the brightly dyed hair on her head? The traveler watched her pass in abject disbelief.

A nasty smell caught his attention. He was able to pry his eyes away from the catwoman in search of the source of the stink. It was easy to find. Here now, following closely (too closely) behind the woman, was a vision directly out of a horror movie – a menacing, lumbering caricature of a villain. It was an absurd sight. The man was wearing a black leather trench coat embellished with spikes, chains, and animal bones. He wore a dirty, tattered top hat and carried a large staff with a human skull affixed to one end. It was not immediately apparent if the skull was real or not. The man's features were entirely obscured by a muddy, brown mask.

The stench grew as the man approached. The traveler realized that the man had a thick layer of feces caked on his face. The man in the poop mask was obviously trying to intimidate those around him. He walked the street like a predator. As he passed the traveler, he lunged in his direction and sneered, revealing sharpened teeth and a modified tongue. The traveler could only stare, dumbfounded, as the ridiculous character walked up the street with an exaggerated, silly swagger, leaving a trail of excrement behind him.

The traveler took a moment to compose himself. He was only 25 years removed from his own time, but what little he had seen of this world was vastly, frighteningly, different. *These people seem so primitive*, he thought. *The technology appears to be sufficiently advanced, yet the populace has apparently regressed.* Everywhere he looked, he could see examples of this unexpected dichotomy.

The cars on the street were, to his eyes, appropriately futuristic, yet the drivers had the appearance of tribal throwbacks – hairy, unkempt, tattooed, near-nude, atavistic specimens with dull expressions on their slack faces. Fantastically sophisticated devices and high technology were abundant, yet all signs indicated an extremely anti-intellectual, escapist culture. Such a strange juxtaposition!

He noticed that many of the pedestrians who passed by were drinking the same beverage. He found an empty can on the ground at his feet. The garish writing on the over-sized can proclaimed the fluid inside to be Narconade, a potent mixture of chemicals promising "12 hours of bliss!" Across the street, a group of children were exiting a clinic. The sign above the door read *LobotoMart*. The children were no more than 12 years old and each had a freshly sealed incision across his or her forehead. They were giggling, drooling, and stumbling down the street.

Above the clinic, a massive billboard announced an upcoming sporting event. The sign displayed animated depictions of graphic violence. Two uniformed teams of men were locked in brutal, close-quarters combat, stabbing, slicing, and disemboweling each other in an obscene display of carnage. Interspersed with these images were shots of deliriously excited, cheering spectators. The next game was scheduled for this very evening. The traveler was appalled. In his short stay, he had gathered enough information to provide a rather grim assessment of the near future to his superiors.

Despite his training and innate strength of mind, body, and spirit, the traveler was beginning to feel strongly uncomfortable – threatened, even – in this hostile, unfamiliar environment. He decided the best course of action would be to find a newspaper, collect as much data as he could from its pages, and then find a safe, quiet place to wait for the engineers to return him to his own time. He spotted a trashcan on the corner. He walked toward it calmly, confidently, attempting to attract as little attention as possible from the other pedestrians on the bustling street.

As the traveler neared the trashcan and prepared to inconspicuously examine its contents in search of a newspaper, he heard voices directly behind him. He quickly, reflexively spun around, ready to defend himself. There before him stood the LobotoMart children, each clutching a can of Narconade, their forehead incisions still oozing pink fluid. A few of them were pointing their mobile devices at him. *Were they filming this encounter?* he wondered. *Why?* Two of the larger children approached him, their black, lifeless eyes locked on his. They were vaguely grinning and leering at him like murderous idiots, breathing heavily from their open mouths.

The LobotoMart children closed in on the traveler. While a few stood back to record the assault, the rest began to strike in a disorganized, chaotic flurry of tiny arms and legs. Despite being half the size of their target, they were furiously aggressive and strangely fearless, like a pack of wild, rabid dogs. The traveler was forced to defend himself. He did so easily, using his training and considerable strength to fight off the feral children efficiently and systematically, until they were piled upon each other at his feet.

The traveler expected the rest to launch an attack, but they simply turned around and walked away unfazed, leaving their bloody and battered companions lying in a heap on the sidewalk. The other pedestrians paid no attention to the sudden violence. No one even looked up from their mobile devices.

The traveler was finally able to continue his search for a newspaper. He examined the trashcan and was not surprised to find it full of empty Narconade cans. There were, of course, no newspapers. For as far as he could see, in fact, there were no newsstands or newspaper vending machines.

There was a bookstore across the street, however, but according to the signage it specialized in pornography of the most lurid and perverse kind. The pictures displayed in the windows were revolting. *Do people even read anymore?* The traveler decided to continue on his way in search of a secluded spot to await his extraction.

He had not gone far when he heard a deafening roar above and behind him. Something was approaching with a thunderous din. He looked up and felt true fear for the first time since he had arrived. Hovering now, mere feet above his head, was a nightmarish contraption. It appeared to be a large, robotic flying machine held aloft by four powerful rotors. It was black and menacing, equipped with a variety of instruments and weapons. The traveler was utterly astonished. A high-pitched, ear-piercing metallic shriek promptly penetrated his head, driving away his thoughts and forcing him to his knees.

Pain and panic immobilized the traveler. The craft then emitted a thick, green mist, which completely enveloped him. His eyes burned. He gagged and frothed at the mouth. He felt like a cockroach at the mercy of some omniscient, omnipotent exterminator. As his consciousness quickly ebbed away, he couldn't help but admire the extraordinary design and magnificent engineering of the machine.

# The Woods

My nightmare began as a simple walk in the woods. It had been a hard day and I just needed a little fresh air and exercise. I thought a short hike through the forest behind the office building would be the perfect remedy for the stress I had been feeling. I had no idea then that I would soon find myself lost and wandering through Hell.

To be clear, I don't *hate* my job. Let's just say that designing software is a lot less fun and creative – and a lot more tedious and frustrating – than I expected. I had been really struggling with a piece of code, ready to pull my hair out and put a fist through the monitor. Iteration after iteration, nothing worked. I was sweating, cursing, and near tears. Bobby, who works in the cubicle next to me, knew I was getting more and more upset. He poked his head over the wall and said, "You should take a walk, buddy. I can hear your frustration. Take a break before you totally lose it." It was good advice. I immediately thought of the trail that winds through the woods behind the building. I thanked Bobby for his wise suggestion and was out of my seat and out the door in a flash. I didn't even bother to back up my work.

It was late afternoon when I stepped outside. It was sunny, but not too hot, and there were big, fluffy clouds moving through the sky – it was a perfect day for a walk. I took a deep breath and walked around to the back of the building, already beginning to feel rejuvenated.

At the trailhead, I paused. I felt a subtle fear sweep over me, as if I stood before the open, gaping mouth of some hideous, ancient creature. The forest, in that moment, seemed to be alive in a way I hadn't noticed before. It was a vast, singular, mighty organism... and I was about to willfully walk right into its belly. I shook off the fear, convincing myself it was unfounded and foolish, and crossed the threshold.

As soon as I entered the woods, I became aware of a shift in the quality and volume of the sounds around me. It was like I had stepped through a portal into another dimension. I could hear birds, the rustling of leaves, twigs snapping beneath my shoes, and the unsettling scurry of small, unseen creatures. The sounds were sharper and more distinct than those I had perceived outside of the forest. My ears suddenly seemed to be more sensitive, my hearing more acute. I stopped to listen, my brain finely tuned to the activity of the woods.

There occurred then a weird synesthesia – I began to actually *feel* the sounds. It was like music – amazing, otherworldly music, and it caused ripples of pleasure to roll up and down my arms and all over my body. My heart fluttered as if I had just jumped out of an airplane. My scalp tingled and a delicious, warm sensation enveloped me. It only lasted a minute or so, then it faded. I assumed that I was simply feeling the powerful healing and restorative effects that come from spending time in nature, which can be especially beneficial for someone like me who spends so much time indoors staring at a computer monitor. I did not suspect that anything unusual or extraordinary was happening. Boy, was I wrong.

Feeling great, I continued along the meandering trail. A few yards in, I stopped and turned around. I was shocked to see that I could no longer recognize the spot where I had entered the woods. The trees had closed in around me entirely. *Have I really hiked that far in?* I wondered. As far as I could tell, I had only been walking for a few minutes, but I had already lost sight of the trailhead and the edge of the

forest. In fact, I could not even see the treeline. The foliage
was so dense that even the light of the sun struggled to pierce
the thick brush. It had grown considerably darker. I
momentarily panicked in my disorientation until I realized
that I had not stepped off the trail. I posited that if I were to
turn around, the path would lead me straight back out of the
woods. I assured myself that I had nothing to fear. Again, I
was wrong.

As soon as I regained my composure, I saw it... If
only I hadn't! I believe now that it wanted to be seen. Perhaps
the awful thing had even drawn me to it. There it was, just off
the trail, growing at the base of a tall pine. It was an obscene
sight! Initially, I thought it was a dead animal, one that had
met a violent demise. At first glance, it looked like a small
creature that had been torn apart and turned inside out. It was
the color, texture, and vague shape of organs and viscera. My
mind recoiled at the hideous thing until I realized that what I
was looking at was not an animal, but a plant of some sort – a
peculiar pod with lobes, flaps, and tentacles. It was the color
of flesh and it was clearly growing out of the ground.

As I stared at the repulsive pod and tried to
understand exactly what in the world it was, it suddenly
seemed to move. *That's just the wind*, I reasoned, but then it
moved again. It did not sway – it *twitched.* I froze. It
twitched again. In that moment, I should have run, as fast I
could without looking back, but instead, I let curiosity get the
better of me. Despite my growing unease, I foolishly stepped
forward to get a better look at the vile thing growing in the
woods. I leaned in and a horrible, repugnant stench assaulted
me. The pod stunk worse than death. I covered my nose and
mouth with my left hand and crouched down beside the
bizarre specimen. I was utterly fascinated by it. It was unlike
anything I had ever seen – a flora/fauna hybrid. It looked
alien. My inquisitiveness compelled me to get an even closer

look. Wanting to touch it, I reached out. Just as I was about to make contact, the pod suddenly sprung open. The last thing I recall seeing before I lost consciousness was a squirming tongue-like appendage inside the pod – it ejected a cloud of yellow dust directly in my face.

When I awoke, I was on my back. It was cold and dark. The sun had gone down. Overhead, the full moon, ominous and dispassionate, illuminated the forest with spectral shades of blue. I tried to sit up, but I could not. For a terrible moment, I was completely paralyzed, my body and limbs numb and unresponsive. My brain screamed: "Move! Get up! Run!" but my body remained prone and useless. I squelched the shrieking voice in my head, overriding it with an internal mantra of calming words: *Relax, breathe, focus...*

Through pure force of will, I commanded first my arms to move, ever so slightly, then my legs. I could feel my strength returning. I wiggled my toes and fingers. Soon, I was able to lift my hands. I used my forearms to pull myself up to my elbows. From there, I was able to assume a sitting position with my legs folded beneath me.

I felt dizzy, dazed, drugged. The memory of what had happened before I had lost consciousness returned to me, as did the fear, which was infused with a surge of strength. I was able to get to my feet and the first thing I did was spin around to get a look at the grotesque pod-plant that had blasted me with spores. I could not see it! I walked over to the spot where I had discovered it. I approached, slowly, cautiously, but it was not there. I could clearly see where it had been, though. The soil was disturbed and there was a small trench, but the *thing* had disappeared. Could it have walked away? *No,* I told myself. *That's impossible... isn't it?*

As it grew darker, I realized that I had more important issues to worry about than the pod-plant. Night was coming and I needed to find a way out of the forest. I wondered if my co-workers thought I had finally snapped and walked off the job for good. I wondered if I had put my employment in jeopardy.

My imagination started to act up: *What if I were truly lost? What if I ended up wandering around the woods for days?* As a bachelor, no one waited for me at home. An extended absence would certainly cause concern among my family and friends, but how many days or weeks would it take before they realized I was missing? I dismissed these thoughts and reminded myself that I was in a small, wooded area close to work. It would be virtually impossible to get lost... plus, Bobby, my co-worker, knew that I had only gone for a walk. I just had to stay calm and find my way out.

My eyes were beginning to adjust to the darkness of the moon-lit woods. To my left, just off the trail, I could see the spot where I had encountered the strange and dangerous plant. It was now gone, but the memory of its ghastly appearance caused me to shudder. Still, knowing where it had been, I was able to orientate myself. I turned in the direction I recalled entering the woods and began to walk.

With renewed courage and the utmost certainty that I would soon find my way back to the comfort and familiarity of civilization – only yards beyond, but seemingly a universe away – I marched on, trying to ignore the spooky sounds around me. I could hear rustling, crunching, whispering in all directions, like an invisible band of wraiths trailing me. The eerie noises, coupled with the pale, bluish light of the moon, soon unnerved me once again. My heart raced and a cold sweat covered my flesh. I quickened my pace.

I scanned the thick, dark woods on either side of the trail, straining my eyes looking for any sign of danger... and I almost walked right into the jaws of the beast. I turned my head and there it was, directly in front of me, blocking the trail – a massive, white wolf with eyes that glowed blood-red.

It was hunched and snarling, ropes of saliva dangling from its exposed fangs. It was a monstrous sight, but it was also impressive, beautiful, mesmerizing. I had never seen such an unusual creature, either in reality or in pictures. Its fur was a pure, untarnished shade of brilliant white and its eyes glowed in such an uncanny way that they appeared to be self-luminous... And its size! Even hunched over, ready to pounce, the beast was nearly as tall as me. It was more a mutant or a monster than a wolf.

Of course, I was terrified. A dizzying, nauseating, mortal fear penetrated and filled the very core of my being. Time stood still. I looked into the eyes of the beast and saw the abyss, where I would soon reside if it chose to attack. I slowly raised my hands in a show of submission and respect. "Whoa. Easy there, big guy," I said gently as I took a few steps back. Without warning, the beast lunged. I gasped as it bounded forward. When it was only a few feet away, the beast stopped suddenly and – here's where it gets truly bizarre – its lips curled into a subtle and very human smile. The wolf-beast, like something out of a surrealistic dream, sat on its haunches. It raised its snout to the moon and laughed manically. Yes, it *laughed.* It did not bark, it did not howl – it *laughed*, loud and heartily, as if it had enjoyed scaring the ever-loving shit out of me... which it had indeed done.

I stopped and simply stared, my mouth agape, my mind struggling to comprehend what I was seeing. As I stood there watching like a dumbfounded imbecile, the great beast got up, fixed me once more with those intense, piercing, blood-red eyes, and shambled off the trail, vanishing into the woods. The trees swallowed the beast and it was gone, leaving no trace. I listened for any signs of its presence in the bush, but the forest was oddly silent. Even the normal ambient sounds seemed to have been muted. I had the feeling that I had just encountered something supernatural. I started to question my whereabouts. I started to question my sanity.

There was no time to waste. I did not have the luxury of pondering the structure of reality, my place in the cosmos, or the fragility of my psyche. It was the middle of the night and I was tired, hungry, and wandering through the forest. I needed to get out. I needed to get home. The trail in front of me was now clear. I chose to ignore the inexplicable nature of the events I had just experienced and soldiered on. I was hopeful that just up ahead was the trailhead – the place where I had entered the woods and unknowingly stepped into a nightmare.

Carefully, I crept up the trail, half expecting, half wishing, to see the bush open up in front of me to reveal the building in which I worked and deliver me to safety. This did not happen. I walked on for what felt like an hour. Was I going the wrong way? Could I have somehow gotten turned around? Was I plunging deeper into the heart of the forest? Panic again clawed at my brain, but I pushed it away with a few deep breaths. Suddenly, there it was! I could see the building beyond the treeline, silhouetted against the night sky.

Relief, sweet and ecstatic, poured over me like a shower from the heavens. I started to run toward the exit, ready to burst out into the glorious open space that awaited me on the other side. I was grinning like a fool and practically crying with joy as I bounded up the trail, but the smile on my face quickly melted away as I realized something most disturbing: I was not getting any closer to the black, rectangular shape of the office building looming ahead. Instead, it seemed to be receding into the distance as I ran. At first, my mind refused to acknowledge this startling fact. I kept running... but the building was moving *away* from me, as if being pulled by some powerful, mysterious force.

I stopped running. The building remained fixed in its position. I started jogging again, slowly at first, attentively observing the objects in front of me. I was making progress on the trail, getting closer and closer to the trees directly ahead, but to my dismay, the office building continued to recede into the distance! I refused to accept this spatial and optical anomaly and barreled forward, switching gears into a full-on sprint.

I was fast approaching the forest's edge. I could see the gap in the trees where I had entered so many hours ago. I summoned all of my strength and pushed toward it. Just as I was about to reach the threshold, the trees on either side of the opening suddenly came alive. In a coordinated maneuver, they moved as a singular entity, bending down and swinging into position. In an instant, the opening was blocked. The forest had sealed me in.

"No!" I cried as my energy and vitality drained away. My mind reeled in disbelief and my soul ached in defeat. I collapsed on the trail, withering into a sitting position with my head in my hands. I sobbed pitiful, wailing sobs as I grasped the hopelessness of my situation. Tears streamed down my face as I whimpered and mourned for the rational world I once inhabited.

In the vicious grip of despair, under the crushing weight of psychological anguish so enormous that I felt nearly suffocated by hopelessness, I had a revelation. It struck at once with resounding force. In my hour of desperation, the truth was revealed to me – a savage and pure truth. The dawning of my understanding coincided with the dawning of a new day. I could see the faint glow of early morning through the gaps in the trees that now served as the bars of my prison.

I got to my feet and, as I rose, my strength returned and my will to survive increased with fresh intensity. My predicament started to make sense, at least in that moment. My mind had been thoroughly tested – expanded, even – by events of the rarest and strangest variety. I decided to confront what I perceived to be the source of my tribulation. In a small, timid voice that grew more powerful as I spoke, I addressed the forest itself:

"Hello, there. I think I am starting to understand what is happening. First, I would like to assure you that I mean no harm... although I'm sure that, even if I did, I would have very little power to do so."

The trees in my immediate vicinity swayed slightly, as if a gentle breeze had caressed them, though I did not feel it myself. I had the distinct sensation that my words were being heard. I continued: "It seems to me that I am the subject of, for lack of a better term, a *game*. Now, normally, I am not one to ruin someone's fun, but I am an unwilling – and until only moments ago, *unwitting* – participant, and *I'm* not having any fun at all. Is that the point? To torture and torment an innocent, ignorant, helpless individual? Is the goal to drive me insane? Do you get off on my suffering?"

The more I spoke, the angrier I became. Indignation filled my voice with courage and conviction. My words resonated through the woods. As if in response, a chorus of birds somewhere overhead erupted into song, the notes plaintive and sorrowful... and almost apologetic.

"I have had enough. I want to go home now. I want to be released."

Again, the trees around me swayed in a wave-like fashion that rippled through the bush. The birds had gone silent and, in the quiet interlude, something else caught my attention: a large, gray squirrel clinging to the trunk of a tree to my left. It was looking directly at me, its tiny, black eyes both wild and wise. It scampered down the tree and ran right up to me. It stopped at my feet and peered up.

"Hi, little buddy," I said.

The squirrel nodded its head and began to trot up the trail. A few feet away, it stopped and turned back to look at me. I realized then that it wanted me to follow it, so I did. I followed the squirrel for a hundred feet or so, until we came to the spot where the trees had closed in on the trail and sealed me in. The squirrel let out a funny little squeak and then ran off into the bush. Before me, the trees began to move. It was an astonishing thing to witness! As I watched, the trees bent back and returned to their original positions, opening the way for me to leave the woods.

Through the clearing I walked. I could see the office building where I worked getting bigger, closer. My thoughts drifted to the code I had been working on the day before – that frustrating little piece of information that I had so clumsily been trying to manipulate and conform to my desire. All around me – and within me, too – nature seemed to operate so effortlessly. Was there a hidden code behind it? Some special, secret algorithm that governed it all? My experience in the woods had made me feel like a toy at the mercy of a masterful programmer. I stepped out of the woods and into the light of a new day, with renewed appreciation for the complexity and beauty of the natural world.

# The Ward

At the age of 30, Samuel lost his will to live. It was not sudden, but rather a slow and steady process of mental and emotional deterioration, culminating in a state of total, abject despair. Samuel had always been moody and prone to bouts of depression, but the internal desolation that overcame him as an adult was despondency of the highest order.

One day, Samuel woke up and thought, *Today is the day I will kill myself.* It was a pure, crystalline idea – the clear and final solution. After years of turmoil he could finally see a way out. The problem of his existence had been solved and the answer was to cease to exist.

For Samuel, suicide had become something much larger than the negation of his life. The concept itself fascinated him. Contemplating its immense profundity excited him. He fantasized about the various ways that he could exit this world with style. Samuel wanted his death to make a statement in a way his life had not.

Samuel was an artist. He painted in an abstract Expressionist fashion with vibrant and energetic colors on large canvasses. The peak of his depression coincided with a period of creative frustration. While staring at a blank and mocking canvas, a delicious idea occurred to him: *I will make my final act a literal work of art.*

It was a wonderfully creative idea for a burned out, suicidal artist: Get a gun, sit in front of a large canvas, and blow off your own head, splattering blood and brain tissue onto the white surface. To Samuel, it seemed brilliant – a perfect way to end both his emotional anguish and his artistic block. It would be the ultimate mode of self-expression. It might even make him posthumously famous.

Samuel spent a few days preparing for his departure, obtaining the materials he required, including a pistol procured from a pawn shop. During the planning and logistics phase of his project, he experienced a surprising sensation of elation. Soon, he knew, his mind and its troublesome thoughts – and his heart, with its inconvenient sensitivities – would dissolve into blissful nothingness. This knowledge filled him with peace. He felt better than he had in a decade.

On the morning of his planned suicide, Samuel loaded and cocked his gun and stood in front of a blank canvas which he had arranged and secured to a wall in his apartment. He had not written a note. His final 'painting' would suffice. He took a deep breath and put the gun in his mouth. He closed his eyes. His thoughts wandered into strange corridors. In his mind's eye, he saw flashes of old friends, glimpses of distant family, and random, disjointed scenes from his short life. The memories filled him with melancholy and longing. Tears welled in Samuel's eyes. His finger closed on the trigger of the gun.

A sudden, forceful knock at his apartment door shattered the moment. "Sam, you in there?" called a voice from the hall. It was his neighbor Nick.

"Sam, I need to talk to you," Nick insisted. "It's important!" *Everything* was important to Nick. He lived in perpetual crisis mode. He was nosy, bothersome, and dramatic, but he was also loyal, dependable, and kind. Samuel considered him to be one of his few true friends.

Samuel removed the gun from his mouth and sighed. "Give me a minute, Nick," he said. Samuel hastily hid the gun under some papers on an end table and went to the door. He opened the door and there stood Nick with a comically exaggerated look of distress on his face. Typical.

Nick immediately began spewing words. "Cathy has totally lost it," he said, referring to a tenant of the apartment building who lived on the floor above them. "I can't *take* it any more. She's driving me *crazy.*" Without waiting to be invited in, Nick walked right past Samuel and into the apartment. He sat on the couch and continued his diatribe.

"She came down this morning to ask for some milk for her coffee," Nick said, entirely oblivious to the scene he had just walked in on... and unaware that he had just interrupted a suicide attempt. Samuel groaned internally and prepared for the long haul. Nick's stories had a tendency to ramble on and on and *on...*

"So I *give* her the damn milk, okay?" Nick continued. "And guess what? She's back down ten minutes later. 'Got any bread? Got any cheese?' God! She's so *annoying!*"

"Yeah, I know what you mean."

"Have you seen her today?"

"No, I..." Samuel paused. "I've been busy this morning."

Nick nodded at the blank canvas hanging on the wall. "Painting?" he asked. In that moment, Samuel seriously considering telling Nick everything that he had thought, felt, and done over the past few days as he moved seemingly inexorably toward a tragic death at his own hands. *Talk to him,* he thought. *Talk to someone. It would be good.* He chose, instead, to keep the gritty details to himself. "I haven't been feeling too hot," he said.

Nick's expression showed genuine concern. "How so? Want to talk about it?"

"Now's probably not a good time. I didn't sleep well last night. I think I just need to be alone for a bit. Rest, maybe eat. Thanks, though."

Nick uncharacteristically took the hint. "Well, then," he said as he rose from the couch, "I guess I should take off.

Feel free to come over later and talk. I'm here for you, man."
Nick's sincerity was touching. "I appreciate that, Nick,"
Samuel said. "I'll try to pop by later."

"Okay, man. See ya." Nick left the apartment. Samuel
closed the door behind him and simply stood there, his
emotions complex. He cast a glace toward the gun beneath
the paper on the table. His enthusiasm for a quick and violent
end had diminished.

Samuel felt a surge of unpleasant feelings –
embarrassment, guilt, fear, and a great sadness, as if he had
peered into the deepest recesses of his soul and discovered it
to be lacking. *I'm a coward,* he thought. He wanted nothing
more than to climb into bed and slide into a dreamless sleep
for the rest of eternity.

He made it to bed before succumbing to
uncontrollable heavy weeping. He lay there and cried,
frustration and sorrow welling up from the bottomless pit
within his defeated heart. Spent, he slid into unconsciousness
and slept for 12 hours.

In the middle of the night, Samuel awoke, sweaty,
hungry, weak, and alone. It was shocking for him to realize
just how close he had been, only hours before, to putting a
bullet in his head. Visualizing the event now filled him with
existential horror. His soul shuddered.

Samuel got out of bed. In his empty apartment he felt
more isolated and depressed than ever. The strange thing
was, he could not identify the real source of his depression.
Where and when had it started? It was as if a dark force had
infiltrated his life at some unknown point in the past, and it
now had total control over his thoughts and emotions.
Subversive and invasive, the malignant influence had crept in
and rooted itself in his mind. After years of psychic
corrosion, Samuel had been left powerless and hopeless.

*I wonder if Nick is awake,* Samuel thought. In his

weakened, vulnerable state, Samuel was able to recognize his need to interact with another person. He yearned to unload some of the mental burden he had acquired. He longed to release the pressure that had built in his overworked mind. Conversation would be good.

Samuel climbed out of bed and left his apartment. The halls were quiet and empty in the middle of the night. He roamed the apartment building like a restless ghost. He arrived at Nick's door and knocked quietly. No answer. He waited for a few minutes before trying again, this time a little more forcefully. Again, no reply. Samuel thought he heard movement in the apartment.

"Nick," he said in a loud whisper. "It's Sam. You up? I need to talk to you."

More movement and rustling from within. "Okay, okay... one sec," Nick said in a strained, distant voice. Faint cursing and strange clanging sounds followed. Samuel dared not speculate on what weird activities Nick might have been up to in the middle of the night.

The deadbolt was released, the door opened, and there stood Nick, disheveled and out of breath. "Hey, buddy," he said. "What's up?"

"Just wondering what was going on with you. I couldn't sleep. Thought maybe you might wanna stop by for a chat."

"Uh... sure." Nick glanced back into his apartment. "How about I stop by in a few minutes? I just need to... clean up."

"No problem."

Samuel returned to his apartment. In a few minutes, he heard a knock at his door.

"You look rough," Nick said to Samuel as he entered Samuel's apartment.

"I know it," Samuel admitted.

Nick took a seat beside him on the couch and lit a cigarette.

"Care to talk about it?" Nick asked. Samuel had hoped to do exactly that, but found it difficult to start. He hesitated, rubbing a spot on his forehead just above his left eye. Honesty, blunt and direct, seemed like the best approach.

"I planned to kill myself today," Samuel said. "Obviously, it didn't work out."

Nick froze mid-puff, clearly shocked. "*What? Seriously?* Shit, man. I didn't know. You should have talked to me earlier."

"Who knows what would have happened if you hadn't interrupted. I'm glad you did, though, because I changed my mind."

Nick was disturbed. "That's some heavy shit, man," he said. "You should talk to somebody."

"I *am*," Samuel said.

"I mean a professional. I'm here for you, buddy, but there are people out there who could *really* help you – doctors, psychiatrists... *professionals.* They got some good drugs now, you know. I've been on medication for almost my whole life. Couldn't imagine living without it. I'd be a mess."

Nick finished his cigarette and stubbed it out in an ashtray on the coffee table. He was a heavy smoker. Samuel could see dark yellow stains on his index and middle fingers. Nick was a weird dude and Samuel was not surprised to find out that he was on medication. He could only speculate on how weird he'd be *off* the pills.

"You're a good guy, Sam," Nick said as he rose from the couch and headed for the door. "Don't let the world get you down. I have an early appointment, so I gotta get some sleep, but I'm here for you, buddy. Any time you wanna talk, let me know... and consider what I said about seeing a professional. It worked for me."

"Will do. Thanks for stopping by."

Nick slipped out the door. Samuel sat once again in solitary silence. Before he had a chance to reign them in, his thoughts wandered to the gun he had stashed under his papers on the end table. It was within arm's reach. Samuel's rampant imagination displayed a graphic scene in his mind's eye – an explosion of skull, skin, hair, and brain. He was losing control over his mental space. His thoughts were betraying him.

Disturbed, Samuel attempted to shake off the suicidal ideation. He paced the apartment. He played music. He wandered into the kitchen for a snack. The visions returned – persistent, relentless, taunting. *Kill yourself,* a low, maniacal voice inside him insisted. *Do it. Do it NOW. It's easy, instant, painless.* Gory images of self-destruction looped in his head.

Samuel's survival instinct, primal and powerful, engaged. His psyche had fractured into two opposing factions, one driving toward total destruction, one fighting desperately for his continued existence. In the wrestling match for his soul, Samuel's lust for the void submitted to his desire for life. He picked up a telephone and made a call.

"911, what is your emergency?"

"I need help. I'm suicidal."

Samuel was taken by ambulance to the regional hospital. His speech and behavior prompted the medical technicians to inject him with a sedative. Strangely, the first real treatment he received for his depression was the administration of a central nervous system depressant. The effect was instantly calming. Samuel arrived at the hospital and was brought to the emergency ward for processing.

After a brief interview in triage, Samuel was escorted to a tiny waiting room with an examination table. He was given a hospital gown. He stripped, put on the gown, and sat on the table. An overweight nurse with malice in her eyes entered the room and slipped on a pair of rubber gloves. "I need to take your vitals," she said, yawning as she spoke.

"Okay," Samuel said.

The nurse's plump hands explored Samuel's body. Vital signs were taken.

"Am I alive?" Samuel joked.

"Yes," the nurse answered as she removed the gloves and disposed of them. She exited the room without another word, leaving Sam on the examination table. He felt vulnerable and violated. All he could do was wait, so he did.

Hours passed. Samuel shifted his position on the table and drifted in and out of consciousness. Sounds from the emergency ward carried through the walls. It was a busy night at the hospital. While Samuel oscillated between sleep and wakefulness, strange audio penetrated the walls of the small room – moans, screams of agony, demented shouts of the senile and desperate. Someone begged for pain killers, another hurled a barrage of obscenities at hospital staff members. It was a long, weird night.

In the early morning, a professionally dressed young woman entered the room. Samuel had been lying on the table in a state of near awareness for many hours. He heard her come in.

"Hello," the woman said in a pleasant voice. "I'm Dr. Harrison. May I ask you a few questions?"

"Yes, of course." Samuel was extremely relieved to have the opportunity to talk to someone.

The doctor sat in a seat next to the table. She consulted a clipboard she had brought in with her. "Samuel," she said. "Or do you prefer Sam?"

"Sam is fine."

"Sam, would you like to tell me what brought you in?"

"Whew, that's a tough question. I guess the simple

answer is that I've been... depressed."

Dr. Harrison began taking notes. "How long have you been feeling this way?"

Samuel began to feel self-conscious. Sharing the details of his private, internal struggle with a total stranger was going to be much harder than he had anticipated. *Have I made a colossal mistake?* he thought. As if in response, a technicolor vision of violent suicide flashed in his mind. He shook it off and attempted to articulate the mental distress he had been experiencing.

Dr. Harrison could sense his reticence to share. "I'm not here to judge you," she said. "I'm here to help you. Any information you can provide will help me determine the best possible course of treatment."

"Well," Samuel said, gathering the courage to expose the inner workings of his mind. "I'm here because I'm seriously considering killing myself. It's an idea I've long been fascinated with, but lately I've been obsessed. I guess I'm talking to you now because, somewhere deep inside, I really don't want to die."

Dr. Harrison looked Samuel in the eye and smiled. "Good," she said. "That's a start, isn't it?"

The conversation continued for close to an hour, mostly covering Samuel and his family's history of mental illness and emotional aberrations, but also meandering into seemingly irrelevant directions. Samuel spilled his guts. He purged himself of years of pent-up frustration and turmoil. The relief he felt as the pressure was released was near orgasmic. Dr. Harrison took extensive notes.

At the end of the interview, Dr. Harrison said, "I think it would be best for you to be admitted to the hospital as an in-patient. How do you feel about that, Sam?"

"I'm officially crazy," Samuel deadpanned. "Certifiably, undeniably *nuts.* It's not as painful as I thought it would be..."

"We don't use terms like that here, Sam, and even if we did, I wouldn't necessarily apply them to you. You *are* depressed, though. That much is obvious. With the right treatment, including medication and counseling, I think you could lead a very normal and fulfilling life."

"I'm not sure if I'll ever be *normal*, but fulfilled, or at least somewhat happy, would be nice."

With a few strokes of the doctor's pen, Samuel became a psychiatric patient. Being admitted to the ward was like gaining admission to an underground world, a secret realm with its own codes, customs, and hierarchies – a bizarre tangential universe filled with misfits and maniacs.

A nurse escorted Samuel from the emergency room to the psychiatric ward. Despite being able-bodied and relatively physically fit, he was transported in a wheelchair. He voiced his objections and was told that it was simply a matter of hospital protocol. The wheelchair made him feel much more ill than he was. It set a disturbing precedent.

Samuel was wheeled up to the main nurse's desk. Introductions were made and paperwork was exchanged. The head nurse at reception was a kind, middle-aged woman with a gentle, patient demeanor.

"Would you like me to take you to your bed, Sam?" the head nurse asked. She spoke to Samuel as if he were a child... or as if he had a psyche as fragile as an egg shell.

"Sure," Samuel replied.

The nurse's desk sat at the center of an intersection of hallways. The nurse led Samuel down one of the brightly-lit, off-white halls. It was late afternoon and very quiet on the ward. The doors to most of the rooms were closed. Samuel could hear faint conversation, snoring, and even soft sobbing coming from the unseen occupants. The nurse stopped at the last door on the left. "This is your room," she said.

Samuel stepped into the room. There were two beds separated by a curtain which was currently drawn. Samuel could see the silhouette of his roommate on the far bed near the window. The nurse gestured at the bed closest to the door and said, "This is your bed."

"Are those your street clothes?" the nurse asked, referring to a large bag Samuel was carrying. He had been given the bag while in the emergency ward. It contained all of the personal items he had brought with him to the hospital.

"Yes, among other things."

"For your safety – and the safety of the other patients – I'll need to screen your belongings."

"Can I change back into my clothes?" Samuel was still wearing the flimsy hospital gown.

"In time, yes. That is usually at the doctor's discretion. For the first few days, patients are advised to wear gowns."

"Okay." Samuel was feeling a little like an inmate already. He emptied the bag onto the bed. It didn't contain much, just the clothes he had been wearing when he arrived, his keys, and his wallet.

"Did you bring any personal hygiene products?" the nurse asked.

"No, I did not. Wasn't sure how long I'd be here or if I'd need anything like that."

"That's okay. We can provide you with soap, shampoo, a toothbrush, and toothpaste. Razors are provided upon doctor's approval. Do you have any sharp items? Pen, pocketknife, pins?"

"Nope. If I really wanted to hurt myself, I'd have done it already. Ha."

The nurse was not amused. "My concern is for the safety of *all* patients," she said. "Do you wear a belt? If so, I'll need to take that as well." The question filled Samuel's head with grim images of patients hanging from the hospital rafters. "No," he said.

"Okay. If you could please bag up your belongings, we will store them until you are cleared to wear street clothes."

Samuel did so. The nurse took the bag and said, "If you'd like to come with me, I can show you around the ward." Samuel followed her out the door and back into the hall.

The first stop was the TV room. "This is where most patients choose to spend their time," the nurse said. The room was full of drugged and docile patients staring blankly at an inane music video. It was a spooky scene.

The nurse led Samuel down another hall, stopping in front of a large, empty dining room. "This is where meals are served," she said. "Dinner will be served very soon, at 4:30. Breakfast is at 7 AM, lunch at 11:30."

They moved on. "Here is the recreation room," the nurse said, stopping at a room with a bookshelf, couches, and a mini grand piano. Two elderly women were playing a silent game of chess. They looked up in unison at Samuel and the nurse.

"This is Sam," the nurse said. "Sam, this is Margaret and Lucy. Feel free to come here to relax, read, or play a game any time you aren't seeing your doctor or participating in a group session."

"Fresh meat! How sweet!" a voice reverberated down the hall. A young man was skipping toward Samuel and the nurse like a child playing a game of hopscotch. His hair was a shaggy brown rat's nest. Instead of a hospital gown, he wore Teenage Mutant Ninja Turtle pajamas.

"Hello, Graham," the nurse said as the young man approached. "We have a new patient on the ward. His name is Sam."

"Sam, Sam, Sam... wham, bam, thank you ma'am!"

Graham sang. Samuel was surprised to see that, upon closer inspection, Graham appeared to be in his late teens or early twenties – his infantile behavior could not hide the fact that he was in serious need of a shave.

"Hi," Samuel said.

"Hi!" Graham waved like a toddler. "Wanna play Transformers?"

"Maybe later, Graham. Let Sam settle in first, okay?" The nurse spoke to Graham patiently and with kindness. An exaggerated pout appeared on Graham's face. He began chewing on his fingernails. "Awww," he moaned, "you're mean."

"I'll play later," Samuel said. "I like Transformers." Graham immediately cheered up. "Sam, Sam, Sam... wham, bam, thank you ma'am!" he cried joyously as he skipped away down the hall.

"Graham has been with us for a while," the nurse said. "He can be a challenge, but he's a good... kid."

The nurse checked her watch. "That concludes the basic tour," she said. "Dinner will be served shortly. If you have any questions, I'd be happy to answer them."

"When does my treatment begin?" Samuel asked. "When will I see the doctor again?"

"There will be a team meeting in the morning – psychiatrists, psychologists, nurses, and social workers. The team will establish the best course of treatment based on your individual needs. I expect that you will meet with a doctor sometime after that. In the meantime, make yourself comfortable. Feel free to stay in your room or explore the ward, but you will need doctor's approval to leave this floor. If medication has been prescribed, you will receive it at mealtimes and before bed."

It was a lot to process. Samuel was beginning to feel more and more like a prisoner. He did feel safe, however. It was good to be somewhere other than his apartment, given the dark and disturbed thoughts rattling around in his head.

"Thank you," Samuel said. "If it's okay, I think I'll just rest in my room for now."

"That's an excellent idea," the nurse said. "If you need anything, just ask me or one of the other nurses at the desk." She gave Samuel a genuinely warm smile and returned to her post.

Samuel made his way back to his room. The curtain between his bed and his roommate's was still pulled across the space, the silhouette of the individual on the bed still visible. Samuel climbed onto his bed. Reclining, he folded his hands over his chest and closed his eyes. He attempted to clear his mind.

Samuel's thoughts wandered, retracing the series of events that had brought him from the brink of total collapse to this strange, new environment – from a close call with death by self-inflicted gunshot to a bed in a psychiatric ward. He wondered about the other patients of the institution – the stories, the pain, the tragedy, the madness...

"What are you in for?" called a voice from the other bed. It was his new roommate. An arm appeared and drew back the curtain. Samuel got his first look at the mysterious individual on the other side – a thin, bespectacled man with a shaven head. It took a moment for Samuel to realize that the man had also shaved off his eyebrows.

"Pardon me?" Samuel asked, slightly shocked at the man's appearance.

"What are you in for?" the man repeated. "Depression? Drugs? General insanity?"

"Oh..." Samuel hesitated. "Um... depression, I guess."

"Exactly what I thought!" the man said. "I can always tell." The man was clearly pleased with himself. "Suicidal?" he asked. The tone in his voice was casual. He could have been asking Samuel about his favorite sports team.

"I thought so, but I'm not so sure now," Samuel replied. "I guess if I really wanted to kill myself, I would have."

"Interesting," the man said, obviously not interested at all in Samuel's philosophical musings. "How were you going to do it? Pills? Rope? Gun? I cut my wrists, see?" The man displayed his wrists for Samuel. Both were wrapped in thick layers of gauze. "Did one and then, while it was gushing blood, used that hand to do the other. What a *mess!*" The man laughed. He was proud of his deed and enjoyed telling the story.

"Yikes."

"The doctors said they were the deepest cuts they had seen in a long time. I think they were really impressed!" The man stood up and extended his hand in greeting. "I'm Trevor, but my friends call me T-bone."

Samuel shook Trevor's hand very carefully, conscious of the wound on his wrist. He allowed his morbid imagination a moment to visualize the damage before introducing himself.

"I'm Sam."

"It's nice to meet you, Sam. You'll like it here."

"Nice to meet you, too."

Samuel returned to a reclined position. Trevor sat on the edge of his own bed.

"It's my family that did it. They drove me crazy." Trevor launched into his life story, oblivious to Samuel's reluctance to engage in deep conversation. "Parents divorced when I was two years old. Lived with mom after that and she drank like a damn fish. Know what I mean?"

"I think so..."

"She always had these awful, abusive men around," Trevor continued. "Got the shit kicked out of me constantly.

Really fucks ya up, y'know?"

"Listen, Trevor..."

"T-bone. Friends call me T-bone."

"Listen, T-bone, I'm really not feeling well. If you don't mind, I'm just going to lie here for a bit and try to nap."

"Don't want to miss dinner, do you?" Trevor's ability to pick up on social cues was severely lacking. "Gonna be served soon. You gotta eat."

"Yes, I know." Samuel was exasperated. "I just need a few minutes. It's been a long day. I am *really* tired."

"Oh, I understand!" Trevor exclaimed, sensing an opportunity to fill the air with his voice again. "My first day here was *brutal!* And don't forget, I was seriously injured! You should have seen the slices on my wrists... cut clear to the *bone.*"

Samuel closed his eyes. Trevor finally got the hint. "You should get some sleep, Sam." he said. "You'll definitely need your rest. This place will drive you crazy if you weren't already!"

"Of that I have no doubt," Samuel said. Trevor kept speaking, but Samuel filtered out the sound of his voice. Trevor's rambling speech faded... faded... until Samuel found a quiet mental space in which to linger. He lay there, peacefully suspended in the timeless place between sleep and wakefulness.

Just as Samuel was slipping into deep sleep, a shrill voice shattered his repose. "Time to *eat!*" shrieked Trevor in pure delight as he bounded by Samuel's bed and out the door. Dinner was being served in the dining room. Samuel was groggy, but hungry. He slid out of bed and shambled down the hall.

The ward was now a bustling hive of activity. Patients of both genders in a wide variety of ages and states of awareness were moving through the halls and congregating in the dining room. Samuel moved among them, feeling like a refugee from a distant land called Sanity.

Inside the dining room, food trays were already in place. Samuel approached the nearest tray. As he was about to seat himself in front of it, a woman with wild hair and vacant eyes pushed him out of the way. "Mine," she said.

Trevor was already seated and eating. He spotted Samuel. "Look for a tray with your name on it," he said. The other patients, who were already familiar with the meal time protocol, were quickly finding their assigned meals and settling into place. Samuel began examining the unclaimed trays and, sure enough, he found one with his name on it.

Samuel sat down and found himself facing a person wearing a rubber mask of Freddy Krueger, the supernatural villain from *A Nightmare on Elm Street*. The robust build and hairy hands of the individual indicated a male. The man was attempting to eat, spooning soup through the mouth hole. Some of the soup seemed to be reaching his mouth, but most of it was slopping and splattering down on to his hospital gown and the table. The man was staring directly at Samuel, his foggy, bloodshot eyes visible behind the mask.

"Hi, Freddy," Samuel said. The man offered no reply. Warm, chunky soup dripped from the rubber chin.

Seated beside Samuel was a young, petite, dark-haired girl. She was crouched over her food in a defensive posture, her right arm curled around the tray as if she were eating in a prison cafeteria. Samuel realized that she was weeping as she ate. Tears were raining down upon her food as she cried uncontrollably. She swallowed between bouts of violent shaking.

"Is everything okay?" Samuel was truly concerned. The young girl continued to sob as she ate, inconsolable and unreachable. The man in the Freddy Krueger mask decided to speak. "She never talks," he said. "She just cries all day...

*every* day."

Compassion and empathy stirred within Samuel's heart. For a moment, at least, his own troubles seemed trivial. He pondered what profound distress, what psychic horror, the young lady seated beside him must be experiencing. Samuel felt genuine sympathy for her and, at the same time, though he was mostly unaware of it, his own healing had begun. *I wish I could help you,* he thought. *I wish I could at least ease your pain.*

A very strange thing happened. Just as Samuel's thoughts turned to the young woman and his desire to alleviate her suffering, her weeping ceased. She looked up from her meal and said, in a voice barely above a whisper, "It's okay." The woman's mouth formed an almost imperceptible smile, and then the tears began to flow again as she returned to her meal.

Samuel went with the flow. He removed the plastic lid from his tray, exposing a meal of sliced turkey and vegetables. He began to eat, and was relieved to discover that the food was palatable.

Samuel dined on hospital food, surrounded by psychiatric patients with a vast spectrum of disorders and conditions. The collection of unusual minds gathered in the room formed a matrix, a mosaic, a tangibly skewed tapestry of strange proportions and oblique dimensions. Samuel felt like a node in a giant, diseased hive mind. Trevor's words returned to him: *This place will drive you crazy if you weren't already!*

A nurse was making rounds in the dining room, delivering medication to each patient. She reached Samuel and stopped. She examined the labels on the tiny cups she carried on a tray. Each cup contained an assortment of pills in a variety of sizes and colors. "I have your meds, Sam," she said, offering him a cup. Samuel was surprised that the doctor had acquired enough information in their first, brief session together to make an accurate diagnosis.

"What *are* those?" Samuel asked, peering into the cup. The nurse also carried a clipboard. She checked the attached paperwork. "The doctor has prescribed Effexor, an antidepressant, lithium carbonate, a mood stabilizer, and clonazepam for anxiety and to help with sleep. You will receive the Effexor and lithium now, and the clonazepam before bed."

"Wow," Samuel said. "That seems like a lot of drugs."

"That's a fairly typical regimen," the nurse said.

"Do I *have* to take the pills?"

The nurse gave Samuel a stern look. "To refuse your medication would be to go against the doctor's orders and that may jeopardize your future treatment. I recommend you take the pills now and discuss your concerns with the doctor when you see her next."

The nurse was persuasive. Samuel took the cup and washed the pills down with a gulp of water. "Good," the nurse said, and moved on to the next person. The other patients took their medication with no objections. Some had been eagerly anticipating pill time and gobbled up their meds happily.

Samuel finished his meal. He observed other patients placing their empty trays on a large, rolling, multilevel cart. He followed their lead and then wandered back out into the hall. Trevor approached. "Nasty meal, eh?" he exclaimed, slapping Samuel on the back playfully. "Greasy, rotten hospital food. Always tastes like sasquatch puke to me."

"It was actually not that bad," Samuel replied. "Best meal I've had in a long time, to be honest." That was the truth. In recent years, Samuel had not been taking very good care of himself. His diet consisted mostly of convenience store junk food.

"So, what kind of drugs are they giving you?" Trevor asked. "Anything good?"

"Psych meds. Pills I've never heard of. Standard stuff, according to the nurse."

"Hmm. Probably just antidepressants and lithium, maybe an anticonvulsant... some benzos if you're lucky. Those are nice."

"Benzos?"

"Benzodiazepine," Trevor responded instantly. It was clear to Samuel that Trevor had a vast and comprehensive knowledge of drugs. "Valium, basically. I take a lot for my anxiety. Couldn't function without it."

"Hmm." Samuel was completely uninterested in carrying on a conversation with Trevor. The two men stood in the hallway, facing each other in awkward silence, far past Samuel's threshold. Trevor was content to hover like a stubborn fly, with a silly grin planted on his face. "So," Samuel finally said. "I think I'm going to relax until bed."

"Going back to the room?" Trevor asked. The idea did not appeal to Samuel. He did not want to be trapped in a room with Trevor right now.

"No, gonna watch some TV for a bit." Samuel slipped away.

"Okay, I'll see you later, Sam!" Trevor called after him.

Through the open door, Samuel could see that the television room was once again full. It was clearly the most popular room on the ward. Rather than risking another encounter with Trevor, Samuel decided to take his chances among the media zombies.

Samuel entered the room. A large, outdated television bolted high up on one wall provided the only light. The patients, tightly packed on couches and chairs, basked in its dim glow. The television was still playing music videos.

Some patients were staring blankly at the screen, their eyes
glazed, their mouths agape. They appeared to be heavily
drugged.

On the screen, a nearly naked teenage girl gyrated and
twisted in an extremely sexually suggestive dance. The
nearly comatose patients drooled, their minds obliterated by
the potent chemicals coursing through their veins.

Moving through the room in search of an open seat,
Samuel noticed a man on a small couch situated at the back
of the room. The man was looking directly at Samuel in an
apparent state of awareness that contrasted sharply with the
dull mass of people surrounding him. The man smiled, put a
hand on the shoulder of the half-awake patient sitting beside
him, and gave a shove. The recipient of the not-so-gentle
push offered no resistance and simply slid off the couch,
ending up in a sitting position on the floor. The eyes of the
patient who had been pushed off the couch remained locked
on the television the entire time. The smiling man gestured to
the now open spot on the couch and beckoned Samuel over.

Samuel, slightly horrified – and slightly amused – sat
down beside the man. "Don't worry about the zombies," the
man said. "Make yourself at home."

"My name is Brian," the man said. "New here? First
time?"

"Yup," Samuel replied. "First time in a pysch ward...
and I'm not sure if I really belong here."

Before Samuel could elaborate on that statement,
Brian said, "Yes, you do. You are here for a reason. As soon
as I saw you, I knew that. I've been waiting for you,
actually."

"Oh?" Samuel said. *Here we go again,* he thought.

"I called for you," Brian said. "And here you are.
Welcome!"

Samuel laughed in spite of the seriously bizarre set of

circumstances that he had endured on this long, strange day. "You know, after all I've been through, that somehow doesn't surprise me," he said, shaking his head.

"You like this shit?" Brian asked, nodding at the television. The gyrating teenager on the screen had been replaced by a comically over-accessorized thug spouting incomprehensible words and gesturing menacingly while posing in front of a sports car.

"Nope. Can't stand it," Samuel replied.

"The zombies *love* it. Look at them eat it up!" With few exceptions, the other patients in the room were still staring blankly at the screen. Samuel felt bad for them.

Samuel made an attempt to change the subject. "How long have you been here?"

"A *long* time. Months. Cops brought me here involuntarily. They're trying to stop me from working. They think that by locking me up they can silence me, prevent the world from hearing my message. Ha! Ridiculous."

Brian turned to face Samuel fully, his eyes wide and radiating intensity. "Now that you are here, the work can truly begin," he said.

"What work?" Samuel asked reluctantly.

"You, my friend, are going to help me write my book – *the* book, *The Final Testament*. We are the chosen ones."

On the television screen, a group of young men sporting black t-shirts and trendy, ridiculous haircuts were pantomiming along to an insipid, tedious rock song. Brian instantly switched gears to comment on the video. "What a goddamn *joke* this music is!" he cried. "Look at these fucking *fools!*"

Brian's previous remarks still echoed in Samuel's head: *Chosen ones... Final Testament...*

"I grew up with *good* music," Brian continued, with a freshly summoned fiery passion. "Zep, Sabbath, Floyd... This new stuff is pure, unmitigated garbage. I'm serious. It makes me literally *sick*."

A nurse entered the room carrying a tray of pills in tiny cups. She made her way through the room, checking labels and administering medication to each patient in turn. She seemed to know everyone in the room.

She reached the couch where Brian and Samuel were sitting. "Hello, Brian," she said as she handed him his cup. "How are you this evening?"

"I'm good," Brian said, gobbling the pills in one gulp and washing them down with a sip of water poured from a jug the nurse carried. "I'm excellent, actually. One of my disciples arrived. Have you met him yet?" He was, of course, referring to Samuel.

"Who, Sam?" The nurse said. Samuel didn't recall meeting her, yet somehow she knew his name.

"Sam, Samuel... that's a good biblical name," Brian said. "Yes, he's one of my disciples. We were just talking about writing *The Final Testament*."

"I see," the nurse said, looking at Samuel and gauging his reaction to what Brian had just said. "And how does Sam feel about that?"

Samuel spoke up before Brian could reply. "Sounds like a fun project," he said, giving the nurse a subtle wink.

"Well then, that sounds just fine," the nurse said. "Sam, I have your evening medication."

The nurse handed Samuel his tiny cup. It contained one pill. "This will help you sleep," she said. Samuel swallowed it, washing it down with water the nurse poured into the empty paper cup. "Thank you," he said. The nurse moved on.

"How does it feel to be a disciple of the true messiah?" Brian asked. Samuel found himself playing along. "I suppose it feels... good," he said. "We've got a lot of work to do."

"Damn right, we do!"

A warm sensation was coming over Samuel. The pills were taking effect already. He felt very relaxed, at ease in his own body. All traces of anxiety dissolved. A pleasant, calming blanket of bliss wrapped around him. It was the most comfortable he had been, mentally and physically, in many years. *Wow,* he thought, *this is what contentment feels like.* For someone who had been deeply, clinically depressed for so long, it was like visiting an alien planet.

Samuel and Brian continued their conversation, though most of it was lost to the abyss. Drowsiness was quickly overcoming both of them. The medication was powerful. Soon they each retired to their respective rooms and succumbed to deep sleep. Samuel had survived his first day and night in a psychiatric ward.

Three days in, Samuel was fast adapting to life on a psychiatric ward. He began to appreciate the routine, the predictable flow of events, and the elimination of all distractions as he and the doctors focused solely on his mental health. His life had been simplified, his world reduced to a single floor of the hospital. He had even become accustomed to the unusual assortment of characters who populated the ward. They were brethren.

Samuel's body adapted to the chemicals he ingested. The effects were subtle, but the medication seemed to be working. He did, in fact, feel better. His mood had greatly improved, although it was difficult to determine whether it was a result of the pills or simply that the hospital was a safe environment. As a patient, his basic needs were taken care of. He was not required to make many decisions. He was now allowed to wear his own clothes, but his movement in and out of the hospital was still restricted. He was told when to eat and when to sleep.

On a deeper level, the doctors were regulating Samuel's emotions and perceptions through the drugs they prescribed. Unaware, he was becoming institutionalized. Scarier yet, he was losing control of his mind, having surrendered it to a team of psychiatrists and psychologists.

Once a day, Samuel met briefly with Dr. Harrison, the psychiatrist he had met upon admittance, to discuss how he was responding to the medication. As his tolerance increased, so did the dosage.

Group therapy sessions helped break up the monotony of the day. These were hosted by a team of psychologists and behavioral specialists, who explored treatment methods beyond the typical psychopharmacological approach. Samuel enjoyed the sessions.

What was conspicuously absent was an examination of the root causes of Samuel's depression. Psychoanalysis – deep penetration and thorough scrutiny of the hidden, inner workings of the mind – was not a real part of Samuel's treatment. There seemed to be an overemphasis – perhaps even complete reliance – on using drugs to treat each and every condition and disorder.

On the third evening of his stay, Samuel had just sat down to eat lunch when something extraordinary and terrifying happened. Seated in front of his assigned tray, across from an elderly man suffering from senile dementia, a new and frightening sensation suddenly washed over him. It was startling in its swift onset and intensity.

Lifting the plastic lid from his tray, Samuel observed roast beef and mashed potatoes, but the appearance of the meal was *off* somehow. The color of the food was too bright, too alive, too *real.* As he gazed at the food, struggling to understand why it suddenly looked so vibrant, so psychedelic, he heard a strange sound, like insects feeding on a fallen corpse in the forest. He looked up and realized instantly that it was the sound of the old man across from him eating, only it was magnified and distorted. It was the soundtrack to a nightmare.

Panic, pure and total, gripped Samuel's mind. *I've been dosed,* he thought. *Poisoned!* What he was experiencing felt just like a bad acid trip. The old man's face was now a warped mask of flesh, throbbing and morphing as Samuel watched. The entire room filled with an inexplicable cloud of dread and menace.

Samuel screamed. The other diners instantly stopped eating and froze. "Help! Help me!" Samuel cried. He was freaking out. A quiet lady with whom Samuel had never spoken before was sitting next to him. "You're having a panic attack," she said calmly.

"I've been poisoned! What are you people giving me?"

The lady seated beside him remained stoic. "Put your head between your legs and breathe, deeply and slowly." It sounded like good advice. Samuel began doing just that. Finally, a nurse arrived.

"What's wrong, Sam?" the nurse asked.

"He's having a panic attack," the woman beside him said.

"I'm fucking tripping out!" Samuel shrieked, his head still between his legs. He continued taking long, deep breaths.

"Take it easy, Sam," the nurse said. "Everything is fine."

"No, it's *not!*" Sam was hysterical. "The goddamn drugs you're giving me are *poison!* I want out of this fucking place!" A scene such as the one currently playing out in the dining room was far from unusual. It was, after all, a psychiatric ward. The vast majority of the other diners completely ignored Sam's outburst and continued eating.

"Sam, would you like to lie down in your room?" The nurse remained calm as she made the suggestion. Samuel began to cry. "I want to go home," he said, getting out of his seat. The nurse led him out of the dining room.

In the hall, Samuel's episode continued. He looked at the nurse and saw a mad scientist, or perhaps a deranged butcher, leading him to a dark dungeon somewhere in the bowels of the hospital, full of torture implements and certain, excruciating doom. "What are you going to do to me?" he begged.

The nurse's expression never changed, but to Samuel's eyes, in the condition he was in, things were moving beneath her skin – bugs, alien parasites, *creatures* – causing her face to bubble and stretch in obscene ways. Samuel moaned. "Water," he gasped. "I need water. I think I'm dying."

"You aren't dying," the nurse reassured him. "You might be having a reaction to the medication, but it will pass. You'll be just fine." Her words were the antidote. Just like that, Samuel began to feel better. He still felt like he was on a psychedelic trip of some sort – colors were still too vivid and the walls seemed to breathe, but the panic had dissipated.

The nurse brought Samuel to his room. He sat on the bed and she brought him a cup of water. He drank it and felt better still. "Whew," he sighed, "I think this medication is too strong for me. I really thought I was going to pass out, or freak out... or maybe die. I couldn't breathe! I don't think I've ever been so scared in my life."

"That sounds exactly like a panic attack," the nurse said. It was the first time Samuel had ever experienced one. "I guess I was in the right place, then!" he said, the irony not completely lost to him.

From behind the extended curtain between beds, a shrill voice called out: "Yup, sounds like a panic attack!" Trevor pulled back the curtain and inserted himself into the moment. "I should know," he continued. "I've been having them my whole life. A real pain in the ass!"

Samuel groaned internally. *I'm too high for this*, he thought.

"Hello, Trevor," the nurse said. "How are you today?"

"Today has been better," Trevor replied. He held his bandaged wrists out for the nurse and Samuel to see. "Not as much pain in my wrists, but I'm still having negative thoughts. I don't think I'm ready to be discharged quite yet."

"That's something you need to discuss with your doctor," the nurse said.

"Will I be seeing her today?" Trevor asked. "I think my lorazepam needs to be increased."

"I don't know, Trevor," the nurse replied, exasperated. "Right now, I'm tending to Samuel. He isn't feeling well."

"I'm okay... I think," Samuel said.

"He'll be fine," Trevor said. "It was just a panic attack. I almost *died!*"

"Yes, I know," the nurse said.

"Really, I think I'll be fine," Samuel insisted. His sense perceptions were quickly returning to normal. The iridescent tracers and disorienting visual vibrations had disappeared. The sound reaching his ears no longer carried an unsettling, demonic resonance. He still felt lightheaded – a little giddy and short of breath – but he no longer felt in imminent danger of losing his mind. For a few moments there, Samuel *did* feel his grip on reality, and his very identity, slipping away.

"I'd really like to step outside and get some fresh air," Samuel said.

"Are you sure you're allowed to do that?" Trevor said.

"I'm not a prisoner," Samuel snapped.

"I'll have to check your file," the nurse said. "Before you can leave the ward you need clearance from your doctor."

"He could be a danger to himself... or others," Trevor said.

"I'm not going to hurt myself – or anyone else. I just need air and sun... and a few minutes to gather myself. The walls of this place are starting to close in on me."

"Trips off ward need to be cleared with your doctor," the nurse reiterated. "Leaving the hospital against doctor's advice could jeopardize your treatment."

"I've heard that before," Samuel said. "Forget it. I'll take a nap or something."

"That's an excellent idea. If you need anything, let me know." The nurse left the room.

Trevor was sitting on his bed staring at Samuel. Despite the lack of eyebrows, Trevor still managed to convey a look of serious concern. "What happened to you?" he asked.

"I think I had a bad reaction to the medication," Samuel said, lying down on his bed. "Scary stuff. Felt like I was on LSD or something."

"That happened to me when I first started taking antidepressants." It was virtually impossible for Trevor to avoid talking about himself at every opportunity. "Zoloft, I think. Or was it Effexor? Maybe Celexa or Prozac. Actually, now that I think about it, I think it was Cymbalta."

It was too tedious for Samuel. He had to escape. "You know, I doubt I'll be able to sleep," he said, rising from the bed. "Gonna find a book to read." He was out the door and halfway down the hall before Trevor had a chance to respond. He went directly to the lounge.

The staff called the recreation lounge the 'quiet room.' On this day, however, Samuel could hear someone playing the piano as he approached. The music was loud and wild. It sounded like someone was bashing the keys randomly and singing – screeching – at the tops of their lungs in accompaniment. Samuel hesitated at the door before deciding to enter.

Brian, the self-anointed prophet, was seated at the piano. He was flailing and bobbing, his eyes closed, as he hammered passionately and relentlessly on the keys. The music was awful, the lyrics asinine. He was, apparently, making it up as he went along. *"Gonna lead 'em to the promised land, gonna hold 'em in a mighty hand..."* Brian sang on, unaware that someone had entered the room.

"Sounds good," Samuel lied as he took a seat in an easy chair by the window. Brian opened his eyes. "Thanks, man," he said, still poking at keys arbitrarily. "I'm working on an album. It'll be released at the same time as *The Final Testament.* The faithful will be able to listen to the songs while they read the truth – a full, sensory experience!"

Brian finally, mercifully, stopped playing and turned on the piano stool to face Samuel. "How have you been, brother?" he asked. Samuel had to seriously ponder the question before he could answer. He had not fully recovered from his drug-induced delirium. The world still retained a surreal veneer. "It's been a weird day," he said at last.

Brian smiled knowingly and nodded. "Three days in, right?"

"Yes."

"I bet you've been experiencing some unusual... sensations. Freaky, psychedelic stuff. True?"

"That is true," Samuel said with a hint of trepidation.

"You probably think the feelings are a side effect of the medication they're giving you – at least, that's what the doctors and nurses are going to say." Brian leaned in, his face stern, his eyes steely. "Don't believe them," he whispered.

"Uh, okay... but I *did* have a reaction to the pills, I think..."

Brian laughed heartily. "No, my brother, it wasn't the pills," he said. "You've been reborn. Three days ago the old you perished and then you were resurrected. Welcome to Christ consciousness. You now inhabit an astral body as well as a vessel of flesh and bone."

Samuel opened his mouth in an attempt to reply, but no words came. He simply stared at Brian, baffled, a quizzical expression stamped on his face.

"How does it feel?" Brian asked. "Is this your first miracle?"

Gazing out the window at the world beyond the hospital walls, Samuel sighed. He had a sudden urge to jump right through the glass. He visualized himself hitting the street running, not stopping until he was far, far away from the psych ward – far from hyper-religious and perhaps dangerously delusional Brian, far from the unsettling sickness percolating within Trevor's shaven head, far from the nurses and doctors and pills. The madness was viral. The depression that had originally brought him in seemed tame in comparison.

Brian was still preaching, still delivering his impassioned, lunatic sermon: "*The Final Testament* will be the last book ever written. It is the final chapter of human history, in this world and the next. You and I will finally reveal the hidden truth of this existence – of *all* existence, spanning this dimension and a vast multitude of others. Aren't you *excited?* The time for the ultimate revelation is upon us... and you and I are messengers! We've been chosen."

"Amazing," Samuel said, still fantasizing about his grand escape. He settled for a minor evasion. "Listen, Brian, I'm still not feeling well. I think I'll try to get some sleep."

"I understand. Resurrection is a painful, tiring process. Go rest. Tomorrow we'll start writing."

"Okay, see ya." Samuel was on his way out of the room before Brian could finish.

"Bless you, brother." Brian made some obscure gesture of anointment that Samuel neither recognized nor understood.

In the hall, Samuel's sense of confinement increased. An anxious restlessness grew within him. To his horror, he could feel another panic attack approaching. Its arrival was preceded by an awful tingling at the back of his head – an unpleasant throb deep within his brain – and a cold shudder like the embrace of an invisible, icy specter. Before the wave of panic overwhelmed and immobilized him, Samuel rushed down the hall toward the nurses' desk.

"It's happening again," he said to the first nurse he encountered, his breath short, his brow sweating.

"What is, Sam?" the nurse asked.

"The drugs..." Samuel stammered. "I'm freaking out again. Whatever it is you guys are giving me here, it's too strong. I'm having a bad reaction."

"Would you like some water? Have you tried lying down?"

"I want to see a doctor. I want to feel like myself again."

"Your doctor is currently unavailable."

"I'm losing my mind!" Samuel shouted. "Don't you understand what I'm telling you? *I want to see a fucking doctor!*" The outburst caught the attention of every nurse and patient within earshot. All sound and motion on the ward suddenly ceased. All eyes were upon Samuel.

"Sam, you need to relax," the nurse said, rising slowly. "I can't do anything for you if you're agitated." Tears were beginning to well in Samuel's eyes. "Please, help me," he whimpered.

"I can give you something to calm you down," the

nurse said. "I see here the doctor has prescribed Ativan for you, to be taken as needed."

"No more drugs!" Samuel protested. His body was vibrating, as if electrified by an unseen power source. His brain was buzzing with psychedelic impressions. The last thing he wanted was to ingest more chemicals.

"Then I suggest you lie down and do some breathing exercises," the nurse stated bluntly.

*What am I doing here?* Samuel thought. He walked away from the nurses' desk without another word. At the door to his room he looked in and saw Trevor in his usual spot on the far bed, reading a magazine and absentmindedly running a hand over his bald head.

Samuel made an instant decision. Instead of entering the hospital room, he kept walking down the hall, all the way to the big doors which separated the psychiatric ward from the rest of the hospital. A nurse saw him as he reached out to push the doors open. "Where are you going, Sam?" she asked. "Are you allowed to leave the ward?"

Samuel stopped to face her. "Yes," he simply said.

Samuel walked right out of the hospital and into the open air of a cool evening. He had not been outside in three days. The fresh air was invigorating. The hallucinatory fog in Samuel's head began to lift. He moved his legs. He moved his arms. His body responded to the commands his brain issued. He was *alive*... and knew it.

Falling into a comfortable stride, Samuel tuned into his surroundings. He felt an intimate connection to the world around him – a renewed appreciation for nature, for the city he lived in and its inhabitants, for his body and mind... and for life itself. Something gentle and glorious stirred within him. Samuel looked up at the night sky. It appeared to him, in this moment of awakening, to be wide open to the space beyond, as if the atmosphere had bled away, leaving the

cosmos bare and exposed. The stars were so bright and close
that they seemed to be hovering mere feet above him. His
thoughts rose from his head and expanded until they filled
the universe... and the universe filled him.

Samuel kept walking until he reached his apartment
building. It may have taken hours or a single instant, he could
not be sure. He entered the building and went to his
apartment. It was as he had left it, yet it seemed so
unfamiliar. His furniture and possessions were exactly where
they should have been. He could even see the remains of the
last meal that he had prepared before leaving for the hospital
sitting undisturbed on the table. The blank canvas still hung
on the wall. The gun still sat under the papers on the end
table.

It was he himself, Samuel realized, who had changed.
Where once he felt only despair and emptiness, he now felt
hope and purpose. Drive and determination replaced
apathetic lethargy. Confidence replaced insecurity. He had
been to the edge – the very brink of destruction – and had
fought his way back to the light, along the way discovering
the strength and resiliency of his character. *Perhaps*, he
thought, *I've been resurrected after all.*

Inspired like never before, Samuel approached the
blank canvas hanging on the wall. He was no longer
intimidated by its empty, white surface. Instead, he saw it for
what it truly was – a wide open expanse of infinite creative
possibilities. He picked up a brush, opened a tube of acrylic
color, and began to paint.

# Paradigm Shift

There are moments in life that are so significant, so momentous, that they completely alter one's perspective on the world. These moments serve as demarcation points, effectively separating the life of the individual into two distinct parts – life before the event and life after. Today, I experienced such an event and, though it has only been a few hours since the occurrence, it is already clear to me that from this day forward, my life will never be the same. Paradigm shift, reality upheaval, worldview or belief system reassessment – call it what you will – I have been changed. It's a story worth telling, so I am going to do just that. Bear with me. It's going to be a weird and wild ride.

  I had classes this morning, just like I do every Monday. I'm in my second year at the university and my course load is heavy. The first unusual thing that happened to me today was that I woke up much earlier than I normally do. It was still dark out and my alarm wasn't set to go off for a few hours. I tried to get back to sleep, but I was already wide awake. I tossed and turned for a while before deciding to just get out of bed. My roommate was still fast asleep. I think he was out late last night partying – no real surprise there. I could hear him snoring away as I went down the hall of our apartment to the kitchen. I put on some coffee and sat at the table.

  The nice thing about where we live is that we have a great view. The apartment building is on a hill and we are on the top floor. From our kitchen, we can see the school and most of the sprawling campus, which sits on a lake. It's actually quite scenic.

When the coffee was ready, I poured a cup and sat gazing out the window. The sun had just begun to come up. I was admiring the sight when I noticed something – a bright light slowly descending from the sky directly above the auditorium. It was clearly visible, a bluish-white point of illumination flashing in a strobe-like manner. It was interesting, but the sunrise was so beautiful that I didn't pay too much attention to the falling light. Considering what happened later in the day and what I know now, I should have. The light seemed to disappear behind the building and I forgot about it.

I still had time to kill before my first class and, to be honest, I didn't want to be around when my roommate woke up and starting babbling about the crazy things he and his drunken frat boy friends had done the night before, so I gathered my stuff and left. I thought it would be a good opportunity to do some studying in the library. By the time I got outside, the sun was up. I felt good. It was nice to get an early start. The streets were quiet as I walked toward campus. It was serene and peaceful being out before most of the city had woken up.

When I got to the campus, I headed directly to the library. There were still very few people around, but I did notice a procession of vehicles moving toward the administration building – a line of black sedans with blacked-out windows. Again, I really didn't think much about it and just continued on my way. My mind was on a paper I had been working on. I was composing sentences and arranging paragraphs in my head. Who knew then that the writing I would end up doing today would be so much more interesting than that sterile academic stuff! Right now, my fingers are having a hard time even keeping up with the flow of thoughts. I must try to get this down before I forget the details.

Once I got to the library, I went to my favorite spot – an isolated desk by a window at the very back of the building. I pulled out my reference material and notebook and started into it. For some reason, it was a struggle. I could not seem to express what I was trying to say. Everything I tried failed. My ideas would not coalesce, the words would not work. Perplexed by my lack of productivity, I became frustrated. I knew that I needed to clear my head, so I decided to stretch my legs. Sometimes it helps if I step away from what I am doing and then return to it with a fresh perspective.

My plan was to go for a walk along the lake, but when I got outside, a sign posted by the entrance to the library caught my attention. I hadn't noticed it before. The sign announced the appearance of a guest speaker that very morning in the auditorium. The name and face of the speaker were very familiar to me, but it took a few moments before I remembered where I had heard of the individual. Then it came to me – the man was a researcher and speaker on some really out-there topics, like UFOs, aliens, government cover-ups, and other strange conspiracies. I had heard of the guy on the internet but had never really paid much attention to what he had said – or what he was selling. I'm a pretty skeptical guy when it comes to stuff like that. The sign said he was on a special tour of universities and that he had new and exciting information to share. I assumed it was a new book he was pushing, but for some reason, I was still curious. According to the sign, the talk was about to start. My paper was giving me grief and I still had time before class, so I thought, why not check it out? At the very least it could be good for a laugh, right? I'll tell you – I'm not laughing now.

For an early morning presentation, there were a surprising number of students gathered in the auditorium when I arrived. I'm not sure how many of them were there to hear the speaker and how many were there just to hang out, but there had to be over a hundred people in the room. As I recall, the man who was scheduled to present has a large online presence and a fairly loyal following of conspiracy geeks and UFO fanatics, but I was surprised to see so many people in attendance. I don't know how many true-believers there were, but I'm sure certain members of the audience – me included – were there simply out of curiosity... or for some laughs.

On the floor of the auditorium there was a small stage with a podium and a microphone. A large screen had been erected on the wall behind the stage. The stage was empty and the screen was blank. There was some quiet murmuring in the audience, but most of the students had their heads down and their eyes firmly planted on their phones and tablets. For some reason, I was drawn to an empty seat in the front row directly in front of the stage. Looking back now, I realize how out of character that was for me. I generally like to sit near the back when I attend a speech or lecture, but this time, I sat front and center. Perhaps I just didn't want to sit among the other students. The truth is, I have a hard time relating to most of them. Perhaps, on the other hand, I was guided by intuition or some other mysterious force. Well, for whatever reason, I sat at the front only ten feet or so from the stage.

The speaker entered the auditorium. He walked onto the stage and approached the podium. There was a small smattering of applause, but most people did not acknowledge his entrance or even look up from their devices. The lackluster welcoming did not faze the speaker. He carried himself with a confident swagger and had an intense, serious expression on his face. He immediately began to speak.

"Hello," he said. "Thank you for joining me this morning. I think you will find this presentation informative and enlightening." The speaker pushed a button on a remote control that had been sitting on the podium. An image appeared on the screen behind him. It was an old and rather famous black and white photograph of a UFO – or flying saucer, as they were called in the days when the photo was taken. It's an image I had seen before and was intrigued by, despite my skepticism. The resolution and detail were quite impressive for a picture nearly 60 years old.

"I'm sure many of you have seen this photograph," the speaker said. "It is one of the earliest pictures of a UFO. It has been the subject of debate for decades. The object shown in this image resembles no known aircraft, then or now. It was taken by a respected and trusted senior member of the Air Force. It is not a hoax. It is a real picture of a real craft."

The speaker used the remote control to switch the picture on the screen to that of another famous shot of a UFO. This photograph was a full-color close-up of a flying disk over a field. It was one I had not seen. The clarity of the image was astounding. "This is not a hoax, either," the speaker said. "It looks too good to be true, but it's real. As is this..."

The speaker began cycling through photographs, each more convincing than the last. "And this... and this... These are actual pictures of unknown flying objects – unknown to the general public, at least. There are those in positions of power who have always known exactly what these things are... but more on that later."

The speaker now had my full attention. He had a commanding, convincing presence and the material was entertaining and totally fascinating. I looked around and was dismayed to see that most of the other students were disengaged. The majority of them were still fiddling with their phones or tablets. Some of the students were taking 'selfies' – obsessively, it seemed, one after the other. Between each shot they would check the result and then pose again, puckering their lips in a ridiculous and totally unattractive pout and making small adjustments to the angle of their head. I even noticed a few people yawning. Their loss, I thought.

The speaker used the remote control to dash through a long series of photographs of UFOs in rapid fire. Not all of them were disks. He showed pictures of ships that looked like luminous spheres, large cylinders, massive black triangles, and some that were shaped like acorns or bells. So many pictures at such a fast rate – I could not process them all. The speaker suddenly stopped his machine gun slide show and froze on an unsettling image. I recognized it instantly as the face and upper torso of a so-called 'Grey' alien, immediately identifiable and incredibly realistic. Was it a photo or CGI image? I couldn't tell. The bulbous head, large, black, insectoid eyes, tiny nose, and slit-like mouth of the creature were shown in life-like detail.

"I'm sure most of you are familiar with this little fella," the speaker said. "A typical, garden-variety Grey alien. We've all been conditioned to accept that this is what an extraterrestrial looks like. When we think of an alien, we think of this. I am here to tell you that we have been lied to. This little guy is nothing more than a standard psy-op, a diversionary tactic to steer you away from the truth. Would you like to know the truth?"

The speaker paused, waiting for a response. Aside from a few murmurs and shrugs, he was largely ignored. Those who weren't locked on their cell phones simply looked at him blankly. Impulsively and sympathetically, I answered him. "Yeah," I said, "I would like to know the truth."

The speaker heard me. He looked me in the eyes, smiled, and said, "Good. That's what I like to hear."

I'm not sure why I spoke up like that. I think I just wanted the presenter to know that *someone* was following his talk and was interested in what he had to say. I'm still surprised that more people weren't curious. It was fascinating stuff! The speaker continued, unaffected by the ambivalence of his young audience.

"I am here today to make an announcement," the speaker said. "This lecture tour is for purely educational purposes and has nothing to do with selling a new book or video. I am not here to obfuscate the truth of the UFO and alien phenomenon by adding yet another theory or angle to the bloated subject. I have been tasked with a simple assignment – disclose the facts. What I am about to reveal has been known to a select few for a very long time, but due to the sensitive nature of the material, it has been kept secret. Those in power believed people simply weren't ready to receive this information. Political, psychological, and religious factors made disclosure a dangerous prospect. However, the cultural climate of the world has changed and it has been decided that the general population is now ready for the truth."

Talk about an effective set-up! I was totally riveted. I glanced around again and was shocked to see that most of the other students were *still* completely preoccupied with their gadgets. Such a self-absorbed, vain, narcissistic, narrow-minded group... Sometimes I fear for my generation.

"The truth is simple," said the man at the podium. "Aliens are real." The speaker paused, waiting for a response from the crowd. A few people shuffled in their seats. There was scattered murmuring and a cough or two. Someone behind me yawned loudly. Overall, the audience barely reacted.

"Yes, aliens are real and they have been with us for a long time. They have, in fact, always been with us. But this," The speaker gestured toward the image of the Grey alien on the screen behind him, "is not what they look like. Here is a photograph of a real alien." The speaker pushed a button on the remote and the picture of the Grey was replaced by that of another humanoid entity, equally as bizarre.

The creature on the screen looked like a cross between a catfish and a man. It had two very expressive, very human, eyes. To me, they conveyed kindness, intelligence, and even a touch of playfulness. I was startled by the personality and character expressed in those eyes. The creature had a nose, but it was small and vaguely feline. The bottom portion of its face was the most unusual feature. Its mouth was large and fish-like and, despite the lack of lips, it seemed to be gently smiling. Stringy tendrils of skin dangled from its jaw like the whiskers of a catfish. The creature's skin was a very light shade of green, with hints of pink. It had long, flowing, silvery hair that obscured the creature's ears. I stared at the vivid and detailed image. Was it real? Was this another elaborate ruse? My mind recoiled and struggled to grasp what the speaker had just said and what I was now seeing.

"This particular individual," the speaker said, "is a good friend of mine. He enjoys blues music, long walks in the woods, Italian food, the occasional glass of red wine, and has a wickedly dry sense of humor. He is very obviously not human, but here's another secret – he is not from another planet. He and his kind are Earthlings, just like you and me. They have lived alongside our race since the dawn of time. We must accept the fact that we share this planet with other intelligent beings."

"What a load of shit," I heard a dude in a Greek-lettered shirt say.

"This is so, like, *dumb*," a gum-chewing girl in a too-tight sweater said.

"That thing is fuckin' *ugly!*" shouted some guy near the back. A burst of laughter from the mob followed. At this point, people began to leave the auditorium. I guess it was too much for most of them to accept... or maybe they were just bored. I stayed in my seat, eager to hear more. I wasn't totally convinced of the veracity of the presenter's claims, but I couldn't dismiss them entirely.

The man at the podium calmly watched as a large portion of the audience cleared out. He waited for the commotion to subside before speaking again: "To those of you who have chosen to remain, thank you. I am well aware that this is bizarre material. All I ask is that you keep an open mind and consider what I am revealing to you as a *possibility*. Think and decide for yourself."

While the man spoke, I found myself staring at the image of the creature on the screen, wondering what it would be like to actually meet it... or *him*, or whatever. I studied its features and allowed my imagination to wander. Would I be scared in its presence? Would I be in awe? Would it be possible to have a conversation? What would we discuss? The more I pondered it and the more I visualized an actual encounter, the more real it became for me.

At this point, I snapped out of my reverie. The presenter was now speaking about the long history of interactivity between the catfish creature's race and our own. He gave some compelling examples of their presence and the influences of their race, going all the way back to prehistory. According to the speaker, they had contributed in profound ways to nearly every aspect of civilization, even though the vast majority of people have been – and will remain – totally unaware of their existence. The man at the podium then said something that gave me the creeps: "Some of you have encountered these entities and were totally unaware. There may be some here on this campus right now."

That statement struck a nerve. A very strange sensation came over me – a sudden feeling of intense psychological distress. I'm not sure what happened, but it was as if the speaker's words had unlocked something buried in my subconscious – a hidden subroutine, a concealed sensory mechanism. My body broke out in a cold sweat and I began to tremble. My breathing became erratic and shallow. My head tingled and a weird pressure built in my skull, making my eyes throb. I inhaled and exhaled slowly, deeply, in an attempt to avert an imminent panic attack. I was successful.

I looked up to see the speaker scanning those who had remained in their seats with an amused sparkle in his eye. "Yes," he said, "there may, in fact, be such entities in this very room."

The words prompted me to turn to look at the people around me. I was alone in the front row. My eyes passed over the empty seats to my left as my neck slowly swiveled. There was a young woman sitting behind me a few rows back. Sitting in the seat next to her, as obvious as could be, was one of the catfish-men. The creature was dressed in contemporary and fashionable men's attire. It sat in a relaxed and confident posture, as if it didn't have a care in the world. The woman in the adjacent seat seemed to be entirely unaware of its presence. The creature returned my gaze and smiled. Skin tendrils dangling from its cheeks twitched.

For many moments, I could only stare. Had the creature been there the entire time? Why hadn't I noticed it before? The bizarre entity grew tired of my ogling. It made a frustrated gesture with its hands, shook its head, and looked away. The actuality of what I was perceiving was beginning to sink in. I looked around at the other people still gathered in the auditorium and was not surprised to see more of the catfish humanoids seated among them. There were just as many of *them*, it seemed, as us. I also realized then that I was not the only human who had begun seeing the creatures. There were a few other equally astounded students looking around the room. Like me, they seemed to be more amazed than frightened at the seemingly instant manifestation of the entities. Some people, I noticed, still had utterly blank expressions on their faces as they continued mindlessly playing with their hand-held gadgets.

"A small minority of you, I suspect, are beginning to understand," the man at the podium said. "The world you thought you inhabited is largely an illusion. There are many aspects of reality that are beyond the scope and grasp of what you have been conditioned to believe. I represent a group of people who feel that the human race is now ready to accept certain truths that were once too much for our immature species to handle. It may take time to adjust to the new reality... and some never will, unfortunately. For those who do, the future will be a very exciting time indeed. Our two races still have much to learn from each other."

I sat in stunned silence as the speaker concluded his lecture. When he was finished, enlivened chatter filled the auditorium. Students – human and catfish-kind alike – rose from their seats. Those who were unaware of what was happening around them filed out of the auditorium, somehow managing to walk while keeping their eyes fixed on their mobile devices. Those of us who could now see the entities among us lingered near our seats, unsure of how to proceed with our day-to-day existences. Finally, after an awkward minute of uncertainty and apprehension, I decided to act. I approached the nearest creature, held out my hand, and introduced myself.

# The Great Divide

"This world has gone totally insane."

Harlan roughly crumpled the newspaper he had been reading and shoved it aside. He picked up his coffee cup from the kitchen table and drank down its remaining contents in one large gulp.

"What's that, honey?" Kate, his wife, called from the living room.

"Oh, nothing," Harlan replied. "Just the same old nonsense. I feel like I'm living in the Dark Ages sometimes."

"Have you been reading the paper again? I thought you were going to cancel your subscription. All it does is agitate you."

"You're probably right... but how else am I going to find out what's going on in the world?"

"Step outside. See for yourself."

Harlan glanced up at the clock on the wall and sighed. "I guess it's about time, isn't it? I wish I could just take the day off and stay home with you and Spencer."

Kate walked into the room. She carried their three-year-old son Spencer in her arms. "It's Friday," she smiled. "One more day to go. Let's do something fun this weekend."

"That sounds good to me. I'm burned out. I need a vacation."

"Is that new client still giving you a hard time?"

"Yeah. These young guys – they want to finagle and negotiate every little detail. They enter the workforce as if society *owes* them success. A bunch of arrogant, entitled children, if you ask me."

"You're starting to sound bitter. Those guys can't be

much younger than you."

"True, I just feel so... out of sync. I have a hard time relating to most of the people I encounter. And now, with all this heated political stuff going on, it's worse than ever. Most of the time I just smile and nod and try not to say anything that might show a particular political alignment. These are crazy times we live in."

Kate nodded thoughtfully. "I do know what you mean. I can't watch TV at all anymore. The rhetoric is just too much... from both sides. I don't know what to believe."

"Don't believe any of it."

Harlan stood up and gathered his keys, wallet, and briefcase. Kate followed him to the front door, still holding Spencer in her arms. Harlan embraced his wife and child and kissed them both on the forehead. "You two have a good day, okay? Don't give your mother too hard a time, little buddy. We're going to have some fun when I get home."

Harlan stepped out the door and into the warm, early morning air. The smell of orange blossoms and the chirping of birds greeted him. Spring in Phoenix – before the brutal, oppressive heat sinks in – is magical. For a moment, Harlan forgot the pressures of his job and the turmoil of the world. As he got into his car, he breathed in deeply and savored the scents and sounds of his quiet neighborhood in the North Valley.

Harlan pulled out of the driveway and turned on the car radio. It was tuned to a popular local station that played primarily classic rock. On this morning, however, he did not hear music coming from his speakers. Instead, the announcer was rambling on about a recent topical issue that had stirred up heated national debate. Harlan listened for all of ten seconds before turning the radio off in disgust. He drove on in silence.

A few miles from home, Harlan reached the interstate

that would take him south to the downtown office building in which he worked. He waited at the light until it was his turn to merge and then he was absorbed into the crawling mass of cars that streamed along like a column of ants. He glanced around at the other drivers. They all seemed to share the same exhausted, defeated expressions on their faces as they inched their way along. Harlan rolled his window down and leaned on his elbow.

Just ahead, on the shoulder to Harlan's right, two cars were pulled over. There had apparently been a minor accident, which was not at all a surprise. Accidents were, in fact, quite common – especially on a Friday, when people were tired and distracted by their weekend plans. As Harlan approached, he looked over with muted interest. The drivers of the two vehicles involved in the minor fender bender were in a heated discussion. The taller of the two men was jabbing a finger in the smaller one's face. The shorter one was holding his ground, his chest puffed out and his fists balled at his side. They were both livid and yelling loudly.

"Geez, guys," Harlan said to himself, "take it easy."

To Harlan's eyes, the damage to either vehicle did not seem too severe. The men, middle-aged and relatively well-dressed, seemed to be comically overreacting. This, too, was not uncommon. Harlan had seen some absurd behavior from drivers on the freeway.

The traffic had slowed to a creeping roll, and Harlan now found himself directly beside the quarreling men. While Harlan was observing, the encounter quickly turned violent and, to his surprise, the shorter of the two men suddenly lunged at the larger man, knocking him down. The short man jumped on the fallen man and began viciously attacking him. It was like nothing Harlan had ever seen – the short man punched, bit, and tore at his victim relentlessly, shrieking inhumanly the entire time. Blood and dirt flew in the furious onslaught.

The larger man fought back. He pushed his aggressor off and then came at him swinging. Harlan could hear the man's punches landing with dull thuds and an awful crunching that made his stomach turn. Harlan became aware that the people in the cars around him were also watching, but instead of stopping to help or attempting to end the fight, they were cheering and laughing at the brutal spectacle.

As the violence increased, so did the excitement of the ogling commuters. Harlan began to get nervous. No one was doing anything to stop the fight, and the fight was getting gruesome. The larger man now had his opponent on the ground. To Harlan's absolute horror, the man on top picked up a large rock from the ground beside him and brought it down hard on the other man's head, killing him instantly. The drive-by audience roared.

*What is going on?!* Harlan thought. *That man is dead and no one tried to help him. In fact, these people liked it! Where are the police?*

Feeling sick, helpless, and totally horrified, Harlan pulled his cell phone out of his pocket and shakily called 911. Traffic had started slowly moving again, forcing him to drive on.

"911, what is your emergency?"

"Hi, I'm southbound on the 51, just past Lincoln Drive, and I think I just witnessed a murder."

"We already have people en route, sir. Thank you for calling."

"Okay, good. I wasn't sure if anyone else was going to call. A lot of people were just watching and not –"

The line went dead. Harlan looked at his phone to confirm that the call had ended and then set the device down in the center console. He was still shaking and his heart was racing. What he had seen had disturbed him deeply. He made a quick, impulsive decision – as soon as he reached the nearest exit, he pulled off the freeway. Once on the surface streets, he found a quiet, shady place to park beneath a palm tree. He shut off the car's engine, leaned back in his seat, and rubbed his eyes, as if subconsciously trying to wipe away the dreadful vision of the assault.

After he had regained his composure, Harlan sat up straight and started the car. "There's no way I'm going to be able to work today," he muttered. He was going to turn around and go home. He would deal with the consequences later.

Coming up the sidewalk now, on the other side of the street, was a young woman. She was staring at her cell phone while she walked, completely unaware of a man who was quickly approaching from behind. Nothing seemed out of the ordinary, until the man, who looked like a transient to Harlan, was within a few feet of the woman – without warning, he pounced on her. The woman screamed and flailed as the scruffy figure wrapped an arm around her neck and began choking her from behind.

"Hey!" Harlan shouted as he instinctively jumped out of his vehicle. "Let her go!"

The transient, still clutching the terrified woman, looked at Harlan with a strange, distorted expression and began to howl manically. Harlan, emboldened by the fear on the woman's face, briskly crossed the street to confront the obviously insane assailant. As Harlan approached, the transient released his grip on the young woman, who jumped out of reach as soon as she was able. The homeless man dropped to his hands and knees and barked like an animal.

"Be careful!" the woman cried. "He's crazy!"

"Are you okay?" Harlan asked.

"Yes, I think so," replied the woman.

"Good. Get out of here. Get help if you need it."

"Thank you," the woman said as she hurried away.

Harlan addressed the growling individual crouched before him: "I don't want any trouble. Why don't we both just go about our business. What do you say?"

The transient charged, coming at Harlan like a rabid dog. Harlan spun around and dashed for his car. The beast-man pursued on all fours, barking and drooling. Harlan got to his car, opened the driver's side door, and slid in just as the transient reached the vehicle. Harlan slammed the door shut, nearly severing the lunatic's hand as it reached for him.

The transient pounded on the car and snapped his frothing jaws as Harlan started the engine. The car peeled away, spun around in the middle of street, and roared past the deranged man, who chased the car down the street until it was out of sight.

"What the fuck?!" Harlan shouted as he watched the transient recede into the distance in the rear view mirror. "What is going on around here?"

Confused and scared, Harlan picked up his cell phone and called his wife. "Hi, honey," he said when Kate answered.

"What's up?" Kate asked.

"That's what I'd like to know," Harlan replied. "I've just had one hell of a morning. I'm coming home. We'll talk about it when I get there."

"Wow... Well, that's interesting that you'd say that. I've had a pretty weird morning so far, too. Something happened up the street. I was actually going to call *you*."

"I'll be there soon."

Intuitively, Harlan remained on the surface streets. Something very strange seemed to be happening and the last place he wanted to be was on the interstate, where he could only change course a mile at a time. He drove north on the surface streets in a high state of alert.

A few miles from home, as he approached an intersection, he noticed another commotion. He could hear honking and shouting from the cars that had stopped for the red light ahead. There was a man in the crosswalk holding up traffic. He was yelling incoherently and shaking his fists at the stopped cars. This man, however, did not appear to be a transient. He was well-dressed and well-groomed... and also totally out of his mind.

"Get out of the road, you idiot!" someone yelled.

"Rrrraaagghhhh!" the man in the street roared. He then leaped onto the hood of the closest car and battered the windshield with his bare hands. The man pounded away, seemingly oblivious to the damage he was doing to his hands, which were quickly bloodied and broken.

The driver of the car being attacked, a young man in urban street clothes, stepped out of the driver's side door. "You bitch-ass punk," he said. "I'm going to fuckin' kill you."

Other people began to step out of their vehicles, but no one intervened. Instead, they cheered on the melee as the two men grappled and threw punches in the middle of the street. It was brutal, ugly, and sickening – at least to Harlan. He reversed his car and sped away to find an alternate route.

Kate was standing in the doorway when Harlan arrived at home. She was holding Spencer and looked distressed.

"Everything okay?" Harlan asked as he got out of his car.

"I'm glad you're home. The police just left."

Harlan walked up to Kate, put his arm around her, and guided her back into the home. "What happened?" he asked.

"The neighbors got into a fight. It was pretty bad."

"Bill and Violet? They always fight."

"No, I mean, it was *really* bad. Much worse than usual. I could hear them yelling at each other from here."

410       The Great Divide

"Nothing new there. We've heard them before. They can both swear like sailors, that's for sure."

"Well, I expected it to blow over pretty quickly, like usual, but it kept escalating. I started hearing stuff smashing over there. At one point, Bill said he was going to kill her."

"He would never do something like that. He's got to be almost 80 years old."

"That's what *I* thought... until I heard the shots."

"*What?!*"

"Yes. I nearly jumped out of my skin. I didn't know *what* was going on. Then I heard her scream, 'You stupid bastard! Where'd you learn how to shoot?' "

"You're kidding!"

"Nope. It was absolute madness. So, I called the cops. Just after I hung up the phone, I heard them screaming outside. I looked out the window and could see her chasing him with a butcher knife in her hand. He was still waving the gun around, threatening to shoot her."

"I can't believe it." Harlan shook his head in disbelief. "What do you think it was about?"

"Politics, from what I could tell. There was a lot of name calling and accusations. Apparently, they do not share the same political affiliation."

"Welcome to modern society. What happened? Where are they now?"

"The police showed up just as I was sure they were about to murder each other. They kept on cursing and screaming even when the cops arrived. When they saw that Bill had a gun, things got pretty tense. Thankfully, Bill dropped it when he was ordered to, but they had to restrain Violet. She was on a rampage. It was like she was possessed or something. Eventually, the cops put them both in the car and took them away. I have no idea what happened after that. It wouldn't surprise me to find out that they were both put in an institution. It was just crazy."

"It seems to be an epidemic," Harlan said. "I saw some stuff today I wish I hadn't."

"Care to talk about it?"

Harlan considered sharing the events of his morning with Kate but decided against it. He was more interesting in moving on than reliving the upsetting experiences. "If it's all the same to you," he said, "I think I'd rather not."

"Whatever it was, it was enough to keep you from going to work this morning. I trust you'll tell me when you're ready."

"Yes."

Their conversation was interrupted by the shrill wail of approaching sirens, which seemed to erupt at once from multiple directions. It was clear that something quite serious was happening. Harlan walked to the window, drew back the blinds, and looked outside.

"What is going on?" Kate asked.

"I don't know," Harlan replied, "but there sure are a lot of people hanging around out there right now."

"Neighbors?"

"Yeah, mostly... There's Rocky with his dogs. I see Skip and some others. A lot of people I don't recognize, too."

"What are they doing?"

"It's weird... Everyone is just wandering around. They look confused."

The sirens got closer and louder. They overlapped and intermingled as more joined in the cacophonous chorus. Kate joined Harlan at the window and peered out. She gasped when she saw the strange scene developing outside. "Oh, my God," she said. "What is *wrong* with them?"

There were now nearly 30 people gathered in the street. Some were standing motionless in their yards and talking to themselves. Some were walking in circles with their heads in their hands. Some were crawling around on their hands and feet. All appeared to be delusional, or at the very least, extremely disoriented.

"I'm scared," Kate said.

"I'm a little freaked out, too," said Harlan.

With the sirens still blaring, the scene outside suddenly and dramatically changed. As if choreographed, the men and women who had been wandering around locked in their own internal worlds suddenly attacked each other. It was complete chaos as each person rushed at whomever was closest and viciously assaulted them. Neighbor on neighbor, family on family – it was a chaotic free-for-all.

Kate screamed at the onset of the explosion of savagery and picked up Spencer, who had been playing with a toy at her feet. Harlan stood staring in disbelief at the mayhem. The battle was irrational, disorganized, and barbaric. People were punching, kicking, tearing, and using anything at hand as a weapon. Casualties were quickly mounting. The injuries were grave.

The sound of an explosion snapped Harlan out of his trance. In the near distance, he could see thick, black smoke beginning to rise. He could also hear the screams and inhuman cries of the hopelessly insane. "We've got to get out of here," he muttered.

"What should we do?" Kate asked. She was frantic, on the verge of hysteria. "Should we wait for the cops? Is someone going to come and stop this? I think we need help!"

"I have a feeling we're on our own right now. We need to pack our stuff and get out of here as quickly as we can."

Harlan and Kate went to work. They understood that the situation outside of their home was dire, and that any moment, the chaos could burst through their front door and invade their safe haven. In a frantic flurry of activity, they packed a few bags with some essential belongings.

"Where are we going to go?" Kate asked.

"At this point, I'm really not sure. I just want to get out of the city right now. I'm thinking north. How does that sound?"

Young Spencer, who had remained silent and observant the entire time his parents had been rushing around the home gathering items, spoke up. "Mommy, are we going away?" he quietly asked.

"Yes, dear," Kate replied. "We're going to go on a drive. Remember when we went camping last summer? It's something like that."

"You mean we're gonna sleep in a tent?"

"Maybe," Kate smiled. "Would that be fun?"

"I like sleeping in a tent," Spencer beamed.

"That's a good idea, buddy," said Harlan. "We'll bring ours just in case."

With enough supplies to last them a few days, the small family prepared to leave their home. They still had to get to their car, which was parked on the street – right in the middle of the absurd brawl still raging in their normally quiet neighborhood.

"How are we going to do this?" Kate wondered. "Look at them – they're like animals. I don't want to be attacked."

"I wish we had a gun," Harlan said.

"You know how I feel about those things."

"Well, let's just hope none of *them* have one."

"Are those people going to hurt us?" Spencer asked fearfully.

Kate picked up Spencer and cradled him in her arms. "No, honey," she replied. "We're going to keep you safe."

"I need you to hold on to Mommy as tightly as you can," said Harlan. "We're going to run to the car."

Harlan grasped the door knob and braced himself. He took a deep breath and slowly eased the door open a few inches. He did not want to attract any attention. "Everyone ready?" he asked. Kate and Spencer nodded in unison.

Harlan swung the door open and, with an over-stuffed duffle bag slung over one shoulder and a small tent under the other arm, he bounded down the steps of the home and across the lawn toward the car. In mid-stride he pushed the button on his key fob, unlocking the car doors with a series of beeps. The sound alerted the bloodied and battered combatants who were still conscious to his presence. Those in close proximity stopped fighting and stared at Harlan as he fumbled with the back passenger door. Like a pack of zombies, people he had known as neighbors and friends only hours before began to move in on him with cold, cruel malice gleaming in their vacant eyes.

"Oh, shit," Harlan mumbled. "Come on..." He composed himself and finally got the door open. "Get in!" he shouted to Kate and Spencer, who had followed closely behind. While Kate buckled Spencer into the child's car seat in the rear of the vehicle, Harlan popped the trunk and stuffed the tent and bags inside. The neighbors were closing in like a phalanx of the undead. "Stay back!" Harlan yelled. "Get the hell away!" That seemed to amuse the approaching mob. They chuckled, drooled, and smiled.

Kate had managed to secure Spencer in his car seat. She opened the front passenger door and slid in. Harlan went around to the driver's side. As he was about to get in, a young man he recognized from down the street rushed at him with a maniacal shriek. Harlan spun around and, before he was even aware of what he was doing, dropped the deranged man with an expertly executed jab to the chin. This signaled the other attackers to rush, but before they could reach him, Harlan was able to get into his seat and start the car.

"Oh, my, God!" Kate cried. "Are you okay?"

Adrenaline raced through Harlan's body. "I think so," he said as he gripped the steering wheel with white knuckles. "I haven't been in a fight since high school. Didn't know I had it in me."

The crowd had formed a circle around the car. With no other choice, Harlan accelerated and plowed right through those who were directly in front of the vehicle. Most were still grinning like homicidal imbeciles as they bounced off the hood and went flying in all directions. The road ahead was now clear, so Harlan accelerated as the rest of the pack tried to catch up. Harlan and his family sped away from their home of many years, not sure when or if they would ever be back.

"Do you think it's like this all over the city?" Kate asked as they drove through their neighborhood toward the road that would take them north. All around them, the chaos had spread.

"Yes, I do," replied Harlan. "In fact, something tells me that it might be like this all over the country – all over the *world*, perhaps."

"I don't understand." Kate shook her head in bewilderment. "What caused this? What *happened?*"

"All I know is that people are getting sick and it's spreading fast. We need to find an isolated place to wait it out... or settle down and rebuild, if we have to."

"Maybe we should turn on the radio and check out the news," Kate suggested.

"In all honesty, that's the *last* thing I want to do right now. I'd rather trust my own senses, my own perception."

"But we could be missing vital information..."

"Or we could end up swallowing a bunch of lies and misinformation. For all we know, this... *sickness*... may have been spread through the airwaves. It could have been perpetrated and perpetuated by the media – technologically induced madness."

"You really think so? That's a bit of a stretch. You don't know what's really happening."

"You're right – I don't. But at least I *know* that I don't know and, at this point, all I trust are my own eyes and my own ears."

"Daddy?" Spencer called from the back seat.

"Yes, buddy?"

"Are we going to find a new home?"

"I don't know for sure, but we might have to. Keeping our family safe is my number one concern right now. Do you understand?"

"Mommy, Daddy, and Spencer – our family."

"That's right, buddy."

"I like our family. I want to stay with you guys."

"We love you, Spencer." Kate smiled, despite the tense situation. "We're going to stay together, no matter what."

The car had now passed through their neighborhood and was on a major street that would take them out of town. Surprisingly, traffic was light.

"It's quiet," Kate remarked. "It's kinda spooky."

"More and more people must be getting sick," Harlan speculated. "We might be some of the few left who can still drive – or function as human beings at all. It's good for us. I think we're going to make it out of here."

"And then what?" Kate asked.

"If we have to, we'll camp out in the Sonoran Desert for a night or two until things settle down. Then we'll head north. I don't plan to come back to Phoenix until I'm certain that it's safe to do so. The insanity seems to be settling down somewhat, so that might happen sooner than later, but who knows?"

"Yay!" Spencer exclaimed. "I like camping. Can we eat turkey dogs and ketchup?"

"We'll see what we can do, buddy," grinned Harlan.

The car carrying the small family joined the procession of vehicles that was leaving the city. The median and shoulders were lined with parked cars, many with their doors open. Kate reached over and took Harlan's hand in her own. Harlan looked at her and nodded sincerely, his eyes radiating deep love for his wife and child. Relief washed over him as he realized that there were others who had not been afflicted with whatever had come over the majority of the city's – perhaps the world's – population. The presence of the other vehicles gave him comfort. For the first time all day, Harlan relaxed as the the sun began to set over the desert. He knew that their adventure had only just begun.

# The Calling

The man awoke in the desert with no recollection of his past or identity. A scorching wind swept across the desolate plains. Clouds of dust billowed and undulated as if animated by spectral entities. The man was lying prone on the hard, dusty ground. Consciousness returned to his body in a slow insertion. Overhead, the sun raged and throbbed, bathing him in its intense, unforgiving heat, indifferent to his predicament.

The man sat up. A sharp pain instantly alerted him to a problem in his lower back. He cried aloud as a bolt of agony shot up to his reeling brain. He reached back and explored his lower spine with trembling fingers. He was shocked to discover a small, metallic lump under the skin attached to a vertebra a few inches above his butt. He immediately understood at least one aspect of his frightening and inexplicable situation – *I've been implanted*, he realized. He found a mental compartment in which to store this disturbing bit of information.

The dense fog that clouded the man's mind began to clear. He could still not access his memories, but his clarity of sensory perception was growing, his awareness of the environment increasing. He looked around and discovered that he was sitting on a patch of earth in a scrappy, remote area. Bizarre, beautiful, and dangerous desert flora sparsely dotted the landscape. The intermittent islands of stubborn life juxtaposed strongly with the vast expanses of dry, dead ground. It was unfamiliar and alien territory.

Thirst, strong and desperate, clawed at the man's throat. *I need water!* his mind screamed. The fearful nature of his body's demand was sufficient impetus. He gathered his strength and attempted to stand up, making it to a crouching position before a wave of vertigo caused him to nearly pass out. He paused, his hands on his knees and his head down, while his brain wavered on the edge of deep black nothingness. The man could feel his consciousness flickering like a loose light bulb.

Finally, the man was able to get to his feet. Something in his peripheral vision glinted in the harsh light of the sun and caught his eye – a small object resting at the base of a strange, spiky, tentacled plant which sprouted from the desert floor like a ragged talon. The man approached the plant and bent down to examine the object. It was a small box roughly the size of his fist with a lid secured by a metal clasp.

The man picked up the box, hesitated for a moment, then released the clasp and opened it. Inside sat a tiny, transparent bottle and a piece of paper. The man picked up the bottle. It was full of little white pills. The label on the bottle read *Hydration Tablets*. The man examined the paper. On it was a typed note, which read *Take one of these once a day if you want to survive.*

"Well, isn't that interesting," the man said. He looked around again, scanning the brutal, inhospitable environment. For as far as he could see stretched nothing but desert, shimmering in the heat. The man's thirst was growing. He pondered the risk of taking one of the pills. *Whoever left me here could have killed me already,* he thought. *If they wanted me dead, I would be.* The logic seemed sound enough. He opened the bottle and popped a pill into his mouth.

The pill instantly dissolved upon his tongue. Within moments, the man began to feel better. He was no longer dizzy and no longer shaky, but he was still hot and hungry. The sun was almost directly overhead, indicating to him that it was midday. It would be a while before the coming evening

brought relief from the cruel, relentless radiance of the sun.
"I need shade and food," the man said to himself. The
complete absence of any signs of human beings or their
habitations made the man feel a little wild in the head.
Talking to himself made him feel better. "I better get
moving," he said.

The man then became aware of his clothing. He was
wearing a simple white T-shirt and a pair of loose-fitting
cargo shorts. On his feet were a good pair of rugged hiking
shoes. He was relieved to find that he was dressed
appropriately for the climate and conditions. He put the small
box in one of the spacious pockets of his shorts.

In the distance loomed a large mountain range, its
appearance hazy and ethereal as it glimmered on the horizon.
"I'd be safer there," the man said. "More shade, more shelter,
more food." He set his sights on the mountains and focused
his attention on reaching them. The immediate problems of
health and safety had temporarily displaced the troubling
issues of who and where he was – survival trumped his
newfound identity crisis.

The man walked. The desert received him. For nearly
an hour, the man encountered nothing but cacti, rocks, and
the occasional skittering lizard. The small reptiles zipped in
and out of view before the man's brain could fully register
their presence. A large bird of prey appeared far overhead. It
swooped and circled as it followed the man's progress
through the brutal landscape. "I'm not dead yet," the man
said. "Go find something else to hunt." The bird screeched,
as if in response.

Just ahead, the man spotted something anomalous. It
appeared to be a wooden box affixed to a pole. "What do we
have here?" the man said. It looked like a mailbox in the
middle of nowhere. He moved in to get a better look, but
before he could get any closer, an eerie sound rose sharply

and caused him to freeze in his tracks. It sounded like an electrical transformer and emanated from everywhere and nowhere at once, its volume increasing until the man's head began to ache.

As the man watched, the air around the mailbox began to ripple and waver. It was like the heat effect of the desert, only much more intense and localized in the immediate vicinity of the box. The rippling, like the sound, grew in intensity and, for a moment, the desert and the distant mountains were replaced with an urban street setting, or more accurately, the two scenes were superimposed.

Suddenly, there was a vehicle beside the mailbox. It appeared instantly, as if it had been cloaked the moment before – or as if it had been teleported from some distant location. The vehicle was long, black, and apparently armored, like a cross between a stretch limousine and a tank. A door on its side opened and a man in a dark suit stepped out. "Hello, Philip," the man said.

*Philip*, the amnesiac thought. *My name is Philip.*

The man in the suit opened the mailbox and put something slender inside. "You'll need this," he said. The man in the suit shut the mailbox and entered the vehicle. The vehicle instantly disappeared in a flash of light. Philip stood for a moment, dumbfounded, before he approached the mailbox.

Inside the mailbox, Philip discovered the suited man's offering – a large envelope. He opened it and found a single sheet of paper. It was a map.

The map was a topographical representation of the desert and the nearby mountain range. This was made clear to Philip by a star near the center with the words *You are here* written above it. "That's helpful," Philip said, "but where the heck is *here?*"

Philip studied the map carefully. There was another

star near the top of the map, marking a location somewhere in the mountains. Philip was no cartographer, but to his untrained eyes, the terrain between his location and the other starred location appeared to be relatively flat, at least up to the tightly spaced curved lines of the mountain range which indicated a steep ascent. "Is that where I'm supposed to go?" Philip asked himself – and the man in the vehicle that had popped in and out of view like a vessel between dimensions. "I suppose I'll play along. Somehow I get the feeling I don't have a choice."

The sun had descended in the sky considerably. The day was slipping away quickly, late afternoon transitioning rapidly into early evening. Philip examined the map again in an attempt to comprehend its scale. Near the bottom of the map, Philip noticed what appeared to be a deep wash – he remembered crossing the wash not long after he had set out on his hike through the desert after awakening. Using his fingers, he crudely measured the distance between it and the star indicating his current location. He then measured the apparent distance from his own star to the star in the mountain range. "No way I'll get there before dark," he surmised. "I need to find somewhere to spend the night." Philip folded the map neatly and put it in a deep pocket of his shorts. He walked on toward the mountains, leaving behind the strange mailbox.

Philip hiked through the desert until bands of brilliant color began streaking the sky. The sun was setting and the evening was gorgeous. Despite Philip's fatigue and hunger, he could not help but admire the singular beauty of the sight. Vibrant shades of purple, yellow, orange, and red – it looked as if God himself was painting the vast expanse above Philip's head in real time, the clouds and sky a massive canvas for His experiments in Impressionism.

"I could learn to like it out here." Philip was

developing an affinity for the desert.

When Philip's astonishment subsided, the inevitability of the approaching nightfall became real for him. The heat of the day had been replaced by a distinct chill in the air. The rapid and extreme drop in temperature surprised and frightened him. He frantically began to look for a place to spend the night. "I don't think I'll be doing much sleeping," he said. Still, he needed to find a spot which would provide him with a semblance of security.

Not far ahead, he spotted a tree silhouetted against the darkening sky. He had only seen a small number of them all day – they were few and far between on the desert plains. Though thin, spindly, and rather insubstantial, the tree had sufficient vegetation to provide a little cover and, most importantly, the sensation of safety.

Philip covered the short distance to the tree in a spirited trot. He cleared a spot at the base of the tree and sat down with his back to its trunk. The sun had now fully set. The brilliant colors of a few short minutes prior had drained from the sky, leaving only inky blue and the vague forms of shifting clouds.

Philip pulled his knees up to his chest and shivered. He made a valiant effort to keep his mind from imagining all the potential dangers that might have been lurking in the dark. He was only nominally successful. Visions of snakes, scorpions, and venomous lizards filled his head like unwanted intruders. "It's going to be a long night," Philip sighed. He put his head in his folded arms and closed his eyes... then promptly fell fast asleep. Exhaustion, total and debilitating, had overridden his fear. His body and mind rested.

In the middle of the night, Philip awoke with a start. Something was moving in the dark – something big, something breathing heavily, something *close*. Philip stood up immediately, ready to defend himself. His body became a taut wire coursing with electricity. His brain was on fire, ignited by pure, primal instinct.

Philip strained his eyes in the darkness, trying to catch a glimpse of the large form that lurked somewhere just beyond the tree, his tiny oasis of safety. The dark was impenetrable. The landscape and its inhabitants were fully cloaked in the thick veil of the moonless night. Philip could still hear the creature. It seemed to be circling the tree at a fair distance – too far to be seen, but close enough for its threatening presence to be felt. Philip could even hear the thing moaning in a low, guttural voice that sounded neither human nor animal. *What* is *that*? Philip thought.

Remaining as still and silent as he could, Philip struggled to remain calm. He was on the verge of panicking and he knew it. He had the sudden and irrational urge to run. *That would be stupid*, he reminded himself. *That thing is waiting for you to make a move.*

The creature in the darkness continued to pace and circle Philip's position. Philip's fear grew until it eventually got the better of him. He picked up a large branch and, before he was fully aware of what he was doing, jumped to his feet and yelled out, "What do you want?! I'll kill you! Go away!"

Silence followed. Philip stood in a combat stance, ready to use the branch as a weapon on whatever was out there apparently stalking him. Nothing happened. He wondered if he had scared it away. It seemed highly unlikely, yet the night was once again still and quiet. Philip stood there for what seemed like an eternity, unwilling to relax his guard and trust the deceptive, eerie calm that had returned to the desert.

Minutes passed and nothing happened. Philip returned to a sitting position at the base of the tree, but kept his grip firm on the stick. There would be no more sleep for him on this night. He waited for the sun to rise. Many hours later, it did. Philip admired the magnificent morning vista while he considered his next move.

When Philip stood up to stretch, he again became aware of the metal object lodged in his spine. He poked at it tentatively. There was no pain, just the uncomfortable sensation of something alien inhabiting his body. "Someone's going to answer for this," he muttered. "I will find you and make you pay."

Philip began to survey the area around the tree, looking for any sign of the thing that he had heard in the middle of the night. He found something much stranger than what he had expected. Ten feet or so from where he had sat all night under the tree lay an object. It had not been there the night before, Philip was sure of that. Philip approached it cautiously.

The object was an oblong box about a foot long, six inches wide, and four inches tall. Philip reached into his pocket and retrieved the smaller one he had found the day before. The boxes were of different sizes, but of similar design. Before satisfying his curiosity about what the new box might contain, Philip swallowed a pill from the vial resting in the small box. The tablets apparently worked – he did not feel any symptoms of dehydration.

Philip inhaled deeply, bent down, released the metal clasp of the new box, and opened the lid. It contained two items – a small foil-wrapped energy bar and what appeared to be a strange, hand-held power tool. "Must be a care package from my secret admirer," Philip said. His stomach began to rumble as soon as he spotted the energy bar. He tore open the wrapper and gobbled up the vaguely chocolate-flavored confection in three ravenous bites. He could instantly feel warmth and strength spreading through his body.

Next, Philip carefully removed the strange tool. It was

like a futuristic cross between a flashlight and a handgun and totally unlike anything he had ever seen before. There was a button on its underside just above the formed grip. The business end of the thing had the flared appearance of a musket barrel. It was like a prop from a low-budget science fiction movie. "What *is* this thing?" Philip wondered. He pointed it at a large boulder. He was about to push the button – the trigger – but uncertainty caused him to pause.

"Fuck it." Philip pushed the button. He braced himself for anything – a gunshot, an explosion, a laser burst, a shockwave, the complete obliteration of the boulder in a flash of lightning, but instead, the 'tool' emitted a faint beam of light which made the boulder appear purple in its glow. "Weird," Philip said. He slid the object into one of his capacious pockets.

Philip was about to walk on and leave the box behind when he noticed something else resting inside. It was another note. He picked it up. *Use this tool in case of an emergency. Aim at your target and push the button. Has an effective range of 100 feet,* it read. "Okay, then." Philip was skeptical, but intrigued. "I'll remember that. Thank you."

Feeling somewhat rejuvenated, Philip moved on, away from the tree and toward his destination in the mountains – toward whatever mysteriously awaited him at the location indicated by the star on the map.

By the time the sun was once again nearing its midday point in the sky, Philip had made great progress. The mountains loomed above him now, practically within striking distance. He was close enough to see faint trails snaking their way through the valleys and up the peaks. Using the map and his apparent position to estimate how much ground he had already covered, Philip calculated that he had traveled approximately halfway from where he had begun his long, arduous, involuntary trek to the mountain location where he hoped to find rest... and answers.

Awareness of how far he had come and how close he was to what could potentially be the end of his lonely and frightening sojourn in the desert filled him with renewed determination. "If I can get into the mountains by nightfall," he said, "I should be able to reach the star tomorrow afternoon." He had no idea what he would find and had no desire to speculate.

Soon, he was at the foot of the closest mountain – a fair-sized formation with a moderate slope. Ascending would not be as difficult nor as treacherous as Philip had anticipated. There appeared to be trails leading all the way up.

Philip pushed his way through some thorny bushes, probing for a trailhead. He was focused on the ground and vegetation directly in his path and did not see the figure hiding in the bushes mere feet from where he stood until he was almost right on top of it. When he did spot the shape of a man crouching in the thick bush, he let out a shocked cry and jumped back. Wide, startled eyes peered at him from the shadows. Philip stared back in horror. The eyes belonged to an individual who looked more like an animal than a human being. Long, matted hair framed a filth-encrusted face, giving the man the distinct look of an anthropological throwback. The crouching savage bared his black, rotten teeth in a feral expression of intimidation.

"Whoa, there," Philip said, raising his hands slowly in a gesture of peaceful intention. "I'm not going to hurt you."

The man in the bushes started to rise, his eyes still locked on Philip's. He growled menacingly through clenched and exposed teeth. Philip lowered his right hand to his hip, where the strange apparatus was resting in his pocket. His fingers found their way to the implement – or weapon, as he had been informed of in the note – and closed around it.

The man in the bushes raised his thin, sinewy arms and clawed his hands up in front of him in a provocative, threatening manner. Philip could sense an attack coming. He had to act *now...* so he did. He pulled out the lightgun, aimed it at the feral man, and pushed the button, hoping for the best. Just as when he had tested the item on the boulder, the strange tool silently emitted a beam of light, illuminating the snarling, sneering, attacker in a weird shade of purple. The man in the bushes froze, confused.

"Bang, bang," Philip joked. "Gotcha."

Before either of them could make a move, Philip saw something extremely unsettling. Behind and above the savage in the bushes, he could see throbbing, translucent, amorphous blobs floating in the air around the man's head. The shapes moved like jellyfish in water, flitting, undulating, and dancing about. The man in the bushes seemed to be entirely unaware of them. Philip then realized that the light of the device he held in his hand had exposed the bizarre entities.

"Looks like you've got bigger trouble than me, my friend," Philip said, gesturing at the creatures floating in the air around the man's head. The man seemed to understand – his posture relaxed and he looked in the direction Philip was indicating. Philip kept the light trained on the creatures. When the man spotted them, they suddenly scattered, as if aware of being seen. The otherworldly entities dispersed in all directions and disappeared. The two men observed the uncanny event in stunned silence.

When the man in the bushes returned his gaze to Philip, Philip was amazed to see that a transformation had taken place. Though still dirty, disheveled, and nearly naked, a spark of intelligence and a sheen of total awareness had replaced the wild, mad look in the man's eyes. His jaw had also loosened and his teeth were no longer clenched. Philip was even more astounded when the man spoke. "What just happened?" the man in the bushes asked. "Who are *you*?"

Philip extended his hand. "I'm Philip, and I think we just said goodbye to some of your invisible friends."

The man in the bushes grasped Philip's hand and shook it firmly and sincerely. "My name is Charlie. Thank you for your help."

Charlie rubbed his eyes and took a series of deep breaths. "I feel like I've been sleepwalking for a century," he said, "or like I just woke up from a very long and vivid nightmare."

Charlie surveyed their position. "Where did you come from?"

"I wish I had a good answer for you. I woke up in the desert yesterday morning. I had no memory. Some weird shit happened. I found out that my name is Philip. I started walking. Spent the night alone under a tree. More weird shit happened. Walked some more until I found you and –"

"Some *really* weird shit happened," Charlie finished the sentence for him.

"Indeed," Philip smiled.

Philip noticed that he and Charlie were wearing practically identical clothes, although Charlie's T-shirt and shorts were stained, tattered, and nearly falling apart. It was a major clue that the two men had endured similar ordeals.

"I don't suppose you happen to have a map, do you?" Philip took a guess.

"Yes, I do, as a matter of fact." Charlie reached into his pocket. He pulled out a piece of paper as torn and tattered as his clothing. Philip retrieved his map and compared it to Charlie's. They were identical, complete with the same star indicating a location somewhere in the mountains Philip had been about to explore. The star near the bottom of Charlie's map, however, was far to the east of Philip's starting location.

"Isn't that interesting," Philip said.

"What do you suppose it *means*?" Charlie asked. "Why *us*? Who's responsible?" He was fully cognizant of the fact that neither of the men had any clue what they were doing or what was happening, but he couldn't help vocalizing his profound confusion.

"I think if we make our way to that location on the map, we may find some answers. That's about all I'm sure of right now. Care to join me?"

"You're the one packing the heat," Charlie joked. "I don't have a ghostbusting flashlight like you do. It would be in my best interest to stay close... plus, you may have saved my life. Thank you, again, for that."

"To be honest, I had no idea what this thing is or what it could do. I just kinda acted on instinct. I thought you were going to tear my throat out."

"It really was like being in a dream," Charlie recalled. "I have vague memories of wandering through the desert like a drugged-up zombie, trying to crawl back to reality from the depths of a deep, black pit – for how long, I have no idea."

"Are you thirsty or hungry?"

"Surprisingly, not really."

Charlie put a hand in his pocket and pulled out a bottle of hydration tablets. It was half empty. Digging further, he found empty energy bar wrappers. "Somehow I had the presence of mind to keep my body sustained," he said.

"Those things were feeding on you," Philip said. It was a leap of insight, but when he spoke, he knew it to be true. "Feeding on your energy – on your lifeforce. I'm sure they needed you alive and at least *physically* healthy."

"Parasites," Charlie shivered. "Invisible fucking parasites. Just when I thought it couldn't get any weirder."

"It can *always* get weirder."

Philip and Charlie bushwhacked their way out of the

tangled underbrush and began to ascend the mountain. After a short but tricky scramble over rocks and around various species of flora of the extremely spiky and painful variety, they reached a well-worn trail that appeared to wind up and around the mountain.

After taking a moment to catch his breath and examine the map, Philip said, "This looks promising. Let's stay on the trail for as long as we can. We should keep going until we find a safe place to spend the night. I think we can reach the star on the map sometime tomorrow afternoon if we make good progress early."

Charlie was winded, but managed to nod in agreement. "Let's do it," he sputtered. The two men moved on.

They had been hiking for about an hour, each man quietly content with his own thoughts, when Charlie spotted something ahead. "Check it out," he said. "A sign."

"I see it."

There was indeed a sign, planted at what seemed to be a fork in the path.

"Looks like a trail marker to me," Philip said.

The two hikers approached the sign. It was a piece of thin, rectangular metal attached to a sturdy post in the ground, but Philip was wrong – it did not indicate which trail they were on, but instead had three simple words embossed on its glossy surface: *SURVIVORS THIS WAY.* An arrow next to the message pointed to the trail leading right – a trail that would take them to the summit of the mountain.

Philip was in the lead as they made their final ascent and was the first to crest the mountain. Charlie was still climbing when he saw Philip freeze at the peak. Philip stood motionless and gazed out at the valley below with a look of utter astonishment on his face.

"Is everything okay?" Charlie asked.

"I can't believe it," Philip said, shaking his head incredulously.

"What *is* it?!" Charlie cried as he sprinted the last few feet to stand at Philip's side. When he reached the summit, he was too stunned to speak and simply gawked at the sight before him with his mouth agape.

From their vantage point at the apex, Philip and Charlie had a clear view of the entire valley, a wide basin which stretched for miles between where they stood and a distant range of mountains far to the north. To the south, the vast expanse of the desert they had spent the last two days crossing was visible. The panorama was spectacular.

What was most incredible, however, was what they could now see spread out on the valley floor in front of them – the ruins of a very large and completely demolished city. It lay cradled among the peaks like the carcass of some long dead and desiccated beast. The totality of the destruction was practically incomprehensible. There were vast swaths in which nothing remained – the structures which once stood in those areas had been completely razed, leaving large pockets of scorched earth. The skeletal remains of the downtown core jutted out of the center of the destroyed city. High-rise towers poked up from the rubble like cracked and sun-bleached ribs. There was no light, no movement, and no sign of life.

"Holy shit," Charlie finally said.

"You took the words right out of my mouth," Philip said.

"Earthquake? Nukes? Meteor?"

"I haven't got a clue, but it sure looks like the wrath of God to me."

The sun was beginning to set. The golden hour had come, painting the mountains on the far side of the valley in warm, brilliant shades of orange and casting deep, ominous shadows on the ruins of the city below. Philip was about to suggest that they move on and find a place to spend the night when he noticed that Charlie was idle, staring into space with a spooky, vacant expression on his face.

"Hey, are you okay?" Philip asked with sudden concern. Charlie did not respond.

"*Charlie!*" Philip yelled. He grasped Charlie's shoulders and gave him a vigorous shaking. "Charlie! Snap out of it!"

As he attempted to communicate with Charlie, Philip began to experience an unpleasant sensation in his head – a distressing buzzing sound accompanied by tendrils of pain which wiggled their way deep into his brain. He began to lose his ability to think clearly and could actually feel his consciousness fading away.

Philip marshaled the force of his will. He was able to retain enough control to reach a hand into the pocket where the lightgun rested. As if from a third-person perspective, he observed himself pulling the weapon out and pointing it at the apparently empty space between Charlie and himself. He pushed the button, instantly revealing the invisible parasites that had gathered in the air around them. The creatures pulsated in the purple light as they fed.

Philip struggled for control of his mind. *Leave us alone*, he thought. *Go back to Hell*. The command worked. The parasites abruptly scattered. Philip's tenuous tether to reality snapped back. He was plugged back in, restored – fully aware and in control once again. Charlie, too, had recovered.

"Those things were sucking on me again, weren't they?" Charlie asked rhetorically.

"We have to be very careful. Those things are nasty, insidious little bastards. I think they are attracted to intense emotion – fear, anger, despair. We need to watch ourselves. Try to stay calm, cool, and collected."

Looking down upon the ruined city was disturbing. Philip and Charlie had a strong desire to move on and leave the shattered corpse of civilization behind. The path indicated by the *SURVIVORS THIS WAY* sign they had passed continued along a ridge that connected the peak on which they stood with a series of others that wrapped around the valley. Philip and Charlie proceeded up the trail in the dwindling light.

"Let's get as far away as possible from that city," Charlie said. *Maybe it's haunted*, he thought. *Maybe those things floating in the air are ghosts...*

Philip pointed to the farthest peak in sight. It was silhouetted black against the deepening twilight. "I think we can reach that hill in a few hours," he estimated. "We can rest there and move out first thing in the morning."

The mountains were fully submerged in darkness when Philip and Charlie made the decision to stop and rest for the night. For the last two hours, they had hiked the ridge with near-zero visibility. Philip had occasionally used the lightgun to check for and ward off parasites, but with no knowledge of the item's power supply or charge, he had used it sparingly.

The various enigmatic dangers that lurked in the murky, blue-black gloom had remained concealed. The mountains had so far granted them safe passage. The hikers arrived at a plateau just off the trail – it was just large enough for the two men to lie down in. Philip and Charlie each cleared a small patch of ground and stretched out.

"I don't know if *I'll* be getting any sleep tonight," Charlie said as he struggled to find a comfortable position on the hard ground.

"Just close your eyes and rest," Philip suggested.

"Easier said then done," Charlie retorted. He closed his eyes and was asleep in seconds. His mind and body had reached their limit.

Philip lay awake, listening to Charlie snore and searching his mind for any clue to his own identity. Incomplete, fleeting memories taunted him from just beyond his recollection. Indistinct scenes formed in the deep recesses of his subconscious but never broke the surface. Tantalizing clues, fuzzy images, snippets of conversation, and random sensory impressions lingered on the outer perimeter of his awareness – so close, yet agonizingly out of reach.

Before Philip drifted off to sleep, he used the lightgun once more to sweep the immediate area for parasites. Finding none, he settled back and allowed himself to slip into unconsciousness. The two men slept side by side on the mountain. In the valley below, the shattered remnants of the city lay silent and barren in its final repose.

Philip and Charlie awoke as the first rays of the sun appeared on the horizon and began to spread over the valley and the mountains. The two men were sore, stiff, and groggy, but rested and ready for the day ahead.

"Not exactly luxury accommodations," Charlie smirked, "but at least I was able to sleep."

"Good. You'll need your strength for – " He stopped mid-sentence as he spotted something sitting at the edge of the clearing – it was another box. It was resting on the ground where they had stepped off the trail.

Charlie followed Philip's gaze and saw it too. "Was that there last night?"

"I don't think so," Philip said as he walked over to the box. "I'm sure one of us would have seen it."

"It was dark when we got here."

"True, but look at the size of it."

The box was much larger than the others they had found on their journey. It was knee-high and nearly three feet across. It very much resembled a footlocker. Philip crouched down, released the metal clasp, and opened it.

The box was full of supplies: new clothes, new shoes, boxes of energy bars, two backpacks, another lightgun, and even two large canteens full of water.

"Wow!" Charlie cried when he saw the contents. "The motherlode!"

"Someone is apparently looking out for us," Philip said.

"Our guardian angel," Charlie mused.

"Something like that."

Charlie immediately stripped down and began changing. The new clothes were identical to what they had been wearing: simple white T-shirts, cargo shorts, and rugged hiking shoes. The clothes Philip had been wearing were nowhere near as dirty and tattered as Charlie's, but he, too, changed. It felt good.

Each man then chose a canteen and a backpack. They filled the backpacks with energy bars and slung them over their shoulders.

"I assume this is for me," Charlie said, picking up the second lightgun.

The large box was now empty, revealing a neatly folded piece of paper at the bottom. "Another note from our anonymous benefactor," Philip said. He plucked it out of the box and read it out loud:

"Congratulations on making it this far! It is a remarkable accomplishment. Here are some supplies to help you on the final leg of your journey. Your ordeal has almost reached its conclusion, but there are still challenges ahead. Stay alert, stay vigilant, stay strong. We look forward to seeing you when you arrive."

The note was not signed. Philip and Charlie contemplated the mysterious message.

"Well, that's intriguing," Charlie said, "and totally

baffling."

"Leaves me with more questions than answers," Philip said.

The two men stepped onto the trail and began walking. They continued to hike in the direction indicated by the sign they had passed the day before. From their current position, the path rose and fell over a series of small mountains, culminating on a high peak barely visible in the hazy morning light.

"I think our destination is the valley beyond that last peak," Philip said as he compared his map to the terrain in front of them.

"That's not so bad," Charlie said. "I bet we can get there by early afternoon."

The hikers fell into their rhythm. Hearts pumping, legs working, eyes scanning, minds relaxing into an introspective drift, they slipped into a state of automatic locomotion. They hiked in comfortable silence. The sun rose in the sky as they made progress, bathing them in warmth and light.

They had been walking for a few hours when Philip, who had been in the lead as usual, stopped suddenly and gasped. The section of trail ran along a ridge that dropped off steeply to one side. "Oh, no," Philip said, "look." He was pointing to something far below the sharp cliff.

Charlie walked to the rocky edge carefully and peered down. He, too, gasped. There was a body down there, smashed against the rocks and burst open in awful shades of black, purple, and red that contrasted highly with the gray stones. The body was bloated and partly devoured by scavengers. It had apparently been there for quite some time.

"That's disgusting," Charlie said.

"Poor soul," Philip said. "He must have fallen."

It was a terrible sight, more sad than frightening.

Philip and Charlie looked down upon the body in solemn reflection, suddenly acutely aware of their own mortality.

"There's nothing we can do for him," Philip said. "Trying to get down there to bury him would be too dangerous. We might end up in the same condition. We'll have to leave him."

"Hey, check it out!" Charlie exclaimed. He had spotted something on the other side of the trail, partially hidden in a creosote bush. "It's a backpack," he said as he pulled it free.

"It must have belonged to the dead man," Philip said. "Open it."

"Someone already did," Charlie observed. "It's empty."

The backpack had been torn wide open and ransacked. There was nothing inside but a few empty energy bar wrappers.

"I have a bad feeling that guy was robbed and killed," Philip said.

"Maybe it was an animal."

"I doubt it." Philip couldn't be certain, of course, but his intuition was strong.

"Let's get out of here," Charlie said.

Philip and Charlie left the empty backpack and the deceased man just as they had found them and moved on. After a few minutes of hiking, they came to a curve in the trail that took them around the mountain. When they got to the other side of the bend, they were again presented with a strange and unexpected sight.

At the side of the trail a few yards from where Philip and Charlie had rounded the bend stood a crude sign, propped up by a pile of rocks. It seemed to mark the entrance to a cave – or perhaps a mine – carved into the side of the mountain. The opening appeared to be illuminated by the light of a fire inside. Shadows danced on the walls of the cave and on the trail in front. Philip and Charlie could hear faint voices emanating from within.

"Be careful," Philip whispered. "Go slowly, quietly."

"Does that cave match up to where the star is on the map?" Charlie asked in hushed excitement.

"I don't think so. Doesn't seem like we've gone far enough yet."

"Listen... there are people in there! I bet they're the ones we were supposed to find!" Charlie was insistent as he moved forward.

"Be careful!" Philip hissed.

Charlie approached the sign. "This is it!" he mouthed.

Philip crept up to the sign. It said: *SURVIVORS HERE*. The words were barely legible and had been scrawled on a rough piece of wood with what appeared to be mud... or blood.

"I don't know," Philip whispered. "I think we should keep going." Philip nodded toward the mountain up ahead. The trail continued past the cave and meandered over more rolling hills before the final visible peak. "I have a bad feeling about this place," Philip said. "Let's get out of here."

The voices in the cave suddenly ceased. Philip and Charlie froze. The fire flickered in the mouth of the cave. After a few moments of intense silence, sounds of scuffling issued forth from somewhere deep within the rock walls.

"We should run," Philip urged. It was too late. A man appeared. He stepped out of the cave and stood on the trail directly in front of Philip and Charlie.

"Greetings, travelers!" the man exclaimed in a booming, cheerful voice. "Welcome!"

The man was extremely tall and robust. On his large, powerful frame, he wore a flowing white robe. His beard was thick and bushy. His hair was long and brown. His eyes sparkled with compassion, humor, and intelligence. He carried a large, hand-carved, wooden staff.

"My name is Ezekiel," the robed man said. "I'm so glad you found us. Please, won't you join us in our humble abode for a warm meal? You must be exhausted." Ezekiel's radiant grin was disarming.

"I'm Charlie and this is Philip!" Charlie's enthusiasm was obvious. "We're so glad we finally made it. We saw a dead man back there. Poor guy. He was so close."

Philip remained silent.

"Yes, it's unfortunate," Ezekiel frowned. "Not all who seek will find. Not all travelers reach their destination. Now, please, come inside. Meet the others." Ezekiel motioned toward the cave opening with an exaggerated sweep of his arm.

Charlie needed no more encouragement. He stepped into the cave. Philip hung back, reticent.

"I know you have a lot of questions, Philip," Ezekiel said. "I can help you find answers."

"Have you ever seen one of these?" Philip asked as he drew the lightgun from his pocket.

"Of course I have," Ezekiel said. "I helped design it."

Philip gave Ezekiel a quizzical look. "I see," he said. "Then you won't mind if I use it. No disrespect intended, of course. It's just that we've had some scares. Better safe than sorry, right?"

"Right, indeed," Ezekiel replied with a smile. "By all means, use the item as you wish. When you are satisfied that we offer no threat, please join us by the fire for refreshments."

Ezekiel ducked into the cave. Philip pushed the button on the lightgun and kept it directed in front of him as he cautiously followed Ezekiel through the opening. Philip scanned the room as he entered, using both his eyes and the lightgun.

The interior of the cave was brightly lit, surprisingly commodious, and full of people and objects. There was a stone pit in the center of the cave containing a rather large fire. Around it, a group of ten or more people were sitting and talking quietly. There were tables, desks, and strange apparatus throughout the expansive interior, which stretched farther back than could be seen. Deeper in, people were milling about, involved in a variety of tasks. No one paid any attention to Ezekiel, Charlie, or Philip. Philip aimed the lightgun in all directions and could find no parasites.

"You're safe here," Ezekiel said. "You don't need that item any more. This is a perfectly clean environment. We have taken steps to ensure that those... *things*... won't survive in here."

"How did you manage that?" Philip asked.

"All in due time, my friend," Ezekiel replied. "All your questions will be answered, I assure you."

"This place is *amazing!*" Charlie cried. "Look at all this *stuff!*"

"Would you care for something to eat? A warm beverage, perhaps?"

"Sure!" Charlie said.

"Jennifer, could you get these gentlemen some tea and biscuits, please?" Ezekiel addressed a young woman who was operating a strange device in a corner of the cave. It appeared to be equipment used in the preparation of food.

"Of course!" Jennifer promptly replied as she manipulated some knobs and pushed a few buttons. Hot liquid began pouring from a spout on the unusual device and Jennifer collected it in cups. A small door opened and out popped fresh biscuits. Jennifer gathered them on a plate and brought the snacks and drinks to where Ezekiel stood with Philip and Charlie.

"Welcome!" Jennifer greeted them genially. "It's always nice to see new faces. I hope your travels weren't too difficult. Enjoy these delicious snacks!" Her smile radiated warmth and hospitality.

"Thank you, Jennifer," Ezekiel said. "I was just about to introduce Philip and Charlie to the family and show them around."

"Oh!" Jennifer cried. "You're going to *love* it here. We *are* a family. I'm so delighted you two survived and found us!"

"All these people are survivors?" Philip asked.

"Yes," Ezekiel replied. "Just like you."

"What *happened*?" Charlie asked. "What happened to the world? Why can't we remember anything?"

"Come, sit with me," Ezekiel said. He led Philip and Charlie to the fire. The assembled crowd shifted, providing the threesome with a bare patch of floor on which to sit. There were men and women in the group, all wearing identical robes – light brown, not the pure white of Ezekiel's, as though of lower rank. Conspicuously, there were no children present. Once Ezekiel and the new arrivals were seated among them, the group sat in hushed reverence.

"Hello, brothers and sisters," Ezekiel said.

"Hello, Brother Ezekiel," the group said in unison.

"Please welcome Philip and Charlie."

"Welcome, Philip and Charlie!" the group cheered.

"Hello," Charlie smiled, "and thank you so much. It's so wonderful to be here."

"Hi," Philip said.

"We truly hope you enjoy your stay here," Ezekiel said. "We would love for you to join us – to join our family."

"Great," Charlie was now grinning widely. "That sounds just great."

"So, who exactly *are* you people?" Philip asked.

"And where did you get all this *stuff?*"

"We are, quite simply, the inheritors of the planet," Ezekiel said. "We are the architects and inhabitants of the New World. We have been chosen to lead mankind into the future – to pick up the fractured and scattered pieces of our species and repopulate this devastated planet."

"Where did all this equipment come from?" Charlie asked in awe.

"Some of it was scavenged, some we built ourselves," Ezekiel explained. "Much was destroyed in the cataclysm, but not everything."

"How were you able to do *that?*" Philip probed. "When I woke up, I couldn't even remember my name."

"Some of us have been awake for a long time," Ezekiel replied, "and I... well, I had one distinct advantage over the other survivors."

"What *kind* of advantage?" Philip continued prodding.

"I woke up with total recall," Ezekiel stated flatly. "I had full recollection of who I had been before the destruction. My memories and skills were intact. It made me the logical candidate for a leadership position."

"I can see how that would give you quite an edge," Philip said.

"Yes, but it was imperative that I not make the same mistakes as the leaders of the old system. You have seen for yourself what *they* did to this world." For the first time, a hint of something less than pure, loving benevolence crept into Ezekiel's voice. His contempt for those who had held power in the old world was evident.

The people gathered around the fire were enthralled, hanging on each and every word that flowed from Ezekiel's mouth. Those who had been occupied in other tasks around the cave also began to congregate around the fire to listen. It was clear that Ezekiel had their complete and utter devotion.

"Naturally, other survivors were drawn to me like moths to the flame," Ezekiel said. "Like the two of you, they too had been given some basic supplies and a few vague hints on where to head upon awakening. Totally inadequate, as you have seen. Whoever created this ridiculous, nonsensical, demeaning little *game* is nothing but a sick, cruel, and vindictive monster. A warped and sadistic tyrant with the mentality of a disturbed child who enjoys torturing small animals." Ezekiel's face had turned bright red and traces of froth had formed in the corners of his mouth. He was now visibly agitated and furiously indignant.

"Please excuse my anger," Ezekiel said as he calmed himself with a deep breath. "When I think about the horrors that have been inflicted upon innocent human beings, I get extremely upset."

"That's understandable," Charlie said.

"So, who exactly *were* you before the shit hit the fan?" Philip asked.

Ezekiel smiled. "Before the... *cataclysm*, I worked in the technology sector, which is how I knew how to re-purpose and reprogram all of this old equipment you see in here." Throughout the cave, on every available surface, were banks of computers of all makes and models and monitors of all sizes. There was an astonishingly wide variety of laptops, tablets, and hand-held devices scattered everywhere. Amazingly, most appeared to be operational.

"You have *electricity* in here?" Philip was skeptical.

"We have a source of power," Ezekiel said. "Once you have settled in and worked with us for a while, you will understand more."

"What do you *do* with all this stuff?" Charlie asked.

"As I mentioned, we are preparing to re-establish civilization. This time, however, it will be in *our* image, of *our* design – far superior to the failed attempts of those who drove mankind to the precipice, to the very brink of extinction. We can – and will – do much better."

The crowd of robed followers had remained silent up to this moment, but upon hearing Ezekiel's proclamation, they erupted in joyous cheers.

"We are united by our singular goal," Ezekiel continued. "We have one purpose. We are, as it were, of one mind."

"Amazing," Charlie gushed. "It's just incredible what you guys have been able to accomplish. This place is awesome. It really is."

"One mind," Philip said. "Kind of like a – what's that term? – *hive* mind?"

"Yes, that's an accurate analogy," Ezekiel nodded. "We are all focused on the same task. We all have the same desires, the same goals, the same vision for the future. United, nothing can stand in our way."

"Am I to assume that if we stay, we can work toward this goal of yours?" Philip made no effort to disguise his doubt. "We, too, can become of 'one mind' with you and the others?"

"Of course!"Ezekiel exclaimed. "By surviving and successfully reaching your destination, you have earned the right to join us in the New World. We would love to have you."

"That would be so cool," Charlie said. "I think I'd really like that."

"You will also have the exciting opportunity to assist me as I continue the work I began before the destruction," Ezekiel said.

"What exactly were you working on?" Philip inquired.

"Genetics, nanotech, robotics – fairly mainstream,

mundane stuff... until I had my greatest breakthrough..." Ezekiel trailed off, unable – or unwilling – to share a deep secret.

"You see, the world simply wasn't ready to accept what I had to offer," Ezekiel continued, "but now the time has come. Humanity is ready for the greatest gift of all."

"What exactly are we talking about here?" Philip asked.

"Immortality, of course," Ezekiel replied. "We have reached the singularity."

"Are you saying that you have developed some kind of technology that will allow people to live forever?"

"Yes, we have defeated death."

"Wow, that's *amazing!*" cried Charlie.

"You have survived the tribulation and you have earned your reward," Ezekiel said. "Your spinal implant, have you wondered about its purpose?"

"It crosses my mind from time to time," Philip admitted.

"I was part of the design team," Ezekiel said. "It is a marvelous invention. It is an RF receiver that allows direct access to all systems – bloodstream, endocrine, muscles, brain. We can even alter the body on a genetic level. All of this is done using a computer interface."

"That's impressive... and frightening," Philip said.

"Not at all," Ezekiel said. "Look at the people around you. They have all received their upgrades. Do they not seem perfectly happy and extraordinarily healthy?"

The assembled crowd murmured in agreement. Philip's eyes passed over them, and each individual was ostensibly fit and content.

"Sign me up and plug me in!" Charlie blurted.

"That's the spirit, Charlie," Ezekiel grinned. "We can start your upgrades immediately, if you'd like."

"Sure, that would be cool!" Charlie said.

"Are you sure you want to go through with that?" Philip asked. "Seems so intrusive and risky."

"There is no risk whatsoever," Ezekiel said. "The technology has been rigorously tested and perfected."

"They are survivors, like us," Charlie said. "We can trust them."

"Charlie, just give it a little thought. You don't have to rush into it." Philip insisted.

"I'm really hungry, really sore, and really tired," Charlie said. "The machine will fix me."

"Yes, Charlie, it will," Ezekiel said. "You'll never feel pain or discomfort again, actually."

"See? Doesn't that sound *awesome*?" Charlie was practically begging to be jacked in.

"Jennifer, would you care to assist Charlie? He is ready for his upgrades."

Jennifer approached Charlie and held out her hand. "If you'd like to come with me, we can begin the process," she said.

"Cool," Charlie said as he grasped her hand and stood up.

Philip stood, too, and put a hand on Charlie's shoulder. "Please, Charlie," he said, "just think it over a little bit. You might regret this."

"It is wrong to hinder the development of another person." Ezekiel was getting irritated. "To be quite honest, it is also foolish to stand in the way of evolution. Charlie is an adult. He can think and act for himself, and I believe he has made his decision."

"Yeah," Charlie said. "It's okay. I want to do this. I think these guys have a good thing here. I want to be part of the New World."

"It's a painless procedure," Ezekiel said. "You won't

even notice the RF transmission and, when it's over, you're going to feel like a new man. You'll still be *you*, of course, only improved."

Philip's intuition was sending out a multitude of warning signals. Though he couldn't put his finger directly on it, or even attempt to articulate it, there was something disturbing, unnatural, and perhaps even evil about what was happening in the cave. Ezekiel, his followers, and their plethora of weird technology scared him on a visceral level. He decided to get out of there as quickly as he could.

"You've made up your mind, Charlie, and I respect that," Philip said, "but if it's okay with you and everyone else, I think I'll be leaving now. I'm feeling a little claustrophobic... and I'm kind of a loner anyway."

Philip got up and moved toward the mouth of the cave. "Thank you so much for your hospitality," he said. "The snacks were delicious."

Before Philip could step out of the cave and get back onto the trail, the robed congregation quickly rose and surrounded him in a synchronized, fluid swarm.

"I'm afraid I must insist that you stay," Ezekiel said from behind the wall of minions.

The small army of automaton acolytes began to close in on Philip, tightening the circle around him in a preternaturally coordinated maneuver. He was running out of options. The window of opportunity for escaping was quickly closing.

"I can sense your fear," Ezekiel said. "So very human... and so very obsolete. We are the future. Don't you see that? Your emotions have clouded your reason."

"Get back," Philip said to the mob. He raised his fists and assumed a boxer's stance. He was prepared to defend himself. "I'm warning you! Get the fuck away from me!"

Ezekiel laughed. "Such aggression! Look at this atavistic throwback. You, Philip, represent everything rotten and filthy in human nature. Individualism, bravado, stubborn attachment to outmoded ideals... Let go of the past. Let go of your regressive tendencies. Embrace evolution or perish."

The crowd of drones stood silently, all eyes locked on Philip. Someone near the back of the cave now spoke. It was Charlie. "It's wonderful, Philip," he smiled. "I feel like a new man." The procedure was over. Charlie had been assimilated.

"Stop fighting and join us," Charlie urged as he merged with the mob that had surrounded Philip.

Philip's intuition was practically screaming: *get away NOW!* He could not directly account for his intense aversion to what was happening in the cave – he was simply repulsed by Ezekiel and his people, as if they represented an ancient enemy. Philip's memory had been wiped and it was as though he recognized the opposition on a subconscious level.

Hands began to claw and grasp at Philip's clothing. The mob was about to subdue him. Philip reacted by swinging at the closest minion, catching the surprised man with a clean blow to the cheek. The man he struck tottered on his feet and fell back. Philip kept swinging, landing a series of punches on the people directly in his way. The robed drones were not fighters, collapsing easily under Philip's frenzied barrage. Soon, he had cleared a path to the mouth of the cave.

Ezekiel sighed as he watched the melee. "Philip, you are a fool. A silly, misguided, stubborn fool. You and your kind will soon be extinct. Farewell."

Philip sprinted for the exit. No one made any more attempts to stop him. Philip left the cave without looking back and began jogging up the trail. The sun was high and the heat was dry and intense. Philip ran along the rocky trail until the cave was far behind him and the last peak was within striking distance. He was so close.

Philip pushed himself to keep going. Drops of sweat fell from his face and hair in time to the rhythm of his stride. He was focused purely on reaching his destination: the top of the last visible hill. Machine-like, he drove toward it, his muscles straining, his heart beating so hard in his chest that it felt like it was about to burst. Philip did not stop or even slow down as he reached the base of the hill – he powered himself straight up its rugged incline.

At the top, Philip stopped and stood, panting. He found himself looking out upon another valley. It was a gorgeous sight – a broad, verdant basin nestled in the arid and rocky mountains that jutted from the desert floor. To Philip's utter amazement, there was a village in the valley. He could see cabins, barns, and other structures arranged neatly along rough, unpaved roads. A large patchwork of tilled fields lay adjacent to the village and stretched for many miles. Consulting the map and comparing it to the landscape he now observed before him, Philip was certain he had reached his destination – the location indicated by the star.

Upon closer inspection, Philip could see people below – men, women, and children – working in the fields and walking along the streets of the settlement. There were no cars or power lines. It was an astonishing scene – a vision of pure, untainted, idyllic beauty as rich in substance and function as it was in form and aesthetic.

A great up-welling of emotion stirred in Philip's chest as he stood quietly observing the people in the village and fields below. Tears formed in his eyes, as if the sight before him had unlocked something deep and dormant coded in his soul. He had instantly recognized the beauty and truth of what he was witnessing.

Philip's elevated vantage point on the mountain allowed him to see the larger perspective. The people of the village were living and working in harmony, co-existing with each other and with their environment. Nature had not been beaten into submission – it had been nurtured and cultivated. Work was being performed by people who cared for their families and for the land that provided for them. Had they abandoned currency? Philip could only speculate, but he had a strong suspicion that the people who had created and maintained the little pocket of paradise were rewarded in other, more substantial ways.

Philip had been called – by whom exactly, he wasn't sure – but his ordeal was over. He had survived a great tribulation and had truly earned a place in the new community. A trail led directly from the peak where he stood down to the village. Philip set out on the final leg of his journey. He headed down the mountain and into the valley.

# BABY
# IT'S YOU

## ALAN COHEN

# BABY
# IT'S YOU

Alan Cohen Publications, Inc.,
P.O. Box 662071, Lihue, Hawaii 96766


ISBN: 978-0-910367-21-9
Ebook ISBN: 978-0-910367-26-4

Cover design: Elena Karoumpali
Interior design: Isabel Robalo

*For Yeshua*

*Fiction often reveals truth the public would not accept if presented as fact.*

*Zvat, Israel*
*12th Day of the Hebrew Month of Nisan, B.C. 1*

---

"Close the door behind you before anyone sees," a raspy voice echoed through the basement.

Shefer glanced over his shoulder onto the windblown courtyard. Satisfied he had not been followed, the olive-skinned Essene drew the thick wooden door closed behind him with a long groaning creak. He barricaded the rough-hewn boards with a wrought iron bar, metal against metal reverberating through the chamber. Shefer unwrapped the brown scarf covering his face, revealing leathery skin and a thick black beard tinged with slender strokes of gray. He surveyed the group of anxious men sitting in a circle. The glow of thirty-three candles spilled through the musty crypt, casting a dozen shadows on the stone walls, stretching the images of hooded figures like long ghostly fingers.

One by one, the men rose and cast steel eyes at the messenger. A tense silence fell as they decided who would speak first. Rain was beginning to fall on the hardened mud roof atop the synagogue, drops spilling loudly onto the cobble-stone street.

"Did you see them?" Yona the elder finally asked.

Shefer nodded.

"Are they ready?" The impatient voice was Nachman's.

Shefer took a long breath and nodded again.

A quiet gasp rippled through the assembly.

"They said that if they wait any longer, the time will be passed," Shefer reported. "It must be during the next three days."

The elders caught each other's eyes, some uneasy, others excited.

"Then tell them to go ahead," Yona ordered, candles flickering with his outbreath.

Shefer nodded. It was time.

# *Brianna 1*

*He is either the smartest person I have ever met, or the craziest.*

Brad's words echoed in Brianna's head as she watched the door of the lecture hall, anticipating the arrival of the infamous Professor Redmond Hathaway. The clock over the door showed ten past ten. True to reputation, Hathaway was late. Sometimes he didn't show up at all. She pulled her phone out of her jeans rear pocket, searched the list of semester courses, and checked the cancellation policy.

"Don't let him see your phone, or he'll take it away," a girl's voice from the row behind Brianna interrupted her search. Brianna turned and shot her stink-eye.

"Good morning, ladies and gentlemen," a deep male voice bellowed in a dignified British lilt. Brianna ditched the phone and looked up to see Professor Hathaway striding toward the stage with theatrical sass. The physicist resembled a handsome sixty-ish Ewan McGregor, thick salt-and-pepper hair overhanging the collar of his herringbone jacket. For all the rumors Brianna had heard about the oddball sage, she found him initially likeable.

Hathaway set his laptop on the podium, connected a few wires, and walked to the whiteboard with the grace of an actor who had honed his performance to a fine art. He picked up a marker and scribed in thick black letters:

# *Giordano Bruno*

"Who can tell me who this man was and what he did?" Hathaway asked the class as he tossed the marker onto the tray.

A hundred students furiously typed into their laptops.

"Come on, now, unglue your eyes from your screens. Someone speak up!"

After a sticky silence, the professor pressed a key on his laptop and an image appeared on the huge movie screen above his head. It showed a massive statue of a monk-like figure, his dark, shadowed face barely visible under a hood.

"Giordano Bruno was an Italian scientist and mystic who lived at the end of the sixteenth century, around the same time as Galileo. Bruno proposed that the sun was a star and that the universe contained an infinite number of inhabited worlds populated by other intelligent beings."

The image on the screen shifted to a colorful painting of a more innocent-looking, young, fair- skinned Bruno with a John-Lennon-like moustache.

"Giordano Bruno was convicted of heresy and burned at the stake. When the Church judges issued his death decree he told them, 'Perchance you who pronounce my sentence are in greater fear than I who receive it.'" Hathaway paused to let the statement ricochet through the hall.

The students stopped typing and looked up. Another image appeared on the screen—an Italian postage stamp depicting Bruno's face, a quill, and an inscription on parchment. "Four hundred years later, the Italian government issued a stamp in his honor."

The professor faced the class squarely, hands on hips. "Now why on earth would I open a twenty-first century quantum physics course by introducing you to a rebel crucified four centuries ago?"

The bewildered students looked toward each other, hoping that someone else would have a clue. Finally a red-headed girl with an eyebrow piercing raised her hand. "'Great spirits have always encountered violent resistance from mediocre minds.'. . . Einstein said that."

Hathaway leaped off the stage and dashed to the girl. As she recoiled in surprise, students in the back of the auditorium stood up and craned their necks to watch. The professor took the girl's hands, squeezed them together, and shot her a penetrating stare. "And how is that relevant to this course?"

The girl made a pained face and shrugged her shoulders. A black guy in a side row called out, "The truth is on the other side of what you think you already know."

"Brilliant!" the professor pointed to the student and shouted, "You, sir, will ace this course." The teacher leaped back on stage and touched his laptop to restore the image on the screen to Giordano Bruno's larger-than-life statue face. Hathaway stood silent, gazing about the auditorium, waiting for his students to absorb the lesson bequeathed to them by a mentor four centuries their senior.

A head-shaved student raised his hand. "So you want us to blow off science as we know it and make ourselves vulnerable to be burned at the stake?"

The professor smiled and stepped back against the projection screen until Bruno's hooded face hovered over Hathaway's head like a great guardian spirit. He placed the microphone close to his lips and uttered in a voice almost sardonic:

"Welcome to Quantum 101."

# Driscoll 1

Lieutenant Driscoll Ames clutched the letter in his hand, shaking his head. The heat on his right temple told him his blood pressure was rising. He read the words one more time and clenched his breath.

"You okay?" he heard Ticia's voice from the bedroom.

"Yeah, sure, babe," he called back. "I'll be right in."

With a long, controlled breath, Driscoll rose and tried to collect himself, hoping to dilute his rage enough to not worry Ticia. When he finally felt more composed, he walked into the bedroom, efforting for poise.

The shelf of amber pill bottles, hypodermic needles, and the commode in the room corner reminded him why he could not upset his wife. Ticia Ames lay on top of the patchwork quilted bedspread, bundled in her terrycloth housecoat, a maroon knit cap covering her crown, disheveled hair straying beneath it. Her pink slippers with the bunny heads offered a welcome contrast to the sober scene. The frail woman was trying to watch a noisy game show on television, but this program, like most others, had lost its power to distract her. She pressed a button on the wand beside her, and the television blipped off.

"How ya feelin'?" Driscoll asked in a phony chirpy voice as he sat down on the side of the bed and took his wife's hand.

"Been better."

"Anything I can get you?"

"A new body."

Driscoll took a breath and forced a small smile. "I'm still holding out for a miracle."

Ticia took a long breath. The somber tone of his voice tipped her off. "Okay, what's up?"

"Nothing, everything's cool."

Ticia clumsily sat up on her elbows. "Driscoll Ames, don't you tell me everything's cool when I know it's not! Now spit it out—what's the matter?"

His jaw squared. "I got a letter from the promotions board."

"Saying?"

Her husband reached into his shirt pocket, drew forth the paper, and laid it on her stomach. Ticia picked it up and read:

Dear Lieutenant Ames,

The Review Board has considered your application for promotion, and we regret to inform you that we are declining to promote you at this time. We do, of course, appreciate your lengthy service to the U.S. Army. You may apply again after one year.

Sincerely,
Major Thomas T. Raines,
Secretary, Promotion Review Board

Ticia dropped the letter at her side on the bed and looked up at her husband. By now he had regained much of his composure, sitting up straighter. Ticia recognized the stoic look she had last observed at his father's funeral.

"So?" Ticia asked in the stern voice she used when she wanted the kids to know she meant business.

Driscoll remained stone-faced. "So now Brussels is out. Our last hope for your treatment is shot to hell."

Ticia required no further explanation. She, too, had hung her hopes on a last-ditch alternative therapy. Yet the prospect of dying felt a little less frightening each day. She was more resigned to her departure than her husband was.

"You think they passed you over because you're black?"

Driscoll shook his head, picked up the letter, and scanned it as if he were reading it. "It's because I told General Dietrich the army should release the files on Flight 191."

"The Aeromexico flight that crashed off the coast of San Diego? The one you think the army accidentally shot down?"

"It's not what I think, Ticia," he replied, his forehead creasing with anger. "It's what I know. I saw the file. The story the army spun was complete bullshit."

Ticia let her head fall back on the pillow as she laughed. "Is there something new about that?"

Driscoll's heart lightened to see his wife retaining her sense of humor, one of the things he loved most about her. He smiled, folded the letter, and stuffed it back in his shirt pocket. "Best you get some rest now," he said as he started to stand.

Ticia grabbed her husband's forearm and pulled him toward her with surprising strength. "Don't worry about me. Just take care of yourself and the kids. You don't have to be some Dudley Do-Right and expose military secrets. Just live your life."

Driscoll lifted his wife's hand to his lips and kissed it. He wished he had her courage.

*The Vatican*
*August 24*

# Leo 1

"The body of Christ. The blood of Christ." Monsignor Leonardo Bonfiglio gazed down at the bent pilgrim in the wheelchair in front of him. Frazzled white hair strayed beyond her indigo kerchief, her severe hunch causing her gold cross to dangle over her lap. The frail old peasant woman was so crippled that she could barely raise her head to receive the Eucharist.

The monsignor squatted and kneeled before the elder until he found her cataract-clouded eyes, little red patches beneath them above tough skin etched with decades of hardship.

The pilgrim, astounded to see the priest looking up at her gnarled face, grimaced in shame of her infirmity. Yet the kindness in his eyes melted her embarrassment, and she opened her mouth to receive the offering. A small smile spread over her lips.

Father Georgio Rissole stood silently at Monsignor Bonfiglio's side, the wheels in his mind churning. It was not the first time he had seen his superior humble himself before a parishioner. At first Father Rissole had been shocked by Father Bonfiglio's unorthodox practices; over time, however, he had learned to respect them. Perhaps Monsignor

11

Leo was following in the footsteps of Christ more diligently than many of his peers who preached the word of God but did not live it.

Father Rissole helped the priest stand and steady himself as he smoothed out his white robe and straightened his purple sash. The elderly woman kept her head bowed while her middle-aged daughter thanked the priest profusely in Croatian, and then turned the elder's wheelchair toward the rear of the chapel. As the two made their way down the aisle, Leo's eyes followed them, lost in thought. Finally Father Rissole tapped him on the shoulder to remind him of the next pilgrim kneeling before him. Monsignor Bonfiglio gazed at the long line of souls seeking reprieve from their suffering. There were so many.

*Shenandoah National Park*
*August 31*

## *Lauren 1*

---

Lauren Delaney stood before the chipped mirror in the smelly rest stop ladies' room, trying to coerce her mascara to mask her tears. Her face had gone pale, the stress rash on her neck glowing an ugly red. She started to feel wobbly, and grabbed the wash basin. *Please, God, don't let my vertigo kick in now.* The bony twenty-something dropped her head forward, her chestnut hair hanging into the sink.

The sound of a toilet flushing gave way to the stall's wooden door slamming shut. She felt a hand on her shoulder. "Are you alright, honey?" an older woman's voice asked in a thick Brooklyn accent.

Lauren turned to see a plump, fifty-ish woman with short, dyed blonde hair with purple highlights. She wore a white-on-black I Cook and I Know Things T-shirt over a bosom that had seen higher days. In contrast to the lady's sassy, almost-caricature appearance, her eyes spoke compassion.

Lauren forced a phony smile. "I'll be okay."

"Sorry, honey—you can't fool the mother of three daughters . . . Are you sick?"

Lauren shrugged her shoulders.

"In trouble with the law? Pregnant?"

She shook her head.

The woman stepped back and sized Lauren up. "It's a guy, isn't it."

Lauren burst out with an awkward laugh. "You must be psychic."

"Not really. Just twice divorced."

The lady put her arm around Lauren's waist.

"Let's go outside. You can tell me everything."

# *Kenton 1*

Standing before the wall of waist-high wheat stalks, Kenton Baine studied his phone for the fifth time in as many minutes. Zero bars. He stretched his arm into the thicket and strained to count the bars again. Now there were three. He pressed the green Dial button and heard his call connect.

"Amazing!" Kenton called to his wife as he heard her phone ringing. "Simply amazing!"

Cynthia Baine, sitting on a low beach chair a few yards from her husband, pressed Decline on her phone, and shrugged her shoulders. "Maybe it's the wind or some fluke because of where the tower is positioned," she called back, adjusting her oversized straw hat to shade her pale Irish skin from the sun.

"The same thing happens at all the edges of the formation," Kenton called back, straightening to his full five-ten height. "There must be some other explanation."

Cynthia shook her head and went back to her Grisham novel. *Why the hell did I agree to be dragged to some trampled wheat field in the middle of nowhere when I could be ravaging Harrods?*

Nose buried in the thriller, Mrs. Baine was oblivious to the dozen self-proclaimed investigators scurrying about the field twenty yards from her. Some wore t-shirts printed with strange geometric designs; others were extending scientific measuring devices at the end of long telescoped poles; others sat cross-legged with eyes closed, meditating on God-knows-what.

A thirty-ish Asian woman wearing a floppy tan fishing hat approached Kenton. "Does your cell phone go dead inside the formation, too?" she asked. Kenton guessed from her accent that she was Japanese.

"Not the slightest signal." He squinted, facing the sun, revealing crow's feet beside his eyes beneath the beginning of a receding hairline.

"My camera doesn't work inside either," she said in pretty good English, lifting her phone to show him the blank screen. "Please would you take a photo of me from outside the circle?"

Kenton took her phone in the metallic purple case and pressed himself through the first few rows of standing wheat, pushing aside several taller stalks to afford him a clear shot. He pointed the phone toward the short, wiry woman with long black hair and oversized sunglasses. He took time to focus, and pressed the round red button. The unit issued a loud *click* and the image on the screen locked. He studied the picture.

"It works from here," he called back.

The lady hopped awkwardly over the bent stalks and looked at the image. "I don't understand why the camera works outside the circle, but not in it."

"Experts say the formations are created by some kind of microwave radiation that scrambles the energy field."

Cynthia Baine dragged her attention from the crucial courtroom scene to check out the woman her husband was talking to. The lady's top with the embedded rhinestones in the shape of a heart was cute, but that hat had to go. And those jeans probably cost the lady twice what she would have paid in the States.

The Japanese woman placed her hands on the hips of her overpriced slacks and turned around slowly in a full three-sixty scan. A robust breeze wafted up and ruffled her fine hair. "Who or what do you think creates these formations?" she asked.

Kenton laughed. "If I could answer that question, I would be a lot more famous than a New Jersey high school science teacher."

The lady stared up toward Kenton's boyish face, her eyes squinting in the sun. He must have been a foot taller than her. His mild paunch told her he wasn't the athletic type, but his blue eyes were kind. "Do you think it's ariens?"

Kenton's forehead wrinkled. "Ariens?"

She rolled her eyes. "So sorry. . . 'Aliens,'" she said, struggling to emphasize the oh-so-unfamiliar-to-Japanese "L." "Extraterrestrials trying to send us some kind of message?"

Kenton shrugged. "That makes about as much sense as any explanation I've heard . . . Sure seems a lot more plausible than the 'ground hogs trampling the wheat while copulating' theory.'"

The lady shot Kenton a quizzical look; she clearly didn't understand that word. He decided not to try to explain.

Kenton felt a firm hand on his shoulder. "Okay, Mr. Copulation," Cynthia interrupted, her beach chair under one arm and her bulky Louis Vuitton pocketbook, Grisham novel protruding from the top, hanging beneath the other arm. "I don't want to be late for dinner and the show at the Palladium. Say goodbye to the girl and let's hit the road."

# Brianna 2

---

"Caramel Macchiato with soy milk and honey?" Brad asked with a dramatic lilt as he set the cardboard Starbucks cup on the table in front of Brianna and slipped into the seat across from her.

She smiled. "You know me too well."

"Big brothers have home court advantage." Brad broke his blueberry scone into two chunks and placed the larger half on a green napkin in front of his sister. She liked his new slightly spiked hair look; he had grown up to be quite handsome, almost a DiCaprio lookalike. "How's the Quantum class going?" he asked.

Brianna rolled her eyes. "Is that Hathaway out there, or what? . . . He talks more like some Shakespearean actor than a science wizard."

"I told you," Brad chuckled. "When I took his course, I thought more about life, death, and meaning than I had in my whole life. The guy's obsessed with ultimate reality."

Brianna reached across the table and gently flicked a crumb from her brother's chin. "Do you think he's some kind of prophet, or just a nut case?"

Brad shrugged and wiped his chin with his napkin. "Maybe both." He took a long breath, leaned forward, and found his sister's eyes. "There's something I need to talk to you about."

Brianna recognized that tone of voice. She stiffened.

"Mom needs to go into a facility."

His sister furrowed her brow.

"Her psychiatrist told dad that she is in danger of another attempt. Leaving her alone at home would be really risky."

Brianna set her cup down and stared into it, trying to process the news.

"Dad and I went to visit the hospital where she would go. Dad's veteran's benefits would cover her there."

"And?"

Brad shook his head and contorted his face. "It was nasty depressing, sis. A locked ward where they stash really crazy people. The doctors and nurses are overworked and grumpy. There's a high rate of violence—someone was murdered a couple of months ago. Most of the patients are stuck there for life. It's like a scene from some horror movie."

Brianna blanched. "We can't let her go there, Brad!"

He nodded. "Of course not . . .We went to look at a private hospital in Abington. It was so much nicer—like night and day. Patients have their own clean, modern, colorful rooms, the staff is qualified and upbeat, and they have art and recreation programs. A high percentage of the patients get better enough to go home."

Brianna's eyes lit up. "So let's put her there, for sure!"

Brad pursed his lips. "Easier said than done. The place is astronomically expensive. Dad's insurance won't cover it, and what he makes at work is a sliver of what they charge. I can chip in from my salary, but there's still a huge shortfall."

"So what will we do?"

Brad clasped his hands behind his head, sighed, and leaned back. "I wish I knew. Dad and I are looking into some state assistance. But with all the budget cuts, it's a long shot."

Brianna sat silently, nauseous.

"Don't worry, we'll figure it out," her brother tried to comfort her, failing to disguise his own angst. "Just do the best you can in school. Make mom and dad proud."

She took a long, pained breath. "I'll have to ace all of my courses to get a scholarship for NYU grad school. The Quantum class is a wild card. I have no idea where Hathaway is going with it."

Brad tapped his fingers on the table, thinking deeply. A glimmer filled his eyes. "I know how you can pass with flying colors."

Brianna scoffed. "Build a warp drive and teleport the professor to a parallel universe for extra credit?"

Brad leaned in and spoke in a secretive voice. "Hathaway has a 'salon' at his house the first Thursday night of every month. By invitation only. I used to go when I was in his class. I can get you in if you like."

Brianna shifted in her chair. "I don't know...The guy's weird enough in class. I can only imagine what he's like at home."

"How much do you want to get into grad school? Mom's pretty worried about you."

Brianna heaved a sigh and found her brother's eyes. "Should I bring wine to Hathaway's place, or weed?"

*The Pentagon*
*August 25*

# Driscoll 2

Driscoll Ames had dined in the Pentagon Officer's Lounge a half dozen times, but today's meeting with Colonel Wendell Henderson was no social call. The Lieutenant found Henderson at a small table in a far corner of the bar with a three-quarters-full Seagram's bottle and a couple of shot glasses before him.

"Good to see you, Driscoll," Henderson said as he stood to shake the junior officer's hand.

"You, too, sir," Ames replied, impressed by the firmness of Henderson's shake, considering he was already a few sheets to the wind. The lieutenant removed his hat and took a seat at the tiny round table.

"How's Ticia doing?"

Ames shook his head. "Not well. The treatments sent her disease into remission for a while, but now it appears to be intensifying."

Henderson sighed. "I'm sorry to hear that, Driscoll. If there's anything I can do. . ."

Ames thought for a moment and leaned in. "Actually, there might be, sir."

Henderson squinted through glassy eyes. "And what might that be?"

"I've been passed over for promotion," Ames explained. "We were counting on the additional income and more time off for me to take Ticia to Brussels. There's a doctor there, Anastaas Prins, who has a phenomenal success rate healing patients that other doctors have given up hope for. We had a phone consultation with him and he feels confident he can help Ticia. We believe it might be her one chance to survive. If there's anyone you can talk to . . ."

Wendell Henderson sat back, crossed his arms, and shot his visitor a troubled glance. "It's a damn shame," the thick-gray-haired senior officer spouted, shaking his head. "I saw a memorandum advising review committees to be more stringent about promotions. Don't take it personally, Driscoll—the recession is crunching the military. They're cutting corners at every turn."

The Lieutenant wasn't convinced. "Maybe so, but I think there's more to it than that."

Henderson squinted.

"I'm pretty sure I rubbed General Dietrich the wrong way when I pushed him to release the flight 191 files."

Henderson nodded. "Another damn shame." The colonel picked up the Seagram's bottle and poured himself another shot. He offered to pour one for Ames. He accepted.

"I just don't know what to do, Wendell," said Driscoll, setting his emptied shot glass on the table. "I've followed all orders for twenty years, put my ass on the line, and worked my way up the ranks with patience and dignity. Now, when I need help from my country the most, they won't give it."

Henderson grunted and downed another shot. "I've never told anyone this, Driscoll, but I have a gripe with the military, too."

Ames leaned back and folded his hands in his lap. He was all ears.

"You know my son, Aaron?"

"I met him at the officers' Christmas party a couple of years ago . . . .Nice guy."

"Yes, helluva nice guy. Selling cars now, in Arlington."

Ames wrinkled his forehead. "Wasn't he in the service?"

"He was in the navy—until his court martial."

The lieutenant made a pained face. "Court martialed?"

The colonel sat up straighter. "Aaron and a few sailors on shore leave went to a bar in Anacostia Park. On their way out, a couple of punks picked a fight with them. One kid pulled a gun on my son's buddy. Aaron jumped the kid, wrestled him to the ground, and the creep hit his head on the pavement. Someone saw the scuffle and called the cops. By the time they arrived, the kid was unconscious. When they took him to the hospital, they found he had sustained nerve damage and lost partial use of his legs. His family hired a hotshot lawyer who pressed charges against Aaron. At the court martial he told the review board exactly what had happened, but they found against him— 'diminishing the image of the military' and all that. He escaped the brig, but they kicked him out of the service dishonorably. All for trying to save his friend's life—can you believe that? Now he's struggling to make a living for his family. That's a stinking pile of shit right there, wouldn't you say?"

Ames shook his head sympathetically. Henderson downed another shot.

"So we've both been shafted, "Ames said soberly. "Sitting here having a pity party isn't going to get Ticia the treatments she needs or your son reinstated."

"Maybe not. But your story just makes me even madder. Ticia's a wonderful gal and I wish I could get you what you deserve."

Henderson swirled some whisky in his glass, lost in thought. His glassy eyes grew lucid for a moment. "I have an idea."

Ames straightened up, a glint of hope in his eyes. Henderson slammed the shot glass on the stable "Meet me in my office in twenty minutes," he spurted. With that, the colonel stood abruptly and, slightly wobbly, departed the room.

# Leo 2

Sister Isabel Rosario knocked softly on Monsignor Bonfiglio's apartment door and waited. When the familiar "please" came, she opened the door and pushed the bussing cart toward the priest's leather easy chair, where he sat behind a small metal tray table holding the dishes remaining from his dinner.

The burly cleric removed his reading glasses and set his newspaper on his lap. For the few minutes each day when the nun was in his presence to deliver his meal and later pick up the dinnerware, he treated her like a respected friend, not a servant, a demeaning habit some of the old-guard priests perpetrated. For at least that reason, Sister Isabel looked forward to helping this reclusive clergyman.

"Did you enjoy your dinner, Monsignor?"

"Very much. Please tell Alonzo to cook the chicken like that again."

"I'll certainly pass that along." The nun issued a polite smile as she began to lift the last few pieces of dinnerware.

When Father Bonfiglio placed his hand firmly on her arm to stop her, Sister Isabel nearly dropped the load. It was the first time in the two years she had been serving the monsignor that he had touched her. Fearing that her face revealed her shock, she lowered her head. Leo withdrew his hand.

"Please just leave the dishes for a moment," the priest requested in a firm voice. Sister Isabel lowered the stack onto the tray, hands trembling.

"Do you ever read the newspaper, sister?"

The nun's mind was reeling. Father Leo had never made conversation about anything other than the food or weather. Efforting to remain calm, she stood arrow straight. "Not much . . . Sometimes I see headlines when I am out shopping, or some television news when I visit my brother's family in Bracciano."

"Tell me—do you think the world is going to hell?"

Never did Sister Isabel Rosario imagine having such a conversation with such a high-ranking authority as Monsignor Bonfiglio. *Is he testing my faith?*

"I . . . I don't really know, Father. There do seem to be many more troubles than I can remember . . . but I trust that Christ will redeem us."

The priest didn't seem to hear her answer. "Do you think Catholics are happy people?"

The nun began to wobble. Sensing her anxiety, Father Leo gestured toward the chair beside him. "Please, sister, have a seat." While under other circumstances Sister Isabel would have politely declined, tonight she accepted.

"Tell me the truth, sister—do you think most Catholics are happy?"

The frail, middle-aged woman had certainly thought about this in her moments of private contemplation. But her line of reasoning was cut short by the memory of her former spiritual director's reproach when she told him that her back hurt her most of the time. "Life is just a sea of troubles with a few shining moments," Father Giaconda had stated dryly. "We are not in this world to enjoy ourselves, Sister. We are here to bear our cross as our Lord did. A life of back pain is a small price to pay for eternity in paradise."

The nun's silent reminiscence dissolved when she became aware of Father Leo's stare. "Happy, Monsignor? . . . I don't know if I would say, 'happy.' Resigned to the life the Lord has appointed for us, perhaps."

Father Bonfiglio picked up the newspaper and showed her a headline:

## Three German Priests Accused of Child Sexual Abuse

"Stories like this disturb me." He tossed the newspaper on the tray table. "The more I read them, the more I wonder if the Church is bringing people to God or driving them away."

If Sister Isabel had known she was to be drawn into this conversation tonight, she would have surely told her supervisor she was too ill to work. But it was too late now.

"I don't know what to say about these terrible occurrences, Monsignor . . . I, too, feel troubled when I hear about them."

Leo offered a fatherly smile. "I'm sorry if I have caused you any distress to discuss this, Sister Isabel. Please feel free to leave if you wish."

Relieved, the nun bowed her head, stood, lifted the tray of dishes onto the bussing cart, and moved toward the door. As she placed her hand on the doorknob, the monsignor's voice caught her again. "Do you believe Christ will return?"

The nun turned and stared for a long, tense breath. "That is what our faith tells us, Monsignor."

"Yes, yes, I know that is what our faith tells us. But what do *you* believe?"

Sister's heart was practically beating out of her chest, "I can't say that I've given the question any thought beyond Catechism."

"Please think about it and let me know what you decide the next time we meet. I want to know if there is life after dogma."

The nun nodded. "Certainly, Monsignor."

With that, Sister Isabel Rosario rolled the cart out of the apartment. As she shut the door, she leaned back on it, closed her eyes, and tried to find a calm place in her soul.

*Shenandoah National Park*
*August 31*

# *Lauren 2*

Lauren's cheeks started to dry as she sat down beside Fern from Flatbush on a knee-high stone retaining wall beside the Blue Ridge Parkway rest area. Tourists stood behind the two, snapping photos of the stunning palette of checkered tan farm fields bordering lush green forests in the sprawling valley below. A purple thunderhead hovered over a distant section of the landscape, dropping a curtain of rain, casting a faint rainbow.

"So what happened with this guy?" asked Fern.

Lauren took a long breath. "I met Todd a year ago and fell for him hard. In many ways, he was my dream guy. Good-looking, smart, communicative, devoted, with a steady job."

"I dated a few guys like that," Fern broke in. "Usually they have a secret family in Connecticut."

Lauren giggled. The joke broke some of her tension.

"Nothing like that," she answered as she leaned against the wall and unbuttoned the top button of her blouse to let a few rays of sunshine soothe her tight neck.

"What then? Good guys don't make their women cry in shoddy restrooms miles from civilization."

Lauren turned to face the woman. "Todd turned out to be a split personality. One minute he would be super present, relaxed, cuddly, funny, and irresistible. Then, without warning, he would get lost in his head, analyzing everything, cold, distant, and critical. Borderline bipolar. I wanted to shake the guy and ask him, 'Will the real you please stand up?'"

Fern nodded. "That would make any woman crazy."

Lauren was thrilled to find someone who understood her; she had hardly spoken of her heartache to anyone. "Eventually I couldn't stand it anymore. We began to fight a lot and the relationship became on-again, off-again. Finally I decided to break it off."

Fern offered a thumbs-up. "Good move, sister . . . So why are you so upset now?"

Lauren reached into her jeans rear pocket and pulled out a folded piece of white printer paper. "A few weeks ago I got this email from him." She handed it to Fern, who opened it and read:

Hi Lauren,

I imagine you're surprised to hear from me. I just wanted to let you know what's happened since we last saw each other.

A few months ago I learned about a community in the mountains. It's called "Project Genesis." I came to visit and I liked it so much that I quit my job and decided to stay.

In the time I've been here I feel like a new person. The fresh air, like-minded people, working in the garden, and sense of common purpose have awakened something inside me that was long sleeping.

Now I realize that I was selfish with you, and I let my moods override our heart connection. I really do love you, Lauren. I always have, but I was afraid to admit it. I want to be with you. Please, come visit. Let's give our relationship a fresh start. That would mean everything to me.

Todd

Fern handed the paper back to Lauren. "So you're on your way to see him now?"

Lauren nodded, eyes still troubled.

"Aren't you excited?"

"Sort of. . .But I'm scared I will get sucked into the same old pattern. How can I be sure he's not in one of his open-hearted moods that make him so irresistible? I've seen him like this before. Then, without warning, he reverts to become an emotionally distant mind-fucker. I was just getting over him. Part of me wants to turn around and drive back down the mountain."

"So why don't you?"

Lauren's face crinkled. "If I do, I'll always wonder if I missed my true life partner. When our relationship was working, we were unstoppable. If we could have that again, more of the time, we could have a great life together."

"And if you see him and it doesn't work out, you will know that you made the right decision and you can move on."

"Exactly. So I have to do it and hope that I will find out."

Fern stood up and smoothed Lauren's hair in a motherly way. The distraught young woman felt a welcome moment of respite. "Thanks for talking to me. You're an angel."

Fern offered a comforting smile. "You're a nice girl. You deserve a good guy. Don't settle for a half-partner." She turned and started toward the parking lot. Then she called back over her shoulder. "Just check Instagram for pictures of him with his wife and kids and dog."

*Chippenham, Wiltshire*
*August 28*

# Kenton 2

The Lucknam Park Hotel and Spa sits on five hundred and three impeccably manicured acres, landscaped with stately hedges and lush gardens befitting the royal family. In room 327 Cynthia Baine lay on her plush white comforter, perusing the mansion's menu of services. "I think today's the day," she called to Kenton.

"Which day is that?" her husband asked, his voice nearly drowned out by the sound of hot water rushing into the washbasin.

"The spa day. The one we came to this hotel for."

The "we," Kenton knew, was presumptive. But he had long ago quit challenging his wife about her projections onto him.

Kenton turned off the water, stepped out of the bathroom, and lifted the tip of his towel to wipe the last bits of shaving cream from his chin. He found his wife stretched out on the oversized pillowtop bed in a posture of queenly command. "Would you care to join me at the spa, dear? Would you like a massage? A facial? A hot stone treatment? They even have a 'decadent chocolate immersion bath.' Lots of men are getting treatments now, you know."

No men that Kenton knew. He feigned needing a few moments to think about his answer. "You just go ahead," he finally replied with a fake smile. "I'll find some way to amuse myself."

"But I could be in for four, five, maybe six hours. They have a *Pamper Yourself like Cleopatra* package that's really speaking to me."

Not to Kenton. Free time was as precious to him as spa time was to his wife.

"I'll be fine, dear. You go and enjoy yourself."

"Oh, all right," Cynthia replied with a sigh. "Stella Tedeschi's husband goes to the spa with her. Maybe one day my dream will come true and you'll get a pedicure with me."

*That's why they call it a dream.* He turned back to check his shaving job in the bathroom mirror.

As soon as Kenton heard the hotel room door shut, he pulled his laptop out of the nightstand drawer. He googled the Higher Design Café, a watering hole he had read about where crop circle aficionados gather. He could easily pop over to the café, an hour drive from the hotel, and get back before Cynthia returned from her treatments. Kenton threw on the flowered sport shirt that Cynthia had purchased in an effort to drag him into the fashion world, then the Calvin Klein button-down jeans he wished he didn't have to unfasten every time he took a leak. As he grabbed the rental car keys, his hand tingled. Finally—an adventure that did not end up in a mall.

# *Brianna 3*

Sipping her glass of chilled Evian, Brianna Marlowe scanned the group gathered in Dr. Redmond Hathaway's living room. Mostly grad students, plus a few science faculty members she recognized. No one else from the Quantum class. Gazing out the picture window of the upscale New Jersey shoreline condominium, Brianna was entranced by the Manhattan skyline sparkling across the Hudson River. A sense of pride swelled in her chest as she considered the strings Brad must have pulled to get his little sister onto the guest list.

The notorious professor was sitting in a corner of the room in a brown leather chair, holding court with a handful of engaged students. Brianna could pick bits and pieces from his part of the conversation, interspersed with spurts of laughter from those within earshot. Finally the low-key chatting around the room was interrupted by a spoon beating against a glass. The group fell silent as the guests turned toward their host.

"Thank you for joining us this evening," Hathaway broadcast in a regal tone. "We never quite know what will happen at these gatherings, but they always prove illuminating." He took a long, slow sip of red wine, prolonging the pause for dramatic effect. "If we stretch your mind, our time will be worthwhile. If we blow it, the evening will be a real success."

A wave of muted laughter rolled through the room.

"Who would like to begin?"

Silence hung as the guests looked at each other to see who would speak first. A pale curmudgeon raised his hand. "Who created the universe?" The audience erupted with a wave of chuckles.

Hathaway remained undaunted, even stimulated. "You did," he answered curtly. "You are fabricating the entire universe every moment with your thoughts."

The young man pursed his lips, trying to make sense of his teacher's odd response. "But don't you believe there is some God or creator behind it all? An intelligence that was here before you or me?"

Heads turned back to Hathaway.

"You make two dangerous assumptions, Nigel. First, that there is some creator outside yourself who operates independent of you, without you, and regardless of you. Second, that there was one act of creation that ceased after the Big Bang. Creation is ongoing, through all living things. The Creator is sitting in your chair, asking the question through you, and answering it through me. So you—like all of us—are ultimately, finally, irrevocably God."

Brianna smiled. Her fears that the evening would be wasted with a dry physics lecture had just been exploded.

"Professor," a young African woman wearing a lime-green headdress called out. "Your words indicate that you are a philosopher as well as a scientist. Do you believe there is a place where science and spirituality meet?"

Hathaway lit up. "Of course, Miss Okeke. When scientists finally arrive at the top of the mountain of truth, there they will find the theologians eating peanuts and laughing like hell."

Another titter rolled through the room.

"Dr. Hathaway," a portly balding man with sallow skin, the only fellow in a suit, called out. "You are teaching theology, not science. Don't you think you should stick to the discipline for which you earned your degree?"

Hathaway's eyes took on an almost diabolical glow. "Ah, Professor Daniken, you finally accepted my invitation," he responded with the confidence of home team advantage. "It's about time that science and religion put down their dueling gloves, don't you think? Science that denies religion becomes itself a religion, with all its inherent evils. Religion that denies science slingshots the world back to the dark ages. How about a marriage between the two that engenders progeny honoring both parents?"

Dr. Daniken's cheeks reddened. "You are licensed to teach physics, sir, not metaphysics. What gives you the right to lure innocent students into your sordid den and fill their minds with new age psychobabble? If you value your credentials, you should stay within the limits of your training!"

Hathaway set his wine glass on the table beside him and stood up like an eight-foot bear intimidating an intruder. "And you, sir, should think twice before denying your students the opportunity to think for themselves. Let them remove their heads from the dark and crusty rear end of a science that is about to tumble and fall of its own dead weight."

Daniken rose and took a step toward Hathaway; Brianna feared the two might come to blows. Yet the renowned author of *Chemistry without Compromise* restrained himself and spoke from his place. "How dare you call your salon 'an evening of illumination?' You should instead advertise it as 'a chamber of brainwashing.'"

Hathaway was clearly enjoying the battle of wits far more than his inquisitor. "Then so be it, sir. The students' brains have been severely soiled by tyrannical poppycock. They can use a good washing."

A burst of applause broke out. Daniken surveyed the group, desperately hoping for some agreement in the temple filled with Hathaway's devotees. Realizing he lacked even one ally, he turned and clumsily stepped toward the door, nearly stumbling over a student sitting on the floor. "Utter, impossible bullshit," he spouted over his shoulder as he stormed out of the room and slammed the door behind him.

All heads turned back to Professor Hathaway, not at all fazed by the confrontation, even invigorated by it. He gazed slowly around the room and added soberly, "True scientists have the guts to cast away shells that once protected them, but now imprison them."

Lacking any students willing to step into the aftermath of the fray, silence ruled for a long, tense minute. Finally Brianna spoke up. "Do you get this kind of reaction from your peers all the time, professor? Does anyone in your department agree with you?"

Hathaway shrugged. "Maybe one or two. But I gave up hope for popularity a long time ago. My search for truth has eclipsed my need for approval."

Brianna sat back, took another sip of Evian, and allowed the professor's declaration to sink in. *This man will either be glorified or crucified.*

*The Pentagon*
*August 25*

# Driscoll 3

Lieutenant Driscoll Ames stood at the door of Colonel Wendell Henderson's office, struggling to imagine how a tipsy senior officer could help him keep his wife alive. Failing the slightest inkling, yet eager with hope, Ames collected himself and entered.

He found Henderson poking through a lower drawer on the left side of his gray metal desk. Even with compromised sensibilities, the colonel was keen to hear Ames enter. Without lifting his head, he called out, "Come on in." Ames approached the desk and watched silently as Henderson scavenged for another minute.

"Ah!" the elder spouted and sat up straight, holding in his hand a small black object. Henderson stood up and, leaning on the desk to steady himself, stepped toward the lieutenant. Ames was put off by the odor of whiskey exuding from his commander's pores. Henderson lifted his hand and opened his palm, revealing a tiny round object, slightly smaller than a dime.

"Any idea what this is?"

"Looks like a button."

"Yes, that's the idea," Henderson replied smugly. "It's a surveillance camera," he said, slurring his words.

Ames touched his finger to the little device. No observer would have any clue it was anything other than a button. A tiny black alligator clip was fastened to its back.

"The body of the apparatus is made of plastic, and the internal circuitry is too small for a metal sensor to pick up."

Fascinated, Ames rubbed the tiny object with the tip of his finger.

"Let me show you how to wear it." Henderson lifted the piece up to chest height on Ames's uniform. He grabbed a button at mid-chest and ripped it from the jacket. The Lieutenant looked down, stunned. *The colonel must really be looped.* Henderson placed the torn-off button in Ames's jacket pocket and told him, "Hang onto that—you'll need it later."

Bewildered, Lieutenant Ames searched the colonel's eyes.

Henderson lifted the tiny camera to the site of the clipped button and pinched it onto the jacket. Driscoll was amazed at how firmly the unit held in place. The colonel reached for Ames's other lapel and slipped the button through the opening. He smoothed the lieutenant's uniform jacket and stepped back to survey his work. "Pretty much undetectable, wouldn't you say?"

Ames looked down at the fake button. It was completely inconspicuous.

"To activate the camera, simply squeeze it from front to back." Confused yet curious, Ames placed his right thumb on the back of the button, his right forefinger on the front. Then he squeezed as instructed. He felt an almost imperceptible click. He looked up at Henderson.

"To take a photo, squeeze the button on both of the outer edges." Ames complied as directed. Again he felt a tiny click.

"That's it. You can take about thirty pictures with the device."

"Pictures of what?"

"Follow me and I'll show you."

*The Vatican*
*August 27*

# Leo 3

Stretched out in his marble bathtub adorned with gold-plated faucets, Father Leonardo Bonfiglio stared at the ornate Venetian plastered ceiling. It was now six months since the questioning voice had begun to distract him. After twenty-four years in the priesthood, Leo expected that his youthful doubts about church doctrine and dogma would have been put to rest by now. But at age forty-nine, in a position of high authority in the Catholic Church, Leo should have outgrown such sophomoric rebellion—or so he believed. *Is some devil attempting to undermine my conviction?*

As Leo reached for the soap in the tray behind his head, he noticed how smooth and soft his bicep had become, with barely any muscle definition, enfolded by a layer of fat that had slowly crept up on him over two decades. His mind drifted to the years between leaving his parents' home at age seventeen and entering the monastery at twenty-two. Young Leo had traveled through Italy, France, and Germany, engaging any labor that would earn him a wage. He had plucked succulent burgundy grapes in Tuscany vineyards, stoked wood on the steam engines of luxury liners cruising the Rhine, and ported the packs of mountain climbers in the Pyrenees. Ah, if he could once again feel the purifying sweat born of honest labor, a manly appetite, and deep, renewing sleep at the foot of windows open to crisp mountain air! But more than twenty years as a sedentary cleric had taken their toll. Too little exercise, too much pasta, constantly being indoors, and breathing polluted Roman air had bestowed the once-robust man with a paunchy gut, stiff joints, constipation, and insomnia. Leo tried to convince himself that his spiritual practice should lift him beyond physical concerns, yet it seemed that his body was daily giving him more signs that he had drifted inexorably far from the hale lifestyle he once relished.

A knock at the door shook the priest from his contemplation. Sister Isabel Rosario had arrived to retrieve his dinner dishes. "Please come in—I'm in the bath," he called in a loud voice, hoping his words would carry through two thick wooden doors. But when he did not hear the chamber door close behind her, he knew the nun did not hear him. Grunting, Leo pulled himself out of the tub, grabbed a towel to hastily dry his body, and donned the thick white robe that seemed to be shrinking more around his middle with each passing winter. Leo opened the bathroom door a small width and repeated his call. This time he was answered by a soft yet firm, "Sorry to disturb you, Monsignor."

Leo kept the door slightly open to lower the room temperature in the aftermath of his steamy bath. In the crack he observed Sister Isabel faithfully walking to his tray of used dinnerware and lifting the plates one by one onto her bussing tray. *I wish I could be as childlike in my faith as her.*

Although the nun had continued to deliver his meals without flaw, Monsignor Bonfiglio knew he had shaken her with his probing conversation. In contrast to the childlike lightheartedness his servant generally displayed, he now sensed a certain trepidation in her demeanor. If there was anything he could do to relieve the good woman of her anxiety, he would gladly do so.

The priest opened the bathroom door and stepped into the living area as Sister Isabel was about to pick up his coffee cup, the last item in her cleanup routine. "Sister . . ." he called to her.

The nun turned with a start and saw her supervisor standing before her in his robe. This was not unusual, since she often arrived as he was entering or leaving his evening bath, and he was always respectfully attired. "Yes, Monsignor?"

"About our conversation the other night . . ."

The nun lowered her head.

"Please, hear me out."

She looked up meekly.

"I did not mean to intimidate you with my questioning, Sister. You have seemed a bit . . . hesitant . . . since that evening."

To Leo's surprise, Sister Isabel did not blush or retreat. Instead, she seemed to find some confidence. "No need for apology, Monsignor. To be honest, your question made me think. I also wonder about the future of the Church and the fate of the world."

Father Leo was pleased at her response. This was the most honest conversation the two had ever had. Suddenly he realized how boring and banal his interactions had become—not just with Sister Isabel, but with his fellow priests, the Church administrators, and practically everyone. It became painfully obvious that dogma, protocol, and politics had eclipsed authentic communication. "Thank you for your honesty, Sister," he replied. "It is a relief to be able to discuss these matters without shame or apology."

The nun set the dinnerware on her cart. "I once asked my confessor why one day it was a sin to eat meat on Friday, and the next day, by a vote of men, that act was no longer a sin."

"And what did he tell you?"

"He gave me a strict penance for questioning the wisdom of the Church elders."

Leo issued a short harrumph. He hated when priests punished sincere inquiry. If a religion's tenets are solid, he reasoned, they should stand the test of questions, not castigate those who pose them.

"How do you feel about— "

Monsignor Bonfiglio's question was interrupted by the telephone ringing. *No one ever phones at this hour.* His mind flew to the Holy Father. Could he be ill?

"Excuse me, Sister," he said as he hastened to the black telephone on the end table beside the couch. He pressed the speakerphone button. "This is Father Bonfiglio."

"I'm sorry to disturb you, Monsignor," came the voice. It was Abramo, the night manager of the priests' quarters. "There is a young man here to see you."

"At nine at night?" The priest did his best to not appear perturbed. "Ask him to phone my secretary in the morning. She'll make a proper appointment."

Sister Isabel, wishing not to intrude on the monsignor's conversation, took hold of the bussing cart and began to roll it toward the door.

"This fellow says he came from Tuscany to see you," Abramo went on.

"Well, that's very nice, but I am not seeing anyone at this hour."

Leo heard the manager place his hand over the phone, muffling a short interchange. Finally Abramo removed his hand from the mouthpiece. "He says he is twenty-seven years old."

"So?"

"He has an important message for you from Kristina Adimari."

Leo took a moment to try to make sense of these odd bits of unrelated information. The lateness of the hour and the Monsignor's glass of after-dinner wine had rendered his reasoning fuzzy. But when his wheels of thought finally kicked in, he grew wary and his stomach began to unsettle. Shaky, he leaned onto the back of the couch to steady himself. He could feel the palms of his hands growing clammy.

"Monsignor Bonfiglio—are you there?"

The priest forced himself to take a long, controlled breath. Finally he told the guard, "Send him up."

*Blue Ridge Mountains*
*August 31*

# Lauren 3

Lauren's once-shiny red Prius, spattered with mud after forging through deep puddles, pulled into the visitor center parking lot. A chill rippled through her as she realized she would soon face the man who simultaneously sent her to heaven and plunged her into hell. Then she recalled Fern from Flatbush's comforting words, "Either way you will know."

The nervous traveler ascended the creaking wooden steps and craned her neck to peer inside the cabin. The space was stark, with but a white two-seat couch against a wall, and a large mahogany desk in front of a window, occupied by a girl with frizzy brown hair and sparkles on her cheek. Her eyes were glued to a large Apple monitor. When the receptionist saw Lauren, she looked up and exuded, "Welcome to Project Genesis!" Her voice was so over-the-top chipper that Lauren was tempted to just say she was in the wrong place and drive home. "How can I help you?"

*Too late to bolt.*

"I'm here to see Todd Alexander," Lauren stated in a business-like voice she hoped would ratchet Little Miss Sunshine down a notch or two.

"Why, of course!" the granola girl replied, exuberant as a puppy. "Todd told us you would be coming . . . Leslie, right?"

"Actually, Lauren."

"Right—Lauren. Sorry about that. I've been on a raw food diet for a month, and details have a way of getting away," she offered with a girlish titter.

*I'll buy you a steak if that will help.*

"I'm Sunflower, the Welcome Center Greeter."

*Please don't hug me. Whatever you do, please don't hug me. If you do, I swear I'll smother you with your frilly pioneer dress.*

Sunflower stood and stepped toward Lauren, who resisted the temptation to reach for the can of Mace in her purse. *Does this stuff work on New Agers?* Fortunately, the greeter did not attempt to hug the visitor, bow in Namaste, or give her a tunic to wear. Instead, she moved toward the door and motioned to Lauren to follow.

*First stage of gauntlet, complete.*

Once outside, Sunflower strode to the side of the cabin and grabbed a large wooden garden cart, which she pulled to Lauren's car and set it behind the trunk. "Do you have any luggage?"

"Just this overnight bag." Lauren pointed to a paisley airline carryon in the back seat of the Prius.

"We can put that and anything else you'll need in this cart."

"Can't I just drive to wherever Todd is?"

"Sorry. . . We don't allow motorized vehicles beyond this point. We're trying to create a sustainable environment."

She motioned toward the surrounding trees, as if proud of their health. "It's just a short walk."

*Breathe, Lauren, breathe.*

"Well, okay. But if anything happens to my car. . ."

Sunflower shook her head. "No worries. The worst thing that could happen to your car would be to collect some bird droppings."

*Would that be from the bluebird of inordinate happiness?*

Lauren opened the left rear door, pulled out her overnight bag, and loaded it into the cart.

"Ready?" asked Sunflower.

Lauren nodded as the greeter began to pull the garden cart down a bumpy dirt path. Lauren looked over her shoulder to get a fix on the Prius's location in case she needed to make a quick getaway.

# Kenton 3

Kenton Baine stopped at the door of the Higher Design Café and studied a long, intricate crop formation replica etched in the glass. The symmetrical design of triangles within triangles drew him in like a *Yantra*, sacred mystical art yogis have used for thousands of years to take them into deep meditation. These crop circles, Kenton had heard, were not just advanced geometry projects; they were portals to other dimensions.

Suddenly the design flew toward Kenton. He jumped back to see a young Goth guy with long dyed-jet-black hair opening the door from the inside. When the kid realized he had almost bashed Kenton in the nose, he mumbled, "Oh, sorry, sir." Kenton stepped back and collected himself. *Feet on the ground, Baine.*

As Kenton stepped inside the café, he saw the interior walls filled with photos of crop formations: simple circles; long, thin designs strung together with hieroglyphic-like symbols; fantastically elaborate webbed patterns; some that looked like jellyfish; others, three-dimensional cubes within pyramids; and one a pixilated portrait of an alien face. Whoever or whatever was creating these images had a flair for depth, variety, art, geometry, and even humor. The drawings were far more than interdimensional doodling, Kenton had long ago surmised; they were cosmic crypto-grams calling humankind to decipher some other-worldly message. *What do they want us to know?*

A few dozen people occupied tables along a wall and stools at a counter. The diversity among the patrons dashed Kenton's presuppositions about the kind of person who would be attracted to this phenomenon. As expected, there were a number of alternative-culture types, women wear-ing muumuus, crystals, and pendants in shapes of some of the crop formations. Yet the woo-woo fringe comprised but a small portion of the customers. There were well-dressed pensioners; backpackers; tourists with loud shorts, knee sox, and cameras; dignified British businessmen in suits; and a few guys wearing blue coverall uniforms from the local tele-phone company. As Kenton strode past several tables, he heard people speaking Spanish, German, and Chinese. At one table, two fellows traced a formation photo with their fingers, pointing back and forth between the image and an advanced calculus book. At the next table, Kenton heard a heated argument about government cover-ups and the illu-minati conspiracy.

When a tall blonde Nordic-looking guy vacated a stool at the counter, Kenton seized his chance to sit down. He took the seat and a pretty Indian girl wearing a red sweater and a small gold nose ring came to wait on him.

"I'd like a coffee, please."

"Just a coffee?" she asked with a thick Indo-British accent. "No fancy Italian-name variations, non-dairy milk substitutes, or personalized instructions on length of heating and height of froth?"

"A simple coffee will be just fine, thanks," he answered with a polite smile.

"Wow, I wish all my customers were as easy as you," she giggled as she turned toward the coffee machine.

*Maybe too easy,* Kenton thought as he considered his suffocating marriage. But, off duty now, he gazed down at a dozen photos of crop formations displayed beneath the glass countertop, including several he had never seen before. Without looking up, he reached for a few packets of cream and sugar in a little bowl at arm's length. Suddenly the sound of glass banging against glass jarred him. He looked up to see that he had knocked over a glass on the counter. Fortunately, it was empty. He quickly set the container aright and turned to the customer next to him.

"Sorry about—," he started to say, but stopped when he recognized the Japanese woman he had met in the crop formation yesterday.

"No problem," the woman answered. Then she studied Kenton's face. "I saw you at Alton Barnes."

"That's right."

"Some synchronicity that we meet again?"

"Maybe the extraterrestrials have arranged it," Kenton quipped with a boyish grin. "Like in *Close Encounters of the Third Kind,* where all those people had a vision of that mountain and were mysteriously drawn to it together." Kenton playfully hummed the *Close Encounters* theme.

The petite woman smiled. "Have you been to any more crop formations?"

Kenton shook his head. "I'm a hostage on vacation with my wife. She's dragging me through department stores and on double-decker bus tours. She's at the spa now, so I escaped for a couple of hours."

"Good for you," the lady offered with a nod as Kenton's coffee arrived. He stirred his sugar into the cup, careful not to knock anything else over. She extended her hand. "My name is Yoshi—but my friends call me *Deru Kugi*." Kenton met her hand with his and shot her a perplexed look.

"It means, 'Nail that Sticks Out.' There is a Japanese saying, 'The nail that sticks out is the one that will be pounded with the hammer.' In my culture, you're not supposed to call attention to yourself. But in school I was always asking questions and challenging the teachers. One teacher told me, 'You are like the nail that sticks out.' So the nickname stayed with me. . . I kind of like it."

Kenton smiled. "My name is Kenton. It means, 'Nail Pounded in for a Very Long Time.'"

Yoshi giggled. "Maybe you'll get lucky and be taken aboard a spacecraft like the guy in *Close Encounters*."

His eyes lit up. "Sign me up! There has to be more to life than waiting outside Nordstrom dressing rooms." Kenton glanced at his watch. "Damn, I need to get back. Cynthia will be really pissed if I'm not there when she gets back." He picked up his check and stood. "Nice talking to you, Sticking Out Nail."

"You, too, Pounded In Nail."

# Brianna 4

Brianna grabbed her steaming cup of Joe and twisted back past the line of bleary-eyed coffee lovers waiting to place their orders. The rainy morning had brought Starbucks aficionados out in force. She took a quick sip and stood in the middle of the shop, searching for an empty seat, looking forlorn.

"There's a couple seats around the corner," a voice called to her.

Brianna recognized the voice and turned. There stood a tall, bald black man wearing a green apron, holding at his side a gray plastic tray of bussed plates, cups, and silverware. His back was slightly bent, his eyes glassy with age. Sparse white stubble dotted his cheeks. "Hey, Ozzie, how's it goin'?"

"Can't complain," he answered, his warm smile revealing an upper front tooth capped with gold. "Even if I did, wouldn't do me no good."

Brianna smiled. She got a kick out of this earthy fellow who always had a kind word and dropped nuggets of simple wisdom she didn't find in her textbooks.

Ozzie pointed to a nook and she flashed him a grateful nod. A table in the corner offered a vacant chair across from a guy sitting with his back to her. An older fellow with a spray of thick grayish hair poking out of a tweed Rex-Harrison-style Elgin hat. Today's issue of *The New York Times* was spread on the table before him.

"Mind if I sit here?"

The man looked up. A jolt ran through Brianna. "Professor Hathaway?"

He studied her face for a long moment. "Ah . . . You're Brad Marlowe's sister. . . Brenda, is it?"

"Brianna."

"Yes, of course. . . Brianna. . . Please, have a seat." He extended his arm, motioning graciously.

Brianna squeezed into the chair wedged between the table and wall. "I can't believe I'm running into you here."

"Life is brimming with synchronicities," he replied with a sneaky smile as he folded the newspaper and placed it on the empty chair at his side. "You were at the salon the other night."

"Yes, I really enjoyed it. You were out there, but brilliant."

He chuckled. "I detest dull interactions and I do what I can to keep myself stimulated."

As Brianna set her cup on the table, she noticed Hathaway's phone, face up. His wallpaper showed a picture of a sheep.

"Do you have a pet sheep?"

He shook his head. "That's Dolly—the first animal that scientists successfully cloned."

Brianna picked up the phone and studied the photo. "I read somewhere that you can freeze your dog after it dies, and then when science perfects cloning, you can regenerate it."

Hathaway nodded almost suspiciously. "That day is not as far away as most people would expect."

"Just imagine if you could bring some great historical figure back to life, like Plato, or Buddha, or President Kennedy. All you would need would be some of their cells, right? How cool would that be?"

A strange glint began to glow in the professor's eyes. He was now far more engaged, almost edgy. He stared at Brianna's face to the point that she started to feel creepy. Finally he spoke. "May I ask your birthday?"

She hesitated, then answered, "January tenth."

Hathaway looked off to the side, as if trying to compute a math problem in his head. "And your city of birth?"

"Philadelphia . . . Are you, like, an astrologer, too?"

Hathaway shook his head. "And Brad is your elder brother, right?"

Brianna nodded cautiously. For the first time since Brianna had encountered Professor Redmond Hathaway, he seemed flustered. He stared at Brianna for another few moments and asked, "May I have your phone number?"

Brianna was befuddled. *Is Professor Hathaway on to some secret about me? Hitting on me? Is he just nuts?* Yet for some odd reason she trusted the man, and nodded. He handed her his phone and she typed her number into his contacts.

"Thank you very much," the professor said as he stuffed the phone into his jacket pocket. He rose and abruptly left the café, leaving Brianna alone with her coffee and a head full of questions.

*The Pentagon*
*August 25*

## Driscoll 4

Lieutenant Driscoll Ames followed Colonel Wendell Henderson into the Pentagon elevator and watched the senior officer pass a key card through a magnetic reader. A hidden panel door sprang open, revealing buttons for twenty floors. Ames had heard there were floors below ground level, but he had no idea there were so many. What those levels contained was known only to a select circle he was about to enter.

Not that the lieutenant did not have respectable clearance. During his three-year tour of intelligence duty in Afghanistan, he had learned secrets about the governments of the world—including the U.S.—that would make most people even more nervous about their safety and privacy than they already are. He had also learned to keep his mouth shut and execute with precision. If anyone was worthy of a journey to the inner sanctum of military secrets, it was Driscoll Ames. *Why* he was here was now the question.

When the light above the door flashed at 18, the elevator came to a quiet halt and the door opened. At the entrance stood two brawny rifle-bearing marines poised at stiff attention. They scrutinized the visitors as they exited the elevator, intimidating the two with practiced stares. Henderson flashed his I.D. and the marines saluted. The guards turned briskly and escorted the two visitors down a long corridor under fluorescent lights that made Ames antsy.

At the end of the hall Driscoll could see a lone door guarded by another pair of marines, equally stern. Though still queasy, he was becoming intrigued. The sentries guided Colonel Henderson to pass his I.D. card through a scanner and then place two index fingers on a reader. Finally he had to lean his head onto a small chinrest for a retinal scan. When the process was complete, the LCD display read, "Colonel Wendell Randolph Henderson #0573987421 cleared for entry." The guards stepped aside, saluted, and the heavy iron door slid open.

## *Leo 4*

After ten minutes that seemed like sixty, Father Leo heard a knock at his door. He stood, smoothed his robe, and walked toward the portal, his breath choppy. He forced himself to reach for the doorknob, and turned it slowly. As he pulled the tall wooden door open, it seemed fifty pounds heavier than usual.

Standing before him he beheld a good-looking fellow nearly his own height, with thick black hair and a trim physique. The young man wore jeans and an open-necked white billowy shirt. With the exception of a light stubble beard, he looked neat and well-groomed. He wore no jewelry, not even a cross or a watch; his only accoutrement was a brown leather shoulder bag. The priest caught the young man's eyes and the two stared at each other for a thick moment.

"Please, come in."

The fellow nodded and entered. Leo gestured toward the couch, and the visitor sat down, scanning the apartment as if he had stepped into some alien world.

"Would you like a drink?"

"Perhaps some water, thank you."

Leo stepped toward a small refrigerator on a counter in the room corner, found a bottle of San Pellegrino, and poured the contents into a tall glass. Then he poured one for himself and, his back to his guest, tossed in a shot of Nero malt whiskey. He turned, delivered the water, and sat down in the maroon leather chair at an angle to the couch.

The nervous priest took another breath and looked the young man directly in his eyes. The visitor reached into his shoulder bag and pulled out an envelope. "Kristina asked that you read this before we speak," he told the monsignor.

Leo hesitantly took the envelope and opened it. Silently he read:

*My Dear Leo,*

*It has been so very long since we last saw each other. I have thought about you many times over the years, and learned about your vocation through mutual friends and some items I read in the news. I am very proud of the honors you have achieved, and happy that you are so close to His Holiness.*

*I know that it must be a great shock for you to meet your son. Paolo is a fine young man. It was not easy for me to raise him by myself, but he has become my best friend. Since he was a little boy, he has wanted to know his father. I told him that his dad lived in a distant land, too far for us to travel. But in light of recent events, I decided that I needed to tell him the truth.*

Hand shaking, Leo set the letter on his knees and closed his eyes. Never in his wildest imaginings did he expect anything like this to occur. He glanced at Paolo, who sat stone-faced waiting for Leo to go on. The stunned priest picked up the letter and continued to read:

*The time you and I spent together during the summer you were in Tuscany was the most wonderful and magical of my life. I fell in love with you then, and I have loved you ever since. When I learned I was pregnant, I struggled deeply with the decision of whether or not to tell you. You had just left Tuscany to enter the seminary. I knew that you cared about me, but I also knew that your real love was your vocation. Even while we were together I felt your spirit longing for the monastic life. After much soul-searching, I realized that I could not compete with God for your affections. I did not want to distract you from your path, or have my child grow up with a father who did not wish to be there. So I decided to raise my beautiful boy by myself, and I do not regret a minute of those difficult but rewarding years. I have never married. Many times I wished I had a partner and I thought of you, but I knew that you could never be a householder. I respected your decision, as I hope you will respect mine.*

Tears welled up in Leo's throat. He was ashamed for leaving a woman with his child, and that his son had to grow up without a father. He looked again at Paolo and studied his face. *He looks just like me at that age.* He felt guilty to sit before the boy he had unknowingly deserted. The monsignor stiffened as he realized the repercussions he would face if news of his illegitimate son leaked to the Vatican. He forced himself to read on:

*A year ago I was diagnosed with Lupus. During the last month my health has deteriorated badly. I do not know how much longer I will be in this world. My doctor says perhaps a few more weeks. I have no regrets about my life, and I am resigned to meet the Lord when He calls me home.*

*Yet there has remained but one thing I had to do to clear my conscience, and that was to tell Paolo about his father. I am very sorry to disturb your seclusion, but he really wanted to know you. I believe he deserves that right, as you deserve to know your son. Perhaps the hand of God is behind this meeting in some way none of us understand.*

*Please spend some time with him and help him get to know you. This would make my life complete.*
*Thank you for your love. I will always love you. Please pray for me and our son.*

*Yours in our Lord Jesus Christ.*

*Kristina*

Monsignor Bonfiglio dropped the letter to the floor. He buried his face in his hands, shook his head, and whispered, *"Lord, please forgive me."*

Paolo watched silently. He had had more time to prepare for this moment, but he still had no idea how to handle the encounter any better than the monsignor. He simply waited for Leo to speak.

Finally Leo lifted his head and reached for some tissues on the table at the side of the couch. He wiped his eyes and nose. The Monsignor took a long sigh and tried to formulate the words he was about to speak.

# *Lauren 4*

As Lauren followed her hippie guide down a bumpy trail through a thicket of Oaks, she wondered if her decision to come see Todd was guided by intuition or she was just plain stupid. Her mother had told her that she was a glutton for punishment; the more guys she dated, the more she feared that her mom was correct. Lost in thought, she stumbled on a thick exposed tree root. "Damn!" she spouted and stopped to check her shoe. "I should have worn flats."

Sunflower the Glad-Hander Greeter turned to her guest. "The path gets easier from here on. Let me know if you need any help."

*A good massage and a cushy bed with 500-thread-count Egyptian sheets would work fine right about now.*

Five minutes later the two arrived at a clearing. In the center stood a large hexagonal wooden building with an array of solar panels spanning the south roof. A wide deck extended around the perimeter, offering several tan-cushioned rattan chairs and a two-person hanging swing chair. A splash of purple rhododendrons and white azaleas enlivened the building's apron. Whoever was in charge was taking good care of the place.

"This is our community center," Sunflower told her guest. "We gather here for meetings, yoga, meditation, and concerts."

*And Kool-Aid fests?*

"I texted Todd. He's on his way to meet you now. Would you like me to wait with you?"

"Uh . . . no thanks."

Sunflower flashed another smile. "Just have a seat and he'll be here in a minute. Enjoy your stay."

*Ya.*

Lauren plopped down in the chair with the thickest cushion and checked her heel again. Minor damage, still functional. She let out a long sigh. Todd's weirdness was enough of a dilemma; now she had to deal with a whole tribe of whackos in the middle of nowhere. She leaned her head back on the seat cushion and closed her eyes. *What the hell am I doing here?*

Just as a weary Lauren Delaney was about to doze off, she heard footsteps on the porch. Someone was approaching from the other side of the building.

"You came!" a familiar male voice called out.

Lauren lifted her head as her body stiffened. She stood and turned in the direction of the voice. There he was. Her heart fluttered.

"I guess so . . . Here I am," she answered, nervously flapping her hands against her hips.

As the two stood facing each other for a long awkward moment, Lauren looked her ex-lover up and down. Todd looked robust and healthy, more grounded than she had ever seen him. A dark stubble beard had replaced his clean-shaven corporate climber mode. She had always liked him in jeans and a flannel shirt; they brought forth the rugged inner man. Suddenly the familiar chemistry started to kick in. Even while Lauren's mind rambled with doubts, fears, and confusion, just being near Todd felt more natural than she wanted to admit. It was as if they had never been apart.

"Thanks for driving all this way," he said, stepping a little closer. "It's good to see you."

She wanted to hug him, but resisted. "You, too," she replied politely, hoping he didn't sense she was melting in his presence.

"You must be tired. I'll show you to your cabin," he said, motioning for her to follow him.

*You didn't just assume I'd be staying with you?*

As Todd pulled the garden cart along a wooded path, Lauren tried to keep up as if her shoes didn't wobble and hurt. "I was surprised to hear from you," she blurted as she caught up. She was always the one who started the real conversations.

He nodded as the two kept walking. "I've been thinking about you . . . A lot has happened since I last saw you."

*Not to me. My life has been a living hell.*

"What are you doing here?" Subtlety was never Lauren's strong point.

Todd smiled. "Let's get you settled and I'll explain later." He extended his hand to help Lauren over a graveled section. It was their first touch since they had met. *Oh, so familiar.*

"Is this some kind of new age hippie-dippie cult where you dance naked around a Maypole and worship an icon of Jerry Garcia?"

Todd laughed. "Not at all. It's just a place where a bunch of sincere people are trying to help the world."

"Do I get a hint?"

Todd stopped, let go of the cart, and turned to face Lauren squarely. "Alright, since you asked. . . We are trying to live in harmony with nature and provide an alternative to the imminent collapse of civilization."

*And all I brought was my overnight bag.*

# Kenton 4

As Kenton approached the cash register at the Higher Design Café, he found a young guy in a leather vest over a white T-shirt, sporting an armful of colorful tattoos of Hindu gods. Talking on his cell phone, he spouted in a loud voice, "No way! Fresh this morning?" The kid went on for a while, ignoring his customers. "Yeah, send it over," he spoke into his phone, and hung up. Kenton expected the cashier to finally let him pay for his coffee, but instead the kid kept pressing icons on his phone, apparently trying to capture an image. Kenton was starting to get irked.

When the picture came through, the guy's eyes bulged. He was now entirely oblivious to his customers. "Excuse me. . ." Kenton tried to get his attention. "I've been waiting—"

Kenton felt a soft hand on his arm. He turned to see the Japanese gal he had met twice now. "Look at that!" Yoshi pointed to the cashier's phone.

Kenton leaned over the counter to get a glimpse of the picture. It was a striking crop formation—perhaps the most complex Kenton had seen—an intricate pattern of stars, ellipses, circles, and squares, shaded and pixelated to make the entire formation appear three-dimensional. "Can I see that?"

The kid handed the phone to Kenton. "It's a new formation they found this morning."

As Kenton and Yoshi studied the photo, the cashier snickered. "Do you think some hoaxsters with ropes and wooden planks could create a sophisticated image like this in a short rainy dark night in plain view from the freeway without anyone seeing them?"

*No, no, of course not.* The symmetry and intricacy were phenomenal.

"Where is this formation?" Yoshi asked.

"Down the A30 near Kentsboro. I'm going as soon as I get off work. Sometimes the farmers plow down the formations before spectators trample their field."

Several customers who had lined up behind the two began to look over their shoulders, straining to get a look at the picture.

"Shall we go see it?" Yoshi asked Kenton as she passed the cashier's phone to the person behind her in line.

Kenton smirked. "I'd love to. But my wife signed us up for a time share presentation. If we survive it, we get a free toaster oven."

Yoshi offered a faux nod. "Of course. Who would possibly choose to unravel the greatest mystery in the history of humanity when you could get a free toaster oven?"

Kenton took another look at the photo and let out a long sigh.

Yoshi pierced Kenton's eyes. "If that guy in *Close Encounters* asked his wife's permission to pursue his vision, he'd still be driving a truck for the electric company."

Kenton thought for a moment. "We can take my car."

# *Brianna 5*

A jittery Brianna Marlowe looked up at the unlit Vantage Theatre marquee above the dark box office. She checked her phone: 7 PM—*exactly the time Professor Hathaway asked me to meet him.* She noticed a sign on the box office window listing the schedule of showings—every night except Sunday and Monday. No wonder no one was here. A senior moment on Professor Hathaway's part?

The drizzle shrouding the evening turned to a downpour. Brianna pulled her hood up over her head and dashed under the marquee, next to a large poster advertising *Frankenstein Lives.* The updated uglier-than-ever monster, standing beside a disheveled deranged scientist, gave her the creeps. *Have I been lured here by a mad scientist?*

Suddenly she felt a hand on her shoulder and she gasped. Brianna turned to see Professor Redmond Hathaway holding a black umbrella over his head. He extended it to cover her. "Ready?"

"The theater's dark tonight."

The professor smiled impishly. "Yes—and no."

Hathaway motioned for Brianna to follow him, and led her back through the pouring rain to the side of the theater, down an alley past a smelly dumpster. Anxiety growing, she looked over her shoulder to map an escape route to the street.

Moments later the two arrived at a large rusty green metal door. Hathaway inserted a key in the lock, pulled the cranky door open, and gestured for her to enter. He collapsed his umbrella, walked past her, and began to disappear down the dark hallway. "Wait here until I turn the light on," he called back over his shoulder.

Brianna strained to see where her weird teacher had gone, but the place was pitch-black dark. She thought she heard motion from somewhere in the building. *Is someone else here?* A chill of fear began to eclipse her. She turned and wrapped her hand around the cold steel bar that opened the theater door from the inside. Suddenly light flooded the hallway behind her, followed by the sound of footsteps. Brianna turned to see Hathaway approaching through the long corridor lined with theatrical props—Victorian chairs, tables, lamps, and a coat rack. The walls displayed faded posters of past plays. The place was dirty and dusty and smelled of mold. "Come this way, Brianna," Hathaway said in a commanding voice, pointing down the hall.

# Driscoll 5

Lieutenant Driscoll Ames flinched as the huge steel door clanged shut behind him. He was now trapped hundreds of feet below the surface of the Earth in one of the world's most secure buildings. After twenty years in the service, he knew what military leaders could do when their control is threatened. Was he now in over his head? Would his outspoken opinion about flight 191, coupled with his knowledge of this secret fortress, make him a liability to the government, and a target? He recalled seeing top-secret documents from intelligence agencies ordering murders of people who knew too much. *Will I be next?*

The rectangular low-ceilinged room resembled a museum, showcasing a dozen grey metal tables, tops encased in glass, a canister light above each, beams shining directly on the objects below. From where he stood, Driscoll could not see what was in the cases, but he smelled formaldehyde. The place felt other-worldly. Ames craned his neck to try to see what was on the table nearest him, about six feet away. Still too far.

As he moved closer, he could make out several small objects inside the case. They looked like pieces of metal, but even in the faint light they gleamed more brightly than any metal he knew. If Driscoll had to guess, he would say they were titanium. But the texture was not so smooth; a subtle pattern of tiny holographic hieroglyphs was imbedded within each surface. The objects, about eight to twelve inches long, bore irregular shapes, as if broken from a larger piece. Extremely thin, but apparently strong. Driscoll scanned the case for an identifying legend, such as he might find in a museum display. None to be found.

Henderson stepped closer to Ames's side. "Figured it out yet?"

Ames shrugged his shoulders.

"These were collected in Dalnegorsk, Russia, 1986. Fragments of the hull of an extraterrestrial craft."

A shot of adrenaline rushed through the lieutenant's lower back. "Seriously?"

"Dead serious. These specimens have been analyzed and re-analyzed by our top scientists, and they contain no known elements from the Planet Earth."

Ames gaped.

"The material is tissue thin, yet its tensile strength is far superior to any that human technology has developed. We've been trying for decades to tear it or reverse engineer it. So far, no luck."

Ames remained speechless.

Henderson cocked his head and moved on, motioning for the lieutenant to follow him to the next display case. Moments later Ames leaned in to see a flat rectangular glassy object filled with small embedded circles, ellipses, and triangles that seemed almost liquid. The geometric forms radiated pure laser-like colors, especially purple, red, and amber.

"This is an instrument panel from the ship's cockpit. Completely flat—no chips, wires, or printed circuits we can discern. Our scientists' best guess is that the pilot activated the panel through some kind of telepathic communication."

Driscoll Ames's mind had no box to hold what he was seeing and hearing. He wondered if this was some kind of trick—perhaps a test or initiation. But he was certainly not important enough for anyone to go to this trouble to test him. Then his attention was drawn to a huge glass case on a long table in the far corner of the room. The display occupied an area perhaps ten feet long by six feet wide by four feet high. When Henderson noticed Ames looking in that direction, he pointed toward it. "Go ahead, Lieutenant. You probably won't be surprised."

Driscoll took a half-dozen steps to the oversized case. There he saw some much larger pieces of what looked like metal, similar to the smaller ones he had observed in the first display case. Maybe three feet each in length. These were thicker and darker in color, almost black, far more intact than the tiny remnants he had seen at first. These specimens had rounded edges.

"Can you guess?"

Ames peered into the case and noticed several old black-and-white photographs, one next to each remnant. They showed the accompanying piece in a desert setting, an army officer standing beside it.

"Roswell?"

"Precisely," Henderson replied with a soft chuckle. "I'm surprised these items are still locked up down here rather than in the Smithsonian. There have been so many security leaks about Roswell that it's astounding that there are still people who believe it didn't happen."

"I . . . I don't really know what to say."

"That's what everyone who comes down here says. But after a while it sinks in as a fact of life. We're not the only kids on the block."

Ames silently surveyed the rest of the room, his mind reeling. His gaze fell upon a door painted with iridescent red and yellow diagonal stripes. A keypad was fixed beside it.

"What's in there?"

"Are you sure you want to know?"

Ames nodded.

"If I show you what's in that room, your life will change and your idea of what the universe contains will never be the same again," Henderson stated soberly.

"That's already happened."

Colonel Henderson walked to the door and pressed his index finger to the first number on the keypad.

*The Vatican*
*August 27*

# Leo 5

Paolo Adimari shifted uneasily on the chair facing his father. Monsignor Leonardo Bonfiglio remained stunned and confused. Yet years of posturing for public presentations had given the priest the capacity to maintain the appearance of composure. He sat back and folded his hands as if waiting for a confession. Meanwhile he felt that he was the one who should be confessing.

"You've had a good education?"

Leo shuddered as he heard those words escape his lips. He realized the jarring incongruity between the deep anguish he was feeling and the stoic manner of his question. But it was a start.

Paolo nodded. "I went to Santa Maria Academy in Montecuore. Mom worked in the vineyards to earn the money to send me."

Leo's heart sank as he pictured Kristina toiling under the hot Tuscany sun while he had been relaxing on a plush leather chair in an air-conditioned palace. Had he known of her burden, he would surely have sent money.

"And you have gone to mass regularly?" The monsignor cringed as the question echoed in his brain. He did not want to set himself up as a religious authority figure to his son. But force of habit kept him trapped in banal church rhetoric.

"I used to go, but stopped. Around age nineteen I began to question church dogma."

Leo nodded, wanting the boy to feel safe to express himself. How ironic that Leo, at age forty-nine, one of the most respected magnates in the Catholic hierarchy, was wrestling with his own skepticism. He felt a certain vicarious relief in Paolo's admission, akin to when he had shared his uncertainties with Sister Isabel Rosario.

"One day I went to church and heard the priest preach about a God of love," Paolo went on. "Then he described the horrific hell to which sinners are consigned. He painted gory details of people screaming in a vat of scalding oil, or freezing without a stitch of clothing in the coldest of winters, or being torn to pieces by vicious lions." Paolo paused for a moment, as if reliving the awful visions. "As the priest went on, I could not reconcile his statement that God is love, with his graphic descriptions of how that loving God would torture you if you did not toe the religious line. I looked around me and saw that everyone in the church was petrified. It was then I realized that my church was based not on love, but fear. As soon as his sermon was over, I walked out of the building and never returned."

Monsignor Leo's gut hollowed as he considered that his son had turned his back on the Church that he himself had chosen as the foundation for his life. Yet in an odd way he was proud of the young man for his courage to act on his conviction. Paolo had the guts to voice the doubts Leo feared to express.

"On my way home from church, I passed a park where children were playing. I observed them in such delight, laughing freely, pure joy beaming from their eyes. They were happy, not afraid, recoiling not in the least from a wrathful God. They were far closer to God than adults programmed by a dogma of terror."

Leo was tempted to spout the stock scripture, "Lest ye become as a little child . . ." But he restrained himself from hiding behind his frock, and did not want to appear pompous. Truth be told, tonight's revelation had humbled him beyond words.

Paolo took a sip of water and went on, his cheeks ruddier, voice firmer. "I took a job as an assistant in the public school near our house, and went on to become a teacher. In a single day I learn from the children more about true living than I have learned from the Church in my lifetime. *They* are my mass." Paolo locked eyes with his father. "I see them as the body of Christ. Their joy is the blood of Christ."

Leo sat speechless, his mind reeling. Was his own son lecturing him on Catechism? Though tempted to engage in a theological debate, he resisted. Paolo sat quietly, his head dropping for a moment as if he were letting his own words sink into his soul.

Leo decided to return honesty with honesty. "Thank you for telling me that, Paolo. I, too, ask myself the same kinds of questions," he confessed. "I, too, am trying to come to peace with the contradictions of my religion." *There, I said it.* To Leo's surprise, no lightning bolt pierced the heavens and struck him dead. To the contrary, he felt relieved.

Paolo leaned forward, elbows on his knees, nervously rubbing the palms of his hands together. He raised his head and caught Leo's grey eyes. It was the first time the two men held eye contact for more than a fleeting moment. "If you knew about me, would you have come back to Montecuore?"

The rattled priest felt beads of perspiration oozing on his forehead. He took a long time to consider his answer, and then shook his head. "I don't know, Paolo. This is all so new to me. I can hardly believe you are sitting in front of me. I need some time to think about all of this. Please forgive me if I don't have quick or easy answers." The priest reached for a tissue and patted his brow.

"I'd like to spend some time with you," Paolo said. "I'd like to get to know my father."

Leo swallowed hard. Thirty minutes earlier he was a semi-sequestered priest furrowed deep in the bastion of Roman Catholicism, wrestling with existential doubts that affected no one but his own troubled psyche. Now he sat facing his illegitimate son and news of the boy's dying mother.

"Certainly, let's spend some time together," Leo finally answered. Then he flushed. "But there are some . . . complications."

Paolo leaned back, listening intently.

"Please do not speak of this to anyone. Let me figure out how to deal with this. For now, let's just say you are a parishioner coming for counseling."

Paolo nodded. "I understand." He sat up straighter. "Can we meet on Saturday morning?"

The monsignor tapped his finger nervously on the arm of his chair. "Saturday will be fine." His mind went tilt as he considered all the ramifications of this bombshell news. Where to go to avoid the eyes and ears of the Vatican? "Ten o'clock at Maria del Amato Park?"

Paolo nodded, "Sure," and rose. Leo stood and showed his newfound son to the door, where the two found one another's eyes one more time, as if trying to reach inside each other. That, Leo realized, would take a lot more time and effort than tonight's meeting would afford.

The monsignor opened the door, the two bowed their heads slightly to each other, and Paolo exited the apartment. Monsignor Leo turned his back to the door and leaned his head against the dark, thick wood, his eyes firmly closed. He had not been taught a prayer for such a meeting.

*Blue Ridge Mountains*
*September 2*

# Lauren 5

Sitting on a lumpy round black cushion on the floor, Lauren scanned the Project Genesis meeting hall. Three dozen people sat quietly, most on the floor, several in flimsy green plastic patio chairs against the knotty pine wall. A few women wore long, billowy skirts; others with yoga bodies sported leotards and spandex leggings; a handful of men bore muscular arms of laborers; some were dressed quite neatly like professionals; a few others were old enough to be retired. Sunflower the Greeter sat by the door, like a high school hall monitor.

At the front of the room a small altar bore a tall, freshly-lit white candle. Beside it stood framed images of Jesus, a round-faced Indian yogi with dark skin and long hair, and a dapper contemporarily-dressed older white man with black-rimmed eyeglasses and a bowtie. Next to the altar, an empty chair faced the room. It was draped with a large cream-colored cloth that made it appear like a simple throne.

Todd, sitting beside Lauren, fidgeted. She knew him well enough to know when he was nervous. No matter how kindly Todd portrayed the commune, Laura remained leery of people who smiled constantly, hugged everyone in sight, and smelled like musk oil.

A tall pleasant-looking man with light brown hair and a neatly-trimmed beard entered the room. In his early forties, he wore a teal pullover sweater and nicely-pressed beige slacks. As he made his way toward the front of the room, he offered a half-smile to those he passed, touching some lightly on the shoulder, and waving to others on the far side of the room. When he reached the front of the room, he settled into the empty chair beside the altar. The man took a long moment to survey the room, making eye contact with each person. When his eyes met Lauren's, she found his gaze intense. Fearing she might get hypnotized, she looked away.

"Good evening, friends," he said in a soft but strong voice.

"Good evening, Jeremy," the group responded. Groups that spoke in unison sent Lauren up a wall. They reminded her of kindergarten and church.

"Have you had a good day?" he asked.

"Yes," most of the audience answered. A few said, "A great day!" Lauren wanted to gag.

"I see we have a guest tonight," said Jeremy, turning toward Lauren. Her hands went sweaty and she wanted to run out of the room. "Welcome. Would you care to introduce yourself?"

*No, I would not. Not at all. Not now. Not ever.*

She forced a phony smile. *God, I'm doing what I hate about them.* "Hi, I'm Lauren. I'm Todd's . . . friend."

"Hi Lauren," several folks called out. *Is this some kind of A.A. meeting?* Others smiled, nodded, and waved at her.

"Thanks for making your way to the middle of nowhere," the leader said.

*I might be heading back to somewhere very soon.*

"Is there anything we can do to make your stay enjoyable?"

A burst of heat shot through Lauren's chest. "You can tell me what you're all doing out here," she blurted out. *OMG, did I just say that?* She looked at Todd to see if he was upset. Absolutely. He attempted to stifle his embarrassment.

"Good question," Jeremy answered, not at all rattled. "Very simply, Lauren, we are here to build a new world." He paused for a few moments to let his words sink in. "The old world is dying. The institutions we have looked to for our safety and security are no longer serving their purpose. There are better ways to live, and we are striving to live them."

"Is this some kind of cult?" Tact and patience were two other qualities not at the top of the list of Lauren's virtues.

The group laughed. "Not at all," the leader answered in a kindly voice as he leaned back in his chair, enjoying the repartee. "Everyone is free to come and go as they please. Independent thinking is encouraged. We are each living our unique path. No knocking on doors, begging at airports, or group marriages."

Lauren nodded silently, as if giving the leader permission to move on. Todd was cringing, but she didn't care.

Jeremy turned his attention back to the group. "Any reports?"

A bulky olive-skinned guy stood. The sides of his head were shaved, longer hair on top. "I was working at the cottage today. The parents are feeling strong. They are prepared. They send their good wishes to everyone."

Lauren leaned to Todd and whispered, "Jeremy's parents? You're taking care of them?"

"Not exactly."

"What then?"

"Ask me later. I'll tell you everything."

# Kenton 5

Kenton pulled the silver Astra out of the Higher Design Café parking lot onto the A30 highway, his face glowing like a little boy about to open a huge birthday present. He glanced at the clock on the dashboard: 3:51. By now Cynthia was back at their hotel room, starting to wonder where her husband was. For the first time in twenty-two years, he would not be home when his wife expected him. After countless banal barbeques, wandering through crappy yard sales, and trying on ugly Christmas sweaters, Kenton Baine was off on his own adventure.

Twenty minutes down the road, Kenton noticed a long line of vehicles parked on a grassy strip beside the highway. "This must be it!" Yoshi exclaimed as Kenton turned off the highway and maneuvered the Astra onto the bumpy shoulder. The two exited the car and trudged along the roadside, passing luxury cars and beat-up old pickup trucks. Motorists whizzed by, craning their necks to glimpse what so many people had left their vehicles to search for. A powder blue sky dotted with puffy clouds formed a quiet backdrop to the bucolic scene while a mild breeze sent soft ripples over the brown wheat stalks spreading as far as the eye could see.

All in poignant contrast to the frenzy growing in Dane and Margaret Waithright's field of cereal grains.

During crop circle season, news of fresh formations spread virally through Wiltshire, via word of mouth at local pubs, text messages, Internet blogs, and the stalwart Higher Design Café. This summer, thousands of pilgrims had flocked from distant lands to England in hopes of sighting fresh formations after they mysteriously appeared overnight. By late afternoon the number of vehicles at this new venue would double, and by the next morning it would double again.

For more than forty summers, farmers had been up in arms trying to prevent circle hounds from ruining their fields. Eager seekers ignored No Trespassing signs, toppled fences, and scattered cigarette butts without regard for the fire hazard. Most farmers were incensed by the invasion of hordes packing video cameras, dowsing rods, and electronic sensing devices; some visitors camped overnight to try to capture infrared footage of crop circles while they were being generated. Many formation-bestowed farmers immediately plowed the stalks still standing, which cut short the pedestrian invasion. But the steady stream of small airplanes, helicopters, ultralights, and drones only fueled their ire.

A handful of farmers were sympathetic to the cause and allowed the pilgrims access. Some property owners felt honored by the choice of their field for a message from some otherworldly source; they offered visitors tea, pastries, lemonade, and conversation. A few hosts charged admission or set up donation boxes. Others permitted entrepreneurs to erect T-shirt and other paraphernalia stands in exchange for a share of the income.

Kenton and Yoshi followed a freshly beaten path along the highway until they reached a gap in the line of trees, revealing a sprawling wheat field with visitors milling around an area a hundred yards from the road. They stepped down the embankment and trekked through a tractor line in the standing wheat until they reached the clearing where the fresh formation had been cast. At ground level it was hard to discern the diagram, but Kenton could feel a tingling energy. He looked up to see a drone buzzing over the formation. Ten yards away, the operator focused intently on the hand control's screen while he manipulated the joysticks. When the man sensed Kenton's presence, he turned and asked, "Would you like to have a look?"

Kenton nodded, trying to keep from jumping out of his skin. The fellow tilted the panel for Kenton and Yoshi to view. From a hundred-foot altitude, Kenton could see the entire crop circle. And magnificent it was! A five-pointed star was laid over another one, surrounded by a circle, inscribed in a hexagon. Radiating out from this formation were ten more five-pointed stars, with lines connecting them that made the circle appear like a mosaic in a mosque. Three huge concentric circles surrounded the artwork with pixelated shading that magnified the three-dimensional effect. The floor of the circle was composed of wheat stalks interwoven with each other in a spiral pattern, the array shimmering in the sun.

"Amazing!" Kenton spouted, thrilled to see the whole formation while standing in its dead center. After a minute he grew concerned that he was hogging the operator's time, so he stepped back and thanked the man profusely.

Kenton felt a hand on his shoulder and turned to see Yoshi pointing toward a small group of people gathered in a corner of the formation. Standing before them, a tall, lanky, sandy-haired man in a maroon sweater and gray slacks addressed the group. "Is that him?" she asked.

Kenton squinted and held his hand above his eyes to block the sun. As he studied the man's face and posture, his heart started to pound.

"My God, it is."

# Brianna 6

Twenty paces down the dingy hall, Professor Hathaway and Brianna arrived at a door marked **PROP ROOM: NO ENTRY WITHOUT PERMISSION**. A small stream of light bled through the crack beneath the door. Hathaway knocked three times, then three times again in shorter spurts. A moment later a loud click signaled that an electronic lock had been released. Slowly the door swung open as if by an invisible hand. Hathaway motioned for his perplexed guest to enter.

The "Prop Room," Brianna discovered, was not that at all. The space was filled with tables topped with beakers, Petri dishes, test tubes, computers with massive monitors, screens showing sine waves, and a cache of sophisticated electronic instruments Brianna couldn't begin to identify. The room was illuminated with bright, state-of-the art lighting, a sharp contrast to the shabby theater and dank hallway. The door clanged closed behind Brianna, the electronic lock clicking loudly. Suddenly she felt trapped.

"What is this place?"

The professor shot his student a coy smile. "You are now standing in a delivery room where noble visions are birthed into reality."

Brianna sensed movement in a far corner of the room. Straining to see through the maze of beakers, she discerned the back of a seated man's head, bald with a skirt of black hair. Covering most of the bald spot was a dark brown knitted skullcap, a Jewish *yarmulke*.

Hathaway took Brianna by the hand and guided her through a thin aisle past a table bearing stacks of old leather-bound books with faded gold-embossed titles. Finally the two reached the man she had noticed.

"Brianna Marlowe, meet Rabbi Dr. Isaac Roth." Roth swiveled on his chair and stood to meet his guest. His round metal glasses and thin salt-and-pepper beard gave him an air of authority. His forehead was smooth for a fifty-ish man, his blue eyes innocent.

"A pleasure to meet you," he said, extending his hand to hers. His grip was firm but gentle, skin soft, his kindly demeanor a welcome contrast to the weird sterile environment and Hathaway's intensity. "Please, have a seat," he offered as he cleared some papers from the edge of his desk. "Sorry about the lack of chairs. We rarely get visitors."

*I'll bet.*

Brianna remained standing. "Okay, gentlemen, shoot. Why did you bring me here?"

# Driscoll 6

As Driscoll Ames approached the open red-and-yellow-striped door, the smell of formaldehyde grew more intense. In a flash he was back in his ninth-grade biology class, the day he had to dissect a frog. He didn't like the smell then and he didn't like it now.

Once inside the room, his sight fell upon four tables, each about five feet long, one against each wall of the clammy chamber. The room was dimly lit by canister lights similar to those in the main exhibition room, intensifying the eeriness of the scene. Each table was covered with a large thick curved glass canopy. From where he stood, Ames could not make out the contents of the cases, but he had an unsettling intuition about what he was about to find. As he approached the case closest to the door, his heart began to pound wildly and his knees grew wobbly. *Hold on, man.*

Driscoll drew closer to the glass casket and stared into it. There it was: the body of a creature from another world. The form was not surprising—it looked remarkably like the many descriptions and drawings he had seen in movies and read in books. The body was about four feet long, the large head narrowing to a thin point at the chin. Its eyes were dark, wide, and almond-shaped, tilted at an angle upward toward the ears. No nose, a tiny mouth, and small orifices for ears. The alien's thin arms were almost as long as its legs, leading to bony hands with four long, spindly fingers each. The skin color was a light greenish-gray, with some areas more pinkish-white, probably from long immersion in the chemical solution. There was no navel or genitalia.

*I am looking at someone from another world.*

The lieutenant took a long breath as he stared at the specimen, attempting to grasp the import of this discovery. Again he wondered if this was some kind of hoax. But such elaborate security and entombment would be spent only on the real thing.

Slowly he moved on to the next casket. The body in this case looked similar to the first one, slightly smaller, with a gaping wound on the outside of its left thigh. Driscoll could make out some tissue similar to muscle, quite smooth. A portion of bone was exposed. He scanned the body up to the head. The open eyes of this corpse seemed alive. A chill rippled through him.

*This is real.*

Colonel Henderson approached Lieutenant Ames and stood beside him, staring at the display.

"So it's true," Ames said in a low voice without turning his head.

"Dead aliens don't lie," replied the colonel.

A million questions flooded Driscoll Ames's brain. "Any idea where they're from?"

"Between these and others, we've discerned four races. Origins unknown."

"Others?"

"There have been a number of crashes. Far more than the public knows about. We have a first response team that gathers the wreckage, including survivors and corpses, cleans up, and silences witnesses."

"Survivors?"

Henderson nodded. "A few. Most didn't live long."

Ames tried to fathom this bombshell. *How has this information been squashed for nearly eight decades?*

"Their technology?"

"Mostly still a mystery, except for a few pieces we've reverse engineered."

"Such as?"

"Lasers, fiber optics, and microprocessors, for a start. All sourced from beyond the stars."

Ames took another long, deliberate breath. He felt a little steadier, but the formaldehyde smell was starting to get to him.

"One thing we've ascertained from their instruments and controls . . . There's nothing in them to take apart."

Ames shot his commander a puzzled look.

"It's impossible to break their guidance system into components. There are none. Their entire mechanism is one indivisible unit."

Ames looked down into the casket nearest him. Whoever had lived in that strange little body was much smarter than anyone on Earth. Maybe by thousands or millions of years.

"How did they run their ships?"

Henderson shrugged. "With their minds, we assume. Physically, their bodies are underdeveloped compared to ours—probably due to less activity—but their brains are twice the size of ours, relatively. You know how they say that Einstein was a genius because he used ten percent more brain than most people? Well, imagine a brain twice the size of a human being's, and using all of it."

Ames just kept staring at the body. "Such a civilization could figure out how to travel across the universe in a flash."

"Precisely," Henderson answered. "And one more thing…"

"What's that?"

"They could decimate an entire planet and everything on it with the touch of a button—or a thought."

*Rome*
*August 29*

## *Leo 6*

---

Father Leo Bonfiglio arrived a few minutes before ten at Maria del Amato Park, a fifteen-minute walk from the Vatican. During the three days since he had met Paolo, the shaken cleric had engaged in constant prayer and introspection, fervently asking the Lord for guidance as to how to relate to his son, and explain his fatherhood to the Church and the Holy Father—or not. He more deeply wrestled with the devastating image of his former lover dying. Amidst his psychic chaos, he started to feel some chest pains, which he had experienced a few times during periods of extreme stress.

Leo sat down on a green wooden park bench and looked at his watch again. On a grassy patch twenty yards to his left, a young father was playing catch with his little boy. *Becoming a father at forty-nine is entirely different than at twenty-two.* Watching the young man enjoy fatherhood, Leo felt a pang of regret he had occasionally entertained about not having children. The priest was touched when parents brought their toddlers to him for a blessing; twinges of envy eclipsed his equanimity as he observed the family's joy, a stark contrast to his drab monastic life.

But that life had changed in one stunning moment. Now the priest had a son, and while Paolo was no longer a toddler, perhaps Leo, too, could still claim some of the rewards that parents owned. *But the shame if this gets out.*

"Good morning," a voice interrupted Leo's contemplation. He looked up to see Paolo standing before him. Today the young man was neatly attired in navy blue dress slacks and a lilac short-sleeved shirt. Unlike their first encounter, Paolo was clean shaven. Leo felt honored that his son had taken care for his appearance in respect for this meeting.

The priest rose and extended his hand. As his hand met his son's, Leo felt odd about acting as if this were a business meeting. He wanted to embrace the boy, but the relationship was still too tender. "Shall we walk?"

The sun's intensity had abated today, a brief reprieve from the oppressive Roman summer. "Sometimes I come here to get away from my office," Leo noted as the two men slowly walked side by side. "I find the flowers very soothing." He stretched his hand toward a ribbon of white poppies lining the path.

"I understand," Paolo replied. "An honest day's work in the school garden brings me closer to the divine than sitting on a hard pew."

Leo's thoughts flew to his summer in Tuscany, when he had worked hard during the day and made love with Kristina at night. For an instant, all the years between that moment and this one evaporated, and the supple woman was in his arms again.

"How is your mother doing?"

Paolo pursed his lips and shook his head. "She is trying to stay strong, but she grows weaker daily. She has lost a great deal of weight and she sleeps much of the time."

Leo's heart sank. He paused to gather some strength, and turned to Paolo. "I am thinking about going to see her."

Paolo stopped abruptly as if he had seen a ghost. Distraught, he turned to his father and told him, "My mother has asked me to make a request of you, Monsignor."

Leo faced his son squarely, eyes full of question.

"Kristina has asked that you please not visit her." Paolo gulped. "She would like you to remember her as she was."

Leo's heart sank. He closed his eyes, trying to process the flood of conflicting feelings coursing through him.

"She also wants to respect the life you have chosen and not put your position in jeopardy."

Leo let his head fall back and gazed up at the sky. There was nothing easy about any of this. He took a long, pained breath and a minute to think. "Very well, then," he finally replied with a resigned sigh. "Please tell her she is in my prayers and I wish her peace."

Paolo nodded and appeared unburdened for the first time since the subject arose.

The two walked on in silence until they arrived at a small grotto dominated by a massive crucifix bearing a life-size statue of Christ. Monsignor Bonfiglio knelt and made the sign of the cross on his forehead and chest. Paolo remained standing and did not move. Leo rose and turned to Paolo. "You don't respect the crucifix?"

"I worship Christ, not his dead body."

Leo failed to disguise his shock.

"Why do you pray to a corpse?" asked the young man.

Another stab. "I do not pray to a corpse," Leo answered indignantly. "I pray to Jesus Christ."

Paolo's eyes grew fiery. "Imagine, father, that you had never heard of Jesus Christ or Christianity. Then imagine you went to some remote island where you encountered a primitive tribe. The shaman takes you on a tour and you come upon a life-size painted wood carving of a murder victim hanging from a tree. The emaciated body has been stripped to an undergarment, his forehead pierced with a crown of thorns. The figure's head hangs lifeless as he bleeds from his head, wrists, ankles, and a wound on his side. The look on the dead man's face is one of utter defeat and desolation. You shudder at the grotesque image as you ask your host, 'Who is that?'"

Leo's face contorted. *Where is he going with this?*

"With solemn devotion the tribesman tells you, 'This is our God.' He bows before the idol and asks you to do the same. Then he asks you to eat his body and drink his blood." Paolo paused purposely, to give the priest a moment for the grisly image and pointed question to sink in. "As an intelligent, educated man, what would you think of this tribe and its religion? Would you not find it barbaric?"

Father Leo's churning gut grew even more agitated. He had hoped to get to know his son today, not engage in a theological debate with a fuming young malcontent. The priest had to marshal all his strength to not retort emotionally. When he regained his composure he replied, "It is not the physical form of Christ I worship, Paolo. It is his spirit that lives on."

"That's just the point, Monsignor!" Paolo spurted. "If we worship the *spirit* of Christ, why do we give so much attention to his dead body? Don't you find it bizarre that Christians have bowed before a crucified cadaver for two thousand years, and adopted as their religious symbol an ancient torture device?"

Monsignor Leo was tempted to turn away from his son, but he forced himself to stay put. He had to muster the training of all his spiritual practices to overcome being so triggered. After twenty-seven years of not even knowing about his son, he could not let a religious dispute upend their relationship—even if the young infidel teetered on heresy.

"Can you fathom what this means, father?" Paolo persisted, "If Jesus Christ were executed today, people would be walking around for the next two thousand years with little gold electric chairs hanging on chains from their necks."

Monsignor Leo Bonfiglio tried with all his might to quell the rage rising in his gut. His head began to throb and he felt faint. He reached for a tree to regain his balance, and placed his hand on his aching heart.

# *Lauren 6*

Stepping cautiously along the forest path in the dark of the moonless night, Lauren grasped Todd's arm. As he laid his hand over hers, she felt comforted and safe. "That meeting was about the parents," she said. "What's the deal with them?"

The muscles on Todd's forearm tightened. "If I tell you, will you swear not to tell anyone?"

"Swear."

Todd slowed to a stop and turned to face Lauren. The white of his eyes stood out in the dark. "Have you ever heard of the Essenes?"

She shook her head.

"They were a mystical Jewish sect that flourished around the time of Jesus. The Essenes were disenchanted with the many rules the religion had gotten bogged down in, along with the hypocrisy among the leaders. So they lived in isolation and purity rather than succumbing to a culture of fearful people laboring under oppressive laws."

Lauren's thoughts ran to her parents, who were avid churchgoers but followed dogma mainly to avoid punishment by a wrathful God. She didn't detect any sincerity or inspiration in their practices. She often wondered if her own compulsive behavior was the offspring of their neuroses.

"The story of Jesus's birth wasn't exactly as the Bible says," Todd went on.

"And you know how it really was?"

A chilly breeze reared up. Lauren pulled up the collar on her jacket and inched closer to Todd.

"The Essenes knew for a long time about the coming birth of Christ, and had received guidance on how to prepare. They prayed continuously, ate pure foods, did intensive spiritual practices, and cultivated a sacred environment. They met secretly in caves and basements, meticulously planning for the sacred event. Jesus's birth was not a surprise, as the Bible tells us, but the result of generations of purposeful preparation."

Lauren tried to grasp Todd's story. Had someone deleted some very important facts from the well-known biblical account?

Todd turned and continued along the path, giving Lauren a chance to digest the radical ideas. Minutes later the two arrived at a small wooden cabin. "This is where I live," Todd told her. Lauren looked the place over. The square structure was simple, yet cleanly built. Todd had always lived by himself—a troubling pattern that caused her to wonder if he would ever trade his independence for an intimate relationship.

"Would you like to come in for some tea?"

Lauren, still feeling protective, started to say "No thanks," but then she noticed how sad she felt to part. She grew angry at herself for her weakness to resist. But, then again, she had come to find out if there was any life left in their love. There was only one way to find out.

# Kenton 6

Kenton grabbed Yoshi's hand and drew her across the trampled stalks until they reached the small group gathered around the speaker. The slender mid-fiftyish man held a long, straight shaft of wheat in his hand, gesturing toward the center of the formation. As Kenton edged his way toward the front of the group, a curly-haired fellow in a blue parka leaned over and whispered with a German accent, "How does this guy know so much about this?"

"Brian Turner is the foremost authority on crop circles," Kenton whispered back, loud enough that a few people in front of him turned around, annoyed. He lowered his voice. "He's a respected university biologist with a half-dozen books on the subject. Researchers take his opinions more seriously than anyone else."

Turner squatted and pointed to the floor of the formation. "Do you see how the stalks on the floor of the formation are bent at a right angle? They are blackened as if burnt, and abnormally expanded at the nodules." The crowd leaned in to see that the elbows were indeed bent and apparently exploded.

"The stalks are bent with some kind of microwave ray," Turner went on, brushing a windblown lock of hair from his eyes. "The elbows are heated and softened just long enough for the stalks to bend. Then they harden in this new position."

The scientist held up the straight stalk he had been holding. "If you try to bend a stalk manually, this is what happens." Turner raised his right knee and bent the stalk over his thigh. It broke into two splintered pieces, issuing a crisp snapping noise.

"You can also see that the wheat in the floor is woven together in a pattern, like a straw basket. Simply trampling down the stalks would not create such a design."

A round-faced fellow in a tweed golf cap spoke up. "If not people, who or what is making these formations?"

All eyes turned back to Turner. "No one knows for sure. Let's just call it an intelligence from another dimension. Extraterrestrial visitors? Angelic forces? Nature spirits? Call it what you like, someone or something has mastered a technology we cannot even begin to understand. 'It' or 'they' are as playful as they are brilliant. These designs have stymied some of the best engineering, mathematical, and physics minds on the planet for over four decades."

The audience remained silent, trying to digest Turner's suggestion. Kenton felt in awe of the man's knowledge and dedication. "Now, if you will excuse me, I must continue my research," the teacher said, and turned away.

The audience applauded politely and began to disperse. Several people ignored Turner's request and pursued him with their questions. Kenton imagined that the man was used to it by now.

# Brianna 7

Professor Redmond Hathaway reached to a swing-arm lamp and redirected the light to shine on a wall. There Brianna saw a large yellowish cloth about six feet long, hanging vertically. On it a number of brown darkened spots suggested the image of a man, as if burnt into the fabric.

"Do you recognize this?" asked Dr. Roth.

Brianna scanned the object. "It looks like the Shroud of Turin. We just studied that in Comparative Religion."

Both men nodded.

"You have Jesus's burial cloth in your lab?!"

Hathaway shook his head and smiled. "A replica."

"My friend Dr. Alim Beshara is a DNA consultant for the Egyptian Museum in Cairo," Roth went on. "He is one of the few people in the world who has been given permission to examine the original shroud."

Brianna leaned forward, hands on Roth's desk, her eyes fixated on the image of the relic. "And you know this Beshara how?"

"I'm Professor of Genetics at Albert Einstein College of Medicine."

"Dr. Roth is being humble," Hathaway interjected, his hand firmly on Roth's shoulder. "He is one of the world's most respected authorities in the field of genetic analysis and manipulation. Two years ago his name was place in nomination for a Nobel."

Brianna, impressed, extended her lower lip.

Unfazed by the accolade, Roth went on. "One fact about the Shroud that has not been publicized: a few samples of organic matter were found on it."

"Plants or animals that touched the cloth?"

"No—from the underside of the cloth, where the body oozed blood from the spikes driven through his wrists and feet, and the spear that pierced his rib cage."

Hathaway and Roth fell silent, giving their guest a chance to connect the dots.

Brianna thought for a long moment. "So you are telling me that you have some organic material from the body of Jesus Christ?"

The two scientists stared at their guest so seriously that their answer could not be denied.

"How can you be sure that the DNA is his, not some schmuck who touched the cloth sometime during the twenty centuries it's been around?"

"A reasonable question," Roth nodded. "We've carbon-dated the sample to the early first century A.D. It was taken from the area corresponding to where Christ's side was impaled. It contains the molecular blueprint of human blood."

Brianna smirked. "Come on, fellas. Now are you going to show me a piece of French toast that looks like Jesus's profile?"

Both men disregarded her joke. "Have a look at this," Roth said as he clicked a few keys on his keyboard. A picture came up on the monitor. "This image was captured by our electron microscope." It was a strand of DNA.

"Okay, so you might have a smidgeon of the savior in your lab."

"We're actually pretty sure," the rabbi answered.

"And what were you nominated for a Nobel Prize for, if I may ask?"

Hathaway spoke: "Dr. Roth is the world's foremost authority on cloning."

Brianna issued a nervous laugh as she looked back and forth between the DNA image and the stone faces of the two scientists. They seemed sincere—totally deluded, but sincere. Then she recalled the photo of Dolly, the cloned sheep, on Hathaway's phone.

"So you guys intend to clone Jesus Christ and bring him back to life? *The Passion of Christ* meets *The X-Files*?"

"Not exactly," Roth answered.

"Well, that's a relief."

"We're going to implant a gamete containing the genetic material of Jesus Christ into the womb of a woman and bring him to birth in the modern world," Hathaway stated dryly.

"YOU'RE WHAT??????"

"We believe we have all the information and technology to restore the physical body of Jesus Christ," added Roth.

"THIS IS NUTS!" Brianna slid off the desk and faced the two men, her arms crossed.

"We also believe that the wisdom and compassion he embodied are imbedded in his DNA," Hathaway went on. "Quantum physics has demonstrated that intelligence and emotion are transmitted with genetic material. So it's not just Jesus's body we are resurrecting, but—even more important—his soul."

Brianna took another look at the screen and shook her head. "Do you guys realize you could be put away for trying something like this?"

Hathaway snickered. "Like Galileo spent the last part of his life under house arrest by the Church, for the heretical assertion that the earth revolved around the sun?"

"And Copernicus's breakthrough astronomy books that were banned?" Roth added. "And the Wright Brothers were condemned by their fundamentalist preacher father who warned them that human beings flying through the air was the work of the devil?" Roth laughed. "We'll be in good company."

"Either that or prison," Brianna came back as she paced back and forth nervously. "What if something went really wrong? You might end up with a religious Jurassic Park, a horde of bloodthirsty raptors with the face of Jesus terrorizing the planet and slaughtering millions of innocent people."

"That's already happened, Brianna," Roth stated matter-of-factly. "They called it 'the Inquisition.'"

Brianna stopped pacing and shook her head. "To be honest, I think you are both delusional. But if you can pull this off, it will be the greatest scientific and religious feat of all time. If not, you will be the laughingstock of the century and your careers and reputations will be in the toilet forever."

Roth nodded. "You're not telling us anything we haven't thought about at painful length." He shrugged. "But where would science be without risk?"

"Consider, Brianna, that the time between the Wright Brothers' first airplane flight and a man walking on the moon was only sixty-five years. If you had predicted that lightning-speed progression when those 'delusional' bicycle repairmen started their experiments, you would have been locked up. It's the crazy scientists who move the world ahead."

Brianna let out a long sigh. "Well, I wish you both luck." She smoothed out her sweater and turned toward the door. "I have to get going now. I'm going to Las Vegas for a date with Elvis. Penn and Teller brought him back to life."

As she stomped through the aisle toward the door, Hathaway called in a firm voice, "Before you go, don't you want to know why I invited you here?"

The young woman stopped and turned. "Are you looking for a laboratory assistant? Some millennial Igor?"

"Very cute," Hathaway replied with a forced chuckle. Then his eyes grew intense. "Actually, Brianna, we want you to bear the Christ child."

# Driscoll 7

Lieutenant Ames forced himself to stop staring at the alien body. He turned to Colonel Henderson. "How many people know about this?"

"Just a few top brass. The guards don't even know what they're guarding."

"And no one has ever leaked it?"

Henderson snickered. "A few did. They became *personae non gratae* and ended up on the speaking circuit for UFO conferences. But they had no hard evidence. Just their word against the government's. That lumped them in the lunatic fringe and no one respectable paid any attention to them."

Ames slowly scanned the room full of extraterrestrial remains. "Did the presidents know?"

"A few, not all."

"Because?"

"The Company is selective about who it reveals its best-kept secrets to."

Ames creased his forehead. "You mean the CIA has higher security clearance than the president?"

Henderson smirked. "The president has Level 10 clearance. The highest is 16."

The lieutenant had heard such rumors.

"The presidents who knew didn't want to set off a national panic. Most of them already had plenty of issues on their plate, so they kept their mouths shut. Especially if they wanted to get re-elected."

*Politics before people. Not surprised.*

"Except for one," Henderson volunteered.

Ames shot the colonel a questioning look.

"Jim Keane was really impressed with this. He had no wars or disasters during his administration, the economy was booming, and he wasn't scared. He thought it would be a positive revelation and he wanted to go down in history as the leader who made the worldwide disclosure. He was preparing for it toward the end of his second term."

Ames wrinkled his forehead. "But he never made the announcement."

Henderson smiled slyly. "The Company had a secret weapon."

Ames's face contorted as he struggled to fathom the secret. Then his countenance shifted to stun. *"No!"*

Henderson nodded. Ames just kept shaking his head.

"Think about it," the colonel suggested. "Presidents rarely have interns close to them while traveling, much less gorgeous 21-year-old slim, tall, blonde, blue-eyed hotties with generous jugs. The CIA knew Keane wouldn't be able to resist, so they Trojan Horsed their heavy artillery."

Ames laughed for the first time since the two had taken their journey to the netherworld. "So they hired some college girl to create a scandal to discredit President Keane, distract the nation, and make the alien disclosure an unthinkable liability for a wounded leader?"

"Right on the second part," Henderson replied. "But The Company couldn't take a chance on some novice screwing up. Nicole was already an operative—the perfect candidate. And she pulled it off masterfully."

Ames snickered. "So you're telling me that the only thing that has stood between humanity and the most significant revelation in history was a couple of indiscreet rolls in the hay?"

"Off-leash libido has shaped more world history than any of us learned in school, my friend," Henderson called back over his shoulder as he turned and headed toward the door.

*The Vatican*
*August 31*

## Leo 7

---

As Monsignor Leonardo Bonfiglio gazed out the western window of his fifth-floor Vatican apartment, he paused to savor the ambient ochre twilight. The quiet moment seemed a soothing balm against the turmoil churning in the hidden places of his psyche. In the distance, streets grew noisier as the city came to life after *riposa*, gearing up for the vibrant Roman evening. *Perhaps I should have just lived a worldly life after all, drinking wine, singing, and laughing with comrades into late hours. Here I sit in my golden cage, riddled with doubt and anxiety. Have I missed the heart of life?*

Leo turned to watch Sister Isabel Rosario setting out his dinner. After placing the last piece of fine silverware, she set a copy of today's *Il Messaggero* to the right of the dinnerware. Whenever Sister went into the city for an errand, she would pick up the popular tabloid Monsignor Leo liked to read after his meal.

"Was there any good news today?" he asked with a dubious smile.

Sister Isabel shrugged. "Not much. The regular murders, wars, and scandals." She smoothed out the tablecloth and removed the cover from the gilded plate of halibut. "But there is an article you may want to read at the bottom of the front page."

The priest opened the newspaper and scanned the page until he found the story:

### Vandals Steal Christ

A large wooden statue of Jesus Christ was removed from the Santa Barbara dei Librai Church on Via dei Giubbonari late last night. Sometime after the church locked its doors at 9 PM, one or more persons broke into the church, removed the carved image of Christ from the crucifix, and absconded with the religious artifact. Nothing else in the church was damaged or stolen. In place of the statue, the vandals left a white lily and a handwritten note pinned to the empty crucifix: "Set me free." Church officials are stumped about how the thieves entered the church, since the door was locked and there was no evidence of breaking in. Police are investigating the theft.

Above the article Leo found a photo of the vacant cross and a close-up of the lily and note left by the robbers.

"Very odd, don't you think, Monsignor?"

Leo shook his head as he dropped the newspaper onto the table. "I have never heard of anything like this."

"Perhaps some kids playing a prank." Sister turned toward the door to exit. "Maybe they will return the statue."

"Let's hope so. We don't want to have to chain Christ to the cross. He's had enough troubles as it is."

As Sister Isabel wheeled her cart toward the apartment door, looking down, she tried to stifle a small giggle.

# *Lauren 7*

Lauren sat at the head of Todd's stiff mattress, her back propped against the rough wooden wall, her fingers wrapped around a gray ceramic tea mug. The warmth of the cup felt comforting against the crisp night air penetrating the rustic cabin. The aroma of peppermint reminded her of the late night talks she used to enjoy with her lover, now sitting just inches away. The scene was so deliciously familiar that the months and tears that had separated the two seemed to dissolve.

"So Jesus was no surprise? And he had a human father?"

Todd nodded. "The nest was well feathered. His parents were carefully chosen and they consciously agreed."

"So the virgin birth goes out the window?"

Todd shook his head. "Not exactly. Physically, Jesus did not have a virgin birth. But the purity in which he was conceived was spiritually innocent in that his parents were completely dedicated to bringing forth a master soul. Their purpose was not simply to have sex or bear a child, but to give venue to a divine being who would change humanity's destiny."

There was that word again. "*Parents*—that's what Jeremy called the people in the cottage."

Todd stared into Lauren's eyes as if waiting for her to get the message. Lauren gazed into her teacup, lost in thought. Then she looked up and shot Todd a penetrating glare. "They aren't Jeremy's parents or the parents of anyone else here, are they, Todd?"

Todd shook his head.

Lauren lowered her cup and turned to fully face Todd. "They're the parents of. . ."

Todd nodded.

"You couldn't be. . ."

Todd nodded again.

"You are trying to replicate the birth of Christ?"

Todd gave Lauren a few moments to be with the idea. She just stared, saucer-eyed.

"Ten years ago Jeremy began to receive messages, first in dreams and then while waking. He was told that civilization was on the verge of collapse and there needed to be a powerful and intense energy of good infused to offset the rampage of evil, or ignorance, or illusion—whatever you want to call it—that has overtaken the Earth. At first he doubted the guidance, but the voice persisted and grew stronger. Finally he wrote down what he was being told. He was given the true story about Jesus's birth as well as specific instructions to establish a community to renew the values and practices of the Essenes. He became obsessed with learning everything he could about the sect. Along the way, he met with extraordinary synchronicities. Someone gave him this land—five hundred fertile acres in an ideal climate. That was just the beginning."

Lauren rubbed her forehead and squinted. "And the couple?"

"Several months after Jeremy started to receive the messages, he was told that the parents would be brought to him. Later that week he was driving out of the ranch driveway when he noticed two hitchhikers—a young man and his girlfriend, both about twenty years old. They flagged him down and asked him if he knew somewhere they could stay. It was out of character for him, but his intuition urged him to offer his place for a while. They accepted and they all got along well. Jeremy invited them to stay on in trade for work around the property. They agreed. As Jeremy got to know the couple, he felt sure they were the ones his dream had foretold. Eventually he told them of his guidance."

"And they agreed? Just like that? Sign on the dotted line to bring back the messiah and save humankind?"

Todd laughed. "It wasn't that simple. The conversation developed over months. The couple told Jeremy they had had visions of birthing a spiritual child together. They didn't think it would be the second coming, but they felt it would be an important event, not just for them, but for many other people."

Lauren twirled her hair with her fingers, a habit she indulged when she was nervous. "I don't know, Todd. This is all a bit hard to swallow." She found his eyes. "You've always been really level-headed. I mean, you were trained as a civil engineer! And with me, you've never been willing to take any risks. Jeez, you must be the world's greatest living master of *coitus interruptus.* I never imagined you'd be involved in something like this."

Todd clasped his hands behind his neck and leaned back. "Neither did I. But when I came here for a visit, I felt like I was coming home. It's where I belong."

Lauren fell silent. *I have never heard him talk like this. He sounds so sure.* "What are these people—the couple—doing now?"

"They have lived in seclusion for the past three years, praying, meditating, fasting, and doing practices to purify their bodies, minds, and emotions. They interact with others in the community only minimally. We bring them their food."

Lauren struggled to digest this wild scheme. "Have you ever met these people?"

"Once, just briefly." Todd exuded a knowing smile. "They are the purest spirits I've ever encountered. They are extremely loving and their eyes shine like innocent children. In their presence I felt the deepest safety. It must be like what people felt when Jesus walked the earth."

Lauren shook her head. Todd was the last person she ever expected to become a Jesus freak.

"And all of this talk about the collapse of civilization—do you really believe it?"

"You don't have to be a psychic to see where the world is headed, Lauren. All the traditional institutions that people have dedicated their lives to, have become dysfunctional. The economy, government, religion, marriage, medicine, law, and education are so corrupted that it's only a matter of time until they fall under their own weight. It's already happening."

Todd had a point. Lauren felt distraught when she saw the world disintegrating before her eyes. "And this community is offering a replacement for the ills of humanity?" she asked, half cynically and half inquisitively.

"In our own way."

Lauren shook her head. "I don't know, Todd. This all sounds pretty woo-woo to me."

"That's what I thought when I first arrived. But the more I think about it, the more sense it makes. Face it, Lauren. The world as we know it is beyond repair. The best thing that could happen would be to let our broken system fail so we can start over."

Lauren tapped her fingers on her thigh and turned to face Todd. "And the name, '*Project Genesis*?'"

"Did you ever see the *Star Trek* movie *The Wrath of Khan*?"

"The one with Ricardo Montalban?"

"That's it. In the story, the Federation conducts an experiment where they infuse life into a dead planet and transform it into an Eden. That was Project Genesis."

"So which dead planet are you going to resurrect?"

"Planet Earth."

# Kenton 7

As Kenton inserted his key in the door of room 327 at the Lucknam Park Hotel, he knew that what he was about to find on the other side would not be pleasant. He was not at all surprised, then, to find a tall mustached British policeman in full bobby array standing in front of the fireplace. Another officer, bald, shorter, and more rotund, faced Cynthia, sitting on the edge of the bed. She was still wearing the luxury spa's white fluffy robe with the hotel insignia. Her makeup was off, hair frazzled. The second policeman held a pen and pad in his hand, taking notes.

"My God, you're back!" Cynthia shrieked. "I've been waiting for you since three o'clock! Where the hell have you been?"

The bobby facing Cynthia put his pad and pen away, while the taller one reached for his hat resting on the mantle. Obviously seasoned by many domestic investigations, the two stepped quietly toward the door. "We'll be on our way, then, ma'am," the taller officer announced.

"Wait a minute!" Cynthia called back, the veins on the side of her neck bulging. "Tell him he has no business worrying me to death like that!"

The bobby kept a deadpan face. "We'll leave this to you and your husband," he replied politely. Cynthia grunted, the bobby offered a nod, and the two exited.

Cynthia turned to face Kenton, hands on her hips, like an irate elementary school teacher confronting a student who threw a wad of chewing gum in her hair. "Where were you? . . . Why didn't you call?"

Kenton shook his head. "Jesus, Cynthia, I'd think you'd be glad to see me. I'm a couple hours late and you go ballistic."

"We're in a foreign country. For all I know you could have been kidnapped by terrorists."

*Not nearly as nasty as the one bludgeoning me now.*

Kenton threw his arms up. "Or maybe I was actually doing something I enjoyed, for a change."

Cynthia heard not a word. "Don't you ever do this to me again, do you understand?!!!"

The beleaguered husband sighed, paced back and forth, and gritted his teeth. Then he turned to face his wife, his carriage unusually erect. "I promise you won't have to worry about that happening again."

Cynthia nodded and offered a satisfied smile.

But instead of embracing her as she hoped, her husband walked to the closet, pulled out his suitcase, and set it on the bed. He went to the walnut dresser, opened the third drawer, removed his clothes, passport, and Eurail ticket, and calmly placed them in the open suitcase. As his wife watched in disbelief, Kenton stepped into the bathroom, gathered his toiletries, and tossed them in the suitcase. He closed the valise, set it on the floor, pulled up the telescoping handle, and dragged it toward the door.

"And where do you think you're going?"

"To live my own life," Kenton answered brusquely as he opened the door, walked out, and slammed the door behind him.

# Brianna 8

Brianna wiped tiny tears of laughter from the sides of her eyes. "You guys really are bonkers! Wait, I know—this is some kind of practical joke. A psychology experiment?" She looked up at the corners of the room where the walls met the ceiling. "Where's the camera?"

The two scientists sat patiently, waiting for Brianna to process the appalling proposition she had just received. They didn't expect it would sit easy.

"This is no random selection, Brianna," Hathaway finally said. "We've spent years researching potential mothers. We are asking you because we believe you are the most qualified of all the women we have considered."

Brianna shook her head and smirked. "Listen, fellas—I'm a career woman. I don't want to have kids. I haven't been to church since I was seven. And—I hate to disappoint you—I'm not a virgin."

Roth opened his desk drawer and pulled out a folder. "None of that matters. You are healthy, smart, and. . . . ." He cast a questioning glance at Hathaway, who nodded.

"Have you ever heard of *gamatria*?" asked the rabbi.

"Some Jewish rap singer?"

Roth chuckled, then his face grew serious. "Gamatria is an ancient mystical science that decodes the universe using the numerical value of Hebrew letters in sacred texts. Kind of like numerology."

Roth had Brianna's attention. She was a sucker for left-brain analytics.

"One level of gamatria is prophecy," Hathaway added. "Thousands of years ago, Hebrew scholars predicted World Wars I and II and the establishment of the State of Israel in 1948. All of that information is in the Bible and clear if you know gamatria."

"Interesting. . . But what does that have to do with me?"

"We have been working with Rabbi Zev Kane, a highly respected gamatria master in Jerusalem. We asked him for clues as to who would bear the millennium messiah. He sent us this information." Roth opened the folder and handed Brianna a printout of an email dated a year earlier:

BIRTH DATE: EARLY JANUARY, DURING DECADE FOLLOWING HEBREW YEAR 5760 (A.D. 2000). BORN IN THE CITY OF LOVE ON EAST PORTION OF UNITED STATES. NAME BEGINS WITH ב (B). OLDER BROTHER'S NAME ALSO BEGINS WITH ב. HE IS LINEAGE OF HOUSE OF JACOB. THE WOMAN IS LINEAGE OF HOUSE OF MIRIAM. SHE WILL APPROACH YOU AND HINT THAT SHE IS INTERESTED IN THE RAISING OF THE DEAD.

Brianna was becoming less amused and more uneasy. Her birthday, birthplace, name, and brother's name, all accurately predicted. In Starbucks she had invited herself to sit next to Hathaway and asked him about cloning. Her eyes spoke anxiety.

Roth pulled another paper from the folder, showing two columns of data. "Based on the DNA sample from the Shroud, we did a genetic projection of Christ's blood type and other physical characteristics. It matched your records on file at the college medical center, compatible to ninety-three percent. You are as perfect a genetic match for the child as anyone could possibly be."

"You got my medical records? Isn't that an invasion of privacy?"

"The whole project may sound unethical, Brianna," Hathaway replied, "but you must understand the crucial nature of our work." He cleared a few more papers on the desk and sat next to her. "We are about to reach a point of no return after which humanity will cancel itself out of existence. Unless we reverse this insane march, all the advances of science and spirituality may be lost. It has happened before. The presence of Jesus walking the earth again can be the tipping point to begin to heal the world. Crazy as we may seem, Brianna, we are far saner than most people. We know the power and potential of what we are doing and we need you to help us. The future of life on Planet Earth may depend on you."

*No pressure.*

# Driscoll 8

---

"Now what?" Lieutenant Ames called to Colonel Henderson as the senior officer made his way toward the door of the macabre museum of fallen aliens.

The colonel trained his eyes on the camera hidden in the button on Ames's jacket. "Do you know what photos of what's in this room would be worth?" Henderson whispered.

Lieutenant Ames squeezed his face. "Millions?"

"And then some."

The lieutenant failed to disguise his shock. "You want to breach the highest level of security in the U.S. government for personal gain?"

Henderson shook his head. "Not for me, Driscoll. I don't want the money and I don't need it. I could have come here years ago and taken pictures up the wazoo. I'm thinking about your wife. If she dies because the military can't spare a few bucks, and my son has to sell cars for the rest of his life because the Navy is more interested in its public image than defending one of its loyal sons, then I say let the military go to hell and let the people of the world know the truth."

Ames stood immobilized, unable to decide which was more disturbing—the existence of aliens on Earth, or career officer Henderson's intention to blow the lid off the greatest story never told.

"A couple mil could get Ticia all the treatments and medication she could ever need, by the top specialists and healers in the world," Henderson added. "You could retire and spend precious time with her and your kids."

Ames knew that the colonel was right. As he looked down at the spy button, his mind flew to the devastating image of his wife's body withering by the day. He remembered how Ticia's face shone before she got sick, playing with the kids on Bethany Beach, tossing a stick for their Golden Retriever Molly to fetch. Now the woman's sunken eyes and hollow cheeks told a very different story.

"I'll distract the guards," Henderson said as he paused before the electric eye that would open the door. "You have five minutes and thirty shots. Make them count."

*Rome*
*September 1*

## Leo 8

---

"Would you like something to drink?" Paolo asked his father, sitting uneasily in the Sorriso del Mattino Caffé, watching students sipping exotic hot drinks, texting, and typing on their laptops. This early evening Leo had donned neatly pressed black slacks and a blue cardigan sweater, to avoid the kind of attention a Vatican priest might draw at a coffee bar. The hot drink names on the blackboard were as foreign to him as Latin might be to the kids surrounding him. "Anything will be fine."

As Paolo made his way to the counter, Leo sat dreading the difficult conversation to come. Now he understood the angst that parents face in raising their children. Leo had but one child, delivered to him as an adult just days ago. Already things were not easy.

Paolo returned and set a small round white mug on the table, steam rising from the brew it contained. Leo savored the aroma for a long moment, and took a sip. Whatever it was, he liked it. He would return on his own and learn the new language of hot beverages.

"You've been well?" asked Paolo.

"Yes, yes," Leo answered unconvincingly. Then he paused, fidgeting with the handle of his mug. "There is something I need to ask you about."

Paolo questioned his father with his eyes.

Leo reached into his wallet, pulled out the newspaper clipping about the stolen crucifix, and set it on the table in front of his son.

The young man scanned the headline and then raised his eyes to meet his father's. "You think I had something to do with this?"

Leo tried to appear nonchalant, but failed. "After our conversation at the grotto, I wonder. Forgive me if I'm wrong."

Paolo took a minute to feign reading the article, then pushed it back across the table. "And what if I did?"

The priest sighed. "I just don't want you to get in trouble, Paolo."

The young man shook his head. "The Church is the one in trouble. I'm trying to get it out."

Leo leaned in and reduced his voice to a whisper. "There are people within the Church who consider themselves above the law, Paolo. They don't hesitate to take matters into their own hands." He lowered his voice even further. "The Inquisition is not so far in the past as you might think. Are you prepared to deal with such a force?"

Paolo's jaw firmed. "I'm not afraid. If I get hurt, it's for a good cause."

Leo grimaced. "The Church already has enough martyrs. We don't need any more."

Paolo's breath shortened. "Where does it end, father? What does it take to stop a religion that glorifies pain and keeps people in poverty and unnecessary sacrifice? Without Christ on the cross, the Church has no power to control the guilty masses."

Leo folded his hands on the table and stared squarely at his son. "You're not going to transform Christianity by stealing a few statues, Paolo. The roots of the religion are deeply implanted in the psyche of its two-and-a-half billion followers. The Church fathers have had two millennia to build massive fortresses. All you will do is anger the elders and reinforce their determination." The priest looked around to see if anyone had heard him.

"I appreciate your concern, father. But I want my life to count. I must make my statement. I trust God to guide me."

Leo's face contorted as he flushed and pounded his hand on the table. "Damn it, Paolo, maybe God is speaking to you now, through me, telling you to watch out. How much clearer could your message be?"

*Blue Ridge Mountains*
*September 2*

## *Lauren 8*

Lauren stood at Todd's cabin window and peered out into the darkness. "I should get going."

"I understand." Todd rose from the bed and set his teacup on the end table. "Thanks for listening. And for coming here."

Lauren turned and faced him.

"Todd, can I be honest with you?"

He laughed. "You always are."

*Subtlety is not on my menu.*

"I came here to see if I could get over you. I'm tired of wondering if we could ever be a couple."

"And now that you're here, what do you think?"

Lauren sighed and made a sour face. "Now I'm more confused than ever. It isn't like you to be involved with something like this." She scanned him up and down. "Yet I like the man I'm seeing now."

Todd took a step toward Lauren and found her eyes. "Would you give that man another chance?"

Lauren looked down at her feet and shook her head. "I don't know. We've had such a hard time getting together."

Todd stepped closer, now inches away. "We're together now." She looked up and found the blue eyes she loved to dive into. The gentle strength she had missed for so long was returning to her in soft waves. Feeling safe, she rested her head on Todd's chest and reached her arms around his back. Her heart, touching his, felt so familiar.

*God, this feels good. Why did we ever part?* Her resistance was fast evaporating.

Todd gently took Lauren's face in his hands, leaned forward, and pressed his lips to hers.

# Kenton 8

A soft rain was falling as Kenton pulled the silver Astra to the curb at the Higher Design Café. There stood Yoshi, military straight under a black and white umbrella, Japanese resigned and resilient. The woman folded her umbrella, opened the door, and slid into the passenger's seat. "What have you been doing since I saw you three hours ago?" she asked, attempting to be funny.

"Not much," Kenton answered, deadpan. "I just left my wife."

"You mean you left her at the hotel?"

"No, I left our marriage."

Yoshi turned to face Kenton, her eyes bulging and jaw agape.

"The relationship has been dead for years," he stated matter-of-factly. "Neither of us had the guts to admit it."

Yoshi just stared out the windshield, trying to make sense of the shocking announcement. Japanese people rarely make such rash decisions.

"There's an old Chinese saying," Kenton went on. "When your horse dies, get off."

"But this is your wife—not a horse."

"You don't need to worry about me or her, Yoshi. This will be good for both of us."

Yoshi sat stunned, as if she had swallowed a grapefruit whole.

"Now tell me how you got us into this meeting tonight," Kenton purposely changed the subject.

Yoshi, relieved to talk about something else, turned to face him. "You know that guy at the cash register—the one who showed us the crop circle picture?"

Kenton nodded.

"When you dropped me off at the café this afternoon, he told me about Brian Turner's private lecture tonight. When I asked him for the address, he said he would give it to me if I gave him my friend's phone number—we went into the café the other day and he thought she was hot."

Kenton chuckled. "Hormones make the world go round."

Yoshi thought for a long moment. "Do you and your wife have hormones?"

Kenton took a breath. "Maybe when we first met. But you need a lot more than hormones to make a marriage."

Yoshi wrinkled her forehead. "What else do you need?"

"Both people have to feel free enough to be themselves."

Yoshi laughed. "That's not what I was taught. My mother said that when I get married I should do whatever my husband tells me to do."

"That's why you're not married."

Yoshi squeezed her forehead. "I used to be embarrassed about that, but now I am proud for following my inner voice."

Kenton offered a comforting smile. "Sometimes a nail that sticks out brings attention to where a house needs to be fixed."

He put the Astra in gear and exited the parking lot.

## *Brianna 9*

---

"That's all very noble, gentlemen," Brianna said as she slid off of Roth's desk and brushed back her long hair with her hand. "But I, as they say, am out of here." She turned curtly and headed toward the door.

Hathaway hustled to follow Brianna and caught up with her at the lab door. He faced her squarely. "Would three million dollars sweeten the deal for you?"

The rattled girl squeezed her forehead and squinted her eyes. "You're going to pay me three million dollars to have a test tube baby?"

"Not just any baby."

Brianna laughed irreverently, arms crossed. "And where would you get that kind of money?"

Roth's voice broke in as he joined them. "We have some grant funding as well as an anonymous benefactor who is highly motivated to see the project succeed."

The girl shook her head. "This isn't how it happened in the Bible, as I remember . . . Didn't an angel speak to the Virgin Mary? I don't think she did it for the shekels."

"This isn't about money, Brianna," Hathaway replied firmly. "It's about redeeming humanity. The money is a way to thank you and make your life—and your mother's—so much easier. You would never have to take a job you didn't like; maybe you wouldn't have to work at all. If you decide to have your own family, your kids would be set for life."

"Hey, with Jesus as their elder brother, how could they go wrong?"

The scientists, unimpressed by the girl's quip, maintained their steady stare.

Brianna sighed. "Well, that's very generous of you, but I don't think so." She stepped toward the door and stood facing it, silently demanding Hathaway to open it. He pressed a button beneath a tabletop, and the lock clicked open.

Brianna walked through the door and then turned around, her face squinted in question. "Why would a scientist and a rabbi be so interested in regenerating Jesus Christ? Isn't he out of both of your departments?"

"Jesus was the ultimate quantum physicist," Hathaway answered. "He used scientific laws to achieve healings and awaken people to their untapped potential. I want that presence back on the planet."

Roth nodded. "Jesus was born a Jew. People called him 'rabbi.' He represents the fulfillment of thousands of years of Jewish prophecies."

"Are you some kind of Jew for Jesus?"

Roth shook his head. "This goes far beyond religion, Brianna. It's about ending human suffering. In the two thousand years since Jesus walked the Earth, the planet is no closer to peace— actually, a lot farther from it. In some ways, technology is destroying the world. But it has also yielded us the ability to provide that master soul with another chance to fulfill the purpose he came for. Wouldn't you help do that if you could?"

Brianna sighed. "You guys have good intentions—but I'm not your gal." With that, the lanky blonde turned and began to march down the dark hallway. Until Roth called, "Brianna Miriam!"

She turned and shot a puzzled look at Rabbi Roth. "Why did you use my middle name?"

"Do you know what it means?"

"I was named after my Jewish grandmother. She died before I was born. It's Hebrew for 'Mary.'"

"Exactly," answered the rabbi as he closed the door behind her.

# Driscoll 9

---

Driscoll Ames slid into the cushy faux-leather bench seat at the Macaroni Grill and scanned the restaurant for any other military. Negative. A short Hispanic waitress approached and placed a glass of ice water and a menu before him. Meanwhile his eyes were trained on the restaurant door. As the minutes ticked by, he drummed his fingers on the tabletop. No sign of Cheryl Lansing. Had she bailed?

Ames tried to remain calm, but he realized he had not succeeded when he took a drink of water and noticed his hand shaking. The server returned and asked him if he wanted to order. "I'm waiting for someone," he answered politely.

Minutes later, a tall late-forties woman in a brown suit and yellow blouse appeared at the hostess station. Driscoll recognized her from her photo in *The Washington Post*. He stood and waved for her to join him.

Cheryl Lansing looked pleasant enough, not the hard-boiled career journalist he expected. Her minimal makeup, long brunette hair down to her shoulders, set off by a gray streak, and light jewelry made her seem available, and distinguished her from some of her image-driven peers. The reporter approached, introduced herself, shook Driscoll's hand, and took the seat opposite him.

"You didn't want to tell me over the phone how you got my private number."

"I've been in military intelligence for over twenty years, Miss Lansing," he replied dryly. "No land line in Washington is safe. Even cell phones are questionable now."

"Point taken."

"Tom Croft," Ames stated in as soft a voice as would carry across the table.

Lansing raised an eyebrow. Croft had won national acclaim and journalism awards for his investigative reporting that blew the lid off bribes for several southern senators, a scandal that unseated them. Croft's integrity was impeccable. Cheryl knew Tom would never give her number out indiscriminately. "What can I do for you?"

"It's more what I can do for you."

Ames reached into a brown leather briefcase at his side and withdrew a large manila envelope with no writing on it. Without a word he slid it across the table. Cheryl picked it up and started to open it. Ames reached over and nudged her to hold the contents close to her so no one else could see.

Lansing drew the envelope onto her lap, suspicion shadowing her face. She slid out a handful of eight-by-ten-inch photos and studied them for a long minute. Her forehead squeezed tight. "Where did you get these?"

"I took them myself. Pentagon Subterranean Floor 18. Above Top Secret."

She flipped through more of the images. "How do I know they aren't faked or photoshopped?"

Ames produced the tiny button camera. "Here's the camera I took them with. The pictures are still in there if you want to download them right from the camera and have them analyzed."

Cheryl examined the camera, rotating it in her hand, shaking her head as if impressed by the technology. She studied the photos for another minute, turned them face down, and looked up at her enigmatic host. "Why are you doing this?"

"I need cash."

Lansing maintained a poker face. "How much?"

"A million."

The journalist pursed her lips, looked down at the table, and had an imaginary conversation with an invisible supervisor. Another long breath. "If they are what you say they are . . . and they pass authenticity tests . . . and we run the story, maybe. But I don't know if my boss is willing to put his ass on the line."

Lansing leaned in and lowered her voice. "Why would a military career man with impeccable credentials—I googled you—blow the whistle on the government? Drug habit? Gambling debt? Got some girl pregnant?"

Driscoll shook his head. "My wife has a rare degenerative disease that no doctor in this country is willing to touch. She's fading daily. We found some treatments in Europe that might save her. I can't do it on my salary. The army passed me over for promotion."

Lansing, quite embarrassed, swallowed. "Sorry—I had no idea." She thought for another long moment. "I'll see what I can do."

Ames nodded.

"You know what this means, don't you?" Lansing followed with a cold stare.

Driscoll folded his hands on the table. "I *think* I know what this means, but let's be honest: Neither of us has any idea how far this might go."

"Absolutely correct, Lieutenant. First off, this will be the most important news story ever revealed to humanity—assuming people believe it. I assure you, no matter how real these photos are or how much authentication we cite, a huge faction of people will find ways to deny them. Next, it will shake the government. The public will be outraged about the decades of cover-up; lots of them already are. The President will come under intense heat since one of his campaign platforms was full disclosure. He'll be caught between a rock and a hard place: *'If you knew, why didn't you tell us? If you didn't know, why did U.S. intelligence hide information of the highest importance from the Commander-in-Chief—and the nation?'* Political ramifications aside, science will take a new direction now that it's confirmed that we are not alone in the universe."

Ames sat stone-faced, giving the reporter space to process the potential sequence of events he had travelled in his own mind a thousand times.

"Or scenario two," she added, lips pursed.

"What's that?"

"*The Washington Post* becomes the butt of international derision and jokes for printing a story that belongs in the *National Enquirer*. I lose my job, and the career I have taken thirty years to meticulously build goes down the tubes with me."

Ames took a moment to consider her morbid vision. When he had set up this meeting, he had no idea how Lansing would respond. She was obviously brilliant at strategizing, including doomsday scenarios.

"And what will they do to you, Lieutenant?"

Driscoll Ames shook his head and shrugged. "I could be court-martialed and dishonorably discharged. I might face prison. My family may be threatened and I might become a laughing stock . . . That's just the beginning."

The reporter leaned back and spread her arms across the top of the booth. "Or you could go down in history as the whistleblower who brought the greatest revelation in history to the masses."

"Are you ready to order, folks?" the waitress interrupted. She stood with a smile, holding an electronic order taker.

Cheryl quickly stashed the photos face down on the seat beside her and, though not hungry, ordered a salad. Driscoll did the same, to justify taking up the restaurant's lunch seats and avoid suspicion.

As soon as the waitress departed, Cheryl asked, "Then why not just keep your name out of this? We do it all the time. 'A reliable government source disclosed . . .'"

Driscoll shook his head. "If no one owns up to this, the revelation will lose credibility. People will say that some hoaxster fabricated the images. There are millions of hokey photoshopped pictures on the Internet and fake videos on YouTube. For this story to get the attention it deserves, someone has to stand behind it." Driscoll grew quiet for a moment, looking pensively out the window beside the table. Then he faced Cheryl squarely. "If I can keep my wife alive and give my kids a mother for a few more years, it will all be worth it."

Cheryl Lansing nodded. "You have good values, Lieutenant. Let's hope the world agrees. If not, we may both be waiting tables at the Macaroni Grill."

*Leo 9*

As Monsignor Leo Bonfiglio threaded his way through the nightlife revelers on Borgo Pio, he felt a moment of respite. In his civilian outfit, no one smiled at him, bowed their head, moved aside to make way, or asked for prayers. He was just another guy amidst the teeming masses, conjuring long-faded memories of his freewheeling youth when his passion was strong and his worries few.

As Leo turned onto Via della Traspontina, he was surprised to see a familiar figure walking toward him—Sister Isabel Rosario. Ill at ease to be seen out of his cleric's garb, he tried to avoid the nun by facing a tourist store selling religious artifacts. He quietly gazed at the statues in the window, as if shopping.

"Monsignor?"

He turned and raised his brow in a weak attempt to feign surprise. "Ah, Sister Isabel . . . I was just taking an evening stroll," he offered, more embarrassed than convincing. "Sometimes it's relaxing to be out of uniform."

The thin woman smiled, unfazed. "I was just on my way to find some gifts for my niece and nephew. . . I am going to see them this weekend."

A middle-aged kerchiefed woman passing Sister Isabel made the sign of the cross, and she reciprocated.

Father Leo stared nervously at the nun. "Would you care to take a walk with me?"

Since their edgy discussion, Father Leo had not confronted Sister Isabel with theological issues. But still he sensed her disquiet. "Just for a few minutes—perhaps on the walkway by the river?"

The nun gathered herself and nodded obediently. Leo could not discern if she really wanted to join him or she was surrendering to duty. Perhaps both.

Leo led the way, working through the motley throng toward Lungotevere Vaticano. Soon the two reached a cobblestone pathway along the bank of the Tiber, where young couples walked hand in hand and old men sat on benches under streetlights playing chess, smoking cigars, and reminiscing about war stories and lovers long gone.

Leo finally stopped at a small overlook bounded by a green metal railing. Sister took a place beside him. The muggy day's air had finally started to ease. Both silently gazed at the river for a long awkward moment. Leo looked from side to side to make sure he was out of earshot of any passersby. He turned to his companion.

"May I speak with you confidentially, Sister?"

The ill-at-ease but willing nun nodded.

Leo took a controlled breath. "Do you remember that newspaper article you showed me about the statue of Our Lord that was stolen from the crucifix?"

"Of course."

"Someone who was involved in that incident has made his confession to me."

Sister Isabel looked up, forehead wrinkled.

"He's actually a fine young man—not really a trouble-maker—he just sees himself on a mission. He believes that the Church should stop glamorizing suffering."

The nun took a thoughtful moment to absorb her superior's revelation. "What did you tell him?"

Leo felt grateful to be heard without being judged or lectured. "I told him to be careful that he does not get in trouble."

"I see." Sister Isabel gazed out over the river and spoke again without turning her head. "Can you leave it at that, or do you believe you need to correct him?"

Leo laughed nervously. "Are you asking the priest you deliver dinner to, or the man in street clothes beside you?"

"I'm asking the person who invited me to talk about this."

Leo nodded and leaned forward, resting his forearms on the railing. "To be honest, Sister, part of me agrees with his philosophy. After twenty-five years in the priesthood, I do not feel closer to God than when I began. I feel more distant. I look around the world and I see the poor, the hungry, and the sick. I see privileged people who smile and appear happy, but in their confessions I hear that their souls are in turmoil, far more than those who lack material wealth. Even the clergy in the Vatican, supposedly men of peace, fight shamefully within the Church government. They are as enslaved by the riches and power of the Church as the corporate greedy we condemn. We present ourselves as holy, but we are no closer to heaven than that man over there sleeping on the park bench—perhaps even farther. If our religion is the way to God, why are so many devout Christians in such guilt and pain? I fear that we have magnified suffering more than we are relieving it."

Sister Isabel studied the homeless man on the bench, the wheels in her mind churning. She turned back to Leo. "Have you taken this question into prayer, Monsignor?"

"I have prayed about this long and deep, Sister. But I get no answer. I simply feel torn."

Sister Isabel remained silent. Leo drummed his fingers on the rail. "Walking through the streets tonight without my priestly attire, I felt free for the first time in a long time. I do not have to be a holy person, have answers, make ecumenical decisions, or save others. I don't have to represent the Catholic Church. I had no idea what a huge burden that identity has become. For a moment I feel young again, as if the open sky is above me, not the heavy dome of the Vatican."

Sister Isabel turned toward Leo and offered a small smile. "Then perhaps, Monsignor, you are receiving the answer to your prayer."

Leo looked at her quizzically.

"Before you can help that boy or relieve the suffering of the world, you must find your own way out of hell."

*Blue Ridge Mountains*
*September 3*

# *Lauren 9*

Lauren Delaney hadn't woken up next to Todd Alexander for six months, three days, and one hour—not that she was counting. As she opened her eyes and scanned the wooden beams on the ceiling, she remembered where she was. She sat up with a start. *My God, what have I done?* Quickly her protective mind scrolled through all the reasons she should not have slept with this man. But her body felt so yummy that the objections melted like ice in the sun.

Todd looked boyish when he slept. *If only he could retain that innocence when he's awake. Maybe he really has changed. Wouldn't that be a miracle?* Lauren slid from beneath the tan and red Native American wool blanket and headed for the bathroom. The early morning chill tingled her naked body. Once inside, she put up with the cold toilet seat and the sight of a few ants at the baseboard. *If I ever marry this guy, we're living in the city.*

When Lauren caught herself on the train to Marriageville, she slammed on the brakes. She had gone down that fantasy track many times, and it always led over a cliff. All she knew this morning was that she had had a fabulous night with Todd. Beyond that, there were no guarantees.

A minute later she closed the bathroom door behind her and dashed toward the bed. But something moving outside the window caught her attention. *A guy looking in the window.*

"*Eeeehhhhh!*" Lauren shrieked as she grabbed the blanket from the bed to cover herself.

Todd sat up with a jolt. His eyes followed Lauren's arm pointing toward the window. The intruder did not run away, but tapped on the window.

"Drew?" Todd called out.

The man at the window disappeared. Lauren dove onto the bed and pulled the covers up to her neck. Todd went to the door. Lauren couldn't believe he would open it.

There stood a guy a bit older than Todd, wearing a ragged black sweater and worn jeans. His thick black hair was long and unkempt. He looked distressed.

"Sorry to bother you," he told Todd, then looked at Lauren. "I didn't mean to scare you." Then back to Todd. "There's an emergency meeting in the hall . . . It's the parents."

"Are they all right?"

"I don't know . . . Jeremy said it was important. I've never seen him this rattled."

Todd nodded. "I'll be right there." He closed the door and turned to his lover. "I'm sorry, Lauren. I have to go."

Todd threw on some jeans, his white Guatemalan poncho, thick sweat socks, and laced his boots. Lauren lay in bed, trying to make sense of what was happening. *Same ole' same ole'. Always something dragging him away. I come all the way up here to see him, we make delicious love, and then he disappears. How many times have I seen this movie?*

When Todd finished dressing, he sat down on the bed beside Lauren, and took her hand. "Last night was amazing," he told her. "I need to leave for a little while but I'll be back as soon as I can." He looked into Lauren's eyes as if he really meant it. *Now **that's** a new behavior.* He kissed her on the lips sweetly. A moment later he was out the door.

Lauren sat up in bed and squeezed her eyebrows together. *Who is this man I just slept with?*

*London*
*August 28*

# Kenton 9

"That's the building there," Yoshi pointed to a run-down, graffiti-covered faded gray brick apartment building. Kenton stopped the car and surveyed the Hackney side street with beat-up cars lining the curbs in front of shops with graffiti-covered boarded windows. "Why would Brian Turner give a class in a dumpy neighborhood like this?" he asked.

"The guy who edits Turner's books lives here. He's in a wheelchair and he has a hard time getting out. Brian does a private lecture here once a month as a way to thank his friend."

Minutes later Kenton and Yoshi found themselves trudging up an old creaking staircase that reminded him of a scene from a Sherlock Holmes caper. The aroma of liver and onions wafting from under a door assaulted their nostrils. Yoshi made a pained face.

Nearly spent of breath, the pair finally arrived at apartment 4B. *I should have kept up my gym membership.* Kenton knocked three times on the door, and a sixty-ish woman answered. Her archaic mousy-brown coiffure, necklace of oversized polished beads, and pointy horn-rimmed eyeglasses reminded him of Dame Edna Everage. Peering over the lady's shoulder, he saw Brian Turner sitting on a stuffed easy chair in the living room. The hostess opened the door and gestured for the guests to enter.

Two dozen people of assorted ages and garb were squeezed into the tiny Victorian parlor, half of them filling a couch and some rickety wooden folding chairs, the rest seated on cushions on the floor. A middle-aged balding fellow in a wheelchair sat at a slight angle to the guru's chair. Brian nodded politely to the two new guests as they threaded through the group and found an empty section on the maroon-and-gray braided rug. Kenton was thrilled to make a moment of eye contact with the sage.

An air of expectancy filled the room, all eyes fixed on Turner. "Okay, let's get started," he said, scanning the assembly. The proper Brit took a final sip of tea and set his black mug on the end table beside him. A stand-up lamp with a large old-fashioned tan shade cast a muted light on the speaker. Kenton took out his phone and, as discreetly as possible, set it on Record. He didn't know if that was allowed, but he didn't want to interrupt. *Better to ask for forgiveness than permission.*

"At the beginning of the current crop circle season, I typed on my computer in a file of notes, 'WHO AND WHY'" Turner began. "I wasn't asking anyone in particular. I had just hit a wall of extreme frustration. I was banging on the door of the universe, imploring anyone or anything out there for a straight answer about the source of the crop circles and their meaning. I showed no one this file, but kept the question in the back of my mind, almost prayerfully, for about a month.

"Then one morning when I opened my email I found a message in my inbox, with the subject: WHO AND WHY. The email had no source or return address. I dug into the program to reveal the chain of sending, but there was none. I showed the email to some geek friends, and they were baffled. Even if someone had figured out how to blank out or disguise their name, email protocol lists a string of data about the sequence of transmission, including all of the servers involved, and so on. Any and all of this identifying information was absent. All of my other emails included the proper transmission information. No one has access to my computer but me, and my files are strictly protected by passwords." Turner paused and scanned the eyes of the audience seated rapt before him. "Until tonight, I have never told anyone about this."

A shiver ran up Kenton's spine. Yoshi turned to Kenton and in a low voice exuded a long *"Uuuuuuuuyyyyyyyy,"* a Japanese expression of amazement.

Turner put on his reading glasses and pulled a paper from a folder. "I will now share with you the message exactly as I received it."

*Manhattan*
*September 7*

# *Brianna 10*

---

Brad Marlowe's yellow crewneck sweater made a statement against the backdrop of thick green trees as he entered Central Park from the 59th street entrance. Stocky yet fit, his squarish face remained pale from sitting too long in his cubicle at ESPN sales. He found his little sister sitting on the grass twenty paces from the children's playground, leaning against a wooden fence post. Her head tilted back, eyes closed, she appeared to be relaxing in the sun, but her clenched jaw spoke her angst.

Brad plopped down next to Brianna, pulled a green Gatorade bottle from his backpack, and offered her a sip. Eyes still closed, she shook her head.

"Don't keep me in suspense . . . How did your rendezvous with Hathaway go?"

Brianna grimaced. "Don't ask."

Brad broke into laughter. "That guy really is a card. Did he tell you some egghead quantum physics joke?"

Brianna opened her eyes and stared into the distance. "Hathaway hooked up with this rabbi geneticist and they want to bring Jesus Christ back to life."

Brad laughed again, louder. "Wow, that's a good one!"

Brianna shot him a long dead serious look.

"Holy shit—you're not kidding."

Brianna sighed. "There's more. . ."

Brad leaned in and cocked his head. "More?"

"Hathaway wants me to be the mother."

Brad threw his head back and roared. "Now I know you're putting me on!"

Brianna shook her head. "I wish I was, Brad. . . I couldn't make something like this up if I tried."

"No way! . . . What did you tell him?"

"I'm no lab rat."

Brad leaned back against a big rock and took a swig of his drink. "The dude is seriously deluded—or the next Einstein."

"Or the next Frankenstein." Brianna turned to face her brother, her eyes burning. "I don't care how smart Hathaway and this other guy are, they're not gonna turn my womb into a mad scientist experiment. I refuse to play nursemaid to some *Planet of the Apes* miscreant for the rest of my life because Hathaway overlooked some crucial chromosome."

Brad scratched his head, trying to process the bizarre news.

"I know there's the money and all that . . ."

Brad's eyes lit up. "Money? Hathaway's offering you cash for this?"

She forced the words out: "Three million."

Blood rushed to Brad's cheeks. "Hathaway's gonna give you three million bucks to rent your womb???!!!"

"More if the experiment is successful . . ."

"Holy Mother of God!" Brad stood up and started to pace. "You're not gonna even consider it?" he asked in a voice so loud that his sister was afraid a couple sitting nearby would hear.

"Of course I'm not gonna consider it," she retorted. "I'm no science whore."

Brad squatted in front of his little sister as if facing an impudent child. "Have you thought about how this could help mom and dad? We could get mom into a really good facility, or round the clock care at home, and dad could retire. You know how his health has gone downhill worrying about mom and how to cover her medical expenses. They've struggled for money all their lives, and now they're both sick. This could be the answer to our prayers."

Brianna shook her head. "I don't care, Brad. It's my body and my life. I'll get a good job and earn the money to help mom and dad."

Brad smirked. "And bust your butt for how many years? Then add paying back your student loans. You'll be in over your head until you're fifty."

Brianna groaned, stood up, and stomped toward the road. "Just get over it, would you?" she yelled over her shoulder. "I need a brother, not a pimp."

Brad hustled to catch up with his ruffled sister. He faced her and placed his hands on her shoulders. "Okay, Brianna, I'm sorry. I didn't mean to pressure you. I just got excited when I thought we can solve our family's money issues and keep mom safe." He caught her eyes firmly. "I'll support you whatever you choose."

Brianna's shoulders dropped. She pressed her forehead onto Brad's chest, and the two fell silent for a few moments. Finally she looked up. "If I ever did do it, it wouldn't be for the money."

Brad squinted. "Then why?"

"If there's any truth to Hathaway's idea that a child with genetically advanced intelligence could help the world, that would be a huge contribution." She gulped. "Do you think there's something to his story?"

Brad shrugged. "I don't know. Maybe. He's probably the most brilliant guy I've ever met."

Brianna's eyes grew teary.

The tallish man smoothed his sister's frayed hair. "Why don't you just sit with the idea? You'll figure this out. Whatever you decide, I'm with you for the distance."

For the first time since the immodest proposal, Brianna Marlowe felt comforted. She exhaled audibly. "Thanks, Brad. When it comes down to it, I know you're there for me."

Brad flashed a naughty grin. "Jesus made me do it."

She punched him on the arm.

# *Driscoll 10*

"Tanisha, Jared, come in here," Driscoll called from the edge of his wife's bed. A fragile Ticia sat up and adjusted her red and white kerchief, efforting to keep her kids from seeing her thinning hair. The curious children dashed in and Tanisha crawled into mom's lap while Jared, ever the stoic like his father, took a seat on the bed. Driscoll took a moment to savor how much like himself the boy was starting to look, even at age ten. His body was wiry but firm, thin face set off by a firm jaw. Tanisha, three years her brother's junior, looked more like her mom, round face, big eyes, wide nose.

"I have good news, everyone—really good news."

Ticia sat up straight. "You got the promotion?"

Driscoll shook his head. "Better than that. We don't need the army for our income anymore. I found a way to get the money for your treatments."

Ticia scrunched her face. "What bank did you rob?"

Driscoll laughed. "No bank necessary. I came upon a news story that's worth a lot of money."

"You better not be b.s.'ing me, Driscoll Ames. I'm in no condition . . ."

"What's the story?" Jared asked. "How much did we get?"

Driscoll paused for a moment as he scanned his family's eyes. "We now have almost a million dollars to get your mom to the doctor and treatments that can save her life."

"A million dollars!" Ticia spurted in a louder voice than anyone in the house had heard in a long time. Her eyes practically bugged out of her head.

"Does this mean that mommy will get better?" asked Tanisha.

Driscoll smiled. "It means she'll have a better chance."

"*Yaaayyyyy!*" the girl called out. Jared looked perplexed.

"You kids go into your room and play for a while. Give me and your mom some time alone."

The kids kissed their mom on the cheek and pranced to their room. Ticia laid her hand over her husband's and looked at him suspiciously. "Let's do a reality check, Driscoll. What do I have left? A month? Two? I need these treatments and I want them. But in case they don't work. . ."

Driscoll placed his finger over his wife's lips. "I know, sweetheart. But we both know people who've come back from a dire prognosis. Julie Hale bounced back from stage four cancer. If anyone can beat this, you can."

Ticia took a long breath, closed her eyes, and kissed her husband gently on his cheek. "Thank you, Driscoll Ames. You are my prince." She took his arm and he held her hand.

"Now, what's this story?"

# *Leo* 10

---

"May I sit here?" a soft voice interrupted Leo as he sat on his favorite bench in Maria del Amato Park, watching a pair of squirrels chasing each other up and down the trunk of a tree. The college girl standing before him was plain but pretty, slim face, no makeup or jewelry. She wore a gray *Earth is our Mother* T-shirt and purple leggings. A camera dangled from a leather strap around her neck, a small tablet computer in her hand.

"Please," he answered, graciously motioning toward the space beside him.

The girl took her seat, opened her iPad, and began to press her index finger against the screen. Leo had seen some people in the Vatican using such devices, but never tried one himself. "Are those easy to use?" he asked the girl.

She sized Leo up for a moment, trying to decide if he was safe to talk to. Apparently. "You can find just about anything you are looking for. Would you like to try it?"

The incognito priest pushed his palm toward the student. "I don't want to invade your privacy."

"Don't worry," she giggled cynically. "There's no privacy anymore anyway. Just touch some icons and they will show you different apps."

Leo took the machine, his face glowing like a curious boy. He pressed a few buttons and saw all kinds of dazzling images and ads. He looked up at the girl, intrigued.

"Go ahead, play with it while I get some photos of the birds."

The student stood and stepped ten yards toward a grove of trees. As Leo grasped the techno toy, he felt like an ape in the movie *2001: A Space Odyssey*, pawing a mysterious monolith sent to Earth from some distant civilization. He found a shopping app, then a rock music feed, and one showing current movie listings—all colorful, but nothing caught his fancy. Then he saw one labeled Breaking News. *Ah, maybe something I'll understand.*

A screen came up displaying stories about a local politician who used a government credit card to hire prostitutes, and Roman citizens incensed about the increased sales tax. *All the same mayhem I read in the newspaper.* As he was about to set the device down, he noticed a photo showing a large crucifix in a church. Next to it a priest pointed to some holes on the crucifix. Leo recognized the priest, Father Joseph Ulario, from a local church. The headline read:

## Crucifix Vandals Strike Again

He scrolled down and read:

The fifth in a series of crucifix defacements occurred at the Sant'Ignazio di Loyola Church on Via del Caravita last night. Like the previous crimes, the statue of Jesus

Christ was removed from the crucifix and replaced by a white lily and a note saying, "Set me free."

Parish priest Father Joseph Ulario reported that the crime was committed sometime after he left the building last night around 8 PM.

Police have stepped up the investigation into the crucifix crimes and have called in a team of detectives from the Central Rome Police Authority to help them stop the vandals from continuing their dirty work.

Internet sites report that similar incidents have occurred in New York, Buenos Aires, Berlin, and Barcelona.

A sickening feeling churned in Leo's gut.

The girl returned, camera in hand, and took her seat. "Do you like the iPad?"

"Thank you very much," Leo answered as he handed the device back to the student, his hand shaking.

"Are you okay, sir?"

Leo's breath shallowed. "Could I please use your phone?"

The girl reached into her hip pocket while Leo took out his antiquated little paper address book with brown-edged pages. Quickly he dialed Paolo's number. When it rang for a long time, Leo feared his son would not answer. Finally he did.

"Paolo?"

"Yes?"

"This is Father Leo. I need to see you—now."

# *Lauren 10*

---

Lauren was sitting on Todd's porch listening to music on her phone when he emerged from the woods. She removed her ear buds. "How'd it go?"

"Not so well." Todd took a few heavy steps on the deck and sat down, letting his head fall back against the wall.

"Anything you'd care to talk about?"

Todd sighed "You know the parents I told you about?"

"Uh-huh."

"After three years spiritually preparing for the child, six months ago they sensed they were ready. Jeremy and the community agreed it was time. So they began to consciously try to conceive—without success."

Lauren scooted over to sit beside Todd. His vulnerability had her attention.

"Finally they had some tests done. We got the results yesterday. Her uterus is severely tilted. She cannot conceive or give birth. She's infertile."

Lauren was at a loss. The whole idea of what these people were trying to do was way out there. Yet she felt for them. "I'm sorry to hear that."

Todd grimaced. "I don't understand. We are trying to help the world. Why would this whole project go south?"

Lauren remained silent, offering the man a chance to vent.

"This isn't just about me and the community, Lauren. It's the entire world we are seeking to save. Can you imagine if Mary in the Bible was infertile?"

If God knew that Mary was infertile, Lauren figured, He wouldn't have chosen her to bear Jesus. Or He could create a miracle to make her fertile. If God really wanted these parents to have the millennium Christ, couldn't He arrange it? But now was not the time to get into a theological debate. Todd was obviously very disappointed and he needed comfort more than philosophy.

"Maybe you can start over, with another couple."

Todd shook his head. "We don't have time. That would take years to prepare, and the timing won't be right. All the factors—astrology, numerology, ancient texts, and shamanic prophecies—say that now is the window of opportunity. Besides, we expect the collapse within the next year. If we wait, it will be too late."

Lauren didn't know what to say. Maybe humanity would figure it out without a savior coming to whisk everyone off to heaven. Maybe the world needed to run its course and destroy itself so it could start fresh. Maybe this community was deluded, and stopping their fantasy mission here and now would be the best thing that could happen to them. Or maybe they truly did have some hotline to heaven, and Satan or whoever commands the dark side of the Force had foiled the plan. It was all a bit too much for her to fathom.

So Lauren did the only thing she could do with confidence. She leaned over and began to softly stroke Todd's forehead. Sometimes men on a quest for world salvation need a woman's touch more than another trophy.

# Kenton 10

Brian Turner's devotees waited breathlessly to hear the mysterious emails he had received. The teacher took a sip of tea, donned his reading glasses, and read aloud:

> We are the image makers who have created the formations that have appeared in your crop fields for centuries. We are extraterrestrials only in that we exist in a higher dimension. We outgrew our need for physical bodies centuries ago. Yet we can manipulate matter to communicate with you. We are far more than any forms we create, just as you are.

Turner set the paper down on top of the folder, removed his reading glasses, and looked around the room at the engrossed audience. "That was the first message. There are many more." He held up a manila folder stuffed with a thick pile of printouts. "Rather than go through all the material, I will be happy to answer your specific questions."

A gaunt, pasty-skinned forty-something man in a blue suit and vest spoke in impeccable British English. "If the circle makers really want us to receive their message, why are they communicating through cryptic forms in fields?

Why don't they just materialize or land a spaceship on the White House lawn?"

"Good question, David," Turner replied. "The formations are a kind of calling card, an initial gesture testing the waters to find out if people are ready to accept and communicate with beings from beyond Earth. Governments are suspicious and defensive, and would respond violently. Such an event might also set off mass panic and cause more problems than the visitors' appearance would solve."

The questioner smiled sadly and nodded as if he understood.

Yoshi raised her hand. "My grandparents were killed by one of the atomic bombs that decimated my country in World War II. UFOs began appearing all around the planet right after that time. Are these visitors concerned about our nuclear power?"

Turner shuffled through his papers, pulled one out, and read:

Nuclear detonations send destructive ripples into the universe that tear the fabric of space and time. You are contaminating far more than just your planet. As your galactic neighbors, we must protect ourselves and the local universe from your aggressive tendencies. We have the means to prevent atomic warfare, and we will. We also have the technology to purify your polluted environment in a few simple steps.

Kenton felt a jolt of energy ripple through his spine. From a physics perspective, the warning about atomic explosions tearing space and time made perfect sense. If what Turner read about disabling nuclear missiles was true, one of greatest threats to humankind had just been defused.

A burly, dark-complexioned man sitting near the door, wearing a black blazer, arms crossed, spoke out. "If it weren't for nuclear power and military strength, a Nazi flag might be flying over both of our countries today," he said in an American accent. "You can't discount nuclear energy just because a few people have gotten killed. Some must be sacrificed for the sake of the many."

Faces tightened as if a skunk had just sprayed the room. A tense silence hung for a long time, folks squirming in their seats. Then a sweet-looking lady in a long white dress broke in, as if she wanted to steer the discussion away from politics. "One crop formation remains the biggest mystery of all. It's a huge pixilated image of Jesus, bordering a circle containing many dots at irregular spacing. They form some kind of encrypted message. Have you asked the circle makers about that one?"

Brian nodded. "The dots represent some kind of binary language, like we use in our computers. The circle makers said that we already have the tools to decode the message, but we have been looking in the wrong place."

"Why do they have to be so vague?" the cash register kid called out, irked. "The world is in horrific condition, on the verge of suffocating ourselves to death. If these advanced beings can heal the environment and prevent nuclear war, why don't they just give us a hand instead of leaving us to suffer in our stupidity?"

"Another good question," Turner replied. "Our interdimensional friends are not here to rescue us, but to educate us. Do you remember the Prime Directive from *Star Trek*?"

The man in the wheelchair called out, "A more advanced civilization is not permitted to interfere with the evolution of civilization in a more primitive stage of development."

"Exactly," Turner replied. "The circle makers can give us clues, but we have to understand why and how their formulas work. Otherwise they would be robbing us of the wisdom the lessons will impart when we do our homework."

Turner turned to a woman wearing a brightly-colored flowered smock. "You're an artist, Glynis. If you wanted to give a message to all the world, what would be the most obvious way to communicate it?"

"Through pictures, a universal language that transcends words."

"Precisely," Turner replied. "And where would you post your pictures so everyone could see them?"

"In the fields of many countries, images acres long, so they would be obvious to everyone."

Brian Turner nodded and took a long breath. "There's one more piece. . ."

He reached to the back of his file and pulled out a paper. "I received this transmission yesterday."

Soon you will receive a final transmission that everyone on your planet will recognize. It will be unmistakeable, and contain what we most want you to know. When you decode it, you will have your instructions. After that your fate is in your hands.

Brian Turner set the paper down on his lap and scanned the silent room. Kenton turned off his recorder. *I knew there had to be more to life than the one I was living.*

# Brianna 11

Dr. Hathaway, I've given your proposal some thought and I just

Brianna sat back and read the text she had just typed. Delete

Your project is noble and if anyone can do what you are setting out to do, it's you. I just don't see myself

"Arrrgh!" Brianna tossed her phone onto the bed and marched into the kitchen. She opened the refrigerator door, pulled out a Coke Zero, and downed a few gulps. *Why does this have to be so hard? It's just a simple note.*

Brianna took her drink to the window and sat cross-legged on the wide sill. She gazed down on the street nine stories below and watched harried New Yorkers crossing Third Avenue, talking on their cell phones, and walking in and out of the Minimart across the street. A pregnant woman in a brightly colored maternity blouse emerged from the shop, pulling a small cart behind her, a little boy holding her other hand, whining.

Brianna picked up the phone and pecked at the keyboard again.

I'm honored that you invited me to deliver the Christ child to humanity. I imagine there are lots of women out there who would love to have a holy baby. I'm just not one of them.

Send

# *Driscoll 11*

Lieutenant Driscoll Ames stood on the blackened stage wing, palms sweating, knees practically jelly. He had seen press conferences televised from the National Press Club, but he never expected to present one. The career military man peered from behind the curtain and scanned the audience. Some were chatting with their peers, others were texting, and a few were sitting quietly with blank looks, wondering what they were doing here. Late-arriving reporters jockeyed for standing room in the back of the hall. Everyone held a laptop, tablet, camera, or some other recording device.

At Ames's side stood veteran reporter Cheryl Lansing, who had called the conference. After pounding the Washington news beat for three decades, Cheryl was known and respected among her colleagues. Had anyone else thrown the party, the audience would have been half the size.

Cheryl placed a firm hand on Driscoll's lower back. "You ready, champ?"

"Not really. At this point I'd trade for deployment in Afghanistan."

"Too late now, soldier. Chasing the Taliban will never accomplish anything like this." She gave Driscoll a firmer pat on the back. "Just tell the truth. . . . For Ticia and the kids."

Andy Wilkinson, President of the press club, stepped to the podium. The crowd settled down and gave him their attention. He began his introduction. The last time Driscoll felt such an adrenaline rush, he was dodging machine gun fire in Kabul.

"Show time," Cheryl said as she released her hand from Driscoll's back and stepped away, like the umbilical cable dropping away from a Saturn rocket at the moment of launch.

Ames felt his heart pumping so hard he thought it would leap out of his chest. Only sheer determination kept him from bolting.

". . . Without further ado I introduce to you Lieutenant Driscoll Ames."

A handful of people offered faint applause. The audience clearly did not know what to expect. They were here either because they trusted Cheryl or they were simply curious. Reporters never know when they might score a scoop; they must show up rain or shine.

The edgy officer stepped to the podium. He placed his notes on the small angled shelf and looked down at them. They were blurry. He looked out at the crowd and started to feel nauseous. He had read somewhere that a lot of people fear public speaking more than death. Now he knew why.

"Ladies and gentlemen of the press, thank you for coming today," he began, trying to disguise the trembling in his voice. He scanned the crowd again. They were listening. Maybe they weren't all ogres waiting to stone him.

"I am here today because I have information that is important for the people of America and the world to know. This information has been withheld for a very long time. I believe that bringing it to public awareness will promote the advancement of our nation as well as all humanity."

Driscoll looked up from his script and saw reporters taking notes. No eggs or tomatoes hurled at him—yet. He returned to his script.

"I am well aware that I may be criticized, mocked, and even condemned for revealing the information you are about to receive. Some groups or nations may grow frightened and take defensive action. As a member of the military for over twenty years, I am committed to the security of my country. If I believed that disclosing these facts would in any way present a threat to our nation or the world, I would not be standing here. I see greater danger in our government withholding the truth. I have thought about this revelation long and hard, and, in my estimation, the value of disclosing this information far outweighs the value of hiding it."

Ames quickly glanced at Cheryl Lansing standing in the stage wing. She nodded, as if to say, "Just keep going."

He motioned to the stage manager to turn down the house lights. A large movie screen descended behind him, the hum of the motor echoing through the room. It seemed to take forever. As soon as it was in place, Driscoll Ames began his recount.

*No turning back now.*

"Eleven days ago I was taken to a highly-secured facility deep in a subterranean section of the Pentagon. There I was shown the wreckage of an extraterrestrial spacecraft and the bodies of four aliens."

The audience started to chatter while some typed furiously on their laptops. Some smiled or laughed, as if they were hearing a joke. Ames extended his hands palm down, slowly pumping them to quell the din. Eventually a hush returned.

"Using a state-of-the-art surveillance camera"—he picked up the little button-like device, extended his arm, and panned it across the audience—"I photographed what I saw. I will now share the photographs with you."

The reporters sat up and leaned forward, eyes riveted to the screen.

Ames pressed the button on his remote-control wand that triggered the projector. How many times had he gone over this moment in his mind? In a way, it was as significant as man's first step on the moon. *No, more.* That step symbolized our connection to a dead sphere floating a few hundred thousand miles from Earth. This step connected us to extremely advanced intelligent life in far reaches of the universe.

The first photo showed the display case Ames had initially seen when he entered the room containing bits of spacecraft wreckage. "These are pieces of debris from an alien spacecraft that crashed in Dalnegorsk in the Soviet Union on 29 January, 1986. When I asked my source how our government had obtained it, he told me that the U.S. had traded some of our captured UFO paraphernalia with the Soviets."

Ames surveyed the audience. Some reporters looked puzzled, others doubtful, some troubled, others excited. Others smiled, as if waiting for the punch line. But it did not come. Instead, Lieutenant Ames went on, "For nearly eighty years, those who have doubted the reality of UFO visitations to Earth have demanded, 'Show us hard evidence.' Well, here it is."

Having gotten through the intro and first photo, Driscoll Ames felt more at ease. *I can do this.* Slowly he clicked through each of the images, explaining to the best of his ability what he knew or thought the objects to be. When he arrived at the large piece of hull, he explained, "Since 1947 there has been a huge hubbub over the alleged crash of an alien spacecraft in Roswell, New Mexico. I am here today to tell you that the crash was not alleged. What you are seeing is a portion of the hull of the spacecraft that fell to Earth."

Another murmur arose from the crowd.

"As you can see, the material contains a holographic pattern imbedded in the metal. To date, our best scientists have been unable to pierce the metal or decipher the symbols."

As the presentation went on, Driscoll dropped into more confidence, his voice deepening with authority. When he approached the slide showing the image of the first alien body, his heart began to beat wildly again. *Bits of metal are one thing. Bodies are another.*

He forced himself to take a long deep breath, and pressed Forward.

When the photo of the first dead alien appeared on the screen, all the reporters stood, stretching forward to see the picture. Cameras clicked wildly, accompanied by flashes and a clamor twice as loud as the last one. Three dozen hands shot up. "Please," Lieutenant Ames begged, extending his arms, palms down. "I will answer all of your questions in a few minutes." For a moment he feared that the group might charge the stage. But the hands went down. The audience remained standing.

Ames showed the photos of all the alien bodies, adding comments about the appearance of the tissue and as many details as he could recall. From that point on, the audience was virtually silent. Ten minutes later the last image clicked onto the screen. As the lights in the hall came on, Ames left the image on for effect, as he had been coached by Cheryl Lansing, who stood in the stage wing with a proud but cautious smile.

# *Leo 11*

It had been more than ten years since Father Leo Bonfiglio had ridden the Rome subway. As he rambled along toward Paolo Adimari's apartment, the musty smell of the hot underground and the hypnotic clack of the wheels transported him to a carefree era when he could travel wherever he wanted, whenever he felt moved, without an image to maintain or religious obligations on his shoulders.

The train came to a noisy halt and Leo trudged up the dirty subway steps. As he emerged onto the street and felt the late-summer sun baking his neck, the Monsignor was relieved that this meeting took him a good distance from the Vatican. He looked over his shoulder to be sure he hadn't been followed. Satisfied, he continued. *This bizarre affair has become a dance of shadows.*

Piazza Bologna was teeming with college kids sitting on porches, skateboarding in the street, blaring rap music from apartment windows, drinking beer and wine, fingering their phones, laughing, and flirting. Gray and red *Università di Roma* T-shirts and fashionably torn jeans seemed to be the uniform of the day.

Standing before a poorly-maintained yellowish apartment building with brown shutters, the priest scanned the list of residents until he found Paolo's name. Reading *Adimari* sent a pang through his heart. *Is Kristina still alive? Is she in pain? Is there some way I can lighten her burden?* And the most disturbing: *Should I have stayed with her?* Leo forced his mind to quit drifting, and he pressed the doorbell button.

Soon a young woman appeared at the door. Tall, thin, pretty, long black hair, silver hoop earrings, and a small colorful butterfly tattooed on her upper arm just below the strap of her pink camisole. "Father Leo?"

He nodded.

"I am Lisbeth, Paolo's girlfriend," she smiled warmly. "Please come in."

The wispy girl guided Leo down a dark hallway with but a thin shard of afternoon light streaming through the window of the entry door. "Paolo told me all about you," she called over her shoulder as Leo followed her past several doors on the ground floor. "I'm very pleased to meet you."

Watching the maiden's gait, Leo felt jarred. She looked jarringly like Kristina at the age Leo had met her. *Have I stepped into some alternate reality showing me my guilty past?* But he had a mission here, and he could not allow himself to be sidetracked by self-accusing fantasies.

Lisbeth opened an apartment door and beckoned Father Leo to enter. He nodded and peered inside. Yet he was not prepared for the chilling sight he beheld: a life-size wooden statue of the crucified Christ lay on the floor, butting against a wall beside a couch. Suddenly Father Bonfiglio realized that he had become a central actor in a very dark play.

Lisbeth gestured for him to step inside before any passerby could see into the apartment.

The priest surveyed the flat. Another wooden Jesus lay on the floor against a wall opposite the couch. To his right, two more statues protruded from an open closet, one atop the other, their feet stuffed into the closet, outstretched arms too wide to fit through the closet door. Leo turned and saw the legs of another Jesus stretched out from beneath a table. All of the statues seemed eerily lifelike, some with eyes open, all with painted blood dripping from the wrists, ankles, side of the rib cage, and down the face below the crown of thorns. A morbid ode to agony.

"What do you think of our museum of ended suffering?" Paolo asked with a sly smile as he emerged from the bedroom.

Leo could barely speak. He simply kept shaking his head. "Why must you do this?"

"Look at the faces on these statues, father. Do you see the light of the world that Jesus urged us to be, or do you see two thousand years of guilt, pain, anguish, and bloodshed?"

Lisbeth plopped on the coach and lit a cigarette. She offered Leo one. He hardly noticed.

"I didn't come here to debate theology with you, Paolo. I came to tell you that you are in serious danger."

"From God?"

"From the Church."

Paulo snickered. "Obviously two different entities with opposite purposes." He shook his head. "I am not trying to hurt the Church. I am trying to free it. Two millennia of misery are enough. Being represented like this—" Paolo lifted the head of the most tortured-looking statue "—does not make our Lord happy. It breaks His heart."

Leo sighed. "Who is doing this with you, Paolo? Is there a team?"

Paolo smiled and pointed to Lisbeth. "This is my team."

Lisbeth giggled. *Does this girl have any idea of what she's gotten into? No, she's just a kid excited to play a daring game with her Robin Hood boyfriend.*

"May I sit?"

"Please," Lisbeth replied, rising from the couch to make space for Leo. "Would you like a beer? Wine?"

"Some water, please." Leo settled into the lumpy dark brown torn couch, guessing the kids had picked it up at some thrift shop. "What about the people in other countries who are doing this? Are you working with them?"

Paolo shrugged. "I knew nothing about them until I read about them on the Internet—just like they read about me."

Leo studied the boy's eyes. He believed him. Lisbeth delivered a glass of water and he took a shaky sip.

"Paolo, do you realize how powerful the Church is to crack down on crimes like these?"

Paolo scoffed. "The same power that has massacred millions of innocent people for not worshipping the God of Suffering?" He took a drag of the cigarette Lisbeth had passed to him. "Don't you see, father? This is an idea whose time has come. If I didn't do this, someone else would. The momentum will continue even if I am stopped. You are beholding the first rays of the millennium resurrection."

Leo closed his eyes as he considered the irony of the situation. How many hours had he spent questioning the sorrow that had burdened his parishioners? In an odd way he was more sympathetic to Paolo's cause than he was to the Church's dogma. But that was immaterial now.

"Has the Church pressured the police to intensify the hunt for me? Is that what you came to warn me about?"

Leo shot his son a cold stare. "It's not the police I am worried about, Paolo. There are people within the Church who look into these things. They take religious license and will stop at nothing to enforce traditions."

"The Christian Mafia?" Paolo laughed.

"You are not so far from the truth," Leo replied soberly. "I've seen what these people can do. I don't want them to find you."

Lisbeth cast a worried glance toward Paolo.

"It's too late now," Paolo came back. "The movement has a life of its own."

Leo rose and set his empty glass on the table beside the couch. He placed his hands on his son's shoulders and faced him squarely. "We have just met, Paolo, but we are family. Your mother will always be in my heart and I love you because you belong to both of us. I beg you, *please stop this crusade*. For your mother's sake. Don't let her go to her grave knowing her son is in jail or maimed."

Leo invoking Paolo's mother's name got his attention. He looked concerned for the first time in the conversation.

"Maybe he's right, Paolo," Lisbeth interjected. "This might hurt your mother."

Paolo took a long breath and stared over Leo's shoulder. "I am going to visit my mother this weekend. She is very ill."

Leo's heart sank.

"I will tell her of our conversation. If she wants me to, I will stay with her."

Leo let out a long exhale. "Please do that, Paolo. Stay away from Rome. Don't touch any more statues. I will pray for you both."

Monsignor Leonardo Bonfiglio turned, exited, and made his way back down the gloomy hall. When he reached the doorway to the street, he saw the frolicking students. They were enjoying the golden age of their youth; the suffering of humanity was nowhere in their reality. *Maybe they are better off.*

# *Lauren 11*

As Todd rested his head on Lauren's lap, he looked up and found her eyes. After a long moment he sat up and took her hands. "I want to be with you, Lauren. I want you to stay here with me."

Lauren's heart lifted for a moment, and then sank. Her dream of Todd committing to her had come true. But this place made it a nightmare. Living with a bunch of saucer-eyed new agers was this woman's idea of hell.

"I need some time to think, Todd. Just with myself."

Todd nodded as if he understood. He pointed past the porch railing toward the woods. "There's a trail through the forest right over there. If you want to take a walk, I have some chores to do. We can connect later."

*OMG, is this the same guy who used to have to control my every move?* "Where is my old boyfriend and what have you done with him?"

Todd flashed a proud grin as he rose without a word and stepped toward the stairs leading off the porch.

Lauren popped on her pink baseball cap, grabbed her water bottle, and set out on the forest trail. Her mind churned as she wrestled with her longing to be with Todd and her deeper knowing she could never stay with him amidst a living conspiracy theory. Soon she felt her face warmed by sunlight filtering through the leaves, amidst a bevy of birds, squirrels, and clucking chickens escaped from the community henhouse. For the first time since Lauren had arrived at this weird place, she started to breathe more freely.

Fifteen minutes into the woods, the path merged with a dirt road wide enough for one vehicle, tire ruts filled in between by grass and wispy white wildflowers. Bordering the road stood a new silver chain-link fence with barbed wire at the top—an anomaly in this haven for peace-loving tree huggers. On the other side of the fence a thinner road veered off out of sight. A black wrought iron gate five feet high, sharp spikes at the top, bore a bold **No Trespassing—Private Property** sign.

*Could this be where the parents live?* Lauren walked past the gate, but twenty paces down the road she turned and gazed into the dark thicket where the road led. *What does this couple look like? Are they really so pure? I would sure like a glimpse of the people chosen as the parents of the millennium Christ.*

Then Lauren Delaney did something totally out of character for her. She walked to the iron gate, set her foot on the cross-bar, and began to climb it. *I must be crazy.* But, coursing with the lingering love hormones from her passionate night with Todd, the determined city mouse scaled the gate, careful not to impale her rear on the pointed spears. Satisfied she still owned her butt, she leaped to the other side, her ankles tweaking with a painful thud as she landed.

The curious sleuth followed the slim road winding through the woods for a hundred yards, no people or buildings in sight. But fresh tire tracks told her the road was often used—all the more reason to expect it led to the parents' home.

Suddenly the sound of a vehicle pierced the forest behind her, tires splashing through puddles from last night's rain. Lauren dashed into a thicket and crouched behind a tree, eyes on the road. Soon a bulky white Ford F250 pickup truck rambled past her, splattering mud to its sides. Peeking from behind the tree trunk, Lauren could make out a short mustached Hispanic-looking man in the passenger's seat, puffing a vape, billows of smoke pouring out the window. The truck's bed was filled with large rectangular-shaped objects covered with a blue tarpaulin, tied down by a yellow-and-black rope. Soon the vehicle disappeared around a curve, the acrid smell of diesel exhaust wafting in its wake.

Lauren was tempted to retreat to the main path, but the tingling in her belly was too tempting to dismiss. She pushed through the grass and twigs, and kept walking along the road, determined to find out why that industrial vehicle was penetrating the silent forest.

Fifty more yards down the bumpy dirt road, she caught sight of the truck. It was parked ten paces from the base of a large earthen mound so perfectly shaped that it had to be man-made. She etched her way through the bush, careful to avoid crunching branches, remaining out of sight of the truck driver and his companion, should they glance in her direction.

Lauren worked her way up a small rise to a vantage point. By that time the men had pulled the tarpaulin off the bed of the truck, and were unloading large wooden crates, setting them down behind the truck. The crates were all different sizes, mostly long and rectangular. *Coffins?* No, not long enough to hold a body. Most of the crates had red stenciled letters on them, but Lauren could not make out the words from the distance.

The rear side of the mound revealed two large steel doors cut into the side of the hill, like a military bunker. *Gentle pacifist hippies would not have such a structure.* The place was probably some kind of earth-berm dwelling, popular among eco-nuts, she had read in a magazine at her massage spa. *Is this where the parents live?* But there were no windows or openings except for the thick steel doors. The place was uninhabitable for any person, let alone a couple who valued pure air and light.

The two men grunted as they unloaded the heavy crates. Then the guy who had been sitting in the passenger seat walked to the doors and began to punch numbers on a keypad to their right. He fiddled with the device for a minute, and looked frustrated. "Hey, Marco, what the heck is the combination? I tried a couple and nothing worked."

Marco, taking inventory of the boxes on the ground, stood up and called back, "I think it's 7315. They change it every month."

The man at the door touched the keypad again, the hefty doors released, and the worker dragged one open. Lauren tried to see what was inside the vault, but from her angle it was impossible. All she could do was watch and wait until the men had completed their task. Half an hour later the workmen had moved all the crates indoors. They exited the vault and closed the metal door with a clang that echoed through the forest. Relieved that their cumbersome job was complete, they made their way to the truck. Soon a plume of dust from the road told her that they were gone.

Lauren was too engaged to stop now. The fact that she had heard the entry combination seemed a sign to her that she was to pursue her commando investigation. She stepped out of the little glen and walked to the road to make sure the truck was out of sight. *All clear.*

Lauren went to the keypad and, palms sweating and temples throbbing, pressed the numbers she had heard. Never before had she indulged in such an escapade—but this was a lot more fun than sitting at a monitor for hours, crunching numbers and scrolling through mindless social media posts. She loved mystery movies, and this scene was up there with the best of them.

The keypad issued three short beeps and she could hear the lock release. Grunting, she pulled the heavy door open.

# Kenton 11

The Brian Turner gathering broke up just before 10 PM, leaving members exchanging phone numbers and bathing in newfound confidence that they were not crazy after all. Amid profuse thanks, Turner politely took his leave and headed down the stairs, his manila folder of other-worldly communication tucked under his arm. Kenton and Yoshi lingered for a moment to thank the host, Dame Edna, and the cash register kid, oddly disparate characters united by a vision that transcended their worldly identities.

Kenton practically floated down the long staircase of the old apartment building. His mentor had explained the most important elements of the crop circle phenomenon, and more. The dispirited high school physics teacher, long burdened by a stifling bureaucracy, unmotivated students, and depressed coworkers, suddenly found himself transported to a world of stunning dimension.

When the two reached ground level, they watched Brian Turner cross the street toward his car, parked a few places in front of the Astra. Kenton decided to seize one more opportunity to connect with his guru, and dashed across the road, wet from a passing shower. Yoshi hustled to keep pace.

"A truly illuminating evening, Mr. Turner," Kenton called, reaching the speaker as he was unlocking his car. "I can't thank you enough."

The Brit offered a small polite smile. "I'm glad you found the discussion valuable."

"Everything you said was—" Kenton began. But Turner seemed distracted, peering over Kenton's shoulder. A shadow of anxiety eclipsed the man's countenance.

Kenton followed Turner's glance back toward the apartment building and saw the fellow in the black blazer conferring with two tall, burly men wearing dark suits. He pointed toward Turner across the street, and the men nodded. They turned and started to cross the street, waiting for a break in passing cars.

Brian Turner suddenly grew quite distressed. His eyes darted to Kenton, then to Yoshi, who had caught up, her laptop under her arm. Nervously he thrust his file into her hands. "Put these in your bag. Safeguard them—I beg you." Yoshi, shaken but alert, unzipped her laptop case, inserted the file, and quickly zipped it back up.

By that time the two suited men had crossed the street and approached the threesome. Fortunately, the combination of night, passing traffic, and Yoshi's back to them prevented them from viewing the file transfer.

"Are you Brian Turner?" one of the men asked with an American accent.

"That's right."

"We'd like a word with you," said the other man, also American.

"What, may I ask, is this about?"

"We'll explain to you when we get there."

"Get where?" he came back angrily.

Suddenly a large black panel van pulled up to the group. A side door slid open while the two goons grabbed Turner by the arms.

"What in bloody hell do you think you're doing???!!!"

The men said nothing as they dragged Turner to the open door and pushed him into the rear seat. One of the men jumped into the seat beside him while the other slammed the door shut, opened the passenger door, and slipped into the front seat. Quickly the van shot off into the night, leaving Kenton and Yoshi standing aghast.

*Provence, France*
*September 10*

# Brianna 12

---

Brianna Marlowe spread her knees apart as wide as she could under the sterile draping. The French doctor's features were hidden behind his surgical mask and his green cap concealing his hair and forehead. Brianna could see the reflection of her disheveled hair in his thick black-rimmed eyeglasses as he reached under the tent toward her birth canal. When he touched the baby's crowning head, he nodded. A swarthy midwife and red-headed nurse beside him watched intently, awaiting the next command.

"Hurry up, would you?" Brianna shouted, sweat rolling off her forehead. "I can't push anymore. I'm exhausted!"

The doctor looked up and found Brianna's eyes. "You're almost done," he said in a reassuring voice with a thick French accent, positioning himself to maneuver better. "Please keep pushing!"

The midwife grabbed a soft white cloth and patted Brianna's forehead. The mother-to-be felt as if someone was pounding her lower back with a sledgehammer while her vagina was ripping to shreds. *Why any woman would choose to do this is insane.* "Dammit, just get it out, would you!!!"

Just when she could bear the pain no more, she felt massive relief. "*Coupez,*" the doctor ordered the nurse. She reached to a side table and picked up a pair of silver scissors that gleamed in the morning light streaming through the window of the French countryside chalet.

Moments later the doctor lifted the baby, and the nurse began to clean it. A broad smile spread over the midwife's face as she positioned the child to hand it to its mother. An unexpected swell of joy filled Brianna's heart. Now, after all that agony, she could hardly wait to see her baby. With new-found strength, she reached to receive the child and drew it to her breast.

When Brianna caught sight of the baby's face, the child did not have the angelic visage she expected. Instead, it had the horrid head of a boar, with crooked yellow teeth, jagged horns, and an evil, tortured look in its eye. It smelled ghastly, as if wrenched from the bowels of hell.

*"Arrrrgggghhhhh!"* Brianna's scream reverberated off the walls of the chalet and shook the bed. She slammed her eyelids shut and turned her head away.

When Brianna opened her eyes, she saw her favorite down pillow beside her. All was quiet. Dazed, she sat up and looked around. There was the night table with her iPad on top of her Mythology textbook. The room was dark except for the thin beam of a blue neon light from a sign across Third Avenue streaming between the crack in her blackout shade and the window frame. No doctor. No nurse. No monster baby.

She sat up and looked at the clock: 3:37. It took ten long minutes for Brianna's breath to calm down. She let out a shuddered sigh, slipped back under the duvet, and tried to get back to sleep. It would not be easy.

*Washington, D.C.*
*September 5*

# Driscoll 12

---

"Lieutenant!" fifty reporters called out, arms shooting up. Driscoll felt overwhelmed. Cheryl joined him onstage for the question-and-answer period. Knowing most of the reporters in the room, she decided who to call on and how to couch the political answers. She pointed to a baldheaded man in a gray suit, sitting at the far left side of the audience. "Sandy, from *USA Today*," she acknowledged him.

"Does the President know about your discovery and the disclosure of this information and these photos?"

"We have informed the White House of our presentation," Cheryl answered. "At this time we have not received a response."

"Ms. Lansing!" A black man with a gravelly voice called from the front row.

"Yes, Greg?"

"Has *The Washington Post* tested the photos for authenticity?"

"Absolutely. We submitted all the photos to Digital Forensics Laboratories, the most respected photographic analysts in the industry. They concluded that these photos are genuine. They also examined the camera that Lieutenant Ames used to take the photos. They found that to be authentic. That report will be posted tomorrow on *The Washington Post* website." Cheryl turned to the right side of the room. "Jorge?"

"Lieutenant Ames, are you concerned that you have breached the highest level of U.S. government security, and what the repercussions from that act might mean for you? Will you be the next Edward Snowden?"

Ames's face grew sober. "I have spent many sleepless nights pondering that very question. My feeling is that by hiding this information, our government has breached its responsibility to be honest with the American people. Which breach is more reprehensible?"

The Lieutenant reached for a small bottle of water on the podium. Fielding the previous question, which he had expected, and answering as he did, made him feel less defensive and more confident.

"Linda from *Newsweek*." Cheryl pointed to a short bony woman with frosted hair, sitting toward the rear of the room.

"One of the rationalizations governments have used to hide UFO information is that such a disclosure might set off a mass panic like Orson Wells' famous 'War of the Worlds' radio scare did in 1938. Do you believe this disclosure will frighten the public into a frenzy?"

Ames was also prepared for this query. "Alien spacecraft have been flying around our planet since 1947—some people say much, much longer—and they have not attacked, invaded, enslaved, or exploited the human race like many science fiction books, movies, and conspiracy theorists have dramatized. I believe they are here to either study us, help us, or protect themselves. If our interplanetary neigh-bors wanted to off us, they could have done so thousands of years ago. Maybe they are here to keep us from destroying ourselves and cause irreparable harm to our planet and the local universe."

To Ames's surprise, a number of reporters nodded in agreement. Had they given this matter some thought?

He went on, "Polls show that two-thirds of the popula-tion believe there is intelligent life in outer space, and over half the population believes that we have been visited by extraterrestrials," Ames went on. "If that's true, even while governments squirm at the prospect of disclosure, most people might just yawn."

More nods from the audience.

A fit young man with a dark brown stubble beard stood and spoke. "Another poll showed that more people believe in the reality of UFOs than those who believe that the govern-ment will be able to pay them their social security benefits when they are due." A ripple of laughter rolled through the crowd, followed by scattered applause.

Cheryl Lansing remained at the lieutenant's side, glowing, bolstered by his cool eloquence and the positive response. She scanned the sea of raised hands and pointed to a tall, thin, sixty-ish woman in a black pant suit. "Lieutenant Ames, I did a bit of research and learned that you were recently turned down for promotion. Is your disclosure an act of spite?"

Ames tightened his grip on the sides of the podium. "I must admit that I was disappointed in being passed over. I was hoping to use my salary increase to get better medical treatment for my wife, who is battling a rare terminal disease. I am not fighting the government. I am making a stand for the rights of citizens to know what the government knows."

Driscoll breathed out and dropped his shoulders a bit. He had fielded the toughest question he expected.

Cheryl called on another female reporter, perhaps the youngest in the room.

"Is it true that *The Washington Post* has paid you a huge sum of money for the rights to your story? And if so, what is that sum, and what rights have you granted?"

Cheryl took the microphone. "We have paid Lieutenant Ames a fee for the story, the amount of which I am not permitted to disclose. He has granted us exclusive rights to the photos, a series of interviews with him, and the option on a forthcoming book."

"Follow-up . . ." the reporter insisted. "So your motives are not entirely altruistic, Lieutenant Ames. Both you and *The Washington Post* stand to gain a huge financial windfall from this so-called 'disclosure.'"

Ames felt rattled for the first time during the presentation. He took a moment to compose himself so as not to appear defensive. "When Bob Woodward and Carl Bernstein broke the Watergate story, they certainly gained prestige and lots of income. But the service they rendered to the American people was immeasurable. It unseated an unscrupulous president and changed the course of history. My hope is that this revelation will bring people together and force governments to reveal what they know about

advanced technology they have captured and reverse engi-
neered. While that technology has been applied to develop
instruments of war, the very same knowledge can be used to
meet our energy needs, advance physical healing, and end
starvation. Yes, I am reaping a benefit. And yes, the people
of Planet Earth will reap far more."

# Leo 12

The knock on Father Bonfiglio's door came just after 9 AM. When Leo opened, Father Georgio Rissole stood rigid, his face solemn. Leo ushered him in and closed the door.

"The Holy Father has called a meeting of the Vatican Security Council at 11 o'clock," Father Rissole stated soberly.

Leo felt his neck stiffen. "He's never attended those meetings, let alone called one. Why now?"

"I don't know . . . Apparently it's important."

Leo's eyes fell for a moment, lost in thought, and then returned to his visitor. "Of course, I'll be there."

Father Leo closed the door, his gut churning. He walked to the window and gazed out over Piazza San Pietro. Thousands of pilgrims were milling about, photographing each other with the Vatican dome in the background. The Church was a source of inspiration to them; for some, their visit was the trip of a lifetime. Many looked toward the Pope's window, hoping they might catch a glimpse of God's anointed messenger. In two hours Leo would be sitting at his side.

The morning went by terribly slowly. Father Bonfiglio made some phone calls and wrote a few letters, mostly to keep his mind occupied. Without success.

At 10:45 AM Leo stood before the full-length mirror in his bedroom, smoothed his red-trimmed black cassock robe with a purple sash, and ran a brush through his thick salt-and-pepper hair. *There, the appropriate Vatican priest.* He stepped into the hallway and threaded through the high-vaulted gilded corridors to the executive conference room, the legacy site where Church policies affecting billions of Catholics have been issued for a half-millennium. Outside the door stood two husky security guards with radio devices attached to their ears, indicating that the Pope was already inside.

Beside the guards stood Father Giuseppe LaCorte, Chief of Vatican Security, confirming those to be admitted. As Father Bonfiglio arrived, Father LaCorte nodded, and a guard opened the door. Leo stepped inside and saw the Holy Father sitting at the middle of one of the long sides of the huge mahogany conference table. A half-dozen council members were seated opposite the Pope. Beside the pontiff sat Father Gabriele Abatangelo, the Pope's personal secretary. The mood was somber.

Father Leo took a seat at a forty-five-degree angle to His Holiness, bowed his head, and the two made brief eye contact. When the Pope smiled, Leo felt his first moment of relief since he had learned of the meeting. One more priest, Father Marcello Bucci, entered, and Father LaCorte closed the door behind him.

The Pope led a brief prayer and made the sign of the cross. "Thank you all for coming on short notice. I wouldn't have disturbed you unless this was important."

The priests exchanged questioning glances. No one knew for sure why they were here.

"As you all know, there has been a rash of crucifix vandalizings in Roman churches."

Father Leo's gut twisted into a knot.

"To date there have been six," the Pope continued.

*No, just five, I read it yesterday.*

"Last night a statue was removed from Basilica di Santa Prassede. The same note, *'Set me free,'* was found."

Leo reached toward the center of the table, grasped the handle of a water pitcher, and poured himself a glass, praying that his shaking hand would not expose his anxiety.

Father Abatangelo added, "We called this meeting today because we learned last night that there have been more incidents in Florence and Paris. And one in the Philippines."

*No, no.*

"At first we believed that the desecrations in Rome were something of an anomaly," the Pope went on. "We expected that the vandals would quit or be caught and that would be the end of it. But now we are concerned that an international ring is behind the crimes. If this is a worldwide movement to undermine the Church, we cannot condone it."

Leo began to feel nauseous. He shifted in his chair.

"Do we have any clues as to who might be behind this?" asked Father Rissole. "A faction from another religion? Muslim? Jewish?"

"No evidence like that," Father LaCorte answered. "Just the lilies and the notes. The police are taking fingerprints."

The priests exchanged troubled glances.

"Have there been any unusual occurrences at the Vatican lately?" asked Monsignor Franco Bottaglio, overseer of the Vatican's famed collection of religious artifacts. "Any disorderly people? Bomb threats?"

"Nothing significant," Father LaCorte replied. ". . . except we did receive a report from the night guard Abramo. Late one night last week a nervous fellow came to visit Father Bonfiglio."

All eyes turned to Leo, who struggled to maintain the semblance of nonchalance. He shrugged his shoulders and shook his head. "Just a distraught young man in a crisis of faith. I feared that he might be suicidal, so I spoke to him for a while. I think he's alright now."

A long silence hung. Finally the Holy Father broke it. "What, then, shall we do? We can't put churches around the world at risk to a ring of terrorists."

Leo's shoulders dropped and a long breath helped him regain some composure. He remained quiet as the discussion grew heated, priests vying for the floor to spout their opinions. Some were angry, others confused, others vengeful. A few called for patience and forgiveness. The debate ran in circles, spiraling into deeper dissension and frustration. The Pope listened carefully, evaluating each idea. Monsignor Bonfiglio raised his hand. "If I may, Your Holiness. . . "

The Pope nodded.

Leo leaned forward, forearms on the table and hands clasped. "Is it possible that whoever is behind this means no harm? Perhaps they are just trying to make a statement. Someone's way of seeking to diminish suffering. They have hurt no one. Perhaps if we could have compassion, even create some kind of dialogue . . ."

Father LaCorte pounded his fist on the table. "Terrorists are not interested in dialogue!" he bellowed. "They are interested in anarchy. I, for one, will not have it. The Church has dealt harshly with anarchists over the centuries, and we need to hold the line now. If we put up with this, who knows what evil acts will follow?"

A murmur rippled through the room. Then all eyes turned back to the Pope, who closed his eyes and took a long, deliberate breath. Father LaCorte leaned over and whispered in his ear. The pontiff took a moment to absorb the message. Then he nodded, opened his eyes, and sat up straight.

"Let's try to deal with this peacefully," he finally said. "Let's give the police a few more days to look into this. I will issue a statement calling for those responsible to cease, out of respect for the Church and our Lord. If the incidents do not let up, we will take stronger measures."

The Pope bowed his head for a long moment, indicating he was finished. Slowly he rose, followed by his entourage. Father Bottaglio opened the door, and the Holy Father's procession quietly exited the meeting room.

The remaining priests stood, commenting to each other about the meeting, and then filed out in order, Father Rissole behind Leo. When the two had stepped a few paces down the corridor, Leo stopped, turned, and asked him, "What do you think Giuseppe whispered to the Holy Father?"

Father Rissole closed his eyes and shook his head.

It did not take long for Father Bonfiglio to get the message. "Those thugs are still doing their dirty work?"

Father Rissole snickered. ". . . A kind description."

"I thought they were banished during John Paul's term."

"Only officially. Inquisitions, my friend, do not belong to the past. They have simply gone underground."

*Blue Ridge Mountains*
*September 3*

## *Lauren 12*

---

A shaft of daylight spilled into the darkened bunker, just enough for Lauren to find a light switch on the wall. She pressed it, and six overhead halogen lights came on, flickering faintly at first, gaining intensity as they warmed up. After a minute, the chamber, the size of a three-car garage, was illuminated, and Lauren could clearly see scores of wooden crates like the ones the workers had unloaded from the truck.

Now she could make out the red lettering stenciled on the outside of the crates. Nearest her a large crate read, Vigilance Rifles Submachine Gun A-M20; the next crate, ABC-M25A2 Riot Control Hand Grenade; and another, Non-Detectable Anti-Tank Land Mine 3A. Two dozen similar boxes were piled in two stacks, all labeled as military-grade munitions.

*Holy shit, these people are preparing for war.*

She walked around the room, examining more of the boxes. Flame throwers. Mortars. Tear gas.

Lauren shook her head, incredulous. These people seemed so innocuous, gentle hippies trying to save the world. Naïve, yes. Violent, no. Was the commune just a ruse for some underground revolutionary army? A front for a Neo-Nazi conspiracy?

She stood frozen, her mind spinning. A sickening feeling rolled through her gut.

*I have to get out of this place.*

# Kenton 12

Kenton Baine gawked down Edevane Road, straining to read the license plate of the vehicle that had just carried away the man he admired most. It was gone. He scanned for a policeman. None in sight. The soft rain that had been falling began to intensify. "I can't believe it," said Yoshi, eyes afire. "What do we do now?"

Kenton locked his eyes on Yoshi's computer case. "The file . . ." He motioned toward their car and the two dashed to slip in. Kenton locked the doors and switched on the map light. Chilled in the raw, rainy night, Kenton turned on the engine and heater.

Yoshi unzipped the laptop case and pulled out the manila file folder, now frayed. She removed a handful of papers, passed some to Kenton, and kept some on her lap. They both leaned in, intently eyeing the contents.

"All email printouts," Kenton said. "No sender's address—just as Brian said." Kenton took a few of the papers and passed them one by one under the map light, scanning them like a jeweler studying facets of a precious diamond.

"Yoshi!" Kenton exclaimed in a breathy whisper. "These are all instructions from the circle makers on how to interpret the circles and apply advanced technology for humanity's benefit."

"Here's one about sacred geometry as a key to the creation of the universe," Yoshi said.

"This one is a kind of riddle. *'When two dimensions become three, all your energy will be free.'* I wonder what—"

**RAP. . RAP. . . RAP.** The two sat up, jolted. Someone was beating on the car window. *"Ayyeee!"* Yoshi shot out. Clumsily she stuffed the papers between her seat and the car door, as did Kenton. "Shit, those goons have come back for us!" Kenton blurted.

He looked out the passenger's window to see the face of a bobby peering in. Yoshi cast a quick glance at Kenton, and let the window down.

"Everything all right in here?" The policeman stuck his head slightly in the window, studying the couple.

"Uh, yes, sure, officer," Kenton answered, wishing he sounded more innocent.

The bobby scanned the back seat, then the front. "All right, just checking," he replied with a nod. "I noticed your motor running and windows all steamed up." He took another moment to size up the occupants. "I imagine you're old enough to not need supervision, if you know what I mean," he added with a wink.

Relieved, Kenton flashed a short insincere smile. Yoshi looked at Kenton with questioning eyes, as if asking if they should report the kidnapping to this officer. Kenton kept a poker face.

"You American?"

Kenton nodded.

"This a hired car?"

"That's right."

The policeman looked up and down the street. "Watch out, then. This section's a bit dodgy, you know."

*I certainly do.*

"All right then, have a good evening," the officer said.

"You as well," Kenton offered as the bobby went on his way.

Yoshi rolled up the window. "Let's get out of here."

# Brianna 13

A siren from the street below jarred Brianna awake. She rolled over, groaned, and groped for her phone. 8:04. *Shit. Less than half an hour to get to Mythology class.*

Brianna dragged herself out of bed, staggered to the closet, and threw on the black Eminem T-shirt at the top of her drawer. She slipped into tattered jeans and hurried to the kitchen, where she tapped buttons on the coffee machine with one hand and extracted the purple travel mug from the dishwasher with the other. *I'll never make it on time. But Manheim likes me. I think he has a crush on me. He'll cut me a break if I'm late.*

Forty minutes later the frazzled senior slid into a chair at the rear of the drab classroom, darkened for some kind of visual presentation. Professor Scott Manheim stood with his back to the class, fiddling with the projector. Brianna took her first long breath since she woke up. *He didn't see me come in late.* Finally the instructor turned to the class. "We're up to the messiah birth myth today."

*Double shit.*

The professor pressed a clicker, and a slide showing a painting of Buddha appeared on the large screen hanging behind him. "Nearly every religion and culture has a messiah birth myth," Manheim began, his annoyingly nasal voice slowly disappearing into the room's poor acoustics. The next image appeared on screen: a tiny golden-skinned infant prancing through a field. "Buddha is said to have emerged from the womb, stood, took seven steps, and declared, 'I alone am the World-Honored One!'"

A succession of images flashed rapid-fire on the screen. "Horus of Egypt. Krishna of India. Dionysus of Greece. Mithras of Persia. The Norse god Odin." With each image and description, Brianna grew more edgy.

"Now, on to the messiah myth you are most familiar with." The screen showed a Renaissance painting of an angel whispering to the Virgin Mary. "You all know the Christ story. Here we see the Annunciation by the Angel Gabriel that Mary was to conceive a child. She was fifteen or sixteen years old."

*I'm, like, an old lady compared to her.*

"Who can tell me why every culture fantasizes about birthing a messiah?"

A girl with white powdered cheeks, black lipstick, and purple fingernails raised her hand. "So they can all have a Christmas kind of holiday?"

Manheim snickered. "Good try, Jennifer, but not quite it."

An Indian guy with a trimmed black beard called out, "The idea of the virgin birth instills and maintains believers' guilt for their own sexuality, allowing the Church to control them."

"Possibly . . . but there's more to it than that."

A skinny kid in the rear of the room hailed the teacher. "People feel lost, confused, and powerless. They can't save themselves or the world, so they invent a savior to believe in."

"Precisely!" Manheim replied, obviously pleased. "Every generation hopes that someone will come and save it from the mess the world has always been. But in spite of all the saviors prophesied and worshipped, the world is still in deep trouble—maybe more than ever."

A round-faced clean-cut girl with short black bangs called out, "But Jesus Christ *is* the Messiah. Believe in him, and your sins are forgiven. Anyone who worships Him will go to heaven."

"Maybe," Manheim answered cynically. "But that hasn't kept people from making up new savior stories. If you watch the news, you will notice that every couple of years some cult leader prophesizes the end of the world, and promises to save his followers from the Great Tribulation and guide them to their special place in heaven. The deluded disciples run to a mountaintop waiting for the flood, asteroid, or nuclear war, convinced that their group alone will be saved. When the disaster doesn't happen, the leader claims that their timing was wrong or that their prayers averted the catastrophe. A few years later the same story crops up elsewhere, with another demagogue and gullible followers. Yet the sordid world just goes on. The model is classic and predictable."

Brianna raised her hand. Manheim called on her. He always did.

"Do you think that one day a genuine spiritual leader will come who will actually make a difference in the world? Maybe, these days, through like . . . genetic engineering . . . or something like that?"

A titter rolled through the room. Brianna felt embarrassed.

"That's a pleasant thought, Brianna," the professor replied, his condescension thinly veiled. "Every culture fantasizes and mythologizes in ways familiar to it. Two thousand years ago people envisioned a religious messiah. Now we believe in science, so we might fancy a savior through chemistry."

Brianna took a long breath, sighed, pursed her lips, and beat her thumb on the heel of her MacBook. She opened Word, found a headline font, and typed:

**Delusional Professor Seeking Escape from Painful Existence Enrolls Gullible Student in Fantasy Scheme**

# Driscoll 13

Reporters banged at the door, the phone rang at all hours, and emails streamed from every corner of the planet. Half the messages were congratulatory, half critical. Some bore death threats. CNN, FOX, and NPR begged for interviews. The empty lot across the street from the Ames house became a camping ground for UFO fanatics, religious extremists, and conspiracy theorists. Oddballs paraded on the sidewalk in alien costumes and rolled homemade flying saucers in the street. When the army refused to supply security, Seven Oaks police kept vigil. Overnight the name Lieutenant Driscoll Ames had become a household word.

Behind closed doors Driscoll printed the tickets he had purchased for his family to fly first class to the Geopend Genezing clinic in Brussels to see doctor Anastaas Prins. *If we can just put up with this insanity for a few more days, we'll be out of the country and Ticia will have her shot at recovery.*

At 2:10 PM Driscoll's text tone (the *Close Encounters* theme, downloaded by Jared) sounded. Cheryl Lansing.

"The President is holding a press conference in one hour—about you."

A jolt of adrenaline shot through Driscoll's lower back. "He has bigger balls than I thought," he texted back. Driscoll made his way into the bedroom, where the kids were on the computer looking at pictures of their house on Internet news sites and reading stories about their suddenly-famous dad.

"This article says you're a spy from China trying to subvert the U.S. government," Tanisha called over her shoulder. "What's 'subvert?'"

"This one says E.T.s took over your body," Jared followed. "Like in *The Invasion of the Body Snatchers*—Cool!"

Driscoll smiled, offered a not-bad zombie impression, and sat down on the bed next to his wife. "I hope this isn't overwhelming you."

Ticia forced a small smile. "You know me. I'm always up for a good party."

"Well, more people are coming. The President's going to comment at three o'clock."

Ticia's eyes bulged. "Then let's get out the popcorn."

*The Vatican*
*September 7*

# Leo 13

---

At 5 PM Father Leo was awakened from *riposa* by his telephone ringing. He answered to hear Sister Isabel's voice. "We have your dinner early as you requested, Monsignor. Would now be a good time to deliver it?"

"But I didn't—"

"Certainly, Father," she spoke in a voice loud enough for her co-workers in the kitchen to hear. "I'll be there in a few minutes." *Click.*

Leo stared at the receiver for another few moments and then hung it up. In the two years the nun had been delivering his dinners, he had never requested his meal early, and he certainly hadn't done so tonight. *Is she losing her mind?*

Fifteen minutes later came the familiar knock.

"Come in," he called out.

The door opened to reveal Sister Isabel and her dining cart, exactly as she appeared nearly every night—except three hours early. The priest eyed her with consternation as she closed the door behind her and wheeled the cart to its position in front of the sofa.

"Sister—"

"Let me show you what we have tonight, Father," she said in a voice as loud as the one she used when she had phoned from the kitchen. "Chef Alonzo has prepared a tomato basil soup, pasta primavera with charred salmon, and a creamy lemon sauce. . ." As she spoke, Sister Isabel took the Monsignor's arm and began to pull him across his living room. He resisted, but then, feeling the adamancy of the nun's tug, followed.

To Leo's greater surprise, she led him into the bathroom and closed the door behind them. By this time Father Leo was completely dumbfounded. Sister looked up and around at the walls and ceiling, and when she seemed satisfied, she spoke.

"Listen to me carefully, Monsignor," she said in a whisper. "I was removing Father LaCorte's lunch tray when he received a phone call. He thought I had left his apartment, but I was still around the corner of his hallway out of sight. I could still hear the conversation on the speakerphone."

Leo tried to imagine what Sister might tell him. He couldn't.

"Father was talking to someone who knows that Paolo is behind the crucifix vandalizing."

Leo's body stiffened. "How?"

"They matched the record of the night Paolo came to visit—Abramo had recorded his name—with your call to his cell phone. They got someone in the telephone company to check Paolo's cell phone call record. He has lots of calls to someone named Lisbeth."

Leo's head started to throb. Obviously the nun knew what she was talking about.

"The Church and police pressured the telephone company to monitor Paolo's and Lisbeth's text messages. There were all kinds of messages about the stolen crucifixes, absolutely incriminating Paolo. This morning Paolo told Lisbeth to meet him at Suore Figlie Della Divina Provvidenza for 'one last mission of mercy.' When I heard that, I left Father LaCorte's apartment so I could call you."

Leo's knees grew wobbly. He sat on the bathtub and grasped the rim with his trembling hands. Sister reached for a washcloth, ran it under some cold water, and dabbed it on the priest's face.

"I must stop Paolo from going to that church," Leo said, staring off into space.

Sister Isabel nodded gravely. "They will be waiting for him."

# *Lauren 13*

Todd opened his cabin door to find Lauren feverishly tossing her clothes into her suitcase. "Where are you going? . . . Did I do something wrong?"

She didn't bother to turn her head to look at him. "You lied to me," Lauren shouted over her shoulder. She slammed her bag shut, zipped it loudly, set it upright, pulled up the handle, and dragged it toward the door.

Todd grabbed the unhinged woman by the shoulders and turned her around to face him.

"Why didn't you tell me what's really going on here?"

"What are you talking about?"

"I'm talking about the guns, Todd . . . Your sweet little pacifist spiritual commune has an arsenal big enough to take out a small city. You're not about peace and love at all, are you?"

Todd stiffened. "How do you know about that?"

"I found your bunker in the woods, loaded with weapons. . . What are you? Nazis? KKK? Working with Isis?"

Todd took a forced breath. "I can explain it all. . . Would you please just sit down for a minute?"

Lauren shook her head back and forth rapidly.

"Come on, Lauren, give me a chance."

She stopped and stared at Todd with sharp, angry eyes. "OK, but no bullshit!"

"No bullshit—I promise."

Lauren sat on the edge of the bed, arms crossed, eyes fuming.

"We're not planning to attack anybody. We don't want to hurt anyone."

"Then what are all those munitions for?"

"They're for self-defense."

"Self-defense? Out here?!!!" she cackled. "Against who? Bigfoot?"

Todd paced back and forth. "Remember I told you that the collapse of civilization is imminent?"

Lauren nodded, her jaw clenched.

"When things go haywire in the cities, it isn't going to be pretty, Lauren. There will be lots of hungry, distraught, angry people. Law enforcement will be useless, people will take to the streets, and there will be mayhem—rioting, looting, and killing."

Lauren shook her head vehemently. "Boy, do you guys have your heads up your butt! You claim to be building a new world, and you're putting your chips on total chaos. What a bunch of hypocrites!"

Todd tried to catch her eyes, but she was staring into the distance.

"Food supply lines will be disrupted, and people will be roaming wherever they can to find food. Some will find their way here."

"Oh, I see. So you're going to just shoot them."

"Not necessarily. But if they come with weapons—one out of three people in this country has a gun—we need to be prepared to defend ourselves."

"So it's all about self-defense, is it? Isn't that how Hitler fooled the Germans into going to war? 'We better attack Poland before they march on us?'"

Todd's tried to take Lauren's hand. She pushed it away.

"We are planting the seeds of the new world right here. We can't afford to have our community overrun or destroyed by fearful people."

Lauren stood up, faced Todd squarely, and practically screamed at him. "Don't you see, Todd—*you* are the fearful people." She tried to ratchet herself back, but couldn't. "How can you claim to start a new world when you are doing exactly what's wrong with the old one? You don't save the world by shooting hungry people, Todd. You save the world by feeding them."

Lauren waited for Todd to shout back, but he didn't. He remained quiet, looking down at the floor.

"I enjoyed being with you, Todd." Her voice grew a bit calmer. "I actually thought we could have a life together. But now I don't think so. I think you and your flower child friends are deluded. You're not helping the world. You're a bunch of meditating narcissists, evil as the people you say you are protecting yourselves from."

With that, Lauren Delaney grabbed the handle of her overnight bag and stomped out the door.

*Beaconsfield, England*
*August 28*

# Kenton 13

When Kenton Baine woke up that morning, he had no idea that by the end of the day his marriage would be over and he would be standing beside Yoshi at the door of her parents' condo. Yet he felt more life force coursing through him than at any time he could remember.

"Did your parents come to England to see the crop circles?" he asked as Yoshi slipped off her shoes and placed them neatly next to two other pairs beside the front door. Kenton took the hint and followed her example.

Yoshi laughed. "They came as my chaperones. They didn't want me to travel alone—you know, everywhere outside Japan is unsafe and I would surely be raped or murdered. But when I told them I was coming this summer no matter what, they decided to come too. In between worrying about me, they play cards and watch *Britain's Got Talent*."

The door swung open from the inside, revealing a munchkin-like couple in their early sixties, eyes bulging at the sight of a man standing beside their terribly single daughter. Yoshi's mother Tomiko stood just north of five feet tall, with short gray bangs and scant makeup. Her long white flowered blouse hung neatly over black stretch pants. Her face was wrinkled, with character. Her husband Takao stood a half-foot taller than his wife. His hair was darker, skin more golden, jaw firm. He looked comfortable in a cream-colored cardigan sweater and gray slacks.

Yoshi introduced her guest in Japanese, and her parents bowed respectfully. Tomiko, jittery in the presence of Yoshi's assumed boyfriend, motioned toward the dining room table. Kenton was not hungry, but he didn't want to insult his hosts, so he acceded. Tomiko set a large black pot on the table and lifted the lid, releasing a waft of steam she fanned toward Kenton. "Miso soup," she said proudly, straining to get her English pronunciation correct.

The shy guest lowered himself to a cushion on the floor beside the knee-high dining room table. With some effort, he was able to stretch his legs beneath the table without bumping his hosts. With coaching, he was able to work his chopsticks to get some of the shrimp over soba noodles into his mouth without dropping too much. Tomiko was chatty and bossy, but likeable. Takao, a disciplined engineer, remained quiet in the shadow of his wife, yet he was keenly observant. Both spoke shaky English, so Yoshi translated most of the conversation.

It did not take Kenton long to figure out that the elders were sizing him up as a future son-in-law. Yoshi was well beyond the Japanese woman's desirable marriage age of twenty-five at most. Although Yoshi cared little about finding a husband, her parents still had their hopes up. Kenton was not about to tell his hosts that he had left his wife just a few hours ago, let alone that he and their daughter were involved in an international conspiracy web. A polite "thank you for the excellent meal" would do for now.

Meanwhile the elephant in the room was the mysterious file Kenton and Yoshi had just inherited. As soon as etiquette permitted, Yoshi told her parents that she and Kenton had some business to discuss, and asked to be excused. She poked her companion to stand when she did, and he awkwardly mimicked her formal bow. "Where are we going?" he whispered.

"To my bedroom."

Kenton's mind went tilt. He hadn't been thinking about Yoshi like that. She read his anxiety. "Relax," she whispered. "It's the only private place in the condo."

"What will your parents think?"

"We'll leave the door open. They'll see we're doing business and they'll like you because you're a good businessman, choosing work over sleep or sex—very Japanese."

# *Brianna 14*

---

Stretched out on the grassy knoll outside Hunter College's north building, Brianna gazed up at the early fall afternoon sky. Some leaves on the trees above her had already twinged a slight orange. *Thank goodness that weird Hathaway proposal is behind me.*

As she closed her eyes and started to drift off, her phone rang. Brad.

"Sis, you have to come meet me at Penn Med."

Brianna sat up ramrod straight.

"Mom was drinking and taking pills. Dad found her passed out when he got home. They took her to the E.R."

Her body stiffened. "Will she be okay?"

"They pumped her stomach. She's pretty woozy, but conscious."

Brianna's solar plexus relaxed a bit.

"We have to do something. If she stays at home, she is going to kill herself. It's only a matter of time."

"What about that V.A. hospital you and dad looked at?"

"I called them. They're filled up. They are referring patients to some facility in upstate New York. I googled the place . . . It sucks as bad as the one near us."

"Brad, this is terrible . . . What are we going to do?"

Long silence. Brianna could hear the wheels in her brother's head turning.

"Oh, no, Brad." Brianna shook her head. "I just blew off Hathaway. I'm not getting involved with his crazy scheme."

"I know you don't want to do it," Brad came back. "It's wacked out, for sure. But it might be our only shot at keeping mom alive and out of some chamber of horrors. I bet Hathaway will give you an advance if you ask him."

"Don't do this to me, Brad. This is my life."

"I understand. But it's mom's life too. I know it's a big ask. You can save her—and our whole family—from a living hell. Please, Brianna, just say yes."

# Driscoll 14

Driscoll Ames propped his wife's pillows behind her and helped her sit up. The kids pulled cushions from the living room sofa and plopped on the floor between the bed and the TV. Driscoll leaned against the headboard next to Ticia, his arm resting lightly around her. A Tupperware bowl of popcorn sat between them, another between the kids, everyone munching eagerly.

At three o'clock *The Young and the Restless* intro fizzled and segued to the White House Press Conference Room.

"We interrupt this program for a live newscast from the White House."

Driscoll shot Ticia a nervous look. *Here we go.*

But the President did not approach the podium. Instead, Press Secretary Gloria Wheeler stepped up. As she readied her papers, Driscoll heard his text message chime. Cheryl. "HE'S TRYING TO DOWNPLAY THE IMPORTANCE BY SENDING HIS AIDE."

"Members of the press," Wheeler began, "the President has asked me to convey his comments on the alleged disclosure by United States Army Lieutenant Driscoll Ames."

*Alleged. They're going to deny it.*

"Lieutenant Ames has presented a story and images of supposed remnants of extraterrestrial crafts and bodies of aliens. He claims that he gained access to top secret facilities in the Pentagon to do so."

The television camera panned the audience of hushed reporters, fingers dancing over keyboards.

"To get to the truth of the matter, the President ordered a rapid investigation of the facilities Lieutenant Ames says he visited. Investigators have found that this room is indeed a museum of artifacts."

Driscoll sat up straight. *Are they going to come clean?*

"The artifacts, however, are not from outside the Earth. They are the remains of various high-level classified projects. The so-called 'pieces of spacecraft' are portions of Soviet satellites that crashed to earth during the cold war. There are also a few sections recovered from the space shuttle *Challenger* disaster. The supposed 'bodies' are remnants of dummies that fell to earth from high altitudes. They were used to test atmospheric conditions unsafe for human beings. The dummies were damaged upon impact with Earth, hence the appearance of torn tissue. So after all, ladies and gentlemen, in spite of the excitement that the idea of alien visitation engenders, we have nothing to report from out of this world."

Text from Cheryl: SHORT, SWEET, AND FULL OF SHIT.

Dozens of hands shot up. Wheeler pointed to a stocky male reporter in the front row.

"The images Lieutenant Ames showed didn't look anything like human beings. Why would the government formulate dummies that looked like extraterrestrials?"

Wheeler offered a contrived smile and nodded as if she had anticipated the question. "The experiments were carried out in the 1950's when the public was engrossed in a flying saucer craze. The scientists who formed the dummies were just having some fun." The Press Secretary seemed confident now. "Andrea. . . "

A young Asian woman in a gray dress stood. "Dummies don't have internal body structure. The photos Lieutenant Ames showed clearly revealed cartilage and bone. How would you account for that in a dummy?"

Wheeler nodded. "The manufacturers inserted organs from animals to test the effects of high-altitude exposure on tissue. They were attempting to replicate human anatomy to determine the effects of changes in air pressure and study damage . . . Jean Luc?"

"Can you give us the name of the equipment manufacturer, so we might research the records?"

"That company is long gone. Besides, that's classified information . . . Mary?"

"What about the strange symbols inscribed on some of the larger pieces of metal? They are clearly, intelligently imbedded in the material, and they do not represent any language known on Earth."

Wheeler nodded. "They were identifiers of the equipment and various data related to the experiment, encrypted so that if the gear fell into Soviet hands, they would not be able to glean any information from them."

A tall, dark-skinned reporter with a brown military haircut spoke next. "Will the government be taking punitive action against Lieutenant Ames for revealing classified information . . . or fabricating it?

Driscoll gulped. *Will I now be crucified?*

"That has not yet been determined . . . The President is considering if and what action is appropriate . . . Jerry?"

A young male black reporter with a shaved head spoke with an air of confidence. "This revelation, true or false, represents the tip of the iceberg of a growing movement among citizens of many nations, demanding that governments make public their hidden files on UFOs, or 'UAPs,' as they are now called, as well as contact with extraterrestrials. Britain, France, Australia, Brazil, and a number of other countries have released all of their files, including compelling photos, videos, and documented testimonies by military personnel indicating encounters with unidentified flying objects that cannot be explained in any earthly terms. Does our government have any plans to release our documents?"

Wheeler began to look uncomfortable. She studied her notes for a few moments as if looking for an answer there.

"Our government deems it necessary to keep classified any information it believes vital to national security, and it will continue to keep those documents secret. As far as the President knows, there are no documents in our archives that verify the existence of alien spacecraft, extraterrestrials, or such contact. . . One more question . . . Mark."

"During his campaign, the President promised a transparent government with full disclosure. The people who elected him expect him to be true to his promise. Do you believe that this incident, and the people who believe

Lieutenant Ames rather than the President, might damage the President's chances for re-election?"

Wheeler's jaw tightened. "The President believes that he will be re-elected because more citizens value his commitment to national security than delving into areas that are more a matter of fantasy than fact . . . Thank you all for your time today."

Gloria Wheeler offered a curt smile and stepped off the stage. Moments later, *The Young and the Restless* returned to the screen.

One more text from Cheryl: THE SPIN DOCTORS HAVE PERFORMED AS EXPECTED.

*The Vatican*
*September 7*

# Leo 14

"Paolo, you must phone me immediately," Leo spoke to his son's voicemail. "It is extremely important. Don't wait."

As he hung up, Leo realized that if anyone tapped that voicemail he, too, would be incriminated. Yet at this point his status in the religion felt less important than keeping his son out of jail or the hospital, not to mention facing public humiliation that would mar the boy for life and send his mother to her grave in shame.

Slowly the late afternoon gave way to evening. Leo looked at the clock. 7:20 PM. The two hours since Sister Isabel had informed him of Paolo's danger felt like two days. Paolo had failed to answer the phone or return Leo's messages in all that time. Leo tossed on a light jacket, going over in his mind the train route to Paolo's apartment. But if Paolo was not home, Leo's trip would be in vain and his rebellious son would be left to the clutches of vicious brutes. *If I can get to the church before he does, I can stop him.*

He picked up the phone again. "Abramo, I need to go out. Please get me a taxi." Leo stood for a moment at the foot of the portrait of the Blessed Virgin on the wall above his couch. He made the sign of the cross across his forehead, shoulders, and chest. *Please protect my son.* Then he dashed out the door. By the time he reached Abramo's security station at the street, a white *Via Roma* taxi was waiting for him.

Leo threw open the rear door and slid into the back seat. "Suore Figlie Della Divina Provvidenza. Please hurry." The driver nodded, threw the vehicle in gear, and launched away from the Vatican. Leo looked at his watch. 7:35. If Paolo's ruse was true to the form he had revealed to his father, he and Lisbeth would go to the church during the hour before closing and hide in a bathroom or utility closet until the church's doors were locked, usually around 9 PM. When they were satisfied they were alone, the two would sneak into the sanctuary, remove the Christ statue, leave their infamous note and lily, take the statue out to their small panel van waiting on the street, and abscond. If Father Bonfiglio could get to them before they entered the church, they would be spared the ugly meeting awaiting them.

*Blue Ridge Mountains*
*September 3*

## Lauren 14

As a fuming Lauren reached the bottom of the cabin's stairs, her paisley overnight bag bumping clumsily down the steps behind her, a black Jeep Cherokee stormed into the clearing in front of the cabin. The driver slammed on the brakes, kicking up a billow of dust that made Lauren gag.

Todd, pursuing Lauren, turned to the Jeep. The driver, a tall olive-skinned guy with a Mohawk haircut, leaned out of the window and yelled to Todd, "Malthus is here."

Todd stiffened.

"What's she doing here?" the driver asked.

"She's my girlfriend."

Lauren shot Todd an icy glance that told him she was anything but that.

"She'll have to leave now," the driver barked.

"No problem," Lauren retorted, and started to drag her suitcase along the bumpy path.

"Lauren, wait!" Todd called out.

She didn't look back, but simply stomped forward, trying to maneuver her bag over rocks and roots.

The Jeep hurtled off, but then stopped abruptly fifty yards down the road. Lauren could see the driver holding a walkie-talkie to his ear, loud squawking noises shooting from the device. Quickly the Jeep turned and rambled toward her. Startled and fearing it would run her over, she jumped toward the bushes. The vehicle stopped short right in front of her.

"You're going to have to stay," the driver shouted.

Lauren shot him an angry look.

"Why?" Todd asked as he approached the truck.

"She was snooping around the ammo dump. Caught on the security camera."

A burst of adrenaline shot through Lauren's lower back. "You can't keep me here, you asshole."

A burly guy with thick tattooed arms opened the passenger door, jumped out, and grabbed Lauren by the arm. She yelled and resisted, until he twisted her arm so hard that she gave in. The creep opened the rear door of the Jeep and pushed her into the seat. Todd forced his way into the seat beside her, and the vehicle sped off.

Lauren gave Todd a glance of utter contempt. This wasn't turning out as she had planned.

# *Kenton 14*

---

After a bad night's sleep on the lumpy futon in the Satos' living room, Kenton woke long before his late-rising Japanese hosts. Yoshi was sitting at the dining room table, her back to him, eyes glued to her laptop. Bleary-eyed, he sat up, a dull pain in his back keeping him from straightening fully. He groaned.

Yoshi heard him and turned around.

"I feel like I just slept on a bunch of billiard balls."

Yoshi made a pained face. "I'm so sorry, Kenton. Would you feel better going back to your hotel?"

Kenton flashed an even more bitter face. "A saucer landing would be more likely."

"I have some news for you."

Kenton wrapped his blanket around himself, stood, and slid into the chair beside Yoshi. As he peered over her shoulder, he saw a BBC news site up on her laptop screen. The headline announced:

**Crop Circle Researcher Disappears**

Below a full-face photo of the missing scientist, Kenton read:

Dr. Brian Turner, foremost researcher and respected authority on the crop formation phenomenon, was reported missing last night. Turner's wife Helen phoned the police around midnight when Turner did not come home after a lecture he presented in Hackney. "He has never not come home before," Mrs. Turner told a BBC reporter. "I'm really worried."

Authorities have questioned some of the audience who attended the program, as well as the host, Mr. Arthur Rayburn. No one has yet provided any helpful information. Dr. Turner was last seen leaving the gathering around 10:00 PM.

If anyone has any information regarding Dr. Turner's whereabouts, please report to the BBC via contact information at bbc.co.uk.

Yoshi turned to Kenton, angst in her eyes. "Do you think we should tell them what we know?"

He shook his head. "Better not, for now. We have the crucial file, and we don't want anyone confiscating it. We also might be implicated. And if we identify ourselves, those goons might come after us."

Yoshi nodded. "So what then?"

Kenton rubbed his chin. "If we can get to Turner's computer, the one he was emailing from, we might be able to capture the final download."

"And we do that how?"

"We pay a visit to Mrs. Turner."

Yoshi wrinkled her forehead. "And you think she'll just let two strangers walk into her house and poke around her missing husband's private computer files?"

"If she believes we can help her get him back, she might."

Kenton tried to muster a confident face. "Do you know the English expression, '*We'll cross that bridge when we come to it?*'"

Yoshi laughed nervously. "Do you know the Japanese expression, '*The goose that honks the loudest is the one that will get shot?*'"

# *Brianna 15*

Brianna's breath clenched as she reached to open the door of Dr. Redmond Hathaway's office, tucked into a far corner of the Hunter College Science Building. *Locked.* She peered through the slim window next to the door. *Lights out.* The printer paper taped to the door read, Office Hours: Tuesday and Thursday, 2:00 – 4:00 PM. She checked her phone. 3:15. She looked again through the window. *Maybe he's in the back somewhere.*

"Hey, Brianna, check this out," a young woman's voice called out.

Brianna turned to see Ashley, a girl in the Quantum class, walking briskly toward her. She was holding a copy of The Envoy, Hunter's student newspaper. Ashley turned the front page for Brianna to read:

### Hathaway Charged with Malfeasance

Below the headline Brianna found an unflattering random photo of the renegade physicist, his eyes bulging, mouth open. She took the paper and read:

Physics Professor Dr. Redmond Hathaway, long-time controversial figure at Hunter, has been notified by the National Science Foundation that he is being investigated for misusing grant monies. Last November Dr. Hathaway received $100,000 from the NSF to conduct experiments on string theory, a leading-edge component of quantum physics. According to Dr. Randall Niemes, Chairman of the NSF Ethics Board, Dr. Hathaway has instead used the funds for genetic engineering experiments. The NSF was alerted to the possible misuse of the monies by chemistry professor Dr. Henry Daniken, who produced copies of purchases orders and receipts for equipment unrelated to the approved experiments. The rumor mill has it that Daniken engaged senior supergeek Erik Bendle to hack into the college's accounting department records.

We couldn't reach Dr. Hathaway for comments, but, hey, if you've taken any of his courses you know that he's out there but cool. Dr. Daniken was, however, eager to go on record: "It's about time Hunter College held Professor Hathaway accountable. He's spending valuable money on crackpot research and teaching theories tantamount to witchcraft."

If the NSF board finds Dr. Hathaway guilty of malfeasance, he will lose the equipment and possibly be dismissed from Hunter, go to jail, or all of the above.

"Everyone is talking about it," Ashley reported. "Erik admitted that he hacked for Daniken."

"What did Hathaway say?"

"Nobody's seen him for three days," Ashley reported. "He didn't show up at his Electromagnetic Waves class. People are saying he defected to Russia."

*Seven Oaks*
*September 8*

# *Driscoll 15*

---

"Liars!" Driscoll spewed, shaking his head.

Ticia offered a sarcastic smile. "Did you expect anything else? The country has spent eighty years covering up a lot more than you disclosed. Do you really think they're going to give it up because of you?"

Driscoll paced beside the bed, fuming. "Does *anyone* in the public eye have the guts to tell the truth?'

Ticia reached up to try to catch her husband's hand. She was too weak. When Driscoll saw her outstretched hand he stopped and took it. "That would be you," she told him with absolute love in her eyes.

Driscoll sat on the bed while Ticia efforted to reach up to stroke his forehead. "You're a good man, Driscoll Ames," she told him. "You've been a wonderful husband and a great father. When I'm gone, have no regrets."

Driscoll placed his finger over her lips. "Don't go there, baby. . . I called the clinic—they can get you in next week."

Ticia smiled and held his hand tighter. Yet when he found her eyes, they looked glassy.

"You okay, babe?"

She lifted her head a bit, but when it became too painful, she rested it back on the pillow.

"I don't know if I will make it to the clinic," she said quietly.

"Oh, come on, sweetheart, it's just a few days more. You can do it."

"My mind says I can, but my body is not agreeing. A woman knows her body. I might be heading home sooner than you think."

Driscoll inched closer to her. "Don't talk like that. Now we have the money to get you fixed up."

Ticia offered a sad smile and shook her head. "There are some things that money can't buy."

Driscoll Ames took a long, slow, pained breath. For all the courage he had to muster in combat, he could not accept his wife dying. "Then what do you want to do? Just tell me."

She smiled ever so slightly. "I want to go home, Driscoll. I want to die where I was born."

"Bimini?"

"Yes, I want to see my family, the house where I grew up, my school, my church, and my friends. That would be the best farewell."

Driscoll tried to fight back the tears. He could no longer deny the reality before him.

"All right, my love. Bimini it is."

# *Leo 15*

Father Leo looked at his watch for the tenth time in five minutes: 7:51. *We should have been there by now.* He lowered the taxi's rear window and stretched his head to catch sight of the street sign at the intersection: Viale delle Milizie. The priest shifted in his seat uneasily. He was no expert on the Roman map, but he knew that Viale delle Milizie was east of the Vatican, and Suore Figlie Della Divina Provvidenza was well north. He leaned toward the front seat of the cab. "Are we heading east instead of north?"

"Exactly, Father," the cabbie replied as if he expected to be asked. "There's a bad road construction delay on Viale Angelico. I am taking you on an alternate route. Trust me—I'll get you there in the fastest way."

Father Leo sighed. "Very well. But please hurry. I have someone I need to meet."

"Yes, sir, I'll do my best."

Leo sat back and tried to relax. Failing that, he glanced at the dashboard of the taxi, where his eyes fell on the driver's I.D., **Philippe di Stefano** printed in bold letters beside the photo. The picture showed a fair-skinned man, thinning hair, with a round face and a double chin. But the driver looked nothing like the photo. The man behind the wheel was gaunt, olive-skinned, with thick curly hair.

He tapped the driver on the shoulder and pointed to the dashboard. "Is that your picture?"

"That's my brother," he called over his shoulder. "He owns the taxi, but he was sick tonight. I told him I would take the shift for him."

As Leo's malaise thickened, the driver kept glancing into the rear-view mirror. Leo turned and looked out the back window of the cab. A police car was trailing the taxi—just cruising, yet enough to make the driver nervous.

Suddenly the taxi made a sharp right turn onto a narrow side street, almost knocking Leo onto the bench's seat. He raised himself and looked again through rear window. The squad car was gone.

"What are you doing?!"

No response from the driver, who picked up speed and kept hurtling down the side street way off course.

"Stop this cab and let me out now!"

The taxi driver paid no attention to Father Leo's plea, but instead accelerated. Leo reached to open the rear door. It was locked. He fiddled with the lock button. It was disabled. Blood rushed to his temples as his heart began to beat wildly.

An idea shot into his brain. Leo reached to his waist and removed the long purple sash cinching his robe. He pulled the cloth belt tight, a two-foot length clenched between his hands. With dogged determination, he reached over the driver's seat and pulled the sash against the driver's throat, yanking his head back to the headrest. The driver began to gag and struggled to protest, but could not get the words out. Desperately he reached up with one hand to try to free himself from the sash, the other hand weakly on the steering wheel. He was losing control of the vehicle.

The cab veered into the opposite lane, directly into oncoming traffic. Two cars blasted their horns as they swerved to avoid a head-on collision. In a crazy instant the taxi veered off the street and crashed into a fire hydrant, spraying wildly as the cab careened off to the side. Still in drive gear, the cab rammed into the wall of a brick apartment building and came to a stop, thick smoke spewing from its grill. Passersby shrieked and ran for cover. The driver, faint but conscious, took the vehicle out of gear. Leo lowered his window and awkwardly crawled out of the cab, crashing to the sidewalk and skinning his hands, bleeding as he broke his fall.

A few pedestrians ran to examine Leo and the driver, who was blanched and gasping for air. Leo raised himself and stood, wobbly, examining himself to see if he was in one piece. He was severely shaken, but still mobile. A man in a navy-blue suit came to Leo's side and offered to take him to a hospital. He refused. When he felt confident he was not seriously injured, the priest looked down the street toward an intersection. A red traffic light at a hundred yards caught his attention. Leo took a few steps to make sure he had his balance, and then increased speed, gaining to a dash.

"Look, mommy, where is that priest running?" he heard a little child call out. But he did not take the time to turn about. He jogged faster, his heart pumping intensely, sweat pouring on his cheeks. After a half-minute he felt a stitch in his side, but adrenaline overrode his stress, and soon he arrived at the intersection. Breathing heavily, he ran to the edge of traffic, raised his arm, and waved. After a few seconds, another *Via Roma* cab stopped and picked him up.

"Suore Figlie Della Divina Provvidenza," he told the driver as he fought to catch his breath. Leo looked back and forth between the driver's photo and the man at the wheel. Satisfied they were the same person, he sat back and tried to calm himself— although he knew that would be quite impossible.

# *Lauren 15*

---

"I'm sorry I got you into this," Todd confessed as the Jeep rattled over the bumpy road. He reached to touch Lauren's shoulder to comfort her.

She pushed his arm away. "Not as sorry as I am."

Todd turned and stared out the window, as if asking some invisible angel how to fix this mess.

Finally she turned her head. "Who's Malthus?"

"You don't want to know," he mumbled over his shoulder.

"Try me."

Todd leaned forward to see if the driver could hear their conversation. His ears were stuffed with Bluetooth ear buds, loud rap music spewing from the speakers.

"Remember I told you that someone donated five hundred acres to Jeremy to start the community?"

Lauren nodded.

"That was Malthus—actually, his real name is John Saynor. He adopted the name after the British economist Thomas Malthus . . . Do you know who he was?"

Lauren thought for a moment. "Wasn't he the guy Aldous Huxley referred to in *Brave New World*? People were wearing Malthusian belts for birth control?"

"Good memory. Thomas Malthus was a nineteenth-century scholar who said that there were too many people in the world, and the food supply would never catch up with the rapidly-growing population. He proposed that poor and sick people should not be allowed to have children. Some of his radical followers believe that masses of the population should be annihilated because they are just consuming resources and not contributing to humanity."

Lauren tried to digest the sick idea. "So what does this Saynor guy have to do with the original Malthus?"

"He believes Malthus was correct. He would like to depopulate the world. He thinks it would be a service to humanity and the planet."

Lauren snickered. "So he's a deluded narcissist . . . Lots of people would like to get rid of everyone but the people they like."

Todd's eyes took on an unnerving intensity. "But this guy is actually planning on doing it."

Lauren laughed cynically. "What does he have, like a bunch of atomic bombs?"

Todd shook his head. "He has a deadly poison that can kill huge masses of people quickly."

Lauren squeezed her face in disbelief.

"Jeremy met Malthus—then Saynor—at some online counterculture chatroom. They both believed the world was going to hell, and needed to be redeemed. When Jeremy found this property as a possible site for a survivalist community, Saynor offered to fund it. He had been a high-ranking chemist for a big agribusiness corporation, developing pesticides for farmers. He made lots of money garnering patents. So he bought the property for the community."

Lauren squirmed. *This is starting to sound too real.*

"There was one other person involved with founding the community—a Chinese doctor named Jian Chung. He is a gifted herbologist and acupuncturist, trained in China by healers who knew secret teachings handed down over thousands of years. Chung also believed the world was in deep trouble. He had a vision to build a community based on natural healing."

"So how did the community go south?"

"Soon after Project Genesis was established, Saynor got into the teachings of Thomas Malthus. He grew more paranoid and changed his name. Then he tried to boss the community. He figured that since he had paid for the land, everyone should do his bidding and go along with his campaign to depopulate the world. He is the one responsible for all the munitions you saw."

*Paranoid people with brains and money. Very bad chemistry.*

"When Chung saw that the community was headed to the dark side, he appealed to the members to avoid a violent direction. A split occurred. Most people sided with Chung, and a few with Malthus. They argued with Malthus to allow Project Genesis to go ahead cultivating the birth of the Christ teacher rather than murdering the masses. When he saw that his followers were outnumbered, Malthus left in a huff and warned that if the birth strategy failed, he would return and strong-arm the community to follow his will. He threatened to sell the property and dissolve the community.

As a compromise, the community voted to let Malthus keep the munitions onsite as a last resort. Dr. Chung could not live under such a sordid prospect, so he left and went somewhere in the Middle East. Malthus moved to Charlottesville, but stayed in touch with his sympathizers in the community. No one has seen him for years."

"So why is he here now?"

"Malthus must have gotten the word that the couple is infertile. Now he is back to take his due."

Lauren squinted cynically. "So he's paranoid and vindictive. Mental hospitals are filled with guys like him."

Todd squirmed. "But this guy is not institutionalized and he has a plan. The poison is colorless, tasteless, odorless, and dissolves easily in water. It's hard to detect with scientific instruments unless you are specifically screening for it. If this chemical was dropped into the water supply of a large city like New York or London, it would go unnoticed and be invisibly distributed to millions of people. Once ingested, the chemical takes about a week to establish itself in the human body. Then it slowly strangles the alveoli of the lungs, so everyone affected will suffocate from the inside out. Great masses of people will be dropping dead on the streets before anyone has a clue as to what caused it."

Lauren blanched. "My God! What kind of mind would even think of that, let alone do it?"

"The chemical also penetrates the body through the pores of the skin. So anyone who bathes or showers in the tainted water will be exterminated as well. Even a few drops on the skin will start to do the dirty work."

Lauren kept shaking her head. "He's just one crazy guy with a lethal chemical. He can't annihilate the population of the world single-handedly."

"One crazy guy who has attracted others. Malthus has assembled an army of paranoids around the world who believe in him and follow his instructions. He intends to station his agents at the water sources of major cities and simultaneously infuse the chemical. Then they can move on to other cities and repeat their horrid task before the poison takes effect and people start to figure out what happened. It will be only a matter of weeks before half the world's population will be gone."

Lauren nervously twirled her hair with her hand. "Isn't there any antidote?"

"None that could be discovered and administered to the masses before the foul deed is done. Just before Dr. Chung left the community, Malthus told him about the poison and how it worked. Chung told his own sympathizers that he could offset the effects with specific herbs that would have to be introduced into an affected person within a week after the drug is ingested. But conventional medicine doesn't want to hear about herbs. They believe in chemicals. And researchers have to go through a long process of government approval. Remember how it took pharmaceutical companies a year to come up with a coronavirus vaccine? We won't have the luxury of that window with this killer. By the time science figures out how to combat this poison, huge masses of people will have been blindsided and it will be too late."

The Jeep came to a sharp halt in front of the meeting hall. The driver stepped out and opened the door next to Lauren. He grabbed her by the arm and started to pull her toward the meeting hall. "You're hurting me, you jerk. Where are you taking me?"

"Malthus wants to see you," he said as he pushed her toward the door.

*London*
*August 31*

# Kenton 15

---

Kenton rang the doorbell beside the front door of Brian Turner's upscale Wimbledon Village house, and brushed his hair back. Yoshi, at his side, smoothed her dress. Moments later a sixty-ish woman with long chestnut and silver hair answered. She wore a plain below-the-knee dark blue dress and a turquoise pendant in the shape of a star. Minimal makeup, looking quite ragged. She questioned the visitors with her eyes.

"Hello, are you Mrs. Turner?"

"That's right."

"We're sorry to trouble you, ma'am. We know what you've been through with Brian's disappearance."

The woman shot the two a piercing stare. "Who are you and what do you want?"

"We're acquaintances of Brian," said Yoshi. "We have some information that might help you find him."

Helen Turner glanced down at the file folder in Yoshi's hand. "That's Brian's file," she exclaimed. "His label and handwriting! Where did you get that?" She eyed the two suspiciously. "I'm calling the police!"

Kenton lifted his hands palms up toward the anguished woman. "Please, Mrs. Turner, we want to find Brian too. We're his biggest fans. Just give us five minutes."

"Are you going to kidnap me too?"

"Do we look like kidnappers?" Kenton replied.

Helen Turner took a long, tense moment to size up the pair, Kenton and Yoshi breathing shallowly. Finally Mrs. Turner sighed, opened the door, and ushered the couple into her living room. The distressed wife directed her visitors to a leather loveseat at an angle to a brick fireplace, while she took her place on a chair facing them. As Yoshi set the file on the coffee table, Kenton scanned the room. The mantle displayed several photos of Brian at various ages, the most recent ones showing him standing in the midst of several different crop formations. On the tabletop sat Turner's latest book, *Crop Circles: Mystery and Majesty*. Kenton felt like a little boy in the temple of a visionary giant.

"We were at Brian's gathering the other night," Yoshi began. "We were speaking with him outside the building afterward. Several men grabbed him, dragged him into a car, and sped away."

Helen Turner issued a short gasp and lifted her hand to her mouth. "Dear me, I knew something like this would happen . . . It was only a matter of time." Her words gave way to tears. Yoshi reached into her purse and pulled out a few tissues. Mrs. Turner politely refused, dipping her hand into her pocket to retrieve a small white embroidered hankie.

"Brian has been receiving weird phone calls for the last few months," Mrs. Turner said in a shaky voice. "Someone with a Middle Eastern accent would phone at odd hours. The calls were short, but when Brian got off the phone he was rattled. At first he wouldn't tell me who was calling, but eventually he confessed that some group was trying to bully him to issue a press release stating that all the crop circles are fake. When Brian refused, the man told him that if he didn't cooperate, his life and his family were in danger. We thought it was just a prank—he's gotten weird calls before, even death threats—but now . . . my God, they've taken him!" Fighting back her tears, Helen touched the tip of her hankie to the side of one eye.

Kenton rotated the file on the coffee table to face her. "Just before he was abducted, Brian handed us this file and told us to keep it safe. It contains printouts from some of his recent emails."

Helen opened the file, studied a few pages, and nodded. "So this is what he was working on."

"He didn't tell you about this?"

"Brian shared a lot of the crop circle information with me, but some pieces he kept secret. He promised he would reveal it when the time was right. I was curious, but I know better than to press him."

"Apparently Brian was somehow communicating via email with the circle makers," Kenton explained.

"You mean the hoaxsters who have made some of the formations?"

Kenton shot Yoshi a questioning look, wondering if they might be pushing Helen Turner too far. But it was too late to turn back now. "As far as we can tell, Mrs. Turner, the emails came from the real circle makers," Yoshi said. "The emails have no return address. That would be very difficult for anyone to fake."

The woman stared at the two in disbelief.

"Even more significant," Kenton went on, "the emails contain advanced scientific information and detailed formulas. I have been a physics teacher for twenty years, and everything I have read on these pages not only checks out, but goes far beyond any technology we currently have."

Helen Turner picked up a few papers, glanced through them, and tossed them back onto the folder. "All well and good. But where is my husband and how can I get him back?"

Kenton sighed. "I wish I had an answer for you, Mrs. Turner. I respect your husband more than just about any person I know." Kenton took the folder and thumbed through the pages until he found one toward the bottom of the pile. "There is one clue that might help us."

Helen Turner's eyes sparked with a glimmer of hope.

"The last email indicates that one more message to come would specifically identify the circle makers and reveal the most important communication of all. That message was to be delivered soon—it may have already come in. If we could access Brian's emails, we could download that information. If his work was threatening to some individual or group, we might have a hint about who kidnapped your husband and how to rescue him."

Helen Turner took the page and read it carefully. She set it down. "So you want me to get into Brian's email program or let you do it?"

Kenton and Yoshi looked at each other nervously.

"That could be our key," Yoshi answered, trying to sound convincing. A long silence hung.

Mrs. Turner scanned her visitors warily. "How do I know you're not trying to trick me or use this information for personal gain?"

"We're not that kind of people, Mrs. Turner. I'm a high school teacher and Yoshi—" Kenton stopped short, realizing he didn't know what Yoshi did for a living.

"I'm an emergency room nurse at a hospital in Yokohama," she said quickly before the pause left Kenton looking foolish.

Helen Turner tried to read her visitors. Brian had always been the woo-woo one in the family, spouting about auras and intuition. Now she was being forced to practice what he preached.

# *Brianna 16*

Brianna pounded on the rusty green metal door in the Vantage Theater's alleyway. "Professor Hathaway! . . . It's Brianna!" She banged the door again, three more times, harder. "I know you're in there!"

No answer. She pounded again, until the side of her fist throbbed. "Damn!" she spewed, and waited. After another minute without a response, Brianna turned and started back through the alley toward the street. After several paces, she heard the tumbling of the door lock. She turned to see the door opening slightly, a Herringbone-clad arm protruding from inside the old theater.

Brianna rushed back to find Professor Redmond Hathaway standing inside the door. In the dark she could barely make out the man's features. His face was drawn, dark circles draped beneath his eyes. Without a word he turned and strode toward his inner sanctum. She followed, the heavy door slamming shut behind the two.

"Is it true?" Brianna called out. "Did you really hijack those funds?"

Hathaway kept walking. "String theory research would have been a far worse misappropriation," he called back over his shoulder. "A bunch of physics nerds mentally masturbating over ideas that bear few practical implications for humanity. Meanwhile, eighteen bloody wars are being waged around the globe, greedy oil companies are raking in billions while elderly people are freezing to death because they can't afford to pay their heating bills, and eight thousand children die each day because their mothers can't find enough food for them to survive. And the NSF thinks it's more important to poke into the ethers for imaginary particles than to keep human beings alive. Do you perceive some error in this formula, Brianna?"

The student hustled to catch up with her teacher as he approached the door to his covert lab. "*The Envoy* said they could take away your equipment, fire you, and put you in jail. Is that true?"

Hathaway opened the lab door and entered, still avoiding eye contact. "Yes to all of it."

Brianna could see the familiar array of equipment on the lab tables, Dr. Roth working intently on the other side of some beakers. Hathaway turned to face her. "It's only a matter of time, now," he said with a mordant smile.

"Until . . .?"

"Until the whole project goes down the drain. . . . *Swiiiiishhhh*." He raised his hand in the air and circled his finger, imitating a toilet flushing.

"So what are you going to do?"

Hathaway sighed. "We'll just have to let the world destroy itself and wait ten million years for evolution to come around to rebuild civilization to the point when we can try to make something of it again." The physicist crossed his arms, held his chin in his hand, cocked his head, and looked skyward in contemplation. "Or will the timeline be longer since we may have to wait 4.5 billion years for the half-life of uranium to run its course after nuclear war? . . . I'll have to get back to you on that."

Brianna grabbed the professor by his arm and pulled him toward her. "Come on, Dr. Hathaway—isn't there anything you can do?"

Hathaway made a sour face. "Well, we had a shot at a good mother to birth Jesus Christ once again. But she didn't want to be a science whore." He turned to Roth. "Isaac, you've studied the Bible more than I have . . . Is there some passage where Moses refused to be a leadership whore, or Noah a ship-building patsy, or Mother Mary . . . ? Oh, never mind. That's all so . . . biblical."

"Stop!" Brianna blurted out. "Just stop!" She grabbed the professor by the shoulders and faced him squarely. "I know you're upset. I know you just had the rug pulled out from under you. But I didn't come to annoy you."

The professor leaned back against a counter and took hold of it. The tension in his face dissipated slightly. "Then why are you here?"

"Do you really think this baby thing will work?"

Dr. Roth, overhearing the conversation, stopped working and approached the two.

"If we didn't think it would work, Brianna, we wouldn't be here," Hathaway answered. "Or put our careers on the line. Or maybe go to jail."

Brianna scanned her teacher's eyes. He was dead serious.

Roth spoke. "The only thing scarier than the experiment not working is not doing the project at all. Then miserable humanity will be left to its own devices. And—let's face it— we don't have the greatest track record."

Brianna looked back and forth at the two scientists. *They might be crazy. But they also might be terribly sane.*

*Bimini, Bahamas*
*September 15*

# Driscoll 16

As Driscoll Ames guided the white minivan along a quiet beach road on the west shore of Bimini, he turned to look at his wife in the passenger seat. Her contented smile told him that her decision to return to the island was a smart one.

"That's it! . . .Turn here," Ticia called out, pointing to a dirt road off Kings Highway. Driscoll turned onto a long rutted driveway that led through a grove of palm trees and opened to a funky little yellow house on an out-of-the-way beach. "After my parents died, my cousins Kendall and Marifer moved in. They do their best to maintain the place, but it's hard. He's a fisherman and she's a seamstress. So don't expect the Taj Mahal."

When Ticia showed up at the door, her cousins greeted her warmly. Kendall, tall and soft-shouldered, looked bent for his age. Marifer's hair had gone half-gray, yet the impish twinkle in her eyes withstood the grueling years. The two could not hide their dismay when they saw how frail Ticia looked. Yet they recovered quickly; after seeing so many loved ones depart, they knew that being together was more important than dropping into worry. "Well, look who's coming to dinner!" Kendall spouted as Marifer and Ticia shared a long, tearful hug. "Come on in for some old-fashioned Bimini hospitality."

As Driscoll wheeled his wife's suitcase into the house, his solar plexus relaxed, knowing that Ticia was in good hands. Kendall and Marifer had set out a colorful traditional Bimini lunch of conch fritters, tostones, and pigeon peas. Jared and Tanisha, more interested in exploring than eating, dashed out to play on the beach. As Driscoll watched them prance through the sand, he felt guilty for his kids having spent their entire lives on army bases and in cities, many moves leaving them unrooted and insecure. Their father being deployed to Afghanistan had only deepened their stress.

After lunch, the adults retired to the tiny living room. Driscoll sank into a shabby but comfortable chair beside the couch. "Seen any more spacemen lately?" Kendall asked with a condescending smile.

"Not really," Driscoll answered with his own polite smile, hoping to change the subject. But he wasn't so lucky.

"UFOs don't really come from outer space," Kendall said with faux authority. "They are angels and demons. The Bible is full of visitations from light and dark entities. Most people haven't studied the Bible, so when they see a light or get abducted, they are really encountering a spirit, usually from the dark side. As for me, my faith is in Jesus."

Driscoll had no desire to get into a religious argument. Ticia had warned her husband that Kendall tended to get preachy. "He's the fisherman, but I have to reel him in," Marifer often joked.

Driscoll replied, "People have all kinds of ideas about aliens, Kendall. I don't claim to know much about them. I just know what I saw." He paused, turned toward his wife sitting beside him on the couch, and placed his arm around her shoulder. "At the moment we are here for Ticia. I will not allow anything else to distract us."

Ticia reached to take his hand. "I need to rest."

Marifer stood quickly. "We have your old bedroom made up for you. We thought you would like to stay there."

Ticia's face lit up. She turned to her husband and held onto his forearm. "I told you I have the best family in the world."

Driscoll gratefully took his leave from Kendall and helped Ticia up to the bedroom. He sat beside her on the bed, his back against the old rattan headboard. His weary wife rested her right arm on his leg, her hand stroking his shin. She looked weaker than yesterday.

"My chest of dolls was over there," Ticia said in a slurred voice as she pointed to a corner of the room. "There used to be two beds. My sister and I fought like the dickens, but we always loved each other."

Driscoll offered a soft smile.

Ticia looked up and found her husband's eyes. "Promise me that when I'm gone, you'll take good care of the kids."

Driscoll hated to talk about when she would be gone. But the idea was becoming more real each day. He fought off a tear. "The best, my love."

Ticia grasped his leg more firmly, as if to acknowledge his promise.

"Thanks for doing what you did to get that money, Driscoll. I know you put your ass on the line."

He just listened.

"Use it for the kids, would you? Put them in fine schools and get them a good college education. Help them to stand on our shoulders." She took his hand and kissed it. "Don't worry about me. I have no complaints. I couldn't have picked a better man."

Driscoll forced a smile as he softly smoothed Ticia's hair. *Is she saying goodbye?*

*Rome*
*September 7*

# Leo 16

Around 8:30 PM the taxi pulled up to Suore Figlie Della Divina Provvidenza, one of the oldest churches in Rome. Father Leo tossed a fifty euro note onto the console beside the driver and hustled out of the cab.

The street was quiet except for a white-bearded man carrying a grocery bag with a wine bottle and a long, thin loaf of bread protruding. Fifty paces behind him a tall, dark-haired woman walked her gray Afghan. There was no traffic on the street. Leo glanced toward the rear of the church and saw a light blue panel van parked a few steps from the door. *Paolo is here. I am still in time.*

He pulled open the huge wooden church door, heavier for his aching shoulder from his taxi disaster. The door creaked with age, bearing the burdens of the many who had carried their sorrows and prayers to the basilica. Once inside, he recognized the familiar musty smell of old wood, cloth, and burning candles.

A faint sound caught his ear—a little girl crying. Perplexed, he followed the voice through the high-ceilinged green vestibule toward the sanctuary. The weeping grew louder. Now it sounded more like a woman. Was she hurt?

As Father Leo opened the door to the sanctuary, an eerie feeling overtook him. Something was very wrong. As he closed the chapel door behind him, he saw in the dim light a young woman kneeling on the aisle floor at the edge of a pew. She was slumped over, her head in her hands. The girl was sobbing heavily, shaking her head, muttering to herself in an unintelligible whisper. As Leo approached her, the smell of vomit assaulted his nostrils. He looked to see the foul puddle on the floor in front of the woman.

As he drew closer, in the dim light he could make out the woman's face: Lisbeth.

The priest lowered himself to one knee, inches from the tortured soul. He lifted her face so she could see him. When he found her eyes, she seemed catatonic, looking right through him. Her eyes were obscured by heavy tears, mascara running down her cheeks, snot dripping onto her white blouse. Lisbeth did not acknowledge the priest, but returned her head to her knee and seemed to go off into a trance.

Stymied, Leo rose and looked around the church to see if he could find Paolo or someone who could help. The only sound in the church was the wailing echoing off the cold stone walls.

He scanned the chapel again, hoping to find some sign of why the woman was hysterical. Everything seemed in order. Now after dusk, the only lights beside those illuminating the entrance were the candles at the altar, shining dimly on the crucifix containing the body of Christ.

But something about the crucifix seemed weird. As Leo slowly approached it, nausea began to fill the pit of his stomach. The closer he came to the altar, the deeper his dread.

At five paces' distance from the altar, he beheld the sight that made his entire body revolt. Heavy sweat broke out under his arms and his head began to pound violently. He felt dizzy and his knees began to buckle. A shot of adrenaline stiffened him.

There, on the life-size cross above the altar, hung the body of his son, Paolo. He had been stripped to his undershorts and impaled through the wrists and feet with railroad spikes. A butcher's knife pierced the left side of his rib cage, the instrument dangling at an angle. Blood dripped slowly from all the wounds. His head hung like the statues that have depicted the crucified Christ for two thousand years. But this was not Christ. This was Paolo.

"God, no!" Leo screamed as he rushed to the horrific scene. Sensing a tiny twitch in Paolo's arm, he reached to see if the boy was still alive. Leo tried to remove the spike from Paolo's ankles, but it was firmly wedged in. "Paolo! Paolo!" he called out. Yet Paolo made no response. Leo tried to find his eyes. They were closed. There was no more breath and no movement in Paolo's body.

Leo looked down to the spike nailing Paolo's feet to the cross. A piece of paper dangled from the spike. He tore it off and read: *Now set yourself free.*

*Blue Ridge Mountains*
*September 3*

# Lauren 16

The man who called himself Malthus looked nothing like Lauren expected. Instead of a menacing terrorist with dark glasses, pocked skin, and a devil's goatee, he seemed more like a nerd. Late forties, clean cut, short blondish hair graying at the temples, brown-rimmed eyeglasses, tan crewneck sweater over a plain white shirt, he could have been any respectable engineer or someone's grandpa. Lauren wondered if Todd's sinister description of the malicious chemist was overplayed.

Malthus sat at the head of the meeting room in the throne-like chair Jeremy had occupied a day earlier. Jeremy sat in a humbler seat a few feet to his left. A cluster of Project Genesis members, fewer than yesterday, sat before the two, some in chairs, others on the floor. The tone was grave.

"Bring her here," Malthus ordered the Jeep driver. The thug tried to take Lauren by the arm, but she pushed him away and walked herself to the front of the room. She stood defiantly before Malthus.

"So, I hear you had a look at our munitions supply."

The woman remained stone-faced.

"It's not illegal, you know," Malthus went on in a soft but calculated voice. "Firearms and explosives are allowed in this state. Lots of people have weapons in their homes." From the lilt in his voice, Lauren guessed he might be gay.

She looked around the room. The audience appeared uneasy, watching Malthus, waiting to see how he would dispose of the nosy guest.

Malthus stroked his chin slowly, wheels in his mind turning. "Has Todd explained to you any more about what this community is doing here, Lauren?"

"He told me you are trying to build a new world."

"Correct," he answered, pleased. "And do you agree with what we are doing?"

"I agree with your purpose but not your method."

Malthus pursed his lips. He seemed stimulated. "Because?"

"You will help more people by feeding the hungry or housing the homeless, instead of isolating yourselves and saving your own asses while others are suffering. Shooting hungry people doesn't quite set the world up for paradise."

Malthus raised an eyebrow. "Then let me explain to you where the world is headed, Lauren."

He stood, turned, and looked out the window for a long moment. Then he turned back to face Lauren. "The world is now divided into two camps: Those hypnotized by technology and serving it as slaves, and those who respect the natural order and wish to live in harmony with the world as God created it. Technology is not inherently bad, but weak and ignorant human beings have made it their god, and worship at its altar most hours of their days."

Lauren was now quite confused. Minutes earlier Todd had painted Malthus as an evil ogre. Now he was touting the benefits of living in accord with natural law. And a chemist who invented toxic pesticides talking about God? *Who is this guy?*

"If humanity is allowed to run its current course, the Earth will suffocate in its own waste. The rich are getting richer and the poor, poorer. Billions of impoverished people in underdeveloped countries just keep having more and more children without forethought for the squalor and hardship those children will face, or the burden they will place on society. People in more developed cultures drudge at jobs they hate so they can pay off mortgages that feed the coffers of banks that own their souls. A handful of families have financial assets that exceed the entire economies of countries where hundreds of thousands of people are starving. Do you really think the world will get better on its own, considering that the people in power have no intention to give it away, and the people without power grow more downtrodden daily?"

Lauren was getting fidgety. Deluded as this man was, he was quite intelligent. "And you plan to change all that?"

"I plan to accelerate planetary evolution by removing the drag of spiritually impoverished people from the gene pool so that those who want to live in harmony with the natural law will be able to survive. This is the only chance for conscious people to defeat corporate greed and military aggression. I worked for many years for one of the world's largest agri-businesses, and I can tell you quite assuredly that these people are entirely soulless."

"Oh, I see. And killing lots of people is a soulful act?"

Malthus pointed out the window to the lush forest. "In olden times, nature culled the population. Disease, famine, war, and natural disasters kept the population stable or slow-growing. But with the advent of medicine, food supply, and minimal wars, the growth curve is getting out of hand. Most people are essentially brain-dead, obsessed with mindless television, silly movies, social media, texting, scurrying about on foolish errands, and acquiring endless possessions that are stripping the planet of its natural resources. "Would you really call that living, Lauren?"

Lauren's angst deepened. Malthus's assessment of a hypnotized humanity was correct. But there was nothing new about scapegoating and eliminating the weak. "Isn't that what Hitler tried to do? He thought he could create a master race by getting rid of the Jews. Is your plan any smarter?"

Malthus paced back and forth, enjoying the repartee. "What we're talking about, Lauren, is eugenics—cultivating segments of the population with positive traits and removing elements with negative traits."

"And you are wise enough to decide who should live and who should die?"

Malthus stopped pacing, grabbed a chair, and set it in front of Lauren. He straddled it and stared his impudent visitor squarely in the eyes. "If a pruning is not done soon, Lauren, *everyone* will die. The world will cancel itself out with a giant nuclear blast. One modern atomic warhead packs three thousand times the killing power of those dropped on Japan. At the moment there are about fourteen thousand deployable nuclear weapons on the planet. If some crazed narcissistic leader presses the panic button, all the progress of civilization for many thousands of years will be lost. My goal is not just to get rid of people acting as a drag on society, but to strategically eliminate the people capable of initiating nuclear war. I intend to empower all that is worth carrying into the new world and get rid of all that is a hindrance."

Lauren sighed. "You are a brilliant thinker, Mr. Malthus—but you are quite deluded. You can't play God."

Malthus grabbed the back of the chair and sat up straight, his eyes afire. "No, Lauren, I am not playing God. I am serving God." Malthus smiled. "You're a feisty young lady—I like that. But you know too much and you now pose a danger to this community. I think we will keep you around for a while." He motioned to Todd. "Todd, would you be your friend's host while she is here? . . . We'll station someone outside your cabin to make sure she sticks around."

As Todd nodded sheepishly, blood rushed to Lauren's cheeks. "You can't keep me here! . . . I'll get out and squeal on all of you. You're not helping anyone. You're nothing but a bunch of fucking fascists."

# Kenton 16

Helen Turner guided her guests into her husband's office, where Kenton laid eyes on a huge Apple monitor on a wide glass-top desk. He felt awestruck visiting his guru's personal space. Yoshi, more Mac savvy than her companion, slid into the desk chair, took hold of the mouse, and found Brian's e-mail program. The screen came up:

Enter Password

Yoshi turned to Helen. "Do you know the password?"

Helen shook her head. "Brian never told me and I never asked."

Kenton, dismayed, pursed his lips. "Does he have a book where he keeps his passwords? A file on his computer? An app?"

Helen Turner shrugged her shoulders and shook her head. "Not that I know of. He is very private about his research."

Yoshi turned to her confused host. "How about his birthday?"

"August 11."

Yoshi typed in Brian0811.

### Password Invalid

"Any favorite expressions?"

"Let me think . . . He says, 'stellar,' and 'synchronicity,' a lot."

Yoshi tried one word, then the next. Neither worked.

Kenton slapped his hand on the desk. "Damn! So near and yet so far!"

Yoshi began to type in various phrases: cropcircle . . . formation . . . circlemakers . . . No response. On to: Brian . . . Turner . . . druid . . . Celtic . . . mystic . . . science . . . on and on. Nothing worked. Helen and Kenton suggested some more. Still no response.

"This is useless," Kenton groaned. "His password could be any one of a billion possibilities. We might need to get a professional hacker."

Yoshi swiveled the chair around. "We don't want anyone else seeing this material. Anyone who has seen the news knows how hot this is. A hacker could pirate this for their own profit, or implicate us."

Suddenly a loud bang, followed by glass crashing, pierced the office. And again. And again. The trio cast anxious looks at each other, and dashed to the front door. Yoshi threw it open and rushed out onto the porch, Kenton a few paces behind.

"Oh, no!" Yoshi shrieked, pulling one hand to her mouth, pointing toward the car with the other hand. Someone had smashed the Astra's windshield.

Fifty yards down the street, a black sedan was speeding away. It turned a corner and disappeared from sight.

Yoshi and Kenton rushed to the vehicle and found the front seats filled with a thousand shards of shattered glass. Kenton circled the car, surveying the damage.

"They know about us."

# *Brianna 17*

---

"Let's say I agreed to have this baby," Brianna forced the words out. "What would I need to do?"

Hathaway and Roth looked at each other, the first signs of light in their faces that she detected. "When do you expect to ovulate next?" asked Roth.

Brianna scrunched her forehead as she did a few mental calculations. "Next week."

"Perfect," Roth replied. "Do you have a passport?"

"Yeah, last winter I went to Cancun with my cousin . . . Why do you ask?"

"Do you remember Dr. Beshara we told you about, the geneticist who has permission to study the Shroud of Turin?"

She shrugged. "Sort of."

"He is in Cairo. He is the one who will perform the implant."

Brianna stiffened. "Come on, guys—I'm not going to Egypt to do this."

Hathaway remained unmoved by Brianna's objection. "Dr. Beshara has been working on this project with us since the beginning. He is a respected gynecologist and expert in in vitro fertilization."

Roth typed a few keys on his computer until a photo showed up on the screen. The man in the image was maybe mid-fifties, dark skin, balding with a thin matte of black hair barely covering his scalp. His eyebrows were thick, like his moustache. His round face was slightly pitted with acne scars. He looked more like a criminal than a doctor. Brianna's stomach twisted into a knot.

"We'll go with you, along with Isaac's wife Aviva, who will take care of you. First class all the way."

Brianna held her hands up as if to push the idea away. "I don't know, fellas . . . I am *thinking* about having this baby—not traveling halfway around the world for some creepy-looking dude to shove some cold instrument up my vagina and get me artificially pregnant."

Hathaway turned to Brianna, took her hands, and found her eyes. "We know this is a big stretch for you, Brianna. Dr. Beshara is a kind man. We wouldn't work with him if he wasn't. We will monitor every step to make sure you are extremely comfortable—if you don't like anything, just tell us. Could you please try to suspend your judgments for the sake of the bigger picture of what we are trying to do?"

Brianna took a moment to consider Hathaway's plea. "What am I supposed to tell my family and friends?"

Roth peered into the distance for a long moment, thinking hard. Finally he said, "A dig."

"What dig?"

"Tell everyone that the Hunter archaeology department received a grant and they are enrolling seniors with good

GPAs to participate in an exclusive dig in Egypt, all expenses paid. Who would turn that down?"

The idea didn't go down easily. "I can't be away from my family for very long. My mother is extremely fragile."

"You'll be away for no more than a week. We have a team of medical professionals here who will prepare you with stimulus injections before you leave and follow up closely when you return. Then you can be at home for your first trimester. If you choose to go through with your pregnancy here, you can. If you would rather have no one know about it, we'll fly you anywhere you like."

Brianna began to feel lightheaded. *This is starting to sound too real.*

"We'll give you some cash up front," Hathaway added. "As soon as we return we'll get your mother into the best facility—better than your family could ever afford."

*Comforting . . . Tempting . . . Crazy.*

Roth turned back to his computer and pecked at the keyboard again. Moments later the monitor showed a time-table. Brianna leaned in to see the *EgyptAir* website.

"There's a flight from JFK to Cairo every evening at 6:30," said Roth. "Shall we say the eighteenth?"

*Bimini*
*September 21*

# Driscoll 17

As Driscoll stood on the beach watching his children giggle as they formed castles in the wet sand, he felt a breath of relief from the nightmare of Ticia's collapsing health.

Jared and Tanisha turned from their playmates and bounded back toward the house. "Dad, can we go watch them make a movie?" the boy asked his father.

"What movie?"

"The kids we are playing with said a crew is filming up by North Point. It's like a ten-minute walk up the beach from here," Tanisha added.

Driscoll turned to Kendall. "You know anything about this?"

Kendall shrugged. "Lots of tourists snorkel and dive up there. There's some kind of underwater road."

Driscoll nodded to the kids. "Sure, just be careful and don't get in anybody's way. Jared, keep an eye on your sister and be back for dinner."

As the kids dashed off, Kendall walked to the refrigerator, grabbed a couple of beers, and motioned for Driscoll to join him on the porch.

"What's this about a road?" Driscoll asked as the two settled into a couple of gray Adirondack chairs.

"I don't know exactly. A couple of years ago the History Channel came and did some documentary. Something about Atlantis."

"The lost continent of Atlantis?"

"That's what they say. . . Beats me."

"Have you ever seen that road?"

"Once I was fishing over there and my anchor got wedged in some rocks. I had to snorkel down to free it. It's only eighteen feet deep. I saw the tops of a bunch of big squarish blocks. They went on for quite a distance. Didn't look natural at all . . . I didn't give it much thought."

The two men sat quietly for a while, sipping their beers and watching the surf roll in. Driscoll couldn't remember the last time his mind was still. Kendall rose and walked into the living room to a bookshelf holding a couple dozen books, mostly tattered paperback novels and a few on fishing. He pulled out an oversized hardcover book and handed it to Driscoll.

He read the title: Amazing Underwater Discoveries. "A British lady stayed here a few years ago when we were renting out rooms for tourists," Kendall recounted. "She came to dive and see the road. We talked about it one night. She left this book."

Driscoll paged through it. Lots of photos of unusual artifacts divers have come upon in bodies of water around the world. A two-thousand-year-old "computer" called the "Antikythera mechanism," discovered off the coast of Greece. The manmade device of stone was capable of sophisticated astronomical calculations. Another showed photos of clearly handcrafted structures on the ocean floor off the coast of Japan. Then there was a story about a Stonehenge-like construction at the bottom of Lake Michigan. Finally Driscoll found the page about the Bimini road. He studied a striking color photo for a while. A long series of rectangular rocks, fit perfectly together, stretched underwater as far as the eye could see.

"This has to be manmade," he said, showing the picture to Kendall.

"Yep, that's what I saw," he confirmed.

Driscoll read the accompanying story:

Nearly 2500 years ago the philosopher Plato recounted the story of the lost continent of Atlantis. While there has been much speculation about whether or not that continent existed, and if so, where, many people believe that Atlantis was located in what is now the Caribbean Sea.

In 1968 three divers were exploring Bimini's underwater north shore when they discovered these rock formations, laid out in a systematic fashion forming an apparent roadway for a length of one-half mile. Geologists date the rocks to be about 15,000 years old. Some people consider this meticulously designed thoroughfare to be proof of the existence of Atlantis. Other unusual artifacts such as what looks like human-built columns have been found underwater around Bimini.

Driscoll looked up. "Do you think you are living on what was once Atlantis?"

"Hell, anything is possible. They call it the Atlantic Ocean. Had to get the name from somewhere."

Driscoll continued reading:

Legend has it that the Atlanteans were a spiritually and technologically sophisticated civilization. But they abused the knowledge they had gained. They experimented with genetic engineering, creating bizarre minglings of species. Their once-pristine world grew corrupt with greed and power. They grew warlike and attempted to subjugate other nations. Then a sudden cataclysmic upheaval, possibly a huge tidal wave as a result of an asteroid crashing into the ocean, caused the continent to sink within 24 hours, taking a once-glorious civilization to a watery grave.

We may never know the whole truth about Atlantis. Yet the Bimini road and other anomalous artifacts give us some clues to the rise and fall of one of the world's great cultures. Perhaps knowing their ill-fated story will inspire us to not follow in their footsteps.

Driscoll closed the book and set it on his lap. His idea of human history was quickly dissolving.

# *Leo* 17

The train ride to Montecuore was much as Father Leo remembered it: Cranky old train cars, cigarette butts dotting cabin floors, rank toilets, and the monotonous *click-clack* of wheel against rail. He gazed out the window at small poor villages, children playing in yards of dry grass, portly women in kerchiefs hanging laundry on clotheslines. Beyond the villages, sprawling hills glowed with olive and grape crops ready for harvest. Seeing Tuscany for the first time in two-and-a-half decades, his thoughts drifted to his carefree days with Kristina Adimari, a memory that delivered a modicum of solace.

Yet there was no solace in the task at hand. Leo was going to tell his dying lover, the mother of his child, that their 27-year-old son had been brutally impaled on a crucifix by zealous Christians. He could not imagine a harder burden. Although the veteran priest had conducted hundreds of funerals and consoled countless grieving families, no amount of theology could assuage the anguish that had worn his soul threadbare.

One act of kindness, however, brought the dispirited cleric a little respite. The Rome Police, in response to a high Vatican official's request on behalf of Monsignor

Bonfiglio, had agreed to wait two days to release the name of the victim, so Leo could tell the boy's mother himself rather than have her learn the dreadful news through public channels. Leo let his head fall back on the train seat, closed his eyes, and rehearsed a hundred ways he might deliver the news. None of them would make the heinous murder any less torturous for Paolo's mother. *Dear Jesus, what a web we weave.*

Finally the train pulled into Montecuore and Father Leo stepped off to find the sleepy village much as when he had left it. Mrs. DeLuca's bakery still sat on the corner of Via Giancolo, next to Franco's butcher shop. The police station was perched at the north end of the town square. The open-air market was vibrant with women shopping for fresh vegetables, seasoned with generous helpings of the day's gossip. In the distance, Leo heard the voices of children playing in the school yard. At first he was tickled by their laughter, but then he remembered that these were the very children who had inspired Paolo to follow his joy—a quest that had turned the darkest corner.

Leo found a taxi (Bruno Crispo's old station wagon—the only one in town) to drive him to Amadio, the tiny hamlet where he had lived with Kristina on a small farm owned by her uncle Felice. The swarthy farmer had inherited the 80-acre property from Kristina's grandfather, and, in family tradition, had kept it in grape production. Felice was atypically open-minded, looking the other way when Leo emerged from Kristina's room in the mornings. Leo was supposedly a hired hand, but everyone knew that his heart belonged to the lady of the manor.

When Leo saw the farmhouse, he wondered if he had slipped into a time warp. The building and grounds looked almost exactly as they did so long ago. Had any years passed at all? Had Leo somehow been transported back to his glorious youth? Yet the boyish headiness of that era was quickly eclipsed by the grim task before him. Not to mention his dread of seeing Kristina on her deathbed, a withered husk of the sensual maiden whose body he had worshipped deep into the Tuscany nights. Perhaps she was already gone. Part of him wished she would already be dead so he could spare her the awful news, and himself the burden of delivering it. He wanted to remember Kristina as she was, not how illness had ravaged her.

Leo straightened his shirt, summoned all the courage he could, and marched to the white farmhouse's door. If the priest could have redeemed all of his good deeds for a reprieve from this moment, he surely would have done so. Yet failing heavenly intervention, Father Bonfiglio uttered a short prayer for grace.

He knocked on the weather-beaten door and waited. After a minute that felt like an hour, he wondered if no one would answer and he would be spared.

"Coming!" a male voice finally bellowed from deep in the house.

*Has Kristina gotten married? Is she with another man?* Leo had not thought much about the possibility. He liked to think of her as young, single, and vivacious—and with him.

Finally the door opened to reveal a bony old man, clad in worn coveralls and a white sleeveless undershirt, his cheeks sprinkled with gray stubble. Dry, brittle skin told of years under the sun. A few lower teeth were missing. "Yes?"

Leo removed his hat. "I'm sorry to disturb you, sir. I am an old friend of Kristina Adimari. I am hoping I could perhaps see her." The weight on Leo's chest belied his words.

The man shook his head. "Kristina Adimari? Haven't seen her for years."

Leo's gut relaxed. "She doesn't live here anymore?"

"Not since her uncle died and Kristina sold me the property."

"Do you know where she is?"

The man rubbed his chin. "I heard she bought a small vineyard in Capella. But that was years ago. I don't know what's become of her."

Leo nodded. "I see. Thank you for your time."

The fellow offered a half-smile and closed the door. Leo turned and made his way back down the cobblestone pathway. The last time his feet had touched this path he had just said goodbye to Kristina and he was off to become a priest. Now the journey had come full circle.

# *Lauren 17*

Lauren sat at the window of Todd's cabin, staring into the night forest. She hadn't slept all night, and the first rays of dawn were lighting the sky. The chirping of the crickets would have been pleasant had her predicament not been so dire. No matter how diplomatically Malthus had couched her sentence, she was a prisoner. At the edge of the clearing surrounding the cabin sat a white Chevy van, a thin Latino guy wearing a Yankees baseball cap in the driver's seat. He, too, had been up all night, keeping watch on Todd's cabin. He was fingering his phone in an effort to stay awake. Twenty yards to the van's side was the entrance to the path leading back to her car—just a five-minute walk, but a world away.

"What will they do with me?" she called over her shoulder.

Todd looked pallid. "I don't know, Lauren."

She faced him, daggers in her eyes. "Level with me, Todd."

Todd sighed. "A few months ago a couple defected from the group. They knew about the arms and Malthus's poison scheme."

"And . . . ?"

"State Police found their crashed car in a ravine to the side of a hairpin curve on Skyline Drive. The brakes had failed—fluid drained from the drums. The husband died and the wife barely survived. I'm not sure if or how long she lived."

Lauren's stomach dropped out.

"I should have deleted your email," she blurted, cheeks crimson. "You've done nothing but make me miserable, Todd. I'm sorry I ever met you."

Todd grimaced, guilt clouding his face. He approached Lauren and tried to comfort her by placing his hands on her shoulders from behind her. She threw them off. "I'm so sorry, Lauren." Todd fell silent for a while. Then he said, "I'll help you get out."

She turned to face him. "And just how will you do that?"

Todd looked down at the floor, in deep thought. Lauren knew that look. Usually she hated it when Todd got lost in his head. But tonight he could use that overworked brain to help free her.

"I'll go out to the van and distract Rico. He's not real smart. You can slip out the side window. Take the trail through the woods back to your car. Check the brakes. Then get out of here as fast as you can. When you get home, keep your mouth shut."

Todd reached under his bed, came up with a small flashlight, and handed it to Lauren. He threw on his jacket and sauntered toward the van. Lauren could see the driver's face lit by his phone. Todd approached Rico and struck up a conversation.

Satisfied the guard was distracted, Lauren went to the side window of the cabin and crawled out. Crouching, she made her way around the back of the cabin and stayed close to the edge of the woods until she found the path, keeping an eye on the van driver to make sure he was engaged. The growing dawn gave her just enough light without turning on the flashlight and signaling her motion.

Stepping as lightly as possible, Lauren began to trace her way back to the parking lot beside the welcome cabin—an ironic name for the entrance to a murder and prison camp. When her foot crunched a large branch on the ground, she stopped and looked back to see if she had been detected. Negative. She kept going and picked up her pace.

Minutes later she arrived at the welcome cabin and worked her way around to where the Prius was parked.

It wasn't there.

*London*
*August 31*

# Kenton 17

Snarled in London traffic, Kenton pulled the wind-shieldless Astra behind a huge dump truck spewing an inky cloud of awful-smelling diesel exhaust into the front seat of the car. Yoshi began to cough so heavily that she pulled her sweater up over her mouth and nose to screen out the toxic fumes.

Just then a gleaming white Tesla sedan pulled into the lane beside the Astra. Kenton took a moment to savor its sleek design. "If the world had listened to Nikola Tesla a hundred years ago, we wouldn't be breathing that truck's noxious exhaust today," he stated. "All vehicles would be electric."

As soon as the light changed, Kenton guided the Astra to a clear lane. Yoshi pulled out her iPad, googled Nikola Tesla, and fixated on her tablet. Kenton remained silent, giving her time to find out what she could about the master of electricity.

"Holy shit!" Yoshi burst out.

Kenton jerked his head toward Yoshi, and giggled. "I didn't know you knew how to curse."

"I know why Brian Turner was kidnapped."

"Why?"

"Do you remember the circle makers' message about free energy?"

Kenton nodded.

"They said that with the right technology, anyone could draw power directly from the universe and transform it into usable electricity at virtually no cost. Any family could invest a few hundred dollars in such a device and have unlimited electricity forever."

"Go on . . ."

"It says here that Tesla was onto this principle as early as 1901. He enrolled the financial magnate J.P. Morgan to fund an experiment where Tesla built a huge tower on Long Island as an experiment to transmit unlimited free electricity. If the experiment succeeded, it could be replicated all over the globe."

"I remember reading something about that. Whatever happened to the experiment?"

"When Morgan realized that such electricity could not be metered and there would be no profit for him or the energy companies, he pulled the plug."

Kenton smirked. "Of course. Profits before people . . . But what does that have to do with Brian's disappearance?"

"Do you remember that riddle from the circle makers' email, 'When two dimensions become three, all your energy will be free?'"

Kenton nodded.

"Before he died, Tesla was working on a zero-point energy machine like the one the circle makers described. It looked like an hourglass, with a cone on top, pointing down, connecting with a cone below, pointing up. Horizontal disks sat the top and bottom of the device."

"Go on . . ."

"This Tesla article links to a news story about an engineer named George Corby, who develops software for 3D printers. Corby had the brilliant idea to take some of the crop formations, tilt them vertically on his computer, apply CAD architecture technology, and show what they would look like fleshed out in three dimensions. Lines become columns, squares become cubes, and circles become spheres . . . Kenton, look at this!"

Yoshi shoved her iPad in front of Kenton. There he beheld a gleaming silver machine resembling an hourglass with circular plates at the top and bottom. Next to it was a cross section diagram, showing complex interior parts. Suddenly a blaring car horn jarred Kenton, alerting him that he had veered into another lane. At first opportunity, he pulled onto the road shoulder.

"Yoshi, this is fantastic! The circle makers have imbedded the formations with the technology to save the planet . . . But what does that have to do with Brian's disappearance?"

"If free energy devices were proliferated now, it would be only a matter of time until power companies would be out of business."

Eyes glowing, Kenton turned to face Yoshi. "That would be the end of the oil, electric, and atomic power industries as we know them. People could just set up free energy transformers in their homes, much like wireless routers, and power all their appliances and electric vehicles. No wonder the guys who threatened Brian on the phone had Arabic accents . . . Big oil."

"But the guys who took him were American."

Kenton drummed his fingers on the console. "Just follow the money, Yoshi. Except for China, the United States uses more electricity than any other nation on Earth. There are huge lobbies in Washington that pressure the government to support traditional energy companies. Whoever is behind the kidnapping is protecting that industry."

His mind churning, Kenton pulled back onto the highway. By that time the obnoxious dump truck had moved back into the lane in front of the Astra, again leaving a foul wake.

"Can you please just get us home before I suffocate?" Yoshi pleaded.

*Cairo*
*September 19*

# Brianna 18

---

Brianna Marlowe rolled down the limousine's rear window and then quickly rolled it up. Cairo's pollution was thick, traffic was a mess, drivers were yelling, a guy on a motorcycle next to the limo was blaring annoying Egyptian rap music, and vendors hawking wares on the street corners gave her a headache. Lots of women were shrouded in thick black *abaya* and *niqaab*, only eyes and hands exposed. *We're definitely not in Kansas anymore, Toto.* She leaned her head back and stared at the vehicle's plush ceiling. Cairo was colorful and exotic, yes. Welcoming, not at all.

When the jetlagged student finally reached her room at Le Meridian Pyramid Hotel, she was never happier to see a soft bed. True to his promise, Hathaway had gotten Brianna a first-class suite with gold-foiled wallpaper, high-thread-count Egyptian cotton sheets, and a wet bar. But at the moment she couldn't care less about the amenities. She plopped down on the bed and fell asleep without even getting undressed.

Sometimes you just have to pull blackout shades on your brain and disappear.

# Driscoll 18

Marifer knocked softly on the open door to Ticia's room. "My neighbor said that the film crew over by North Point is going to do a live TV broadcast in an hour," she told her cousin. "Maybe we'll see Jared and Tanisha."

"Are you up for it?" asked Driscoll, sitting on the bed at his wife's side.

Ticia lifted her head with effort. "We'll see in an hour."

Marifer picked up the remote wand on the table next to the bed and handed it to Driscoll. "Let me know if you need anything." Quietly she departed.

Ticia turned to her husband. "Do me a favor and text Laney the house sitter. I want to make sure the dog and cat are okay."

Driscoll frowned. "You don't need to be thinking about that. I'm sure they're alright. Save your strength."

"Don't argue with my motherly instinct, mister."

Driscoll knew better than to do that; God knows he had tried. He picked up his phone and composed a text. But when he pressed Send, nothing happened. He tried a few times, to no avail. He switched to phone mode and dialed. No signal. FaceTime, same.

"That's weird—I have had good reception ever since we've been here."

Driscoll went into the living room, where he found Marifer on her computer, looking befuddled. "Do you ever have any problems with service?" he asked.

"I was online and the page froze," she replied. "I'll check the wireless." She walked to the router and pressed a few buttons. "The router's fine. Must be a problem with the island transmitter. Sometimes it goes down for a little while. . . Island life. We'll just have to wait."

Driscoll returned to the bedroom and switched on the television. No picture or sound. "Is your TV on wireless too?" he called to Marifer.

"No, that's on cable," she replied. "There's no reason for that not to work. It never goes down."

*Montecuore, Tuscany*
*September 9*

# Leo 18

As Leo closed the courtyard gate behind him, he noticed that the old San Michele Church had had a facelift. The moldy blackened walls had been power-washed, restoring the stone façade to an earthy gray. A small addition, probably a fellowship hall, had been attached to the side of the building. The modest lawn was neatly mowed, a row of ruby-red geraniums bordering the sidewalk.

Leo found his way around the side of the church to the priest's study. The door was open. A stocky man sat at a desk looking over some papers, his back to the door. The fellow's thick dark hair hung slightly over his white collar, gently whisking his black shirt. "Good day," Leo called politely.

The priest turned and the two men eyeballed each other for a long moment.

"Matteo?" Leo asked, surprise in his voice.

The man peered into Leo's eyes and studied his face, trying to figure how the visitor knew him.

"It's me—Leo Bonfiglio."

A stunned look washed over the parish priest's face. "Good God, it's been forever!"

Father Matteo Delvecchio rose and welcomed his guest with a hearty embrace. The two men planted kisses on each other's cheeks, cemented by firm slaps on the back.

"Was it the Bergamo conference? . . . Twelve years ago?"

Leo laughed and began to relax in the presence of his comrade. "More, I think—but let's not try too hard to count . . . I stopped aging at thirty-eight."

Father Delvecchio smiled and pulled an empty chair to one side of his desk. "Please, sit down. Would you like a glass of wine?"

"Just what I could use." Leo took a seat. The stable wooden chair felt like a relief after riding on bumpy country roads.

Father Matteo poured a glass for himself and one for his guest. "Where is your robe? I heard you're a hotshot at Big Town."

Leo shook his head and smiled stoically. "I assure you it's not all that people say it is."

"I see you haven't lost your humility." Father Matteo raised his glass, and the priests toasted.

"Terrible about the crucifix murder," said the parish priest, shaking his head. " . . Any leads?"

Leo felt as if he had been kicked in the stomach. He took a long moment to compose himself, then just shook his head. He was not about to deliver the tragic news to anyone before Kristina.

Leo changed the subject before Father Matteo could inquire further. "Actually, I came up here to visit an old friend—Kristina Adimari . . . Have you seen her?"

The priest pursed his lips and shook his head. "She used to come to church, but I haven't seen her for a long time. She was living out in the country on a vineyard."

"Do you know which one?"

"It's the Saporito Vineyard," Father Delvecchio replied. "Just go out Maggiore Road to the village of Capella. From there, anyone can tell you where it is."

Leo forced a smile. "Thank you, Matteo. It's good to see you again."

Father Matteo leaned forward and placed a hand on Leo's knee. "Are you all right? You look a little pale."

Leo stood. "As good as can be expected. I have some hard news to deliver."

Matteo rose, set his hands firmly on Leo's shoulders, found his eyes, and offered a sympathetic look. "Then be strong, my friend. Be strong."

# *Lauren 18*

---

Lauren found her way back to Todd's cabin, crouching to avoid the guard detecting her. She tapped on the rear window.

Startled, Todd jumped out of bed and opened the window to let her in.

"What are you doing back here?"

She crawled in. "I couldn't bear to leave you," she said, faux-dramatically.

Todd smirked. "You're full of shit."

She smiled cynically. "You're right." Her faced turned sober. "My car is gone."

Todd shook his head. "I can't believe all the trouble these guys would go to, to keep you here. Malthus must see you as a big threat."

"Now what?"

Todd paced to the front window and looked out toward the guard's van. Then back at Lauren. "Didn't you tell me you heard the combination for the keypad on the munitions dump?"

"7315."

Todd went to his closet, slipped on a sweatshirt, and grabbed the flashlight.

"You stand at the window with the light on so Rico sees you are here."

"What about you?"

Todd made his way toward the side window. "Give me half an hour."

*Beaconsfield*
*September 3*

# Kenton 18

"I've gotten nowhere," Yoshi sputtered, pushing back from her laptop, making a sour face Kenton didn't think she was capable of. Her cheeks were whitish, eyes bloodshot, housecoat disheveled around her shoulders. "I even downloaded a 'How to Hack a Password' program and phoned a geek friend in Japan for advice. No dice . . . I don't know if we'll ever find that email with the final transmission."

Yoshi's parents looked on, distraught to see their daughter so upset. In the three days she and Kenton had been working on getting into Brian Turner's emails, the Satos had grown fond of their guest and enjoyed seeing their daughter come to life working with him on this bizarre project. Takao, recently retired from a long engineering career, found common ground discussing science with Kenton. Meanwhile Tomiko continued to fantasize about her daughter in a wedding dress.

"We might have to turn the files over to the authorities," said Yoshi.

Kenton grimaced. "The same authorities that send armed helicopters to monitor the crop circles and intimidate anyone who believes they are real? I don't think so. . . If they got a hold of this material, they would deny it, destroy it, or—"

"—or use the circle makers' technology for military purposes," Mr. Sato finished the sentence as he approached his daughter at the kitchen table.

Yoshi looked up, jarred. Her dad was usually quiet and unassuming. He knew what Yoshi and Kenton were trying to do, but had refrained from getting involved. Until now.

"When I was a little boy, my class took a trip to Nagasaki after the bomb had dropped," he recalled. "The entire city had been leveled—all that remained was charred concrete. I saw photos of disfigured people dying in agony, children my age. That memory has haunted me for my entire life. Every day I pray to *Kami-sama* to never let anything like that happen again. Please, if you can put technology in the hands of people with good intentions rather than warmongers, you may be able to prevent that kind of atrocity from causing such unbelievable suffering."

Yoshi studied her father's downcast face. His display of emotion was as rare as Yoshi's newfound passion. She took his hand.

Mr. Sato drew a long breath. "If I go to my grave knowing that you made even a small contribution in that direction, my soul will be at peace." He leaned closer to Yoshi and whispered, "I don't care if you ever get married, *Deru Kugi*. Just make your life count."

*Giza*
*September 20*

# Brianna 19

After a brutal 5 AM wake-up call, Brianna found herself in a taxi with her companions heading toward the pyramids of Giza. An eerie fog, typical of Cairo mornings, shrouded the passage, reducing visibility to practically zero—symbolic, perhaps, of Brianna's doubts about going through with this weird undertaking. Hathaway, Roth, and his wife Aviva—a quiet, plain, unassuming woman—had been extremely congenial and generous, making sure Brianna was comfortable at every turn. But the reasoning sector of Brianna's brain was sounding huge alarms that she had gotten in way over her head.

The rising sun gradually burned off the mist, and the vehicle came to a stop. There, almost close enough to touch, towered the Great Pyramid of Giza, the subject of mystery, poetry, and controversy for at least five thousand years, ten by the count of more radical Egyptologists. Brianna stepped out of the vehicle and craned her neck to gaze at the capstone, still largely intact even after desert winds had pummeled it for eons. A tourist book in Brianna's hotel room said that the over two million blocks in front of her weighed up to eighty tons each. All of the ancient stones were fitted together with impeccable precision, impossible to pass even a sheet of paper between them. While many theories abound, no one has yet to prove how these mammoth blocks were lifted and placed together so perfectly—a feat modern technology has been unable to replicate.

"Amazing, wouldn't you say?" Brianna heard Roth's voice from behind her.

"How did they do this?" she asked without turning her head.

Hathaway approached from the other side, and stated in a matter-of-fact voice, "Sound."

"Sound?"

"The Egyptian mystics knew how to harness the power of sound to move objects."

Confused, Brianna squeezed her forehead.

"You know how a musical tone projected at a certain pitch can break a glass?" Roth asked, stepping to Brianna's other side.

"Like when my dentist cleans my teeth with a sonic instrument?"

"Exactly," Hathaway replied, pleased that Brianna had latched onto the principle.

"Moving huge rocks with sound is just a matter of degree. The dynamic behind the process is the same," Roth added.

Brianna tried to absorb the idea. "I read that the pyramids were tombs for the pharaohs."

Roth smiled and shook his head. "Another mistaken conjecture. Most Egyptologists don't understand the spiritual principles the ancient Egyptians had mastered."

"Then what were the pyramids for?"

"They were massive energy collectors and focalizers," Hathaway answered.

"The geometric design of the pyramid drew power from the universe and lasered it to a specific point," Roth added.

"Which was?"

"The king's chamber, at the heart of the structure," Hathaway replied. "But, contrary to the popular belief that the inner chamber was the tomb of the pharaoh, it was actually a platform for the priests to attain dimensional shift."

Brianna was getting stimulated. The intersection of science and mysticism was a metaphysical erogenous zone for her.

"The priests—and occasionally the pharaoh—would lie in the enclosure and be transported to other realities where they received revelations and training from higher sources. This was the font of vision and guidance that made the Egyptian dynasty the longest-lived, wisest, and most powerful culture in the history of the world."

Brianna's mind was spinning. The book she had read said nothing about all of this. "If this culture was so connected to the wisdom of the cosmos, what happened? Why is it such a mess now?"

Hathaway sighed. "For the same reason that all the golden civilizations, like the Greeks and Romans and Maya, fell. At some point ego, or illusion, or greed, or whatever you want to call it, overtook the culture, and the quest for truth was eclipsed by the pursuit of worldly power."

"Sort of like what's happening in the world today?"

"Very much like what's happening in the world today."

Just then a group of tourists traipsed in front of the trio. Posing for photos with the pyramids as a backdrop, the women were holding up their new Gucci handbags while the men displayed their Rolex watch knockoffs. One guy reached around from behind a woman and grabbed her breasts just as the photo was being snapped. Others were fingering their phones while some flipped cigarette butts and candy wrappers on the ground.

"The enlightenment of humanity functions in cycles," Roth explained, carving an invisible graph in the air with his index finger. "Twelve thousand years of connection to higher wisdom, followed by an equal span of disconnection, characterized by alienation, despair, and suffering. We now sit at the rock bottom of the age of darkness, when humanity has sunken to the deepest level of depravity."

A group of Arabic students passed in front of the trio. One kid carried a boom box playing loud gangsta rap while another took a can of spray paint and started to write graffiti on a pyramid stone, until a security guard chased him away.

"When civilization hits a low, nature is set up with two failsafe mechanisms to ensure its survival," Hathaway went on.

"Which are?"

"Humanity cancels itself out of existence—"

"Or?"

"Or people get fed up with misery and reach for a higher way. When the volume of people hungry for healing reaches a critical mass, they begin to reverse the dark cycle."

"So what would it take to put a civilization over the tipping point?"

"A teacher shows up who serves as a role model so compelling that people recognize there is more to life than fighting for survival. That is the effect Jesus and Buddha had on people two thousand years ago, and the effect someone like them would have today."

Brianna felt a huge click in her brain, as if she were lying in the king's chamber under that laser ray. "So that's where I come in—and the baby."

"That, Brianna, is what everything in your life, and all of our lives, has led to. You, my dear young lady, are standing on the launch pad of the restoration of humanity."

The wireless and cable failure lasted exactly one hour. At 11:27 AM, the television in Ticia's bedroom flashed on, white static filling the screen. "The TV's working again, Marifer," Driscoll called out.

Ticia's cousin made her way back to the bedroom. "The Internet's back up, too." She picked up the remote-control wand, pointed at the television, and pressed some buttons. "That's weird. The channel isn't changing . . . Must be the battery." As she started to leave the room to search for a new one, Ticia called, "Wait, Marifer . . . Look at this."

An image appeared onscreen. "That looks like the shore of North Point, where the kids are," Marifer said. "But what's—?"

Offshore from North Point, perhaps a quarter mile, an ancient city stood on a land mass. The settlement was surrounded by a series of crescented harbors formed by concentric rings of earth separated by water. The small houses dotting the firmament were square and grayish, white dome roofs gleaming in the sun. Marifer looked out the window at the dismal sky thick with gray clouds, and tried to make sense of the radically different weather the screen showed just a few miles away.

"Must be some movie," she said as she stepped to the TV to change the channel manually. But for all her attempts, the same image appeared on every channel.

At the entrance to the city stood huge gold statues of the god Poseidon driving six winged horses. The grounds around the statues were vibrant with purple, yellow, white, and red flowers in glorious full bloom. The landscaping was immaculate, tall green hedges artistically complementing the stunning foliage.

"That sure doesn't look like any place on this island," Marifer commented.

At the center of the city a great temple sat atop a high hill. Inside, visible between the stately marble columns, stood a huge crystal with a multitude of sparkling facets. Tall as three persons, the crystal emitted laser-like rays of light in many colors, extending beyond the temple to the city, sparkling on the walls of the houses.

Kendall walked into the bedroom. "I just went online, and some strange picture appeared. It was on every website. It—" He looked at the television monitor. "You're seeing it too?"

"Every channel," replied Marifer.

*Capella, Tuscany*
*September 10*

## *Leo 19*

Father Leo gazed up at the rusted wrought iron arch marking the entrance to the Saporito Vineyard. The top of the arch formed black metal letters: *"God's bounty is our inheritance."* A twinge of cynicism contracted Leo's heart as he considered the horrid progression of events that had led him to this moment. Or was his deeper angst the sadness that the life of faith to which he had devoted himself was now crumbling?

As he stepped through the arch, the priest felt a sense of respite. Even as a child he was drawn to gardens. Now they testified to the elegant simplicity of creation, a virtue absent in the bureaucracy in which he had become ensnared.

Scanning the vineyard, he could see a dozen workers scattered about the acreage as they harvested luscious deep blue Sangiovese grapes. At the end of the row in front of him he could make out the figure of a woman leaning to pluck fruit. She was short and stout, dark complexion, perhaps early thirties. Leo made his way through the row, touching the leaves as he passed, in an effort to ground himself. When the woman saw him approach, she straightened up and turned toward him. A green and white kerchief covered her raven-black hair tied back in a small bun.

"Are you here to buy wine?" she called out. "The store is on the other side of the house." She pointed in that direction.

"No," he answered as he approached her. "I am looking for Kristina Adimari. Does she live here?"

The woman did not answer. Instead, she gazed over Leo's shoulder.

"Kristina Adimari—do you know her?" Leo repeated, wondering if perhaps the woman had not heard him.

The woman nodded, yet did not speak. Instead she cast her eyes over Leo's left shoulder.

Curious, Leo turned to look behind him. Another woman followed his steps down the row. She was taller and thinner, her long, dark hair falling over her left shoulder. She wore a long-sleeved white blouse and jeans.

Leo caught her eyes. They seemed familiar. A feeling of safety began to ease his angst. He studied the woman's face. High cheekbones. A long but graceful nose. Wide lips. A strong chin. Some wrinkles, with character. *Could it be? No, of course not.*

The woman approached and studied his face. She dropped her basket, grapes scattering at her feet. She stood immobilized. The two stared at one another for a timeless moment.

"Kristina?"

She nodded. "Leo?"

"I thought I would never see you again," he blurted.

Incredulous, he stepped closer. Leo felt an impulse to embrace her. But the moment was too fresh and he was too stunned. "You are . . . well?"

She squinted as if to question his question.

Leo took a step closer. "Paolo told me—"

Kristina blanched. "You met Paolo?"

Leo gulped. "Of course. He gave me the letter you wrote me."

The woman's face wrinkled in consternation. "My letter?"

"Yes, the one introducing me to my son."

Kristina shook her head. "I didn't write you a letter, Leo."

Leo struggled to make sense of her response. "You wrote that you were very ill and you wanted me to know my son before you died."

Kristina's head fell back as she broke into laughter. "Do I look sick to you?"

Leo looked her up and down. "No, not at all . . . You look as radiant and beautiful as the last time I saw you—even more."

Kristina Adimari's tears burst over the dam that had held them back for almost three decades. Leo was at a total loss. Without thinking, he took her hand and closed his eyes. God, he knew that hand. His heart fluttered like a schoolboy.

Kristina moved within touching distance from Leo. Awkwardly he reached around her shoulders and gently pulled her close to him. She rested her head on his chest. His mind was spinning out of control.

Finally she looked up and found his eyes. "I couldn't bear to tell you about Paolo," she confessed, wiping her tears. "I knew it would ruin your life, and I loved you too much to do that."

Leo felt as if his heart would burst with gratitude. *How could I have ever left you?*

"So you met Paolo?" she giggled lightly. "He always wanted to know his father. When he was a little boy I told him that you were working in a faraway country. When he became a young man I told him the truth, with the strict instruction that he was to never contact you. But, stubborn as he is, he didn't listen." She smiled proudly. "How is he, Leo? I haven't seen him for months."

Leo stiffened. When Kristina felt his body clench, she pulled back and looked at him intensely. Something was wrong. Very wrong.

"Let's take a walk," he said.

# *Lauren 19*

---

After an hour that felt much longer, Lauren heard Todd tapping at the window. She opened to let him slip through, and searched his eyes. He reached into his jacket pocket and pulled out a small brown glass bottle with a black cap.

"What's in there?"

"A sample of Malthus's poison. He has a stash in the munitions dump."

Lauren studied the vial, stiffened, and stepped back. "You want us to commit suicide?"

Todd shook his head. "You being here has made me rethink what I am doing." Todd held the bottle up to eye level. "We need to stop Malthus before he mobilizes his plan."

"How?"

"We'll dump the poison in his water supply."

"You mean kill him?"

Todd nodded. "It's either him or half the population of the Earth."

Lauren shook her head, face paled. "I can't be involved in something like this, Todd."

He snickered. "Lauren, you are already involved—deeply. At this point, there is no easy way out. If we don't do something now, you will be the next body in the ravine."

*How the hell did I get into this?*

"The morning group meditation meeting will start in half an hour. Malthus will be there. This is our only chance."

# Kenton 19

"I can't keep doing this," said Yoshi, dropping her head onto her arms crossed on the kitchen table. "My brain is fried. We're just going down a bottomless rabbit hole."

Kenton, equally frustrated, shook his head. "Let's take a break and then we can decide what to do."

Yoshi stood up from the table, plopped on the couch, and stared at the ceiling. "Arrrgh! So near and yet so far!"

Kenton smoothed her hair in a fatherly way. "I'm going out to get some coffee with a kick. . . What can I get you?"

"A magic wand with the password printed on it," she answered, pulling a blue and white throw cushion over her eyes.

Kenton smiled. "I'll see what I can do . . . I'm off, then . . . Shamai."

"Shamai," Yoshi called back, her voice muffled through the cushion as Kenton walked out the front door.

As the word ricocheted through Yoshi's brain, she pulled the pillow from her face and looked at the ceiling, bug-eyed.

*No way.*

The woman sat up with a jolt, walked back to her laptop, and opened the email login page.

Enter password:

Carefully she typed:

S...h...a...m...a...i

Yoshi set her right index finger on the Enter key, closed her eyes, and held her breath. She slowly pressed the key and opened her eyes.

The screen morphed from the password page to a list of emails.

"Kenton!" she yelled, "We're in!"

Yoshi's parents, who had never seen their daughter exude such a boisterous display, dashed in from their bedroom, frightened, as if she were yelling "Fire!"

Yoshi rushed to the front door and threw it open. Kenton was halfway along the path to the street. *"We're in!"* she yelled. *"Kenton, we're in!"*

Kenton turned around and stared at Yoshi, bewildered.

"I found the password!"

Kenton hurried back along the path and up the steps.

"It's SHAMAI!!!" Yoshi blurted out as Kenton approached. She jumped up into his arms and wrapped her legs around his waist. Tomiko and Takao looked on, shocked. Maybe their daughter *was* crazy, after all. But Yoshi didn't care. Some things, she had discovered, are more important than what your parents think about you.

*Cairo*
*September 21*

# Brianna 20

Brianna slid cautiously onto the gynecological examining table in Dr. Beshara's office. Aviva Roth sat beside the nervous girl and helped secure the back of her hospital gown. The surgical suite was not nearly as neat and sterile as an American counterpart. Some cardboard boxes were unevenly stacked in the corner, a few surgical tools lay on the counter in a less-than-orderly fashion, and the windows' exteriors were grimy with film from the polluted city air. Her exposed back was cold from the noisy air conditioning unit. Soon a callous-looking Arab man with a unibrow and unruly moustache would sedate her, work some weird tool up her birth canal, extract one of her eggs, mix it with some mysterious crud from a cloth that had been lying around for two thousand years, and implant it in her uterus. *How did I get myself into this?*

A nurse entered the suite and introduced herself in Arabic. She weighed Brianna, took her temperature, and placed a cuff on her arm to check her blood pressure. The nurse was pleasant enough, but she did not speak any English, adding to Brianna's angst of being a stranger in a strange land. She forced herself to take a deep breath as she held Aviva's hand.

The wall phone rang and the nurse picked it up. As the conversation ensued, she looked surprised and confused. After a minute, the nurse hung up and left the room, uttering some kind of apology, leaving the two women alone and stumped. As minutes ticked by, Brianna began to worry. *Has something gone wrong?*

The door opened and Dr. Beshara entered. He looked older than his photo, hair grayer, gut paunchier. He had dark circles under his eyes, his cheeks and neck slightly unshaven. He looked more like a gangster or a seedy politician than a doctor. A chill ran up Brianna's spine.

"Hello, Brianna." His voice sounded softer than he looked. "Thank you for participating in this project. You are a courageous young woman."

*More than you know.*

"Something has come up."

Brianna and Aviva shot each other questioning looks.

"I just received a phone call from Dr. Ashraf Ahmad, Minister of Antiquities, the department that oversees the pyramids and all the historical sites in Egypt."

*What could that possibly have to do with my uterus?*

"There will be an unexpected television shoot at the Great Pyramid later today. I am a member of the board that governs that department. The Minister wants all the board members to be present at the shoot."

"So you are not going to do the procedure?"

"Not today," Beshara answered soberly, "I am very sorry for the delay. I know you have come a long way and this is a big step for you. With your permission, we can start again tomorrow."

*Shit. But at least a reprieve.*

Someone was knocking at the door. The nurse opened slightly to reveal Hathaway and Roth. "May we enter?"

Aviva cast a small blanket over Brianna's exposed legs, and she nodded.

"We're really sorry about this, Brianna," Dr. Roth spoke as he approached, obviously flustered. "We had no idea this would happen. The whole scenario is very unusual. Usually if someone wants to do a film or television shoot at the pyramids, they have to apply for a permit months or years in advance. Very few are granted. For some reason this shoot was permitted in one day's time."

"The entire area will be cleared of tourists," Dr. Beshara added. "That is equally unusual. Whatever is happening, it's big."

Brianna tried to absorb the news. She looked to Aviva for some sign of guidance. The woman was equally clueless.

Dr. Beshara went on, "The good news is that the Minister has given permission for you to join me at the site."

Brianna remained unimpressed. "Can't you just tell them you have a previous commitment?"

Beshara shook his head. "It wasn't a request from the Minister. It was an order."

The frustrated young woman slid off the table. "I can't believe the conception of the world savior has been upstaged by some stupid TV show."

Aviva offered Brianna a motherly look. "We're in a foreign culture, dear. We have to go along with their customs."

Brianna made a sour face. "How soon can I get out of here and back home? I am really worried about my mother."

"We understand," Roth replied in as kindly a voice as possible. "After Dr. Beshara extracts one of your eggs, he will take it into his laboratory and infuse Jesus's DNA. It will remain in vitro for a five-day incubation period for the embryo to grow. Assuming that everything goes well, at the end of that phase he will implant the embryo in your uterus. Then we are on our way . . ."

Brianna scrunched her face. "Aren't you missing one crucial element?"

"What's that?"

"Isn't there supposed to be a sperm involved? . . . Could you maybe contact Justin Bieber?"

Hathaway smiled. "We've given this procedure a great deal of thought, Brianna. Jesus was originally conceived without a biological father. We are counting on replicating that process. We don't want another person's genetics involved. We believe that his DNA merged with your ovum should be enough."

Brianna sighed and rolled her eyes.

*The Virgin Mary didn't go through all this. Nobody took her to some creepy double-chinned gynecologist who poked at her private parts. All she did was hear a message from an angel. Couldn't we just keep it that simple?*

*Bimini*
*September 21*

# Driscoll 20

"Wait a minute," Kendall spouted as he pointed to the image of the ancient city on the TV monitor. "I've seen that place before. . . in that book." He dashed into the living room and returned with the Amazing Underwater Discoveries volume he had shown Driscoll. He fingered through the pages. ". . . It's Atlantis."

Kendall turned the book to show Driscoll. On the page following the photo of the Bimini underwater road was an artist's rendering of the ancient city of Atlantis. Not exactly the image on the TV screen, but close enough. There was the harbor of concentric rings, the gleaming buildings, the great temple, the sculpted trees, and the artistically land-scaped flowers.

"Who's doing this?" asked Marifer, pointing to the TV. "Some smartass kids playing a trick?"

The onscreen image zoomed, as if by drone, to show citizens in loose-fitting, light-colored garments strolling on the streets. Wooden ships with tall white billowing sails were cruising into the harbor while others at the dock were being unloaded. Fisherman sold their catch beside the pier. Then the focus shifted from the dock, over the houses, and up the hill to the temple, where a huge flame burned on an onyx altar at the base of the massive crystal.

A young man and woman wearing white robes ascended the steps to the temple and kneeled in front of the altar. Their skin was fair and smooth, almost shining. They closed their eyes to meditate. A soft smile grew over their faces as they sank into themselves.

Suddenly two rays of brilliant light shot from the crystal toward the couple, the beams penetrating their chests. Their bodies glowed, the light filling them. Their smiles widened as they entered an ecstatic state.

Soon the image of the couple faded out, replaced by a random pattern of thousands of tiny pixels of blue, white, green, and brown. The arrangement had no form and made no sense. The image stayed on the screen for a minute, and disappeared.

The group watching in the bedroom looked bewildered. Ticia was glowing. "Those people looked so happy!" she spouted. "It's as if their energy was jumping off the screen to me. Wait. . ." She placed her hands on the side of her waist. After prodding it in different spots, her face lit up. "My pain is gone."

*Capella*
*September 10*

# Leo 20

Leo Bonfiglio and Kristina Adimari sat on a ridge overlooking the sprawling hills of Tuscany as they had done so many times in days long gone by. Yet this morning a dense silence eclipsed the song of the crested lark that had once brought them so much joy. The little makeup that Kristina had worn was smeared on her cheeks and blouse. By now she had no tears left. The thrill of sitting with one of the two men she considered the loves of her life had been decimated by the loss of the other one.

For all his priestly experience, Father Leo found no words of comfort to offer. If he had been less devastated by the atrocity, he might have been able to soothe the anguished woman. All of the Catholic principles of forgiveness he had learned felt empty now.

Kristina took Leo's hand and held it firmly. "Paolo said many times that he wanted to know his father before his father died," she remarked with a bitter snicker. "At least he got to know his father before he himself died."

Leo simply listened. He could do no more. Kristina rested her head on his shoulder. He wrapped his arm around her shoulder.

"Do you think Paolo's death will mean anything to anyone, Leo?" she asked. "Or will he just be written off as a deranged angry young man?"

Leo took a long sigh. "I don't know, Kristina. Many brilliant souls have been cast off as heretics in their own time, only to be glorified or sainted decades later."

"I don't need Paulo to be a saint," she came back. "I just want him to be understood." Kristina pulled away from Leo and turned to face him. "I don't want him to be condemned and remembered as a criminal . . . Can you keep his name out of the newspaper?"

Leo pursed his lips. "I pushed the Church as far as I could, to delay until I could speak to you first. I expect they'll want to use him as an example."

Kristina stared off into the distance. "So the religion based on brotherly love brutally murders anyone who disagrees with it? Is that how it works?"

Leo took a long breath. "Yesterday I received a call from my friend Father Gabriele Bianci. He's the liaison between the Vatican and the Rome Police Department."

"And . . .?"

"The Catholic Church was not behind Paolo's death."

Kristina pulled away from Leo and stared into his eyes. "Then who?"

"A small, right-wing underground group called *Tueri Ecclesia*. The name means 'Protect the Church.' The Church decries them, but they take matters into their own hands."

Kristina shook her head. "I really don't see any difference . . . Murder in the name of God is still murder. What kind of sick mind would twist a faith into a tool of evil?"

"Just the devil," Leo came back. "His soldiers have infiltrated every religion."

# *Lauren 20*

At 7:45 AM Todd stepped out of his cabin and walked across the graveled parking area to the guard sitting in the van. A minute later Lauren heard the van's engine turn on, followed by the crunch of tires over loose gravel.

Todd dashed back to the cabin. "What did you tell him?" asked Lauren.

"I told him he could trust me to keep an eye on you while he goes to the meeting . . . Like I said, he's not real bright."

Todd slipped on his jacket and grabbed the bottle of poison. He handed Lauren her jacket. "Where are we going?"

"Malthus's cabin. He'll be at the meeting, along with everyone."

Even while Lauren's intuition screamed at her to stay put, she followed Todd out the door. The two continued through an overgrown path through the woods, ducking branches, Lauren brushing spider webs from her hair. Her heart raced faster as she walked. Ten minutes later the two emerged into a small clearing around a simple wooden cabin with weathered cedar shakes siding. A round black metal exhaust pipe jutted two feet above the roof, a few wispy plumes of smoke wafting from last night's fire. Todd motioned for Lauren to follow him around to the back of the cabin, where she saw a large round redwood water tank.

"This is the water supply for his cabin. It catches rain from the roof."

Lauren stared at Todd, her eyes filled with question. Todd took her hand and led her to the far side of the tank, where a ladder leaned against the warped wood, extending almost to the top of the tank at about eight feet in height. Standing at the base of the ladder, Todd reached into his pocket and took out the brown bottle.

Lauren's eyes bulged. "Todd, you can't. You wouldn't!"

Todd smiled irreverently. "I can, I would, and I will."

"You are going to murder a human being, Todd."

"Actually, Lauren, I am going to prevent the murder of millions."

Todd opened the bottle and handed it to Lauren. "When I get to the top, I'll reach back for the bottle. Then hand it to me, okay?"

Lauren's hand trembled as she received the vial. "I don't know, Todd . . ."

"Just be sure to keep the bottle upright." He stared fiercely into her eyes. "If you get even a few drops on your hand, your skin will absorb it, and you will die a slow and painful death. Do you understand me?"

Lauren watched aghast as Todd slowly scaled the makeshift wooden ladder. When he reached the top, he peered into the water tank through a six-inch space between the wall and the roof. He nodded, as if confirming there was water in the tank. He reached back down to Lauren as she held the brown bottle of lethal liquid.

Lauren withdrew her hand. "This is crazy, Todd. I'm not doing this. I will not participate in killing a man. My soul is already tortured enough without have a human being's death on it."

Todd glared at her. "If you don't do it, the death of vast masses of innocent people will be on your soul. You are stopping a very bad man from destroying much of humanity. Don't be fooled by his soft demeanor, Lauren. I assure you, Malthus is pure evil."

When Todd saw Lauren's hand trembling, he took a step down the ladder. "If you could have gotten rid of Adolph Hitler before he started the Second World War that led to the deaths of seventy-five million people and unbelievable destruction, wouldn't you have done it?

*In a heartbeat.*

Todd hopped down to the ground and faced her squarely. "Okay, Lauren, I need to tell you this: If you don't do this, Malthus will surely do away with you. I didn't want to freak you out earlier, but the couple they found in the woods were not the only ones Malthus eradicated. There have been others who knew about his plot. They have been found dead or they mysteriously disappeared."

Lauren tried to take a breath to calm herself, but she was too scared. "How do I know you're not making this all up? Groups like this are paranoid."

Todd shook his head adamantly. "This is not paranoia, Lauren. It's reality. Even if Malthus doesn't succeed with his plan, you will be looking over your shoulder for the rest of your life, wondering if and when and how he or his cronies will hunt you down."

Lauren stood frozen.

"We have to hurry before anyone comes."

Todd ascended back up to the top wrung and reached his hand down for the second time. Holding the open bottle, Lauren stretched her hand until the container was inches from his fingertips.

# Kenton 20

As Yoshi opened up Brian Turner's enigmatic email program, Kenton and her parents hovered over her. "Hurry," Kenton implored as she clicked on Get Mail. Forty-nine emails loaded. The spam filter immediately tossed nineteen into the trash. Eighteen of the remaining messages were from business associates and groupies. Another eleven were from people who had heard that Brian had disappeared and suspected he was holed up on a private retreat. The remaining one read Circle Makers, with no @ or domain name.

"That's it!" Kenton burst out.

Yoshi clicked on the message and read aloud:

> The security of this communication channel
> has been breached. No further messages
> will be delivered to this address.

"Shit!" Kenton slammed his hand on the table, fuming. "We worked so hard to get this far, and now this." Yoshi groaned and spun around on her chair to face Kenton. The Sato parents looked on, bewildered.

"Whoever's trying to stop Brian has hacked into his email," Kenton surmised, his neck reddened. "The circle makers figured this out and put the kibosh on the transmissions."

"But how would they know?"

Kenton snickered. "Our email system is as rudimentary to them as a string and paper cup is to us. If some under-handed human can figure out how to hack incoming mail, the circle makers can surely detect it."

"*So, so* . . .Now what?"

Kenton brushed his hair back from his forehead. "I don't know . . . I just don't know." He stood and walked to the window, as if asking some invisible source for guidance.

Mr. Sato approached Yoshi and leaned in toward her. "Excuse me for the interruption, but I heard you say that no more emails will be delivered to this address."

Stunned that her father was taking an interest, Yoshi turned to face him. "That's right, dad."

"Perhaps there is a clue in the message." All eyes turned to Takao as Kenton returned to his side. "Perhaps the sender is hinting that messages will be delivered to another address."

"What makes you say that, Mr. Sato?"

"The message does not say, 'No more emails will be sent.' It just says, 'No more to this address.' I am an engineer. Technical communication must be very precise. It must not say any more than it needs to say, but it must also not say less."

"So the messages might come to some other recipient?"

Takao shrugged his shoulders. "I cannot say for sure. It's a possibility. I'm just an old engineer taking a guess."

Yoshi's eyes lit up. "No, dad, you're a genius."

Mr. Sato smiled coyly. "Old Japanese saying: 'The older the child gets, the smarter parents become.'"

# *Brianna 21*

---

Brianna held firmly to the wobbly handrail as she ascended the stairs of the makeshift wooden platform facing the Great Pyramid of Giza. When she reached the top, she turned and gazed out at the blazing crimson sunset, bathing the desert in an other-worldly glow. The rippled sands, stretching as far as she could see, shimmered as they welcomed the cool evening after the scorching day. On the horizon, Bedouins on camels formed silhouettes against the setting sun. *A thousand years ago I would have seen the same scene.*

Just ahead of Brianna, Isaac Roth turned to Dr. Beshara. "What have you found out?"

Beshara shook his head. "Not much. This morning a crew from Al Resalah TV set up their equipment. They have three cameras for a live feed, plus the huge monitor you see before you, for our viewing. No one is telling us what's going on. They say they don't know. I am inclined to believe them. Usually someone leaks a secret if someone crosses his palm with enough *baksheesh*."

Professor Redmond Hathaway stood on the other side of Beshara, hands on hips, quietly contemplating the scene. The previous morning, tourists were crawling all over the place. Now the area was ghostly.

"You will be sitting with some of the most prestigious dignitaries in Egypt," said Dr. Beshara as he pointed to two dozen chairs arranged in two rows behind him. Older men in traditional white *dishdara* robes occupied the front row. A few younger men in the rear row wore modern business suits. A slender woman in an *abaya* sat beside one of the younger men.

Beshara extended his hand toward five empty chairs at the end of the second row. "Shall we take our seats?"

As Brianna and her companions settled into their chairs to view some weird event that had muddled everyone associated with it, her mom's face flashed before her. Brianna was not surprised, then, when her cell phone went off. Brad. "Hey, sis, where are you?"

"Actually, you won't believe—" Suddenly the call dropped. *Inferior cell service in an underdeveloped country.* She tried to call back, but No Service flashed on her screen.

Brianna looked to her right and saw an Arab man in a business suit fiddling with his phone. "Did you lose your signal too?" she asked.

"Very strange," he answered with a thick Arabic accent. "Giza always has good reception."

She tried again. Still no service.

Brianna turned to Aviva Roth, sitting at her side. "Does your phone work?"

"I think so. . . I used it a few minutes ago."

Aviva removed her phone from her purse, and saw on the screen, No Service. "Oh, my—it looks like the system is down."

Brianna looked around. One of the men in the viewing gallery was tapping his iPad, lifting it in different positions, trying to get reception. None of the wireless devices were working. *This can't be an accident.*

# *Driscoll 21*

---

"What was *that*?" Marifer asked as the Atlantis broadcast disappeared and a children's show replaced it. She clicked the wand to power off the television.

"I have no idea," Ticia replied. "All I know is that my body hurt like hell before the show started, and it doesn't now."

Driscoll gently set his hand on his wife's forearm, his eyes teary.

"Satan has taken control of the television!" Kendall spouted.

Ticia snickered. "Nothing new about that, cousin. Satan seized that industry the moment it was invented."

Kendall was unamused. "The evil one also shut down all wireless communication for a full hour."

Ticia shook her head. "That wasn't the evil one, Kendall. Maybe humanity was getting a break from mindless screen time. Teenagers might have had to actually interact with a live human being. Maybe other people besides me felt better after watching that picture."

"Our pastor has been preaching about this for years. It's the end times," Kendall retorted. "Only those who believe in Jesus will be saved—the Book of Revelations predicts there will be one-hundred-and-forty-four thousand people pure enough for redemption."

Driscoll grimaced. "Why can't you just let good things happen to people outside your religion, Kendall? 'The rest of the world deserves to go to hell, but my club is special and we will be the only ones in heaven.' How can you call yourself a man of God when you cast yourself as superior and you take perverse reward in the suffering of people who don't believe as you do?"

"But Jesus is the only—" Kendall started to argue, until Marifer poked her brother in the ribs to silence him. She turned to Ticia. "Seriously, cuz, what do you think that was?"

"Maybe a reminder of how good it could get if we let it."

Kendall pulled his Bible from a shelf and started to page through it to further his argument. "Listen to the woman," Marifer told him in a stern voice as she pulled the Bible out of his hands. "She's making sense."

## *Leo 21*

---

The townspeople of Montecuore gathered for Paolo Adimari's memorial service at the school where he had taught. Out of respect for what she knew would have been Paolo's wishes, Kristina did not hold the funeral in the local church. Father Delvecchio, sympathetic to Kristina's request, had formulated a scheme to evade the many reporters who had flooded the little town to exploit the event. The priest announced that the service would be held in the church on Saturday afternoon at 2 PM. While the paparazzi gathered there, the townspeople met covertly at noon in the elementary school auditorium. Paolo's students had put together a scrapbook filled with photos of their beloved teacher, pictures the children had drawn, and their personal letters of thanks and goodbye. As an anguished Kristina watched the kids file past Paolo's coffin, placing their innocent gifts next to his body, she felt a grain of solace. Her son had left his mark.

By the time the service was completed, the reporters, waiting at the empty church, found no Paolo or guests, and they went looking for action. But it was too late. The body had been taken to the vineyard to be interred in the presence of a few family members. When the angry press found children filing out of the school, they asked some of the townspeople why they had colluded to deceive them. "You did not know Paolo and you did not care for him," a school-teacher told one reporter. "Paolo was a son of Montecuore. His goodbye was too precious for nosy cameras to mar. Here we do not capitalize on the sorrow of others."

# *Lauren 21*

As Todd was about to grasp the bottle of poison, Lauren dug her heels into the ground to steady herself. Suddenly she heard the bushes behind her rustle. Startled, she turned to see a huge black and tan Rottweiler, head piercing the bushes, barking fiercely. The ugly beast growled, showed its teeth, and charged Lauren. Her hand shook until the bottle tipped backward and spilled before she could right it. As she felt the splash of liquid on her wrist, her heart started to race and her body shook violently.

"Oh, my God!" she yelled as she dropped the bottle onto the ground and scurried up the ladder to a rung just below Todd, grabbing onto his thigh.

Todd leaped off the ladder and planted himself on the ground between Lauren and the beast. "Here, Lucy, come, girl," he called in a friendly voice. The dog relaxed, wagged her tail, and nuzzled her head into Todd's thigh. He reached down and began to stroke Lucy on the back of the head. "See, Lauren, she won't hurt you."

"I spilled that shit on my hand, Todd!" Lauren shrieked.

"No, no, no, don't tell me that!"

Shivering, Lauren clutched the ladder while Lucy sniffed her ankles.

Kenton looked at the dining room table to see what he knew he would see: Yoshi's laptop was gone.

"I'm sorry," Takao said to his daughter. "I tried to help."

# Brianna 22

At 5:27 PM the giant monitor in front of the Great Pyramid fired up to a widescreen view of all three pyramids and the Sphynx. But the picture on the screen did not show what Brianna and her companions were seeing behind the screen. Instead of the eroded windblown monuments, the brownish rocks were covered with a smooth white limestone veneer. The Great Pyramid was crowned with a golden capstone gleaming in the sun. Rather than the arid desert surrounding the structures, verdant lawns and lush palm trees set them off, enhanced by white and purple lotus flowers in shimmering ponds beside stone pathways. Even more astounding, the River Nile flowed within a hundred yards of the site.

"Extraordinary!" Hathaway exclaimed.

"What are we seeing?" asked Brianna.

Roth, transfixed, answered, "Egypt at the height of its glory."

The audience in the viewing gallery sat perplexed. Most were silent; some babbled nervously.

"Why is the river so close to the pyramids?"

"The Nile was not always in its current location," Dr. Beshara answered. "The ancient Egyptians recognized water as the source of life, so they constructed the pyramids on the banks of the Nile. Over thousands of years, the river has meandered six miles to the east."

The onscreen image shifted to one of the pyramids still under construction. Thousands of sweaty bare-chested men were rolling huge stones on a system of logs and ropes.

Brianna turned to Dr. Roth. "I thought you said the pyramids were constructed with sound?"

Roth smiled coyly. "Just keep watching."

The workers dragged one of the massive building blocks to the base of the pyramid, and stepped away. Then a group of men in white robes marched into the area, carrying musical instruments, some trumpet-like, others stringed, and others drums. As the musicians formed a semicircle around the stone, more men and women, dressed in colorful garb, joined the group. An older man with a shaved head began to chant a prayer. He went on for a minute. Finally he stopped, nodded, and raised his right arm, signaling the others.

The musicians lifted their instruments and began to play a high-pitched monotone, piercing Brianna's ears. Others chanted a single tone with harmonics. The sound was shrill but entrancing. It reminded Brianna of a concert she had attended where Tibetan monks rubbed a softened stick around the edges of brass and crystal bowls. The hypnotic music and chanting went on for a few minutes.

"Look!" Brianna called out. "The stone is moving!" Hathaway and Roth rose to their feet, along with all the other observers.

As the audience watched in awe, the huge stone began to ascend and hover above the ground, vibrating slightly. Slowly it continued to rise, casting a shadow over the side of the pyramid.

Dr. Roth chuckled and slapped Hathaway on the back. "I knew this is how they did it. They could never have gotten those massive stones to huge heights manually."

As the music went on, the granite block rose to about fifty feet above the ground. Then something even more amazing happened: a beam of brilliant light descended from above, somewhere offscreen, and engulfed the rock, the dazzling column throwing off a shower of white and golden sparks.

Brianna stood entranced as the music accelerated and the block ascended faster. After a few minutes it reached an opening near the top of the pyramid. Slowly, with meticulous control, the rock slipped into the space prepared for it, guided by an unseen force. Then, as quickly as the beam of light had revealed itself, it disappeared. The singers and musicians fell silent. The priest initiated a new chant, presumably a prayer of gratitude.

Brianna turned to Dr. Roth. "What was that beam of light?"

"A little help from our friends," Roth answered, exuding the joy of a little boy who had just opened the best birthday present of his life.

"What friends?"

Hathaway answered. "The construction of the pyramids was a joint venture between humans and extraterrestrial civilizations."

*And I thought the baby idea was out there.*

Suddenly the pyramid scene disappeared, replaced by an abstract pattern of tiny irregular shapes colored blue, white, brown, and green. There must have been thousands of them. Brianna turned to Dr. Hathaway. "Some kind of test pattern or transmission glitch?"

Hathaway shook his head. "I assure you that whoever engineered the program we just saw is beyond test patterns and glitches."

# Driscoll 22

While Driscoll was playing cards with the kids in the living room, he was jarred by a loud thud from the bedroom. He dashed up the stairs to find Ticia lying on the floor, her body doubled over. Quickly he moved to pick her up. "No, just leave me," she pleaded, her face contorted. "I need to catch my breath."

Her husband took a pillow and propped it under her head. Her face relaxed. "I shouldn't have gotten up so quickly. My side grabbed and I went down."

He stroked her face. "I thought you were feeling better after that transmission we saw."

"I was," she nodded, "but then my side started to hurt again. I didn't want to scare you. I know you were happy about my improvement . . . But I can't fake it anymore, Driscoll. I'm hurting."

Though he hated to admit it, Driscoll knew quite well what was happening. Over the last few days he had watched his beloved wife's body weakening. The man struggled to be strong, not just for himself, but for his children. He had seen soldiers die in combat, but it's different when the person you love most is withering before your eyes.

Over the next few days, as Ticia's physical form faded, her spirit grew brighter. The less she was in her body, the more she was in her soul. Driscoll was astounded that of all the people in the house facing Ticia's death, she seemed to be the one in least fear.

On Friday around sunset, Ticia called Driscoll and the kids into her room. Marifer and Kendall joined them. She took Driscoll's hand. "I don't think I can hold on much longer," Ticia said with a small forced smile. Driscoll shook his head, as if to deny her prophecy. But he knew she was telling the truth. A small tear ran down the soldier's cheek. He didn't want his wife to go, but he didn't want her to stay in pain.

Ticia turned her head on her pillow to face Driscoll. He held her hand tighter.

"You know how we've been asking for a miracle?"

He nodded.

"We got it, Driscoll. When I was sleeping, mom and dad came to me, then our first dog Tucker. They were all glowing with such a beautiful light. They were young and vital, like when I knew them at the peak of their aliveness. They told me they were waiting for me and they were looking forward to welcoming me home. Then they opened a door to a room filled with a bright, almost overwhelming golden light. It was so beautiful, warm and wonderful and inviting. Driscoll, I know where I am going. I'm going home."

Driscoll, fighting back the tears, stroked his wife's hair and forehead.

"You don't have to worry about me, you tough soldier with a heart of gold. I am in good hands."

Ticia lifted her head and reached to stroke Jared's forearm, and then Tanisha's. The kids looked at each other, lost to what was happening.

"Just know that I love you."

With that, Ticia Ames closed her eyes, took a long, cavernous breath, and left this tired world behind.

# *Leo* 22

---

Leo walked up the farmhouse steps and found Kristina on the veranda sipping coffee at a small wooden table. Before she saw him, he took a moment to savor her radiance, his heart filled with gratitude that he could be with her once again. Without a word he spread a newspaper before her. Kristina read the article headline:

### Is the Old Rugged Cross Too Old, Too Rugged?

She scanned the paper and looked up at Leo. "This is the international edition of *The New York Times*," she said, stunned. She read aloud:

The debate in America over Paolo Adamari's mission and death is growing, the clash within Catholic churches rapidly escalating to a war of ideologies. The younger, more free-thinking church members are siding with the "set me free" vision, while the older, more conservative congregants are dead set against it. Factions are protesting at Sunday services, and Internet blogs are ablaze with the argument. To add fuel to the fire, a number of Protestant churches are questioning the symbol of the simple cross. Some have removed the icon from their sanctuary walls. Bloggers are proclaiming "the second reformation."

Kristina shook her head in amazement.

"Paolo has touched many more people than we imagined," said Leo.

The woman turned her eyes from the paper and stared out over the courtyard for a long moment. Then she turned back to Leo. "I just had the oddest thought."

"What's that?"

"In a weird way, Paolo has brought us back together."

Leo pondered the idea. *She is right.*

"I'm going to ask you a hard question, Leo . . ."

His breath clenched.

"If you had it to do over again, would you have left me those many years ago?"

Leo's eyes dropped as he explored some very sensitive inner territory.

"I believed that the priesthood would bring me peace," he finally answered, looking up at Kristina. "In some ways, it has." He locked into her eyes. "But, to be totally truthful, the fondest memories of my life are the times I was with you."

Kristina's lips turned up in a quiet smile.

Leo stepped closer to her and placed a hand on her shoulder. "I can't turn back the clock, Kristina, but I know where my heart lives today."

"And where is that?"

Leo moved to the railing of the porch overlooking the vineyard. He swept his hand across the lush green land-scape, and paused to let the image sink in. Kristina rose to join him gazing at the panorama. He turned to face her.

"It's here, Kristina. With you. With this land, this village, these people. I find honesty and family in Montecuore that I have never found in the pomp and power of the Vatican. My soul is at home here." He turned to face her directly, his eyes filled with determination. "I'm not going back."

Kristina reached up, took hold of Leo's face, and kissed him on the lips. Firmly, strongly, sweetly. He seemed flus-tered at first, and then settled into the softness of her touch. It had been a long time. A very long time.

*Blue Ridge Mountains*
*September 5*

# *Lauren 22*

---

"You've got to pull yourself together!" Todd yelled at Lauren.

"What for? So I can die a slow and painful death?"

Todd took the unhinged woman by the shoulders and commanded her eye contact. "Listen to me, Lauren . . . There may be a way."

Her eyes lit a bit as her forehead furrowed in question.

"Remember I told you that Jian Chung said he can make an antidote?"

Puffy-eyed, she nodded like a little girl.

"If you can get to him, he may be able to help you."

Lauren looked down at the brown bottle, emptied on the ground. "Where is this doctor?"

"Somewhere in the Middle East—Iran or Iraq or some-place like that."

Her eyes grew dark. "Oh, great, that makes it really easy to find him. . . .What the hell is he doing there?"

"No one really knows. He left quickly and didn't give any explanation."

Lauren shook her head vehemently. "I'm not going to the Middle East. I'll find a doctor here."

Todd reached both arms to take her by the shoulders. "Lauren, you won't be able to find a doctor here that can help you—at least not during the week you have to live. This poison is insidious and undetectable until it is too late. It's unknown to the medical world. By the time they diagnose you, you will be dead or close to it. Your only chance is Jian Chung. When he said he can cure the effects of the poison, I believe him."

Lauren's mind went tilt. She didn't know what to believe. A creepy chill rolled through her as she considered that Todd might be telling her the truth.

"How am I supposed to find this guy?"

"He has an organization you can google. His students know how to contact him. Tell him exactly what's happened. He is your only hope."

*Salisbury*
*September 8*

# Kenton 22

Kenton and Yoshi found the patrons of the Higher Design Café abuzz with the news of Brian Turner's disappearance. Some said he had been murdered by the British government. Others "channeled" that he had gone into seclusion to communicate psychically with the circle makers. Others were certain he had been abducted by aliens. The intrigue was amplified by the arrival of a BBC reporter and film crew covering the story from the inner sanctum of the "croppies."

Kenton pulled a chair up to one of the public computers on a counter against a window. To his left, a bony white-haired woman was surfing cropcircleconnector.com, the premier website for diehard fans. On his right, a teenage boy with barrels piercing his earlobes was looking up the Phoenix Lights. Several people sat on a couch and a plush easy chair, pecking away on their laptops.

Yoshi grabbed a stool and wedged it between Kenton and the Phoenix Lights kid. Looking to one side, then the next, to be sure no one was snooping, Kenton opened up his webmail page.

Seventeen emails showed up, none of which he was interested in. Except the one from Cynthia. "Where the hell is our

Eurail Pass?" was the only message. No "Where are you?" or "Can we talk?" or "I hope you're okay." *Not a surprise.*

Kenton pressed Compose and typed Circle Makers in the To box, exactly as he had seen on Brian Turner's emails. In the subject column he wrote: We're ready. He shot Yoshi a nervous glance. She nodded.

Send.

Kenton watched the monitor for a while and then turned to Yoshi. "That's weird," he said.

"What's weird?"

If anyone tries to send an email without an "@"sign, the email program should reject it. But this one went out."

"That *is* weird."

Kenton and Yoshi hovered over the monitor for five minutes that seemed like an hour, anxious for a response. *Nada.* But there was also no return "cannot be delivered" email—a good sign. Kenton nervously rotated the mouse against the counter until Yoshi took it away from him. Finally he made a sour face, stood, and turned to her. "Maybe it's just not meant to be."

Yoshi shrugged. She had no more idea what to do than he did. She sat on the stool Kenton had vacated.

A short "ding" indicated that a message had come in. Kenton turned back excitedly, hoping to see a missive from the circle makers. Yet all he found was an ad for booking airplane flights. Kenton shook his head, moved the cursor to the Log Off button and clicked on it. But the computer did not respond. Again he tried, and again the page was frozen. He furrowed his brow and pressed Ctrl-Alt-Delete to reset the device. Still no response. He started to stand to get someone from the café staff to help. As he turned, he heard another "ding." He faced the computer one more time.

There, at the top of his list of emails, appeared a message from: Circle Makers. He seized the mouse and clicked on it. "Yoshi, look at this!" Yoshi leaned in, her eyes riveted to the screen.

The message simply said:

21 September 15:27 UTC

N 51°10'43.83", W 1°49'34.29"

"What are those numbers?" Yoshi asked.

"Latitude and longitude coordinates. A precise location on the planet." He rushed to Google Earth to paste in those coordinates to find the spot they pinpointed.

"Hey," the Phoenix Lights kid called out, irked. "What's this?"

Kenton ignored him, but Yoshi turned to look at the boy's screen. "Kenton, look at this."

Kenton refused to look up. "Wait . . . The map is loading."

"No, Kenton, you have to see this—now."

Kenton tore himself away from the monitor and looked at the kid's screen. The Phoenix Lights site had disappeared and was replaced by a page showing:

21 September 15:27 UTC

S "13°09'5.64 S", W 72°32'45.65"

Kenton's face lit up. He compared those coordinates with the ones he had received. They didn't match. "Do you know how to navigate Google Earth?" he asked the kid.

"Sure."

Meanwhile Kenton's page had loaded. The map on his screen showed: Southern England.

Zoom in.

County of Wiltshire.

Zoom in. Zoom in. Zoom in.

Kenton dropped his hands. *The center of Stonehenge.*

"What the hell?" a guy in a yellow jersey and maroon jogging shorts called out from the couch. "Who's hacking my email?"

Meanwhile the Phoenix Lights user zeroed in on his coordinates.

*Machu Picchu.*

Kenton moved to Google search and entered *21 September 15:27 UTC*. Immediately a list of websites popped up, one phrase common to them all: *Fall equinox this year.*

"What happened to my phone?" a college-age girl sitting in a tattered overstuffed chair whined.

Kenton moved to the girl and looked over her shoulder onto her phone. Over the wallpaper of her boyfriend's face, bold black script was imposed:

21 September 15:27 UTC

N 29°58'45.03" E 31°08'03.69"

"Google Earth," Kenton told her.

The girl complied as Yoshi leaned beside her and watched the image load: *The Great Pyramid of Giza.*

By now other patrons were gathering around those on the computers, while the reporter and camera crew hurried to those affected. A guy in a plaid flannel shirt and blue jeans opened his laptop and went to cropcircleconnector.com. There was a photo of yesterday's fresh crop circle overlaid with huge red letters:

21 September 15:27 UTC

N 31° 46' 41.11", E 35° 14' 7.32"

The BBC reporter, a pretty thirty-ish woman with fair skin and short brunette/reddish hair, wearing a stylish navy-blue pant suit, ordered her assistant to switch his camera on. Instantly a bright spotlight flooded the area. The reporter took her place in front of the camera and hastily primped her hair while the cameraman counted aloud, "Five . . . four . . . three . . ." then a silent shake of two fingers, then one.

*"Here at the Higher Design Café, a Mecca for crop circle devotees, an astounding phenomenon is taking place. Someone or something is jamming the signals of Internet users and transmitting latitude and longitude coordinates of numerous ancient sacred sites from around the world. So far the Great Pyramid of Giza has been identified; Machu Picchu, the lost city of the Incas in Peru; and our very own Stonehenge have appeared. These mysterious transmissions have been accompanied by a cryptic notice of 21 September, 15:27*

*Greenwich Mean Time, the precise moment marking the upcoming fall equinox.*

The camera panned around the café, focusing on the people who had received the messages. Meanwhile everyone else furiously opened up their laptop or phone, hoping to receive their own communiqué.

*"Could these cryptic messages be coming from the other-worldly makers of the crop circles, issuing some kind of directive to humanity? Or has some clever hacker hijacked the wireless system of the Higher Design Café, perpetrating yet another hoax in the tradition that, some say, has spawned all the crop formations?"*

The reporter moved to a tall, nice-looking fellow wearing neatly pressed jeans and a light blue knit shirt. He was standing behind the couch, leaning his hands on the backrest, surveying the frenzied scene. The camera followed.

*"Or has café owner Simon Barrington set up a pseudo-event as a publicity stunt to draw attention to his establishment?"* The journalist turned to the owner. *"Mr. Barrington, it seems rather fortuitous that these messages conveniently arrived at the precise moment a television crew happened to be on premises. Did you have a hand in this event?"*

Barrington laughed. "I couldn't have thought this up if I tried. Whoever's doing it is absolutely brilliant!"

The reporter turned back to face the camera. *"Whoever is behind this bizarre phenomenon, fans here are practically jumping in—pardon me—circles with the alleged revelations. I guess we'll just have to see what happens on September twenty-first . . . Megan Jeffries, BBC news, Wiltshire."*

# *Brianna 23*

The huge screen in front of the pyramids went blank, leaving some of the audience buzzing, others silent. Brianna turned to Dr. Roth. "What did we just see?"

Roth was glowing. "A history lesson we never learned in school."

Brianna didn't know what to believe. This could have easily been some techno prank or publicity stunt. Whatever it was, it sure looked real. She felt her phone vibrating. Five bars, restored after exactly one silent hour. FaceTime—Brad.

"Brad, you're not going to believe what I just saw!"

"You're not going to believe what *I* just saw! Check out the recording." Brad pressed a few icons and a video image came up—precisely what Brianna had just seen on the large screen in front of the pyramids. "You saw it too?" she asked.

"Every detail."

A shiver ran through Brianna's back.

"Not just me, but Vanessa on her tablet." Brad tilted his phone to reveal his girlfriend sitting up in bed next to him. *He was never shy about his love life.* "Hi Brianna," she waved as she smiled and pulled a sheet up over her chest.

"I called dad and my buddy Jack," Brad went on. "They all had the same show going on their phones, laptops, and TVs. *Everyone everywhere* saw it."

"What do you make of it?"

"This is the kick in the ass the world needs, sis. '*The Day the Web Stood Still.*'" Brad stood, stretched his phone at arm's length for a selfie, and imitated a massive robot. "Klaatu barada nikto."

"Very funny, Gort. Now please put your pants on."

Her brother tilted his camera to waist up.

"Seriously, Brad, who do you think is behind this?"

"I don't really know. Maybe some kind of warning that there are forces out there bigger than we know. Or a throwback to show us how cool things were before we messed it all up. Whatever this is, it's gonna get lots of people trying to figure a lot of stuff out for a long time . . . Gort out."

*Bimini*
*September 24*

# Driscoll 23

Ticia's memorial service was short and simple, in the graveyard behind the church she attended as a child. Just the family and a few friends who remembered her as a bright, precocious girl in her blue plaid Catholic school uniform, and pigtails. The dark-skinned, white-bearded, glassy-eyed preacher, Reverend Rolle, a few orbits on the other side of eighty, recounted how Ticia and her sister got into mischief by taking home a stray dog and hiding it under their bed covers. While everyone laughed, Driscoll's tears fell as he was reminded of what a devoted mother his wife had been. He forced himself to regroup so as not to rattle his children. He knew this dark turn would take its toll and the kids would probably need a good part of their lives to process their mom's death at their tender ages. *Ticia was right. There are some things that money can't buy. We never know how long a loved one will be with us, so we have to make the most of every moment.* Driscoll silently reaffirmed his vow to be there for his kids at every turn.

After the service, the small group drove to the beach house for food and consolation. A few minutes into the gathering, Tanisha had a coughing fit that Driscoll knew was stress related. He picked up the girl and held her in his arms, trying to comfort his daughter like her mother did. "Are we going to live on an army base again, daddy?" she asked.

Her father shook his head adamantly. "No, no, Tanisha. We're never going back to army life again. One way or another, your daddy will be out of the military. I will be home with you. We'll get a nice house with a big yard in a fine neighborhood and you'll have fun friends to play with. I'll send you to the best school and you'll be able to learn whatever you want."

The child's eyes brightened. "Can I learn the tuba?"

Driscoll laughed, a welcome relief in the roughest of days. "You can learn whatever instrument you like, my princess."

A sullen Jared drifted over to his dad and sister. Driscoll pulled the boy onto his lap. "How are you doing, son?"

Jared shrugged. "Okay, I guess." *Not convincing.*

Driscoll placed his hands on the boy's shoulders and looked him firmly in the eyes. "This is a tough time for all of us, Jared. But we'll get through it, okay?" *I'm talking to myself as much as him.* "I'm going to need your help to take care of your sister. Can you do that?"

Jared nodded, feeling proud that his dad would entrust him with responsibility. The child stared deeply into his father's eyes. "Why does God take away people we love?"

Driscoll issued a long, heavy sigh. "That's a question everyone asks, son. I wish I had an answer. It's just a fact of life we have to learn to cope with."

The boy's face remained stark.

*I don't think he got it. . . Well, neither do I.*

# *Leo 23*

Carlo Baldacci's house was one of the few in Montecuore that sported a satellite dish, so it made sense that the villagers would gather at his place for the big event. The early evening crowd grew so large that Carlo's son Franco had to move the wide-screen monitor—also a rarity in the region—onto the porch and let the audience watch from the lawn. The atmosphere was festive, townspeople sitting on beach chairs, blankets spread across the grass. Guests passed wine bottles and cheese plates around while children played in the grove.

"Everybody be quiet!" Franco called out. "The show's coming on."

A wave of "shooshes" rolled through the assembly.

Franco's younger sister Catarina stepped up to the porch and took hold of a microphone connected to a cheap p.a. system donated by Antonio de Rosa, who had spent a brief foray in Milan as a disc jockey. Catarina had gone to college in New York, and she was the best—make that the only—translator in the village. "Hallo, hallo?" she tested the system, the tinny echo providing a hint as to why Antonio was back in Montecuore rather than Milan.

When the intro music came on, the crowd leaned forward to read the show's logo: *The Tim Corey Hour.*

"Who the hell is Tim Corey?" Lorenzo Bertanoli called out.

"He's a hot shot interviewer," Catarina answered. "Everybody in America watches his show."

The music faded and the camera closed in on the host, a fortyish black man with strong shoulders and short hair. His eyes were clear and intense. "The crucifix is the symbol of Christianity, bringer of hope and healing to billions of people over two millennia," he began. The screen image shifted to a Catholic crucifix with a painted porcelain Jesus hanging on the cross. Then a photo of a kerchiefed woman kneeling and praying at the foot of a huge cross.

"It is also the dreaded symbol of inquisitions and genocide." The screen showed a painting of Spanish conquistadors brutally murdering native Incas, a rendering of a woman being burned at the stake, and a photo of a Ku Klux Klan rally in front of a huge blazing cross.

"Today that symbol is under fire from many Christians who claim it is antiquated and an image of violence, torture, and suffering. Other Christians defend the cross as God's chosen symbol of the sacrifice made by their savior Jesus Christ. Is the crucifix a sign of life, or death? Tonight two spokesmen will state their case for each side of the debate blazing across America. Father William Byrne of Woodland Hills, California, and Bishop Wilford Boswell of Cleveland, Ohio will put forth their reasons for wanting to get rid of the cross or keep it. Thank you, gentlemen, for joining me."

Catarina struggled to keep up with the translation, people in the back of the crowd straining to hear.

"Father Byrne, why would you want to change a symbol that has sustained your religion for over two thousand years?"

The camera focused on the fair-skinned priest's face, sandy hair, soft blue eyes, and boyish countenance. "A living religion must change with the times, Tom. It wasn't very long ago that Catholics believed that masses had to be said only in Latin and it was a sin to eat meat on Fridays. A meeting of Cardinals overturned all of that, and more. It's time to revisit the purpose and meaning of the cross. Our Lord Jesus Christ was murdered on it. Every time we look at the cross, we are reminded of Jesus's horrific death. Jesus said, 'I have come to bring you abundant life.' If that is so, why cling to a picture of gruesome death? It's time to let go of the suffering that Catholics have borne for over two thousand years, and get on with living with greater joy."

A murmur rippled through the crowd. The people of Montecuore clearly had their own opinions. "Shhhh!" Franco stood and called out.

"Bishop Boswell," the host turned to the other guest. "Are you ready to say goodbye to the crucifix?" The pale sixty-ish bishop, portly and bald, wore thick black-rimmed eyeglasses, a red uniform shirt, and a white skullcap. He shook his head vehemently.

"Certainly not, Tom. The crucifix has long been the symbol of our faith with good reason. Jesus Christ died to redeem us from our sins. To make light of his death, overlook it, or distract us from it, would deny the purpose for which he was born. Every moment of his ministry, even his entire life, was a prelude to his final sacrifice so we don't have to suffer. He paid the price for all of us. When Jesus rose on the third day after the crucifixion, he demonstrated that we, too, will overcome death if we believe in him."

"But Bishop," the young priest cut in, "would you say that Catholics have escaped suffering because Jesus suffered for us? Many Catholics continually labor under guilt, overwhelming obligation, self-sacrifice, and fear of going to hell because they cannot toe the unattainable standard of holiness the religion has prescribed for them. By painting a picture of a suffering Christ and then reminding us of his agony and death every time we walk into a church or look on a wall in our house, we have not eliminated suffering, but perpetuated it."

The television flashed a series of photos of crucifixes from traditions around the world, some ornate like the cross of St. Francis, and some a simple wooden form or even straw. The final image panned a huge European military cemetery marked by thousands of small white crosses.

The Bishop squeezed his forehead, accentuating the vertical crease above his nose. "There is nothing in the doctrine of our religion that says Catholics will escape suffering. Because of original sin, we all bear the stain of Adam. In heaven we will be redeemed, but we must follow the precepts of our religion to earn it. You can't just go around reinventing the religion because its symbol makes you uncomfortable. Life is painful. A priest can't stick his head in the sand and tell people, 'Don't worry, life is fun.' Jesus didn't have fun on the cross, and we must emulate the example he showed us."

The host broke in: "We have to go a break now. We'll be right back to take your calls." Fade to music.

Again the crowd murmured. Asking a group of staunch Catholics in a remote Italian village to consider letting go of the cross is no small task. Even if one of their beloved sons died for that very reason.

Minutes later the show resumed. "Do you believe the crucifix should be retired?" Tim Corey asked his television audience. "Is there some better way to honor Christ? What do you think should happen to people who remove crucifixes? If you have a question or comment, give us a call."

The audience on Baldacci's lawn grew quiet.

"Edna Rae from Hot Springs, Arkansas . . . You're on the air."

"I think it's just horrible what these people are doing," the woman spouted in a thick southern accent. "I'm not Catholic, but I do go to church every Sunday at First Baptist. I'd lie down and die before I'd let anyone take the cross off my church wall. Trying to take the cross from Christians is like . . . like . . . spitting on the Lord's grave!"

A buzz went through the audience on the lawn, followed by scattered applause. Kristina, seated beside Leo in the front row, turned to see who was clapping.

"Bob from Seattle . . ."

A young man spoke. "I was raised in the Catholic religion and I have spent the last thirty years of my life trying to get out from under the guilt that was laid on me. I was told that food, money, sex—and pretty much everything I like—is sinful, and if I do anything to make myself happy I am robbing good from someone else. I think it would help millions of Catholics like myself—and, more importantly, our children—to quit focusing on the Jesus who died because I'm a sinner, and to become acquainted with a Jesus who loves me as I am."

Another round of applause, more tentative, issued from the group on the lawn, mostly younger people.

Tim Corey turned to Father Byrne. "You began this—I guess we can call it a movement—in America because of the tragic murder of a young man in Italy who was removing Christ statues from crucifixes in Rome, correct?"

Father Byrne nodded. "That's right, Tom. His name was Paolo Adimari. He was an elementary school teacher in a small village in Tuscany."

Kristina reached across the arm of her chair and gripped Leo's forearm. A buzz rippled through the crowd.

Tim Corey turned to face the camera. "To give you an idea of the fate that befell this young revolutionary, we've received from the Rome Police Department previously unreleased photos of the crime." Without further warning, the screen flashed a photo of Paolo hanging lifeless on the cross, the horrendous sight that Father Leo had beheld in person. At that time, he had seen the corpse only in dim light, but now, fully illuminated under a police floodlight, the image was even more gruesome. Blood was still flowing from the five wounds where his body had been pierced, and his eyes were open, frozen in the moment of his execution.

Leo reached toward Kristina to shield her eyes. But it was too late—she had seen the horrible image. To Leo's surprise, she did not burst out hysterically. Instead, she sat stone-faced, catatonic.

A wave of "My God!" and "Paolo!" shot through the audience. Women began to weep and husbands tried to comfort them. Several mothers rose and pulled their young children away from the viewing area. Tragically, the television show held the horrific photo on screen for a long time. When Franco Baldacci realized the mayhem the image was causing, he pulled the plug from the television monitor. But the damage had been done.

## *Lauren 23*

Lauren Delaney found her apartment just as she had left it. But now everything was different. When you may have just a week to live, your priorities change. While she continued to wonder if Todd's prognosis was fact or fiction, she could not afford to wait around to find out.

She fired up her Mac and googled *Jian Chung herbologist*. Sure enough a website, "chi-for-life.org" came up. There she found a photo of the master, much as she had expected: mid-fifties, darkish skin wrinkled with character, a round face, vibrant eyes, thick black hair with traces of gray. True to Todd's word, the healer's bio was impressive—two doctorates from respected Chinese universities, many years of study with famous healers, significant stints in prestigious clinics, and a long list of testimonials from credentialed sources.

She scrolled down the page and read:

Dr. Chung is currently on a medical mercy mission in the Middle East. He is unavailable for consultations, and our communication with him is sporadic. If you wish to contact Dr. Chung, you can email us and we will do our best to contact him. We cannot promise a response, or when.

Her heart sank.

Lauren stood up from her computer and plopped on her bed. *If I can't contact Chung, I'm screwed.* She stared at the ceiling for a long time, mentally going over the bizarre events of the last few days. *I should have deleted Todd's email.*

A knock on the door jarred her. *Shit, they have found me.* Her heart raced as she walked to the window of her garden apartment with a view of the front porch. *Just the UPS guy–thank God.* Lauren opened the door and received her Amazon order with a phony smile, nervously looking over his shoulder at the black car parked curbside. *Kids in the back seat. Not Malthus.*

Lauren shut the door, leaned against it, closed her eyes, and took a heavy breath. *I can't live like this.* She returned to her computer at the kitchen table, sat, and typed:

Dear Dr. Chung,

I have just returned from the Project Genesis community in the Blue Ridge Mountains. There I accidentally spilled on my hand a lethal poison formulated by the man called Malthus. I heard that you are familiar with the substance and you can provide an antidote. **Can you please help me?!!!** I may have only days to live.

Lauren Delaney

As Lauren's finger reached to press Send, she stopped. *This is absolutely crazy. I have no idea if any of this is true, or if I will ever reach this doctor in the hell hole of the world.*

At that moment she began to cough. As she tried to recover, she remembered Todd's prediction: *The poison strangles the lungs.*
Send

# Kenton 23

As quickly as they could, Kenton and Yoshi made their escape from the frenzy in the café and dashed under the twilight sky to the Astra. They climbed in, rolled up the windows, and locked the doors. Kenton turned on the map light, Yoshi's eyes fixed on her iPad.

"How many GPS locations were transmitted?" Kenton asked.

"Five," Yoshi answered. She read the list out loud:

*Stonehenge*
*Machu Picchu*
*Great Pyramid of Giza*
*Bimini*
*Tell Abu Shahrain*

"The first three are well-known ancient sacred sites," Kenton reasoned aloud. "But Bimini? . . . And who ever heard of Tell Abu Shahrain?"

Suddenly the two were jarred by a bright light shining in the driver's window. Kenton turned with a start to see the face of the BBC reporter who had recorded the news story inside the café, her cameraman beside her. Kenton shook his head and sighed, torn between opening the window and driving away. Against his better judgment, he pressed the Down button.

"Sorry to disturb you," the reporter began, crouching to see into the car. "Some people in the café said that you were the first to receive a message."

Kenton raised his hand against the light to shield his eyes. The reporter motioned to the cameraman to move the light away.

"That's right."

The reporter shoved the microphone closer to his mouth. "Why do you think you were chosen to receive the first message?"

Kenton shrugged his shoulders and shook his head. "I have no idea." *No way I am going public with the story now.*

"Are you crop circle researchers?"

"Just amateurs on a holiday."

The reporter rested her left hand on the top of the car door and leaned her face closer to Kenton's.

"Who do you think is making these formations?"

Kenton took a moment to think, hoping to choose the right words. "An intelligence from beyond the known world."

The reporter nodded. Kenton wasn't sure if she was agreeing with him or humoring him. "What do you think this intelligence wants us to know?"

"It's a wake-up call. We're not alone. Somebody out there wants to help us. Maybe show us a way out of the mess we're in."

Kenton started the car engine. "One more question," pressed Ms. Jeffries, her hand firmly against the windshield as if she could stop the car. "Do you really think these messages can help humanity?"

A smug smile grew over Kenton's lips. "If you newspeople gave this phenomenon as much attention as war, crime, and politics, we might have a chance." With that, Kenton Baine rolled up the car window, stepped on the gas pedal, and curtly left the reporter and crew in the darkened parking lot.

*Cairo*
*September 22*

# Brianna 24

Dr. Alim Beshara's waiting room was not especially user-friendly. Small footprint, stuffy, drab gray walls, hard-on-the-butt chairs, and a guy smoking a smelly cigarette next to his wife. A TV droned on in the corner while Brianna paged through a magazine flaunting photos of the first women recently licensed to drive in Saudi Arabia. *What century are we in?*

Professor Hathaway, flanking Brianna on the other side, was glued to *Yahoo News* on his laptop. "That army lieutenant who released the alien photos is sure generating a lot of buzz," he looked up and commented. "The story in the online *New York Times* has gotten more clicks than any article in the newspaper's history."

Roth chuckled. "The closet believers are coming out of the woodwork."

An announcement on the TV interrupted the conversation. "We now bring you breaking news from Washington."

A male reporter with thick curly brown hair and a ruddy complexion stood on the steps of the Capitol building. *"Since yesterday the entire world has been abuzz after the global silencing of wireless communication and the transmission of images of ancient civilizations, followed by enigmatic abstract patterns. Immediately after the incident, the Federal Communications Commission announced it would launch a thorough investigation to discover the source of the blackout and transmissions, blatant violations of international communication protocols."*

The screen image shifted to a rapid-fire series of short video clips showing frustrated people in different countries unsuccessfully trying to use their wireless devices, followed by snippets of the broadcast of the sacred sites.

*"This morning, the U.S. Army Office of Intelligence revealed that our country's military was responsible for the incident. Public Information Director Major Peter Wade called a press conference, where he read a statement that the events were part of an army experiment to maintain control of wireless transmissions in the event of an attack by Russian, Chinese, or other hackers."*

Brianna looked toward Hathaway, his lips turned up in a suspicious smirk.

The screen showed a trim, middle-aged, black-haired army officer in dress uniform. He stood behind a podium bearing the U.S. Army insignia. "Cyberspace is the battlefield of the new millennium," Major Wade stated soberly. "The people of America and the free world cannot afford to be vulnerable to other countries or terrorists interfering with our communications systems. Yesterday's blackout was our message to hackers that we can take charge of global wireless systems if we need to."

Hathaway and Roth shot each other cynical looks.

A lanky male reporter called to Major Wade, "What was the purpose of depicting ancient civilizations?"

Obviously prepared for the question, the officer replied, "We wanted to show the people of the world how easy it is to use computer-generated imagery to fabricate images to deceive the masses."

A young female Asian reporter asked, "How about those abstract patterns of blue, white, brown and green that followed each of the five transmissions?"

The major shrugged nonchalantly. "Just some random digital residue from the immense effort to transmit the broadcast worldwide."

*"So, ladies and gentlemen, the mystery has been solved,"* the reporter concluded. *"We can all quit wondering now, and get back to business as usual. Maybe sleep a bit easier tonight knowing that our country is protecting us on the new battlefield of cyberspace. I'm James Whitley, CNN Washington."*

Brianna turned to Professor Hathaway to check his reaction. He sat with his hands folded on top of his head, eyes closed, shaking his head as if he had just bitten into a piece of rancid meat.

# *Driscoll 24*

Driscoll Ames stepped out of the huge wooden doors of the Department of the Army courtroom, Cheryl Lansing at his side. As expected, two dozen reporters were waiting, shining floodlights in his eyes and shoving microphones in his face.

"What was the result of the court martial hearing, Lieutenant Ames?" a female CNBC reporter in a maroon pant suit asked.

Ames stopped, planted his feet, and faced the group directly. "It's not Lieutenant Ames anymore," he said, the relief in his face obvious. "I am now simply Driscoll Ames, civilian."

The reporters jostled each other, jockeying for position to get the celebrity's attention.

"What was the army's verdict on charges of breaching security or fabricating evidence?"

Ames stood tall. "The United States Army has officially discharged me honorably." A buzz rippled through the assembly. "That is all that I am permitted to say, according to the agreement I have signed with the army's attorneys."

"Will you be permitted to keep the monies paid to you by *The Washington Post?*" the *USA Today* reporter probed.

Cheryl stepped between Driscoll and the journalist. "The fee that Mr. Ames has received from *The Post* will remain his." She paused for a moment, her brows dropping a bit. "He will not, however, be permitted to write the book we have planned, or offer any further interviews or information related to his experience."

More chattering and a barrage of questions.

"That is all that I have to say," Driscoll stated curtly. "You will not be hearing from me again."

With that, Driscoll and Cheryl pushed through the mob, the reporters still pursuing them. Then down the wide gray granite steps to a black Lincoln limousine waiting at curbside.

Once in the rear seat, the two breathed a long sigh of relief. Driscoll turned to his colleague. "What do you think about how it went?"

Cheryl smiled smugly. "Exactly as expected."

"You knew how this would turn out? Did some mole leak the decision to you beforehand?"

"I don't need a mole, Driscoll. I've been in this business for almost thirty years. I know how the government thinks. The last thing they want is for you to stay on international radar. A long trial would generate a tsunami of attention they dearly want to avoid. The photos you took and your testimony would be splashed on every newspaper in the world. You would be the hot topic on all the news shows, video clips of you would go viral on social media, and you would be in the public eye a hundred times more than you have been. If you were convicted, every ACLU, free speech, counterculture, conspiracy, and UFO group would be up in arms, making a huge stink that the spin doctors have been praying to avoid."

"You really think I would raise such a ruckus?"

Cheryl laughed. "You already have! Add to the fray the blacks who would play the race card and argue that a white officer would have been acquitted; single parents who sympathize that you are now a widower dad; and child protection advocates who, if you went to jail, would call your children orphans. A trial, conviction, or any form or punishment would generate a sensation the likes of which the nation has not seen since the impeachment hearings. I promise you, my friend, letting you off the hook now is by far the government's most efficient way to close the book on your disclosure and go back to a 'we know nothing about UFOs' position."

Driscoll took a moment to take in Cheryl's comments. He looked out the window, watching the streets of Washington scroll by. "Well, it's done. Tonight I will be on a sleepy little island with my kids, and the nightmare will be over."

At that moment Driscoll felt his cell phone vibrating. Unknown caller. Langley, VA.

"Do you know anyone in Langley?"

Cheryl smiled suspiciously. "I certainly do—better take it."

"Lieutenant Ames?" a mature deep male voice spoke.

"Yes?"

"This is Carlton Pierce, Assistant Director of the Central Intelligence Agency."

Driscoll knew the name and the position. "What do you want with me now? The army dropped the court martial. I just became a civilian."

"This is about a different matter. Can you meet with me now? I have a car right behind you."

Driscoll turned to look out of the back window of the limo. Sure enough, there was a big black Cadillac SUV, government plates.

"Sorry, Mr. Pierce, I'm on my way home. My kids are waiting for me."

"I'm sorry to disturb your plans, Lieutenant. I know you've just been through a huge ordeal. But we have a potentially catastrophic situation on our hands that may cause irreparable harm to a very large number of people. You may be able to head that off. Can you give us an hour? After that, we'll take you to Bolling Air Force Base and fly you directly to Bimini."

Driscoll looked to Cheryl. She nodded.

"Keep talking."

"There is a bank parking lot ahead on your right," Pierce went on. "If you pull in there, you can make the transfer."

Ames sighed and leaned forward to tap the driver on his shoulder.

# *Leo 24*

If anything less than a papal order had called Monsignor Leo Bonfiglio back to the Vatican, he would have refused. Yet as long as he was still a priest, he had to obey.

Wearing his robe for the first time in a week, a limousine picked up the priest at *Roma Termini* and whisked him off to Vatican City. Sitting in the plush leather rear seat amidst a television, telephone, sophisticated sound system, and liquor bar, he pondered the contrast between the humble world he had just departed and the luxury surrounding him.

The Vatican Security Council met in the conference room where Leo had last seen the Holy Father. The previous emergency meeting was about his son, as he was sure this one was to be. *Three weeks ago I did not even know I had a son. Now he is shaking the Church from his grave.*

There were more security staff at this gathering than the last one, along with more papal assistants, plus Monsignor Alfonso Molinelli, the Vatican Director of Public Relations. All announcements of church policy had to be passed through Monsignor Molinelli, who spun them to the media. The last time Father Leo had met with Father Alfonso, he was trying to tone down Vatican Astronomer Reverend José Gabriel Funes, who issued the landmark announcement that belief in extraterrestrial life is not incompatible with Catholic doctrine.

The room was quiet, the clergymen's faces sober. Father Bonfiglio took the seat reserved for him and scanned the stone countenances. Today, like the previous meeting, he was nervous, but he was more deeply indignant. He had no sympathy for a religion or any faction that would stoop to murder. He considered how naïve he had been to accept the slaughter of millions of people by crusaders and inquisitors, while now he was irate about the killing of one young man. Finally the Pope arrived, and everyone rose and offered him proper abeyances. The Holy Father took his seat, made the sign of the cross, and uttered a short prayer.

"Your Holiness, we have a . . . situation," Father Molinelli began. "You are aware of the furor in America over the crucifix?"

"Yes, of course."

"The situation, I regret to report, is aggravating. Catholics and Protestants in other countries are saying that due to what happened to the Adimari boy, they want to choose a symbol for our religion other than the crucifix."

Monsignor Leo felt his chest tighten. The Pope absorbed the information and quietly deliberated. "I understand that these people are upset. But we are not going to change the cornerstone of Catholicism for a few malcontents."

Half of the assembly shot each other looks of relief. The other priests exchanged troubled glances.

"Unfortunately, your Holiness, there are more than just a few malcontents," Father LaCorte added. "Apparently there are hundreds of thousands, perhaps many more. Reports are coming in from Europe and South America, where people have been following the controversy on television and the Internet. They are protesting on the steps of churches and mimicking what is happening in the United States."

The Pope sat quietly, stroking his chin. The situation was more serious than he had realized. "What if we just let them speak their piece, issue a statement that we, too, decry and mourn the loss of the young man, and that the Church remains fully committed to maintain the two-millennia symbol of our religion?"

Father LaCorte looked pained. "With all due respect, your Grace, that might have worked twenty years ago. But with modern communications, movements like this and—I hate to say it—revolutions—spread like wildfire. The downfall of the Soviet Union was orchestrated through fax machines, and the longtime oppressive Egyptian regime was overthrown by people communicating through Facebook." Father Rissole, who had been looking down at his notes, looked up until he caught His Holiness's eyes. "Do you know what that is, sir?"

The Pope laughed. "Of course I do! I have my very own Facebook page! Monsignor Molinelli convinced me to do it when he found out the Dalai Lama has fourteen million followers. Now I only need four hundred thousand to catch him!"

The group burst into welcome laughter. Father Leo relaxed for the first time since he had left Montecuore.

"I agree that the situation is grave," the Holy Father continued, more seriously. "What are our options?"

Father Giacondo Rossalino spoke. "For one, you can issue a statement declaring that worshiping Christ on the crucifix is not a matter to be debated. You can order all Catholics to continue to attend mass and keep crucifixes in place, regardless of the critics."

The Pope took in the advice. That was the obvious route, at least at first.

"Reasonable," Father Vittorio Mancini replied, "—but soft. We're dealing with a huge number of emotionally charged people. They already know we want them to keep going to church and to keep the crucifixes in place. We need something stronger, more solid, more persuasive."

A short silence followed. "We can organize an ecumenical meeting of Christian leaders," Monsignor Molinelli suggested. "Then announce a joint resolution declaring that the cross is the universal symbol of Christianity, affirming the solidarity of the entire Christian world."

The Pope nodded.

"That's also a good idea," Father Mancini replied, "but time is of the essence. Some people are threatening to take down the crucifix themselves, and others are starting their own new churches."

"Good God, we may have another Protestant reformation on our hands!" Father LaCorte bellowed, pounding his fist on the conference table. "We could lose thirty or forty percent of our parishioners, maybe more. You all know how much church attendance and donations are down already.

The British Church is practically dead. This could be a huge blow for churches all around the world."

The priests, baffled and disconcerted, searched each other's eyes.

"I have an idea," Father Mancini suggested. He turned to the Pontiff and asked, "What kind of sin is desecrating the crucifix?"

The Pope raised his index finger. "That would be a venial sin."

Mancini folded his hands and sat up straight. "What if we made it a mortal sin?"

The priests looked around the room, searching each other's eyes. Some looked surprised. Others nodded in agreement.

Monsignor Leo felt like a rock had been dropped into the pit of his stomach. "You can't just create a mortal sin to suit the Church's political agenda, Vittorio!"

Father Mancini shook his head adamantly. "It's not political, Leo; it's spiritual. If people fall away from the Church over this issue and they are alienated from the Lord, we shall see a wave of damnation unlike the world has ever known. We're not manipulating souls. We are saving them."

Cardinal Antonio Firenze, the only cardinal on the council, spoke. "In 2008 the Catholic Church added seven mortal sins to the list of the previous seven mortal sins that stood for fifteen hundred years. The new ones are, as I remember them . . . polluting, genetic engineering, drug dealing, abortion, pedophilia, causing social injustice, and . . . what was the other one?"

"Being obscenely rich," Father Rissole answered.

Leo gazed up at the gold-leafed rafters, then at the original Renaissance paintings on the walls. He looked out the window onto the parking lot, where a dozen limos awaited the beck and call of priests and Vatican administrators. He considered the Vatican museum of art pieces, etchings, sculptures, and artifacts collected over two millennia, only a small portion of which are on display. Add to the coffers huge bequests and all the land donated to the Church, which makes the Catholic Church's net worth, by some estimates, over two hundred billion dollars—one of the wealthiest institutions in the world. *If lavish wealth is obscenity*, Leo considered, *the Church is one of the world's guiltiest sinners.*

"We could easily add defilement of a crucifix to the list of mortal sins, as an act of creating social unrest that would damage souls," added Father Molinelli.

"I need to speak here," Leo interrupted, his cheeks flushed, breath heavy. "I've been sitting here doing my best to listen to all of your suggestions patiently and impartially. But I can hold my tongue no longer."

Heads turned toward Leo, and then to the Pope, who sat stone-faced.

"Does the Lord really want us to twist dogma to suit our agenda? The religion based on brotherly love and forgiveness is one of the worst perpetrators of fear and punishment. The notion of creating a new mortal sin to curb the crucifix protestors is indecent and in itself sinful. Do you really think you're going to scare people back to church with yet another threat of hell? How long do you think that intelligent people will put up with this? Every time you add a new sin to the 'scary' list, we lose more Catholics. People cannot be frightened into knowing God. They must come to God through love, not threat. Look at the 2008 list you—sorry, I take responsibility, too—*we* created. Are we ourselves not all guilty of many of those sins? Pollution? Take a look out the window at the exhaust from the limousines that drive us all around, running now just to keep the air conditioning going until we return. Drug dealing? When you scare people into coming to church, you are addicting them to fear, the most dangerous drug of all. Social injustice? How many starving babies around the globe could we feed if we sold off even ten percent of our holdings? My brothers in Christ, if those sins we enumerated have the power to damn, then I assure you that we are all going to hell—and the good, innocent people who want to worship a Christ of love, not blood, will find their way to heaven in our stead."

# *Lauren 24*

Lauren peered over the receptionist's shoulder at the Mercy Hospital Emergency Room. The digital clock on the wall read 10:43—now more than a full day since she had dropped the poison on her hand.

"How may I help you?" a tall, thin receptionist nurse in multi-colored flowered scrubs asked.

"I need to see a doctor. I spilled some poison on my right hand."

The nurse's eyes shot to Lauren's hand, squinting to see the damage. When she saw none, she looked confused.

"What kind of poison?"

Lauren shook her head. "I don't really know its name."

"Are you in pain?"

"No, but I am starting to be short of breath."

The nurse cast a suspicious glance.

"Come with me." She guided Lauren to a white-curtained examining area, where she motioned for the patient to sit on the stiff gurney. The nurse drew the curtain and departed.

As minutes ticked by, Lauren grew nervous. *What if they can't find the poison, they release me, and I die like Todd predicted? What if they find the poison and there is no cure? What if this is all bullshit?* She slid off the gurney and reached to part the curtain to see if anyone was coming. At that moment a hand nearly touched hers from the other side of the curtain. The curtain slid to the side, revealing a short Indian doctor, dapper, dark black hair slicked back. Maybe Lauren's age, late twenties. On his white lab coat Lauren read in embroidered blue letters, Dr. Ramesh Mehta.

"Please, have a seat," Dr. Mehta invited Lauren. She complied.

"Tell me about this poison you spilled on your hand."

Flustered, she tried to pace her words, but failed. "I went to visit a friend up in the mountains. A guy there is a chemist who developed a poison that suffocates you within seven days. I was pouring the liquid and it spilled on my hand."

The doctor squeezed his thick eyebrows toward each other. "Do you know the name of this poison? Was there any label on the bottle?"

"No, it was plain."

"Did the substance have a color or a smell?"

"It smelled a little like cough medicine."

Dr. Mehta furrowed his forehead. "Let's have a look at your hand."

Lauren lifted her right hand as the doctor slipped his hands into blue nitrile gloves. He reached for a silver gooseneck stand and pulled a bright light to shine intensely on the back of her hand. He leaned in, focused his eyes on the hand, and softly prodded the area.

"Any pain?"

"No."

"I don't see any discoloration or damage to the skin . . . Any itching? Nausea or vomiting?"

"No."

"Dizziness or fainting?"

"No"

Dr. Mehta pulled a small flashlight from the pocket of his lab coat, and asked Lauren to open her eyes wide. He examined her retinas, then touched his stethoscope to her heart, and took her blood pressure. All the while he remained silent, which made Lauren even more edgy.

"Have you had any symptoms at all?" he finally asked.

"My breathing started to get shallow . . . That got me worried—the guy who told me about the poison said it would disable my lungs."

Dr. Mehta reached for his stethoscope and pressed the tip against Lauren's back just below both sides of her rib cage. He listened carefully, his eyes looking down at the floor.

"Who was this guy who told you about the poison?"

Lauren could feel her heart start to palpitate. "My boyf—. . .My former boyfriend."

Dr. Mehta thought for a moment and placed a comforting hand on her shoulder. "Have you been under any stress lately, Lauren?"

*Duh.*

"Quite a bit."

The doctor nodded, as if he finally hit on something he could work with. He reached for his clipboard, wrote on a piece of paper, tore it off, and handed it to Lauren. She read, *Dr. Arthur Levy.* "Go up to the fourth floor and see Dr. Levy," said Mehta. "He will be able to help you. I will phone ahead to let him know you are on your way."

*Thank goodness. There is hope.*

Lauren found her way out of the E.R. and took an elevator up three floors, nervously drumming her fingers on her hip. The elevator door opened and she stepped out. There, before her, hung a large sign, red letters on white background: Psychiatric Services.

She closed her eyes, shook her head, and stepped back into the elevator.

# Kenton 24

Ten minutes down the A30, Kenton switched on the radio, hoping to hear some news about Brian Turner. Instead, all he heard were reports of rising petrol prices, a terrorist bombing in Lisbon, and bankrupt governments. He turned it off.

Meanwhile, Yoshi surfed the web on her iPad. "I found it!" she called out. "Bimini's an island in the Bahamas, fifty-three miles east of Miami."

Kenton had heard of the place but knew nothing about it. "Why would it be lumped with ancient sacred sites?"

"Hang on . . . I'm looking."

Kenton glanced in his rearview mirror and noticed the headlights from a vehicle behind him following at a close distance. *Some kid with a lead foot.* As soon as he could, Kenton moved into a slower lane. When he looked in the mirror again, the vehicle had changed lanes behind him.

"Ah!" Yoshi spurted. "Bimini is at the western tip of the Bermuda triangle. Some people say there is a huge crystal buried offshore that was once a part of Atlantis. That's why navigation goes haywire in the triangle and lots of planes and boats have mysteriously disappeared. There's also an ancient underwater road that is obviously manmade. Do you want to see a picture?" Yoshi turned the tablet toward Kenton.

Kenton's eyes were fixed on the rearview mirror. "Maybe later." He changed lanes again. The headlights mimicked his move. "Looks like we have a tail."

Yoshi looked out the rear window and turned back to Kenton, worried. "What shall we do?"

Kenton didn't bother to answer. Instead, he jerked the steering wheel to the left and pulled abruptly onto the highway shoulder, almost thrusting Yoshi into the driver's seat. The lights behind him followed. Screeching brakes pierced the night. Kenton threw open the door.

"Kenton, don't!"

But he was already out of the car. The otherwise meek physics teacher marched to the rear of the Astra and strained to make out the vehicle and who was in it. All he could see were the vehicle's headlights, diffused by the thick fog. "Here I am!" he called into the shrouded void, his arms open. "You have something to say to me?"

*Silence.*

"If you're following me for a reason, have the balls to show up and look me in the eye!"

*More silence.* Then, as quickly as the vehicle had pulled onto the shoulder, it lurched back onto the highway, leaving a trail of dust and smelly exhaust. Kenton made out the form of a green truck, a British Army insignia emblazoned on its door. His eyes followed the truck until it disappeared into the night.

He dropped his shoulders and made his way back to the rental car. "You're brave," Yoshi told him as he slid into driver's seat.

"I'm actually a coward," he stated. "But I'm fed up playing games with these people. I wish they would just come out and tell us why they are so threatened by a 'hoax.'"

"A coward wouldn't have stood up to those people like you did."

Kenton shrugged and turned to face Yoshi. "Let's have a look at that underwater road."

Yoshi turned the tablet toward him. He studied the picture for a while, and then noticed on the opposite page a black-and-white photo of a frail man with thin graying hair and wire-rimmed glasses. He looked like an old-time country preacher. "Who's that guy?"

"Edgar Cayce, the famous psychic. In 1940 he predicted that Atlantis would rise again in 1968 or 1969."

"When was this road discovered?"

"1968."

Kenton sat for a long moment, staring into nowhere. "Secret destinations," he finally said.

Yoshi looked at him, question filling her eyes.

"It's a quote I read: 'All journeys have secret destinations of which the traveler is unaware.' I thought I was coming on a vacation with my wife."

# *Brianna 25*

---

"Why did that army news report rattle you so badly?" Brianna asked Dr. Hathaway as he made a pained face in Dr. Beshara's waiting room.

The professor shook his head and snorted, "A massive crock of disinformation."

"You think the story was fabricated?"

Hathaway reached into his jacket pocket and pulled out his phone.

"Who are you calling—the President?"

Hathaway chuckled cynically. "There are people in the government who know a lot more than he does."

"Like who?"

"My friend Harrison Ray was my classmate at Cal Tech. He is now one of the top-level digital communications engineers at NASA—responsible for transmissions between mission control and all space flights. If anyone can tell us the truth about what happened, he can."

Hathaway pressed a few numbers and a phone rang three times. "Hello, Harrison? . . . Redmond Hathaway here. . . . Fine, fine . . . And you? . . . Yes, I figured you guys have been up to your eyeballs since what happened yesterday. I hate to bother you, but I have a curious student here. Can I put you on speakerphone?"

Brianna, Isaac, and Aviva leaned in.

"Harrison, who or what do you think was responsible for those incidents, and what's your best guess on how they did it?"

A raspy voice spoke with a slight southern drawl. "If I could answer that question, Redmond, I would be the recipient of a Nobel Prize—or on some hit list."

"So you don't think the army did it, like they announced?"

Ray snickered. "There's no way they could have done what they say they did, Redmond. I am privy to the most sensitive information about our technological capabilities, and I can tell you that to pull off yesterday's stunt would require scientific knowledge far beyond any that we have."

"Could it have been done by our government or hackers?"

Ray laughed. "Hackers or the government would have to bypass the firewalls of every server in every nation on Earth. They would have to break into all the Internet-beaming satellites orbiting the Earth, each of which is imbedded with a unique highly-secured code. They would have to seize control of every home and business wireless system on the planet, of which there are about a billion. They would have to know how to leave intact the internal wireless systems of hospitals, police, and fire stations. Hell, whoever did this even halted transmissions from our Mars Rover and Jupiter probe! Show me one hacker on Earth who can mess with our entire solar system! I can't imagine any individual or country capable of pulling that off, let alone create the realistic production values of those ancient civilizations. My buddy Henry Hale does advanced AI for DreamWorks. Even he was astonished. The most sophisticated geeks are going to be pulling their hair out over this one for a long, long time."

Brianna leaned forward, elbows on knees, and swirled her coffee in a touristy mug with cartoon camels wrapped around it. *This makes conspiracy theories look amateur.*

"And what about those abstract patterns that showed up at the end of the transmissions? Were they just digital garbage?"

Ray chuckled cynically. "Yeah, they were so unimportant that our military's top geeks have been working around the clock trying to decipher them. Washington pulled one of my best techs off his job to work on that project. They're worried it might be some kind of virus to scramble the entire Internet, break down military communication, and leave us vulnerable for some kind of cyberattack."

Roth broke in. "Hi Harrison, Isaac Roth here. Were your wireless transmissions at NASA also interrupted?"

"Every single one."

Ray's side of the conversation went quiet for a while.

"I'll tell you one more thing, fellas . . . but if anyone asks, you didn't hear it from me."

"Have I ever let you down?" asked Hathaway.

Ray chuckled. "Well, there was that time in college when you told my girlfriend that I was gay and she should go out with you instead."

A quick laugh broke the gravity of the conversation. Even Aviva smiled.

"I've been monitoring intra-government communications since the incident. The Pentagon is in chaos."

"Because?"

"When everyone's electronics went down, all of our nuclear missile silos were totally disabled. Not just wireless systems. Failsafe operating systems with backup generators independent of the public grid. The same shutdown occurred in all the other nuclear-armed countries. Whoever pulled this off has the power to neutralize mankind's ability to launch nuclear warheads. That, my friend, is who or what we are dealing with."

# Driscoll 25

A short female Latino aide in white pleated slacks and a dark blue blouse opened the door for Driscoll Ames to enter the meeting room on the sixth floor of CIA headquarters. The interior was stark—light gray walls posted with large-scale photos of the city of Washington, surrounding a long walnut conference table. A wide LCD monitor was fixed on the wall, audio visual equipment on a black metal stand below it. At the head of the conference table sat Carlton Pierce, sixtyish, neatly-combed thick brown hair, his lean body a statement of daily trips to The Company's fitness center. To Pierce's right, a slightly paunchy army elder four-star general loaded with medal ribbons; and a tall, gray-haired black marine commander, also well-decorated. To Pierce's left, two young bleary-eyed, stubble-bearded guys, one pasty-skinned and the other Indian. Beside them, a pretty woman about their age, smooth skin, green eyes, short brown hair with blonde highlights. Everyone looked serious.

Pierce stood, approached Ames, and shook his hand. "Thank you for coming, Lieutenant. I know this was not on your agenda . . . Please, have a seat." Pierce gestured to an empty chair between him and the marine commander. Ames cautiously took it.

"This is General James Watson and Major General George Hazelden." Ames saluted and they returned. "To your right, meet Spencer Pilvey, Navneet Adkar, and Ms. Leora Wentworth, three of our most gifted IT wizards."

Driscoll scanned the gathering and turned to Pierce. "Why did you call me here?"

Pierce swiveled his chair to face Ames. "You are, of course, aware of the global interruption of wireless service and the broadcasts that occurred earlier this week?"

Ames nodded.

"And you remember the colorful abstract patterns transmitted for a minute at the end of each broadcast?"

Ames nodded again.

"They were not random elements, Lieutenant."

Ames smiled irreverently "Of course they weren't . . . What were they?"

Pierce motioned with his hand, and Pilvey clicked a remote-control wand that lowered the overhead lights. The monitor flashed on, showing a matrix of five squares on the screen.

"These are copies of the end-of-broadcast patterns, captured while they were being transmitted. They may look alike, but when we magnified them, we found a lot more."

Driscoll leaned forward, elbows on the table, hands clasped together, focusing intently on the images.

Navneet Adkar stood, pointed a red laser onto one of the onscreen boxes, and circled it. "Each cluster contains just under twenty-nine thousand individual elements." He worked the mouse beside his laptop below the screen and zoomed in to show a blow-up section. All the shapes were irregular, as if torn from a larger source.

"A massive jigsaw puzzle," Ames surmised.

"Exactly," Adkar replied. "Altogether, they add up to one-hundred-forty-four-thousand pieces."

*Where have I heard that number before?*

Pilvey went on, "Nearly all of the segments are blue, brown, white, and green—the colors of the Earth as seen from space."

"I see," said Ames. "Are we supposed to somehow put the Earth together?"

"That's what we figured," Spencer replied. "But there is no key to how to fit the pieces together. All the blues are exactly the same color, as are the whites. The browns and greens have some slight detail and variation, but there are so many of them and they are so similar, with radically different shapes, that we can't figure out how to interlock them."

"So we are looking at a shattered, irreconcilable world," Ames suggested.

"In more ways than one," Ms. Wentworth added.

All eyes turned to Pierce. "But there was one element we could put together," he stated gravely.

Ames scanned the room. Everyone looked uneasy. Pierce nodded to Pilvey.

"There were a small number of black pieces. They were easy to fit together because of their contrasting color, squared edges, and matching curves." Pilvey pointed the laser at some of the individual black pieces amidst the larger group.

"We copied the black pieces into one file and put them together. Here is what they formed."

Pilvey scrolled down to show the black letters super-imposed over the muddled group of fragments. Driscoll flinched as he read,

**THE END IS NEAR**

# $\mathcal{L}eo$ 25

A dense silence hung over the Vatican Security Council meeting room as the eyes of nine priests turned to the Holy Father. At no time in known history had any member of the Vatican staff laid into the Church as irately as Monsignor Leonardo Bonfiglio just had—and certainly not in the presence of the Holy Father. Would the renegade priest be rebuked? Silenced? Excommunicated?

Instead, the Holy Father simply raised his hands, palms down, and made a small downward motion, as if to say, "Let's all calm down here."

No staff member had the guts to speak. The ball was clearly in the Pope's court.

"I understand your upset, Monsignor Bonfiglio," the Pope finally said. "But Father LaCorte is correct. We have to do something about this. If we simply stand by and hope this will go away, the Church will be further criticized for weakness and apathy. Strong measures must be taken."

Father Tommaso Bucci turned to Monsignor Leo. "You knew the Adimari boy, didn't you? You were the one who found him dead. Rumor has it that you knew he was behind these desecrations. Perhaps your personal feelings about him are getting in the way. Did he influence you with his radical talk?"

Father Leo, still boiling, forced himself to contain another outburst. "Yes, I knew the boy. He was rebellious, but sincere. He meant no harm. He wanted to make a point—and he did."

"That point has become an arrow piercing the very heart of the Church," Father Bucci retorted.

"Or perhaps piercing the armor that has grown over the Church's heart," Leo shot back.

"Fathers, please," Monsignor Molinelli called out. "What has been done has been done. We have to decide what to do next."

"I agree," said the Pope. He scanned the gathering of priests, thinking deeply. "How many of you are in favor of making crucifix desecration, removal, or replacement a mortal sin?"

Leo fumed as the priests searched each other's faces. Father LaCorte's hand went up immediately. Then Molinelli. Then Cataldi. One by one, more hands were raised. Of nine papal advisors, seven hands went up.

"Very well, then," said the Holy Father, turning to Monsignor Molinelli. "Prepare a release." He looked around the room and bowed his head. "Thank you, gentlemen. That will be all."

Under a shroud of silence, the council members began to rise and move toward the door.

"No, that won't be all," Father Leo said as he stood up. Everyone turned to him. Some appeared afraid he would grow violent. "I am ashamed to be part of a church that wields the sword of fear to control its followers. That was not Christ's idea and it is not mine. You can take this hypocritical religion and shove it up your holy asses."

With that, Monsignor Leonardo Bonfiglio removed his gold ecclesiastical ring and tossed it onto the table. Some priests looked on aghast, others with pity, others with indifference. Many shook their head. After a long, thick silence, they filed out of the room without a word.

Father Leo walked to the window and gazed out. Vatican City looked much as it did before the meeting. A crowd was still gathered beneath the Holy Father's balcony. Visitors lined up for tours, anxious to see the Pieta, the Sistine Chapel, and Michelangelo's famous ceiling portrait of God reaching to touch Adam. The line of limousines sat with engines running, air conditioners at full throttle, committing the now-mortal sin of pollution. Nothing in the Vatican or the Catholic religion had changed. Nor would it.

Leo felt a hand on his shoulder. He turned to see Monsignor Pietro Sabatino, the only other priest who did not raise his hand for the mortal sin vote. The men caught each other's eyes.

"We tried," said Monsignor Sabatino. He smiled sadly, patted Leo's shoulder, and left the defeated priest alone in the room.

# *Lauren 25*

Lauren closed her apartment door behind her, hoping no one from psychiatric services had followed her. All she wanted to do was crawl under the duvet and make the world disappear. Maybe Dr. Mehta was right. Maybe she *was* crazy. Maybe she had just dreamed up the whole Todd and Project Genesis story.

*I'll google that Malthus guy. Maybe I'll find out he's a looney—like people think I am now.*

She opened her phone and saw she had email. From: Dr. Jian Chung.

*My God, he wrote back!*

Dear Lauren,

I am very aware of the poison you mentioned. It is indeed dangerous. I can help you, but you must come immediately. Time is crucial. I can get you into Iraq on short notice. I have friends at the U.S. Embassy. Let me know your flight and I will take care of the paperwork and pick you up at the airport. I repeat, *do not delay*.

Dr. Jian Chung

*Beaconsfield*
*September 10*

# Kenton 25

Just as Kenton was dozing off, his phone rang. He reached for the device and read through bleary eyes: 11:04 PM. Caller I.D. showed a London number. *Cynthia at some hotel? The last person I want to talk to. Maybe she's in trouble. Better take it.*

"Is this Mr. Kenton Baine?" Female voice, British accent.

He made a face at the phone. "Who's this?"

"Megan Jeffries, BBC. I did the story on you at the café."

He shook his head disdainfully. "Didn't you bug me enough at the café? . . . How did you get my phone number?"

"From the rental car company. I wrote down your number plate. . .The BBC has connections."

Kenton grunted. "If you think you're going to grill me again. . ."

"Wait—don't hang up . . . I want to help you."

He sat up and pulled the comforter over his shoulders, his forehead creased. "How?"

"I can't tell you over the phone . . . Can you meet me at Stonehenge? Tomorrow morning at ten?"

Sigh. Long pause. Very long pause.

" . . . Are you there?"

Kenton shot the phone a harsh look. "No cameras or crew."

"Just me, I promise."

Kenton shook his head, mentally berating himself for caving. "Okay, ten."

"Thank you, Mr. Baine. You won't be sorry."

He tossed the phone onto the carpet.

"Are you alright?" he heard a voice ask. Kenton turned to see Yoshi entering the living room. She was wearing a short blue silk robe, her shiny black hair cascading over her shoulders. *OMG, she's a woman.*

"Yeah, sure," he answered, scratching the side of his neck. "That was the BBC reporter. She wants to meet me at Stonehenge tomorrow."

Yoshi lowered herself to sit at the edge of the futon. Her exposed legs were soft and sleek. He tried not to stare, unsuccessfully. "What does she want?"

*Focus, Baine.* "She didn't say. But it sounded important."

"So is this." Yoshi held up her iPad. "Before I went to bed I did some more exploring—*Tell Abu Shahrain.*" She turned the tablet to Kenton. A map displayed.

"Iraq?"

"Iraq today. Ten thousand years ago, Sumer."

"Sumer?"

"A mysterious culture that achieved a quantum leap in civilization practically overnight. In a short time, the Sumerians introduced astronomy, architecture, mathematics, the written word, and all manner of sophisticated knowledge that went far, far beyond what the world knew.

Historians are still trying to figure out how they grasped these skills so quickly."

Kenton reached for his shirt beside the futon and pulled it over his undershirt. *Still shy.*

"Maybe they were just smart people."

"More than that." Yoshi slid her finger to open a new tab on Safari. A picture of an elderly white man with a roundish face, silver hair and moustache, and black eyeglasses appeared. "A scholar named Zechariah Sitchin was a modern-day Sumerian expert. He could read and write the lost language, and he devoted his life to figuring out what the Sumerians knew and why."

"And . . .?"

"The Sumerians were in regular contact with a race of extraterrestrial visitors called *Annunaki*. Apparently the Annunaki gave the Sumerians vast technology and information that accelerated the evolution of the human race at light speed. Thousands of years earlier, the Annunaki had genetically manipulated the native ape hominids to become what we now know as humans."

Kenton folded his hands behind his neck and leaned back. "That's fascinating . . . but as a scientist I would need more proof."

Yoshi nodded. "Check this out." She slid on the futon next to Kenton. As her leg touched his, he felt a tingle he hadn't felt in a long time. His sex life with Cynthia had dwindled to nil years ago. He distracted himself with his work, but wondered if he would ever be attracted to a woman again. Now he had his answer.

Yoshi opened another tab. "For one, the Sumerians had a map of the solar system that depicted all of the planets in their correct size, orbit, and relationship to each other—all swirling around the sun. A hundred centuries before modern science figured that out."

"And there's hard evidence for that?"

Yoshi spread her fingers to expand a picture on the tablet. "Archaeologists found this Sumerian wall carving." Kenton studied the image of a tall, bearded god-like figure sitting on a throne, instructing two human beings. On the wall between the people was a map of the entire solar system as we now know it. "This was carved around 8,000 B.C.—a time when only three planets were known, let alone the fact that the Earth revolves around the sun."

Kenton raised an eyebrow. "And how does Tell Abu Shahrain fit into this?"

"That is the epicenter of where the Sumerian empire thrived."

Kenton reached for his jeans beside the futon and slipped them on under the covers. "If this is true, and the Sumerians were interacting with extraterrestrial guides, that place ranks as one of the most significant sites on the entire planet."

"Maybe even the *most* significant, if that is where visitors from the stars cultivated the seeds of humanity."

Kenton stood and buckled his belt. "Now for the million-yen question: Why did we receive the GPS locators for those five sites?"

Yoshi crossed her arms and made a face that only the Japanese make, furrowing the brow, squeezing the eyes almost closed, tilting the head to one side, gazing at the ceiling, and looking pained. It means, *I am thinking hard about this and trying to come up with an answer. Please wait.*

"Maybe we are supposed to study the cultures that created those structures?"

Kenton shook his head. "There has to be more to it than that . . . The circle makers also gave us the fall equinox time."

"Something will happen at those places then?"

"Probably. . . and maybe we are supposed to do something about them."

"Like?"

"Like go there."

"Well, you are going to one of them tomorrow."

Kenton took Yoshi's hand and thought silently for a while. "I'm not going without you."

She looked surprised. "But the reporter invited you, not me."

"Nope," he replied firmly. "We're in this together."

Yoshi smiled. "Wow, you're starting to think like you're Japanese."

*Cairo*
*September 25*

# Brianna 26

Exotic as the pyramids were, after six days Brianna was tired of looking at them through her hotel window. *I wish I could just get this over with and get home.* Daily calls to Brad about her mom assuaged some of her guilt, but mom's fragile state until they got her into her new facility distressed her daughter.

She slipped into the one dress she had brought, long silky silver, bare shoulders, V-neckline that made her feel more like a woman than a science experiment. After a few make-up touch-ups, Brianna made her way down to the hotel dining room where she found Hathaway, Roth, and Aviva sitting in a corner booth. Brianna slid in beside Aviva and smiled.

When neither man returned her smile, she realized something was wrong. "What's up, fellas?"

Hathaway and Roth looked at each other, trying to decide who would speak. Roth nodded, as if to give his partner the go-ahead. "We are concerned about the embryo, Brianna," Hathaway began. "It is not developing."

Brianna didn't know what to say. This whole affair was way beyond her. All she knew was that her sponsors looked terribly confused and disappointed. "So what now?"

"We still have two more days," Roth answered "Sometimes it takes a while for the chemistry to click. And with the unusual element of no sperm, the progression is highly unpredictable."

Hathaway breathed long and deep. "We may have to repeat the procedure. We are watching for signs."

Brianna looked at Aviva Roth, hoping to get some clue. She looked as stymied as the men.

"Okay, but if this doesn't work, I'm out of here. I'll give Jesus one more chance to pull off a miracle. If he can't do it in two shots, he's out of luck."

# Driscoll 26

---

"The end of what?" Driscoll asked, staring at the ominous warning on the monitor. "The world?"

"That would seem to be the intent," answered Pierce. "The segments that form the words are mixed with pieces that would form an image of Planet Earth if we knew how to connect them."

"But we can't be sure," Leora Wentworth broke in. "It could be some kind of code or metaphor."

Driscoll shrugged. "So what do you want from me? You have the best cryptologists in the world under this very roof. What you're talking about is way out of my wheelhouse."

Pierce scanned the eyes of his staff. They all looked tense. Then he continued: "There is something about your visit to the extraterrestrial artifacts collection that you should know."

Ames snickered. "So you're admitting that what I saw was real?"

"If you quote me, I will deny it. The powers that be are not ready for disclosure."

*Of course not.*

"A number of intelligence operatives have been shown the artifacts over the years," Pierce went on, still edgy.

"Some of them emerged with. . ." Pierce surveyed the stone faces of his associates.

"With?"

"With enhanced extrasensory abilities."

"You mean, like 'psychic?'"

"More than that. They gained heightened faculties of telepathic communication, clairvoyance, and remote viewing."

Driscoll folded his arms. *Extraterrestrial bodies are one thing. Fortune telling is another.*

"There seems to be a relationship between belief in the alien artifacts and receptivity to paranormal information about them," Ms. Wentworth added. "The agents who were convinced that the artifacts are genuine displayed the greatest enhancement in their intuitive powers. The agents who doubted, demonstrated little or no improvement."

Pierce leaned in toward his stymied guest. "The fervor you displayed by sharing the information with the entire world would lead us to expect that you have a high potential as an extraterrestrial communicator."

Ames shook his head and issued a nervous laugh. "This takes the cake. In a red-hot moment I go from being the evil whistleblower to the alien whisperer?"

Driscoll chuckled at his own joke. No one joined him.

"So you think little gray people from outer space are going to tell me what the warning means?"

Major General Hazelden spoke. "You may be closer to the truth than you know, Lieutenant."

General Watson leaned in toward Ames. "If there's any way we can get an explanation of 'The End is Near,' we may be able to avert a global catastrophe."

Ames laughed. "So let me make sure I'm getting this straight . . . The agency that knows the most secrets about everybody, teaming with the top brass of our country's two most powerful military arms, plus three renowned supergeeks, want me to talk to aliens so we can figure out how to save the world?"

Pierce sat back in his chair and tossed his pen onto the table.

"Yes, Lieutenant . . . That is pretty much what we are asking you to do."

# *Leo 26*

---

As Leo emerged from the Montecuore train station, his eyes fell on the welcome sight of Kristina Adimari sitting on the tailgate of her old white farm truck. After Leo had been ripped to shreds in the den of sour priests, the radiant woman in jeans and a light blue short-sleeve top, long hair fluttering in the breeze, was a vision of grace. Kristina scanned him up and down. "You left in your robe and returned in farm clothes."

"From the palace of illusion to the manger of simplicity," he said with a stoic grin. "Shall we grab an espresso?"

Twenty minutes and one dark recount later, the two sat at Donato's café clinking their tiny cups in a toast. "To our new life!" Kristina's face shone brighter than Leo had seen since the morning he had delivered the grim news.

"And to our brightest dreams," he added. As the two sipped their drinks, Kristina gazed glassy-eyed for a long moment out the window. Leo touched her arm as if to wake her up. "Where did you go?"

Embarrassed, Kristina forced herself to speak. "When I was a little girl I had a recurring dream of living in a white city at the top of a mountain, surrounded by majestic green peaks. Looking down, I could see a river a thousand feet below. I could hear it roar as it caught the rain from waterfalls cascading down from the heavens."

Leo smiled softly. "Sounds magical."

"Years later, my high school teacher Miss Bari gave a lesson on Machu Picchu, the lost city of the Incas, high above the clouds in the Andes. When she showed us pictures of the city, I was stunned. It was the place I had dreamed about . . . Leo, I *knew* the place, as if I had lived there my whole life."

"And you've never gone there?"

Kristina shook her head. "I was raising Paolo, and when he grew up he was struggling for money. I gave him what I could, and saved a little bit. I just couldn't justify going off on a whirlwind vacation. It seemed so . . . self-indulgent."

Leo took Kristina's hand and gave it a gentle squeeze.

"I never forgot about the place. Sometimes I still dream about it."

Leo pulled Kristina's hand toward him and looked her squarely in the eyes. "Then let's go."

"Go where?"

"To Machu Picchu . . . You and me. . . I have some money saved."

Kristina leaned back, wrinkled her forehead, and laughed nervously. "Are you crazy?"

"Maybe. But maybe it's time for something crazy, Kristina. Both of our lives have just turned upside down. Paolo's gone and so is my vocation. We're both starting over. Let's make up for the time we've been apart. Let's live the life we wish we had lived. What do you say?"

"I don't know what to say. . ."

"Then repeat after me: 'Yes, Leo, I would love to go to Machu Picchu with you.'"

Kristina looked around the café as if to be sure no one was listening. Then she stared down at the table for the longest time. Leo reached across the table and gently lifted her chin until he found her eyes. Small tears were forming. Finally she nodded. "Yes, Leo, I would love to go to Machu Picchu with you."

Leo smiled. "There! That wasn't so hard, was it?"

"Not if you don't count the twenty-seven years I have been fantasizing about you asking me that."

*Baghdad*
*September 10*

# Lauren 26

Baghdad Airport was surprisingly modern, clean, and pleasant. Even in the wake of the abominable Hussein regime, incessant war, and social turmoil, the terminal appeared to be functioning, business as usual. That is, until Lauren noticed American soldiers slowly patrolling, rifles over shoulders. Apparently the U.S. was not out of the country, despite what the public had been told.

Lauren's culture shock thickened when she observed Arab women in line for immigration clearance. Most were clothed in thick, dark *abaya*. The idea of hiding her body or kowtowing to a patriarchy was totally foreign to this sophisticated millennial. Yet she was in no position to protest now. Having been warned to keep her arms and legs covered, or else she might not be granted entry, she reached to pull down the arm-length sleeve of her beige blouse.

When the immigration officer saw Brianna approach his window, he blanched as if he'd seen a ghost. The few white women in the country were in the military, and they flew in on army planes. No American civilian, especially young, female, blonde, attractive, with a butterfly tattoo on her neck, would dare walk the streets of Baghdad alone. After the officer ran her passport through the electronic reader, he turned to his computer monitor and spent a long few minutes reading something suspiciously. Finally he turned back, offered a forced small smile, and stamped her passport. *Dr. Chung has done his homework.*

As Lauren exited customs, her stomach twisted into a knot. *What if Chung doesn't show up? What if he can't cure me? What if I die in Iraq? God, what a horrible way to end a life that I thought was just beginning.*

Before she could dig herself any deeper into a pit of despair, Lauren was relieved to see the figure of Dr. Jian Chung standing at the lobby gate. True to his photo except for a few added pounds and more gray hair, his face exuded a kind, fatherly demeanor. The tears on her cheeks told her that she had been more anxious than she had realized.

Dr. Chung smiled and waved. She approached him and, to her surprise, reached out to hug the man. Lauren was not a hugger, but her defenses had been nearly decimated and her desperation outflanked reason.

The healer accepted her hug modestly. "Welcome to The Country Most Off the Tourist Map," he said with an impish smile. His voice was soft yet firm, his Chinese accent noticeable but not overwhelming.

"Thank you so much for answering my email and seeing me," she blurted, wiping her cheek with the back of her hand. "You don't know how hard this has been for me."

The doctor reached into his pocket, removed a purple cloth pouch, and emptied a dozen little tablets into Lauren's hand. Some were small, gray, oblong, and porous; others black, spherical, shiny, and hard; they reminded Lauren of the BB's her brother and his friends used to shoot in the back yard. Chung reached into his other pocket and pulled out a small plastic bottle of water. "Take these now," he said. "We can't waste any time." Lauren was tempted to ask him what she was ingesting, but decided to just go with it; jeez, her whole trip was an act of faith. The little pills tasted awful, but she forced herself to down them; it took several swigs of water to do the job.

"Very good," said Dr. Chung. "Now, let me take your bag and we can get on with getting you well."

Sweeter words, to Lauren Delaney, were never spoken.

# Kenton 26

Kenton Baine quivered as he gazed up at the enormous gray monoliths of Stonehenge. The towering rock formation seemed to have a life of its own, ringing with echoes of the sacred rituals of the Druids who erected the giant stones nearly five thousand years ago. Ten paces away, a tour guide told a group, "To create this mysterious solar calendar, thirty-ton slabs were quarried and transported more than a hundred miles—an astounding achievement even by today's technological standards."

Kenton pulled up his collar to offset the raw, windy day. As he watched a foreboding rain cloud approach at a distance, he marveled at how thick-skinned those ancient people must have been to endure the bone-chilling British climate.

"Good morning, Mr. Baine," he heard a woman's voice speak. He turned to find the BBC reporter in a maroon knee-length coat and a matching beret. She offered a smile that Kenton sensed camouflaged a more serious agenda. "Welcome to our national treasure."

"Hello, Megan," Kenton returned with a cautious smile as he gestured toward the woman at his side. "This is my friend Yoshi."

Megan reached out and politely shook Kenton's hand, then Yoshi's. Yoshi bowed her head slightly.

"Why are we here?" Kenton asked, locking eyes with the woman.

"Just give me a moment." Megan walked to a guard posted at the rope railing that kept tourists a distance from the stones. She showed him a paper, he nodded, and Megan motioned for her guests to follow her as she held up the rope while they ducked under it. "Press privilege," she smiled as she stepped ahead to take the lead. "Just don't touch any of the stones."

Thrilled at the private entrée, Kenton followed his guide to the center of the enigmatic formation. He extended his arms and made a slow, silent 360-degree sweep, imagining he was a Celtic priest surveying the mythic astronomical computer so very long ago. Megan and Yoshi looked on respectfully, watching the serious scientist morph into a little boy.

When Kenton completed his ritual, Megan led the pair to a spot behind a huge slab that shielded the trio from the eyes and ears of tourists. She looked from side to side to make sure no one was within earshot. "We don't have much time, so I'll be brief. I was impressed by what I saw at the café the other night. I, for one, do not believe the information you received is a hoax. If it is, it's a very good one."

Kenton tried to read her eyes. She seemed sincere.

"Someone high in the BBC wants to follow up on the data you received. I can't tell you his name, but he has the power to move the BBC in any direction he chooses."

Kenton and Yoshi shot each other curious glances. "What does he want to do?" asked Yoshi.

"He wants to do a simultaneous live television feed from the sites you downloaded—at the moment of equinox."

A chill ran the length of Kenton's body. "Smart move . . . What do you want from us?"

Megan's face grew more intent. "You seem to have a unique connection with whoever is communicating this information. If you get any more details, we ask that you pass them along to us." She stopped and squeezed her face together like a child about to step into a body of cold water. "If this is a hoax, I would really appreciate you telling me now before we make complete asses of ourselves, and my boss and I lose our jobs."

"As far as we know, this is for real," Kenton stated firmly. "If it's fake, we've been fooled too."

Megan nodded. "That's what I thought. You don't seem like the hoaxing type."

The guard approached. "I'm afraid your time is up," he announced, British-politely.

Jeffries nodded to the guard and turned back to the pair. "I'll be in touch with you. Please don't leave London." She handed Kenton her business card. "This could be very, very big." Then she grimaced. "Or very, very embarrassing."

*Cairo*
*September 27*

# Brianna 27

"Are you ready for take two, Brianna?" Aviva Roth asked as the uneasy student emerged from her suite's bedroom, smoothing out a wrinkle on her tan slacks.

Brianna mustered a fake smile. "No more than I was for take one, Mrs. Roth. But I will do what I said I would do. Then I will get the first flight out to go home to take care of my mom."

Aviva placed a comforting hand on Brianna's shoulder. "You're a brave young woman, Brianna. I wish I had your guts when I was your age. I did everything my parents told me, including marry the man of their choice when I was eighteen." She pursed her lips. "I'm not complaining, mind you—I couldn't find a kinder husband than Isaac. But if I had it to do over again, I would take some time to get to know myself and find out who I am before diving into marriage."

Brianna was taken aback by the woman's honesty; this was the first time she had volunteered personal information. Just then Aviva's phone rang with her *Jerusalem of Gold* ringtone. She paused and studied Caller I.D. Isaac. Speaker on.

"Where are you?" he asked.

"Just leaving Brianna's room."

"Don't go anywhere. Redmond and I are coming up."

Five minutes later Professor Hathaway was panting as he stepped into Brianna's suite, as if he had jogged down the long hotel corridor. His brow was sweaty, cheeks flushed, gray laptop tucked under his arm. Isaac Roth labored to catch up. Aviva rushed toward the professor. "Are you alright?" she asked.

"Ladies, please sit down."

The two women shot each other confused looks as they took a seat on the white leather couch. Hathaway squeezed in between them and opened his computer.

"This morning I found a YouTube video in my feed, posted by an Israeli professor," Hathaway began, starting to catch his breath. He clicked the touchpad and a video appeared, showing a thin, pale, mid-thirties man with smooth skin and a light brown beard. He wore a yellow short-sleeve button-down shirt atop jeans. The man stood at a lectern, behind him a blue wall bearing the Tel Aviv University insignia in white lettering. A movie screen hung center wall. Below him a caption read, "Dr. Zvi Epstein, Professor of Linguistics." He began to speak in Hebrew, the English translation scrolling at the bottom of the screen.

"When I saw Stonehenge on yesterday's worldwide broadcast, I noticed a crop formation in a field in the distant background. I have been interested in the phenomenon for years, especially the one with apparent binary code." Epstein clicked a remote-control wand, and the binary formation photo appeared on the screen. "That circle is contiguous with the formation that resembles the face of Jesus." The Christ image formation appeared on the screen. "To date, no one has been able to decode the pattern." The professor zoomed in on the dotted markings within the circle.

"Everyone who has tried to decipher the code has been working in English, the default global language of science. Jesus did not speak English. He spoke Aramaic, an ancient language very similar to Hebrew."

Dr. Epstein motioned to someone off-camera, and another man approached the podium. He was younger, round-faced, wearing thick brown-framed glasses. Epstein placed a hand on his shoulder.

"I contacted my colleague here, Dr. Nachum Cooperman, a highly respected programmer at the university. His book *Code Write Now* has become a standard textbook in many college courses."

Cooperman picked up the thread. "Working together, we approached the binary pattern as if it were written in Aramaic, rather than English."

"Here is what we discovered," said Epstein as he clicked the wand again.

Brianna watched a series of white Aramaic letters overlay the dark green formation background:

ܟܝ ܟ ܕ ܐܪ ܐ ܝܬ ܒܝܝ ܝܝܡ ܒܝܘ

ܟܝ ܐܪ ܐ ܝܬ ܟܝܡ ܝܝܡ ܛ

ܟ ܐܬܩܥܚ ܚܬܗ ܪܠܗܝܬ ܐ

ܝܒܝ ܚܬܗ ܒܠܣ

"Here's the English translation," said Epstein. The letters on the screen morphed to:

**I will not return as one.**
**I will return as all.**
**Don't look for me in a body.**
**Look for me in your heart.**

# *Driscoll 27*

Driscoll Ames stared up at the CIA meeting room ceiling for a long time, then turned to face his host. "This is a bit too out there even for me," he answered Carlton Pierce. "Maybe we should leave close encounters to Spielberg."

Pierce ignored his suggestion and pulled a small blue jewelry box out of his jacket pocket. He slid it across the table to Ames.

"What's this? . . . A magic Flash Gordon ring that will call the mothership when I rub it?"

Pierce motioned with his head as if to say, "Just open it."

Ames opened the box to find a gray USB flash drive.

"You will find files containing all the segments broadcast at the end of the transmissions, separately and also in one file with all the pieces," said Adkar. "We've added the image Spencer showed you with the 'End is Near' message."

"If you could open the files and have a look at them, you might get some ideas," Leona Wentworth added.

Ames held the flash drive up to the light and studied it. "Sure, I can look at it." He placed the drive back in the box and stuffed it in his jacket pocket. Ames crossed his arms and thought for a long moment. He turned to Pierce. "I'll make you a deal."

Pierce cocked his head, curious.

"Two things: There is a scientist in England, Brian Turner, who was kidnapped a month ago. Word on the street has it that you know who was behind the job . . . I want you to spring him."

Pierce went stone-faced, but Driscoll could see the wheels in his head turning. He opened up his laptop, clicked a few keys, and studied a screen for a length of time. Finally he looked up. "Can do."

Ames turned toward General Watson. "Next, I want the army to release the files on Aeromexico Flight 191."

Watson grimaced. "Those files are Top Secret, Lieutenant. You've worked in Intelligence. If we reverse our public statement on that crash, the army will lose all credibility."

Ames laughed sarcastically. "That already happened with your rookie 'protecting cyberspace' yarn. Not to mention the 'crashed weather balloon' tale. Who thinks up these things?" He paused for a moment. "But I understand. How about if you leak the files anonymously to Cheryl Lansing? She'll publish them. Then the doubters will be able to argue, but the people who want to know the truth will be satisfied."

Watson crossed his arms and shook his head. "That's a huge ask, Lieutenant."

Ames rose and slowly headed toward the door like a customer walking away from a car salesman who made him a crappy offer. "Very well, we can just let the end that is near come, and you will see how respected the army is—if it still exists." He kept walking.

"Lieutenant, wait," Watson called out. He took a heavy breath. "I will put the mechanics into motion."

Ames continued toward the door, and then turned around. "One more item for your laundry list." Everyone in the room, already quite upended, faced Driscoll. Pierce spoke. "Wait, don't tell me—you want us to tell the world who killed JFK."

Ames snickered. "I'm sure that would satisfy a lot of people, but this is a lot simpler." He turned to Major General Hazelden. "I want you to contact Navy top brass and have them reverse the dishonorable discharge of Aaron Henderson, reinstate him, and promote him."

Hazelden thought for a moment, and nodded. "Done."

"Thank you all," Ames said as he turned toward the door with a smug smile. "Wow, this day turned out even better than I hoped."

## Leo 27

The train ride from Ollantaytambo to Aguas Calientes, the tiny town at the base of Machu Picchu, was more of a journey through dimensions than geography. The noisy steam engine pulled a chain of red passenger cars down the thirty-mile downward slope, penetrating into thicker and thicker jungle. On the left, the sacred river Urubamba roared more boisterously with each passing mile. Peering out the wide glass picture window, Leo observed small villages of native Peruvians sporting their signature brown bowler hats and colorful shawls. A hundred years had not altered the scene.

When the train arrived at Aguas Calientes, the story changed. The moment Leo and Kristina stepped off the train, they were besieged by men, women, and children shoving jewelry, carved wooden totems, hats, post cards, T-shirts, and snow globes in their faces. When Leo stopped to purchase a carved statue of Mother Mary he thought Sister Isabel might like, he noticed that the little vendor boy, maybe seven years old, had a twisted arm. Leo winced as he recalled the fellow on the train who told him that some beggar parents maim their children so they will garner tourists' sympathy and fetch more sales. He gave the boy a few extra coins and kissed him on the top of the head. The child lit up. "God bless you, mister," the boy spouted in rickety English.

Soon the couple found themselves crammed in the back of a crowded bus, suitcases on their laps, scaling the switchback up the steep mountainside to the once-obscure but now global destination city. All the passengers were tourists, speaking many different languages, cameras pointed out the open-air windows below rolled-up khaki cloth shades. As the creaking rusted vehicle negotiated sharp hairpin curves, Leo grew queasy; one false turn and the bus would plummet hundreds of feet to the river below. But when he saw little boys running up the hill in a straight line, meeting the bus as it reversed on each successive switchback, he relaxed.

Up, up, up the old bus cranked, a thirteen-hundred-foot rise from the valley floor (already at a seven-thousand-foot elevation) to the summit. Yet the ascent was no challenge to the locals. Leo had read about native guides leading visitors over the legendary twenty-six-mile Inca Trail, ascending as high as fourteen thousand feet, ending at Machu Picchu. While tourists huffed and puffed, begging for time to rest, the five-foot-tall Peruvians gingerly carried their guests' massive heavy packs, wearing only T-shirts, shorts, and rubber flip-flops.

Finally the bus arrived at the top of the mountain and the passengers streamed out. Leo and Kristina turned to find themselves standing before the Machu Picchu Sanctuary Lodge, the only place to sojourn at the summit. Operated by the government and in high demand, the inn is booked a year in advance. Yet a phone call from the Vatican to the Cusco church had magically caused a vacant room to appear.

Leo wandered twenty paces from the bus and turned toward the west. There it was: Machu Picchu, the lost city of the Incas. Shrouded in clouds like the mists of history that still veil its secrets, the place seemed to float like an other-worldly vision. The many tiers of rock-walled terraces seemed to form a staircase to heaven.

A bus pulled up and a group of Australian tourists poured out, pointing their cameras. The guide, a short frosted-haired woman in a yellow jumpsuit, adorned with large round sunglasses and a big floppy white hat, corralled their attention. "The city was constructed so high and remotely to protect against Spanish conquistadors and invasions by native tribes," she projected in a well-practiced voice. "Yet historians still cannot tell us how and why the culture disappeared almost overnight, leaving the complex settlement fully intact. It was overtaken by dense jungle until British explorer Hiram Bingham stumbled upon it in 1911."

The tourists jockeyed for position to get the best pictures of themselves with the classic scene in the background. Leo was more interested in the story. "Legend has it that the ghosts of the ancients still roam the ruins, frightening tourists who sneak into the city at night," the guide went on. "So I don't recommend you enter without a guide. If the guards don't catch you, the evil spirits will."

As the tourists laughed, Leo wondered if there might be more to the joke than the audience realized. As the Australians scattered, he took a slow breath and tried to absorb the staggering scene. In two days the fall equinox would signal the balance of light and darkness. *Will this troubled world ever see the light of kindness outshine the darkness in men's hearts?*

*Nasiriyah, Iraq*
*September 10*

# Lauren 27

The three-and-a-half-hour drive from Baghdad to Nasiriyah was anything but pretty. Mercilessly hot; dry, dusty desert in all directions; barely a green living thing. Thank God that Dr. Chung's car had air conditioning and he let Lauren lie down in the back seat and sleep.

When the station wagon finally pulled up to the physician's home on the outskirts of town, Lauren was immensely relieved to get out of the car. She scanned the neighborhood of a handful of run-down tan mud-like houses with dogs barking and kids playing on grassless yards. Chung grabbed Lauren's bag and guided her through a side door. The place was simple yet clean, part living quarters and part make-shift clinic. In the private area Lauren laid eyes on a rickety kitchen table with wooden chairs, a threadbare burgundy couch, and a few thinly-padded chairs in the living area. That was it.

Dr. Chung motioned toward the clinic door. "I know you want to sleep, Lauren, but I need to check your vital signs." He ushered Lauren into the small side room and asked her to lie down on an examining table. There he lifted Lauren's right wrist and quietly held it between his thumb and forefinger for half a minute, his eyes closed as he gauged her energetic pulses.

Then he asked her to show him her tongue. She felt silly sticking her tongue out, but then remembered she used to do that when the local doctor visited her elementary school and pressed her tongue down with a thin wooden stick. Chung seemed quite intrigued with her tongue—she couldn't imagine what was going on there that could be so interesting.

"You are showing signs of heavy fatigue—but that's natural after the trip you made and what you've been through."

She looked at him nervously. Dr. Chung didn't have to be a mind reader to figure out her question.

"I detect some effects of the poison; your lung meridian is weak. But your constitution is strong and I think we can stay ahead of the issue. If you are willing to stay here this week, I can treat you several times a day with herbs, acupuncture, and diet. With some luck, you will be okay."

Tears again. *This man is saving my life.*

"What were you doing at Project Genesis?" he asked as he stepped back and leaned against a small glass-doored wooden cabinet containing jars filled with colorful powders, herbs, and teas.

"I was visiting my former boyfriend Todd. Do you remember him?"

Chung nodded. "A tall, thin fellow with sandy hair. Talks a lot."

"That's him," she laughed.

"How did you contact the poison?"

*The one memory I wish I could forget.* "Todd found some and we wanted to get rid of it. I was pouring it on the ground and my hand slipped."

Chung just listened. Lauren knew he was not convinced. She never was a good liar. *Can he read my mind like my invisible pulses?*

"You'd better get some sleep," he said dryly. Even if he knew she was lying, he didn't seem to care. "I'll show you to my 'luxurious' guest room," he said with a playful smile. "We can continue your treatment in the morning."

*Beaconsfield*
*September 21*

# Kenton 27

At 11 AM on the fall equinox, Kenton Baine walked out of the Satos' condo and unlocked the driver's door of the Astra. His mind flew to the thousands of people who had converged on Stonehenge that morning to capture the first ray of sun as it struck a precise point on the central monolith like a laser. The spectators would find the BBC film crew and believe they were on a routine shoot. Megan Jeffries and the BBC executive who had ordered the project would remain in place for the entire day, anxiously awaiting the cryptic 4:27 PM moment. Would the circle makers materialize and explain the crop formations? Would a spaceship land and give humanity technology that would save the planet? Or would they inform us that the world is just too far gone, and there is nothing more they can do to help us? Or maybe this was all just a big nothing burger. Kenton pictured himself and Megan slinking away from the huge gray blocks, tails tucked between legs, apologetic pawns in some cosmic practical joke.

"Kenton!" Yoshi called from the steps of the condo. "Come quickly, please!"

Kenton turned and ran to her. "What's the matter?"

"It's mom . . . her asthma. She gets attacks when she is nervous."

"What can we do?"

"We need to take her to the hospital. Dad doesn't drive."

Kenton's heart sank. The biggest thrill of his life had just given way to the deepest disappointment.

Yoshi looked so sad. "I know this is such an important day for you, Kenton. The whole TV shoot is because we found those GPS markers. If you don't show up, people will think we are liars or cowards."

Kenton sighed and then issued a kind smile. "So what? We know what we are. Your mom is more important."

A glow of gratitude spilled over Yoshi's face. She leaned up and kissed Kenton on the cheek. The nerdy teacher stood quietly for a long moment. He didn't remember ever having been kissed so sweetly.

# *Brianna 28*

---

Brianna stared at the words overlaying the crop circle on Professor Hathaway's laptop screen. "'Don't look for me in one body'—Does this mean that your idea to rebirth Christ is out the window?"

Hathaway sighed and nodded. "Apparently his appearance on Earth in the body of Jesus was a one-time visit." The professor, though obviously disappointed, looked relaxed for the first time since he had proposed this bizarre experiment.

"What about all the people waiting for the second coming?"

Hathaway issued a wistful snicker. "If you visited a place to help and heal as many people as possible, and you were brutally murdered, would you be quick to drop in again?"

"And if people still haven't lived the message you taught them two thousand years ago," Roth added, "would you teach them more?"

Brianna smirked. "I see your point."

"Isaac and I have discussed this at great length. We asked for a sign, and we got it. We have been too focused on his body, while it is his energy that made him who he was. So, my dear Brianna, in spite of how much we wanted this to work, we're going to have to let the project go."

A huge wave of relief washed through Brianna's body. She had no idea how tense she had become. She leaned back on the couch, looked up at the ceiling, and whispered loud enough for all to hear, "Thank you, Jesus. You just saved my ass."

*Bimini*
*September 27*

# Driscoll 28

---

Driscoll Ames stood on the weathered wooden deck behind the old beach house and gazed at the white-capped Caribbean Sea. The smell of salt air and the song of seagulls soaring through twilight reminded him of the walks on the beach he took with Ticia before she died. *God, I wish she was here.*

He turned to go inside and noticed that Marifer had left her computer turned on in the living room before she and Kendall had gone out for the evening. The flash drive that Carlton Pierce gave him continued to haunt him. With no one home, Driscoll went to his room and pulled the small blue box from under his shirts in the dresser drawer. He returned to the computer, inserted the drive in the USB slot, and began to study the scrambled images.

Just then Driscoll heard the front door slam, followed by heavy footsteps on the creaking wooden floor. He turned to see Kendall.

"I thought you were going out."

"Marifer forgot her phone." Kendall noticed the images on the monitor. "What's that on the screen?"

"Some data I got from the military."

Kendall placed his hands on the back of Driscoll's chair, leaned forward, and studied the picture. Driscoll wished the man had showered.

"You know the Wi-Fi interruption and broadcast?" Driscoll asked.

"Sure."

"These are all the closing segments."

Kendall stretched forward to study the pictures more closely. "Looks like a million odd pieces."

"A hundred-forty-four thousand, to be exact."

Kendall looked jarred and leaned in farther as Driscoll kept clicking through the images, until he pulled up the final image with all the pieces dumped into one file.

"What do they think it is?"

"Some kind of jigsaw puzzle of the Earth."

Kendall read down to the bottom of the picture.

"'*The End is Near*' . . . Where did those words come from?"

"They were the only pieces imbedded in the mess that the analysts could fit together."

Kendall fell silent for a while, lost in thought. Driscoll turned to see his cousin's eyes glowing. "You okay?"

"Yeah, yeah, I'm cool," he answered almost nervously. "Sorry, man, I have to go. Prayer meeting starts soon."

*Machu Picchu*
*September 20*

## Leo 28

Dinner at the Machu Picchu Sanctuary Lodge required guests to dine family style at long, colorfully draped tables where waiters delivered generous terrines of mysterious but tasty local dishes. Seated beside Leo and Kristina were five British guys who didn't seem much like tourists, their talk dotted with electronic tech lingo. The blokes seemed amiable enough, repeatedly toasting mugs brimming with frothy *Cusqueña* beer. One of the men invited the rest of the guests at the table to raise their glasses toward a successful project.

"What are you guys doing here?" Leo asked in his best English.

"We're from the BBC, on a shoot."

"A tourist documentary?" Kristina asked.

The fellow's face contorted. He turned to the guy sitting next to him, who shrugged his shoulders and cocked his head as if to say, "Sure, go ahead."

"Well, to be honest, we're not exactly sure what we're shooting. That's pretty embarrassing for me to tell you, since I'm the director. Ian's my name." He extended his hand to Leo.

"You traveled all the way from England and you don't know why?"

"That's pretty much it, mate," Ian came back with a soused laugh. "It has something to do with the fall equinox. Tomorrow morning at 10:27 something is supposed to happen. What that is, we have no idea. Our instructions are simply to station ourselves around the settlement and shoot. Whatever we see will be broadcast back to England and around the world."

"How odd that they would send you here and not tell you what you are going to broadcast!" Kristina commented.

"Weirdest assignment I've ever been on," he said, downing another swig of beer. "When I pressed my boss for details, he said he couldn't tell me."

"Sometimes I feel the same way," said Leo as he raised his glass.

# *Lauren 28*

---

When Lauren opened her eyes, it took her a while to figure out where she was. She sat up on her elbows and scanned the room. The faded yellow stucco walls, sparse décor, heat penetrating the windows, and barren desert outside the bedroom window reminded her that she was very far from home.

She rubbed her arms to make sure she was still alive. Affirmative. If Dr. Chung knew what he was doing, she would stay that way. If not, she might have the dubious honor of being the first victim of a holocaust that would blindside humanity.

Lauren slipped out of bed, used a primitive bathroom she would never be caught in elsewhere, threw on her black shorts and purple tank top, and found her way into the kitchen. Her host stood at the stove, his back to her, lifting a tea kettle from the burner. He gracefully poured water into two teacups set on a counter beside the stove.

Dr. Chung turned and carried both cups to the kitchen table, as if he knew Lauren would arrive at that moment. The healer smiled and motioned for her to sit as he poured tea. In a smaller cup she found another collection of pills like the ones she had taken yesterday. She downed the group in three stages, washing them down with the bitter tea.

"How are you feeling this morning, Lauren?"

Her eyes widened. "What a difference a day makes."

Her host nodded and sat down in a chair opposite her.

"May I ask you a personal question, Dr. Chung?"

"Of course."

"What are you doing here? This place is way off the beaten path. I know you said you are in Iraq on a medical mercy mission, but this is the middle of nowhere. I imagine there are lots more people you could help in Baghdad or Beijing."

Chung took a long, slow sip. "You are very perceptive, Lauren. The sign of a clear mind."

*Well, that might be going a bit too far.*

"Yes, I am here to help people in pain. But I have another purpose."

"Are you, like, a spy?"

He laughed. "I would make a terrible spy. If I try to lie, I get a headache."

"Then what?"

"I'm here to witness something."

"Such as . . .?"

Dr. Chung stood and walked to a small altar he had set up in the living room. He picked up a weathered wood-framed photo of an old Chinese man with a bald head, thick eyebrows, and white Fu Manchu beard. Chung studied the photo for a long moment, as if he was conversing with the soul behind the image. Then he set the picture on the kitchen table facing his guest. "In China I studied with Master Hue-Tsu, the most gifted and respected practitioner of Chinese medicine in the last century."

Lauren examined the picture. It was very old, faded, and cracked. Yet even through the imperfections Lauren detected the same glow in the master's eyes that she recognized in his disciple Chung.

"I was with Hue-Tsu before he died. He gave me teachings no one else received. If he had gone to the grave without imparting these truths, the world would have lost such precious jewels forever."

Lauren gazed more intently at the man in the photograph. She felt his presence.

"Hue-Tsu revealed to me certain ancient Chinese prophecies passed down through the ages. They are based on many elements, including astrology, numerology, the energetic configuration of the Earth, choices humanity was making, and messages from invisible sources."

*Oh, man. Here we go. . .*

"Master Tsu told me that at a place near here, an event would occur that would shake the world. When the Iraqi war broke out, I thought that was what he meant. But he said that the event would be very positive. For a moment a portal would open that would give humanity access to wisdom that could change its destiny. The veils of illusion would part, enabling human beings to see into the heavens and be lifted from the dregs to which the world has descended."

Lauren leaned forward, elbows on the table, chin on her hands. "What kind of event?"

Dr. Chung shrugged. "I wish I knew. That's all my mentor told me. But since so many of his other prophecies have come true, I don't question this one."

Lauren looked out the window at the stark terrain. *Might as well be the moon.* "Why here? This place seems so . . . lifeless."

"It wasn't always that way. A very long time ago this area, especially where the Tigris and Euphrates rivers meet—now Baghdad—was a lush paradise. Some anthropologists believe this was the original Garden of Eden, where the human race originated."

A shiver ran up Lauren's spine.

"Then why aren't you in Baghdad?"

"Another significant event occurred just miles from where you are sitting."

Dr. Chung went to the window and pointed toward the desert. "This land was once called 'Ur.' There are many references to it in the Old Testament. Even more important, it was the epicenter of the civilization called Sumer, where a miraculous event occurred."

"Such as?"

"Unprecedented and unexplainable advances in human knowledge and civilization. Some people believe that was the result of intervention from galactic visitors."

Lauren struggled to overcome her urge to make a smart-ass comment. "But that was a very long time ago. What does that have to do with us sitting here today?"

Chung sat and faced Lauren squarely. "Master Tsu said there is going to be another intervention of some kind and that it was extremely important that I be here at this time."

Lauren sat speechless.

"And now you are here too, Lauren. All the events that led to you being here are no accident."

She made a face. "Oh, come on . . . Spilling that horrible poison on my hand was no accident?"

"No accidents, Lauren. None."

# Kenton 28

The waiting room at the Macy Medical Centre was homey with wood paneling, cushioned chairs, a tea dispenser, and colorful magazines on the coffee table. A TV was broadcasting cricket finals at low volume. One other person sat in the area, a skinny long-haired kid about seventeen, leather jacket, skull tattoo on the back of his hand, absorbed in his phone. Kenton looked at his watch: 3:25. A little over an hour until the bombastic—or utterly disappointing—event.

He opened his phone and scanned for news of the Stonehenge broadcast. *Nada.* Apparently Megan's boss had decided to play it safe and leak nothing to the media. If something happened, it would be a surprise. If not, his reputation would be spared.

Kenton took a pained breath and dialed. He hoped he would get a voicemail and leave a message. But then, "Hello?"

"Megan, this is Kenton."

"Where are you? We're waiting for you."

"I'm so sorry, Megan, we have an emergency. Yoshi's mom had an asthma attack and we had to take her to the hospital."

Silence. Kenton could feel the reporter struggling to gather herself.

"So you're not coming?"

Kenton sighed. "We can't leave Yoshi's mom now."

Another thick pause. "You're sure you didn't make up this whole story?"

"Of course not. You know as much about this as we do."

*Sigh.* "Okay, I'll tell the producer. He'll be disappointed."

"So are we. Please convey my apologies."

Kenton started to hang up. "Kenton," he heard the woman say, almost desperately.

"Yes?"

"If this flops, I'm coming back to New Jersey with you. You'll have to get me a whole new identity like they do in the witness protection program."

Kenton laughed. "I'll have to drop out too. But then I can live out my secret fantasy of being a rock drummer."

Yoshi, returning from her mom's examining room, leaned over and chimed in, "And I will do body painting."

As Kenton hung up, he chuckled. "Why do we need a disaster to give ourselves permission to live the life we love?"

# *Brianna 29*

---

As Brianna zipped her suitcase, she scanned the luxury suite her sponsors had provided for her. *I don't imagine I'll see a place like this again anytime soon.* She turned and gazed out the window at the towering pyramids. Fascinating as her trip had been, she would not miss Cairo. A blanket spread on the grass at Central Park would be the holiest pilgrimage for her.

Brianna picked up her phone and texted her brother: Procedure cancelled. Coming home tomorrow.

As she wheeled her bag toward the door, her phone rang. Brad.

"What happened?" he asked, nervous voice.

"It's a long story, Brad. I don't feel like going into it now. I'm pretty beat. The experiment is off. Can I tell you when I get home?"

"I was going to call you anyway," he spurted. "Mom had some kind of breakdown. When dad came home last night he found her sitting in the bathtub under the shower in her clothes, crying. She's a basket case, Bri. I've never seen her like this before."

Brianna's gut clenched. "Now what?"

"She needs someone to be with her 24/7 until we get her into a facility. I'm taking a week off of work. I'll stay at the house so dad can go to work." *Now for the elephant in the room.* "What are we going to do without the money Hathaway was going to give you? That was the answer to our prayers."

Brianna felt her neck and shoulders stiffen. "We'll just have to find some other way. He gave me five grand up front off his credit card. The college froze his salary until they resolve the charges against him. The money for the experiment isn't his, anyway. He has some investor who paid all the expenses until now, but the big bucks are contingent on the result. They're not gonna pay me for something that didn't happen."

Long tense silence. "If we can't get mom into a facility, we're screwed."

*He never melts down like this.*

"I'll be home soon, Brad. We'll figure it out. I can take the semester off and put off grad school. Mom comes first."

Brad issued a sigh of minor relief. "Text me your flight info. I'll pick you up."

*One crazy scene gives way to another.*

# *Driscoll 29*

With blurry eyes Driscoll scanned the time on his phone. 6:15 AM. *Who the hell is calling at this hour?* He looked again. Cheryl. "Why are you waking me up?"

"Turn on CNN."

He shot the phone an annoyed look and pressed a few icons until the news site came up. A jolt thundered through his spine when he saw the image of the scrambled Earth he received from the CIA, complete with the "End is Near" message. He sat up ramrod straight.

The picture dissolved to a split screen showing a female Asian reporter on the left and his cousin Kendall on the right. Driscoll's stomach started to drop out.

"You are the cousin of Lieutenant Driscoll Ames, who recently made the famous alien photos disclosure?" the reporter asked.

"That's right," answered Kendall. Driscoll was shocked to see their Bimini living room in the background. He could hear Kendall's voice wafting up from downstairs.

"And Lieutenant Ames indicated he received this image from the military?"

"That's right. Researchers dumped all the little pieces from last week's transmission into one file. It appears to be pieces of the Earth all blown apart, along with a message."

Driscoll's gut clenched. *How stupid could I be to leave that flash drive in the computer?*

"Please explain to our viewers why you contacted CNN."

Kendall nodded smugly. "We now have the smoking gun proving that we are living in the end times. The world will soon be destroyed. The hundred-forty-four-thousand pieces symbolize the number of people who will be saved because they believe in Jesus Christ. Everyone on the planet should know about this so those who want to be saved can repent."

"No, no, no, no, no," Driscoll moaned as he offed the phone, fell back onto the bed, and pulled a pillow over his head.

*Machu Picchu*
*September 21*

# Leo 29

When Leo and Kristina arrived just after 9 AM at the entrance to the Machu Picchu ruins, they found the entrance blocked off with a rope railing, guards standing behind it. A large handwritten sign had been posted in Spanish and English: **We Sorry. Ruins Closed. Open Tomoro Morning**.

A throng of grumbling tourists milled about, stretching to see inside the ruins. Some tried to bribe the guards to let them in, without success. "What could be so important that they would close Machu Picchu?" Kristina asked.

The two worked their way to the railing and craned their necks to peer inside, hoping for a glimpse of something to explain the mystery. Just then, TV director Ian stepped out from inside the ruins to talk to one of the guards. As they spoke, he looked over the guard's shoulder and noticed Leo. Without a word, Ian lifted up the rope and beckoned the couple to slip under. When some other folks in the crowd tried to follow, the guard dropped the rope and said, "Sorry, these people are with the crew."

As they gained some distance from the crowd, Leo placed a grateful hand on Ian's shoulder. "Thank you."

"Least I can do for a drinking buddy," the Brit came back.

The couple followed Ian to a large flat grassy field near the middle of the ruins. Leo guessed that the place was a site for ancient community meetings or some kind of sports. Four cameras were set up on the outskirts of the field, two pointed at the field and the other two at the ruins from different angles. Whatever was going to happen, this crew wasn't going to miss it.

The couple seated themselves on a knee-high wall off to the side of the action and watched the crew checking their equipment. Kristina's eyes glowed like a little girl waiting for the town parade. Leo looked at his watch: 9:27—an hour until the great unknown event.

"Hey, what's going on?" he heard one of the cameramen call out.

Ian emerged from the control truck. "Did somebody just pull a plug?"

"I lost my signal too!" said a crew member who had been adjusting lighting.

In the distance, Leo could hear murmuring from the crowd outside the ruins. Through an archway he could see lots of people fidgeting with their smartphones and tablets, shaking them, trying to get them to work.

"Every damn wireless piece of equipment has failed!" Ian yelled, exasperated. "If we've lost our transmission signal, we're toast," he barked at the crew. "Go check inside the hotel. See if they have a signal." A young technician nodded and scampered off toward the building.

Ian approached Leo and Kristina. "Damnedest thing!" he spurted. "Never saw total transmission failure before."

He turned to Leo. "Did I hear you say you were a priest, or was I drunk?"

"Both."

"Can you put in a good word for us with the Bloke above? If we blow this shoot, they'll send us to Australia like convicts of old."

Leo laughed. "I'll see what I can do."

The crew kept tinkering with their equipment, growing more nervous as the countdown proceeded. The crew member returned from the hotel. "They have lost all Internet capability too. They are on cable. So it's not just our wireless signal."

"Shit!" the director spurted as he kicked a big rock.

# *Lauren 29*

"A lovely evening, isn't it?" Lauren heard a voice speak softly.

Dr. Jian Chung stepped onto the porch and sat on the rickety brown wooden bench beside her. Lauren gazed out at the amber and purple sunset, spread like a Maxfield Parish painting on the sprawling canvas of the stark desert. She turned to her host. "Thank you for taking such good care of me, Dr. Chung. For five days now you've given me herbs, acupuncture, good food, and kindness I've never known . . . I don't know how I will ever repay you."

He shook his head. "No need, Lauren. Seeing you get healthy is the best reward." He smiled softly. "This also helps me balance out my karma."

Lauren wrinkled her forehead. "What karma? You seem like such a good person."

The doctor continued to take in the stunning scene without turning his head. "When Malthus joined the Genesis community, I knew he was infusing dark energy. I should have spoken up before he influenced people there, but I remained silent. By the time I warned the community, he had brainwashed too many gullible minds. My helping you now is one small way of offsetting the evil he has wrought, which I might have prevented."

*OMG, I am part of his healing like he is part of mine.*

Lauren didn't want to push Chung any further on the dark story any more than she wanted to revisit it. *Best to change subject.* "Do you have a family?"

He nodded pensively. "An ex-wife and son."

Lauren squinted. "I didn't think of you as being married and divorced . . . You seem more like a monk."

"Even healers have family hardships," the elder answered with a sad smile. He took a long breath and fell silent, as if deciding whether or not to say more. Finally he said, "I had a daughter, but she died."

Lauren was stunned. She figured that Dr. Chung's daughter might have been about her own age had she lived.

"Lifen was eight years old when she caught a cold that gave way to pneumonia. There was no doctor in our little mountain village. We took her to a hospital, three hour's drive. Too late."

Lauren's heart sank. "I'm so sorry. That must have been devastating."

Chung stiffened as he tapped into the painful memory. "Soon afterward I began to study Chinese medicine. I learned that I could have healed Lifen with herbs from the forest near my village. I blamed myself for her death. But eventually I redirected my anger into a desire to help others. It brings me some comfort to think that my daughter's death led to saving other people's lives."

Lauren was at a loss for words. *Even this great soul is not immune to the sorrows of the world.*

Chung relaxed a bit as he got the bitter memory off his chest. He turned toward his guest. "How about you, Lauren? Do you have a family?"

"My mother lives near me. I see her once a week. She is not healthy or happy. My father was an alcoholic. He left when I was five. I was glad. All he did was fight with my mother. He used to beat me. I never saw him again."

Chung listened carefully, taking in her account, compassion filling his eyes. "Then I'm glad we have met," he replied, leaving a long pause. Then he turned to face Lauren and told her, "I would like to be the father you never had."

Lauren could hardly believe what she was hearing. Tears began to well up in her throat. How many nights had she cried herself to sleep as a little girl, wishing she had a real father? Over the years, she had given up ever expecting a man to be there for her. Maybe that was why she kept attracting wishy-washy commitment phobes. With each failed relationship, another layer of protection grew over her heart. To hear a man tell her that he wanted to care for her, even in a fatherly way, was way out of her reality. Her shock must have been obvious.

Dr. Chung gently reached his arm around Lauren's shoulder. As a single tear cascaded down her cheek, she rested her head on his shoulder as he smoothed her hair— something her dad had never done. *Did I have to nearly die and fly halfway around the world to some forsaken place to find a man who would be kind to me?*

*Beaconsfield*
*September 21*

# Kenton 29

"Excuse me, can I log on to your router?" Kenton asked the hospital receptionist. "There's no signal in the waiting room, and I have a business emergency."

The receptionist fiddled with her computer, eyes squinting at the monitor. "That's so weird! I have no wireless signal, but I can get data and send messages to and from the other hospital departments. It's all on wireless."

Kenton's scientific mind tried to put all the pieces together. It couldn't. He threaded his way through a maze of white-curtained cubicles until he found Mrs. Sato lying on a gurney with an oxygen tube in her nostrils. Color had returned to her cheeks and she appeared more relaxed. Yoshi stood at the foot of the gurney, her father planted in a chair beside his wife. Kenton took her hand. "I'm glad you're feeling better, Mrs. Sato."

The woman smiled softly and nodded. "We're waiting for the doctor," said Yoshi.

Kenton found a chair in the adjoining empty cubicle and set it next to Mrs. Sato. While Yoshi went out to gather some snacks for the hungry family, Kenton struck up a conversation with Takao, who told him intriguing stories about how the Japanese rebuilt their country after World War II.

Kenton got lost in the narrative and didn't realize that almost half an hour had passed.

"Kenton, come look at this," Yoshi called to him as she entered the cubicle. He looked at his phone: 4:42. Yoshi took him by the hand and guided him back to the waiting room, where a group of people were gathered around the television. There was Stonehenge.

"It's on every channel," the kid with the skull tattoo said. "And on my phone. And these people's phones too. It's everywhere. There's nothing else on."

Kenton turned back to the monitor. It wasn't present-day Stonehenge on the screen. Instead of the deteriorated version he had toured, with posts missing and lintels dropped, all the megaliths were perfectly intact.

A group of people dressed in plain brown tunics entered the scene, carrying a body wrapped in white linen on a rudimentary stretcher formed of wood and animal skins. They proceeded to an open trench that revealed scattered bones. The pallbearers let the stretcher down to the ground and the group gathered around for a prayer. Then several men lowered the body into the ditch. They picked up some large antlers fashioned into a shovel-like tool, and transferred soil to cover the body. Another prayer followed, and the group solemnly marched away.

"Is this some educational documentary?" Kenton asked the kid.

He shook his head. "I've never seen anything like this."

The onscreen focus shifted to the center of Stonehenge. A large group of people, maybe a thousand, were gathered for dawn at the summer solstice. At the precise moment, the sun rose and shined through a series of apertures in the stone columns. The light fixated like a laser on the center of a stone in the middle of the great stone cathedral. The group closed their eyes and chanted.

As soon as the chant ended, the scene was illuminated by an intense light that turned the grayish early morning into a blazing spectacle, the huge rocks sparkling. Above the stone circle a disk-shaped silvery craft rotated rapidly with multi-colored lights on its underside, spinning so quickly that they seemed to merge. Rays of intense white light beamed down upon the structure and the people within it. The worshippers stood still and erect, absorbing the light as if this was a regular event for them. The faces of the elderly grew younger and more vital. People with infirmities loosened, and a child with a crippled leg straightened. Suddenly the craft issued a burst of light so bright that all the forms, stone and human, merged into one spectacular flash. Then the light disappeared in an instant, the scene returned to a grayish tint, and the ship hurtled off into the sky, gone in a blip.

All that was left on the screen was an unintelligible pattern of blue, white, brown, and green pixels.

# *Brianna 30*

---

As Brianna and her companions approached the EgyptAir security checkpoint, she was appalled at the massive queue snaking down the corridor. "What's going on?" she asked Hathaway. He scanned the crowd and made an "I have no idea" face.

A fellow standing near Brianna overheard her question and turned to her. "Since that terrorist group was busted, the U.S. has intensified security."

"What are you talking about?"

The fellow pulled out his phone and scrolled to a video showing an FBI SWAT team storming into a bunker containing a huge cache of military weapons, and then stuffing a dapperly-dressed handcuffed middle-aged man into the back of an FBI van.

"Some cult in the Blue Ridge Mountains was railroaded by this weirdo called Malthus. He amassed a huge stockpile of illegal munitions and started a sick plan to kill millions of people by poisoning the water supply of major cities around the world."

Brianna made a pained face. "My God, how demented!"

"It gets even stranger," the man went on. "When Malthus's aide realized how brainwashed she had become, she and her husband defected from the commune. Soon after they drove off, they discovered they had no brakes. Their car crashed into a ravine at a hairpin curve. Her husband was killed, but she survived in a coma. When she woke up two months later, she spilled the beans and gave the FBI all the details, including the names and contact information for all the people around the globe that Malthus had enrolled to dump the poison he sent them. When the State Department learned of the plot, they announced a code red security alert and they are hyper-screening all travelers into the country."

Dr. Hathaway leaned forward to hear the ghastly story.

"Well, aren't we glad that woman woke up from the coma," Brianna commented.

"For sure," the passenger added. "She said that while she was in the coma she had a near-death experience. Jesus appeared and stopped her from going into the light. He told her that she still had an important mission to complete."

When the fellow saw the security line starting to move forward, he turned to catch up.

Dr. Hathaway smiled impishly. "I guess the Nazarene doesn't need to be in a physical body to deliver his messages."

# Driscoll 30

Driscoll's sleep escape from Kendallgate was broken by a knock on his bedroom door. "Just get out of here and go to church or anywhere out of my sight, would you?" he called out.

"It's me, dad," he heard Jared's voice. The boy opened the door softly and Driscoll sat up.

"Where's Kendall?"

"He got into his car and drove somewhere."

*Maybe Jesus will give him a personal rapture off the Earth to save us all.*

"What are you doing up so early?"

"I heard Kendall on the computer. He left that flash drive with the Earth files showing on the monitor."

"Good. Now please just throw it in the ocean."

"Not just yet . . . Look what I found." Jared approached the bed holding several small, colored, ragged-edged pieces of paper in his hand. He gave one to his dad. "Hold this up to the light."

Driscoll lifted the paper toward the open window streaming sunlight, and studied it. It was a printout of one of the blue tattered pieces from the scrambled Earth jigsaw. "So what's the big deal?"

"I zoomed in on some of the pieces, printed them, and cut them out on paper. Just then, a sea breeze blew a few pieces on the floor. One went upside down. When I picked it up, I saw this black line."

Driscoll flipped the paper he was holding and found a thin curved black line on the back. "Maybe just a fluke in the program or a flaw on the paper. Or left over from the black words they found."

"No, dad," Jared insisted. "Someone left the printer on the setting to print two sides of a page. When I turned them over, most of them have a marking." Jared dropped a dozen pieces into his father's hand. Sure enough, each of them bore a curved black line against the white background. They appeared to be intelligently designed.

"What do you think they are?" asked Driscoll.

Jared reached into his pocket and pulled out a larger page of many small paper pieces cellophane taped together. "Here's what happened when I matched up the pieces."

As Driscoll examined it, he could clearly make out an eye.

"Hand me my phone, son. I have to make a call."

# *Leo 30*

The failure of wireless service at Machu Picchu gave way to pandemonium. Thousands of tourists were tapping and shaking their devices, tilting them in different positions, and moving around the plateau, hoping to find a reception spot. The crowd was completely wigged out.

Inside the ruins, Leo heard Ian call out, "We've got a signal!" A cheer went up from the cameramen as they turned to their camera viewfinders, and the staff took their positions at the monitors in the control truck.

"What the hell ?!!!" Ian yelled.

Leo grabbed Kristina's hand and drew her up the steps to the television control truck. Amidst crackling electronic equipment, they positioned themselves behind the director, gaining a view of the monitors displaying the images transmitted from the three cameras.

But what Leo saw on the screen didn't match what he had seen moments earlier outside the truck. Instead of ruins with walls crumbling after six hundred years of brutal weathering, the buildings looked bright and fresh as if they had just been constructed. The wide, flat stones, rather than dingy gray and pocked, were white and smooth. All the buildings were fully intact, with thatched roofs and windows draped by dark green cloths. Confused, Leo stepped out of the truck and scanned the ruins to be sure that someone had not done some miraculous restoration. No, they looked as old, faded, and broken as they had a minute earlier. Stymied, he stepped back up into the truck.

"Look, there!" Kristina pointed to one of the monitors. Leo leaned in to see a large group of short, dark-skinned people, men dressed in sleeveless tunics and women in long colorful dresses. Some of the men bore large plugs expanding their ear lobes. They resembled the portraits Leo had seen in the hotel lobby, Incas who had populated Machu Picchu in its days of glory. *Is this some trick of technology? Or is it a miracle?*

In front of the assembled group stood a shaman wearing a long red and purple robe draped with a white sash. His embroidered pointed cap bore flaps hanging over his ears, extending to thick multi-colored tassels touching his chest. The sage was mixing some kind of tea in a large vat, as he prayed intently over it. Three men surrounded the bowl, pouring powdered green plants into the brew. The shaman took a large hollowed-out coconut shell, dipped it into the vat to collect the tea, and held it up for the crowd to see. They all joined in fervent prayers. When the chanting reached a fever pitch, the shaman tilted his head back, opened his mouth, and downed the concoction.

The camera capturing the interaction zoomed deep into the shaman's eye. Then the view reversed and the screen depicted his vision of the group in front of him. At first the crowd appeared as normal physical people. Then they started to glow, a light within them expanding and extending beyond their skin. Everyone radiated auras, at first whitish-golden, and then morphing into bright, rainbow colors. As Leo and Kristina watched, rapt, he placed his arm around her shoulder and she reached her hand up to take his.

The people in the crowd grew brighter and brighter until sparkling light eclipsed their bodies, transforming them into translucent angel-like beings. The foliage and trees behind the group grew more and more vibrant, as if effervescent spirits were animating them. The flora took on the rainbow colors of the shaman's robe, while everything onscreen seemed to be dancing with delight. Leo, mesmerized, was drawn into the scene as if he were the shaman in ecstasy. Kristina, observing Leo in a kind of trance, reached to steady him.

After a timeless moment, the vision began to fade. The other-worldly energy animating the trees seemed to diminish, and the auras of the people gradually shrank. Eventually the crowd looked normal again, and the camera's view once again showed the shaman standing before the group. Leo, still not sure what to make of the vision, looked once again outside the sound truck, only to find the drab ruins.

"What did we just see?" Kristina asked her beloved.

"Ourselves as God sees us," he replied.

# *Lauren 30*

Lauren awoke with a start when she heard the thud of the front door closing. She looked out the window and saw Dr. Chung walking to his car. He opened the rear hatch and tossed in a small travel bag. Anxiety welled up in her chest. *Have I created another father who disappears?*

Lauren quickly slipped into her jeans and beige T-shirt, dashed through the living room, and out the front door.

"Where are you going?" she asked as she reverted to a frightened five-year-old girl.

Chung closed the hatch and turned toward her. "Late last night I received a phone call from a friend who works at CNN in Baghdad. He urged me to go to Tell Abu Shahrain today."

"What's going on there?"

The doctor shook his head and shrugged. "My friend wouldn't tell me. He just said something was happening I should know about . . . Would you like to come?"

"Do you think I am well enough?"

The doctor reached for Lauren's hand and wrapped his thumb and two fingers around her wrist. Silently he looked down at the floor. After a half-minute he said, "Your pulses are stronger. I think you can go."

"That's good," she said, slipping into the passenger seat. "I would have come anyway. You're not leaving me here alone."

A dry and bumpy half-hour later, the pair pulled up to what was left of the oldest city in Mesopotamia. Not much to see. Just some square, waist-high, windblown rock remains of an ancient temple set against the backdrop of a sprawling, arid desert. Important as this place was supposed to be, there was scant hint of the civilization that had supposedly initiated a quantum leap in the evolution of humanity. Lauren roamed around the ruins for a while and quickly grew bored. No shelter, no bathrooms, no food, no signs, no guide. Nothing.

Dr. Chung was far more engaged. As the surprisingly spry man examined the temple from many different angles, he seemed to be conversing with invisible spirits. This was no casual trip for him; the mystic was in his glory.

The morning sun beat on Lauren until she wobbled. Fearing she might be setting her health back, she sat down on a large rock and fanned herself, trying to quell her tender system. Dr. Chung noticed and pulled himself from his exploration. "You can sit in my car," he offered. "I'll put the air conditioning on."

Chung placed his arm around Lauren's back to steady her as he guided her to the car. "How long will we be staying here?" she asked as she slipped into the faded cracked brown leather passenger's seat. The moment Lauren heard those words escape her lips, she felt selfish. Here this gracious mentor had taken her in, devoted many hours to healing her, and literally saved her life. Now she was pressuring him to leave.

The doctor appeared unfazed. "I expect my friend will arrive before too long."

"Sure, take your time," Lauren replied, hoping to redeem herself. "I'll be fine in the car."

Chung turned on the motor and air conditioning. When Lauren felt the cool air wash over her arms, she breathed a sigh of relief. She tilted the vents toward her face, closed her eyes, leaned her head back, and began to doze off.

When a shrill car horn pierced the silent desert, Lauren sat up with a start. She turned to look through the car's rear window and saw a sand-crusted gray Land Rover hurtling through the dunes, kicking up huge billows of dust. The vehicle's windshield was so caked with grime that she could hardly make out who was driving.

Behind the Land Rover, a U.S. Army troop carrier rambled, a green and brown camouflage cloth draping its bed. Close on its heels followed a tan panel truck bearing a satellite antenna on its roof, the vehicle's side painted with large red Arabic letters. The desolate space, until now quiet but for the sound of the wind and the crunch of Dr. Chung's footsteps on pebbles, was suddenly shattered with frenzied activity.

Chung turned and waved to the Land Rover's driver. Excited, the doctor hustled to meet the vehicle pulling to a sharp halt twenty yards from Lauren. She rolled down the stubborn car window, swatting dust from her face.

"Just like you to make a dramatic entrance!" Chung called to the driver as he opened the door and emerged. The man was light-skinned with a blonde-gray moustache, his face round. He wore dark wraparound sunglasses and a tan safari hat. Lauren guessed he had weathered about fifty orbits.

"Now will you tell me what we are doing here?" asked Chung.

The driver shook his head. "I wish I knew. Three days ago I received a call from Atlanta ordering me to assemble a television crew and show up here today, ready to shoot at 4 PM. We wrangled Aletejah TV to put together a remote broadcast crew. The army goes with us wherever we go now. Damned if any of us have any idea what this is all about." He removed his tan floppy hat, wiped some sweat from his brow, and looked around. "Man, this must be the most barren place on the planet."

Lauren opened the creaking car door and stepped out, efforting to put her hair back into place as she approached the two men. The driver seemed surprised to find an attractive young woman in this lonely outpost. "Lauren, meet Avery Stone," said Chung. "He's the CNN correspondent in Baghdad—one of my best friends here. He is a stubborn, pig-headed skeptic, but I've penetrated his thick skull and planted some tiny seeds of appreciation for Chinese medicine."

Stone chuckled, removed his sunglasses, and extended his hand to Lauren. His skin was soft and his touch jittery. When she caught a glimpse of his blue eyes, the first she had seen since she had arrived in this land of dark-featured people, she felt a moment of comfort. "Ever since the Gulf War, my ears were ringing to the point that I could hardly sleep," said Stone. "Dr. Chung cured that, and then my arthritis. I owe him a great debt."

*I know exactly what you mean.*

A young Arab man stepped out of the TV truck and approached Stone. "Where do you want us to set up?"

Stone placed his hands on his hips and scanned the area until he noticed a small hill affording a view. "How about over there?" he pointed. The technician nodded and dashed back toward the TV truck, followed by a dozen soldiers piling out of the rear of the army transport. At first Lauren thought they might be policing the television crew, but instead they hustled to help them.

Stone patted Chung on the shoulder and stepped away to guide his crew. "What is going on here?" Lauren asked the doctor.

Chung looked at his watch. "It's now about 4:30. In two hours we will find out."

*Stonehenge*
*September 21*

# Kenton 30

Dusk was falling when Kenton pulled the Astra into the Stonehenge carpark. At the far end, the television crew was loading their equipment onto a long white BBC truck. Beside the lorry he saw Megan Jeffries talking to a tall, well-dressed man with a thin black beard.

When the reporter caught sight of the Astra, she turned abruptly from her conversation. "Your timing is a little off," she called to Kenton with an impish grin as he pulled to a halt.

"We saw the whole spectacle on TV at the hospital," he came back.

"I can't tell you how relieved I am." Megan shook her head as if to indicate how dire the situation would have been if the event was a flop.

"So you still have your job?"

"Not anymore," she said with a feigned frown, which gave way to a smile. "I have a better one," her eyes lit up like a little girl who just got a pony for her birthday. "My producer is over the moon. The BBC has the exclusive rights to all the footage from all the shoots around the world. We will turn it into a major documentary." She glanced at the men loading camera equipment onto the truck. "This will be a huge shot in the arm for the company." Megan struck a pose. "You're now looking at the Investigative Reporting Producer . . . I can't believe how lucky I was to be at the café when the GPS coordinates came in." Pause. "How is Yoshi's mother?"

"See for yourself." Kenton stepped aside as the left rear window rolled down to reveal a docile Mrs. Sato, an oxygen tube in her nostrils. She offered a kindly smile as she waved to the reporter.

"Yoshi's mom looks so sweet!"

"Just don't get around her when she's had some sake," Kenton whispered.

Megan took another look at Mrs. Sato, who smiled again, innocent as a newborn babe.

She turned back to Kenton. "Can you come to the studio tomorrow for an interview?"

Kenton looked down at the ground for a long moment, then shook his head. "I don't think so, Megan. My fifteen minutes of fame were quite enough. Count me off the media radar."

Megan sighed. "I understand. Good for you. You've helped me more than you can imagine."

Mrs. Sato leaned over and called out the window, "Come by the condo sometime and we'll watch *Britain's Got Talent*, dear. I'm rooting for the black guy with the tight butt."

## *Brianna 31*

During the long flight from Cairo to New York, Brianna tried to sleep, but she couldn't shake the dreadful image of her mom crying under the shower. *Will she ever get better?*

Brianna looked at Professor Redmond Hathaway in the seat beside her, absorbed in Rupert Sheldrake's book, *Science Set Free*. Her throbbing head began to feel so heavy that she leaned on his shoulder, something she would not have considered doing just days ago. The moment she touched his shoulder, she broke into tears.

Hathaway at first looked quite ill at ease, but then he dropped into a fatherly mode. He reached his arm around Brianna's shoulder and rested his hand firmly on her upper arm. Then he took a napkin from his tray table and placed it in her hand. "Do you want to talk about it?" he asked.

She took a weighty breath. "My mom is getting worse. She had a major meltdown. We can't get her into a decent facility. I just don't know what to do."

Hathaway listened attentively, taking in her account. "I know it can be really hard to deal with a parent who seems unhelpable."

Brianna looked up. "How would you know? You came from a good family who gave you a solid education."

Hathaway snickered. "My dear Brianna, the first rule of science is to not make assumptions without facts to support them."

"What facts am I missing?"

"You don't need to hear my facts at the moment. I am willing to listen if you want to say more."

Brianna sat up straight and gathered herself. "Thanks, but I'll be okay. I just needed to vent. My brother and father and I will figure it out." More settled, she turned to face her teacher. "Why are my assumptions about you incorrect?"

"Very well, then. . ." He took the Sheldrake book off his lap and set it on the tray table.

"My dad was a science teacher at a private Christian school in Devonshire. My mom worked there as a secretary. Dad loved science and had brilliant insights about how the universe works. He was a self-taught quantum physicist ahead of his time. I have the fondest memories of him sitting in bed with me before I went to sleep, spinning visions of parallel universes and time travel and free energy. That's when I developed a passion for science."

Brianna smiled. "Sounds like a great relationship. You were lucky to have such a dad."

"I was." The professor's voice tensed. "That changed when my mother became pregnant. Both of my parents were delighted. The baby came early, around seven months. My mother started to hemorrhage and they rushed her to the hospital. There were serious complications. They tried to save her and the baby, but they couldn't. In one horrific moment they were both gone."

"My God," Brianna gasped. "That must have been devastating for you and your dad."

Hathaway stared off into the distance, as if he were reliving the trauma. When his faced morphed to a sad little boy, Brianna took his hand.

"At first my dad dealt with the loss stoically—stiff upper lip, detached scientist, you know. Then he started smoking and drinking. Just a little at first, but then more and more. Initially he would down a few beers while watching the telly at night. But then he got into hard liquor, beginning when he came home from class."

Brianna just listened. She couldn't decide which was more of a surprise—Hathaway's shocking childhood, or him spilling his guts to her.

"Then dad started to take out his suppressed rage on me. If I did the slightest thing wrong, he would yell at me. He started hitting me—hard. Mostly on my behind and thighs. He was smart enough to know that if anyone saw bruises elsewhere on my body, he would be implicated. A half dozen times he put a lit cigarette to my rear end."

Brianna, shaken, began to softly weep.

Hathaway took her hand and smiled gently. "My dear girl, you are having a hard enough time. I don't want to add to your stress."

"No, this is important. It's the first time I've seen you be a vulnerable man rather than a cerebral heretic. . . How did you cope?"

Hathaway sighed. "At first, not very well. Part of me felt like it was all my fault, and I deserved to be punished. Then something happened that changed all that."

"Like what?"

"In a small garden outside the school chapel there was a life-size statue of Jesus standing with his arms open. I was drawn to that image in contrast to the awful crucifix with a limp corpse hanging over my bed, that gave me nightmares. This statue's eyes were alive. When I looked at him, I felt like he understood what I was going through. I talked to him and I could hear him talk back in my mind."

Just then a flight attendant came by offering drinks. Brianna politely waved her on. Hathaway, lost in recollecting his childhood, hardly noticed. He went on:

"One night in a dream, Jesus came to me. Not the stern, punitive Jesus that my school had planted in my mind, but the kindest, most forgiving, most compassionate soul I could imagine. I sat on his lap and he embraced me with pure, tender love. He told me that he was always with me and he would walk with me through this horror show and take me to higher ground. That was the first time I felt at all comforted since my mother died."

"What a beautiful vision!"

"It was then that I developed a relationship with my invisible guide far beyond any I had with any person in my life. It wasn't religious, but personal, like a protective big brother."

"What happened with your father?"

"One day all the students had to go to the school nurse's office for a polio vaccine injection. In those days they stuck the needle in your rear end rather than your arm. When the nurse saw the cigarette scars on my butt, along with black and blue marks, she knew exactly what had happened. Aghast, she asked me if it was so, and I burst into tears. The nurse reported my dad, who faced criminal charges and was dismissed from the school. I became a ward of the state. I was placed in a foster home, then another, and another. I must have been in a dozen homes until I turned eighteen."

Brianna just kept shaking her head. "Professor Hathaway, I had no idea. . . I am so sorry you went through all of that."

"It was a rough ride. I wouldn't wish that childhood on anyone. My one consolation was my encounters with Jesus. I had a few daytime visions, as well. As I grew up, they faded away entirely. Ever since then, especially when I have been in pain, or lost, or confused, I have yearned to meet him again."

*This is all starting to make sense.*

*Langley*
*September 29*

# Driscoll 31

Driscoll Ames never expected to be sitting in CIA head-quarters again. But here he was, his son Jared beside him. Carlton Pierce turned to the boy. "Jared, you discovered something our best cryptographers couldn't figure out."

Jared issued a small nervous smile.

"Would you like to see what all the little pieces add up to?"

The boy nodded.

Spencer Pilvey turned down the room lights and projected an image onto the large monitor on the wall.

"We did a virtual simulation of all of the pieces being turned over, as if they had been printed on the opposite side of a paper." Pilvey clicked the mouse, and the screen was filled with thousands of tiny ragged-edged fragments on a white background, most with a curved black marking.

"Navneet wrote a program that would help each piece find the others it fit with. He used to write algorithms for Google, so that was easy because most of the pieces were uniquely marked, unlike the other side that had no markings."

Driscoll watched the pieces on the screen start to move around as if searching for their mates. The process looked like someone doing a jigsaw puzzle fitting small sections of a puzzle together, each growing larger by joining other sections until they formed a whole.

"Look, daddy, there's a hand!" Jared called out.

"I can see a mouth," Driscoll added.

The picture grew clearer as it neared completion. "It's a man," Jared said in a loud voice, pointing at the screen.

Yet it was no normal man. Two additional legs were superimposed, spread out a bit to each side. The two arms extended at a ninety-degree angle to the torso, augmented by two more arms slightly raised above them. The long-haired man, about thirty years of age, was naked. A circle and a square were inscribed around him.

"This picture was drawn by Leonardo da Vinci around the year 1490," Navneet Adkar told the group. "It's called 'Vitruvian Man.'" Adkar took the red laser pointer and outlined the man's body. "DaVinci tried to depict the most perfectly formed man with divine proportions representing the harmony of the cosmos."

Jared didn't quite get the meaning, but he listened politely.

"Now, just watch what happens," said Adkar enthusiastically. "When we flipped the intact man over to the other side of the pieces, here is what we found." He clicked the mouse a few times, and on the screen appeared the Earth, fully intact, with all the oceans and land masses perfectly intact. The seemingly random blues, greens, whites, and browns had all found their right places.

Ames smiled and shook his head in amazement. "Why would the image creators require us to solve the man puzzle before we could solve the Earth puzzle?" he asked.

Ms. Wentworth spoke. "It's symbolic. Trying to put the world together is overwhelming. There are just too many broken pieces, and lots of them look alike. But when you get your own life together, you are in the perfect position to connect the dots to help the world."

Driscoll considered the notion. "But what about the "End is Near" message?"

"It's not the end of the world the image makers are talking about," Ms. Wentworth went on. "It's the end of the shattered world we've been living in. The transmissions are a huge planetary wake-up call. Our lives have been interrupted to stimulate us to make a course correction. That was what it took to get our attention."

Driscoll leaned back and folded his arms, forehead squeezed. "I find it hard to believe that the CIA figured out such a metaphysical plot twist."

Ms. Wentworth replied, "We had some help."

"From genius cryptographers?"

She shook her head. "My yoga teacher."

*Cusco, Peru*
*September 24*

# Leo 31

"How did you find out about this place?" Kristina asked Leo as she looked up at the painted wooden sign hanging over the old yellow stone building's front door: Orfanotrofioff di S. Martin de Porres.

"Father Matteo told me about his friend Father Roberto, the orphanage director. Matteo asked if we would stop by and say hello before we leave Peru."

As Kristina entered the hallway, a pang of anxiety shot through her. Ever since Paolo was gone, whenever she saw children, especially young boys, she was reminded of her son when he was a boy—joyful memories now eclipsed by his tragic death.

"Ah, you must be Father Leo!" a thin, light-complexioned man in a brown Franciscan robe approached, extending his hand. His graying hair was short-cropped, his nose large. He looked tired, but a certain peace emanated from his eyes.

"Yes," he replied. "This is Kristina Adimari, also from Montecuore."

Father Roberto bowed his head. "I am so happy that you chose to visit us. Please come in and let me show you our facility."

The priest guided his guests through a hallway to a dormitory containing two dozen gray metal-framed bunkbeds. The beds were neatly made, with a brown blanket neatly folded at the foot of each bed. A boy about ten years old sat on a bed reading a comic book, while a few younger boys played with a wooden train set on the floor in a corner.

After a brief chat with the boys, Father Roberto led his guests to a door at the far side of the dorm. "Here is our little chapel." Just then a nun approached, wearing a white and black smock-like habit and long white headdress. "I am sorry to disturb you, Father. One of the construction workers has a question. Could you please give him a moment?"

Father Roberto turned to his guests. "Would you excuse me? We are building an addition to accommodate more children. I will be right back." He opened the door to the chapel and gestured with his hand. "Please, have a seat."

The nun spoke up. "Perhaps this would be a good opportunity for me to show our lady guest the girls' quarters."

"Yes, I would like that," Kristina answered, as the nun took her hand to guide her down the hall.

Leo entered the humble dimly-lit sanctuary, gray walls, a dozen burning candles on a wooden altar draped with a red and gold cloth. As he took a seat on a pew to the far right, he noticed a black-haired woman, maybe mid-thirties, kneeling, praying, clutching a large wooden crucifix against her heart. Tears were running down her cheeks. Leo was tempted to intervene, but his intuition told him to just let her be.

After a few minutes, she kissed the crucifix, rose, and turned toward the door. "Are you alright?" Leo asked.

She smiled. "Oh, yes, sir, I am very blessed."

"I mistook your tears for sadness. Why were you clasping the cross so dearly?"

She nodded, glad to be asked. "Last year my six-year-old son was diagnosed with cancer. My whole family and village prayed and prayed and prayed, but he only grew sicker. Finally the doctor said he had but a few days to live."

Leo listened respectfully.

"When it seemed that all hope had been lost, I got down on my knees in the hospital room and prayed to Jesus on the cross over my son's bed. Suddenly the cross began to glow. I saw a bright light shoot from the center of the cross to my son's lungs, where the cancer was. A beautiful smile spread over his face. I called the doctor, who examined him and took him for x-rays. The cancer entirely disappeared. My son is totally healed. Every day I thank Jesus on the cross, who healed my beloved boy."

"I am very glad to hear that. May you and your son continue to be blessed."

As the woman exited the chapel, Father Roberto entered. He took a seat beside Leo and studied his ashen face. "Are you alright?"

Leo took a few moments to gather himself. "I've been thinking a lot about the crucifix, Roberto. Kristina is the mother of Paolo, the young man who was murdered for his crucifix robberies."

Father Roberto raised an eyebrow.

"I have come to sympathize with Paolo," Leo went on. "I began to agree that we should remove the cross from churches. But now, after hearing that woman's story about how her son was healed through the cross, I wonder if I have underestimated the power of the cross."

Father Roberto nodded slowly and rubbed his chin, taking time to formulate his response. "Faith is the power that draws healing, Leo. That woman's faith called the blessing of God to her son, through the crucifix. If she was Jewish, the healing might have come through a star. Or Muslim, through a crescent moon. The Almighty works through many symbols."

Leo tried to take in the priest's idea.

"The cross is an object onto which we project our faith," Father Roberto went on. "It is what we make of it that gives it power. The real healer is love."

Just then Kristina returned. When she saw that Leo was visibly moved, she took a seat beside him. Leo turned to Father Roberto. "Would you please give us a minute, Father?"

The priest bowed his head respectfully, quietly rose, and exited the chapel. "What's going on?" Kristina asked as she took Leo's hand.

Leo took a long breath. "I just had a huge realization," he answered, a tear forming in the corner of his eye.

"Please tell me. . ."

"Ever since we've been at this orphanage, my soul feels at peace. The gentleness that Father Roberto exudes and the compassionate way he and the staff care for the children remind me why I became a priest. I believed that Christianity was about kindness and helping relieve humanity's suffering."

Kristina nodded. She understood.

"It just hit me that I have drifted so very far from that vision. My eyes were clouded by the pomp and power and dogma of the Church. What these kind people are doing at this place is what Jesus wants us to do. . . take care of each other. I got caught up in Paolo's rebellion. In a way he is right. The Church places too much emphasis on suffering. But lots of sincere people are making an effort to practice Christ's message. We can't throw away a religion just because some of its ideas are warped or some leaders are corrupt."

Leo began to sob. Kristina had never seen him like this before. All she could do was remain silent and give the man a chance to feel. Finally he lifted his head and found her eyes. "God could have destroyed an evil world a long time ago if He wanted. . . But there are enough good people in all religions—and outside of religion—that make life worth continuing. Maybe there is hope for us."

Kristina wiped Leo's tears with the sleeve of her shirt. Now her own tears were flowing. "That, my beloved, is what we all need to remember."

*Tell Abu Shahrain, Iraq*
*September 21*

## *Lauren 31*

---

Lauren tried to remain patient while Dr. Chung attempted to calm Avery Stone after the failed video shoot. Stone sat on a rock beside the ruins, elbows dug into his knees, head buried in his hands, perspiration staining his khaki shirt's underarms. He lifted his head, looked back at the silent sound truck, and nervously etched his foot back and forth in the sand.

Suddenly the sound of a generator motor pierced the silent desert. Stone stood, hands on hips, and peered toward his careworn crew, still scurrying about, beleaguered after struggling to restore their signal. One crewman emerged from the truck and waved his hands, "We're back, boss!"

Dr. Chung took Lauren's hand and guided her toward the ruins. As the two approached the entrance, the ruins suddenly seemed to come to life. Instead of the sand-beaten remnants of low rock walls occupying a few hundred square yards, a huge vibrant city appeared, oddly transparent, almost holographic, clearly visible, yet not physically solid.

The city sprawled into the desert far beyond Lauren's field of vision. In its midst stood a huge rectangular brown building, walls angled in at a few degrees so the roof was smaller than the base. Two long stone staircases ascended from the ground on the left and right corners, meeting in the center near the top, leading to a wide portal. On the ground, a series of tastefully-designed pools and fountains softened the sharp architecture. In contrast to the harsh desert, lush greenery abounded.

Beside one of the pools stood a spacious gazebo-like structure where Lauren could see an extremely tall bearded man standing at its head, lecturing to a group of students. Lauren guessed he might have been ten feet in height. The students were the size of normal people. The teacher was pointing toward a wall containing etchings of many symbols. Some looked like astronomical charts of stars and planets, and others appeared to be mathematical equations. She did not recognize the letters or numbers.

Lauren turned to Dr. Chung, huge questions in her eyes. He placed his arm around her shoulder and gently drew her toward the class building. As they approached, Lauren grew nervous, fearing she might be stepping into some alternate reality she would be unable to return from. *But hey, there's not much I would miss if I never came back.*

The two joined the group of students listening to the teacher. The giant noticed the visitors and beckoned them to come forward. "What would you like to know?" he asked. But Lauren did not see his mouth move. Yet his words were clear, and in English. *Some kind of telepathy.*

"Why did you come to Earth?" Chung asked. Neither did his lips move.

The teacher pointed skyward. "Our planet was suffocating due to atmospheric pollution from a natural disaster.

Your planet is rich in monatomic gold, an element we needed to purify our atmosphere. We came to Earth to mine the element, and we genetically manipulated the primitive indigenous species to serve as slave miners."

Chung nodded as if he was already aware of the story. "Was this the origin of the human species?"

The teacher looked off into the distance, as if peering into ancient history. "It was." He paused for Chung to absorb the answer. Then he added, "This is also the origin of religion on your planet in which you worship a God out-side and above you."

Chung furrowed his brow. "Then what is our true rela-tionship with God?"

"The Creator lives within you, as you, through you. You are extensions and expressions of your divine Source."

Chung nodded as if his intuition had been confirmed. "Do you still visit us?"

The teacher smiled. "Far more than you know."

"Why?"

"You have evolved to a point where you must advance to your next level of planetary maturity. We are doing what we can to nudge you forward. Let's call it our way of reconciling what we started."

Chung nodded. "Can we advance without annihilating ourselves?"

"That is the crossroads at which you now stand."

The doctor spoke quickly, as if he sensed that the time with the teacher was running out.

"What can I tell my people that would help us?"

The teacher seemed pleased to be asked. "It is time for you to grow beyond a slave mentality. Instead of looking up for salvation, look within yourself. Cultivate your higher nature, rather than conquest of nations and the planet, and you will find your way out of the mess you have made."

Lauren mustered the courage to speak. She swept her arm toward the sprawling city before her. "This place isn't real, is it?"

The teacher moved to the railing of the gazebo and looked out pensively. "At one time it was. Many civilizations that you consider primitive were infinitely more spiritually advanced than those that characterize the planet today. We have recreated a vision of the splendor so you can see what is possible for humanity. You can make it real again, if you choose."

Suddenly the hologram disappeared. The city, the massive structure, the gardens, the teacher, the class—everything was gone. Dazed, Lauren found herself and Dr. Chung once again standing before battered ruins in the middle of a scorching desert, the scantest remnant of a golden civilization gone by.

# *Kenton 31*

Kenton, Yoshi, and her parents gathered around the condo's television. None of them had seen the Jack Manning show before, but tonight they had a reason to watch. At 10:40 PM the show's intro came on, giving way to a slightly-plump blondish Scottsman with a round face and sparkly eyes. He sat on a high-backed leather chair before the full-wall backdrop of a penthouse-view photo of London.

After the applause died down, Manning began, "My usual guests are famous actors. Tonight I am going out on a limb to interview a man not in the entertainment industry, who has attracted a great deal of attention lately. Brian Turner is a crop circle researcher who was recently kidnapped by, some people believe, energy industry extremists. Mr. Turner was held against his will for almost a month at a secret facility in a warehouse in Harlesden. For some unknown reason, his captors released him on Tuesday. He has agreed to one final interview. Manning turned to his guest. "Brian, thanks for joining us. You've been through quite an ordeal."

The camera moved to Turner, who looked haggard. He nodded politely.

"The crop circles have been appearing in England and around the globe for over forty years," Manning went on. "Some people believe they are a form of divine or extraterrestrial intervention, and others believe they are a hoax. Last week's mysterious worldwide transmission from Stonehenge plus your kidnapping has brought the phenomenon into the public eye once more. After all your research, Brian, who do you think is making these formations, and why?"

Kenton leaned forward, his elbows on his knees, chin resting on his hands, almost in prayer position. Yoshi and her parents were equally absorbed.

"We are, Jack."

Manning looked surprised. "So now, after four decades of taking the phenomenon seriously—almost religiously—and serving as its chief spokesman, you are admitting that hoaxsters have been creating them?"

Kenton's mouth went dry and his heart started to race. He glanced at Yoshi, also quite disturbed.

"No, Jack, that's not what I'm saying. Sure, hoaxsters have made some of the formations, but most of them are genuine."

"Then why do you say that we are making them?"

Turner reached into his shirt pocket and pulled out a piece of paper.

"Don't tell me you have a message from the circle makers?"

The audience laughed. Kenton shot Yoshi an anxious look.

Turner smiled coyly. "Actually, Jack, I do."

"Well, that's certainly exciting," said Manning, leaning back and crossing his arms. "Did a spaceship land on your lawn and a bunch of little green men get out and hand you a note? If so, can you ask them how Brexit got voted in?"

The audience laughed again, this time Kenton with them.

Turner remained serious. "Actually, the circle makers have been emailing me for several months."

Snickers rose from the audience. Kenton's heart started to sink. *Is this turning into a train wreck?* Manning went on, "So now the 'e' in 'email' stands for 'extraterrestrial?' Where can I get that account? Google is so . . . earthy." More laughter.

"I have two recent emails I would like to read, if I may."

Manning graciously extended his hand. "Please do. Most of my actor guests tell funny stories about their directors. I can't wait to hear about your director."

More laughter.

Turner remained steadfast. "I received this communique on Wednesday, the day after I was released. 'You will be given the microphone by a funny man in a leather chair who has the ear of England. Take it."

Manning sat up straight. "But we didn't invite you onto the show until yesterday. So you are telling me that you received this message before you heard from us?"

"That's right, Jack."

"Now this *is* getting interesting. Pray tell, what was the next message?"

Turner sat up straight and held the paper squarely in front of him. A camera panned the audience, now silent.

Turner read: "Many of you believe that we are extraterrestrials or interdimensional beings. In a way, that is true. We are indeed a discrete independent society living beyond the realm of the physical senses. But that is not the whole truth."

The image of Brian Turner onscreen was replaced by a series of photos of intricate crop circles. The parade of images continued as he spoke a voice-over.

"You, members of humanity, are the real circle makers. We have extracted these images from deep in your subconscious and magnified them in the most obvious places for your attention. They are archetypical forms that represent the loftiest potential of the human spirit. They stand for harmony, balance, nobility, poetry, vision, and even humor. It does not matter how we make them. What matters is what you do with them. As you study them, walk in their fields, and meditate on their shapes, they lift you to an expanded state of mind that transcends the daily slog that characterizes the lives of boredom, fear, depression, and discouragement that so many of you live."

The images on the television screen shifted. A homeless woman sleeping on a cardboard mat in a city doorway, snow drifts piled around her. Starving African children with bloated bellies. A sorrowful man with dark eyes peering through prison bars. Men in business suits waiting for the train, their faces pale, eyes vacant. The bloody aftermath of a terrorist bombing.

"We have generated these forms in your fields to stir your memory of the magnificent place in the cosmos for which you were intended. We are your future self, reaching into your present to remind you who you are at your best, and who you can and will be. Your struggles and suffering have launched a massive call for help into the universe, and we have responded. But we cannot do for you what you must do for yourselves. The answer to your prayers will not arrive from the far reaches of the universe. All the wisdom you need is within you. The Earth will provide for all of your needs if you cooperate with it. A Higher Power will guide you as you turn to It. When you finally make use of what you have been given, your world will become what you have always hoped it could be. Now it's up to you. This is our final transmission."

*Bimini*
*September 30*

# Driscoll 32

Driscoll Ames stood pensively on the long windswept beach at Bimini's North Point, small waves lapping over his bare feet. The sky remained overcast as a chilly breeze moved in from the east. He pulled up the collar on his jacket and watched some pelicans land on a large rock protruding from the water a dozen yards from the beach. In the west, a crimson sun peeked through the sliver of sky between the low cloud ceiling and the ocean.

A quarter mile offshore, a series of blocks lay at the ocean floor, perhaps the road to the legendary Atlantis. A month ago this career military officer would have dismissed the idea as rubbish. Now his world had taken on a stunning new reality. Those blocks trailed not simply into the depths of the sea, but to the portal of another dimension.

Down the beach fifty yards to the west, Jared and Tanisha picked shells. *Thank God I still have them.* Now these two little souls were his priority; he would do all he could to buffer them from the struggles he and his wife had endured. The money from the newspaper story would give his children a life they never would have known. *Maybe this crazy ride has been worth it.*

The kids dashed to catch up with their dad. "Come, sit with me," he beckoned, gesturing to the brown blanket spread beside him on the sand. The children, fragile since their mom's death, snuggled up to his sides as he wrapped his arms around them. For a long time the three sat in silence, watching the evening drop its thickening curtain.

"Look!" Jared pointed upward. "The first star of the night!"

"Good eye," his father replied. "I think that's actually Venus."

The three studied the light in the sky. "Do you think those guys you saw were from Venus?" Tanisha asked.

Driscoll leaned back on his elbows and gazed up. "I have a feeling they come from a place much farther away."

"How far does the universe go, daddy?"

Driscoll laughed lightly. "No one really knows. It just goes on and on and on. Some scientists say that no matter how far we see or go, it goes on way farther than that."

"Whoa!" said Jared.

Tanisha looked up at her dad with questioning eyes. "Where do you think mom went?"

Driscoll took a labored breath. He knew that question would come sometime, just not so soon. He had no choice but to field it. "I think she went home to God."

"And where does God live?" asked Tanisha. "Way far away on one of those distant stars?"

"No, sweetheart. God lives in your heart, and mine, and everyone's. The same place your mom lives now."

The child looked puzzled. "If that's where God lives, then why are we sending all those rockets into outer space?" Jared asked. "Why don't we just look inside our heart?"

Driscoll smiled proudly. "That's probably the best question I ever heard." He kissed both his kids on their forehead, leaned back on his elbows, and gazed into the mystery of the cosmos.

*Cusco*
*September 24*

# Leo 32

"Come, let's finish our tour," Father Roberto said as he guided Leo and Kristina to a large day room where a few kids were doing homework, others about their cleaning chores. Leo remained deep in thought about the revelation he had experienced in the chapel. Kristina smiled at the children and said hello to a few. The kids, tickled to have visitors, waved and giggled.

Just as the couple was about to leave the room, Leo noticed a young boy with a twisted arm. He stopped, studied the child for a minute, and remarked to Kristina. "That's the boy I talked to at the train station—the one I bought a wooden carving of Mother Mary from."

Leo walked to the child, Kristina at his side. "How are you doing today?"

"Pretty good," the child looked up and answered. "How are you, sir?"

Leo was impressed by the boy's politeness.

"Didn't I see you at the train station? You sold me a carving, I think."

The boy looked surprised and embarrassed. He leaned forward and said in a low voice, "Please don't tell Father

Roberto I was there. They don't like us going to Aguas Calientes and bothering tourists."

Leo nodded, leaned down, and asked in a soft voice, "What do you do with the money you make selling gifts?"

"I bring it back here. We have a birthday cake fund."

Kristina squatted to meet the boy at eye level. "How long have you been in this place?"

The boy looked down at the floor, apparently ashamed. Then he looked up and found her eyes. "Since I was three. My mother left my father after he hurt me. Then she got sick and couldn't take care of me. I went to live with my aunt and uncle, but my uncle drinks all the time and they already have six kids, so they sent me here. We don't know where my mother is."

Kristina shot Leo a pained glance.

"I promise not to tell I saw you at the station. Just don't get into any trouble, okay?" Leo patted him on the head.

"Okay," the boy smiled, and dashed off.

Leo walked to the door, Kristina beside him. Just outside the room, Kristina grabbed Leo's arm and faced him.

"Leo, you know how we talked about somehow continuing Paolo's work when we got back to Montecuore?"

Leo nodded.

"Then let's keep taking Christ off the cross."

Leo pursed his lips and squeezed his forehead. "We can't go around removing statues from the crucifix like Paolo did, Kristina."

"No, but we can take real people off the cross."

Leo looked even more confused.

"That little boy was crucified by his father who mangled him, and then he was tossed out by his family. He will carry that broken body and rejection for the rest of his life. He may stay in this orphanage for all of his childhood, and who knows what he will do when he grows up? He may become a beggar or get into trouble. Or die at a young age."

Leo listened intently.

"I know this may sound crazy, Leo, but . . ."

"But what?"

"Let's take him home."

Leo's eyes bulged. "You want to adopt him?"

"Yes, let's give him the life he would never have if he stays here. He can be the child you and I never raised together. It will be like us picking up where we left off so many years ago."

Leo thought long and hard. He turned and watched the boy doing his chores. He was a bright-eyed child, laughing with the other kids. He seemed gentle.

After a long silent minute, Leo Bonfiglio closed his eyes, smiled, and nodded.

"Father Roberto, may we speak to you for a moment?" Kristina asked.

The priest approached.

"You see that little boy over there, wiping down that table?"

"Yes?"

"We'd like to give him a good home."

A soft smile grew over Father Roberto's face. He closed his eyes and nodded. "If you are serious, it can be arranged. There is a lot of paperwork, but if you are intent, we can do it."

"Thank you, Father," Kristina took his hand and then gave the frail man a hug that Leo feared might knock him over.

All three took a long breath. Leo turned to the priest.

"By the way, Father, what is the boy's name?"

"His name is Paolo."

## *Lauren 32*

Lauren Delaney set her suitcase on the floor and threw herself onto her bed. Exhausted, she stared at the ceiling, mentally reviewing the bizarre events that had ruled her life for the past month. *I can't tell anyone about this. It's too crazy.*

Lauren reached into her jeans pocket and pulled out the vial of tablets Dr. Chung had given her. She trusted his promise that she would continue to regain her health if she kept up with the herbs and got acupuncture from a local doctor. She popped a handful of pills into her mouth, took a swig of water from her purple jug, and closed her eyes.

As she started to drift off, her phone issued a loud text ping. *Dr. Chung with more instructions?* As much as she wanted to just zone out, she thought it prudent to check.

From Todd Alexander:

I miss you. When can I see you?

*Unbelievable.*

Her head throbbing, she typed in the text field: When hell freezes over.

As her finger was about to touch Send, she heard Dr. Chung's voice in the back of her head. When she had told him she intended to get even with Todd, the doctor quoted Confucius: "When planning revenge, be sure to dig two graves."

Lauren chuckled and deleted Todd's text. Then their entire history of conversations. She went to her list of contacts, found Todd, and deleted it, and all of his emails. She touched the photos icon, found the folder with pictures and videos of her and Todd, and deleted it. Then she went to the blocked calls list and added Todd's number.

*That should do it.* The trustworthy man she had been searching for was not her absent father, or Todd Alexander, or any of the long string of disastrous relationships that had culminated in this uncanny moment. Her salvation came in the form of an elder acupuncturist who loved and accepted Lauren for who she was. Now her task was to do the same for herself, and quit looking to men to prove she was loveable. If she ever had another relationship, it would be different because *she* was different.

She lay back on the bed and let out a long sigh of relief. For the first time in a very long time, Lauren Delaney felt free.

# Kenton 32

Kenton and Yoshi stood in the center of the freshly-formed crop circle, Brian Turner at their side. The mist that had shrouded the morning was starting to dissolve, revealing a patchwork of golden and green fields stretching across Wiltshire. Brian, hands on hips, scanned the upright wheat that formed the walls of the massive formation surrounding them. Just over his shoulder at a distance stood the stately, ever-enigmatic Stonehenge.

"Most crop circles have come and gone by the end of August. A few carry over into September," Turner stated. "But a new formation at the end of September is virtually unheard of. Maybe this is a message from the circle makers thanking you for your help."

Lost in thought, the compliment sailed over Kenton's head. "Where do you go from here, Brian?"

Turner smiled boyishly. "I might fulfill my dream to put a Japanese garden in our back yard. Helen doesn't want me in the public eye anymore. I don't blame her. I'm tired of trying to convince people of what they are not ready to believe. There are others who can take up the torch." Turner stared firmly at Kenton, silently urging him to read between the lines. "What will you two do now?"

Kenton clasped his hands behind his head and peered out over the sprawling plain. "I emailed my principal and told him I want my job back. I miss my students. They remind me of the innocence I lost along my way. I teach them physics, but they teach me honesty."

Yoshi nudged Kenton, as if to egg him on to say more.

"My wife asked for a divorce. She met a diamond broker at a Sussex wine tasting, and swears he's her soulmate." Turner searched Kenton's face for some sign of distress. None could be found.

Turner turned to Yoshi. "And you?"

"I quit my job. I thought my parents would be angry, but they told me to do what makes me happy."

"And what makes you happy?"

Her eyes brightened. "I bought a plane ticket to visit New Jersey. Kenton says there are lots of crop circles there."

Kenton made a mock-serious face. "Ancient Japanese saying: 'Small white lie allowed when man would miss woman very much if he did not tell it.'"

Turner smiled. Sensing Kenton and Yoshi wanted some alone time, he turned and began to stroll toward the far end of the formation.

Kenton took Yoshi's hand and guided her to the center of the formation, where he lay down and invited her to join him. Holding hands, the two surrendered to the soft wheat beneath them and gazed skyward. A circle of blue opened above the couple amidst the otherwise murky sky.

A man's voice broke the silence. "Hey, my phone works outside the circle, but not inside."

Kenton and Yoshi sat up to see a young guy and his girl-friend trying to make sense of the phone anomaly. "Have you guys noticed that?" the fellow asked, turning toward the couple.

"As a matter of fact, we have," Kenton replied in a dead-pan voice.

"And what do you make of it?"

Kenton rose and approached the fellow. "Just point your camera directly at the formation." The man, grateful to be guided, followed the instruction.

Kenton stepped around to the man's side and studied the image on the screen along with him.

"What do you see?" asked Kenton.

The man stared at the screen. "A crop formation."

"Good." Kenton reached toward the phone and touched the button that changed the camera focus to the face of the man holding it. "Now what do you see?"

"I see myself."

"Ah," said Kenton. "Full circle."

# *Brianna 32*

---

Brianna Marlowe picked up her Caramel Macchiato from the counter, stepped past the line of people waiting to order, and sat down beside Professor Redmond Hathaway. "Now will you tell me where you were going to get the money to finance the experiment?"

The professor raised an eyebrow. "You might be surprised."

The student scrunched her forehead. "Is your benefactor some eccentric recluse, hiding out on a private island, barking orders on the phone to fawning yes-men managing his empire?"

Hathaway milked the moment with a long sip of Earl Gray tea. "To the contrary, Brianna, he is very involved in humanity, closer to you than you might imagine."

*"Uuuuunnghhh!"* Don't tease me! Just tell me, would you?"

Hathaway waved his hand toward a table ten feet away. "Excuse me, Ozzie, would you mind coming over here for a moment?"

Ozzie set down his gray bussing tub and folded his green towel neatly over his shoulder. "Yes, professor, how can I help you?"

"Brianna is trying to figure out who has been putting up the money for my project. Do you have any ideas?"

Brianna sat with her arms crossed, stymied. Ozzie stared at Hathaway with questioning eyes. The professor nodded.

The elder busboy turned to the kitchen window where Brianna saw a pair of hands dragging dirty dishes in from a shelf below it. "Yo, Salvador!"

"Wha's up, Ozzie?" a voice with a Spanish accent called back.

"What's my last name?"

Brianna sat dumbfounded.

"You're the Carver, bro."

Ozzie turned back to Brianna with a mischievous look.

"You're a woodworker?" she asked, more confused by the moment.

"No, Brianna. I'm a Carver. Does that name mean anything to you?"

Brianna tried to think, but by now her mind had short-circuited.

"History, Brianna," Hathaway hinted. "Do you remember high school American history? Another African-American named Carver?"

Brianna squinted. "George Washington Carver? The guy who studied peanuts?"

Ozzie pulled over an empty chair from a nearby table, straddled it, and faced the bewildered student.

Hathaway spoke. "George Washington Carver—a former slave who wanted to get the south off of a cotton economy to give his people a reprieve. A genius who discovered hundreds of uses for the peanut, sweet potato, and lots of other plants. Respected as one of the greatest botanists who ever lived."

Brianna leaned back, stunned. "George Washington Carver was one of your relatives?"

Ozzie smiled, his eyes sparkling in the afternoon sun streaming through the café window. "He was my grandfather, Brianna."

Brianna drummed her fingers on the table and looked back and forth between the two men. "Sorry, guys, I'm still not tracking this." She turned to Hathaway. "I asked you who the donor was, and you're telling me about George Washington Carver, who died, like, what, eighty years ago?"

Hathaway and Ozzie stared at Brianna for a long time, waiting for her to get the punch line.

"Now wait a minute . . . You don't mean to tell me . . . "

Hathaway laughed. "Yes, Brianna, we do mean to tell you."

Ozzie looked kindly at Brianna, as if he wanted to relieve her distress. "By the time my grandfather died, he was a wealthy man. Having been born into slavery, he was very careful with the money that came to him. He was never enamored with fame, and wanted to do good with his fortune. So he started a trust, with strict instructions that his descendants invest wisely to serve philanthropic causes."

Brianna sat open-jawed—one of the few moments in her life she was speechless.

"My parents had good financial advisers. They built the trust fund and told me that when I grew up I was to do good things for the world with the money I stewarded."

"So you're, like, a rich guy?" she replied, saucer-eyed. "What are you doing bussing dishes in Starbucks? Did you give all your money away?"

Ozzie shook his head. "I have plenty to live on. My wife and children are well taken care of. When I was rubbing elbows with other philanthropists, I found that a lot of them were snooty and knew their charities only on paper. I figured that if I dove into the heart of the city I could keep my finger on the pulse of who really needs help. All kinds of people walk through these doors—college students, suits, single mothers, retirees, kids on drugs, the homeless. When I meet someone who has the potential to change the world like my granddaddy did, I am all in."

Brianna shook her head and laughed. "Are you guys putting me on? This is a lot to swallow."

Hathaway leaned in, forearms on the table. "We're perfectly serious, Brianna. Ozzie and I have known each other for over ten years. From the day I first walked in here, we hit it off. We're each a maverick in our own way."

Brianna just kept shaking her head. "This takes the cake."

"Ozzie added the funding over and above the grants I received. Now he has generously offered to pay back the money the National Science Foundation is accusing me of misusing."

"So this will keep you out of jail and get your job back?"

"Yes to the jail part, probably no to the job part. But that's okay. I'm tired of working for a public institution—too many rules and narrow-minded people who don't understand the power of vision. Ozzie and I are talking about starting a private school for kids who don't fit into the mainstream and are trying to find their own voice."

Brianna sat quietly, struggling to absorb the unbelievable account. She couldn't decide which was more amazing—her bizarre escapade to almost bear the Christ child, or finding out that her favorite local busboy was a multi-millionaire philanthropist.

"One more thing, Brianna," Hathaway added as he turned to face her directly.

"What's that?"

"Even though we didn't complete the project, we really appreciate your willingness to help us, and we'd like to help you."

Curiosity spread over the coed's face. Still, none of this seemed real.

"We know your mother has lots of medical needs that rack up costs your family can't possibly meet. So we are setting up a fund for your mom. We will get her into the best care facility and pay all of her expenses for the rest of her life."

Brianna gasped and reached up to wipe the tears streaming down her cheeks. "You guys would really do that?"

Hathaway and Ozzie looked at each other, smiled, and nodded.

"I really don't know what to say . . . How could I possibly thank you?"

Hathaway took Brianna's quivering hands in his. He leaned forward and locked eyes with her. "If you ever have a baby, please just do this: Look into your child's eyes, and before that perfect little soul learns to seek the outer world for saviors and answers, tell that child without a trace of doubt, 'Baby, it's you.'"

# ACKNOWLEDGMENTS

While this book is a work of fiction, it contains many metaphysical truths and principles I have gleaned from dedicated masterful teachers over many years of intense spiritual exploration. Jesus's role as a central figure in the plot tells a deeper story that he holds a paramount place in my heart as the voice of God's love and power to heal. If I could clone him and bring him back to life, I surely would. Yet, as Professor Hathaway and his entourage discovered, the gift of Christ is his spirit more than his body, with whom I connect daily. And I rejoice that we all have that capacity.

I am ever grateful to my beloved partner Dee, for her ongoing love and support of me and my writing. Her enthusiasm for this book reminds me why I write, and her encouraging comments affirm the principles this story seeks to impart.

I humbly honor the many crop circle researchers who have forged a path to understand and illuminate a hugely important phenomenon that the world has largely ignored. Yet I find the event to be impeccable proof of benevolent intervention from powers beyond the world we know. My long-time friend Suzanne Taylor is one at the vanguard of such studies, for which I respect her immensely. Others whom I have learned from include Michael Glickman, Colin Andrews, Charles Maxwell, Charles Mallett, Barbara Lamb, and Polly Carson.

I applaud the courage of many UFO (now called UAP) and extraterrestrial researchers, many of whom have risked their reputations, careers, and in some cases their lives to study and make a stand for the fact that we are not the only kids on the block, and our elder peers may be here to help us. Some of the brave individuals I respect are Bob Dean, Leslie Kean, Major David Grusch, Bob Lazar, Lt. Colonel Wendelle Stevens, George Knapp, Linda Moulton Howe, Dr. Steven Greer, Bashar, Darryl Anka, Dr. Edgar Mitchell, Jaime Maussan, Ryan Graves, and David Fravor. There are many more who are worthy of honor, but these are the individuals with which I am most familiar.

I appreciate a number of friends who offered comments on the manuscript. Gratitude to Rachel Chan, Alyssa Freeland, Arlene Julie, Pat Kneisel-Brown, Barbara Lovejoy, and John Mifsud.

Several knowledgeable individuals were kind enough to provide helpful scientific and geographical information. Thanks to Scott Van Voris, Juli Vermillion, and James Whiting.

Cover artist Elena Karoumpali is a rare gem in my world, a talented and gracious soul who brings my books to life with stunning covers that capture the essence of the material. Gifted interior designer Isabel Robalo is an amazing artist who magnifies the quality of the content, and is a delight to co-create with. I feel so blessed to share this presentation with exceptional professionals with heart.

As always, I am deeply grateful to you, the reader, who is open to a greater reality than the one we have been taught is the only one. Your expanded mind is the doorway through which the light of greater truth uplifts the world. Your confidence in a Higher Power that speaks to your heart, and from it, is the fulcrum for the personal and planetary transformation we all yearn to enjoy in our lifetime.

# ABOUT THE AUTHOR

**ALAN COHEN, M.A.,** holds degrees in psychology and human organizational development.

He is the author of 32 popular inspirational books, including the best-selling *A Course in Miracles Made Easy* and the award-winning *A Deep Breath of Life*. He is a contributing writer for the #1 *New York Times* best-selling series *Chicken Soup for the Soul*, and he is featured in the book *101 Top Experts Who Help Us Improve Our Lives*. His books have been translated into 32 foreign languages.

Alan has taught at Montclair State College, Omega Institute for Holistic Studies, and en*Theos Academy for Optimal Living.

He is a featured presenter in the award-winning documentary *Finding Joe,* celebrating the teachings of Joseph Campbell. His work has been presented on CNN, Oprah.com, and in *USA Today, The Washington Post*, and *Huffington Post*. His monthly column *From the Heart* is published in magazines internationally.

Alan is the founder and Director of the Foundation for Holistic Life Coaching. He presents programs on themes of life mastery, spiritual development, and vision psychology.

For information on Alan Cohen's books, seminars, life coach training, videos, and audio recordings, visit:

**www.alancohen.com**

Facebook:
**www.facebook.com/AlanCohenAuthor**

YouTube:
**@AlanCohenAuthor**
**www.youtube.com/user/Cowinn327**

# Learn More with Alan Cohen

If you have enjoyed *Baby It's You*, you may want to deepen your understanding and inspiration by participating in Alan Cohen's in-person seminars, online courses, life coach training, or online subscription programs.

### Inspirational Quote for the Day
An uplifting idea e-mailed to you each day (free)

### Monthly e-Newsletter
Insightful articles and announcements
of upcoming events (free)

### Alan's YouTube Channel
Live and recorded presentations
for practical spiritual living (free)

### The Miracle Room
Weekly online lesson and live one-to-one
coaching with Alan (free)

### Webinars
Interactive programs on topics relevant to spirituality,
self-empowerment, and holistic living

### Online Courses
In-depth experiential exploration of healing, relationships,
prosperity, prayer, metaphysics, and stress management

### Life Coach Training
Become a certified professional holistic life coach or
enhance your career and personal life with coaching skills

### A Course in Miracles
Ongoing study group and retreat to empower you to master
the principles and skills of this life-changing program

For information about all of these offerings, and more, visit
## www.alancohen.com

www.ingramcontent.com/pod-product-compliance
Lightning Source LLC
Chambersburg PA
CBHW051634050726
47502CB00011B/92